INFORMATION MANAGEMENT IN PUBLIC ADMINISTRATION

An Introduction and
Resource Guide to Government
in the Information Age

Edited by FOREST W. HORTON
DONALD A. MARCHAND

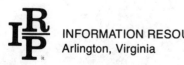

INFORMATION RESOURCES PRESS
Arlington, Virginia

Available from
Information Resources Press
1700 North Moore Street
Suite 700
Arlington, Virginia 22209

Library of Congress Catalog Card Number 81-85897
ISBN 0-87815-038-2

To Carol, Michael, and Bill
and
To Joyce, David, and Todd

THE EDITORS

FOREST "WOODY" HORTON, JR., is an independent consultant specializing in information management. Since retiring from the Federal Government in 1974, Dr. Horton has undertaken a wide variety of consultancy assignments for both the U.S. and foreign governments, as well as both domestic and internationally based private sector companies. From 1975 to 1978, he directed the landmark Information Management Study for the Commission on Federal Paperwork, which led to the Information Resources Management (IRM) concept.

Dr. Horton is the author or editor of five books in the information management field and has been a contributing editor to a half dozen information-related publications. He is the author of several hundred articles in the fields of management analysis, information management, management information systems, operations research, and public administration.

He received his Ph.D. from the University of Lausanne, Switzerland, and an M.S. from the University of California at Los Angeles. He has also held full- or part-time teaching tenures at the University of Maryland, Syracuse University, American University, and others.

DONALD A. MARCHAND is Associate Director, Bureau of Governmental Research and Service, and Associate Professor, Department of Governmental and International Studies at the University of South Carolina. He has served as the principal investigator on a wide range of research projects concerning information management in the Federal Government; office productivity and automation in state government; and planning, procurement, and management of information technology in state agencies, the impacts of information systems in local governments, and the uses, social impacts, and politics of criminal records on interstate and national computerized law enforcement information systems.

Dr. Marchand has contributed, to both scholarly and applied

publications, a number of articles on information policy and the management, social impacts, and use of information technology in the public sector. He is the author of a book entitled *The Politics of Privacy, Computers, and Criminal Justice Records: Controlling the Social Costs of Technological Change.*

In recent years, Dr. Marchand has served as a consultant and adviser to the Commission on Federal Paperwork and Office of Technology Assessment of the U.S. Congress, as well as to the Executive Office of the President. He received his Ph.D. in Political Science from the University of California at Los Angeles.

FOREWORD

The Commission on Federal Paperwork, which I served as chairman, made its final report in October 1977 and presented to the Congress and the president 770 recommendations for reducing the burdens that Federal Government paperwork and red tape impose on the American public and on state and local governments. These recommendations are a blueprint that the commission felt was necessary to enable the Federal Government to serve the American people responsively and to interact with state and local governments effectively.

Although many of the commission's recommendations dealt with specific forms, reports, or record-keeping requirements in federal agencies, others addressed the need for more fundamental reforms in the Federal Government's approach to forming information policy, managing information resources, and establishing appropriate career paths for government information managers and specialists. The commission's strategy was to treat both the symptoms and the causes of paperwork and red tape problems. For example, the Senate has already amended its rules to require that a "paperwork assessment statement" accompany proposed new legislation. I expect that the House will follow suit.

The commission also emphasized that government bureaucrats must stop regarding data and information as a "free good." That idea was termed *information resources management*. Its core is very simple: Policymaking and operating-level officials must begin applying the same management discipline to planning and controlling data that they do to dealing with the other government resources—people, money, facilities, supplies, and so forth. Although this statement of the basic idea behind information resources management is straightforward, its implications for public policy and public administration are profound and far-reaching.

Forest W. Horton, Jr. and Donald A. Marchand, who were members of the staff of the Commission on Federal Paperwork, have brought together in this book some of the key background papers on which the commission based its information management recommendations. Some of the papers included herein were written as a direct result of the commission's investigations and studies. Others were drawn from the literature on public administration and information science. Still others were written especially for this book.

Underlying all these papers is a basic notion: It is critical that public administrators at all levels of government regard data as a valuable resource, not simply as some ill-defined abstraction or mundane commodity like paper clips. I believe that Horton and Marchand have done a valuable service by compiling this collection of important papers. I commend this book not just to government officials, but also to legislators, teachers, researchers, technical information professionals, and information scientists. The application of information management to public administration comes at a time when our nation is searching for solutions to seemingly insoluble domestic and international political, economic, and social problems. Congress cannot do the whole job itself; it must have the guidance and help of information professionals, informed citizens, and technological entrepreneurs. For these audiences, *Information Management in Public Administration* will be a valuable tool in their pursuit of approaches to public policy.

FRANK HORTON
Congressman (R-N.Y.)
and former Chairman,
Commission on Federal Paperwork

PREFACE

This book of readings was conceived and nurtured in its early stages at the Commission on Federal Paperwork and developed and completed at the University of South Carolina. Attention has been given to integrating scholarly and practical concerns, since the challenges and opportunities offered by the convergence of information management and public administration are a blending of new concepts and applied interests and needs. We hope that this book will find an appropriate place in the classrooms of students of both public administration and information science. Without early exposure to the concepts and concerns presented here, the practitioners and scholars of tomorrow will not be stimulated to confront significant issues and questions on the management of information in the public sector.

The selections in this book come from diverse sources. Several were written especially for the book to develop themes and concepts in areas where no suitable work had yet been completed or to present important developments in the field that merited inclusion. We gratefully acknowledge the contributions of James F. Berry, Office of Personnel Management; Craig M. Cook, Arthur Young and Company; Robert Lee Chartrand, senior specialist in information sciences, Congressional Research Service, Library of Congress; and John J. Stucker, associate professor, and Mark Tompkins, assistant professor, Department of Government and International Studies, University of South Carolina, Columbia.

We wish to thank Shirley Geiger, our research assistant, for the invaluable assistance she provided in helping complete abstracts of the selections for the earlier drafts and in providing cogent commentary on the organization of the work.

We also wish to thank Charlie B. Tyer, Director, Bureau of Governmental Research and Service, and the staff for providing administrative support and, above all, a supportive, creative environment for the development of the book.

We also wish to thank Saul Herner and Gene Allen for their abiding professional interest in the improvement of the management of information resources—both nationally and in operating enterprises. To them and to their skilled editors, Nancy Winchester and Maureen Stotland, we owe a special measure of gratitude.

CONTENTS

INTRODUCTION

This is a book of readings in two rapidly converging fields: information management and public administration. To the best of the editors' knowledge, this book is the first work of its kind. Its publication reflects the increasing confluence of ideas in the two fields; the variety and richness of practical and conceptual activity already underway and planned for the next decade; and the rapid and extensive application of modern information technologies in public agencies affecting day-to-day operations, management decision making, and policy analysis and evaluation. The number of divergent paths along which conceptual and practical activities are proceeding makes the present review necessary and compelling.

This work brings together new and old trends of activity and research focused on the meaning and implications of information management for public administration. Included are some new and original contributions as well as more familiar and even classic readings. The interdisciplinary nature of the book means that some readings will be familiar to individuals with a background in public administration, whereas other readings will be familiar to those with a background in information technology or records management. The aim of this work is to break from traditional, narrowly focused perspectives and begin considering a more integrative picture of information management in public organizations and possibilities for future change and innovation. Therefore, the whole is intended to be more than the sum of its parts. This work seeks to cut new paths and establish new horizons for the public administrator, records manager, and information specialist. The book is also oriented to the scholar and citizen, since concern with information management in public administration has far-reaching implications for both that transcend technical and administrative concerns and raise significant economic, social, and political questions and issues.

INFORMATION MANAGEMENT IN PUBLIC ADMINISTRATION: CONVERGENCE AS A NEW POINT OF DEPARTURE

Each day we are confronted with the fact that specialization of knowledge and tasks is a basic requirement of society. The complexity and uncertainty arising from economic, political, and social structures and processes require what Max Weber might have called the "routinization" of the generation and use of knowledge. Given this situation, the idea that fields as significant as information management and public administration are converging may be viewed by some as a radical notion, since it implies that a new reality is emerging that requires changes in traditional perspectives and a willingness to consider new concepts and approaches whose finer points and details are not fully worked out. Convergence implies opportunities and challenges for those persons who are willing and able to break out of traditional molds as well as unpredictable, if not entirely unforeseeable, consequences and difficulties.

The selections in this book examine both the causes for and the bases of convergence between information management and public administration. At the practical level, the need for convergence between these two fields has been perceived for some time. Public administrators, political leaders, and analysts in public agencies have long complained that they need accurate, timely, and complete information on which to base their decisions and formulate public policy. But such information, if forthcoming at all, is often too late to help, is garbled and distorted, or is packaged in ways that make it incomprehensible or difficult to use. The need to understand and deal with social complexity in the development, management, and evaluation of public policy has focused increased attention on the vital role of information in public affairs.

The application and use of information technology, such as computers, telecommunications equipment, duplicating machines, micrographic devices, and word processing equipment, have caused a quiet revolution in public administration in recent years. Modern government and public administration can no longer do without information technology. Many current programs and services that are taken for granted, such as Social Security, medical care and welfare benefits, tax administration, and national defense, can no longer function at an acceptable level without the extensive use of information technology. Many future programs and services are being designed with the application of new information technology in mind. Thus, it is inconceivable that modern public administration can function adequately without technology. Modern society has become increasingly dependent on technology; at the same time, however, the consequences of such changes for public administration have not always been evident.

Therefore, the field of public administration seems both unprepared for these changes and yet ready to begin the task of integrating its concern with information management and its general concern for effective management and policy development in the public sector. Practitioners and scholars in the field of public administration can no longer afford to avoid the reality of convergence. Understanding the changes that are occurring and their consequences and implications is the imperative to which this book responds.

Before proceeding to a general review of the specific contents of the work, however, one should look at the broad economic, political, and social dimensions of the topic that have served as the backdrop for more specific interest in information management in public administration.

HISTORICAL BACKGROUND

Fritz Machlup is generally credited with the earliest effort to place information and knowledge in an economic context. His 1962 classic, *The Production and Distribution of Knowledge in the United States,* stands as a beacon on the horizon of economic treatments of data, information, and knowledge. Machlup moved from a classic, conventional attitude of looking at the economy as a goods-and-services machine in the sense of transformation of raw materials to a position from which one could look two ways: first, to the manufacture of physical and tangible goods and services and, second, to the production of information and knowledge goods and services. Or, as expressed in the words of his disciple, Marc Uri Porat:

An economy can be separated into two domains. The first is involved in the transformation of matter and energy from one form into another. The second is involved in transforming information from one pattern into another. The two domains are linked and inseparable. Manipulation of matter and energy would be impossible without a sizeable input of knowledge, planning, coordination, and control information. And the production, processing, and distribution of information would be impossible without a sizeable input of matter and energy. The systematic marriage of these two domains is absolute. The question is the relative contribution of each partner in producing economic wealth.[1]

The Department of Commerce's nine-volume landmark publication, *The Information Economy,* was released in the summer of 1977, almost simultaneously with the Final Summary Report of the Commission on Federal Paperwork. Congress established the Paperwork Commission in 1975, because federal information requirements had "placed an unprecedented paperwork burden upon private citizens, recipients of Federal assistance, businesses, governmental contractors, [and] State and local governments." The Congress directed the Paperwork Commission to study and investigate statutes, policies, rules, regulations, procedures, and practices of the Federal Government relating to gathering, processing, and disseminating information, and to managing and controlling information activities.

The Paperwork Commission was not long in coming to the conclusion that one of the root causes of the enormous and costly government paperwork burden placed on the American public was not too many pieces of paper—forms, records, reports, and all kinds of miscellaneous documents—but that many public administrators had come to look on information as a "free good." Whenever Congress passes a new law, a flood of paperwork is released on citizens by officials at all levels of federal, state, and local governments who are not held accountable for the cost-effective use of the data and information they collect. The commission found that information is not regarded as a costly asset—a valued resource that needs to be managed—just as government is regarded by the taxpayer as the steward to whom he entrusts taxpayer dollars, public lands and waterways, and other assets and resources. The Paperwork Commission, the Department of Commerce, the General Accounting Office in its many audits of agency program effectiveness, and other groups in both the public and private sectors seem to have come to the same conclusion at the same time: Information must be regarded as a valuable asset or resource that deserves and needs the same kind of management disciplines given to other resources—financial, physical, human, material, and natural.

For nearly two decades, Senator Hubert H. Humphrey (to paraphrase President John F. Kennedy) admonished the information science community not to ask the Federal Government what it can do for the community, but rather what information science can do for the Federal Government. In 1974, Humphrey said,

To find solutions to these problems [the crises of modern society faced by America and the rest of the world] we must do a much better job of establishing goals and setting priorities for our nation, backed up by effective systems of information collection, analysis and dissemination.[2]

Humphrey had been in the forefront, challenging information science and technology to find ways to help public policy officials do their jobs better. For example, he was a key architect of and served on the advisory/overseer board of the Office of Technology Assessment, which helps legislative policymakers anticipate and plan for the consequences of technological change.

Congressman Jack Brooks (D-Tex.), chairman of the House Government Operations Committee, also has fought for improved use of information-handling technologies (particularly the computer and automated technologies) to support public management and policymaking. The so-called Brooks Act is the central legislation dealing with the planning, use, and evaluation of computer technology in government. With Brooks, Congressman Charlie Rose (D-N.C.), chairman of the Ad Hoc Subcommittee on Computers of the Committee on House Administration, has fought for more effective and efficient use of computers and modern office machines, not only to move paper faster but also to ensure that information is made available to senators, congressmen, and congressional staff in the forms and at the times needed.

Among all the initiatives and trends emphasizing the significance of information management in the public sector, the passage of the Paperwork Control Act of 1980 stands as a milestone. The act was preceded by several key studies that outlined the problems associated with the way the Federal Government manages information resources.

In addition to the work of the Commission on Federal Paperwork, studies by the General Accounting Office and the Federal Data Processing Reorganization Study of the President's Reorganization Project provided the necessary background and support to implement significant policy and managerial changes.

The objectives of the Paperwork Control Act of 1980 are to

1. Reduce the information-processing burden on the public and private sectors by requiring the development and implementation of uniform and consistent information policies and practices
2. Increase the availability and accuracy of agency data and information
3. Expand and strengthen federal information management activities
4. Establish a single focal point for information management within the Federal Government
5. Decrease the paperwork burden on individuals, businesses, and state and local governments

To accomplish these objectives, the act established an Office of Federal Information Policy in the Office of Management and Budget with the responsibility for overall direction of the Federal Government's information policies, standards, and guidelines. The bill also revised the Federal Reports Act, passed in 1942, to strengthen the reports clearance function by making all federal agencies subject to review. The act established a Federal Information Locator System, which will contain descriptions of all information requests made by federal agencies and any reports or analyses derived from such requests. The locator system is intended to be used to identify duplication in agency reporting and record-keeping requirements; locate existing information that may meet the needs of Congress, executive agencies, and the public; and assist the new office in deciding which agency requests for information collection should be approved.

The Paperwork Reduction Act of 1980 represents a major revision of the way the Federal Government manages information technology and information as a resource. Although it is too early to assess what impacts this act will have, it nevertheless represents a major step toward recognizing the confluence of information management and technology in public administration.

Despite these advances in government policy and managerial reforms, however, the political and economic problems attending the evolution of information technology applied to public administration still represent phenomena about which elected officials and public administrators have mixed feelings. For example, until recently, Congress and state legislatures were leery of "that machine." They have been suspicious of its applicability to "the politics" of public management and decision making. They have been cautious in trusting secrets to the machine—perhaps with just cause, given the daily headlines of computer abuses and invasions of privacy. In the words of a staff report, prepared for the Select Committee on Committees of the House by the Science Policy Research Division of the Congressional Research Service of the Library of Congress, entitled "The Congress and Information Technology,"

It should be noted that the attitude towards information tools and techniques, as manifested in governmental circles, has ranged from skepticism early on, to a rather ingenuous view that computers offered a panacea for the Nation's, and indeed the world's ills, followed by a predictable reaction in the face of these devices' limitations. By the 1970 decade, a more sophisticated clientele had emerged, with a fairly clear understanding of the benefits (ADP). No longer need the governmental decision-maker fear that some robot would deliver decisions, rather he learned that the computer, if programmed and operated by knowledgeable human beings, could provide him with helpful background information. Professor Kenneth Janda underscored this critical facet of understanding and using ADP-control capabilities when he wrote that: "information systems are not...devices for grinding out policy decisions, and they are not designed to replace human judgement. Rather, they are intended to provide the human decision-maker...with knowledge for making informed choices.[3]

In addition to the broad economic and political aspects of this topic, significant social issues have been raised by new technological developments and their application. The most visible social issue has been the now-classic debate between the public's right to know and the concern with the citizen's right to privacy. The last 10 years have been marked by a growing interest in the standards and practices governing record keeping in our society by public and private organizations and the possible negative impacts on citizens of the information technologies used by these organizations.

The abuses of Watergate and intelligence agencies, such as the CIA and FBI, represent the most recent highlights of a long and difficult process of problem identification, policy development, law making, rule making, and court testing. Indeed, the cases now before the courts relating to the questions of access and entitlement to government-held information under the Freedom of Information Act and the authorized disclosure of personally identifiable information under the Privacy Act will most certainly stretch through the 1980s and possibly beyond. Moreover, state legislatures are just now venturing into this area. Already, state and local laws passed hastily are being withdrawn; rules are being found unworkable or impracticable; and practices are being described as unfair, or confusing, ambiguous, and in need of being reworked. At the national level, the views of two major commissions, the Privacy Protection Study Commission and the Commission on Federal Paperwork, are at odds on the extended use of so-called universal identifier numbers, such as the Social Security number, in federally funded programs. The Privacy Commission voted for a moratorium on extending the further use of these numbers, whereas the Paperwork Commission felt that a moratorium would be both unwise and unnecessary and suggested that greater efforts be devoted to strengthening technical, administrative, and procedural safeguards over government's vast information holdings. In addition, the Electronic Funds Transfer Commission, the Public Documents Commission, and perhaps a half dozen or so other prestigious bodies have recently studied and investigated the problems attending entry into the information age.

Not all the problems are related to invasions of privacy, however. As society seems bent on a course that is increasingly service oriented, government finds itself more in need of information on which to base eligibility decisions and to determine appropriate compliance recourses. In short, agencies at all levels that plan, administer, and evaluate government programs simply need more information because there are more programs, laws, regulations, and procedures. All these programs mean more information handling—more files and records, both manual and automated. The proliferation and compartmentalization of minifiles, minirecords, minidossiers, and minidockets therefore seem inevitable. The social dimensions of the problem are obvious.

Who will control all this information? What new roles and functions must be brought into play? Will information brokers be needed who can act as mediators between the providers and the users of information? Will an ombudsman be needed to help the average citizen find out what government is all about and what it can do for him? Will an ombudsman be needed to answer complaints, locate needed data, and speed up and expedite cases pending? What of the role of the information manager? Are data-base administrators needed? Will they be information czars or simply information custodians?

Of course, this discussion just scratches the surface of these issues and problems. The purpose of this book is to stimulate the dialogue of public officials, record managers, and information specialists. To the extent that the cross section of selected materials herein is rich, varied, and representative, *Information Management in Public Administration* will have contributed to that dialogue. The reader must be the judge.

OVERVIEW

The selections in this book came from diverse fields and sources; however, all the readings fit together in response to two general and related questions: What is the relationship between information management and public administration? What are the most significant implications of this relationship? The first four chapters attempt to answer the first question, whereas the last four chapters respond to the second.

Chapter 1 addresses both the need for and scope of information management in the public sector. The chapter begins with selections aimed at identifying the magnitude and nature of information processing, paperwork, and reporting in government and proceeds to selections suggesting that past approaches to records management are seriously deficient and must be replaced by a more integrative concept of information management.

Chapters 2 and 3 continue to elaborate on the two key dimensions of information management in public organizations: management of the information process and management of the information resources, including the use of information technologies. Chapter 2 focuses on the way in which individuals become informed and use symbols to do so. Selections here highlight the good and bad effects of organizational structures and processes on the quality of individual and collective information processing and communication.

Chapter 3 identifies the major tangible products and aspects of information processing in public agencies, including the coalescence of information technologies, such as computers, word processors, micrographics equipment, and duplicating machines, and suggests that a new method of managing information resources is necessary to deal effectively with such changes.

The question of how information resources can be managed is addressed in Chapter 4. The approaches and methods for planning, budgeting, and accounting for information resources are not yet defined and accepted. Various new ways for treating information as a resource are needed and must be integrated into current agency and program planning, budgeting, and accounting processes to be effective.

In Chapter 5, the emphasis shifts from practicing information management to dealing with its implications for public policy formulation and analysis. What is the role of information management in public policy analysis? How have policymaking groups, such as Congress and state legislatures, been able to use information technologies and manage information to enhance their effectiveness?

In Chapter 6, the implications of information management for organizational change and design are examined. In recent years, various significant proposals have been suggested for changing organizational structures and relationships to use and manage information resources more effectively as well as to reduce the tensions and burdens imposed by the Federal Government and by state governments on local governments, the private sector, and individual citizens. This chapter examines some of the leading proposals.

In Chapter 7, the impacts of using information as a resource in political and organizational life are examined from the perspective of citizens. The privacy, political, and distributive aspects of those impacts are examined. How is society to cope with the information poor in America? What are the implications for public policy if government agencies and interest groups use information as a resource in political action? What problems and constraints do organizations and individuals face in dealing with the privacy issue?

Finally, in Chapter 8, the relationship between information and knowledge management is explored. How can more effective information management in the public sector enhance knowledge production and use? How can knowledge and information management in the public sector be integrated into the framework of democratic government and administration? What significance does the emphasis on information and knowledge management have for the field of public administration and the roles of information specialists and technologists?

Notes

[1]Porat, Marc Uri. *The Information Economy: Definition and Measurement.* Washington, D.C., Office of Telecommunications, U.S. Department of Commerce, May 1977, p. 2. Special Publication 77-12(1).

[2]Humphrey, Hubert, H. "Information for Government: Needs and Priorities." *Bulletin of the American Society for Information Science,* 1(1):7-8, June–July 1974.

[3]Library of Congress, Congressional Research Service, Science Policy Research Division. *The Congress and Information Technology Staff Report.* Washington, D.C., U.S. Government Printing Office, May 5, 1974, pp. 5–6. No. 5270-02355.

Chapter 1

WHAT IS INFORMATION MANAGEMENT?

The systematic and purposeful acquisition of information and its systematic and purposeful application are emerging as the new foundations for work, productivity, and effort throughout the world.

—Peter F. Drucker, *The Age of Discontinuity*
(New York, Harper Colophon Books, 1968, p. 266)

As was suggested in the "Introduction," the aim of this book is to determine the implications for public administrators and government officials of managing information resources more efficiently and effectively to achieve collective goals and interests and to be more sensitive and responsive to human needs and problems. The selections in this chapter explore the reasons why the topic of managing information in public organizations has become so significant in recent years and offer several different, but interrelated, ways of defining information management in the public sector.

In the first reading, "The Public Bureaucracies," Marc Uri Porat describes what he calls the federal information industry to demonstrate the significance of information resources to government. Using the classic input-output model of economic analysis, Porat reviews the operations of the federal bureaucracy as "essentially an information producing, distributing and consuming organism." He suggests that in 1967, about 31 percent of the total federal budget was used for information inputs and that this proportion is rapidly increasing. In 1967, the federal bureaucracy accounted for $50.5 billion in information outputs, and, in 1970, the figure was as high as $52.8 billion. This trend highlights the significance of information resources to government and raises some important questions for public policy and management.

In "The Paperwork Problem," the Commission on Federal Paperwork reports on part of its extensive two-year effort to deal with the paperwork and red-tape problems in government and their effects on business and the public. The commission suggests that mismanagement of information resources and the concomitant burdens and problems placed on public management, the private sector, and the public are caused by the growth of government, overlapping government programs, proliferation and fragmentation of information and program requirements, vague goals and objectives, and the rising costs of data- and information-handling technologies. Each year, the Federal Government collects between 130 and 300 billion individual data items at a cost of $50–$100 billion to governments and $25–$32 billion to respondents to government requirements. In spite of these startling statistics, however, the commission suggests that public administrators tend to regard information as a "free good" and do not manage information as a valuable resource. The commission also maintains that advances in information technologies, such as computers, duplicating machines, and micrographics equipment, have rendered ineffective traditional approaches to information management. Not all paperwork and information collection should be classified as bad, but the burdens of unnecessary paperwork and information proliferation are tremendous. The commission concludes that information must be managed like other resources and that the principles, tools, and methods to do so must be developed.

In the two remaining selections in this chapter, the authors assume the need for public organizations to develop a method of information management and state various ways to define the method and its requirements. In "Needed: A New Doctrine for Information Resources Management," Forest W. Horton, Jr. suggests that a new body of principles is needed from which to draw new approaches to managing information resources. Traditional ways of controlling information resources through paperwork management are inadequate for today's problems. The central-forms clearance approach, long the mainstay for control at the federal level, focuses on the most visible effects of the paperwork problems and is essentially a knee-jerk reaction. To attempt to identify and control the problem of information mismanagement, a different approach is needed that concentrates on the content and not just the physical manifestations of the paperwork problem. Horton advocates a "resource management approach" that attempts to treat information as a manageable resource like labor, equipment, supplies, and funds. He argues that the "information explosion" in the public sector and the need to control the paperwork burden on states and local governments, businesses, and the public require the evolution of a new approach to management comparable to the evolution of new approaches to financial, manpower, materials, and property management beginning in the 1920s in this country. Horton also recommends that an organization developing a method for managing information resources should account for and budget these resources to determine the relationship between their use and cost. Horton warns that without proper controls information management can evolve into "information manipulation," threaten individual privacy, and constrain creative work or bar the free flow of ideas in a democratic society—points that will be developed in later sections of this book.

In "Information Management in Public Organizations: Defining a New Resource Management Function," Donald A. Marchand carries the concern with information management into another significant area of an organization and thus extends the themes of the Commission on Federal Paperwork—the application of information technology in public organizations and the need to concentrate on information rather than hardware before extensive commitments are made to use such technology. Marchand contends that before organizations can use information technology effectively, they will have to focus more attention on information value and use in two dimensions: management of the information process and management of the data resources. Management of the information process is concerned with how well members of an organization interact with data resources and supporting technology for decision making and analysis. The emphasis of this dimension is on the value of data resources that are used in an organization for problem solving and analysis.

Management of data resources corresponds to Horton's definition of management of information resources and focuses on the quality and use of the tangible products and tools of the information process to support the requirements and needs of organization members. These dimensions are mutually complementary and highlight the challenge of information management in the public sector. If the latter need is to be met, certain constraints will have to be handled. The same need that compels an organization to seek information to reduce uncertainty and resolve internal and external problems makes information management difficult. As Marchand concludes: "The realization of the promise of such an approach is highly dependent upon a clear and realistic perception of the problems and issues."

The Public Bureaucracies*
Marc Uri Porat

The market system approaches the government through the legislature. This relation-ship, though highly visible, is with the branch of government which has been declining in importance. The technostructure and the planning system have their relationship with the public bureaucracy. This association is far more discrete; it is also with the branch of government which, as public tasks become more complex, is strongly ascen-dant.

—John Kenneth Galbraith, *Economics and the Public Purpose*
(Boston, Houghton Mifflin, 1973)

Bureaus specialize in the supply of those services the value of which cannot be ex-changed for money at a per-unit rate. . . . As a consequence of the above, bureaus can-not be managed by profit goals and "the economic calculus."

—Ludwig von Mises, *Bureaucracy*
(New Haven, Yale University Press, 1944)

Bureaus are non-profit organizations which are financed, at least in part, by a peri-odic appropriation or a grant. . . . They specialize in providing those goods and ser-vices that some people prefer be supplied in larger amounts than would be supplied by their sale at a per-unit rate.

—William A. Niskanen, Jr., *Bureaucracy and Representative Government*
(Chicago, Aldine-Atherton, 1971)

An essential feature of a technocratic society is the bureaucracy. Bureau-cratic enterprises appear both in the private and public sectors. Their hierar-chical structure insures that the alter ego of the head is reflected throughout the chain of command. It also insures, however, that a change in the head will not cause a radical change in the operating rules and standards of the bureaucracy. This tension is built on purpose. A bureaucracy is at the core conservative—preserving a sense of continuity with the past—while superfici-ally attendant to the direction given it by policy leaders. A good army fights and communicates the same way regardless of the field of battle. It is the leader's responsibility to decide which battles to fight; it is the bureaucracy's

---

*In: *The Information Economy: Definition and Measurement.* Washington D.C., Office of Telecommunications Policy, 1977, pp. 136-147.

duty to execute the decision in a predictable, if not creative, fashion. Karl Marx's delight with bureaucracies is clear:

Bureaucracy is a circle no one can leave. Its hierarchy is a *hierarchy of information.* The top entrusts the lower circles with an insight into details, while the lower circle entrusts the top with an insight into what is universal, and thus they mutually deceive each other....

A bureaucracy is essentially an information producing, distributing, and consuming organism. Bureaucracies plan, coordinate, command, evaluate, and communicate. They process information. They survey, gather intelligence, write reports.

...The Federal Government is conceptualized as an enormous and elaborately organized multiproduct firm, producing both information and noninformation outputs. The informational inputs and outputs of the firm are measured in detail for 1967, and a time series (1958 to 1970) is built. State and local government bureaucracies will not be discussed here, although they exceed the Federal Government in terms of total budget. The reason is pragmatic: the Federal budget is consolidated, systematic, and relatively straightforward to analyze, whereas the State and local budgets are hopelessly unique.

The Federal Information Industry

The Federal information industry can be conceptually described as a multiproduct firm, with a definable stream of inputs and outputs, operating in a market environment that determines the supply, demand, and price of its services.

The "marketplace" in which the firm operates is drawn in Figure 1. A demand for a variety of services is transmitted to the firm through constituent or special interest preferences. These demands are revealed directly (through the vote) or indirectly (through a variety of private lobbying activities). In addition, a demand for bureaucratic output is generated internally by the bureaucracies themselves, for reasons that may be only loosely coupled with externally felt demand.

In 1974, the Federal Government spent $111 million advertising itself, placing it somewhere between the amounts spent by Colgate-Palmolive Company and R. J. Reynolds. This is in addition to the $260 million worth of free advertising offered as a public service. The government knows quite well that it is selling its output, even though no explicit market transaction occurs other than mandatory taxation.

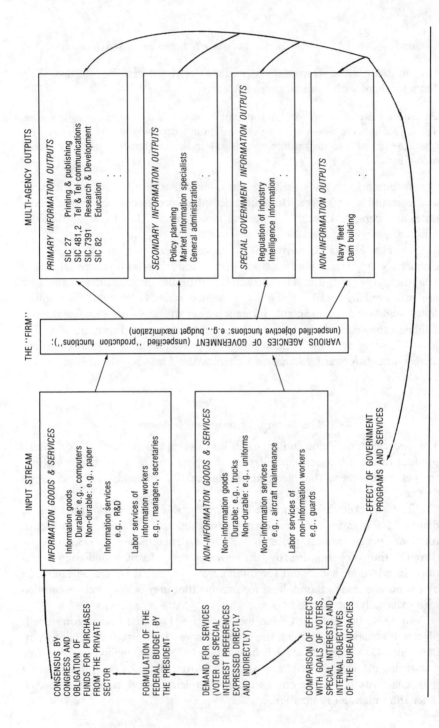

Figure 1 The Federal information industry.

These real or perceived demands are translated into a budget, formulated by the President and negotiated with the Congress. Once a consensus is reached regarding the types and levels of outputs that the firm will produce next year, an obligation for the purchases of inputs enters. Whereas firms in the private sector must await the decision of the marketplace before they can determine the level of output for the next time period, the Federal firm removes the market uncertainty *ex ante,* and can hence know the total cost before any output is "sold."

The multiproduct firm is organized into agencies, although the outputs of the agencies are far from homogeneous. The various agencies purchase a variety of goods and services from the private economy, which are divided into purchases from the primary information sector...and purchases from noninformation industries. The firm may buy computers, facsimile machines, file cabinets, and paper clips from the primary sector; and it may hire managers, lawyers, economists, and secretaries. This bundle of resources enters the firm as the "information inputs." By symmetry, the firm may purchase trucks, fuel oil, uniforms, and beefsteak from the noninformation industries; and it may hire guards, janitors, tank drivers, and pilots. The bundle enters the firm's production function as the "noninformation inputs."

The various divisions of the firm can each be characterized by a unique production function, although for the purpose of this chapter those functions will remain unspecified. Similarly, the divisions of the firm behave according to an unspecified objective function. One objective may be to maximize the division's budget; another might be to minimize risk; a third might be to accelerate the welfare of its top management—with size, prestige, and celebrity status replacing salary as the numeraire; a fourth might be to maximize the present value of the top management's lifetime income, with expected future salaries in the private sector entering into the present decision making processes. Another objective might be to maximize social welfare, or total surplus for the economy as a whole. This analysis is indifferent as to the actual objective function assumed, although more detailed studies of bureaucracies can reveal distinct differences in behavior depending on which objective is used. The binding constraint is assumed to be either financial or labor resources.

The informational and noninformational inputs enter the firm's production function and are converted into a variety of outputs. Some outputs have clearly defined analogs in the primary sector. For example, the Government Printing Office is the Federal version of a large private printing and publishing firm....The telecommunications networks built and maintained by the Defense Communications Agency and the Federal Telecommunications

System together constitute a firm....In addition, the Federal information firm produces a variety of "secondary" outputs....These are information services of a strictly planning, coordinating, and managing sort—activities that take place in all firms, regardless of whether they are members of the primary information sector or part of the noninformation sector. Also, the Federal information firm produces outputs which are unique to itself, and have either weak analogs in the private sector or none at all. For example, the domestic and foreign intelligence communities generate a tremendous volume of information for internal consumption. Unless one counts industrial espionage as a secondary activity of the private sector, this type of information is strictly a government function. Lastly, the Federal Government produces a number of strictly noninformational outputs. The construction of the Tennessee Valley Authority dam system is a prime example, the U.S. Navy carrier fleet is another. Income transfer and redistribution programs are a third. These outputs are noninformational public goods for the most part, or noninformational private services in others. Note that the informational *costs* of administering these programs are embedded in the secondary information sector of our accounts.

A major simplifying assumption is made. We cannot know precisely which input costs are allocated to each output. Hence we assume that the informational inputs *in toto* represent the total cost of providing all information services; the noninformation inputs by assumption are converted into noninformational outputs. This assumption is not as crude as it may seem at first glance. In private sector multiproduct firms, the precise cost allocation between different lines of business cannot be precisely stated either. It is currently a matter of severe contention between the Federal Trade Commission and large corporations whether these data can even be generated. For example, the FTC needs line of business data to establish the profit levels associated with each output, and to determine whether any internal cross-subsidies result in anticompetitive practices. The Federal Communications Commission is contending with the Bell system over internal cost allocations, again to assess whether a cross-subsidy is occurring, and if so, which way the subsidy is flowing.

The cost allocation problem in the Federal information industry is just as intractable. For example, although we may not be able to determine the unique amount of information processing costs allocable to each output, we can state with certainty that the *total* computer budget is jointly consumed by all the informational activities of the firm, whether the resources are used to produce R&D, accounting services, library search, or planning and strategic gaming.

This is a useful assumption because we can immediately restrict the output price of the information services to just equal the input price of the labor and capital resources. If these services were "sold" in a real marketplace, the price (or valuation) would necessarily be the total cost including profit; but with profit equaling zero, the price reduces to total input cost.

Inputs of the Federal Information Industry. Table 1 shows a summary of the informational inputs of the Federal Government. In 1967, the total cost of information resources was $50.5 billion, of which only $11.8 billion was in the form of direct purchase of goods and services from the primary information sector....The Federal information industry purchased $13.1 billion in R&D from the private sector, mostly in development of new weapons and space systems for the Department of Defense and NASA.

The next item in Table 1 is "employee compensation to information workers," accounting for $16.6 billion in 1967. This estimate was derived from Civil Service Commission data on the occupational and compensation structure of Federal employees....Only those workers who perform purely informational tasks are included in this figure. Military workers who performed essentially administrative, planning, communications, or clerical duties were also included.

The next item shows Federal transfers to State and local governments for educational, training, or related purposes. These are considered as a purchase of educational services from an outside vendor, another government.

A portion of the debt service charges are also included as informational inputs. Debt service is mostly associated with deficit spending for income transfer, military purchases, foreign aid, and a variety of domestic programs. However, a portion of the program budget pays for the informational activities associated with planning, coordination, and management. We estimated these informational costs associated with general administration and allocated a portion (31%) of the debt service to information....It is included here only as a rough estimate of the Federal budget portion used for information. In the GNP accounts, only the employee compensation of Federal workers is accounted.

In 1967, approximately 31% of the total Federal budget was used for informational inputs—goods and services purchased from the primary sector, R&D services purchased from noninformation firms, educational services purchased from other governments, and so on.

The time series in Table 1 shows that the informational costs have been slowly increasing as a percentage of the total Federal budget. The fairly rapid increase between 1958 (22%) and 1966 (34%), when the informational ac-

Table 1 Inputs of the Federal Information Industries 1958-1970

	($ Millions, Current)						
	1958	1961	1963	1966	1967	1969	1970
Total information inputs[a]	19,311	27,058	37,049	48,142	50,483	57,589	62,833
Purchases of goods & services from primary information industries[a]	4,063	5,550	10,088	12,670	11,808	13,392	12,726
Purchases of R&D from private industry[b]	3,196	7,185	10,216	12,098	13,133	12,200	12,669
Employee compensation to info workers[c]	9,673	10,678	12,061	15,085	16,588	20,790	23,861
"Purchases" from state & local govt's[a]	453	574	684	2,923	3,117	3,607	4,412
Education	326	446	551	2,724	2,924	3,338	3,867
Other informational	127	128	133	199	193	269	545
Information purchases on transfer account[d]	783	1,381	1,559	2,323	2,498	3,870	5,066
Debt service allocated to general admin.[d]	1,207	1,745	2,492	3,109	3,400	3,835	4,203
Government information enterprises[d]	−64	−55	−51	−66	−61	−105	−104
Addenda							
Total Federal budget expenditures[e]	88,870	102,086	113,857	142,750	163,594	189,207	203,927
Total purchases of goods & services[a]	53,594	57,408	64,244	77,773	90,706	98,781	96,182
Ratios							
Information as % of total budget	21.7	26.5	32.5	33.7	30.9	30.4	30.8
Information employee compensation as % of total information inputs	50.0	39.5	32.6	31.3	32.9	36.1	38.0

[a]BEA, Input-Output Matrices for 1958, 1961, 1963, 1966, 1967, 1969, 1970, and estimates....
[b]NSF, *Federal Funds for Research, Development and other Scientific Activities*, e.g., Vol. XVII, Table C-97.
[c]Selective Service Commission, *Occupations of Federal White-Collar Workers*, October 1967.
[d]BEA, *National Income and Product Accounts*, Table 3.10, "Government Expenditures by Type of Function."
[e]OMB, *Budget of the United States*, FY 60-72, and *Appendix*.

tivities increased by 50%, was temporarily halted as the Viet Nam war heated up. It will likely resume its upward march through the 1970's, as the Federal Government intensifies its dependence on information resources.

Outputs of the Federal Information Industry. The outputs of the Federal information industry have been organized into primary, secondary, and special government functions, shown in Table 2....

The 17 primary information industries listed in Table 2 accounted for $34.6 billion in output. The two largest industries, R&D and education, were mostly purchased directly from either the private sector or other governments. The other primary outputs were produced in-house, using government information workers and resources.

The secondary activities include those functions which are specifically concerned with policy planning and top management (e.g., Office of the Secretary), or as a general management function not tied to a particular primary output. This category also includes a small residual category of unallocable information resources.

The special government functions, such as regulation of industry, intelligence information, and economic information services, accounted for $9 billion in 1967. As a percentage of the total Federal information outputs, these special functions have actually declined, from around 24% in 1958 to about 16% in 1970. However, in absolute terms, they have grown very rapidly—economic planning and information gathering activities have increased eightfold in current dollars, regulation of industries has increased tenfold, diplomatic information gathering has multiplied sevenfold, and information services provided *gratis* to the private economy (such as FAA airport control) [have] increased elevenfold.

Paperwork. The public bureaucracy is a planning and coordinating resource. Part of the Federal Government's bureaucracy necessarily communicates with "outside" entities—private firms and State and local governments. The bureaucracies "talk" to each other in managing the economy. And that volume of bureaucratic chatter has grown to stupendous heights in the past 50 years.

The National Commission on Federal Paperwork reports that "Federal agencies are today churning out forms, reports, and assorted paperwork at the rate of over 10 billion sheets per year. That's 4½ million cubic feet of paper. All of this paper costs the American economy $40 billion per year."[1] Senator Cranston estimated that there are 12,000 laws requiring reports from the public resulting in 10,000 different forms; and that there are 10,000

Table 2 Outputs of the Federal Information Industries 1958–1970

TOTAL FEDERAL BUDGET EXPENDITURES[a]	88,870
Total budget less transfer payments & net int paid	61,935
TOTAL INFORMATION OUTPUTS	19,311
Info as % of total budget	21.7
Info as % of total budget less transfers	31.2
Total Primary Information Outputs	9,274
SIC 27 Printing & publishing	183
SIC 481.2 Telephone & telegraph communications	1,284
SIC 60 Banking	55
SIC 61 Credit agencies	58
SIC 63, 4 Insurance carriers and brokers	284
SIC 6531 Real estate agents, brokers, managers	239
SIC 7311 Advertising agencies	2
SIC 7351 News syndicates	98
SIC 7361 Employment agencies	76
SIC 737 Data processing services	200
SIC 7391 Research & development	4,570
SIC 7392 Management & business consulting	99
SIC 8011 Physicians' offices (prorated)	73
SIC 811 Legal services	141
SIC 82 Education	1,590
SIC 8231 Library services	30
SIC 8931 Accounting and bookkeeping services	292
Total Secondary Info "Quasi-Industry" Outputs	5,469
Policy planning	133
Market information specialists	32
Gen'l administration & management	5,304
Of the civilian bureaucracy (net primary)	3,394
Of the military bureaucracy (net primary)	1,910
Total Special Government Functions	4,568
Regulation of industry	77
Intelligence information	4,011
Foreign intelligence information	3,525
Domestic intelligence information	486
Economic planning info and data	40
Diplomacy & foreign policy info	242
Info services provided gratis to private sector	198
Ratios	
Primary info as % of total info	48.0
Secondary info as % of total info	28.3
Special function info as % of total info	23.7
Total	100.0

($ Millions, Current)					
1961	1963	1966	1967	1969	1970
102,068	113,857	142,750	163,594	189,207	203,927
68,425	76,977	97,572	111,117	123,682	126,127
27,058	37,049	48,142	50,484	57,589	62,833
26.5	32.5	33.7	30.9	30.4	30.8
39.5	48.1	49.3	45.4	46.6	49.8
16,020	20,580	32,436	34,579	37,557	43,145
192	224	238	236	252	409
1,368	1,660	2,257	2,970	3,159	2,969
95	180	112	151	155	131
621	524	679	706	857	928
644	536	763	900	966	1,684
533	589	690	458	410	450
10	9	20	15	18	48
105	125	143	161	169	185
165	229	312	510	601	773
541	785	1,148	1,445	1,908	2,273
9,059	12,495	15,320	16,529	15,847	16,448
119	165	233	240	309	226
257	239	309	386	831	835
165	230	223	306	384	616
1,872	2,321	9,595	9,218	11,299	14,543
33	39	71	69	77	214
241	230	323	279	315	413
5,499	10,381	8,711	7,499	10,881	9,517
218	231	343	370	428	387
73	156	206	138	252	442
5,208	9,944	8,162	6,991	10,201	8,688
3,244	7,928	5,764	4,138	6,590	4,526
1,964	2,066	2,398	2,853	3,611	4,162
5,539	6,088	6,995	8,406	9,151	10,171
212	230	348	486	601	706
4,415	4,599	5,061	5,255	5,824	6,227
3,692	3,819	4,096	4,220	4,626	4,875
723	780	965	1,035	1,198	1,352
88	97	119	147	209	346
214	344	552	1,531	1,369	1,466
610	818	915	987	1,148	1,426
59.2	55.5	67.4	68.5	65.2	68.7
20.3	28.0	18.1	14.9	18.9	15.1
20.5	16.5	14.5	16.6	15.9	16.2
100.0	100.0	100.0	100.0	100.0	100.0

[a]All outputs are estimated from *The U. S. Budget*, the *Appendix*, and *Special Analyses*.

government attorneys who draft, revise, and enforce government regulations. This does not include the private attorneys who work on filling out forms, complying with Federal regulations and otherwise coordinating with the public bureaucrats.

Anecdotes are not research, but they can be fun. The Aircraft Owners and Pilots Association complained that the 1974 Code of Federal Regulations was 45,000 pages long and filled 7½ feet of shelf space. The 1975 edition, to no one's relief, was 60,000 pages long and filled 10 feet of shelves. Current Federal laws require that X-rays used to inspect the welded seams of nuclear power plants be kept for 40 years. But the X-ray film deteriorates in about seven years and becomes unreadable. And the State of Maryland refused to accept a $60,000 grant from HEW for a consumer education program because the cost of completing the necessary forms would chew up about $45,000.

Some anecdotes are more serious. It takes 21 separate documents to get one Indian into a nursing home. It recently took 800 pounds of paper to inform a tribal official of one new law. An oil company spent $17 million and used 475 full-time workers to file government reports other than taxes. From recent testimony following the oil embargo, it seems that the government still knows very little about the operations of oil firms. The Department of Agriculture has 989,000 cubic feet of records. Last year, USDA increased its paper store by 64,000 cubic feet—or 36,500 file drawers. The department spends $150 million a year just printing forms.

The Chairman of the Board of Eli Lilly and Company complained,[2] "...we spend more man-hours filling out government forms or reports than we do on research for cancer and heart disease combined."

The index of information submitted by Lilly to the EPA on one product was 153 pages long. Each entry in the 153 pages refers to a document from 3 to 3,000 pages in size.

The Paperwork Commission estimates that about $15 billion is spent by the Federal Government in processing paperwork. Small businesses spend about $18 billion completing required forms; the printing bills for federal forms is about $1 billion per year; another $1 billion is spent on directives accompanying the forms; and another $1.7 billion is spent to file and store forms. These figures do not even include the paperwork costs of large corporations and State and local governments.

Incidentally, the Paperwork Commission employs 140 information workers. The House hearings on the Federal paperwork burden produced a 7-volume 2,285 page treatise.

We draw no conclusions, since we have done no analysis. This is simply a description of how large the Federal bureaucracy has become, and it raises the question of how effective these resources are in planning, coordinating, and managing the economy. Is this staggering informational machine a drag on the economy? Do we need such a large bureaucracy to deal with the private sector? Are the bureaucracies a source of mischief, or a necessary check and balance on the private bureaucracies? These kinds of questions are not easily answerable, but should be asked again and again as both corporate and governmental abuses are exposed, and as we begin to form images of governance in an information economy.

Notes

[1] R. D. Wood, "Paperwork, Paperwork," in *Washington Post,* July 9, 1976.
[2] M. Mintz, "Drug Firms Oppose U. S. Price Audit," in *Washington Post,* July 9, 1976.

The Paperwork Problem*
Commission on Federal Paperwork

Government is often insensitive to the burdens it imposes on the public, including the economic and psychological costs as hidden taxes...

You can't understand government: what government wants, what government can do for citizens, or what government rules and regulations mean...

Government is unresponsive, uncoordinated, impersonal and distrustful; the bureaucracy is defensive and seems to be hiding behind paperwork...

Government is a conglomerate of multiple organizations, laws, rules and regulations causing conflicting, confusing, overlapping and duplicative requirements. Government has vague goals, objectives, standards and requirements which lead to defensive paperwork and red tape...

Government's programs are poorly designed and lead to unnecessary, complex and costly information requirements...

Government's information management is incredible—information demands are unjustifiable, there are few data processing standards, data are consistently duplicated, reporting forms are poorly designed, and universal reporting is used where sampling is possible...

Government does not adequately use modern information-handling techniques and technology...

Statements such as these express the mounting public irritation with excessive paperwork and red tape that has been relayed to the Commission. Witnesses at public hearings of this Commission held that the cost of paperwork to the public was steadily rising—rising beyond the capability of the respondent to comply and beyond the apparent value of the information to the Government. The paperwork costs include not only the salaries of personnel needed specifically to handle paperwork, but the costs associated with designing programs for computers, computer time, increased printing plant capacity, etc. It has been estimated that the costs of handling a form (personnel and machine time needed to fill it in, verify and process it) can amount from 20 to 50 times the cost of the paper and printing.[1]

To assess the enormity of Federal paperwork, the Commission reviewed

*In: *Information Resources Management*. Washington, D.C., U.S. Government Printing Office, 1977, pp. 1-18.

a sample of 5,002 "public use reports"[2] at the Office of Management and Budget (OMB). The sample represents not 5,000, but approximately 7,500 individual forms that must be filled out by the public. These 7,500 forms contain over 520,000 "data elements"—individual items such as name, age, assets, number of employees, and so on. The review also showed that about 15 percent of the forms required multiple submissions per year, or roughly 975,000 data elements per year rather than 520,000. Given the total number of respondents to these forms, the Government receives approximately 43 billion items of data per year through the forms approved by OMB.

OMB-approved reports represent less than 30 percent of the total Federal public use reports. Reports of the regulatory agencies—such as the Securities and Exchange Commission (SEC), Federal Trade Commission (FTC)—are cleared by the General Accounting Office (GAO). Several agencies, most notably the Internal Revenue Service (IRS), are not required to clear their forms. Conservatively estimated, the Federal Government collects approximately 130 billion individual items of data per year. When this figure is extended to include the many *ad hoc* reports required by Federal agencies, the amount may reach 300 billion data items per year. By any standard, Federal paperwork requires the reporting of an enormous amount of data.

Like taxes, compliance with government regulations and paperwork requirements is mandatory and expensive. But, because governments are not required to identify their own costs of collecting, storing or handling information, much less the costs borne by the public in preparing and furnishing this information, there is little realization of the financial consequences of this aspect of government. Most businesses as well, though aware of the paperwork burden, have never looked closely at the costs and staff hours involved in complying with Federal reporting requirements. One major company, Kaiser Industries, undertook to determine its paperwork costs in 1975. Annual Federal reporting and recordkeeping costs were originally estimated at $168,000. A year and a half later, after extensive examination, Kaiser believes the costs are $4,540,000. This revised figure still does not reflect either the "front-end" or reporting system development costs or the indirect costs. The Commission estimates that the total cost of Federal paperwork to the business community is $25–32 billion annually.[3]

No less difficult to obtain [are] the total paperwork costs in the Federal Government; they are hidden in agency overhead and program accounts. However, Commission research into the annual costs of paperwork and information within the Federal Government demonstrates that the figure is in excess of $50 billion.[4] These figures are estimates and do not include all costs, nor do they take into account State and local government reporting. Thus, the actual cost of government paperwork/information is substantially greater than these tentative estimates—perhaps as great as $100 billion or even higher.

Nature of the Paperwork Problem

The Commission found that the tendency of Government officials to look upon information as a "free good" is an important cause of excessive paperwork. Further, the mismanagement of information resources requires that a distinction be drawn between "good" and "bad" paperwork. In the past, almost all Government paperwork and information was considered "good," or at least "harmless." This is not the case. There is, indeed, much paperwork which is simple, effective and valuable as a source of information. But there is also another class of paperwork which stifles communication between Government and the people, misleads the decisionmaker, clogs information channels and suffocates officials. The Commission realizes that many of the causes of paperwork are immutable, but in distinguishing between these two classes of paperwork in its various studies and reports, it has suggested ways of eliminating much of the "bad" paperwork.

In addressing the broad causes of paperwork and red tape the Commission directed its efforts to a review of some of the factors precipitating these causes:

- Growth of government;
- Overlapping governmental programs;
- Proliferation and fragmentation of information and program requirements, the knowledge explosion;
- Vague goals and objectives;
- The application of information technology capable of handling massive quantities of data; and
- The rising costs of data and information-handling equipment, software, and personnel who run this equipment.

Growth of Government. Government at each level has experienced explosive growth over the past thirty years. This growth can be measured by various yardsticks—programs, budgets, employees, services, etc. The demand for government services and the resulting legislation have required governments to create and operate increasing numbers of programs. Paperwork is a central and indispensable element of these programs which provide services to citizens and serve national needs. This growth, when coupled with the availability and application of modern information-processing techniques and tools, has fostered the demand for more and more information and hence excessive paperwork and red tape.

To appreciate fully the growth in Federal programs, one has only to look at the history of the Federal domestic assistance programs. In 1950, the Federal Government had 71 grant programs totaling $2 billion. By 1975 there were approximately 1100 programs listed in the *Catalog of Federal Domestic Assistance,* totaling $55 billion in Federal funds. All of these grant programs require paperwork—applications, quarterly reports, final reports and audit reports.

The explosive growth in domestic assistance has also produced overlapping responsibilities which cut across different Federal agencies, requiring differing eligibility criteria, administrative machinery, and reporting requirements. Extreme examples of this can be found in the equal employment opportunity programs and the application of the National Environmental Policy Act on various Federal agencies.[5] These two programs are not centrally directed; instead, each Federal agency must develop its own regulations. There are no standardized procedures, forms or guidelines, and therefore considerable overlap and duplication exists.

Domestic assistance programs are operated with little consideration for potential interrelations or a coordinated, planned approach to overall societal needs, let alone information needs. Among the recurring criticisms directed to the mushrooming Federal assistance programs are the following:

- The myriad of programs, developed piecemeal, are inconsistent in policy and administration, duplicative and in conflict with each other.

- They were developed without consideration of the impact on the relationship to State, regional and local needs, programs and plans and had no means of intergovernmental coordination.

- They gave rise to Federal, State and local functional bureaucracies beyond the control of the executive and legislative bodies.[6]

Some contend that public demand for additional Government services follows the emergence of new knowledge which documents the existence of a need. In short, growth of government programs is traceable in part to a sharpened perception of how complicated the "real" world actually is, not just the "demand for more services."

Overlapping Governmental Programs. Dramatic growth contributes to government "layering," the proliferation and diffusion of laws, rules, regulations, paperwork and information systems including reporting, recordkeeping and delivery systems. Each level of government—Federal, State, regional, local—has in some manner the ability to legislate, regulate, and enforce. Often, each level of government legislates, regulates, or enforces in the same field. There is very little coordination of their views. Thus the paperwork associated with their individual laws and rules has different emphases, different requirements, and different time frames. The ultimate burden falls on the public which must report separately and differently to each level of government.

Consumer credit is a good example of the overlapping and multiplicity of rules and procedures. Prior to 1968, legislation was enacted by the various States rather than the Federal Government. Most States had laws setting ceilings on the price of loans to consumers. To this basic legislation, most States have added a multiple layering of special conditions and rules. In 1968, the Federal Government entered the field with the Federal Consumer Credit Protection (Truth in Lending) Act. Since 1968, there have been seven amendments and three separate Federal disclosure statutes involving credit terms. These statutes and amendments led to Federal regulations, interpretations and court decisions. The end result is that State and Federal laws do not fit well together. Instead they produce substantial conflicts and difficulties. The entire consumer credit regulation framework is complex and difficult to understand, administer, and comply with. There are many instances where State law is pre-empted by Federal law and examples where State law is exempted from Federal law. Nor are these intricacies of the State-Federal relationship the only source of complexity. The economic practices and customs of every facet of American society are more varied and different than any law or regulation can anticipate. A rule designed to meet one need often produces unexpected consequences in another situation. The result is perfecting amendments and administrative regulations, designed to reduce inequities, and invariably requiring extensive reporting and paperwork to permit precise application of the "tailor-made" legal provisions. [7]

Still another example of overlapping and multiplicity of rules and procedures is shown in Table 1. Each State has its own Unemployment Insurance Laws with wide variations in benefits and coverage, yet all States must work within the framework of the Federal Unemployment Tax Act which is constantly being altered through interpretation and legislation.

Proliferation and Fragmentation of Data. Welfare programs in the United States are generally considered to have been an outgrowth of the Social

Table 1 Example of Overlapping and Multiplicity of Rules and Procedures

U S DEPARTMENT OF LABOR
1976

EMPLOYMENT AND TRAINING ADMINISTRATION
Unemployment Insurance Service

Significant Provisions of State Unemployment Insurance Laws, January 3, 1977

PREPARED FOR READY REFERENCE. CONSULT THE STATE LAW AND STATE EMPLOYMENT SECURITY AGENCY FOR AUTHORITATIVE INFORMATION

State	Qualifying wage or employment (number x wba or as indicated)[1]	Waiting week[2]	Computation of wba (fraction of hqw or as indicated)[1,3]	Wba for total unemployment[4]		Earnings disregarded[5]	Duration in 52-week period				Size of firm (1 worker in specified time and/ or size of payroll)[16]	1976 Tax rates (percent of wages)[9]	
							Proportion of base-period wages[6]	Benefit weeks for total un-employment[7]					
				Min.	Max.			Min[8]	Max.			Min.	Max.
Ala.	1-1/2 x hqw; not less than $522	0	1/26	$15	$90	$6	1/3	11+	26		20 weeks	[9]0.5	[9]4.0
Alaska	$750; $100 outside HQ	1	2.3-1.1% of annual wages, + $10 per dep. up to $30	18-23	90-120	Greater of $10 or 1/2 basic wba	[c]34-31%	14	28		Any time	[9]2.3	[9]4.8
Ariz.	1-1/2 x hqw; $375 in HQ	1	1/25	15	85	$15	1/3	12+	26		20 weeks	0.1	2.9
Ark.	30; wages in 2 quarters	1	1/26 up to 66-2/3% of State aww	15	100	2/5	1/3	10	26		10 days	0.5	4.4
Calif.	$750	1	1/24-1/31	30	104	$18	1/2	[7]12+-15	[7]26		Over $100 in any quarter	[9]1.4	[9]4.9
Colo.	30	1	60% of 1/13 of claimant's hqw up to 60% of State aww	25	116	1/4 wba	1/3	7+-10	26		20 weeks	0	3.6
Conn.	40	0	1/26, up to 60% of State aww + $5 per dep. up to 1/2 wba	15-20	116-174	1/3 wages	3/4	[7]26	[7]26		20 weeks	[9]1.6	[9]4.5
Del.	36	0	1/26, up to 60% of State aww 14/	20	125	Greater of $10 or 30% of wba	1/2	17	26		20 weeks	1.6	4.5
D.C.	1-1/2 x hqw; not less than $450; $100 in 1 quarter	1	1/23 up to 66-2/3% of State aww + $1 per dep. up to $3	13-14	[4]148	2/5 wba	1/2	17+	34		Any time	2.7	2.7
Fla.	20 weeks employment at average of $20 or more	1	1/2 claim-ant's aww	10	82	$5	1/2 weeks employment	10	26		20 weeks	0.7	4.5
Ga.	1-1/2 x hqw	2,	1/25+$1.00	27	90	$8	1/4	9	26		20 weeks	[9]0.05	[9]4.03
Hawaii	30; 14 weeks employment	[10]1	1/25 up to 66-2/3% of State aww	5	120	2	Uniform	[7]26	[7]26		Any time[17]	[9]3.0	[9]3.0

Security Act of 1935. Since then approximately 168 federally supported income security programs have been enacted to assist the poor. Thus a destitute person must apply separately for Supplemental Security Income, Food Stamps, Medicaid, public housing, Aid to Families with Dependent Children, etc. Each program in turn requires a detailed application which produces proliferation and fragmentation of data.[8]

To facilitate the collection of much needed information, laws generally contain language such as:

The Secretary is directed to collect, evaluate, publish and disseminate information ...(P.L. 90-445 as amended)

The administrator shall collect, assemble, evaluate, publish and disseminate information...(P.L. 93-275 as amended)

The administrator shall collect, assemble, evaluate and analyze...information by categorical groupings...of sufficient comprehensiveness and particularity to permit fully informed monitoring and policy guidance...(P.L. 93-275 as amended)

The administrator is authorized...to collect, evaluate, publish and disseminate statistics and other information...in the several States. (P.L. 90-351 as amended)

Such language, in effect, authorizes the responsible agency to collect not only "needed" information (which, incidentally, is not usually defined in the statute) but also any other information that may be of use.

To be sure, Government decisionmakers and agencies must have information to be able to make decisions, solve problems, and account for the expenditure of funds. But the need for information to make all of the decisions for all of the Federal laws, programs, regulations, rules, procedures and forms, has left us with a labyrinth of conflicting, confusing, overlapping and duplicative information requirements. As one source said:

There can be no question to a major extent, industry's skyrocketing paperwork costs can be attributed to the plethora of new regulatory measures enacted by Congress during the past several years. Increased regulation must necessarily result in added paperwork. While many of these new laws have economic objectives, there has sometimes been a tendency to extend the web of Federal controls in a shotgun fashion or to require reams of paperwork in an attempt to make compliance self executing.[9]

Of course,...just as not all paperwork is "bad," so not all duplication is "bad." But many claims of duplication are not valid; the information requested by different agencies is, indeed, not quite the same, and the differences may be critical from the standpoint of the requesting agencies. Where there is duplication, the response cost may be very small relative to the unique new information which is needed. Finally, elaborate and complicated coordinating mechanisms may be less cost effective than permitting agencies broad flexibility to judge what data they believe are appropriate. After taking all these factors into account, the Commission in this and in other reports offers specific recommendations for reducing overlap and duplication.

Vague Goals and Objectives. Government's goals, objectives, standards and requirements are, on occasion, so broad that they become vague. Examples of this might be the "elimination of slums," "reduction of crime" or "training the unemployed and underemployed." This fact is not cited to suggest that Congress become more specific in its legislation and thereby constrain management initiative, but rather to point out the problems associated with vagueness. . . . Because of this vagueness of goals and objectives, plus the easy availability of computers to handle massive amounts of data, there is the temptation on the part of the Government to collect all possible data "just in case" they might be needed at a congressional authorization, appropriation or oversight hearing. There is little distinction made between "good" and "bad" data, or between reusable data and one-time data. Scant effort is made to determine if the same data already exist in another agency. There is a glut of irrelevant, obsolete and inaccurate data produced by the computer which is clogging communication channels.[10]

Vague goals and objectives also lead to defensive bureaucracy, that is, a great deal of data gathering serves little purpose except to allow the gathering agency to answer questions from congressional or executive branch overseers. An agency that cannot produce "the facts" in budget hearings in response to a question, however trivial, is treated as if it is performing badly. It is analogous to the defensive practice of medicine that leads doctors to order many expensive tests and to prescribe unnecessary medications to avoid possible charges of malpractice. In government, a tremendous premium is placed on factual information that can be brought quickly to hand. Agencies gather data to answer every conceivable question, and they construct management information systems to store and recall them. This kind of defensive data-gathering is responsible for a great deal of the response burden placed on the private sector. It hardly seems to be in the national interest to impose a heavy reporting burden on the private sector solely for the protection of government bureaucrats, but such behavior is inherent in government at all levels and in all branches, and must be recognized as a basic fact to be dealt with in judging efficiency.[11]

Application of Information Technology. As one authority put it, "until fairly recently paper was the primary medium of all organizational information flows, thus, paperwork management was synonymous with information management. By-and-large, information flowed through the organization on paper—it was compiled on paper, manipulated on paper, stored and re-trieved on paper, and disposed of and destroyed on paper. It was reasonable to assume that controlling the medium of information flow through forms, records, and microfilm management, was the same as controlling the flow of information itself."[12]

The reality of yesterday is no longer. Where information once flowed primarily on paper it now flows on electrons. Over the past twenty years, ad-vancements in information-handling technology management...have sub-stantially increased the Government's ability to collect and process data into information products and services. From the basic computer we have wit-nessed the evolution of a whole family of information machines, large and small, powerful and flexible. Through its efficiencies this technology has of-fered a steady decrease in the unit cost of handling data; more data can be handled at less cost per unit than was possible twenty years ago.

This, however, fosters a deceptive view of the economy of computers, because the total costs associated with computers and data handling have steadily increased. By using the economy-of-scale arguments, government has tended to ignore the economy of management. If the unit of measure of effectiveness of a printing plant is the total number of units produced, then the longer the run, the lower the unit cost. So long as the unit cost of storing is lower than the unit cost of taking a document out of the storage system, the record will be retained.

Because overhead is generally more expensive than direct labor costs, volume is increased so that the unit cost is decreased by distributing overhead across the units replicated. There is little incentive to reduce the amount of data handled. Rather there are strong incentives to collect more and more data, not less.

Given the incentive to gather, store and recall data, the methods used can be more or less efficient. Budget controls being what they are, particu-larly controls that limit personnel, the natural tendency of agencies is to substitute equipment for people. Government agencies have bought inor-dinate numbers of computers that generally are inadequately used because of poor staffing and often are kept too long.

The Commission applauds President Carter's "New Look At Federal ADP," a major Reorganization Project launched June 7, 1977. But the Com-mission is concerned that the objectives of this important study may be, once again, too heavily slanted to "efficiency" considerations, instead of looking at the fundamental uses to which the computer is put. In the Commission's view, "the efficient and economic use of data processing resources" must begin with the implicit assumption that information processed on the computer, data needs and uses, must be subject to the most rigorous kind of zero-based justification. It cannot be assumed that information needs and uses are a "given."

In short, the paperwork management programs of the past are unable to control the data explosion engendered by the computer. A simple bureaucratic reorganization of traditional records and paperwork management disciplines to meet the challenges of the information revolution would simply be overwhelmed in attempting to control the mass of complexity presented by modern computer/telecommunications technologies.

Computers and their associated technologies are at once the most important, the most expensive and potentially the most productive information-handling tool in modern society. It has been estimated that, in the private sector, data processing and its associated costs amount to an estimated expenditure of $26 billion per year.[13] It has been estimated that approximately 4 percent of the entire Federal budget, or $15 billion, is the current annual Government expenditure for its 9,500 computers and associated special purpose equipment.[14]

Rising Costs of Data and Information. Thus far in the discussion of the causes for the growth in Government paperwork, we have seen inferences to the cost associated with that paperwork and even an estimated total cost. These costs represent only the tip of the iceberg. The total cost of information-handling cannot easily be ascertained because it is hidden and buried in both overhead and program accounts in Government and ignored for the most part with respect to the public.

Over the last decade Congress and the President have been increasingly conscious of the rising costs associated with constructing new Federal and agency records centers, the capital investment and the huge operating budgets required for the development and operation of computerized information systems[15] and data banks, and the never-ending purchase of filing cabinets. Government and the public are beginning to realize that information is not a "free good." (If there are lingering doubts, just dial 411.)

Information is a valuable national resource no less essential to the survival of government, industry and the individual citizen than are human, material or natural resources. Information is a resource that is in need of conservation, recycling, and protection. In short, it is a resource that must be managed. The Commission has found that treatment of information as a free good by government is a root cause of excessive paperwork and red tape. As long as public officials are not held accountable for proper management of information, they are able to impose paperwork and information burdens on the populace indiscriminately and with fiscal impunity.

As a resource, data and information can and must be managed just as we manage human, physical, and financial resources. Data and information must be subject to the same budgetary, managerial, and audit disciplines as any other resource. To do this there must be both a theoretical and a practical policy/operational framework within which governments acquire, enhance, exploit, conserve, and dispose of their information resources.

Information Resources Management

The Commission recognizes that Government, along with business and everyone else, needs "good paperwork" to design and operate its programs effectively. A principal purpose of the Commission therefore has been to distinguish good paperwork from bad and to make recommendations for eliminating the latter. The Commission found that the need for reform goes beyond individual agencies, individual forms, and individual rules and regulations. Commission studies of paperwork problems have demonstrated that, not only are specific rules, forms and procedures not working properly, but also that the organizational structures, management policies and operating systems for delivering citizen services and benefits are oftentimes obsolete, weak, or misdirected in emphasis and priority. These flaws and deficiencies are the root causes of excessive paperwork and red tape. Thus there was a need for the Commission to go beyond individual program and agency studies, to recommend reforms that could be applied across Government.

In its earlier reports, the Commission has made a number of specific recommendations to strengthen agency management and control machinery, including recommendations to:

- simplify Federal organization and administrative procedures;
- design specific programs and regulations to minimize paperwork while maximizing effectiveness;
- make government understandable and responsive;
- provide consultation with respondents and other interested parties, such as public interest groups, during the drafting of legislation and regulations and during the design and evaluation of programs;
- eliminate duplication and unnecessary differences;
- make complete reviews of information requests using expertise of statisticians, records managers, ADP and other information specialists;

- permit appropriate sharing and limit inappropriate collection; and
- fix accountability for the paperwork burden on the Congress, the President and agency heads.

This report of the Information Resources Management study focused on one of these underlying flaws in government's control machinery which is at once pervasive, long standing, and difficult to reform: weaknesses in the management of reporting and recordkeeping requirements and in the development and operation of information systems. Government can produce relevant or irrelevant information in small or large quantities. Because the production processes can produce information relatively easily, whether or not it is demanded or needed, agencies may have only a limited perception of what information it collects and produces, how it is used, and what its value is for their members, managers or clientele.

In the past, the typical response to problems of this kind was to institute paperwork or records management programs. These were directed at dealing with the physical manifestations of the information proliferation problem and not the content of the paperwork or records. Generally, such programs have sought to simplify and consolidate forms and records and to reduce the total amount of paper and files circulating throughout the organization's message streams. But the problem of information overload in an agency is not just a "how to" problem, it also involves "what" and "why" problems. That is, the questions that are raised by the concern with information collection, use and value touch not only the procedural problems of how information can be more efficiently collected, stored, processed and disseminated, but also the substantive problems of why information is collected and used the way it is, what value it has in the success of an organization's programs and missions.

Although the term "paperwork management" has been around a long time and is readily understood in a general sense by almost everyone, the Commission found that the term *information resources management* more accurately describes what should be the main target of control machinery. That is, the target should be on *information requirements planning, controlling, accounting and budgeting,* not simply the *physical paperwork* such as the forms and reports, which, after all, are just the carriers of information. Paperwork is the vehicle that moves data and information[16] from sender to receiver.

Not all information is transmitted by means of paperwork, however. Indeed, the document is losing ground to electronic and other advanced information-handling technologies. More and more information is being transmitted by wire, communication satellites, radio, computers, microfilm readers and printers, word processing machines and many other related technologies which do not involve paper at all. In short, if the Commission had limited the scope of its investigative studies to traditional "hard copy" paperwork, it would have overlooked both paperwork bottlenecks that do not involve paper at all and the very great potential of modern, automated information-handling technologies and approaches for eliminating "hard copy" paper-work problems.

It was with these considerations in mind that the Commission undertook this study and used the more descriptive title, *information resources management.* It is important to make the distinction between paperwork and information in certain contexts, but generally speaking, throughout this report "paperwork management" as Congress and the public generally understand those terms can be roughly equated to *information resources management.*

The Role of Information Resources Management

A substantial amount of Federal paperwork can be laid at the door of unplanned, uncoordinated and unevaluated requirements. Information, and consequently paperwork, is easily abused because officials can collect, hoard and proliferate it with impunity as costs are hidden in program and overhead accounts. The biggest cost of all, the direct cost to the citizen-respondents, does not even show up in the accounts.

Thus the real culprit of the paperwork burden is mismanagement of information resources. Government has tended to regard information as a relatively free and limitless commodity, like air and sunshine, simply ours for the asking. We must realize, where we have not already done so, that this is not the case. Information is a vital resource to the public and private enterprise alike. Moreover, it is a resource in limited supply, often costly to locate, extract and refine. It exists in a variety of raw forms (data), and may or may not be cost-efficient to acquire and deliver. Like its mineral resource counterparts, it is sometimes not as valuable as we may think.

Management in industry or government requires the careful consideration and selection of the best mix of resources and tools from the wide array usually available. For example, when a program manager decides to employ a questionnaire in lieu of other methods to collect information, he is making a *resource* decision. The decision to employ manual, paperwork-intensive methods—involving substantial recordkeeping and reporting requirements rather than computer-intensive methods—is not unlike the decision to use steel rather than poured concrete.

Historically, when a resource is identified, a management function has been established to deal with the problem. Officials in charge of management function planned, programmed, budgeted, accounted for, audited and evaluated the resource according to prescribed principles and practices. That set of principles and practices (a body of doctrine) is called *resource management.* For data and information resources, no central, cohesive body of doctrine exists today, there is not even good information, advice or guidance to offer top management. . . .

Resource Allocation Management

The central question in resource allocation is choice among alternatives. In the case of Government, for example, actions generate benefits and incur costs. The General Accounting Office has said

These benefits and costs should be broadly defined to include both social and private aspects. The key elements in choice among resources are:

government objectives are achieved by developing, adopting, and implementing policies and by creating and operating programs, all of which consume or transfer resources—tangible and intangible.

there are many public needs. These needs are large and constantly changing. Demands for resources are much greater than the resources available.

decision-makers must choose among competing objectives and among the alternative programs and policies capable of meeting the choices of the chosen objectives at desired and affordable levels of achievements. [17]

It should be clear that the application of information resources management can go a long way toward rectifying the causes of excessive paperwork and red tape. But information resources management must be applied across government, not in one or two agencies alone, and not solely in the Executive branch. For the application of information resources management, there must be established an Information Resources Management function incorporating and integrating many disparate but related information activities, such as:

- paperwork management programs, including correspondence, forms, directives and related programs;
- reports control programs, including public-use, inter-agency and internal programs, and the report inventories therein;

- statistical programs and statistical data series of both the major statistical agencies and other agencies;
- records programs and records depositories, and the files and records therein;
- computers, computerized data banks and automated information systems, including storage and retrieval systems;
- libraries, information centers, scientific and technical information systems and technical data depositories and documentation centers;
- printing and reprographic programs;
- word processing equipment and centers;
- microform programs; and
- other information-related activities.[18]

It needs to be emphasized that the physical consolidation of these functions is *not* what is contemplated in bringing these activities together under a single management coordination umbrella. In some organizations this may make sense; in others, perhaps not. But common sense tells us that we should first look at what is being done now, why it is being done, and who is doing it. For example, an agency's public-use reporting program, its telecommunications activities, and its computer center operations are indeed separate activities, but with one shared purpose: to collect, organize, store, and disseminate information.

Not only must we integrate the functions of the many "information worlds," we must begin to integrate the many information resources available within the Federal Government with the management of other resources so that, in our decisions about how to run a program, we select the best mix of resources to do the job. If we are to manage information as a resource we must first understand the resource, its role, its uses, its limitations, its opportunities and its functions within a program. . . .The problems are obvious but codifying them is difficult. There is no single cause of paperwork, there is a complex of factors, including the structure of government itself which contributes to burdens of paperwork and red tape.

With this in mind the Commission focused its attention on three problems within government today which tend to proliferate paperwork and red tape:

- There is no accountability in Government for the costs either in dollars or burden, to the Government or the public, of paperwork/information;

- Government fails to treat information as the valuable resource it is and thus does not manage it as it should;

- The responsibility for managing or controlling paperwork is fragmented not only within agencies but within the Government....

Information resource management will not only serve to control the proliferation of "bad" paperwork, but will add to the overall quality of program design. The addition of information resource management to the tool kit of general managers who are responsible for the effective use of *all* resources not only presents management with a variety of deployment choices, but also serves to make government more effective, efficient and responsive to the needs of the Nation and citizens....

Information resources management cannot be implemented immediately. It will take time and extensive cooperation at all levels of government. But if the Federal Government is to gain some measure of control over the factors that precipitate paperwork and red tape—growth, proliferation and fragmentation of data and information, the rising costs of data and information, etc.—information resources management must be started now. As this study shows, we have tinkered with the system of paperwork management for almost two hundred years and still the problem remains. It is time to view the problems of paperwork and red tape, not as documents to be managed, but rather as information content to be treated as a valuable resource. By applying the principles of management to this valuable national resource we not only get at the root cause of paperwork and red tape, but cause a rippling effect in the application throughout Government: the design of programs is improved; government becomes more sensitive to the burdens it imposes on the public, becomes more understandable, and develops clearer goals and objectives. In the end, government improves the delivery of services to people as well as fulfills its other functions of regulation, defense, enforcement and revenue collection more effectively.

Information resource management is not the only solution to insensitive, complex and unresponsive government. It can, however, make a significant impact in reducing the economic burdens of paperwork on the public by reducing duplication, clearly justifying information needs, improving reporting forms and collection processes, and effectively and efficiently utilizing modern information-handling techniques and technologies.

The full impact of Information Resources Management will be realized when it is put into place as a part of the Commission's broader concept of "service management." There, once combined with the additional dimensions of more intensive public participation in governmental processes, a more complete cost accounting of the proposed impacts of government's actions to all parties concerned, and the assurance that information, once collected serves the legitimate purposes for which it is intended, Information Resources Management will have the greatest opportunity to fulfill its promise.

Notes

[1]Gottheimer, Debra, "Options in Forms Design," *Administrative Management Magazine,* April 1977, p. 3.

[2]The term is unfortunate. It does *not* mean reports used by the public, but rather Government-imposed reports *on* the public.

[3]Commission on Federal Paperwork, staff report on *Federal Paperwork Impact on Small and Large Business* (Washington, D.C.) July 1977.

[4]Commission on Federal Paperwork, staff report on *Our Shadow Government: The Hidden Cost of Paperwork and Red Tape* (Washington, D.C.) August 1977.

[5]See CFP reports on Environmental Impact Statements (February 1977) and Equal Employment Opportunity (April 1977).

[6]GAO report, "Fundamental Changes Are Needed in Federal Assistance to State and Local Governments," August 19, 1975.

[7]Statement by Philip C. Jackson before Consumer Affairs Subcommittee February 9, 1977, *Federal Reserve Bulletin,* February 1977.

[8]CFP Report on the Federal Paperwork Burden in Welfare, May 1977.

[9]Letter from David C. Kuhn, Air Products and Chemicals Inc., February 8, 1977.

[10]Interview with Donald Scantlebury, Director, Financial and General Management Studies Division, GAO, January 19, 1977.

[11]Letter from Paul Feldman, Director, Public Research Institute, July 14, 1975.

[12]Snyder, David P., "Information Systems—Creating a New Discipline to Manage the Information Revolution," *Records Management Journal,* Spring 1973.

[13]Strassman, Paul A., "Managing the Costs of Information," *Harvard Business Review,* September 1976.

[14]House Report No. 94-1746.

[15]GAO Report FGMSD 77-14, "Problems Found With Government Acquisition and Use of Computers from Nov. 1965–Dec. 1976," March 1, 1977.

[16]The reader should note that throughout this study the terms "data" and "information" have been used more or less interchangeably. Of course, technically, there is an important distinction between them, but the need for a general synonym for the term "information" makes the interchangeable use of the two words almost unavoidable. Therefore, where the word "data" is used, unless the context explicitly makes it clear otherwise, the broader connotation of "information" should be inferred.

[17]GAO Report, "Evaluation and Analysis to Support Decision Making," PAD 76-9, September 1976.

[18]See seminal works of Adrian McDonough, Wharton School, University of Pennsylvania, for a thorough review of the entire field.

Needed: A New Doctrine for Information Resources Management
Forest W. Horton, Jr.

Framework

The time has come to formalize the treatment of information and deal with data as a manageable and budgetable resource, in the same way that organizations must deal with human, physical, financial, and natural resources. Dealing with the information explosion piecemeal simply is not working. Information and data costs are increasing, and individuals and organizations are not getting the information they need. Instead, they are being inundated with data to the point where the data cease to be information. Sophisticated information-handling technologies, including data base management approaches, are leading individuals and organizations into a quagmire of information overload.

As society approaches the leading edge of the minicomputer revolution, employees on the lowest rungs of the organization ladder defend and justify their need for newer, bigger, and more expensive information-handling hardware and software on the grounds that the unit cost of processing information is continually dropping. This defense is true whether it refers to hard-copy records and filing equipment, microform technology, digital equipment, optical scanning approaches, or the more exotic and advanced holographic and related technologies. Therefore, the capacity already exists to proliferate, miniaturize, and splinter data collection, planning, management, and control, down to the level of individual employees in an organization.

How can organizations, whether in government, private enterprise, academia, or elsewhere, control ever-increasing information costs in the face of these pressures?

1. The head of the printing and reproduction plant tells his superiors that his performance should be judged on the total number of units printed—the longer the print run, the lower the cost per unit.

2. The administrative records officer tells his boss that in storing the organization's records, he should be judged on how cheaply and in how small a space the records can be stored; as long as the unit cost of storing records is

lower than the unit cost of backing the record out of the system, the record should be retained.

3. The files chief tells his director that the primary performance-evaluation criterion that should be applied to operating the file room is how often a document is referred to. If a document is referred to less than once a month, for example, it should be considered for transfer to a records depository; if it is referred to more than once, it should be retained.

4. The small-jobs duplication department manager advises his superior that overhead costs are generally higher than direct-labor costs; therefore, if volume is increased, the unit cost is reduced by distributing overhead across the total number of units replicated.

Similar situations occur in the computer room, the library, the mail room, and elsewhere.

The information explosion can be dramatized and illustrated in many different ways. In addition to the specious use of economy-of-scale arguments in the preceding examples, another favorite practice is to consider the following chain of events. A technical report comes into the organization's mailroom. If only one copy arrives, it is automatically replicated. One of the copies goes to the library. The librarian decides that extra copies are needed (not knowing how many copies were received initially or who got them), so he orders them for the bookshelves. Another copy of the same report goes to an official. He decides that several chapters will interest an immediate superior, so the report is sent to a printing plant, where master plates are made and additional copies reproduced. Then, an analyst sees the report and decides that some data may interest various groups, so some data are keypunched, digitalized, and then sent to the computer department, where they are entered into the organization's data banks. At the same time, the micrographics department notices that the report is bulky, so someone decides that it should be microfilmed and entered into the micrographic holdings.

Then an addenum to the report comes in, and the cycle is repeated. By this time, however, some of the same persons who read and processed the original report have left the organization or have been reassigned to other departments. New employees read the addendum; their decisions do not take into account decisions already made. Therefore, the data are inevitably splintered, fragmented, compartmentalized, and dispersed to the point that problems of incompatibility, overlapping, duplication, and inconsistency are almost unavoidable because no single person or unit can locate, identify, correlate, and organize the original data. Some redundancy may be necessary for expediency. But is all of it?

Information, No Longer a Free Good

The organization can no longer afford to treat data and information as free goods. The reader, on faith, does not have to accept this assertion; a central purpose of this section is to substantiate that assertion.

At one time, everyone believed that clean air was a free good to which all were entitled. But pollution, and the environmental protection movement, changed that. What has happened to cause information, like clean air and clean water, to become a valued commodity? Some possible factors will be reviewed.

The need for data and information by officers in private enterprise, at all levels of management and control, has exploded:

1. Company products and services have increased in number and variety; they are increasingly difficult to design, develop, advertise, market, manufacture, and sell.

2. Company markets also have increased in number and variety; they, too, have become stratified, geographically dispersed (sometimes multinationally), and more critical in their discrimination of products as movements, such as the consumer protection movement, catch hold.

3. Company organization charts reflect an increasing trend toward staff specialization as markets become more complicated and products become more complex to produce and market. Each unit requires employees and has its own unique perspectives and interests; employee rolls and organization charts "feed" on data.

4. Stockholders and directors are demanding greater accountability for the efficient and effective performance of company officials. Accountability demands, in part, information on the record to substantiate what actions and decisions were taken and why, when, and where.

5. Social and economic problems faced by the company are increasingly complex and pervasive as the mood of social accountability continues to grow. Equal employment opportunity programs; health, safety, and security regulations; and licensing and regulatory rules and regulations all require data and information.

The same situation is occurring at all levels of government. The problems faced by government are increasingly complex, technical, and specialized. Since 1887, with the Cockrell Committee, which dealt with the high cost of copying data in government, a succession of committees, commissions, boards, and legislation has tried to deal with the information explosion. But the central focus of these efforts has been on physical paperwork instead of the data content of reports, records, forms, and regulations; that is, their main target appears to have been streamlining, simplifying, and mechanizing paperwork rather than dealing with fundamental questions of whether the data collected through the paperwork were used, were useful, contributed to the achievement of positive results, and so forth.

Traditional Approaches to Information Management

Congress authorized creation of the Commission on Federal Paperwork by enactment of P.L. 93-556 on December 27, 1974. In this legislation, Congress said:

The Congress hereby finds that Federal information reporting requirements have placed an unprecedented paperwork burden upon private citizens, recipients of Federal assistance, businesses, governmental contractors, and State and local governments. The Congress hereby affirms that it is the policy of the Federal Government to minimize the information reporting burden, consistent with its needs for information to set policy and operate its lawful programs. The Congress hereby determines that a renewed effort is required to assure that this policy is fully implemented and that it is necessary to reexamine the policies and procedures of the Federal Government which have an impact on the paperwork burden for the purpose of ascertaining what changes are necessary and desirable in its information policies and practices.

In reviewing earlier efforts to deal with the paperwork and information burden, the commission found that undue reliance had been placed on forms clearance as a primary control mechanism. The central forms clearance machinery in the Federal Government was established pursuant to the Federal Reports Act of 1942, which is the primary statute in this area. That act was passed during World War II, when new government agencies were proliferating, each tending to generate new reporting requirements on businesses and the public. Although the act may have been adequate to deal with the war and post-World War II environment, it has long since outlived its usefulness in terms of the expectation that it continue to serve as the central control machinery. This author contends that the act is no longer useful because its focus is on physical paperwork—the public-use report form—rather than on information and information management. Traditionally, government has tended to focus its attention on physical paperwork, rather than on substantive data content (e.g., the attempt by former President Ford to control paperwork before he left office).

President Ford tried, with little success, to reduce the impact of government information requirements on the public. In spring 1976, for example, with great fanfare, he announced his government-wide program to reduce, by 10 percent by June 30, 1976, the total number of government forms at the federal level. He did, indeed, succeed in eliminating 14 percent of the reports by that date. But his program had little impact on reducing the public's total monetary burden in preparing these reports. During the brief time between the announcement of his program and the target completion date, the actual burden on the public, in terms of manhours and cost, increased 4 percent! That increase was primarily the result of adding only two new forms. But these forms were more than enough to offset the collective reduction in all the forms that were eliminated.

President Ford's experience was not atypical—quite the contrary. Research completed by the Commission on Federal Paperwork indicated that the results were representative of what might be called the "quota limit" approach to management and control of federal information requirements affecting the public. The commission concluded, and this author concurs, that traditional approaches to controlling and managing data and information are obsolete. Such attempts may offer temporary savings and relief, but they rarely, if ever, result in lasting and permanent control. Why? Because conventional approaches to managing data and information fail to develop the tools to control information within a formal resource management framework; that is, to manage paperwork and, more important, the data content of that paperwork, an approach must be devised that will help in identifying and measuring the full and true costs of data and information at each stage of the information life cycle—requirements determination, collecting, processing, storage, use, and disposition. The traditional approach is a classic case of too little, too late. By the time a report form is developed, requirements are already established and it is almost impossible to revise or scale down the requirement.

A Resource Management Approach

How does the resource management approach work? The demand for data and information, like the demand for labor, supplies, or office and plant space—all of which are other resources required by management—tends to exceed the supply. Economists say that when this situation occurs, it is usually necessary to assign a price to bring buyers and sellers together in the marketplace. It is comparatively easy for a company to put a price on its needs for raw materials or for physical plant and office space. It is more difficult to price human resources, particularly an organization's professional, technical, and managerial staff. It is even harder for an organization to price data and information, because both the usefulness and value of data are difficult to define and measure objectively. Data's utility, as the economist is wont to say, is much more subjective than that of any other resource. Finally, while *data* might be viewed as a commodity, asset, or resource, *information* is derived from the qualitative use of data and involves value judgments.

Therefore, it is understandable why information has not been regarded as a commodity. To do so would pose both a philosophical and a pragmatic dilemma. If we are to deal successfully with information as a resource, we must reconcile two different ways of viewing information: on the one hand, as abstract concepts or ideas and, on the other, as physical commodities (such as reports, records, forms and computer printouts). A few information scientists and others have attempted that task, but with indecisive results. One problem is predetermining relevancy, which is extraordinarily difficult. Another problem is defining the use to which information is put. A third problem is packaging the information units that are to be priced.

Despite these difficulties and the current methods of dealing with them, information can no longer be treated as a free good. Try dialing 411. Or send out a survey questionnaire to 500 potential customers. Or ask 70 million taxpayers to fill out a government form 1040.

Treating information as a resource means looking at information as

1. Something of fundamental value, like money, capital goods, labor, or raw materials

2. Something with specifiable and measurable characteristics, such as method of collection, utilities and uses, a life cycle pattern with different attributes at each stage, and interchangeability with other resources

3. An input, which can be transformed into useful output(s) that is (are) beneficial to achieving the organization's goals and objectives

4. Something that can be capitalized or expensed, depending on management's purposes

5. An expense for which standard costs can be developed and cost accounting techniques, such as variance analysis, can be used to control

6. Something that presents to top management a variety of deployment choices (e.g., making trade-off decisions between information-intensive and manpower-intensive investments, between teleprocessing and manual processing approaches, or between producing an information product or service in-house or buying it from an external source)

Figure 1 schematically depicts the evolution of the treatment of conventional resource categories. In each case shown in the figure, there was some

Resource	Management Function	Evolution Began	Causes
Money/capital	Financial management	1920s	Heightened investment awareness, capital shortages, and depression
People	Manpower management	1930s	Advances in behavioral sciences and social forces (unions, working conditions)
Raw materials	Materials management	1940s	Critical shortage forecasts for key strategic stockpiles
Land and buildings	Space and property management	1940s	Assure prudent use of office/plant/laboratory space
Information	Information management	1960s	Information explosion, and the need to control the paperwork burden placed on the taxpayer
Documents and procedures	Service management	1970s	Need for improved delivery of public goods and services with less red tape to the citizens

Figure 1   Historical parallels in government.

felt need for the requirement. With information, the need is to manage overload and the proliferation of data.

Why would such treatment of information be useful? The answer is that, like other resources, information could be

1. Identified, measured, and costed at each stage in its life cycle: requirements determination, collection, processing, storage, use, and disposition
2. Planned more explicitly, to ensure that requirements are realistic and receive top management attention
3. Budgeted for, to ensure that information costs are properly balanced against other resource costs, not buried in overhead accounts or somewhere else

4. Managed, by balancing the value received from the use of the information against the costs incurred in planning, collecting, managing, and controlling it

5. Accounted for and audited, to ensure that costs do not get out of hand and that designated organization officials can be held accountable for the efficient and effective use of information

The utility of viewing information as a resource can also be illustrated by a simple analogy to a mineral resource. Coal, for example,

1. Has an acquisition cost

2. Comes in several different grades (some are tougher and more expensive to mine than others)

3. Comes in various degrees of purity (in general, the more impure, the cheaper; often, however, the less pure grades have a bigger and more lucrative market than the relatively purer grades)

4. Must be refined and processed to enhance its value and usefulness

5. Passes through many channels in transport from point of acquisition to point of use

6. Has many synthetics to compete with it—some cheaper, some more expensive

7. Can be bought and processed in its raw form and thus integrated vertically, or costs can be cut by buying it in more refined and processed forms

8. Is subject to the value-added principle at each stage in its life cycle; also, transfer-pricing principles can be applied as it proceeds from acquisition to use and disposal in waste form

As in any analogy, there are important differences between a mineral resource like coal and information. Minerals are physically consumed when they are used. Information often is not, although it does become obsolete.

A New Management Function

Organizations typically respond to ballooning resource costs, when they are first discovered, with what some persons have called the "new jerk" reaction; that is, they deal with the effects of the problem instead of with the causes. In the case of information, the most visible effect of the problem is paperwork—forms, records, reports, and so on. Organizations launch attempts to handle out-of-control overhead expenses, for example, by imposing arbitrary quotas on these documents, as former President Ford did in the case of federal reports. But as has been seen, these reports grow back like weeds; therefore, setting limits may keep the situation from getting worse but will not control underlying causes. Are there alternative approaches?

One alternative is to establish a management function, that is, a discrete function on the organization chart, and assign the necessary authorities and responsibilities to a specific official and a designated unit to

1. Develop the necessary organization-wide policies, procedures, systems, and working guides to deal with the problem.
2. Make the necessary internal organization adjustments to ensure that currently dispersed and fragmented units with pieces of the information problem are brought together in a planning and control framework so that they are all working toward a common goal. This does not necessarily mean the physical consolidation of units into one large information organization headed by an information czar, nor does it necessarily involve the centralization of all the organization's data into one gigantic, centralized data bank (in this regard see Figure 2).

Organizations that Are Data Handling in Character	Activities that Are Data Handling in Nature
1. Computer centers	1. Design and development of information systems, statistical data systems, data bases, and statistical series
2. Printing and reproduction services	
3. Mailrooms and message centers	
4. Libraries and information analysis centers	2. Records creation, maintenance, and disposition
5. Reports control offices	3. Reports creation, maintenance, and processing
6. Communication and telecommunication centers	4. Data base management
7. Statistical services	5. Development and maintenance of directives and instructional materials
8. Record centers and repositories	
9. Clearinghouses and information referral centers	6. Development and maintenance of training and educational materials
10. Data centers and documentation centers	7. Docket and dossier creation, maintenance, and disposition
11. Paperwork management offices	8. Stenographic and court reporting in creating records that are printed and filed (e.g., administrative, legal, medical, financial)

Figure 2 Illustrative data-handling organizations and activities.

3. Set priorities for the organization as a whole. Where is there duplication? What should be reduced or eliminated? Where are there gaps in existing information flows such that the legitimate information needs of some people and units are not now being met?

4. Establish specific standards and guidelines for the definition, measurement, use, and disposition of information so that the entire organization is operating within the same agreed-on definitional framework.

5. Coordinate the development of necessary tools to manage the data resource, for example, an organization-wide information directory and a data-element dictionary.

6. Create the necessary training, education, and career-progression opportunities for information specialists and journeyman-level information managers so that they can accept greater responsibilities.

As shown in Figure 1, when resources do get out of control, a new management function is established.

Budgeting and Accounting for Information Resources

Perhaps the most important task confronting organizations that elect to manage their information resources as suggested here is how to deal with data in their accounting and budgeting systems and processes. To manage data and information, costs of information resources must first be extracted from existing expenditure "objects" and then combined to institute effective controls. One approach that can be used is a bottom-up approach, that is, to proceed step by step.

1. With Figure 2 in mind, identify and extract preidentified costs associated with information-handling activities at the object-of-expenditure level (personal services and benefits, equipment, supplies, and so forth).

2. Construct a total information line-item cost for each organization cost center and work product aggregation (e.g., for companies, by product or service aggregated to product line; for government, by program or comparable activity).

3. Construct a simple ratio of information costs to total costs by cost center, organizational unit, product, or program, and then for the organization as a whole.

This approach, simplified, would allow at least a rudimentary attempt to get at those organization activities that tended to be "information-intensive" and therefore information costly. See Figure 3.

1. *The Formula*

$$\frac{\text{Information} + \text{Paperwork Costs}}{\text{Total Program Costs}} = \text{Information/Paperwork Intensity Ratio}$$

2. *The Intensity... Where to Analyze*

Product	Ranking	*Information/Paperwork Intensity Ratio*
B	1	1:3
C	2	1:6
A	3	1:7
D	4	1:8

3. *Possible Trade-offs in Budget Review*
   Between Information Resources and Other Resources
   —Ratio of Information overhead to direct activities of the program (or product)
   —Information intensity of program (or product)
   —Source of intensity (e.g., people systems vs. hardware systems; complex directives)
   —Frequency of data
   —Quantity of information collected
   Among Information Sources
   —Existing information vs. newly developed information
   —Intermediate vs. original
   —Derived vs. absolute/specific
   —Summarized vs. detailed

Figure 3 The information/paperwork intensity ratio.

A second alternative is a "top-down" approach. This approach would begin with an examination of the mission of each cost center—its goals and objectives—what it is charged to do, and what it contributes to the organization's overall mission. Then the role of the information resource would be defined. With this approach, it would also be necessary to deal with the expenditure object level, but the route—and therefore the results—would be different.

Other approaches are also feasible. For example, should we operate under the principle that in addition to his salary, everything an employee is required to do in creating and processing data and information should be counted as a cost, regardless of physical format, handling medium, or organization location? Or, for an organization like the training department, or an entire state university within a broader organizational framework, should that unit be treated as "informational"? There can be legitimate differences of opinion on how to deal with these situations, depending on one's philosophy and approach to accounting and budgeting.

Comparisons of information costs over time, growth, stability, or decline can be made by cost center, by program or product, by object of expense, and by other organizational standards. But to track these, one must first be able to identify, measure, and specify their attributes. Arraying the data as suggested obviously will not provide the answers to the questions. But at least such arrays should provide a point from which to undertake a rigorous analysis that will lead to causes.

Summary

Treating information as a manageable resource in organizations and budgeting for it as a line-item can be done; however, there are no guarantees that

1. The right questions will be asked
2. The best sources will be consulted
3. Data and information will be used correctly and efficiently
4. Even if data and information are used correctly and efficiently, positive results will be achieved

But such treatment should help managers and others ask more efficient questions, evaluate alternative information sources on firmer and more cost-effective grounds, and weigh more carefully and judiciously the benefits expected against the costs incurred. Treating data and information as a resource should

1. Provide a rigorous and disciplined framework for evaluating information benefits versus information costs in achieving organizational goals
2. Provide managers at all levels with an incentive to reduce to a minimum the information needed to make decisions
3. Make information a highly visible commodity within the organization
4. Give management a working tool, instead of an abstract theory, to deal with increasing information costs
5. Follow the historical pattern of dealing with resource problems that tend

to get out of hand (in short, there is precedent for dealing with information in this manner)

6. Apply management-by-exception principles by focusing on preventing data and information abuses

Of course, various data and information standard costs would eventually have to be developed to have a normative baseline against which to measure actual costs. In so doing, one should be in a position to undertake what accountants call *variance analysis.*

Many persons, including this author, share the concern that managing information may be viewed by some as tantamount to manipulating information, thus posing a threat to privacy, a constraint to creative work, or a barrier to the free flow of ideas in a democracy. Information is indeed power, and the line between managing information and manipulating it to gain power and control is often a thin one. When the efficiencies in information handling are counterproductive to man's creativity, quest for knowledge, and protection of privacy, or to checks and balances in a pluralistic society, that line has been crossed and one should turn back.

If society is ever to realize the full potential of automation, telecommunication, and micrographic, reprographic, and other information-handling technologies, information managers must make sure, particularly in this era of budget deficits and inflation, that money is well spent. To unleash the full power of modern information-handling technologies, information managers must plan the use of data resources more carefully. Treating information as a manageable resource in an organization will help achieve that goal.

Information Management in Public Organizations: Defining a New Resource Management Function*
Donald A. Marchand

Introduction: Why the Need for Information Management?

Paperwork is an ubiquitous aspect of the modern public organization. In contrast to the production processes of a manufacturing firm which change raw materials into finished goods, the public organization's primary characteristic is that of an "information factory"[1] which collects many types of raw data, processes this data through a network of people, procedures, and machines, and produces a variety of finished products in the form of memoranda, letters, records, newsletters, reports, bulletins, and more information requests. The problem with the typical public information factory is that it can produce relevant or irrelevant information, in small or large quantities. Because the production processes of the public organization can produce information relatively easily, whether or not it is demanded or needed, a public agency may have only a limited perception of what information it collects and produces, how it is used, and what its value is for the organization's members, managers, or clientele.

Paperwork Management Programs

In the past, the typical response to problems of this kind was to institute paperwork or records management programs. These were directed at dealing with the physical manifestations of the information proliferation problem and not with the content of the paperwork or records. Generally such programs have sought to simplify and consolidate forms and records and to reduce the total amount of paper and files circulating throughout the organization's message streams. In recent years, an additional factor in the information control problem has been the widespread and extensive use of various

*Reprinted by permission of *The Bureaucrat,* Vol. 7, pp. 4–10, Winter 1978.

types of electronic technologies in the public organization, which have altered significantly the manner in which information is collected, maintained, disseminated, communicated, and used by organizational members. While paper still retains its dominant place as the major medium of communication and information processing in the public organization, increasingly its use is being altered and, in some instances, supplanted by the technology of computers, telecommunications, microfilming, word processing, and duplication. We are dealing today not only with a paperwork problem, but also with a technological problem. How can these new technologies be used most advantageously by the organization? How are they changing the way the organization conducts its affairs? Do these new technologies necessarily mean a reduction in paperwork and better information use in the organization, or are we simply moving to another level of information overload at the same time that we complain about the need for better information to confront our social, political, economic, and environmental problems?

Information Management

It seems clear that what is missing is a viable concept of information management in the public sector which is premised on the notion that information is a valued resource in the organization and should be managed in a similar manner as we manage our human, fiscal, material and natural resources.[2] That is, we can no longer afford to act on the assumption that information is a "free" good. In addition, we can no longer proceed on the assumption that the information problem is susceptible to some "technological fix." Despite the notable advances made in the area of communications, data processing, word processing, duplicating, and microfilming, it is clear that these technologies alone will not solve the problem. This is because the problem of information overload in the organization is not just a "how to" problem, but a "what" and a "why" problem. That is, the questions that are raised by the concern with information collection, use, and value touch not only the procedural problems of how information can be more efficiently collected, stored, processed, and disseminated, but also the substantive problems of why information is collected and used the way it is, and what value it has in the advancement of an organization's programs and mission.

In this context, I will define what I consider to be a viable concept of information management in public organizations and review some of the constraints on the real world acceptance and application of this concept. In doing so, it is necessary to emphasize that the real impact of such a concept derives not simply from its relative newness, but, more importantly, from its integrative character. That is, it is clear that the literature in public administration, organizational theory, information science, business administration, and economics has been pointing in this direction and focusing on aspects of this theme for some time. The missing ingredient has been an integrative concept which permits the forging of links between areas of research and practical activity which have traditionally been viewed as quite separate and distinct.

What Is Information Management?

The basic purpose of information management is to promote organizational effectiveness. Goal attainment by the organization, as James D. Thompson has suggested, is defined not in terms of a maximum efficiency criterion, but as "satisficing," that is, the organization tries to accommodate itself to the demands of its internal and external environments.[3] The need for data and information processing arises from the need to reduce uncertainty concerning the organization's internal and external environments. In stable environments, this process of accommodation involves activity in the performance mode (that is, routine adaptation to changes within the existing perceptual structures of members of the organization).[4] In complex and dynamic environments, this process of accommodation involves activity in the developmental or learning mode (that is, reassessing the adequacy of existing perceptual structures and searching for new data).[5]

Behavioral Regression

As Dunn notes, not all organizations can operate in the developmental mode. Two kinds of problems can arise. The first he calls "behavioral regression" which is the tendency to deal with high level information requirements with low level information processing.[6] Organizations which are dealing with pressures for change in a complex environment may not shift to information processing in a developmental mode, but instead, may regress to lower levels of information processing than they currently use.[7] A second problem which Dunn perceives to set in often is what he calls "entity fixation" which he defines as the tendency to deal with problems through a fixed set of perceptual "windows": "to cling to established forms of symbolic data and fixed entity representations."[8] In its extreme form, entity fixation can lead to the reification of data:

When management is confronted by the fact that its traditional processes are not well enough to deal with current disturbances, it often demands more "information." This is often interpreted as a need for more of the same kinds of data accumulated in the same way. When coupled with the enlarged data processing capabilities of computers, the result can be a flood of detail leading to an actual reduction in meaning and to further loss of control consequent to an overload of meaningless data.[9]

Organizational Effectiveness

The aim of information management is to promote organizational effectiveness by enhancing the capabilities of the organization to cope with the demands of its internal and external environments in dynamic as well as stable conditions. Information management, therefore, as Figure 1 suggests, includes two dimensions: (1) managing the information process, and (2) managing the data resources of the organization. The purpose of the first is to assure the adequacy of the process for organizational decision making, analysis, and planning, while the purpose of the second is to assure that the various types of data an organization uses and the various ways that data is handled and processed can support the needs and demands of the information process. McFarlan, Nolan, and Norton have defined the distinction between these two elements of information management, data processing and information processing programs, as follows:

The types are distinguished by their inputs and outputs. Data processing programs assemble, process, associate, and structure data into information. Data is defined as observed facts. A data element is independent and true at the point in time it is observed. Information is defined as the basis for action to affect the status and environment of the organization. Data processing programs accept data input and output information.

Information processing programs act upon information and alter the status and environment of the organization by objective setting, resource allocation, operating on resources, and control. Accordingly, information processing programs can be further broken down into four subcategories: Objective setting programs, resource allocation programs, operations programs, and control programs. Information processing programs accept information and output action.[10]

Each dimension of information management involves, therefore, a somewhat different, but related concern. The management of the information process has to do with how well the members of the organization interact with the data resources and supporting technology for decision-making and analytical purposes. The emphasis of this dimension is on the value of data resources that are used in the organization. What is the relationship between the perceived needs and demands of individuals for information and the state

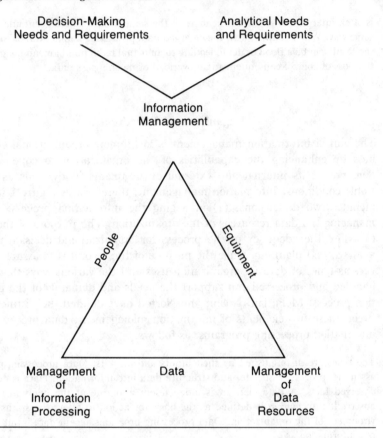

Figure 1   What is information management?

of the available data resources? In addition, how well do organizational members and managers use these resources in the programs and tasks of the organization?

Management of Data Resources

The management of the data resources is, on the other hand, instrumental to the information process. That is, the quality of the data resources, the efficiency with which they are employed, and the skill and expertise with which they are applied, all contribute to the quality and effectiveness of the information process. Data processing and data resource management are, therefore, simply means to an end. Indeed, when data processing is not directly related to information processing in an organization a number of problems can arise. One difficulty is the tendency of the data generating sources, services, and systems to produce too much data.[11] A second and related problem is the tendency to produce inappropriate data for the information processing needs of organizational members. A third problem arises from the tendency to concentrate on the management of data handling technology such as computers as an end in itself or to the exclusion of the concern with the use and value of the data and technology for individuals in the organization.

In contrast to the management of information processing which focuses on the interactions between people and data, the management of the data resources emphasizes control of the physical manifestations of the organization's information processes. The management of the information process includes both the formal and informal dimensions of information processing and communications in the organization. On the other hand, the management of the data resource relates to the control of records, reports, and general paperwork, as well as the management of data processing, word processing, communication, duplicating, and microfilming technologies and their uses.

Managing the Information Process

Management of the information process represents the more dynamic aspect of information management. It focuses on the quality of the interactions and relationships between people and data in the organization. As such, it tends to emphasize the more people-oriented problems and issues related to the effective use of information resources, and requires attention to several key factors.

First, there is the need to focus on the quality of the interaction between individuals and the kinds of symbolic data used in the organization. How well do individuals in the organization process different types of data? To what extent do they have adequate knowledge and training to use and manipulate data, to communicate it to others, and to assimilate or search for new types of data when it is necessary?

Second, there is the concern with how well messages and other data are communicated in the organization. Does pertinent information circulate rather easily in the organization either formally or informally? What aspects related to the social, cultural, and/or educational backgrounds of the members or of their work environments and informal relations result in significant distortion of information in the organization?[12]

Third, to what extent is information processing in the organization coordinated among members and managers? Do individuals share information in the organization? Is there a great deal of unnecessary duplication of information processing in the separate units of the organization? Does the use of various data processing and communications technologies facilitate efficient transmission and processing of information or are the current uses of these technologies exasperating the problems of information overload and duplication?

Finally, what is the relationship between data collection, use, and value in the organization? To what extent is the information that is collected used and to what degree is the information that is used of real value for the organization and its members?[13]

Managing the Data Resources

Management of the data resources emphasizes the data and "hardware" side of information management in the organization. Its main focus is on the quality and use of the tangible products and tools of the information process and their effective management to support the information requirements and needs of organizational members.[14]

Traditionally the tangible products of the information process have been treated as functionally separate. The production of correspondence, reports, forms, directives, mail, files, and messages has demanded distinct management approaches. The result has been a lack of coordinated assessment and use of these information products in the organization.

Similarly, the uses of data handling equipment have also been perceived as distinct. Different approaches have been used to manage manual files, computers, microfilm, telephones, printing, word processing, duplication, and audio/visual equipment with little sensitivity to or appreciation for the interrelatedness of such technologies in the organization's information processes.[15] One result of this approach to information technology has been a failure in many organizations to use the technology to facilitate and even enhance information quality and processing by organizational members.

Thus, management of the data resources requires that specific attention be given to the quality and reliability of information products in the organization as well as the effectiveness and efficiency with which various data handling technologies are employed to support the needs and demands of organizational members. In this way, data resource management can enhance and facilitate the management of the information process. The concept of information management is directed at bridging the gaps in these activities and introducing a sense of coordinated management of processes and products that is of value to organizational decision making. The latter concern with information value represents the key idea that suggests why the concept of information management can be so significant and vital for organizational life. Unless we learn to properly account, budget, plan, organize, and evaluate information as a resource, we will continue to use up valuable resources for information production, use, and handling with no clear sense of the utility of the information thus generated. In the context of the increasing proliferation of communications and information technologies and in the face of increasing demands for usable and relevant information for decision making, such a course becomes increasingly unacceptable.

Constraints on Information Management

Introducing information management as an activity in public organizations will have important implications for the procedures, processes, structures, and goals of the organization. A number of problems or constraints must be clearly recognized if information management is to be effectively incorporated into the organizational environment. In this section, I would like to review seven constraints which may influence in important ways the success of information management in public organizations. As Figure 2 suggests, these seven constraints are overlapping and interdependent. As such, they represent the significant dimensions of the real world context within which information management will have to be conducted.

Theoretical Constraints. The first constraint on information management has to do with the theoretical or conceptual dimensions of the activity. The concept of information management covers a broad range of activities in the organization. As such, it includes both the process and objects of information exchange and data production and use in the organization. Such a definition seeks to move beyond simply a concern with paperwork, records, and data processing equipment to a broader, more integrative picture of the process of information exchange and the many different objects and modes of information exchange in the organization. Looked at in this way, information management implies, as I suggested initially, a broad multidisciplinary, if not interdisciplinary, approach to information processing and data resource management in the organization. Such a generalist perspective

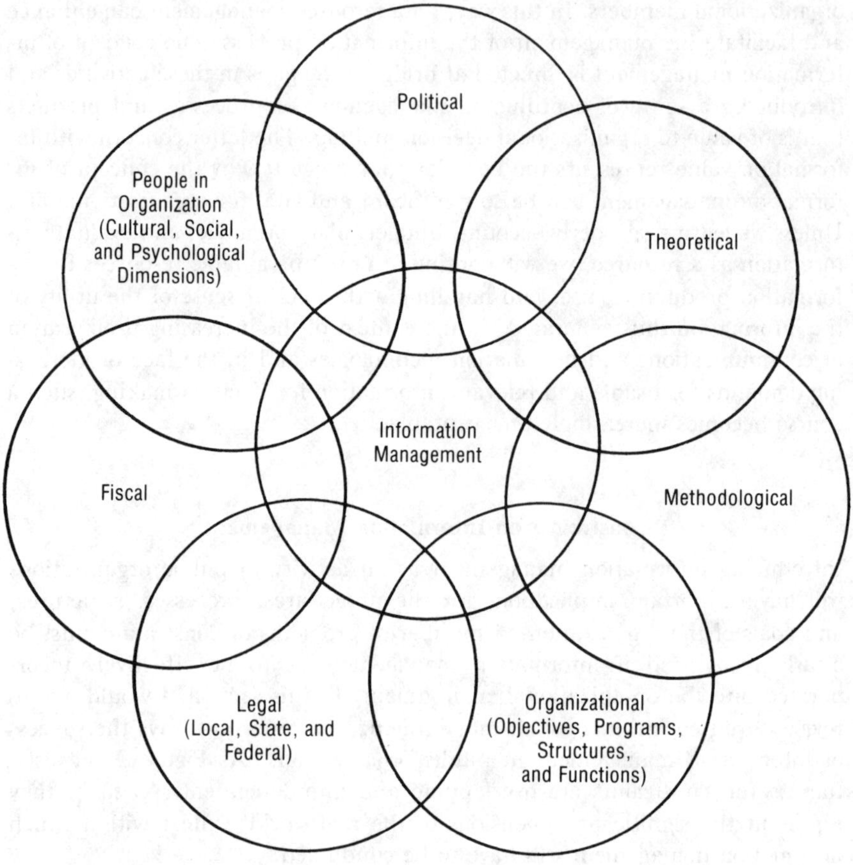

Figure 2   Constraints on information management.

necessitates the incorporation of fields of expertise which have traditionally been viewed as quite distinct, if not completely foreign, from one another in purpose and technique. Therefore, as an innovative concept in organizational management, information management poses a distinct challenge to begin integrating what have previously been rather distinct disciplinary concerns.[16]

Methodological Issues. Related to the conceptual challenge and problems that the concept of information management suggests are the methodological issues concerning the adequacy of available tools for assessing and measuring the uses, value, and costs of information processing and data resources in the organization. We are clearly very far from the point of having a well-established body of standards and criteria to apply to the assessment of the uses and value of information. In addition, the task of measuring the costs of information is a formidable one which demands new applications of cost accounting principles and methods as well as new ways of thinking about the problem of budgeting such a resource in public organizations.[17]

Organizational Constraints. Third, the existing structures and functions of public organizations at the local, state, or federal levels may place significant limitations on the introduction of effective information management concepts. In addition, existing record control and data processing practices may conflict with the more integrative approach of information management.[18]

People in Organizations. Fourth, people in organizations may not be receptive to an approach to information management which alters their existing practices and habits and which may expose their individual job performance to management review in the organization.

Legal Constraints. Fifth, the existence of laws controlling the nature of reporting requirements as well as public record and confidentiality statutes at the state and federal level may increase the costs of methods of information processing and data resource control in public organizations. We cannot assume that the introduction of information management will result, at least immediately, in appropriate changes in the laws governing reporting and disclosure requirements. Indeed, once the problems and practices associated with information processing in the public sector are more clearly identified, there may be even more reason to redefine and tighten such policies and administrative requirements.

Fiscal Constraints. Sixth, budgeting the data resource in the information process is subject to the existing practices and rules of budgeting in organizations and these budgeting processes and procedures of state and federal governments may not be well suited to accounting for the data resource. In addition, it is not clear that relatively minor adjustments to the current incremental approach to budgeting data resources will accomplish a great deal of good in this area.[19]

Maintaining Status Quo. Finally, information management will inevitably mean the introduction of changes in the procedures, policies, processes, and structures of organizations. Such changes must gain acceptability and support. One obvious problem in doing this are the "sunk costs" of the status quo.[20] Many people in organizations have personal and professional interests in *not* changing data handling procedures and policies. Data processing technologists, for example, may regard the concept of information management as a threat to their existing policies, practices, and resources. Beyond these difficulties, information management may point to performance gaps in the organization's activities.[21] The perception of such gaps may cause disruption and change in an organization which may be more interested in the maintenance of the status quo.

The role of information management is to aid in the critical assessment of the information processes and data resources to promote organizational effectiveness. In assuming this responsibility, it is important to consider and keep in mind the real constraints upon such an innovative approach in the public agency environment. The realization of the promise of such an approach is highly dependent upon a clear and realistic perception of the problems and issues.

Notes

[1]Trevor Bentley, *Information, Communication and The Paperwork Explosion* (McGraw-Hill, London, 1976), p. 7.

[2]The first systematic articulation of the concept of treating "information as a resource" in the context of organizations was in Adrian M. McDonough, *Information Economics & Management Systems* (McGraw-Hill, New York, 1963). In recent years, the U.S. Commission on Federal Paperwork has taken up this theme in an effort to reveal the underlying causes of the paperwork problem. See, for example, Commission on Federal Paperwork, *Information Resource Management* (U.S. Government Printing Office, Washington, D.C., 1977).

[3]James D. Thompson, *Organizations in Action* (McGraw-Hill, New York, 1967), p. 32.

[4]See Edgar S. Dunn, *Social Information Processing and Statistical Systems— Change and Reform* (John Wiley & Sons, New York, 1974), pp. 32-33.

[5]Ibid., p. 33.

[6]Ibid., pp. 63-64.

[7]Dunn notes that the cause of such a phenomenon in organizations is rooted in individual psychological responses:

"If an individual is presented with an environmental change requiring the development of psychological structures of a level substantially higher than previously achieved, the developmental mode may be unable to bridge the gap. When the attempt fails it is quite common for behavioral regression to set in. The individual is often unable to maintain even established levels of information processing. There is a tendency to retreat to lower more primitive levels." Ibid., p. 38.

[8]Ibid., p. 88. See, also, the work of Harold Wilensky, *Organizational Intelligence* (Basic Books, Inc., New York, 1967) for examples of this phenomenon in the intelligence and military community.

[9]Op. cit., p. 89.

[10]F. Warren McFarlan, Richard C. Nolan, and David P. Norton, *Information Systems Administration* (Holt, Rinehart & Winston, New York, 1973), pp. 36–37.

[11]Herbert Simon has advocated the design of information processes and systems in organizations that recognize the limited attention span of actors within organizations. See Herbert A. Simon, "Applying Information Technology to Organizational Design," *Public Administration Review* (May/June 1973), pp. 268–278.

[12]See, for example, Downs, *Inside Bureaucracy*, op. cit., pp. 112–131; Gordon Tullock, *The Politics of Bureaucracy* (Public Affairs Press, Washington, D.C., 1965); and Wilensky, op. cit., pp. 41–74.

[13]For a proposed methodology for assessing the uses and value of information in public organizations, see U.S. Commission on Federal Paperwork, *Information Resource Management Study* (Washington, D.C., 1977), Chapter III.

[14]This definition of information resource management is also reflected in the work of the U.S. Commission on Federal Paperwork, see Ibid., Chapter 1.

[15]For an excellent assessment of the technological merging or linkage of data processing technologies in organizations, see C. W. Getz, "Coalescence: The Inevitable Fate of Data Processing," *MIS Quarterly* (June 1977), pp. 21–30.

[16]See, also, Forest Horton, Jr., "Inter-disciplinary Approach Sought For Information Management," *Information Action* (February 1977); David P. Snyder, "Information Systems—Creating a New Discipline to Manage the Information Explosion," a paper presented at the *Information and Records Administration Conference*, Washington, D.C., February 16, 1973.

[17]See Woody Horton, Jr., "Budgeting the Data and Information Resource," *Journal of Systems Management* (February 1977), pp. 12–14; Richard L. Nolan, "Controlling the Costs of Data Services," *Harvard Business Review* (July–August 1977), pp. 114–124.

[18]See U.S. Commission on Federal Paperwork, *Federal/State/Local Cooperation*, op. cit.

[19]See Donald A. Marchand and John J. Stucker, *Information Management in the State University* (Commission on Federal Paperwork, Washington, D.C., 1977), pp. 26–78.

[20]Anthony Downs, *Inside Bureaucracy*, op. cit., pp. 191–210.

[21]Ibid., p. 191.

Additional Readings

Diebold Group, Inc. "Information Resource Management—Part One." *Infosystems*, *26*:1–24, June 1979.

———. "Information Resource Management—Part Two." *Infosystems*, *26*:41–90, October 1979.

Galbraith, John K. *The New Industrial State*. Boston, Houghton Mifflin, 1976.

Horton, Forest W., Jr. *How to Harness Information Resource: A Systems Approach*. Cleveland, Ohio, Association for Systems Management, 1974.

———. "Information in Search of a Manager." *Government Data Systems*, *8*:23–25; 34, September/October 1979.

———. *Information Resource Management: Concept and Cases*. Cleveland, Ohio, Association for Systems Management, 1979.

Kaufman, Herbert. *Red Tape*. Washington, D.C., The Brookings Institution, 1977.

Lamberton, Donald M., ed. "The Information Revolution." *The Annals of the American Academy of Political and Social Science, 412*:1–162, 1974.

Machlup, Fritz. *The Production and Distribution of Information in the United States*. Princeton, N.J., Princeton University Press, 1962.

McDonough, Adrian. *Information Economics and Management Systems*. New York, McGraw-Hill, 1963.

Mitler, Lawrence. "Law and Information Systems." *Journal of Systems Management*, *28*:22–29, January 1977.

Simon, Herbert A. "Information Can Be Managed." *Think*, *33*:8, May/June 1977.

Snyder, David P. "Information Systems—Creating a New Discipline to Manage the Information Revolution." *Records Management Journal*, *11*:16–24, September 1973.

U.S. Comptroller General. *Federal Paperwork: Its Impact on American Business*. Washington, D.C., General Accounting Office, 1978.

Chapter 2

MANAGING THE
INFORMATION PROCESS

Our day is fraught with informational problems. To deal effectively with these problems we need to understand [the] dynamics of information.

—Frederick B. Thompson, "The Dynamics of Information"
(*Engineering and Science*, *36*:324, October 1972)

The preceding chapter concludes with the idea that information management in a public organization can be divided into two separable but closely related concerns: managing the information process and managing the information or data resources. The selections in Chapters 2 and 3 examine both dimensions of information management.

As Marchand observed in the final reading in Chapter 1, management of the information process is concerned with how well the members of an organization interact with the data resources and supporting technology for decision-making and analytical purposes. All the readings in Chapter 2 indicate that this interaction is problematic at several different levels. Organizations are not machines. Their components are not nuts and bolts but individual persons. Therefore, to understand how information is processed in organizations, one must begin by asking some fundamental questions about how persons process information, both as individuals and as members of organized groups or units. How do individuals process and communicate information? What types of languages and symbols do they use? How well do they use languages and symbols in the setting of an organization? What are the prerequisites for effective use of information technology to enhance information processing in organizations? How do the maintenance and survival instincts of organizations affect the quality and value of information processed for both insiders and outsiders? These and other questions are explored in this chapter.

Although they present divergent approaches to management of the information process in organizations, the authors of the readings in Chapter 2 clearly agree about the need for such management. The primary purpose of an information process or system, no matter how simple or complex, is to aid the user in achieving goals and objectives. The central, collective message of the authors is that the effectiveness of information processing in organizations is influenced by many complex variables that go far beyond concern with the sophistication of the information technology used. The key concerns focus on the use of symbolic data by individuals who are affected by a host of linguistic, sociological, and motivational factors. Motivational factors tend to dominate organizations and influence significantly the effectiveness of information processing by an organization's members as well as by outside actors, such as legislators, interest groups, clients, and citizens.

In the first selection, "The Dynamics of Information," Frederick B. Thompson investigates the process by which individuals become informed. He points out that two variables are particularly important in understanding the dynamics of information: language and community. Language allows a person to interpret the meanings of observations and experiences in the world. Different languages reveal different amounts of information about the same observations or experiences. Community, on the other hand, helps individuals deal with the "fractionalization" of information attending the use of different languages in the world or the use of the same language by different individuals with varying values and interests. Therefore, in Thompson's view, organizations provide a powerful means for ordering information processing among individuals in a world characterized by rapid information growth and specialization. Thompson also suggests that the use of information technology in organizations will accelerate control over information and facilitate communication and creativity.

In *Information in Business and Administrative Systems:* "Summary and Postscript," Ronald Stamper provides a less optimistic perspective on the use of information by individuals in organizations and the impacts of information technology. Like Thompson, Stamper notes that the health of an organization depends on how well its members generate and use information. He contends, however, that organizations fail to use information effectively because there is no clear understanding of how an organization's members use information or of what information technologies like computers can accomplish. He proposes the development of a general theory of information, called *semiotics,* as a tool to understand how individuals process information in organizations and how information technology can be used to support, rather than frustrate or prevent, more effective information processing and communication. Organizations are complex, dynamic entities that must be understood before information technologies are introduced. Otherwise, the technologies may do more harm than good.

How then can one ensure that organizations process information effectively? In the last two selections in this chapter, various approaches to dealing with information problems are suggested.

Both Anthony Downs in "Search Problems in Bureaus" and Jacob A. Stockfisch in "The Bureaucratic Pathology" focus on what Stockfisch calls "bureaucratic pathologies"—learned patterns of responses to the internal and external environments that make it rational for an organization's members to distort and manipulate information in various ways. Mismanagement of information resources is wasteful and inefficient but may be rational for the bureaucrat interested in the organization's maintenance, adaptation, and survival. Both Downs and Stockfisch suggest that the solution lies as much in the political as in the administrative area. Inertia on the part of administrators, politicians, and the public must give way to frank recognition of the need to understand information processing in organizations and manage that processing more effectively.

The Dynamics of Information*
Frederick B. Thompson

Each of us feels somewhat informed about his individual corner of the world. At the same time, we are aware that our understanding is incomplete. Each of us in his own way seeks to make sense out of his experience. Some spend their entire lives in increasing our understanding; they are scientists and scholars, not because of what they know but because of their persistence in seeking to know more. And indeed this innate curiosity is a ubiquitous part of all of us. Since these informational activities of others are themselves part of our experience, we seek as well to understand each other. And thus, the dynamics of information.

But the results of these separate acts of knowing are not converging. Our time seems marked by a growing sense of being out of touch, of a too rapid growth in what there is to know. Creativity itself seems suspect when so much that is created is beyond our ken. Our day is fraught with informational problems. To deal effectively with these problems, we need to understand these dynamics of information.

The process of becoming informed can be factored into two parts. The first of these is experiencing. It is by interacting directly with the reality that is around us that we gain the raw materials of information. But raw experience is not enough. We must organize experience into a conceptual structure before it is meaningful to us. Nor does this structure come from the experience itself. Rather, we must impose structure on our experience. The knower must actively participate in the act of knowing. The matter was put vividly by the American philosopher-scientist William James:

The world's contents are given to each of us in an order so foreign to our subjective interests that we can hardly by an effort of the imagination picture to ourselves what it is really like....Is not the sum of your actual experience taken at this moment and impartially added together an utter chaos? The strains of my voice, the lights and shades inside the room and out, the murmur of the wind, the ticking of the clock, the various organic feelings you may happen individually to possess, do these make a whole at all?...We break it; we break it into histories, and we break it into arts, and we break

*Reprinted from *Engineering and Science,* Vol. 36, pp. 4–7, 27–29, October 1972. Published at The California Institute of Technology.

it into sciences; and then we begin to feel at home....We discover among its various parts relations that were never given to sense at all; and out of an infinite number of these we call certain ones essential and law giving, and ignore the rest.

It is our subjective habit to organize the individual elements of our experience, to cross-correlate these elements to others distant in space and time. It is only after this process of imposing organization that we feel informed.

Notice the essential role of abstraction and projection beyond what we have confirmed. Each moment of our experience is peculiar unto itself. It is only by ignoring differentiating aspects of past experience that we can see its application to current concerns. And these patterns that we exploit are not proffered by experience, which does not choose between the infinity that are there. They arise only when we back off and let the shadows of our own subjective structure cast perspective on our cluttered view. I am not questioning the objectivity of these patterns, once perceived. I am emphasizing the essential role of the subjective selection and imposition of organization that determines to as great an extent as experience itself the information that it yields.

Language is the embodiment of conceptual structure. We share our information with others. But to do so we must settle collectively on a structure into which our several experiences can be codified. It is this tacit, common structure that we exploit in communication. The essential characteristic of language is structure, as found in its word forms, its grammar, and its intrinsic logic. The study of language reveals the common conceptual structures of a community.

I should like to use the notion of language in this more precise form as synonymous with conceptual structure. In particular I am not restricting it to verbal language. Think of the language that a person is using at any instant as the embodiment of the organization that he has imposed upon his experience and as the means for framing his current information. I should like to introduce the notion of an informational community as a group of people who share a common language, whose conceptual views are based upon a common structure. An individual can be considered as a special case of such a community. When looking at the dynamics of information, it is the community and its language which is the central focus.

Now let us imagine a situation where we have a certain fixed body of observations or experience. Let us compare what would happen if we were to organize and conceptualize this experience in terms of one language or another. Each language would reveal certain information from its peculiar point of view. The concepts and means of expression in one language might be just so as to be quite inadequate for the experience at hand, while another language may be ideally suited to elicit revealing insight.

One can construct for a formal language a measure of information. Thus given a language and a body of observations, we can define the amount of information that can be elicited from the given observations in terms of the conceptual structures provided by the language. Different languages yield different amounts of information about the same observations.

Languages can be compared in the amount of information they provide. When we say that one language (L_1) is at least as powerful as another (L_2), we mean that whatever distinctions between possible states of the universe can be made in L_2, they can be made in L_1. On the other hand one can show that for any formal language (L) there is a much more powerful language (L') which can express things not possible in L. As a consequence there is no most powerful language.

Let's examine the situation wherein we have a family of more and more powerful languages. Again we will assume that we are considering a family E consisting of a number of observations. Thus for each language L, we can determine the amount of information $I(L, E)$ that can be obtained from E in terms of language L. Let L_0 be the least powerful language in which all aspects of the observations E can be fully expressed. In L_0, the experiences E can be completely described. The question is: What happens to the amount of information as we move to either more powerful or less powerful languages than L_0? What can be shown quite convincingly is somewhat surprising.

Consider a more powerful language, L_1. The observation E can be completely described in L_1, and more. Indeed, L_1 opens many issues which cannot be decided on the basis of E; it gives rise to ambiguities and uncertainties that cannot be resolved. It is not only the case that it distinguishes between two states that were indistinguishable in L_0, but it permits states that violated the logic of L_0, that could not exist as far as L_0 is concerned. A language is essentially a means of correlation of otherwise disparate experiences; thus it perforce must impose assumptions not inherent in the experience it explicates. It is this drastic extension of alternatives in the areas germane but unresolved by the experiences at hand that disrupts the correlations assumed in L_0, and causes information to fall.

What happens when we move to the left? Obviously, if we move all the way to the one-word language, we lose all information. Suppose there are certain aspects of each observation that do not reoccur in any systematic way in the other observations, thus appear random; one assumes them irrelevant. Others may occur quite regularly without perturbation in all the observations; whereupon one assumes their universal regularity, thus equating differentiable characteristics. This indeed is the process of induction, moving us

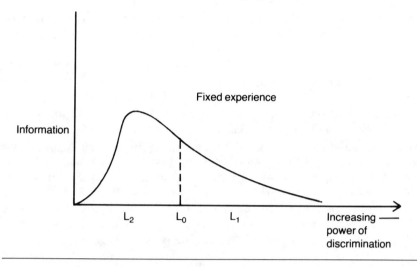

Figure 1 Information as a function of the conceptual structure made available by the underlying language. Each language determines the amount of information that can be obtained from a fixed body of experience.

to higher levels of abstraction. Thus there is an intermediate position in which information is maximized.

We maximize our information at a level of conceptualization above that of our raw experience. The very essence of science has been to find those highly abstract first principles and laws which encapsulate broad stretches of our experience.

Our experience is not fixed but ever extending. In the face of changing experience, that language which maximizes our information also changes. Indeed, this is our simple model of cognitive processes, a model of the dynamics of how we are informed. We constantly change our language in such a way as to maximize the information we can elicit from our experience. We constantly modify and adjust the forms and relationships into which we encapsulate our experience in such a way as to keep us maximally informed.

Information processes, the processes by which we are informed, can thus be viewed as language change. Creativity is precisely such a process. To be creative is to impose upon experience a new structure which suddenly reveals insights which were obscured before. A poet's turn of phrase, a musician's variations on a simple melody, a painter's juxtaposition of shape and color, a dancer's mime in motion, all interpret anew things common to us all; and from these new interpretations we strangely draw a sense of knowing more.

The great moments of scientific advances are just such moments of new conceptualization. Copernicus moved the conceptual center of the universe from the earth to the sun. Kepler gave order to the confusing observations of the planets by placing them on an ethereal ellipse, tacked at a focus to the sun. Dalton observed the integral combinations of the elements in chemical compounds. Bohr gave us the basic model of the atom. Einstein grasped the absolute character of the speed of light. Each enormously expanded our information and opened highways for its further extension only by insightful shifts in conceptual structure.

But the innovative community is not an isolated thing. It exists in a wider culture. In this wider sense, the effect of creative change can be negative as well as positive. Great conceptual change calls for deep reverberating changes in the central conceptual structures that underpin whole cultures. For example, the Copernican shift shattered the image of man as central to the universe and thus opened [to] question the basic assumptions on which the religious institutions of the day were established. As we have already seen, this "opening to question" increases enormously the number of alternatives which have to be dealt with and thus reduces the information these expanded conceptual structures contain.

When one recalls that the previous views had themselves been constructed to be maximally informing in face of existing evidence, one can see how such a shift of view in one area can be a grave threat to the over-all conceptual accommodation of a society. As the cultural pattern of a society is built, a balance is maintained across the growing community that permits and enhances communication. If that balance is destroyed by an alien concept locally extended to account for local experience, it can drastically lower the information in the total society even while it increases sharply the local information. The global effect of a creative act must be analysed quite separately from the analysis which accounts for its local introduction.

A creative act is like an earth movement, an adjustment of local structure to the stresses built up by on-going processes of change, an accommodation to account for local experience. Like earthquakes, such creative adjustment of structure propagates throughout the conceptual structure of the society. And all along this propagating change, information falls as new alternatives are opened and uncertainty is increased. In a culture such as ours, there are continual occurrences of microquakes, thousands of quakes felt in local communities, and from time to time major conceptual quakes such as Darwin's announcement of evolution and the explosion of the first atomic weapon, which reverberate their unsettling implications throughout the society's cultural view.

A common language, a common conceptual view provides a community with a powerful tool. On such a basis, it can coordinate its activities, marshal its skills, share its experience. As a community increases its information, it thereby increases its capabilities to meet its needs and to successfully adjust to its environment. It also increases its capability to gain information. The invention of the telephone added a small item of information to human knowledge, but this small piece of information, how to design a telephone, was multiplied manyfold by its impact on the information its use made readily available in the society. The processes of becoming informed are self-accelerating.

What are the implications of this fact, the self-acceleration of information? As innovative change takes place in a community, it must be communicated throughout the community. The community's language must absorb the change, and all members of the community must recognize and adopt it. Communication takes time. The larger the community, the more time and effort are required to assimilate the result of innovative change. Thus the first conclusion we can draw is that community size must be inversely proportional to the rate of innovative change.

But information processes are self-accelerating; the rate of innovative change is increasing. As the community builds up a strong base of information, this base can be exploited on all sides. Innovation is stimulated at many places in the community. And if the community is to maintain itself, these changes must be communicated and absorbed. At some point in time, the rate of innovation becomes too great. People get out of touch. Some groups in the community are privy to information others do not have. Conflicts in view develop. The community fractionates. The seeds of its own fractionization are sown at the very birth of a community in the self-acceleration of its information.

But the fractionation of a community need not be catastrophic. In fact one can look at the evolution of social mechanisms as the development of means of retaining high levels of information in a society even while it fractionates into a multiplicity of communities. Diversity of views and skills can be tolerated by a society if there are maintained avenues along which communication can take place. Let us review several ways society has learned to accommodate orderly fractionization.

The acceptance of a common medium of exchange is one. In the economic sphere we call it money, in the political sphere it is the vote. Social organizations also accommodate orderly fractionization. It is a common presumption that an organization has a goal and all of its members work toward its accomplishment. The myth of its goal does indeed give common coinage to the activities of its members but it is hardly more than myth. Indeed the very essence of organization is to create channels of communication which allow groups and individuals with diverse skills and goals and values to realize high levels of total information without the too costly maintenance of a single encompassing language. Think for a moment of the immense amount of information to be found in, say, the Department of Defense. The coordination of activities is worldwide and ties together in rational sequence such diverse affairs as the negotiation for the design of a new weapon system and its employment by men trained in its use years later on an unanticipated battlefield. But how few aspects of that information are to be found in any single Pentagon office, or at the fingertips of any single officer. Organization is thus a powerful means of maintaining orderly fractionization of a society.

Mechanisms such as the marketplace and social organizations are one way in which a society maintains higher levels of information in face of the self-acceleration of information. But there is another more basic one. Fractionization occurs when rates of innovation exceed the ability of the community to communicate the results of innovation. Thus if the technological means of communication can keep pace, the moment of fractionization can be postponed.

What activities of an informational community determine this fractionization? It is its data gathering and communicating that ties a community together, maintains the cohesiveness and consistency of its underlying conceptual structure. It is the activities of structuring and theorizing that are innovative activities that tend to fractionate the community.

Ever since the invention of the printing press there has been one major technological innovation after another that enhances our capabilities to communicate and to observe; the telegraph, radio, television, in fact the whole electronic revolution—the microscope, camera, linear accelerators, and bathyspheres—all support the gathering and communicating activity. As far as technological support of structuring, little has been done beyond pencils and paper.

We can record and communicate enormous amounts of data. As a consequence, the commonality of conceptual structure and the confirmation of that structure are very high. At no time in history has there been the commonality of human culture that exists today. The same popular music, the same kinds of transportation, the same values, the same technology are found almost everywhere. We virtually exist as a single informational community.

Into this situation has come the computer. So far it has been used largely to apply known theories and models to special cases in engineering and business. But the potential for technologically supporting the processes of structuring and theorizing, the innovative processes, are here.

Let me enlarge upon this somewhat. Suppose I have a large body of data or find myself in an experimental laboratory and I try to make sense out of what I find at hand. I try to construct a conceptual framework that accounts for the data or the experimental results in an insightful way. This is precisely the process we discussed earlier in the paper, the process in which one seeks to find that higher level structure that maximizes one's information. To do this I examine some small sector of the data or I conduct a limited sequence of experiments. On the basis of these, I form a hypothesis, which I proceed to test by further examination of data or further experimentation. In this way I build up an increasingly complex model or theory. But the process is not only one of accretion of structure. There comes a time when the model becomes unwieldy and unaesthetic. I try a variant on the theory, I simplify the model in a novel way that I could not have seen prior to its construction. I begin to change the model in quite creative ways, much like a sculptor takes a bit of clay off here and puts a bit on there. And at each stage I must step back and assess the implications across the entire theory, and see if the change still fits the data or the results of my experiments. This reverberating adjustment of the conceptual model is the tedious, time-consuming part of research. In the past, each research step was small, simply because checking out the implications of small changes in theory was already taxing.

In such a laboratory as I have described...the construction of models has always played an important role. If we could make an actual physical model of what we were working on, then we could poke it, warp it, and change it here and there, and the implications of our change would be evaluated quickly and immediately by the model itself. But there has been no apparatus in which the abstract conceptual theory itself could be held and manipulated; there has been no way short of tedious calculations with pencil and paper to change the theory in one area and check the implications of these changes in other areas—capability to build complex models and then to set them in motion and see how they work. That is, there has been no such apparatus up to now. But this is precisely what the digital computer is suited to provide.

For example, in our laboratories at Caltech we build complex conceptual models of nerve cells. We then take many of these simulated cells and build them into networks similar to those found in the nervous system, all of course in the computer. The computer is also hooked up to tiny electronic probes that are inserted into the nervous systems of living animals and that can sense their nervous activity. Both our conceptual model and the actual living nervous system feed the same analysis programs. We can thus compare them, adjusting the parameters of our model in immediate interaction with computer analysis, to fit the reality we are trying to understand. In this process the computer is handling data rates from the model and from the animal of 50,000 to 100,000 items a second.

Let me cite another example. Caltech anthropologist Thayer Scudder is studying a Tonga population of about 50,000 individuals in Zambia. Ten years ago they lived as simple farmers in an isolated valley. The Kariba Dam was built at the head of the valley, and these people had to be relocated. Recently industry has come to the area into which they were moved. Professor Scudder and his associates have extensive field notes covering this entire period, giving family relationships, vocations, education, property, etc., of hundreds of these people. We are now putting these data in the computer. In this computer system, Professor Scudder can ask questions and build conceptual models of culture change, testing these models against the data, all in natural English and in direct conversation with the computer. This capability accelerates the processes of understanding and theory building manyfold.

The introduction of the computer is for the first time giving major technological support to structuring and theorizing. What is its effect? There will be a large return in information for this movement. Thus the economic coercions for this change can be expected to be great. And indeed they are, as evidenced by the extremely rapid growth of the computer market and the application of computers in all aspects of our life. We should not underestimate the ubiquitous effect computers have already had. Our highway program, as well as our space program, could not exist without them. The effect on industrial inventories is a major factor in our economic stability. But it will be in expansion of our information frontiers that they will have their greatest effects.

As greater use is made of computers, the balance between conceptualizing and communicating changes. And this change will be such as to reduce drastically the size of the viable informational community. The rate of fractionization will be greatly increased. We should expect a time of rapid divergence in points of view and values. Because innovative change in conceptualization of our environment will be accelerated, we will feel more and more out of touch with others; and their effectiveness in dealing with affairs in ways we neither understand nor value will threaten even more our sense of being informed.

I have mentioned methods a society may use in attaining orderly fractionization. In this regard we discussed the marketplace and the use of social organization. These social mechanisms can be drawn upon and strengthened under current conditions too. However, what are the roads open to a society when faced with catastrophic fractionization of context? There are two, and we stand at the crossroads of these two paths today.

The first is to slow down the rates of conceptual change. Cut the national research budget. Reduce the support of public education relative to the general economy. Repress divergent groups. Enforce conformity to established codes of behavior. But the explosive forces of change cannot be controlled by half measures. This road leads to dictatorship.

The second road is characterized by the tolerance for diversity. It seeks a new, more enlightened conceptual base for our culture—one that recognizes that divergence of views can be enriching to a culture. What a challenge there is to society when innovation runs high! Are there deeper wellsprings of humanity on which we can base a new communication, one that revels in the richness of human diversity and welcomes the kaleidoscopic patterns of a creative culture? It is this choice between the challenge of the innovative society and the grim maintenance of a single conforming world that we face today.

But let us turn away from this crucial issue. Let's suppose we take the challenge. And indeed there is no question in my mind that we ultimately will, even if that ultimate follows a difficult period for free men. What is in store for creativity in an automated society?

It has taken the best brains and a prolonged and intense effort to forge our single science. Today science stands as a single edifice of astonishing complexity, yet yielding stunning simplicities of view. With the limited tools for conceptual structuring we have had in the past, the belief in science's uniqueness of objective view has been a necessary discipline.

Science is the result of those forces that maximize the information that we can obtain from our experience. The intolerance of science of its own history is evidence that it dared not recognize its many changes. The belief that there can be only a single science, that truth lies in only one package, has been necessary when the effort to uncover that truth has taxed our ablest minds.

Yet even now the humanistic aspects of science are well recognized, at least by our scientific leaders. Conant referred to science as policy, not truth, policy to guide further experimentation. Schrödinger, while acknowledging the objectivity of science, called attention to its highly subjective aspects as well. The great expanses of unexplored reality leave open to the subjective curiosity of the individual scientist what corner he will examine, what ex-

periments he will perform. Whatever our philosophical views on reductionism, as a practical matter the scientific landscape is sparsely settled. There
are no bridges today between political science and psychology, individual
psychology and psychobiology, psychobiology and molecular biology.

But what of the future? As we augment radically the technological support of the process of conceptual structuring, each community can build its
own science. From its accumulated experience it can distill that conceptual
view that best expresses its own inner feelings, its values, its aesthetic taste.
Science itself will become our greatest art form. With the material affluence
of our automated society, we can turn our full attention to that which is most
peculiarly human, the building and communicating of conceptual structure.
The humanities—philosophy, the arts, literature, and science too—these will
be the proper province of creative man in the automated society.

Information in Business and Administrative Systems: Summary and Postscript*

Ronald Stamper

SUMMARY

Semiotic is thus an interdisciplinary exercise. In this study we have hardly entered into man's rich symbolic life. We have been concerned mostly with the language needed to talk about this realm.

—Charles Morris, *Signification and Significance*

No corner of man's rich symbolic existence has more practical importance today than the part in which he uses symbols to direct the affairs of government, industry and commerce. As his forbears toiled in vineyard and field, so modern man works in office and committee room; the hoe is replaced by the pen, the even furrows give way to lines of print; and the fruit of his labour springs not from his well-sown seed but from his carefully drafted plans, schedules, proposals and instructions. From words and numbers, man creates his future, and organisation is the name of his task.

We have taken this kind of work as much for granted as the peasant regarded his regular agricultural round. But tractors and computers have changed all that. Quite a new kind of organisation is now possible through the use of technology; to develop it we must understand more exactly what we have been doing unthinkingly for so long. We have been using signs or information to get things accomplished. What signs? How do they inform? How much information do they carry? What carries them? How efficiently?

Semiotics tries to answer these questions. Charles Morris, in his treatment of this subject, places greatest emphasis upon the behavioral sciences and the humanities. I have tried to indicate the relevance of the machine-like use of signs as well, because I am concerned about our failure to use information technology effectively in business and administration.

---

*Excerpts from Ronald Stamper, *Information in Business and Administrative Systems,* London, Batsford, 1973, pp. 324–343. (Reprinted by permission of B. T. Batsford Limited.)

We fail because we do not understand clearly enough how organisations use information. Too often, elaborate systems are devised by people nurtured on a diet of computer programs, people who have never lifted their eyes from their plates long enough to realise that business systems are rather more than "common sense" or "mere O. & M."

We fail because we do not perceive clearly enough what machines can accomplish. Too often, slavish automation of an established clerical system has been demanded by managers and administrators, who have never imagined what might be accomplished by the human intellect and information machines in a new partnership.

[My]...aim...has been to place some ideas from the whole of the relevant field of knowledge in a single panoramic display. I should like the reader to feel that, despite their very great differences, all the views are essential to form a complete picture. The whole is semiotics, which I feel sure can help the man facing practical problems if only because it embodies a variety of perspectives rich enough to match the complexities of real life....

Pragmatics

What is a Sign?...[Signs] exhibit the variety of ways in which people convey messages to one another, not only in words but also silently. The full language is our culture. We communicate it from generation to generation with a great degree of accuracy which depends upon the complex interdependence of one stream of cultural messages upon another. The cultural anthropologists have attempted to describe this interdependence in terms of a syntactic structure,[1] but it seems to me more like the relationship of mutual information between sources of signals. However it arises, the result is that by pulling on one thread of our cultural web we can convey messages about another. These silent messages communicate emotive information: approval, dislike, threat, allegiance, aspirations. Everything that a person does, what he owns and how he uses things radiates these messages; they are easily misread by anyone who does not understand the precise cultural background from which he learnt them.

How Do Signs Acquire Their Stability? All our cultural signs, silent or vocal, derive their stability from the social groups in which they are used....Norm-formation...is one of the most important concepts in social psychology. Any departure, by an individual, from the norms of the group will be censured, whereas his conformity will be rewarded by a display of group approval. Censure and approval are forcefully expressed without words. This mechanism serves to control the individual and to provide the group with the stability essential for effective communication. Norms govern not only our wordless behaviour but also our beliefs, value judgements and even our perceptions, all three of which are usually expressed in words. Thus, deeply embedded in the matrix of a cultural system, language is able to achieve the consistency of usage essential for communication. Although the cultural foundation is slowly shifting, the social mechanism is able to re-align and extend the edifice of natural language to suit the contours of new problems.

How Do We Respond to Language Signs? Most of the information transmitted in organisations is carried by language.... There is a great difference between the language we speak and the language we write; the subtle, silent messages from body posture, facial expression and vocal inflexion add a richness to face-to-face communication that makes it indispensable for transmitting affective information. It is almost beyond the power of a human being to refrain from communicating affectively, thereby influencing attitudes, judgements, expectations and morale. When people try to be precisely descriptive, their judgements intrude and modify or even falsify the picture they report. Sensitivity to the affective overtones of language extends to written words; nonsense syllables will acquire an emotive colouring by chance association with expressive words. This colouring of words can be measured using Osgood's method of semantic differentials. Language has power over what we perceive: a word can predetermine how a person will interpret an ambiguous picture or a muffled voice. Even the apparently trivial nods and how-do-you-do's of recognition (phatic communion) serve to establish communication channels which are open to more serious use, should the need arise. The health of an organisation depends upon how its members communicate.

Semantics of Language

What Can Be Done to Raise the Standard of Communication? Most of our knowledge of signs and how to use them is rooted in the pragmatic level of cultural norms. At this level our linguistic behaviour may be highly sophisticated, but the sensitive interplay between words and thoughts suggests we should exercise caution, lest we should be betrayed by the magic of words. Semantics is a canon of critical methods by which we can establish the legitimacy of the imputed relationships between signs and what they represent.

The significations of signs cannot all be established in the same way. Some signs point to what can be observed objectively by many people; these are *designative signs*. Past and future things can also be designated, but the signs which represent them are more difficult to justify than signs for what can be observed at present. *Appraisive signs* convey judgements about things that can be designated; they must be related to expressions of human feelings. Designative and appraisive signs all serve to describe how things were, are or might be in the future, either objectively or as people respond to them; broadly speaking, we can say that *descriptive signs* convey factual information or value judgements. A different kind of information is conveyed by signs that serve to provoke actions, these are *prescriptive signs* and they can be subdivided into *instructions*, which denote the actions to be performed, and others which signify the threat of punishment or the promise of reward. To be effective, instructions must be supported by *inducements* which indicate the power behind them, not necessarily from the same source, perhaps from a centre of authority external to both giver and receiver of instructions, perhaps from the receiver's own conscience. To complete the classification, designations and instructions can be called *denotative information* while appraisals and inducements are called *affective information* . . . .

How Do Words Denote Things? Words convey very general information. Words select stable patterns from experience, label them so that they stand out as clear concepts in the mind, and provide handles by which concepts can be shifted to form new patterns that have never been experienced. They are the components from which we construct the imagined worlds of the past, the future and the inaccessible. The patterns which we deem worthy of being named are selected because, by common consent, they are the ones most useful for solving practical problems, getting things done, attaining satisfaction and avoiding discomfort. Apart from their necessary connection with the requirements of the human organism in its social setting, words are somewhat arbitrary. Our language embodies a host of metaphysical assumptions about the nature of the world we live in and the problems we have to solve. In a rapidly changing world we must prevent language from placing a straitjacket on our minds. It is salutary to remind oneself that other cultures, such as the American Indians', have languages which embody radically different assumptions about the world. It is often helpful to introduce subscripts, superscripts, hyphens, et ceteras, brackets and inverted commas, as devices to extend our language, and draw attention to the arbitrariness and vagueness of crucial words used in an argument. Starting from words which can be defined ostensively through experience, we can ascend a ladder of abstraction. To construct a secure ladder we must join each conceptual rung to firmer, less abstract rungs below by means of definitions. In the middle of the ladder we can use operational definitions but at the top theoretical definitions will be unavoidable. Unless we are careful to do this, our concepts will be supported only by verbal habits; we may then enjoy a beautiful floating feeling and a kind of mental exhilaration; but when we step off our verbal rung, back into the world of action, we shall fall on our faces.

How Should Statements Be Tested? We use statements to express particular ideas by assembling patterns of general word-tokens. Statements are models of the world as it is, as it was or as it may be. Information about the worlds past and present can be generated from observations, aggregated to a suitable level of abstraction. This information is important in running an organisation but it is not enough. It is the task of managers and administrators to construct the world of the future so they need also statements about the possible worlds they might create. These are generated in the minds of men. Reasoning begins, always, with a stage of conjecture, creation or *abduction*. This provides an indispensable but neglected input of information to all decisions. Conjectures can be nonsense or they can be sound. How do we distinguish between them? We can test them for logical self-consistency, perhaps with the aid of mathematics. We can apply the aesthetic test of Occam's Razor which pares the statements down to their most economical formulation. This helps to make the empirical tests of the next stage more severe; from the hypotheses being tested, we derive statements which can be checked by observation; if the result is negative we can reject the hypothesis, if it is positive we cannot say that the hypothesis is proven, only that it has been corroborated. Finally, we must inspect the evidence used to check the observational statement; in the natural sciences this can be done by making the observation repeatedly; in other decision-situations it can only be done by checking the reliability of the source of evidence, as a lawyer or historian would. Despite all these tests, it is impossible to make sure that the kinds of statements used for making organisational decisions are segregated into facts and value judgements. Decisions, on the vast scale which is normal in big business and government, are outside the scope of purely rational and objective argument. Operational research, economic and accounting models may look coolly reasoned but they will be based upon assumptions embodying someone's value judgements.

Semantics of Number

How Can We Check the Meaning of Numerical Information? Large organisations must use numbers to cope with the scale of their operations. Words can only be aggregated if a person assimilates them and then condenses them into general, subjective conclusions, but numbers can be aggregated arithmetically and objectively. The meaning of the resulting numerical information depends upon the operational procedures by which the numbers are assigned to things: the process of measuring. Some measurements are firmly rooted in structural properties of the real world, these are the *fundamental measurements*. There are *derived measurements* which are obtained by arithmetical manipulations of fundamental measurements. There need be little doubt about the meaning of these in operational terms. Many other measurements used in business are hard to justify. They are the *pointer measurements* which assign numbers to things by an arbitrary procedure or by using an instrument which cannot be calibrated by reference to any fundamental measurement. The key to the distinction between fundamental and pointer measurements is the concept of a scale. When a fundamental measurement is defined, it is *essential* to set up a system of operational relationships among the things being measured; *these relationships do not depend upon the numbers to be assigned* because they can be demonstrated by making empirical tests or by asking a person for his judgements. A scale is then defined which consists of a system of numbers *plus* certain arithmetical relationships, and the measurement is completed by assigning numbers to the things, in such a way that the operational relationships are mirrored by the arithmetical relationships. Pointer measurements have no objective scale because they have to assign numbers *before* any relationship can be defined, instead of the reverse being true. It can be very difficult to justify the use of a pointer measurement, as it can only be done experimentally by showing that the measurement can serve as a predictor. However, if you do not ask awkward questions about the basis of the numerical data (and who does?) it all looks beautifully reliable when garnished with a sprig or two of mathematics!

How Do We Ascend the Ladder of Numerical Abstractions? Numbers can be combined in many useful ways that are clearly meaningful, at least when fundamental measurement underlies them: totals, sub-totals, means, medians, modes are well-known. Also statistics provides a host of techniques such as regression, factor analysis, the method of principal components and cluster analysis, which draw attention to apparent patterns in the data. Sometimes one invokes "objective," statistical tests of the significance of these patterns, dismissing them if the test shows that they might have arisen just by chance. The only adequate test of significance in the final analysis is in terms of their usefulness in solving a practical problem: this is a matter of human judgement; statistical tests can only serve to elect candidates for the accolade of significance.

How Do We Measure Statements?...Common sense suggests that "information" is the name we give to some kind of intrinsic property of statements or messages or signals. A person may be asked to judge how reliable certain statements are as a basis for action, on a scale from "perfectly" to "not in the least." If he is asked first before and then after you give him a message, it is possible to associate the changes in his opinion with the "information content" of the message. The trouble with this method is that a person will make inconsistent judgements and so make it difficult to attach any clear meaning to the resulting measurement. It is possible to show a person that, to be consistent in his judgements in circumstances where it makes sense to place bets on the statements, he should obey certain rules. These rules are the axioms of probability. Once again you can give him a message and use the change in his subjective probabilities to measure the information in the message. There is yet another improvement. If you can persuade the subject to make probability judgements about all the different messages he might receive, you can impose a further rule of reasonable judgement: the conditional probability rule. This gives rise to another measurement of subjective probability and some better measurements of information, one of them even displaying the precious additivity property:

$$\text{Info}(E_1 \ \& \ E_2) = \text{Info}(E_1) + \text{Info}(E_2)$$

when the messages E_1 and E_2 are "independent" of one another.

Can Information Compel "Reasonable" People to Reach Agreement? The answer, regrettably, is "no." Two people, individually, can remain quite consistent in their judgements and as sharply opposed as ever, even though they adjust their separate opinions to each new item of information in the most reasonable manner. The trouble stems from their very different judgements of the evidence. You may get them to agree on a general rule for interpreting evidence but, when faced with it, each may decide that the only thing proven by the evidence is that their rule for judging it was wrong. It may be better to let both sides believe the evidence to be biased, provided, thereby, that they are able to feel that it lies within the bounds of credibility. There is another strategy: undermine, separately, the confidence of each in his prepared position before adducing the evidence they must share. Then, as can be shown by the Principle of Stable Estimation, anyone's prior opinion will be irrelevant when confronted by very exact and reliable information provided that he was not too strongly committed in the first place....

What Information Counts as Truly "Objective"? People may come to agree how certain evidence should be interpreted, by forming a consensus, through social interaction: as though they were establishing an evaluative norm. This is the only method in many practical situations but, where possible, it is desirable to employ further normative rules which any "reasonable" man can accept as guides to his judgement. One such principle can be invoked when the evidence can be derived from repeated observations or replicated experiments. Provided that all the processes of sampling and the procedures of observation and experiment can be *randomised*, then, as reasonable men, we are adjured to accept the *relative frequencies* of events as accurate guides to the probabilities we should attach to statements about them. In these very special circumstances the evidence has an objective force that cannot be denied. Provided that enough information can be obtained we can also cast our first, private opinions to the winds and invoke the *maximum likelihood principle* as a basis for our inductive reasoning. Probability based on relative frequency is appropriate in engineering, where it serves as a basis for yet another measurement of information. It is important, however, not to confuse the relative frequencies actually derived from observations with numbers spoken of as though they were relative frequencies, but derived from a mathematical model of a set of possible events. These are logical probabilities, their semantic standing, if any, being derived from the plausibility of the model, not from the observation of relative frequencies....

Syntactics

What Is Information Processing? From signs, words, statements, numbers and mathematical expressions, we construct models of the world. How do we assemble them and take them apart? What operations can we perform on these models? Such questions require answers which relate only to the signs; the real world, to which semantics attaches them, we can forget. By doing so, we enter the beautiful clear world of mathematics and formal logic, divorced from the untidy world of action. The only objects of interest are the letters, numbers and other symbols which we shuffle about on pieces of paper and inside computing machinery; there is a limited number of *types* of symbol but an endless supply of *tokens*, should we need them. We distinguish between these *object symbols* from which a formal system is constructed and the *meta-symbols* in which the object system is defined. The bases of these systems are the formal languages, each comprising strings of symbol tokens all produced according to a precise set of rules. Depending upon the kind of production rule, the resulting language is called finite-state, context-free or context-sensitive. From simple languages complex ones can be generated by substitution, from complex ones we can isolate simple component languages that make them easier to understand. All this seems remote from everyday life until we notice that some of these formal languages have grammars like ordinary English and that the production and recognition of sentences can be performed by computers. It is also possible to process information from a multitude of practical problems in exactly the same way by using the rules of a single formal system but with different semantic interpretations. That, as a way of increasing productivity, should gratify the most exacting manager!

How Can the Procedures of Formal Logic Be Used in an Organisation? Bureaucracy is built upon a system of formal procedures for making decisions and taking actions. By using a kind of logic called the propositional calculus, many parts of a bureaucratic system can be cast into the shape of a formal language which can be processed with greater efficiency by computers than by clerks. The propositional calculus is a simple component of our natural language but not a part that most people manipulate with much skill and accuracy. Using decision tables and algorithms (which are like computer programs), the tortuous prose of the bureaucrat can be hammered into neat rows of questions with "yes" and "no" answers. If you can assign the answers correctly (a semantic problem) the other procedures can be performed automatically and the tax demand or pension-book can be generated by a machine....

Can Machines Perform More Than Simple Routine Work? They can. They are able to display a kind of rudimentary intelligence by virtue of their power to store thousands of millions of characters of information, any part being within reach in a small fraction of a second. Machine intelligence depends upon the formal manipulation of signs. The first step in building a suitable system is to extend the *propositional logic,* so that each *elementary proposition* is like a simple English sentence with a subject and a predicate. These so-called *basic sentences* form the elementary units of information in another formal language-structure known as *predicate logic*. A computer store, filled with basic sentences, can yield the answers to numerous questions. However, even at a computer's fantastic speed, some questions, which seem quite straightforward, cannot be answered in a reasonable time if the memory is organised on the basis of a predicate logic. More elaborate *data-structures* are required to enhance the machine's performance. The formal language-structures are all one-dimensional, being based upon strings of symbols, but other data-structures can be multi-dimensional. Despite their greater complexity, they can be accommodated in the structure of a computer store in a form known as a *memory-structure* or *file-structure*. The result is a machine with a memory for detail, with a size and speed of operation able to match the needs of a large organisation.

Does the Formal Analysis of Signs Suggest More Ways of Measuring Information? If a formal system can behave with a degree of intelligence, then it seems natural to use it as an objective standard for measuring information. The simplest way would be to count the numbers of symbols employed in the message; another step would be to count the numbers of basic sentences it contains. In all but the simplest problems these methods are either inappropriate or unworkable. Another method can be developed for a simple predicate logic. It is based upon a set of statements that are the least informative ones which can be made in that logical language; these are the *content elements*. Any message can be translated into a set of content elements; the size of this set can be used to measure the information in the message. This method also gives rise to logical probability measures, emphasising again the close relationship between probability and information. Unfortunately, the method has a serious defect because it takes no account of the processing required to analyse the message; it simply assumes that this can be done instantaneously. There is yet to be discovered a way of measuring information that takes into account the work needed to derive it from a memory structure.

Empirics

Given a Communication Channel, What Limits the Information It Can Carry? This is an important question which syntactics disregards because it assumes that signs can be re-arranged instantly with perfect precision. Information, in the context of communication, can be regarded as a stream of signs which must be transported from one location to another, regardless of what they mean, but taking account of the speed and accuracy of transportation. Semantic questions can be disregarded, as in syntactics. Instead, attention is directed towards the statistical properties of the events at the source of signals and at their destination. The result is a branch of engineering analysis called the *statistical theory of signal transmission*. It uses measurements of information based upon relative-frequency probabilities. It defines the information generated by a source of signals in terms of its *variety* of actual behaviour, which is measured by a statistic called *entropy*. It measures the capacity of a channel in terms of the variety of its potential behaviour, taking account of the chance corruption of signals or *equivocation*. The theory shows how to measure, in terms of *mutual information*, similarities in the random behaviour of two or more sources, and it guides the engineer in the design of codes which overcome, as far as possible, the effects of *noise* in the communication channel.

Is the Engineering Theory of Communication Relevant Only to Machines? Not at all. Strictly speaking it is a branch of statistics and it can be applied wherever a sustained pattern of random activity communicates its effects to another place. In fact a person who is speaking, using a keyboard or filling in forms is operating as a channel and his behaviour can be measured statistically. It is found that human channel-capacity is about $2\frac{1}{2}$ bits per stimulus for a very simple task, increasing logarithmically with the complexity of the stimulus. Speed of transmission by a human being can approach 30 bits per second but is normally about 10–20 bits per second, compared with machines which can transmit at ten million times that speed. This engineering analysis is only just beginning to be applied to organisational problems of information-handling.

Topics Which Link the Branches of Semiotics

Design of Forms. This is a commonplace task that is much more difficult than first appearances suggest. It poses problems in the design of codes, the use of correlated questions and check-digits for detecting errors; these belong to the field of empirics. Syntactic problems arise in the choice of the sequence of questions, the grouping of forms for clerical operations, and in the use of forms in a filing system. Semantic questions concern the definition of any procedures of observation or measurement, when a form is used as a source of information; they also arise where the information on the documents is to be used for decision-making or for compiling a report. Pragmatic knowledge must be used to decide how people will respond to the form and the instructions for using it.

Decision-Making. Repeated decision-procedures such as those used in controlling the quality of a product can be studied by the methods of empirics.

Most important organisational decisions are only made once; the result of the decision (the building of a new motorway or the launching of a new product) changes the organisation or its environment to such an extent that the same problem can never occur again. In these circumstances logical models, such as linear programming or critical path analysis, can be used. They are generalised, formal, syntactic solutions but they cannot be employed without a semantic analysis to justify them. Every organisational decision of any importance will involve a number of people arriving at a consensus about values and priorities and sometimes about matters of fact. This process must be understood in terms of pragmatics.

Meaning....the concept of "meaning"...is as vague a term as "information" and it can be interpreted at all four levels of semiotics. "Meaning" can always be interpreted as a relationship between a sign and a "thing" or between one sign and another; the "thing" may be an object, a property, an event, an action or a state of affairs. The relationships can be established in many different ways, resulting in many different kinds of meaning. A few illustrations can be given from each level of semiotics.

At the pragmatic level, almost any object or pattern of behaviour can be invested with meaning by virtue of its regular employment in a social context. Any pair of "things" which are frequently found in association with one another tends to acquire a meaningful relationship thus: dog–subservience; Fleet Street–newspapers; ceremonial–power; the armchair by the fire–father. Usually the relationship "x means y" requires x to be, in a sense, more specific than y. Some of these relationships are rooted in the physical nature of things (storm–trouble; red–danger), others are sustained only by the social process (dark blue–Oxford; handlebar moustache–RAF 1939–45). In all these cases people will come to regard x as a sign for y. This pragmatic meaning will be a kind of mental habit in which they are rehearsed either by observing actual events in nature or by the widespread social use of the habit.

Semantics...is concerned with meanings established by a chain of *operational procedures* linking a "thing" and a sign. In a world where pragmatic meanings can be established so easily by the repetition of two things in association with one another, semantic analysis has the important task of sifting the reliable meanings from the unreliable. When using information to organise a business or administer public affairs, it is wise to check that the signs are related or can be related to "real" things. The operations through which the relationship is established determine the semantic category of the sign. These categories are shown in the table. It must be remembered that any information used in running an organisation seldom falls into only one

Intention of: SIGNIFICATIONS mode of:	Descriptive signs *represent the world and serve to augment our senses* *"thing"→sign*	Prescriptive signs *are used to provoke actions and serve to extend our grasp on the world* *sign→"thing"*
Denotative signs *are related to the objective world of common experience external to the human organism*	designation $\left.\begin{array}{l}\textit{object}\\\textit{property}\\\textit{event}\end{array}\right\}\rightarrow \textit{sign}$ *"I am showing you this."*	instruction $\textit{sign}\rightarrow\left\{\begin{array}{l}\textit{action to}\\\textit{be carried}\\\textit{out}\end{array}\right.$ *"Don't do that!"*
Affective signs *are related to the subjective world of personal feelings within the organism*	appraisal $\left.\begin{array}{l}\textit{feeling about an}\\\textit{object, property}\\\textit{or event}\end{array}\right\}\rightarrow \textit{sign}$ *"I like it."*	inducement $\textit{sign}\rightarrow\left\{\begin{array}{l}\textit{feeling which}\\\textit{will result}\\\textit{from action}\end{array}\right.$ *"You will be hurt if you do."*

category. Words and statements, especially rather abstract ones, have multiple significations.

Information about the hypothetical future is interesting. Its meaning cannot be tested operationally by linking *"things"* to *signs* except by demonstrating that the prospect of doing so is not contrary to our present knowledge. Some justifiable descriptions of the future never come about, others result from the flux of time, and others are brought about through the use of prescriptive information. We generate our future by selecting a suitable description and translating it into instructions and inducements.

Syntactic meanings are relationships between signs at a formal level. If a mechanical process can translate code x to code y or sentence x to sentence y, this can be taken as a definition of "x means y." Also at the syntactic level we can associate the word "meaning" with a system of relationships: imagine a complex file containing details of interrelated jobs, work-in-progress, orders, tools, machine centres and men; the "meaning" of a message about a machine breakdown could be understood in terms of its effect on the structure of the file.

Meaning at the empirical level can be established by a relationship of cause and effect. You can determine the meanings of the signals received from a communication channel by discovering which input signals might have caused them.

Probability and Measurements of Information . . . .the amount of information conveyed by a statement, signal or message can be measured in many different ways, some of which have scarcely been explored, as yet. One method is by evaluating signs on many scales simultaneously, as in Osgood's technique of semantic differentials. These are intensive measurements; extensive measurements, which have an additivity property, can be obtained by using probability as a fundamental measurement. All probability measurements have the same mathematical structure, which can be used to reflect various empirical structures. By changing the empirical relationships a variety of measurements with different meanings can be obtained. A relationship based upon human judgements of statements gives rise to a subjective probability; formal relationships can be used to generate a variety of logical probability measurements; and observations of the relative frequencies of events provide the objective relationship from which statistical probabilities are derived.

Information measures of various kinds can be obtained from these probability measures in two different ways. There is a measurement, relative to a set of statements, which depends upon the change of opinion caused by the information being measured. There is also a way of measuring a statement, S, directly, in terms of the probability attached to it, using a function such as

$$\text{Info}(S) = 1 - \text{Prob}(S) \text{ or } \text{Info}(S) = -\log \text{Prob}(S)$$

Except in the field of communications engineering, very little use has yet been made of information measures, so it will be some years before we learn which ones are important.

Semiotics and Four Levels of Knowledge. Organisation is only possible because we can employ signs to coordinate the work of many hands and eyes. The information systems that we create seem to resemble great machines like communication networks with computers at their nodes, but the analogy is dangerous. It is quite beyond the capacity of men to understand the functioning of an organisation in the same way as a team of engineers can comprehend the functioning of a machine. There may be anything from ten to 100,000 human components in an organisation; each one may respond to signs in his own way, but we cannot describe how a single one behaves, except in performing some simple, repetitive tasks. If we could describe an organisation in detail, our knowledge would be outdated after a few hours because some people working in it would have changed their goals or their perceptions of their tasks. An engineer's kind of knowledge alone will not serve an information specialist. Semiotics, therefore, studies the nature of information on four levels.

Empirics is the engineering level. Some problems in routine, repetitive data-handling will succumb to this type of analysis. Examples are the distribution of the work-load among clerks or machinery, the design of codes, and the optimisation of repetitive decisions.

Syntactics is the computer-programming level. Languages can be designed and used to perform elaborate tasks on computers. These formal systems may be so elaborate that they never do exactly the same thing twice. They depend only upon a knowledge of the structural properties of systems of signs. Examples are the algorithms for scheduling of production or for the storage and retrieval of information.

Semantics is the business analyst's level. Economic analysts, financial analysts, systems analysts and others, in various circumstances, establish the connection between signs and what they signify in the real world. Examples are the description of a market, the compilation of a budget and the design of an information system.

Pragmatics is the operational level. Everyone in an organisation responds to signs; he must know how to do this intuitively or the organisation would cease functioning. Such knowledge cannot always be made explicit, and some people might not wish to regard it as a part of the knowledge of an information system, but, in practical affairs, it is the most important part.

Limitations of time and resources are enough to force a manager, confronted by a complex and unique problem, to rely upon his pragmatic knowledge. This should be no excuse for failing to use critical semantic analysis, or general syntactic solutions, or even the principles of empirics, where circumstances permit.

Our knowledge resides in the signs we use and how we use them. It would be surprising, therefore, if the study of information did not raise serious philosophical problems. The solution...is to acknowledge that we can know about signs in four ways: intuitively, critically, formally and empirically. One must have recourse to all of these when solving a practical problem about the use of information in an organisation.

POSTSCRIPT: INFORMATION AND SOCIETY

Semiotic has for its goal a general theory of signs in all their forms and manifestations. It provides one more wedge for entering into the tissue of man's symbolic life.

—Charles Morris, *Signification and Significance*

We are faced, in the social sciences, with a full and complicated interaction between observer and observed, between subject and object.

—Popper, *Poverty of Historicism*

...By concentrating upon business uses of information, it has been possible to investigate one part of the "tissue of man's symbolic life," a part which is undergoing rapid changes as a result of the increasing use of information technology. Computers and communication networks are being grafted onto organisations of all kinds. These information machines can be used either to enrich man's elaborate symbolic life, or to tie society to a rack of formal systems which will be tightened in the cause of order and efficiency.

If society is not to disable itself in the name of progress, by thrusting the instruments of information technology into its organs of decision-making and control, then it should stop brandishing the picks and shovels of computer technology as though they were magic surgical instruments. There is a dangerous belief that anyone who can grasp these rudimentary new tools is competent to anaesthetise an organisation with his aura of modern knowledge and tomorrow's jargon and then proceed to rip out the arteries clogged with paper, lance the gathering of committees, loosen the paralysis of indecision, all with the edge of a punched card and a little common sense. Some patients have died and others have suffered agonies recovering from these operations and, moreover, they have paid heavily for the service.

Common sense is not an adequate guide to the anatomy of an organisation. In the days before computers we were only able to administer gentle massage to the stiff parts of a system through management education and some carefully directed personnel work. The advent of the computer has inaugurated the age of organisational surgery. Technology has created machines which can respond to and employ language, behave almost intelligently and supplement the human intellect in areas where it is weakest. These remarkable machines, if they are to serve any useful function, must be grafted with great skill into the tissue of society. We have not yet learnt how to do this. One thing is clear: we cannot leave this job to the machine-makers—there is too great a difference between the functioning of a machine and the functioning of a human information system. We need professional information specialists whose knowledge spans the whole of semiotics, the anatomy of man's symbolic life.

No analogy between the information specialist and the surgeon, no comparison of his work and the work of the engineer or architect, will serve to explain its most difficult characteristic. It is a characteristic shared with all social sciences: "a full and complicated interaction between the observer and the observed." The natural scientist, who can make repeated observations under nearly identical conditions, who can regulate the conditions in which he conducts experiments, can plot his field of discourse with a precision denied to anyone surveying our social environment. The Uncertainty Principle in physics forces the investigator to recognise that any attempt to observe a sub-atomic system is likely to be impossible without disturbing it, to such an extent that the process of observation will automatically invalidate its own results. This difficulty can be escaped by investigating gross phenomena. The natural sciences are able, therefore, to underpin the work of the surgeon, the engineer and the architect with a secure framework of objective knowledge, derived from reliable experiments which can be repeated as often as accuracy demands.

The social sciences cannot provide the information specialist with a similar framework of knowledge. Repeated observation and controlled experiment can be used only to a limited extent by social scientists. The information specialist who tries to use these methods to investigate an organisation must recognise their limitations. Social structures, unlike most structures of the physical world, are in a continual state of flux, so that it is difficult to discover about them much that is valid at other times or places. Social structures, unlike physical structures, respond intelligently by deceiving the observer, anticipating his results or changing into something quite different when his conclusions are revealed. There are two problems here: the diversity and flux of social systems, and the interaction of observer and observed that so often nullifies knowledge and action.

The perpetual flux of the universe has been a philosophical problem since Heraclitus, but ordinary language solves it: we *are* able to step twice into the same river provided that we use the word "river" as ordinary men do; it is when we start to label every drop of water that we go wrong. If we step beyond the operational bounds of our concepts they will not support our understanding but that step must be made. Physics can label the drops of water in the river of Heraclitus without falling in, because it first erects a platform of new concepts; instead of talking about the invariance of the river banks and the cold, wet properties of the water, physics talks about the invariant character of the *process of flowing* and uses a set of hydrodynamic equations instead of the ordinary word "river." The flux of a social system does not prevent us from talking about an "organisation" but trouble arises when we try to label parts or properties of an organisation. We should not expect the micro-structure of an organisation to be capable of being explained in the same way as its macro-structure. We need to find new concepts which correspond to invariant properties of its inner processes, not hydrodynamic equations in this case, but descriptions of the sign-processes through which organisation is accomplished. Semiotics is to organisations as physics is to rivers.

As the engineer can use the hydrodynamics of rivers to design the piers of bridges, so one might expect the information specialist to be able to use the semiotics of organisations to improve their functioning. He can, but not in the same way. The engineer can design a bridge and then assemble the component parts according to his design. The passive materials from which a bridge is built do not question the designer, wilfully change their proportions or reassemble themselves into a boat! The components of an organisation behave in just such perverse ways when anyone tries to force them into a form which they dislike.

Insight into the nature of information should make it possible to exploit information technology to the fullest extent by creating entirely new kinds of organisations. This will only be done successfully if we acknowledge that people, the components from which organisations are built, have the capacity to organise themselves. Information systems will not, then, be imposed upon people; instead, they will be designed to enable social systems to organise themselves more effectively. This can be done at the *empiric level* by matching the capabilities of men and machines; at the *syntactic level* by devising formal languages that are economical and adaptable; at the *semantic level* by showing people how to sustain a firm connection between the symbols they manipulate and the real world; and at the *pragmatic level* by training people to use information with sensitivity.

Organisations create themselves according to their ability to use information. That ability can be enhanced by the use of machines. Semiotics, the general theory of information, is one of the tools we shall need for creating the organisations of the future.

Note

[1] See Claude Levi-Strauss. *Structural Anthropology*. London: Penguin Press, 1968.

Search Problems in Bureaus*
Anthony Downs

The Basic Processes of Decision and Action Related to Search

...We assume that the decisionmaker starts in a position of equilibrium with no performance gaps. His steps in generating a new nonprogrammed action are as follows:

1. *Perception.* He obtains new information as a result of his automatic search.
2. *Assimilation.* The information he has received alters his image of the world.
3. *Performance Assessment.* When he compares this altered image of the world with his goals, he discovers a performance gap large enough to exceed his inertia threshold. In short, he believes he ought to do something.
4. *Formulation of Alternatives.* He designs a number of possible actions directed at reducing the performance gap.
5. *Analysis of Alternatives.* He then analyzes each possible action by testing it against his image of the world in order to discover its likely consequences.
6. *Evaluation of Alternatives.* He evaluates these consequences by measuring them against his goals.
7. *Strategy Formation.* If one or more of the actions appears likely to eliminate the performance gap, he incorporates it (or them) into a strategy of action under various conditions.
8. *Action Selection.* He then reexamines his image of the world to discover what conditions exist, and carries out the appropriate action in accordance with his strategy. (He may decide to do nothing, in which case he next acts as in step 13.b....)
9. *Continuous Data Acquisition.* His information inputs during steps 3 through 8 are as follows:

In: *Inside Bureaucracy.* Boston, Little, Brown, 1967, pp. 175–190. (Copyright © 1967, 1966 by The Rand Corporation. Reprinted by permission of the publisher, Little, Brown and Company and The Rand Corporation.)

a. He receives a stream of information from his automatic search which constantly alters (or confirms) his image of the world.

b. He may engage in special-project search aimed at discovering additional facts relevant to any of these....

10. *Action Impact.* His action affects the world in some way, giving rise to new conditions therein.

11. *Action Feedback.* He receives information about these new conditions.

12. *Assimilation of Feedback.* This feedback information alters his image of the world once more.

13. *Performance Reassessment.* He compares this revised image of the world with his goals to determine whether any performance gap still exists.

a. If the gap has been eliminated, he is once more in a position of equilibrium and returns to his automatic level of search intensity.

b. If a performance gap still exists but is below his inertia threshold, he will probably continue some special-project search. However, he will not go through the action cycle again.

c. If a performance gap still exists and it exceeds his inertia threshold, he repeats the action cycle until either condition a or b...prevails.

The Specific Economics of Acquiring Information

The basic principle of rational action involved in search is that the individual should procure additional information so long as its marginal returns exceed its marginal costs. However, this proposition is an empty tautology unless we specify the returns and costs involved.

The Returns from Acquiring Information in General. The function of information is to help the decisionmaker improve his selection among possible actions. These actions are evaluated in terms of their likely impacts upon the performance gap, which can be stated in terms of changes in his utility. The net impact is the net gain or loss in utility caused by any action.

In many situations, uncertainty makes estimating the net impact of an action extremely difficult. However, the decisionmaker can use two concepts to grapple with such uncertainty. The expected value of an action's net impact constitutes a quantitative estimate of the action's likely effect upon his utility. Its variance measures his confidence in the accuracy of that estimate. Thus, the higher an action's expected net impact, the more promising the action appears. However, if the net impact also has a high variance, the decisionmaker may have low confidence in his estimate.

The individual decisionmaker is likely to use net-impact estimates both in analyzing the consequences of potential actions and in evaluating their impact upon his performance gap. Deciding how much information to procure in analyzing an action is intrinsically related to the potential impact of that action upon utility. Unless the action appears to offer some possibility of increasing utility, there is no point in finding out anything more about it. On the other hand, if it appears to offer such promise, one is justified in trying to obtain enough additional information about its effects to compare its net impact with those of alternative actions.

This means that in practice the person analyzing the consequences of any possible action is also continuously evaluating their net impact upon his utility. Only by doing so can he estimate the likely returns from further analysis, thereby deciding how much effort he should make to procure additional data. This leads to the important conclusion that it is impossible to separate the analysis and evaluation steps in the decision and action process without causing the allocation of either too few or too many resources to analysis.

The Returns from Acquiring Particular Pieces of Information. Up to now, we have shown how information derives general value from its roles in decision-making. Yet the choices actually facing the individual do not involve obtaining more information in general, but obtaining particular pieces of data. Clearly, he should acquire any piece with a marginal return exceeding its marginal cost. Its marginal return depends upon the effect it is likely to have upon his estimate of the net impact of an action. It could have any of the following effects:

—It might alter his opinion about what the action's consequences are likely to be without changing his degree of confidence in that (new) opinion. This means it would change only the action's expected net impact.
—It might alter his degree of confidence about the action's likely consequences, without changing that opinion. This means it would change only the variance of the action's net impact. Such a change in confidence alone could have very significant effects upon his behavior. For example, if the information raised his confidence enough, he might stop looking for more data about that action. Conversely, if the information lowered his confidence drastically, he might suspend any decision until he had further data.
—It might change both the expected value and the variance of the action's net impact.
—It might change neither.

The Costs of Acquiring Particular Pieces of Information. Whether the deci-sionmaker will translate his needs and desires for data into actual procure-ment depends in part upon the costs of doing so. These costs include the following:

—*Resource costs* of search, such as time, money, and effort.
—*Costs of delay*, such as the costs of carrying any operations that must be suspended while further information is sought and assimilated, and losses of the utility that would be gained from taking action immediately.

How Organizational Decisionmaking Differs from Individual Decisionmaking

Decisionmaking within large organizations differs from that conducted by a single individual for the obvious reason that it involves many persons instead of one. As a result:

—The various steps in the decision and action cycle are carried out by dif-ferent persons.
—An organization must generate numerous conflict-controlling and con-sensus-creating mechanisms because its members have widely varying perception apparatuses, memories, images of the world, and goals.
—Organization decisionmaking involves the following significant costs of internal communication that have no analogs within an individual:
  a. Losses of utility due to errors of transmission.
  b. Losses of utility (for the ultimate users of the data) due to distortion.
  c. Resources (especially time) absorbed in internal communications.
  d. Losses of utility due to overloading communications channels in the short run.

On the other hand, organizations have such advantages over individuals as much greater capacity to carry out all steps in the decision and action cycle, extensive internal specialization, and simultaneous maintenance of a diver-sity of viewpoints.

We have made explicit these rather obvious differences between organi-zations and individuals because we will also use our basic conceptual scheme for individual decisionmaking in our analysis of organizational search.

Basic Problems in Organizational Search

The basic problems of organizational search include some that are not relevant to individuals. These problems are generated by tensions arising from four factors:

1. *The Unity of Search, Analysis, and Evaluation.* Search, analysis, and evaluation cannot be separated from each other without creating needs for almost continuous communications, irrational allocations of resources, or both.

2. *The Need for Consensus.* Bureaus operate on such a large scale that any significant decision almost invariably affects many bureau members and their activities. These intra-bureau repercussions are unlikely to be fully known to any one member (even the topmost official) unless he specifically seeks the advice of others. In essence, no one bureau member encompasses all the goals relevant to the bureau's whole operation. But evaluation requires measuring possible actions against one's goals (via the performance gap). Hence, evaluation is necessarily fragmentalized in every bureau.

3. *The Economies of Delegation.* Organizations can achieve huge economies of scale in search by assigning some of the steps involved to specialists. But this requires separating some of the steps in the search-analysis-evaluation cycle from others.

4. *Nontechnical Divergence of Goals.* Both delegation and the fragmentalizing of evaluation require giving certain powers of discretion regarding a given decision to many different officials. But officials always use some of whatever discretionary powers they have to benefit themselves and the bureau sections to which they are loyal rather than the bureau as a whole, thus introducing partly inconsistent goals into the theoretically unified search-analysis-evaluation cycle. This point is different from the need for consensus. The latter is required because a bureau is so large that no single member knows what all its relevant goals are. Hence consensus would be necessary even if all members had identical personal goals and ambitions. But nontechnical goal divergence arises from conflicts of interest that cannot be eliminated by knowledge alone.

...We will explore specific aspects of the search processes in bureaus arising from tensions among these four factors.

How the Biases of Individual Officials Affect the Search Process

As each official goes through the decision and action process, he behaves somewhat differently from the way he would if his goals were identical to the formal purposes of the organization. Among his biases relevant to search are the following:

1. His perception apparatus will partially screen out data adverse to his interests, and magnify those favoring his interests.[1] The probability that important data will not be screened out by such biases can be increased by assigning overlapping search responsibilities to persons with different and even conflicting interests and policy preferences, or assigning search tasks to persons who have no particular policy preferences and whose interests are not connected with the advancement of any bureau section.

2. In formulating alternative actions, each official will tend to give undue precedence to alternatives most favorable to his interests, and to those about which adequate consensus can most easily be established. The purpose of decisionmaking within a bureau involves significant costs. Some of these costs probably rise more than proportionately with the number of alternatives considered. Hence it is often more rational for a bureau to choose from a set of alternatives it has already assembled than to expand that set, even if such expansion might provide it with additional choices markedly superior to those now facing it.

This implies that the order in which alternative actions are assembled and evaluated may have an extremely important impact on what an organization eventually does. If the first set of alternatives considered contains at least one that closes the performance gap, the bureau may never discover other alternatives that would not only close that gap, but also provide a new higher level of performance.

As a result, any biases among officials that cause certain types of alternatives to be systematically considered early in the game will cause those types of alternatives to be adopted more often than they would be if officials were unbiased. Among such biases are the following:

—Since relatively simple proposals are much easier to discuss and obtain consensus about than complicated ones, officials will tend to consider such proposals first. This implies that over any given period, a bureau will tend to choose policies that are simpler than those it would choose if its members had perfect information about all possible proposals. Part of this simplification is a rational response to the costs of deliberation, but part results from officials' biases.

—Officials will tend to consider those alternatives that benefit their own interests before those adverse to their interests. Thus, a bureau will tend to select alternatives that are unduly favorable to the particular officials who are in charge of proposing alternatives. Incumbents are usually favored by actions that do not radically alter the *status quo*. Staff members are more oriented toward change so long as it does not injure their own interests or those of their line superiors. Hence bureaus in which incumbent office holders design proposals will tend to make unduly conservative choices. Those in which staff members design proposals will not exhibit this bias unless the proposals concern their behavior or that of their line superiors.

—The evaluation process in bureaus is fragmentalized; so officials proposing policies often need to obtain support from a number of others only marginally concerned. These officials usually bargain for a *quid pro quo* in return for their support. A common *quid pro quo* is including something in the alternatives that benefits them, even though it does not directly affect the performance gap concerned. Another is omitting from these alternatives anything damaging to their interests, even though it would benefit the bureau as a whole. The *existence of such "territorial bargaining" has the following implications:* [2]

(1) A bureau will choose actions that unduly favor continuance of the existing allocation of resources and power among its subsections.

(2) Officials shaping alternatives will try to exclude marginal effects from their proposals so as to reduce the amount of consensus they need to achieve. [3] This will unduly narrow the impact of actions taken by the bureau. We refer to such behavior as the *shrinking violet syndrome*. . . .

(3) The alternatives formulated will be irrationally affected by the particular organization of the bureau.

—If the initial set of alternatives assembled by an official has been rejected, he can either abandon the project, search for wholly new alternatives, or try to reformulate the rejected ones. If the latter include proposals strongly supported by powerful officials, he will tend to devote too much effort to reformulating those proposals.

—Officials will tend to propose alternatives involving as little uncertainty as possible in order to avoid complicated and conflict-engendering negotiations. Thus, over any given period, a bureau will tend to adopt actions that do not take sufficient account of future uncertainties.

The. . .analysis indicates that the need to establish consensus before making decisions has a tremendous influence upon the processes of search within a bureau. The more officials involved in a decision, and the greater the diversity of their views and interests, the more factors must be taken into account, the more alternatives must be explored, and the harder it is to get a consensus on any alternative.

This creates a dilemma for bureaus regarding search. On one hand, those who formulate alternatives often try to restrict the choices they consider to those that affect as few other officials as possible. This renders decision-making both faster and easier. But bureaus will systematically tend to consider narrower alternatives than they would if officials were unbiased.

On the other hand, if officials extend their range of search to encompass alternatives affecting a great many others, they will generate both extremely high costs of reaching a decision and a strong probability that the decision will support the *status quo* to an excessive degree. Thus it appears extraordinarily difficult to create incentives for the officials involved so that (a) they will extend their search for alternatives far enough to encompass all significant interdependencies, (b) they will make decisions relatively quickly and easily, and (c) those decisions will incorporate really significant changes in the *status quo* when warranted.

This situation results partly from a correct perception of the costs of change. If each part of a bureau merely had to consider changing its behavior every time an official anywhere else was making a decision that might affect it, the bureau would lose a great deal of its operating efficiency. Furthermore, it would become almost chaotic if it actually made changes in a high percentage of such cases. Hence resistance to suggestions of change is partly a rational behavior pattern for officials. But the biases of officials make this resistance excessive in terms of efficiently achieving the bureau's social functions.

There may be a partial escape from this dilemma for more significant decisions if the bureau's top officials can create some outside agency that will be free from direct operational responsibilities within the bureau, but quite familiar with its goals, rules, behavior, and routines. Such an agency can be used as an aid in searching for alternative courses of action, and for information useful in analyzing and evaluating alternatives. Ideally, its members should be familiar enough with the bureau to understand the inter-dependencies therein, but detached enough to propose changes involving major departures from the *status quo*. Such detachment normally results only when men have no direct operational responsibilities. The payoffs from such an arrangement can be very large.

The Impact of Time Pressure upon Search

Search is greatly affected by the time pressure associated with a given decision. The cost of delay—that is, procuring additional information—rises sharply with pressure to act quickly. Under such pressure, a rational decisionmaker will decide on the basis of less knowledge than he would if time pressure were lower. Conversely, when there is little pressure to decide quickly, he can acquire a great deal of information before reaching any conclusions. Thus there is an inverse relationship between the extension of search and the time pressure on the decision. Whenever time pressure is high, the following will occur:

—A minimal number of alternatives will be considered. The more complex the decision, the smaller the number.

—Whenever only a few alternatives are considered, all the biases influencing the order in which possible alternatives are formulated become accentuated. Moreover, officials will tend to give primary consideration to "ready made" alternatives that have been thought out in advance. Since zealots will offer the pet policies they have been promoting for a long time, their ideas will have a much greater chance of being implemented than usual.

—The decisionmakers involved will try to restrict the number of persons participating in the decision and the diversity of views among them. Hence secrecy may be used simply to prevent knowledge of the decision from reaching persons who might want to be included in the deliberations if they knew the decision was being made. Furthermore, secrecy may enable more complex decisions to be made. If a great many people must be consulted in making a decision, it becomes difficult to communicate to each person the issues involved, the possible alternatives, and the responses and views of other consultants. But if secrecy restricts the number of persons consulted, those persons can consider much more complicated possibilites.

Clearly, the degree of time pressure has critical impacts upon decisionmaking. High time pressures usually spring from either crises or deadlines. The former are normally of exogenous origin, but deadlines are usually deliberate, hence they can be manipulated to exploit the effects of time pressure. For example, if a high-ranking official wants to restrict the number of people his subordinates consult on a given decision, he can place a very short deadline on it. Conversely, if he wants wide-ranging deliberations, he can give it a long time horizon.

"Gresham's Law of Planning" may nullify this strategy if subordinates are assigned both short deadline and long deadline tasks.[4] In order to complete their short deadline tasks, they may keep on postponing work on longer-run problems until once-distant deadlines loom in the near future.

Therefore, extending search across a really wide and deep spectrum of possibilities normally requires assignment of long deadline tasks to officials or organizations separate from those responsible for short deadline tasks.

Search Extension and Organizational Policies

The foregoing analysis suggests a number of policies organizations can use to influence the degree of search extension in making a decision. These policies are set forth briefly in Table 1.

Our analysis also implies that the optimal degree of search extension depends both upon the nature of the problem and the time pressure for solving it. Other things being equal, the bigger the problem, the more likely that extension of search will be valuable, since potential savings from finding better alternatives are much greater.[5]

The Effects of Separating Search, Analysis, and Evaluation

When Separation is Rational. Because of the inherent unity of search, analysis, and evaluation, there is strong pressure to keep the specialists carrying out these steps for any particular decision relatively close together in "organizational space." In many cases, each department has its own specialists in search and analysis assisting the people actually making decisions. Then the decisionmakers can advise the searchers about how much and what kinds of data they need. Moreover, there can be frequent communications between the producers and consumers of these data during the decisionmaking process. Even more important, the consumers of information must pay the costs of search. Hence such an arrangement minimizes misallocations of resources to search.

However, in certain situations, the economies of scale in search become enormous. Then nearly complete separation of the producers and consumers of data is almost mandatory. Such economies occur when three conditions exist simultaneously.

First, the sources of relevant information are remote from the decisionmakers. By remote we mean relatively inaccessible in terms of space, technically specialized knowledge, cultural unfamiliarity, secrecy, or extreme fragmentalization in diverse locations. Second, the data required by persons working on one type of decision are also useful for persons working on other types. Third, the means of access to remote information can be used to procure data useful for different kinds of decisions.

Table 1   Organizational Policies that Extend or Contract Search

Policies that Tend to Extend Degree of Search and Increase Diversity of Alternatives Considered	*Policies that Tend to Contract Degree of Search and Narrow Diversity of Alternatives Considered*
Allow a long time before conclusions must be reached	Enforce a very short deadline
Bring many people into decision-making	Restrict decisionmaking to a small number
Insure that those involved have a wide variety of views and interests—even conflicting	Insure that those involved have similar views and interests
Reduce number of persons to whom final decision must be justified or intelligibly communicated	Increase number of persons to whom final decision must be justified or intelligibly communicated
Increase proportion of analytically skillful or highly trained persons participating, or to whom it must be justified or communicated	Decrease proportion of analytically skillful or highly trained persons participating, or to whom it must be justified or communicated
Isolate those making decision from pressures of responsibility for other decisions, especially short deadline ones	Assign the decision to those immersed in making other decisions, especially short deadline ones
Reduce proportion of extremely busy persons to whom decision must be intelligibly communicated	Increase proportion of extremely busy persons to whom decision must be intelligibly communicated

The remoteness of data sources means that a large, indivisible capital investment of some type must be created in order to gain access to them. This investment can be a network of scattered foreign observers; the education of certain technical specialists; creation of linguistic, sociological, or political expertise; or a group of clandestine agents. The need for this large initial investment constitutes a forbidding "entry fee" which forces small-scale users to eschew such data altogether, or else to band together and establish joint search facilities.

Once the high initial cost of gaining access has been paid, a certain capacity is generated that exceeds the needs of any one user. In the case of spatial and cultural remoteness, access facilities can be used to gather a wide variety of specific data. An example is the network of State Department embassies abroad. Different users who have diverse data needs can be served by—and help pay for—these facilities. Other access facilities may produce a large quantity of a certain kind of information. This quantity may exceed the needs of any single consumer, but be useful to enough different customers to pay its total costs. An example is the global radio and press surveillance service of the Central Intelligence Agency.

When these conditions prevail, the development and operation of a jointly used search facility is the only economical way to provide for the many varied consumers involved. This facility can be operated by any one of the users alone, or it can be established as a separate agency. In our analysis, we will assume it is an autonomous search bureau.

The Impact of Separation upon Policy Formation. What types of problems does an agency face in deciding (a) what to search for with...existing facilities, (b) how many resources to expend searching for each item or type of item, and (c) what investments to make in creating additional access facilities?

Some of its major problems occur because it cannot judge the relative importance of acquiring any given piece of information. It is not the ultimate consumer of such information, nor can it charge the ultimate consumers money prices. No profit-making firm is the ultimate consumer of its products either, but such a firm can rationally allocate resources because it charges its consumers money for whatever it gives them. We will assume that the central search agency cannot use this mechanism. Instead, it asks the bureaus it serves to describe the relative urgency of their data needs.

Each bureau has no way of estimating how urgent its requests are in comparison with those of other bureaus, and the natural advocacy of each bureau's officials leads them to exaggerate the importance of their own needs. Hence the central agency is forced to make its own judgments about the relative importance of the needs of different bureaus. This it cannot do accurately unless its own personnel start becoming involved in the policy decisionmaking of its bureau clients. Since many officials within the search agency seek to increase their own power and that of their agency, such involvement is quite likely.

In this involvement, members of the central search agency may exhibit the following viewpoints regarding policy making in other bureaus.

1. In many matters they may act like statesmen. There is no *a priori* reason why the central search agency should have any particular substantive policy biases. Furthermore, the agency's members are encouraged to develop a broad viewpoint in order to choose among competing demands for information made by the various bureaus they serve.

True, insofar as this agency is attached to a particular political entity (such as the chief executive), it will be influenced by the political perspective of that entity. Even so, the search agency is partly prevented from becoming an advocate of any particular policy by its need to serve many different advocates of a wide variety of conflicting policies.

2. Members of the central search agency will inevitably seek to augment their own and the agency's power, income, and prestige. As a result:

—The agency will attempt to establish a monopoly over as many remote data sources as possible, partly by advocating "eliminating unnecessary duplication" of search facilities.

—It will exaggerate the need for secrecy in its operations to conceal discovery of how efficiently it operates.

—Its reporting will exaggerate those types of information likely to contribute to its significance. This significance derives from its usefulness to other bureaus, which will consider information most useful that both justifies existing policies and indicates enough change and instability to make larger appropriations desirable. The existence of external threats often performs the latter function. On the other hand, the governing party wishes to present a public image of competence and control of the situation. Hence the central search agency will tend to supply excessively alarming data to individual bureaus and excessively soothing data to the public in general.

—It will exaggerate the importance of expensive forms of search and analysis, and underplay that of inexpensive ones.

—It will overemphasize forms of search involving a great deal of analysis and evaluation by its own specialists.

3. Members of the central search agency may act as advocates for bureaus within the search agency. This will probably occur only if promotion of these liaison officials is controlled by the agencies in which they are working.

The Impact of Separation upon Resource Allocation. The bureau "customers" of the central search agency will have an ambivalent attitude toward it. They will ask it to furnish all information of any positive value, regardless of cost, since they do not have to pay for it. This conclusion has the following implications. First, no matter how large a data gathering and handling capacity the central search agency possesses, its facilities will always be overloaded. This results from the Law of Free Goods: *Requests for free services always rise to meet the capacity of the producing agency.*

Second, officials of the central search agency will develop nonpecuniary prices for their services. These are devices for imposing costs upon members of other bureaus who request information. They will be designed both to discourage requests and to provide rewards to central search agency members. Such "quasi-prices" will include demands for reciprocal favors, long delays, and frustrating barriers of red tape. This illustrates the Law of Non-Money Pricing: *Organizations that cannot charge money for their services must develop non-monetary costs to impose on their clients as a means of rationing their outputs.* Hence much of the irritating behavior of bureaucrats often represents necessary means of rationing their limited resources so they will be available to those truly anxious to use them.

Third, such rationing systems may result in irrational allocations from the viewpoint of society in general. Information seekers persistent enough to penetrate "quasi-price" barriers may not have needs that would be considered most urgent if all concerned had perfect information.

The other part of each information-using bureau's ambivalent attitude is its desire to "capture" some of the search agency's activities and incorporate them into its own program. This would bring its decisionmakers closer to their data sources as well as add to its total resources.

"Spreading the Word" and the Noise Problem[6]

The Fragmentalized Perception of Large Organizations. Since an organization has no personality, only individual members can perceive or search. Therefore, organizational perception and search are inherently fragmentalized. Information is first perceived by one or several members, who must then pass it on to others.

Thanks to the ubiquity and speed of modern communications some information is perceived almost simultaneously by all members of even very large organizations. For example, over 90 per cent of the entire population in the United States knew of President Kennedy's assassination within four hours of his death.[7] Similarly, if members of a bureau all read the same newspapers or watch the same TV programs, they may learn about a wide range of events almost simultaneously. Nevertheless, such high-exposure sources transmit only a small part of the information important to any bureau. A large proportion of the data it needs is initially perceived by only one or a few low-level members, who then transmit it upwards through channels.

Yet it is not clear just when the organization has perceived any particular item of information, for a statistical majority does not by any means comprise the substantive decisionmakers. We can say that the organization has been informed when the given information has become known to all those members who need to know it, so that the organization can carry out the appropriate response.

The Problem of Assessing the Significance of Data. There is a great difference between knowing a fact and grasping its true significance. The radar supervisor in Hawaii whose subordinate picked up returns from unidentified aircraft on the morning of December 7, 1941 knew that fact, but he did not grasp its significance. The number of facts gleaned every day by any large organization is immense. In theory, the screening process...transmits only the most significant facts to the men at the top, and places them in their proper context along the way. But, as we have seen, considerable distortion occurs in this process. Each part of the organization tends to exaggerate the importance of some events and to minimize that of others. This naturally produces a healthy skepticism among officials at the top of the hierarchy.[8]

An inescapable result of this situation is a rational insensitivity to signals of alarm at high levels. This may have disastrous consequences when those signals are accurate. It is the responsibility of each low-level official to report on events he believes could be dangerous. However, the real danger of the supposed threat is not always clear, and his messages must therefore contain suppositions of his own making.

In organizations always surrounded by potentially threatening situations (such as the Department of Defense, the State Department, and the Central Intelligence Agency), officials at each level continually receive signals of alarm from their subordinates. But they are virtually compelled to adopt a wait and see attitude toward these outcries for three reasons. First, they do not have enough resources to respond to all alleged threats simultaneously. Second, experience has taught them that most potential threats fail to materialize. Third, by the time a potential threat does develop significantly, either the threat itself or the organization's understanding of it has changed greatly. Hence it becomes clear that what initially appeared to be the proper response would really have been ineffective. Therefore, initial signals concerning potential threats usually focus the attention of intermediate-level officials on a given problem area, but do not move them to transmit the alarm upward.

Only if further events begin to confirm the dire predictions of "alarmists" do their superiors become alarmed too, and send distress signals upward. But higher-level officials also have a wait and see attitude for the same reasons, and it takes even further deterioration of the situation to convince them to transmit the alarm still higher. Therefore, a given situation may have to become very threatening indeed before its significance is grasped at the top levels of the organization.

This is one of the reasons why top-level officials tend to become involved in only the most difficult and ominous situations faced by the organization. Easy problems are solved by lower-level officials, and difficult situations may deteriorate badly by the time they come to the attention of the top level.

As Roberta Wohlstetter argued in her study of the Pearl Harbor attack, fragmentalization of perception inevitably produces an enormous amount of "noise" in the organization's communications networks.[9] The officials at the bottom must be instructed to report all potentially dangerous situations immediately so the organization can have as much advanced warning as possible. Their preoccupation with their specialties and their desire to insure against the worst possible outcomes, plus other biases, all cause them to transmit signals with a degree of urgency that in most cases proves exaggerated after the fact. These overly urgent signals make it extremely difficult to tell in advance which alarms will prove warranted and which will not.

There are no easy solutions to this problem. With so many "Chicken Littles" running around claiming the sky is about to fall, the men at the top normally cannot do much until "Henney Penney" and "Foxy Loxy" have also started screaming for help, or there is a convergence of alarm signals from a number of unrelated sources within the organization. Even the use of high-speed, automatic data networks cannot eliminate it. The basic difficulty is not in procuring information, but in assessing its significance in terms of future events—from which no human being can eliminate all uncertainty.

Notes

[1] Leon Festinger, *A Theory of Cognitive Dissonance* (Evanston, Illinois: Row, Peterson, 1957).

[2] This subject is explored in more detail in our analysis of Bureau Territoriality (Chapter XVII). [*Inside Bureaucracy,* Boston, Little, Brown, 1967.]

[3] This is related to the desire of decisionmakers forming a coalition to restrict mem-

bership in the coalition to the smallest number required to "win" in a given contest. Such restriction is a central theme in William H. Riker's book, *The Theory of Political Coalitions* (New Haven: Yale University Press, 1962). However, Riker confined his analysis to zero-sum-game situations; whereas the restrictions we are talking about also apply to non-zero-game situations.

[4]This "law" is set forth in J. G. March and H. A. Simon, *Organizations*.

[5]This principle is opposite to the situation described by C. Northcote Parkinson in his "Law of Triviality." It states that "The time spent on any item of the agenda will be in inverse proportion to the sum involved." However, the behavior depicted by Parkinson's law may actually embody rational short-run responses to the fact that items involving large sums are complicated and research into complexity is expensive, whereas small items are usually simple and often involve data already known to the persons concerned. See C. Northcote Parkinson, *Parkinson's Law and Other Studies in Administration*, pp. 24–32.

[6]Most of the ideas in this section have been developed by William Jones, to whom I am greatly indebted.

[7]Paul E. Sheatsley and Jacob J. Feldman, "The Assassination of President Kennedy: A Preliminary Report on Public Reaction and Behavior," *Public Opinion Quarterly*, Vol. 28, No. 2 (Summer 1964).

[8]We discuss this skepticism at length in our analysis of counter-biasing. See Chapter X. [*Inside Bureaucracy*, Boston, Little, Brown, 1967.]

[9]Roberta Wohlstetter, *Pearl Harbor: Warning and Decision* (Palo Alto: Stanford University Press, 1962).

The Bureaucratic Pathology*
Jacob A. Stockfisch

Introduction

Implicit in modern government is the idea of a sharp distinction between policy makers, on the one hand, and the specialists who carry out policy, on the other hand. The specialists may also be described as "operators," or those who literally carry out specialized tasks that require a high degree of expertise. Operators may also be described as "bureaucrats," in the sense that formal institutions or sub-organizations emerge with their necessary trappings of formal procedures, record keeping, and special personnel selection and indoctrination. These trappings might be regarded as the institutionalization of the special brand of expertise that a bureau is created to practice.

It is a credo in modern government that policy makers make policy, and that operators (or bureaucrats) carry out and implement policy. However, for a variety of reasons unique to governmental and bureaucratic processes, bureaucrats consciously or unconsciously make policy; and policy makers frequently seek to operate. There is seldom a clear division of labor. The lack of clarity regarding functions creates tensions, the tensions generate suspicion, and the suspicion promotes struggle.

An important aspect of the struggle centers on budgets. Bureaucrats, as dedicated specialists, must also struggle to get dollars, and the resources dollars can buy, from reluctant taxpayers. They must also compete with rival bureaucrats in the budgetary process. From this complex struggle, a peculiar "secrecy" syndrome emerges. Through their specialization and expertise, senior bureaucrats are able to maintain an element of secrecy about their operations or production processes. This quality is the source of a bureau's power relative to both its executive and legislative branch superiors, and is the key to the "bureaucracy problem." In its broadest sense, the bureaucracy problem has three dimensions. They are: (1) The secrecy that is a by-product of bureaucratic or operational expertise can lead to an abuse of authority; (2)

---

*In: President's Commission on Federal Statistics. *Federal Statistics*, Washington, D.C., U.S. Government Printing Office, 1971, Vol. II, pp. 459–475.

the abuse of authority poses special problems for the "sovereign" who must control subordinate officials; and (3) those individuals and groups who are affected by the decision-making of officials (bureaucrats) operating to influence administrative procedure and decision-making.[1]

Because of the critical role of "secrecy," the subject of bureaucratic behavior necessarily has a very high information or "intelligence" content. It would be astonishing, therefore, if the statistical information programs of bureaus were not greatly affected by bureaucratic motivations. The purpose of this paper is to focus explicitly on these information consequences of bureaucratic behavior.

The Nature of Bureaus

Bureaus consist of operators who perform complex jobs. Performance of any specialized function requires the development of a high degree of expertise. If the bureau itself is large and if the function is highly complex, it also develops fairly rigorous procedures and promotes a high degree of specialization between individuals and sub-agencies. Large elements of the job, therefore, become routinized and standardized. A further characteristic of creating such an organization, to the extent that it involves a number of specialized functional areas and divisions, is that the leadership attempts to impart esprit and create a sense of dedication on the part of its diverse members. It is important that people have pride in the work that they do. A specialization inherent in a given task will often become the focal point for generating that pride. Thus Air Force people, and particularly air crewmen, take great pride in the fact that they fly airplanes. They become "dedicated" to the airplane and more broadly to an abstraction called "strategic air power." This kind of pride and dedication is vital, if not necessary, if the job is to be done well. It is dangerous business at best even if the instrument is never used; when and if it is used, there is a very good chance that many of the people who operate it will be killed. Thus aviators truly have to have faith in airplanes, submariners in submarines, and so forth. Pride and esprit, both in one's self and in the organization with which one is associated, are therefore necessary ingredients to create and sustain an organization that performs any function. The intensity of these qualities may be particularly extreme in military organizations, but they are necessary qualities for all organizations.

A part of developing this kind of feeling is that each agency evolves its own image and style, which in any given time are a product of its past history. It simultaneously espouses its role and mission in such a way as to fortify and enhance its institutional status. At a minimum, a bureau will seek stability (it does not like to see its mission or function degraded or reduced in importance). For this reason it will resist any broader policy change which it judges, either rightly or wrongly, may contain the possibility that its function will become less important. At a maximum, a bureau will seek to expand its mission and function. Every man likes to see his organization grow in size and prestige. If its size grows, the probability of personal advancement is better; if it grows in prestige, the individual enjoys an enhanced feeling of personal self-esteem.

Because bureaus normally perform complex tasks and must employ ordinary people, and because they seek stability, they also develop their own procedures and doctrine, or "decision rules." These decision rules, usually in large organizations, often become "institutionalized." It should be pointed out, however, that the evolution of decision rules often reflects a compromise between the power blocs within the organization itself. Organizations like the Army, the Coast Guard, or the Internal Revenue Service in themselves are by no means monolithic. They consist of subgroups who struggle among themselves. There is (and has been) a perennial struggle in an army among infantrymen and artillerymen and cavalrymen. Within a tax collecting agency there are struggles among auditors, lawyers, and enforcement specialists. The implications of this kind of struggle are that the organization's image of itself, as well as of its procedures and decision rules, is the product of a compromise among internal power blocs. Such a compromise is almost necessary if the larger organization, with which everyone identifies, is not to be shaken with divisiveness. The compromise maintains organizational stability and individual security, and hence esprit. But a frequent consequence of this kind of compromise is that an organization tends to resist change in their way of doing things, because change involves the uncertainty that some segments of a bureau might experience a decline in their relative importance. Hence decision rules and procedures may not be modified promptly and expeditiously so as to implement whatever new policies the executive office may announce, or in response to technological change.[2]

For these reasons the bureau develops a special posture toward the executive office, and, indeed, toward outsiders generally. That posture is one of autonomy seeking, obfuscation, and suspicion. Let us discuss each of these qualities.

Autonomy. The bureau prefers to be left alone in its day-to-day operations, to perform them efficiently in terms of its own decision rules and effectiveness criteria. Operating demands in themselves are usually capable of consuming all of the energy an organization's members possess. The relationship between the bureau and the executive office which the bureau seeks to promote is that of assuring the executive that the job it is performing is vitally important, and that it is being done "efficiently." To the extent that it succeeds in creating this image, it may also create a powerful advocate for its own advancement, particularly in the form of larger appropriations and hence the means to foster the organization's growth. This outcome would be the best of all worlds.

The second best and most prevalent world is one where the executive is passive toward the bureau. In this case the bureau is likely to build up its own independent constituency. It establishes contact with Congressmen, particularly key committee chairmen and members who have cognizance over the particular bureau's authorization and appropriations legislation. Simultaneously, the bureau, either through the specialized services it provides private groups, or its spending for procurement of products and services, impacts upon constituents of Congressmen and simultaneously acquires advocates in the "body politic" for its endeavors. Thus a "triangle" consisting of senior bureau officials, special private sector interest groups, and Congressmen supported by those interest groups who in turn support the bureaus—conduct much of the day-to-day business that gets done in the capital.[3]

Obfuscation. This is a tool that enables a bureau to maintain its autonomy. It will indicate to the executive, in broad general terms, that its mission is to "fight the ground battle" or "to administer the tax system efficiently," or to "maintain law and order." Most bureaus also endeavor to convey a similar impression to citizens. If pushed on particular matters, assuming that the executive has the energy or ability to raise questions, the bureau is capable of coming up with many reasons why it is doing things its way. At this point the executive (or any other influential outside critic) is apt to be confronted with a mass of detail linked together with reasoning that reflects the bureau's own brand of logic, which can at best only be rationalized in terms of its self-image. Under the worst circumstances, it may employ biased samples or downright erroneous numbers to justify its case. Great powers of persuasion are employed to assure the executive or other skeptical outsiders that it is doing its job efficiently and effectively, and that its behavior is in harmony with the executive's own policy objectives or the "public interest." Unless the executive has the staff capability to analyze these offerings in great detail, the dialogue ends. The bureau is therefore left alone and it can get on with doing its job without interference, and with the task of building and enhancing the future stability and growth of its budget.

Suspicion. These problems are intensified by the nature of the executive branch or office where the main orientation is toward policy formulation. Executive offices experience much personnel turnover, particularly at the upper levels. This turnover is necessary and even desirable as administrations and policies change. But as a result there is apt to be a lack of operations or technical expertise in the policy organization. The latter kind of knowledge necessitates concern with minute detail. Top policy officials find it difficult to take time to learn this detail. Moreover, as they acquire it with lengthening tenure, the probability that they will leave increases. Personnel turnover, therefore, exacts a toll. For this reason the executive is usually forced to rely upon the offerings of the leaders of the bureau.

Another quality of the executive office is that it is the source of changing policy. But policy changes often create trouble for the bureau. They may cause a downgrading of its role or mission. At a minimum, a bureau may have to reexamine its function, and perhaps undertake changes that upset the internal balance of power. The executive office is thus a source of annoyance. At best, it epitomizes to the bureau the fact that here are some people they must "educate." At worst, the people "up there" will be the source of trouble which will necessitate going on the defensive (or the offensive) in order to preserve the status quo.

Bureaucrats as Budget Maximizers

Although the behavior described...may seem to have a pathological quality, it nevertheless has understandable motivation. First, it is characteristic of most human beings to resent extensive probing by "outsiders" about their specialized activity, particularly if it is not done with great patience, tact, and skill. Many husbands have experienced this reaction on the part of their wives on matters related to managing the household budget. Second, and much more important in the case of the senior governmental bureaucrat, is the motivation to maximize his budget. Like all experts, he takes pride in his expertise and he is secretive about it. Because he comprises and strongly identifies with a subculture within a larger society, he strives to maximize the role his subculture plays in the social system. He can only do this, however, by getting resources from the society of which he is a part. His operations—and in some cases technical expertise—enable him to perform this maximizing function by virtue of the monopoly of knowledge his expertise endows him with.

Conventional economic theory can demonstrate that a monopolist operating in the business sector of the economy, if he operates under the constraints of linear cost and demand functions, will produce one-half the output that a competitive industry will produce. Essentially, the private monopolist sets a price that maximizes his profits. He enjoys excessive profits—i.e., a larger return from his activity that exceeds the opportunity cost of producing the product. Society gets less output of the particular product, and in the process pays more per unit than would be the case if it were produced competitively.

A bureaucrat/monopolist who is an instrument of the state cannot exploit a monopoly position to reap personal profits. However, it has been observed that the bureaucrat/monopolist is motivated to maximize the size of his agency or bureau, and in this fashion to derive personal fulfillment. By presenting to his superior a joint budget-output package, he can manage to obtain from the society the value equivalent that a business monopolist could mulct from consumers. What would be "excess profits" to a private monopolist are used by the bureaucratic monopolist to enlarge the size of his agency or service. By means of the calculus (or model) with which it can be demonstrated that a private business monopolist would produce only half the output as would an industry composed of competitors, it can be demonstrated that a bureaucrat monopolist would produce up to twice the output as would be called for by equating the relevant demand and cost functions.[4]

Now no bureaucrat literally offers the sovereign a strict budget-output package on a take-it-or-leave-it basis. Such behavior would be impudent if not downright insubordinate. Rather, a variety of techniques are employed, which in most instances are utilized in good faith and sincerity, but which are also self-serving. First is the assertion of the "requirement." The argument runs that failure to program adequate resources to cope with the need bodes ill for the country's safety. There is a tendency to exaggerate the threat or the problem that must be coped with. This exaggeration can be advanced in perfectly good faith on the part of military professionals since they are indoctrinated to be winners rather than losers in war, and numbers or size of force are the major determinant of the outcome. Moreover, in the judgment of historians and politicians, it is the generals who lose the battles if not the wars, not the political decision-makers who determine the budgets.

There are techniques employed with regard to the relation between "inputs" and "outputs" that serve the objective of maximizing the budget. The insider tends to be conservative about the capabilities of existing systems, if only because he knows something about their shortcomings. When budgetary cuts are suggested, they are countered with the query as to which outputs should be reduced, rather than with an effort to cut back overhead or to energetically seek more efficient ways of doing things. In military affairs, the insider also tends to be conservative about doctrine and organization, especially if they were successful in winning a past war. To be sure, one would like new, higher performance equipment that can be substituted for the old, but nevertheless one continues old doctrine. Thus innovations (as contrasted with technological inventions) are not apt to be forthcoming in a manner commensurate with our self-image of being progressive. There is also a tendency, when advocating new equipment systems, to underestimate their costs. This, too, is understandable, both for natural human and bureaucratic reasons. We are all bargain-hunters at heart, and hope is eternal that cost (which is unpleasant to contemplate) will be low. Moreover, the assertion that cost will be low serves to sell the program; once the program is underway there is hope (and not a little pressure) that additional money will be found to complete the development.

Implications of Bureaucratic Behavior for Bureaucratic Information Systems

The pathological aspects of the bureaucratic behavior pattern should not be regarded solely as a result (or the "fault") of bureaucrats themselves. Rather, they are a product of, and simultaneously a vital contributing ingredient to, the perennial struggle between the executive and legislative branches, on the one hand, and between the varied private interest groups that comprise a pluralistic society, on the other hand. Given the nature of the "game," pervaded as it is with self-serving on the part of all concerned parties, it is amazing that the Republic is served as well as it is by the professional civil servants and the uniformed officer corps that constitute "the" bureaucracy. But whatever the roots or causes of the behavior pattern, whether it be inherent in the human or political condition, prime casualties of the process are the information and statistical systems internal to the bureaus themselves. Another casualty is the ability of bureaus to engage in critical program evaluation and, especially, experimentation.

A bureau's information system, including its generation of statistics that are a by-product of its operations, tends to reflect its self-serving motivation to survive and to maximize its budget. Its internal statistics program, which can extend to the reporting requirements it places upon whatever private groups over which it exerts a controlling or regulating function, will mirror an inertia that characterizes the inherently conservative nature of an established organization. The self-serving motive means that seldom will information be gathered that can be used to show that a bureau's programs or operations might not be going well, or that they may be creating unpleasant by-products. The conservative trait means that statistics and information are often gathered, at a cost to those required to keep records to report it, which have limited or no usefulness. An important cost of this latter effect is that an opportunity is foregone, or lost, to elicit information which may be of much greater use to policy makers and the general public, including scholars who need data. Finally, bureaus are frequently adroit at passing off numbers that may in large part be fabricated or the products of various manipulations when those data can be used to support the political-budgeting case a bureau seeks to make. We thus have the "avoidance," "inertia," and "fabrication" problems that afflict the statistical programs of bureaus. These elements interact and mutually reinforce each other so as to affect the government's overall statistical program.

Avoidance is responsible for a failure to gather data on program effects which may reflect unfavorably on a bureau's programs, either by way of showing that particular programs may not be achieving their objectives or that a program may be creating unfavorable side effects. Thus the Department of Agriculture—over many years of administrating agricultural price support programs—did not vigorously pursue gathering data on the attributes of farmers benefiting from these programs. The Urban Renewal Agency seldom followed through to determine what happened to low income individuals uprooted by the renewal programs. Highway commissions and port authorities do not pursue the matter of the possible traffic congestion their projects deliver to central urban areas. Although such agencies are often in the best position to gather these kinds of data, the information that is available is usually obtained piecemeal from diverse other sources, combined with whatever can be ferreted out or inferred from the agency's operating data.

For similar reasons, bureaus are reluctant to pursue program experimentation or field testing. It is perhaps the military departments that have the greatest opportunity to do field experimentation. Yet very little is done, and what little that is done is done poorly or in such a way as to yield ambiguous findings.

This problem seems to spring from inherent qualities of the experimentation process itself. An experiment may show or suggest that a doctrine or weapon favored by one or more powerful people may not be as good as touted. If prior decisions were made, involving either large amounts of resources and/or the personal prestige of decision-makers or staff advocates, the results of the experiment can be embarrassing or personally damaging to powerful individuals. Such individuals may be either professional military officers, or civilian policy makers, or prominent scientists who have "staked" their professional reputation on a particular technical approach to an equipment or tactical issue.

This attitude toward field experimentation has its roots in the budgeting process. Budgets of military departments, for research and development and procurement, are aggregations consisting of individual items and are advocated at low levels of the hierarchy. Each department is motivated to maximize its share of a given total defense budget. New weapon concepts became a means of getting dollars. As long as this incentive prevails, it is difficult for military users to take a critical view of individual systems. Indeed, an opposite view is taken, and exaggerated claims of system effectiveness and optimistic cost estimates pervade the "data base" of a military service. Field experimentation, which is critical in its nature, is not a welcome activity in this kind of setting.[5]

Inertia is often responsible for not exploiting existing statistical sources or collection mechanisms where either relatively small modifications in the statistical program or extra effort would yield very large information payoffs. For example, by modifying business tax forms (through eliminating requests for certain kinds of information—like advertising expenditure) and requesting other kinds of information (e.g., total wages paid, as contrasted with executive salaries) it would be possible to obtain value added data, by industry and identified by major factor payments, for the entire economy. Such information could serve greatly to improve the quality of the National Income and Product Accounts, which are currently very laboriously built up piecemeal (and by a rather large staff) by the Office of Business Economics. But the Internal Revenue Service is reluctant to make what seems to it a "drastic" change of business tax forms, the design of which is determined by a committee on which is represented the various internal power blocs that comprise the Service.

A badly needed type of information necessary to understand the workings of the tax system is how taxpayers' income and taxable income behave through time. Existing data records show how the system behaves each year. Inferences from these data are apt to exaggerate, therefore, the proportion of individuals who are *consistently* in very low and very high income brackets. Information could be gathered that would portray behavior through time of a sample of individuals, and by means of such data the economic effects of the tax system and many of its complex features could be better understood. But it is laborious and costly to produce this kind of data—as contrasted with annual cross-section treatment—within the framework of a statistical program that is viewed by the Service to cost $10 million or so a year. The Service has no internal incentive to produce this information since its primary use would be for tax policy formulation as contrasted with administration of the existing system. Only if a higher authority, like the Office of the Secretary of the Treasury, directed it to be done would results be achieved. However, that higher Office has not pursued this matter, mainly due to other demands upon its energy.

Fabrication of data is widespread and achievable by a variety of subtle techniques. Military organizations have been known to exaggerate the capability of possible opponents and to understate friendly capability. One way to do this is to count only the equipment (e.g., tanks or aircraft) in friendly *combat organizations* and to compare that number with the other side's total equipment procurement, which also includes items in repair depots, those used for training, and stocks procured for combat consumption allowances.[6] Recently, the Senate Armed Services Committee noted that the U.S. Army's statements of rifle assets and requirements behaved in strange ways whereby the amount required was decreasing as the size of the Army increased during the early period of the Vietnam buildup.[7] One explanation of this behavior is that the Army might have been seeking to minimize its purchase of M16 rifles which the Army did not conceive and design, while it was trying to develop on a crash basis a newer and more exotic weapon of its own conception. Finally, modern cost-effectiveness studies spew out vast amounts of "numbers" by employing the technique of computer simulations. Frequently, the numerical inputs for these activities are either the "fudged" numbers generated by the bureaucratic process, or are derived *a priori* from engineering equations, many of which might be irrelevant to system effectiveness or, at best, related to effectiveness in an unknown way.

One of the discouraging implications of these points is that mere "analysis" of systems and programs is not adequate to assist rational decision-making. Policy makers (and bureaus) may acquire analytical staffs, as was done extensively in the federal government during the 1960's as a result of adopting the Planning, Programming, and Budgeting System (PPBS). But the bureaus, by virtue of their "control" over the data available as "inputs" to the analytical studies, can greatly influence the "outputs" of the study process. Thus the managerial innovations instituted in the Defense Department were frustrated if not soundly defeated by the military departments they were imposed upon.

The process by which a bureau fabricates data, or avoids collecting it, can occur unconsciously and spontaneously. It is a consequence or by-product of trying, on a day-to-day basis, to counter the penetration of a bureau's affairs by "outsiders." One of the results of these poor information systems is that the senior officials of the bureaus themselves may not have adequate information to run their own organizations effectively, even though they may have a deep and sincere desire to do so.

Senior bureau officials are not happy about the situation. Bureau heads do want their organizations to be effective. To achieve this end, the workings of an organization must be visible to its leaders. But any workable auditing and inspection procedure that serves the bureau head can also serve the energetic staff of a superior headquarters, which in this case is a civilian secretariat and (in some instances) Congressional committees. To stave off penetration and possible detailed control by such outsiders, bureau heads must therefore pay a price. That price is the creation of information systems that generate information for advocacy and political purposes. There has been a great surge in cost-effectiveness studies and the development of com-puterized headquarters information systems, which, not incidentally, have greatly benefited the research and data processing communities.

The social value of much of this activity, however, is not clear. Its worth is particularly suspect as long as bureaus seek to avoid and prevent penetra-tion by superior headquarters, because the basic data fed into the analytical models and information systems can be generated, doctored, and "fudged" to serve political and advocacy objectives.

Bureaus might thus be compelled to try to maintain two sets of informa-tion and communications systems: one system to deal with the external world as it is with regard to operations; the other system to serve its functioning in the budgeting/political process, which includes providing information that policy makers like to hear. However, it is a rare organization that can pull off such a feat for an extended period of time. Usually, the outputs of dual information systems become mixed. Much relevant and real informa-tion is ignored; much propaganda and folklore come to be accepted as real-ity. Such duality provides the ingredients for occasional massive "intelligence failures."[8]

The Problem and What Can Be Done About It

It might be observed that bureaucratic behavior as we have described it af-flicts the internal workings of all organizations, including private business firms. The point is correct. But there is a vital difference between the public, government bureaucracy on the one hand, and its private counterpart on the other hand. This difference centers around the way in which the two major classes of organizations are "financed."

The private business organization generally is financed by selling its output in the marketplace. In this setting, the consumer is free to take as little or as much as he wants at a per unit price that tends to converge toward production costs. Consumer demand thus places a constraint on the total "budget" available to the private business organization, or to entire industries comprising the private sector. If competition among producers prevails in the market, the consumer also has the option of choice. In this context, the internal bureaucratic pathology of a particular firm is of no concern to the general consumer. The firm's budget is constrained. Price and quality of the firm's output can be the consumer's sole focus.

With the government bureaucracy, however, financing is carried out through taxation or inflationary monetary techniques. Both financial devices are intimately dependent on the coercive power of the state. The "consumer-taxpayer" is caught up in the workings of a complex political-budgeting process, in which his preferences are only indirectly and imperfectly made felt and where they must compete with the preferences and aspirations of powerful producer groups, elected officials, and—finally—those of career bureaucrats. This difference in financing between the private and public bureaucracy, therefore, is sufficiently great so as to render the private one a "special" but not too interesting case.

It can be properly argued that the problem of the public bureaucracy is actually the problem of the democratic political process, including policy evaluation and policy making, public administration, and social conflict in its broadest sense. The point would be correct. But it should also be forcibly emphasized that this broader problem and the conflict it entails have a very high information content. And for many purposes, they can be fruitfully approached as information and statistical production problems.

Regardless of one's taste on how the subjects of politics, bureaucratic behavior, and related subjects are to be approached, the main force of this offering is to emphasize that the subject of government information systems, including the production and use of statistics, cannot be intelligently dealt with, let alone understood, if treated abstractly and hence devoid of an awareness of the complex interactions between producers and users of government statistics. These parties are also political "actors." An abstract approach to government statistics leads to platitudes or generalities that take the form of urging that "more" and "better" statistics be provided. Or it may be suggested that some "centralized" agency undertake the task of better "integrating" existing statistical programs, and laying down quality control standards. Yet if the bureaucratic animal is as hardy as it appears to be, and if the various self-serving private interest groups are as vigorous as they always have been, a centralized agency is unlikely to improve things much, and it is even possible that it might worsen them. The latter possibility is suggested by some of the consequences of the advent of the...PPBS in the Defense Department during the 1960's.

This pessimistic picture suggests that the problems associated with statistical programs might not be coped with unless there is simultaneously more rationality, candor, openness, and skepticism in the political process itself. In their way, all parties—users and producers—are contributors to the present unhappy state of things. Indeed, a case can be made that the "bureaucrats," whom it is tempting to label as the "heavies" in the scenario, are products if not victims of the deeper and broader system. Society gets, in effect, the kind of bureaucratic behavior (and bureaucratic information systems) it demands and deserves.

Yet the information system, including the integrity and validity of the statistical system, is a good point upon which to focus critical (and constructive) scrutiny. And in this regard all users can play a key role. But not many do. For example, academic economists are extensive users of government produced statistics, particularly in the contemporary setting which places an emphasis upon mathematical economics and econometric techniques. The professional journals are full of papers presenting econometric findings. But few members of the profession probe behind the numbers for the purpose of gauging their quality, let alone to offer suggestions on how quality might be improved or to expose shoddy production.

Legislators and executive branch policy makers (and their staffs) could and should devote energy to developing and voicing skepticism regarding any statistics that are presented to them. They should also insist, whenever it is feasible, upon purposeful program experimentation. In the process, all parties should give special attention to designing new institutional and, especially, associated incentives impacting on bureaucrats that operate in a healthy way. For example, in military affairs, there might be a hard requirement that claims of a need for high technical performance of new weapon systems be backed up by field trials that generate hard evidence, that validate the claim. Steps would also have to be taken, by way of establishing independent review boards, to monitor (not direct) such testing processes so as to be able to certify that the test was done in accordance with well-established standards governing the conduct of experiments.

Visiting boards could also be set up and encouraged to review critically, and in depth, the statistical production processes of other operating agencies, like the Internal Revenue Service, the Public Health Service, and so on.

Some agencies do have "advisory boards" on statistical matters. But more often than not the individual members of these boards either represent special groups in a self-serving way, or give little time or energy to the effort, or both. Consequently, they are little more than a "rubber stamp" apparatus—a role generally pleasing to their bureau mentors.

These and other techniques for generating skepticism can go a long way toward improving the present situation. Another major source of improvement may spring from a recognition on the part of all parties that the present system's behavior is a creature of mutual self-serving on the part of the diverse interest groups and a large dose of "gamesmanship." To the extent that everyone comes to realize that this is the likely condition, then the parties who try to bluff and fabricate will know that others know the nature of their game. Such a mutual understanding might be both refreshing and healthful. And with the different attitudes, the process of ventilation could proceed expeditiously and fruitfully.

Notes

[1] Reinhard Bendix, "Bureaucracy," *International Encyclopedia of the Social Sciences* (New York: Macmillan, 1968), Volume 2, p. 214.

[2] For an account of one such case, see Edward L. Katzenbach, Jr., "Twentieth Century Horse Calvary," in *Public Policy,* Carl J. Friedrich and Seymour E. Harris (eds.), (Cambridge: Harvard University Press, 1958), pp. 120–50.

[3] For a treatment of some of these ingredients, see Richard E. Neustadt, "Politicians and Bureaucrats," in *The Congress and America's Future,* ed. by David B. Truman (Englewood Cliffs, N.J.: Prentice-Hall, 1965), pp. 102–120; for a well-documented case study, see Vincent Davis, *The Admiral's Lobby* (Chapel Hill: University of North Carolina Press, 1967).

[4] See William A. Niskanen, "Nonmarket Decision Making: The Peculiar Economics of Bureaucracy," *The American Economic Review*, May, 1968, pp. 293–305 for a rigorous demonstration and extension of this view.

[5] For a further discussion of the status of field experimentation in the U.S. Defense Establishment see J. A. Stockfisch, "Operational Testing," *Military Review* (May, 1971), pp. 66–82.

[6] For an account of one such example relating to the Royal Air Force's estimates of the German air order of battle, after the Battle of Britain, see R. F. Harrod, *The Prof* (London: Macmillan, 1959), pp. 3–5.

[7] U.S. Senate, Committee on Armed Services, "The Army's Rifle Procurement and Distribution Program" (Washington: Government Printing Office, May 31, 1967).

[8] For a number of case studies of such intelligence failures, see Harold L. Wilensky, *Organizational Intelligence: Knowledge and Policy in Government and Industry* (New York: Basic Books, 1965).

Additional Readings

Blau, Peter. *The Dynamics of Bureaucracy.* Chicago, University of Chicago Press, 1963.

Feltham, Gerald A. "The Value of Information." *The Accounting Review, 43:*684–698, October 1968.

Galbraith, Jay R. *Designing Complex Organizations.* Reading, Mass., Addison-Wesley Publishing Co., 1971.

Hershleifer, Jack. "Where Are We in the Theory of Information." *American Economic Review, 63:*31–39, 1972.

Inbar, Michael. *Routine Decision-Making.* Beverly Hills, Calif., Sage Publications, 1979.

Katz, Daniel, and Kahn, Robert L. *The Social Psychology of Organizations.* New York, Wiley, 1966.

Kaufman, Herbert. *Administrative Feedback.* Washington, D.C., The Brookings Institution, 1973.

Koehler, Jerry W.; Anatol, Karl W. E.; and Applbaum, Ronald L. *Organizational Communication.* New York, Holt, Rinehart and Winston, 1976.

Lindblom, Charles E. *The Policy-Making Process.* Englewood Cliffs, N.J., Prentice-Hall, 1968.

Lindblom, Charles E., and Cohen, David K. *Usable Knowledge.* New Haven, Conn., Yale University Press, 1979.

Rappaport, Alfred, ed. *Information for Decision Making.* Englewood Cliffs, N.J., Prentice-Hall, 1970.

Simon, Herbert A. *Administrative Behavior: A Study of Decision-Making Process in Administrative Organization.* 3rd Edition. New York, Macmillan, 1976.

Skjei, Stephen S. *Information for Collective Action.* Lexington, Mass., D. C. Heath, 1973.

Thompson, James. *Organizations in Action.* New York, McGraw-Hill, 1967.

Walton, Thomas F. *Communications and Data Management.* New York, Wiley, 1976.

Chapter 3

MANAGING THE INFORMATION RESOURCES

...[T]he sheer ability to process massive volumes of information cheaply and efficiently has sandtrapped officials into concentrating on data processing at the expense of data management.

—Forest W. Horton, Jr., "Computers and Paperwork"

Management of information or data resources focuses on the data and equipment side of handling information in an organization. Information resource management, or IRM, as the Commission on Federal Paperwork has called it, is essential to the information process in an organization. The quality of the data resources, the efficiency with which they are used, and the skill and expertise with which they are applied, all contribute to the quality and effectiveness of the information process. Therefore, managing the information process and information resources is the means to an end—the effective use of information to support organizational needs and social interests.

The selections in this chapter explore the history of information resource management in the United States and the effects of rapid changes in information-handling technologies on established management tools and approaches. A recurring theme in these readings is the significance of developing new management approaches to deal with the changes in information technologies and program responsibilities in organizations. From an organizational standpoint, as Joseph L. Kish and James Morris observe in "Paperwork Management in Transition," the trend has been to manage at a distance. One result of this policy has been an increase in the use of written communications to replace traditional face-to-face meetings of managers and staffs in bureaus and with their clients.

Political events led to the growth of government after World War II and a concomitant shift in the manager's role. Ascribing cause and effect to these developments is difficult because, as C. W. Getz notes in "Coalescence: The Inevitable Fate of Data Processing," im-

135

provements in handling data have spawned other changes in the organization.

Getz suggests that the traditional organization response to improvements in data handling has been to create the separate positions of reports management specialist, paperwork or forms management specialist, and records management specialist, despite the similarities in responsibility. An unfortunate result of this distinction has been the absence of any coherent policies of data management. Each set of specialists has pursued conflicting and contradictory goals.

Although, as Getz notes, the tendency to specialize is not new, it has become more pronounced with each technological innovation. He writes, "Persons who have the knowledge to communicate with the computer have become a special class of experts...." Kish and Morris also notice a disturbing transition—data-handling responsibilities are being taken from the generalist administrator and given to the computer expert.

Getz observes that, instead of promoting more efficient use of the information resource, the expert may exacerbate the problem of inefficiency. Managers who diligently and effectively manage an organization's other resources have been content to abdicate responsibility for managing data resources. Have these managers been intimidated by the computer's mystique? Have they been lulled to sleep because many information-handling costs are hidden? For whatever reason, the computer expert has emerged as the data manager.

Getz identifies several problems that organizations face because of data handlers with parochial views on information technology. One problem is the experts' aversion to new ideas and their opposition to innovation. Another is the computer experts' tendency to keep the layman ignorant of data processing and to surround the computer in mystery that only the initiated can penetrate. Must one observe the admonition, "Beware the expert"? Probably not. Data expert is a necessary and useful job. As Kish and Morris suggest, however, a shift in management thinking is required. For Getz, the shift is to an information resources manager who has a broad view and perception of the total organization environment.

This view is shared by Forest W. Horton, Jr. In "Computers and

Paperwork," he observes that much of the problem is the nature of the computer and communications technologies. It is cheaper to store data in large amounts, whether or not the information is needed or relevant. Cost cutting has not entered into the calculus because the way to justify the enormous fixed cost has been to expand data output and, by extension, data input. True, the economist would argue that, in the short run, data-equipment costs are sunk costs and are irrelevant to decision making. What has happened in the long run, as the Commission on Federal Paperwork observes in "Managing Information Resources," is that the cost of equipment is often the only data-processing expenditure that is calculated for budget purposes in many organizations, public and private. Horton also contends that paper costs may be relatively low, and increased use of this input places no immediate burden on the organization. What is overlooked is the cost of handling the data. The Commission on Federal Paperwork maintains that the real costs of paperwork are hidden in administrative overhead.

There is merit in developing techniques to hold down costs associated with the quantity of paperwork. At the same time, as Horton and Kish and Morris point out, management must be concerned with data quality. As Horton accurately notes, when data banks are bulging with irrelevant information, major costs are incurred—the opportunity lost by not having reliable, relevant information available and the delay caused by waiting for the necessary data to be located and retrieved. Data stored in computers are not information, for, as Getz succinctly observes, information is data made useful.

Paperwork is a political as well as a human and technological problem. This point is cogently made by Horton and by the Commission on Federal Paperwork. The job of keeping records and collecting data for government agencies to use involves considerable expense. Many requirements are imposed in the political arena when laws are drafted. Legislators who frequently bemoan the paperwork burden on their constituents share the responsibility and have the opportunity to evaluate the effects of new bills and to assess paperwork costs as direct expenditures rather than as indirect administrative overhead. The temptation and tendency is to pass these costs to those persons who must respond to government bodies and their requests. The authors in this chapter suggest that increased paperwork need not be an inescapable by-product nor an evil of bureaucratic centralization and advances in computing technologies. Large-scale organizations can manage the information resource by promoting conditions that reward managers not for hiding information costs but for treating information as a valued resource.

Paperwork Management in Transition: The Impact of Automatic Data Processing*

Joseph L. Kish and James Morris

Paperwork management is a system of controls over the life cycle of business records—from their creation, through their maintenance, and to their eventual destruction as obsolete or their preservation as records of permanent value. It is a relatively new concept, for only 30 years ago the control techniques which presently comprise paperwork management—forms, reports, and correspondence controls and records retention and protection systems—were in formal use in only a handful of the nation's business and governmental offices.

Today, however, paperwork management is a tested and accepted staff activity in nearly every enterprise. A wide variety of management consulting firms are spending a large portion of their time in providing services to their clients in one or more aspects of this area. In addition, professional organizations whose sole purpose is the advancement of paperwork management concepts are rapidly finding new members in every section of our country.

How can this tremendous growth of interest in paperwork management be explained? How can it be that an activity virtually unknown three short decades ago is today nearly universal in practice? To answer these questions, we must first examine the changes which have taken place in the size and scope of business and governmental organization as well as the changes which have occurred in paperwork handling and processing itself.

The typical American company of the 1930's was considerably smaller than its current counterpart. Generally, its product lines were less diversified than those of today's corporation. The span of control was smaller; and, as a result, communication between various levels of management was simpler. Indeed, in many pre-World War II companies, it was not uncommon to find that the president knew most of his executives by their first names.

*In: *AMA Management Bulletin #56.* New York, American Management Association, 1964, pp. 3-15. (Reprinted by permission of the publisher.)

After World War II this situation changed. Companies grew through merger and acquisition. Existing plants were expanded in an effort to increase production, and diversification became commonplace. Consequently, the span of control widened—so much so that communications became slower and more complex. And last, but far from least, government itself, at both the state and Federal levels, went through a tremendous growth, increasing its size and adding to its regulatory powers.

These two developments, growth and diversification, coupled with the increased size and regulatory activity of government, led to an increase in the volume of paperwork generated and retained. With space costs continually rising and the costs of files maintenance (equipment, supplies, and personnel) soaring, it soon became evident that the cost of creating and maintaining records and reports was a major expenditure of every business and governmental agency. It became apparent that, in the interests of efficiency and economy, controls had to be placed over paperwork, much in the same manner that controls had been placed over manufacturing functions.

The findings of the U.S. Commission on Organization of the Executive Branch of the Government (popularly known as the Hoover Commission) dramatized this need for effective paperwork controls. The two reports of this Commission, the first issued in 1951 and the second in 1955, described the overall costs incurred by the Federal Government in the creation and maintenance of records and developed detailed proposals for reducing these costs. The savings that resulted from the Federal Government's implementation of the Hoover Commission's recommendations provided further evidence to the business community that similar recommendations would, to a large extent, apply to its own clerical activities.

The second major factor leading to the growth and acceptance of paperwork management techniques was the change which took place in methods for processing and storing paperwork. In the pre-World War II company, the paperwork processing cycle was rather simple. Most forms were prepared in fewer than three copies. Data were manually entered, in pen and ink or by typewriter or other key-driven office machine. These records were then forwarded for processing and subsequently filed, in their original form, in metal filing cabinets. When the available space in these filing cabinets was used up, clerks would go through the files and remove the older records, those less frequently referred to. These records would then be either destroyed or stored in a warehouse or some other low-cost repository.

In the postwar period conditions changed radically. Plant expansion led to a widening of communications links, and the average number of form copies required to notify all interested parties of a single transaction grew.

The number of transactions involved in a single function likewise increased as companies expanded. For example, a billing department in the 1930's which prepared 800 invoices weekly frequently found itself processing 5,000 invoices weekly a decade later. This increased clerical activity—and ever-mounting clerical salaries—led to the greater use of mechanized processes for preparing and processing forms, reports, correspondence, and other paperwork. As a result, the 1940's saw the increased use of conventional tabulating equipment and office reproduction equipment in business and government. This led in the 1950's to the adoption of more sophisticated paperwork-processing systems, such as electronic computers, automatic typewriters, and new applications of microfilm. The impetus to improve mechanized paperwork systems continues today, as businesses look with interest at photo-memory systems and even larger and faster computers than were available in the past.

Paradoxically, the ability to handle an enormous volume of records at a lower unit cost is actually proving to be the root of many companies' paperwork problems. The very ease with which reports may be created by computers, from microfilm or by one of the other high-speed data-processing systems, has led to requests for more and more reports, which in turn requires more clerical help to prepare, distribute, analyze, and file these reports, more filing equipment in which to store these reports after they are generated, and more floor space in which to place the file cabinets containing the reports. Consequently, most companies realize that mechanization has not reduced their paperwork management problem but *added to it.*

Records Creation

Considerable attention has been given in the past to the management of paperwork through the use of techniques designed to limit the type, number, and distribution of forms, reports, and correspondence generated. Savings realized through programs designed to control records creation are easily measurable, and it is probably as a result of this that we find such universal acceptance by management of records-creation control programs.

We must remember, however, that the basic controls on records creation were established during a period when most data were processed manually or by relatively unsophisticated key-driven office machinery and equipment. It would pay to re-examine these traditional controls to determine their degree of effectiveness today when more and more data processing is being handled by computers and other high-speed systems.

Forms Design and Control. Forms are the key to the success of nearly every business system. Efficiently designed forms can facilitate the entry and processing of data and reduce greatly the reporting of incorrect or extraneous information.

Since forms are used in nearly every business operation, the production and sale of them has grown into a very large industry. At a recent workshop on forms and reports management sponsored by the University of Minnesota, it was estimated that forms had an annual sales volume of $500 to $750 million in the United States alone. Initial cost represents only a small fraction of the total expense connected with forms. The big factor—clerical expense—is at least 15 to 20 times that of forms procurement. This is substantiated by the experience of a large aerospace company, which found that of each dollar spent for procuring, processing, and filing forms $.044 was spent for procurement, $.112 for filing, and $.844 for processing. All this means that American business and governmental organizations are spending between $10 and $15 billion annually on forms.

With expenditures of this magnitude, it is little wonder that programs for controlling the design and procurement of forms have gained wide acceptance in both industrial and governmental enterprises. Such programs usually review a company's existing and proposed forms for the purpose of:

1. Eliminating unnecessary forms, copies of forms, and items on forms.
2. Preventing the issuance of unnecessary forms.
3. Consolidating duplicating and overlapping forms.
4. Improving forms design to allow for ease of data entry, reference, filing, and so on.
5. Increasing the number of general-purpose forms, while reducing the number of forms whose use is limited to one or two departments.

The place where an organization's forms are brought together for study to accomplish these ends is normally a group of control files. One such file arranges all forms by their *function,* another by their *construction features,* and a third by their *numerical designation.* Originally, such files were actually maintained as physical entities by forms analysts. Mechanized data processing, however, allows them to be mechanically maintained. A tabulating card—coded to reflect the functional, classification, and construction features of each form—may be used in place of the massive files of actual copies of the forms.

A second major change in forms-control practice brought about by the increased usage of automatic processing equipment is in the area of forms procurement. Previously, when forms were largely prepared by manual means or by key-driven office equipment, most forms were ordered on a spot-bid, as-needed basis. With the growth of paperwork processing by automated or semiautomated equipment, purchasing methods have undergone drastic change. Since most forms used on such equipment are merely one link in a procedure and are often the source documents for data entry to another form, it has become common practice to issue and revise all forms involved in a given procedure at the same time. This has made it advisable for companies to design and request vendors to submit bids on many forms simultaneously. This combining of orders has the added virtue of enabling companies to obtain the lower prices that accompany volume orders.

Many organizations have also found it feasible to enter into blanket purchase contracts for forms. These contracts generally provide for the purchase of a single form, or several related forms, at a specified price across a specified period of time (generally 90 days, 6 months, or 1 year). The purchaser agrees to order a stated quantity of forms during the life of the contract. If he exceeds or falls short of this quantity, it is customary for an adjustment in price to be made.

Both the customer and the vendor benefit from such an arrangement. The vendor, knowing that the form under contract will not be revised during the life of the contract, may effectively utilize his equipment by scheduling production of the forms during slack periods. Also, he can buy paper for the contracted forms in greater quantity, thereby reducing both his materials costs and internal paperwork. The customer benefits by knowing that the prices in his blanket contract will remain firm during the contractual period. He also may be able to eliminate much of the clerical detail and cost involved in forms procurement through the use of an informal verbal or handwritten release order against blanket contract. This informal system is quick, convenient, and a real cost cutter, since it bypasses much of the clerical detail and costs involved in processing forms orders.

The ability of mechanized data-processing systems to produce paperwork at high speed has also led to marked changes in the methods of forms handling. Whole new lines of equipment have been developed to reduce the time required to prepare forms for data entry as well as to process them after data have been entered by the mechanized system. Specialized forms-handling equipment has been developed to perform such costly and tedious tasks as removing carbons from between copies of the form, removing the margins containing the pin-feed holes, and separating one copy of the form from the others. Before this specialized equipment was developed, these operations were performed manually, at greater expense.

Radical changes in the organization and administration of the forms design and control function itself is also evolving. Before the widespread use of mechanized data-processing systems, forms design and control was the responsibility of the forms analyst. With the increased number of mechanized data-processing applications though, this responsibility is shifting to the data-processing people. It is readily apparent why the change is occurring. As part of their normal routine, data-processing personnel plan for the total conversion of a manual paperwork system to a mechanized data-processing system. They evaluate the source document, lay out the forms which will be used, and coordinate the purchase of such forms.

Specialists in the field of data entry and transmission by mechanical means, they know probably better than any other persons what is the most effective format for information to be transcribed by their equipment. Therefore, they are logically assuming complete responsibility for designing the forms used in mechanized systems. Little by little, the forms-control function is slowly becoming the data-processing man's responsibility as well. At the time of initial installation, he examines the forms which will be part of his mechanized system and then revises or consolidates them to assure efficient, economical transmission and transcription of data from form to machine and back to form again.

The traditional forms analyst is fast fading from the picture as far as forms for mechanized data-processing application are concerned. His chief responsibility today is in the control of those forms which are prepared by hand or by key-driven office machines. Since the majority of paperwork procedures converted to mechanized data-processing methods are those in which sizable processing of data is involved, it is fairly safe to assume that the forms analyst's importance will further diminish as more and more paperwork procedures are mechanized. In the not-too-distant future, the forms-control function may disappear altogether. With only those forms used in manual or low-volume office machine applications remaining as his responsibility, the forms analyst would find himself controlling only forms used for such specialized applications as visitor passes or employment applications. The resulting inability of the forms-control function to pay for itself will cause it to be discontinued in many of the large companies and governmental organizations where it still exists.

Reports Management. Formalized systems for written reports are one of the results of modern corporate growth. When companies were smaller, employees fewer, and all administrative and production functions often located under the same roof, there was less need for written reports. Face-to-face contact was the rule rather than the exception. The executive seeking information would be more likely to get up from his desk, walk into the office or shop area, and obtain verbal answers to his questions, rather than request a written report.

As businesses increased in size, this practice became increasingly difficult to continue. The typical executive of today works for a multilocation company which employs thousands of people. He cannot possibly know which of these thousands of employees can give him the answers to his questions; and if he did know, it is probable that the employee questioned would, in turn, have to question others to obtain all or part of his answers. The parallel trend toward specialization has also led to divisions of knowledge and responsibility. For these reasons, formal written reports have become increasingly important to modern business operations and to government agencies.

A report is probably the most expensive category of records a company normally prepares. This is the result of the very nature of the report itself. A report is usually a formal presentation of summary information from one management level to another, or from one organization to another, which appears at recurring intervals. It contains statistical and other operating information which reflects such matters as utilization of resources or status of operations or which provides other administrative information useful in judging progress, formulating management policies and decisions, and directing operations. The cost of such efforts is naturally high.

One of the reasons managements have looked so favorably upon computers is that such equipment enables them to receive reports, needed to operate their companies, faster than manual systems. This increased speed makes it possible to learn about problem situations sooner and to take corrective action sooner. Use of computers makes possible better and more timely reports but does not, in itself, make them cheaper.

With the ability to prepare reports greatly facilitated by the computer and automatic office equipment, managers began to request report after report. Complaints about excessive paperwork flowing across the executive's desk soon became commonplace. Costs, both of the data-processing operation and records maintenance function, began to soar. One marketing director complained, "The computers are producing so much paper that management is forced to spend the bulk of its time reading and analyzing that data. This is time which could be more profitably spent in planning for future expansion."

As a further indication of how reporting can get out of hand, consider the result of a survey conducted by a prominent management consultant who found that the average middle- and upper-echelon executive spends 30 per cent of his time preparing, analyzing, and reading reports. In companies in which the span of control is large, this figure can climb as high as 60 per cent.

Yet not all the expense of reports is measurable in terms of personnel time for a particular report. Much is also spent in gathering information for the report. As a summary of information, a report usually draws upon many sources or "feeder" reports. Consequently, sizable clerical effort and expense are involved in assembling data for source reports that will be later summarized into a final report. The cost of a report might well be compared to the proverbial iceberg, only a small part of which is visible above water.

A sizable opportunity for cost reduction and increased management efficiency lies in the area of reducing, as far as efficiently possible, the number of reports prepared and distributed within a company. For every report which is eliminated, it is safe to assume that additional source reports will also be eliminated. Fewer reports being prepared means a decreased workload for a company's data-processing operation, lower distribution and filing costs, more clerical and executive time freed to perform other tasks. The key to obtaining such cost reductions, however, lies in:

1. Stopping unnecessary reporting.
2. Trusting employees.
3. Delegating responsibility to subordinates.

The simplicity of creating and distributing additional copies of machine-prepared reports has led to the indiscriminate creation of report copies. In many companies, information is sent not only to those persons who need that information to discharge their responsibilities but also to many other persons who have little or no interest in the data. Unnecessary distribution both increases report preparation, distribution, and filing costs and adds to executive workload since we can be reasonably sure that the typical executive will at least scan any company report which comes across his desk.

Most reports prepared within a company may be classed as "operational" in nature—they describe the progress or status of a project, and so on. They indicate that the situation is normal or is better than anticipated or is worse than anticipated. Normal situations rarely require a decision or action on the part of the report's recipient. There is, therefore, no reason for him to be told that things are progressing according to plan. However, if things are better than expected or below expectations, the recipient should definitely be advised so that he can take whatever line of action may be indicated.

The concept of reporting only those situations which reflect other-than-normal performance offers companies an opportunity to reduce sharply their reporting workload and expense. Adoption of *reporting by exception* or, in the case of situations in which close control must be kept over costs or production, *tolerance reporting* procedures will assure management that reports of situations requiring prompt attention will not be buried in masses of reports on normal situations. Many companies which realize the benefits which are obtainable from exception and tolerance reporting have not adopted these techniques to any great degree. Their reluctance may be due in large part to two factors: a basic mistrust of employees and a reluctance of management people to delegate responsibility to their subordinates.

The following situation is a typical case of waste brought on by lack of confidence in employees. A company, which did not pay exempt employees overtime, still required them to prepare and submit weekly time cards. When the proposal was made that attendance for exempt employees be reported on an exception basis (only absences would be reported), management rejected the idea for fear that supervisors might be tempted not to report the absence of favored employees. The company continued to require highly paid personnel to prepare time cards and forward them to the payroll department where they were examined, posted to an attendance register, and filed away. Because of this useless procedure, the company incurred unnecessary clerical, managerial, distribution, and filing expense.

Another company put its accounts payable file on magnetic tape so that it might reduce the time, expense, and paperwork involved in processing and paying accounts payable invoices. As a side effect of this computer application, the company also envisioned the early destruction of receiving reports, purchase requisitions, and similar records involved in the purchase of an item or service from an outside source. It was reasoned that this information could be reconstructed from the magnetic tape records reflecting such transactions. But once the system was installed and the accounts payable department submitted a revised retention schedule calling for the destruction of accounts payable invoices, the request was denied. Management changed its mind and decided to retain the original records—documenting the authorization, receipt, and payment of the expenditure—in order to guard against fraud. Sometimes, such an attitude may have as its source an outside influence, like an auditing agency. In others, it may reflect a basic disbelief in the honesty of employees. Yet unless management agrees to accept its employees' word where advisable, it will incur heavy and needless reporting expense.

A third deterrent to economical, efficient reporting can be found in the hesitation with which managers delegate authority to subordinates. This hesitation may have as its roots a lack of faith in the abilities of the subordinates (a poor reflection upon the company concerned) or a basic sense of insecurity (the feeling that if a manager lets everyone do the job, someone might wonder why he is kept on the payroll). Whatever the cause, failure to delegate responsibility makes it necessary for the manager to keep his fingers in too many pies. He will have many people coming to him with problems of a routine nature which could be effectively (or even more effectively) handled by subordinates.

Paperwork mountains being thrown up by computers will continue to grow in the future where management does not change faulty concepts of control and supervision. It might be well for management to consider that more control can sometimes result when actual controls are exercised less. This seeming paradox might be compared to the tremendous success of supermarkets in moving goods by allowing housewives to rummage around in their shelves. Some jars may get broken; a few items may be stolen; but the important function of selling is served mightily. Clearing corporate channels and files of excess paper through the delegation of authority in properly thought-out exception and tolerance reporting techniques might have equally salutary results in freeing management to concentrate on its main function—making profitable business decisions.

Correspondence Control. Of all the techniques of records management, none is so neglected by most businesses and governmental agencies as correspondence control. This is an area which can yield substantial savings for the organization willing to devote the time. While not related directly to the mushrooming volume of reports generated by automatic data-processing equipment, the excessive writing of letters and memos does much to add to the cost burdens of the present situation. Correspondence control programs have the following objectives:

1. Improving the quality of letters and memorandums originating within the company.
2. Developing correspondence standards and guides.
3. Reducing time and costs involved in the preparation of large-volume correspondence.
4. Simplifying and reducing correspondence.

Correspondence represents a sizable portion of any organization's paperwork cost. Conservative estimates have placed the cost of the average business letter or memorandum at $1.50 each. Through installation of correspondence control techniques, this figure can be sharply reduced, as evidenced by the accompanying chart developed by the National Archives and Records Service of the General Services Administration of the U.S. Government. [See Table 1.]

Correspondence control programs are relatively easy to establish. Each department is requested to prepare one additional copy of each memorandum or letter generated within a specified period of time. These additional copies are then forwarded to the person setting up the correspondence control program. He reads each letter and memorandum and classifies it according to the subject discussed. At the end of the collection period, he reviews each group of letters discussing the same subject to see if the letters are basically repetitious in nature. If he finds they are, he then attempts to develop a standard letter covering the situation. If the volume of letters dealing with the same situation permits, he prepares this standard letter as a form letter; if the quantity is too low to justify the expense of printing and stocking form letters, he prepares it as a guide letter, which the originator may refer to when preparing his letter.

Mechanized data-processing systems have now made it possible to realize still further savings from correspondence control programs. Through the use of tape-fed automatic typewriters, repetitive letters may be individually prepared in seconds. . . . the constant (fixed) information which goes into the letter is punched into a paper tape. This is then filed away. When a letter concerning that subject is required, the tape is removed and fed into the automatic typewriter. The tape speeds through the automatic typewriter, and

Table 1 Time and Cost Factors in Creating a Typical Half-Page, 175-Word Letter

	Minutes Required For:			
Function	*Steno Dictation*	*Machine Dictation*	*Guide Letter*	*Form Letter*
Planning what to say	10	10	0	0
Dictation	10	5	0	0
Looking up a letter	0	0	2	1
Transcribing—typing	7	8	6	1.5
Reviewing—signing	2	2	1	.5
Total minutes	29	25	9	3
Cost in Terms of Salary	$.70-2.45	$.60-2.25	$.20-.30	$.08-.15

its code is converted to letters which print out on the letterhead. Whenever a point is reached in the letter where variable data must be entered (such as shipping dates in a sales-confirmation letter), the typewriter stops. The typist then manually enters the variable data and presses a button signaling the typewriter to begin its automatic typing again.

By designing repetitive letters as form letters, an organization can take full advantage of the data-entry capabilities of its high-speed computers, tabulating equipment, and so forth. This practice will enable a company to reduce the time and cost involved in preparing letters and memorandums.

Installation of a correspondence control program, which combines the tested technique of using form and guide letters with the relatively new idea of preparing repetitive letters by a high-speed device such as an automatic typewriter, can prove to be an effective way of holding the line on correspondence preparation costs. However, savings are likely to evaporate if the automatic equipment is used to generate unnecessary correspondence.

Directives and Instructions Management. Every person needs to be aware of his responsibilities, as well as the procedures which apply to his job. To assure that he is, many companies issue a series of written directives and instructions.

Like many other good things, written directives and instructions can be overdone—and they have been in several instances. Consequently, employees may be faced with a variety of written guides telling them when and how to discharge this or that responsibility. Many of these instructions may duplicate others, some may be overlapping, and others even contradictory. This is typical of companies in which no one central group coordinates the issuance of directives and instructions. Other employees may find written instructions difficult to read because of the use of technical jargon, or they may find them open to various interpretations (a dangerous situation) because of sketchy or unclear wording. In today's typical company—characterized by job specialization, high clerical turnover, and tight profit margins—a smooth-flowing paperwork cycle is a necessity. Yet without adequate instructions and directives, this smoothness is difficult to achieve.

It is becoming essential, as more and more paperwork procedures are programmed for computers and other high-speed data-processing systems, that companies review their existing directives and instructions. To achieve economic and efficient mechanized procedures, they must systematize their manual procedures before proceeding with automation.

Most companies and governmental agencies have found it desirable to assign responsibility for the review, coordination, and issuance of directives and instructions to a specific group or individual. This has proven to be a satisfactory method of assuring efficient control over the contents, editorial quality, and distribution of directives and instructions.

Mail Management. Closely related to the creation of paperwork is a company's internal mailroom operation. The potential of work-saving forms and procedures, automated data entry, efficient filing systems, and other records management improvements can all be negated by a slow, inefficient internal distribution system.

Considerable attention was focused upon mail management in the early and middle 1950's, following the Hoover Commission study which pointed out that $30 million of the Government's incoming-mail processing costs could be saved through the installation of new and streamlined procedures, including the following:

1. Time stamping held to essentials.
2. Routing promptly adjusted to changes.
3. Machines used where volume warrants.
4. Review of mail limited to essentials.
5. Sorting, delivery, and pickup of mail efficiently planned.

With the growing use of reports prepared by computers and other high-speed data-processing systems, new mail management problems were created. Printouts from computers, tabulating equipment, and other data-processing systems are generally oversized and bulky. This creates a handling problem, since the printout will not fit easily into standard mailing envelopes. In addition, the sheer weight of the printout sends postage costs spiralling upward.

Many companies have turned to microfilm to enable them to efficiently and economically handle the internal distribution of the printout. Through the use of specialized microfilm cameras, they are able to feed the printout into the microfilm camera as it comes off the printer. The printout is instantaneously microfilmed. The microfilm is then processed and forwarded to the location where it must be distributed. Then a continuous microfilm printer can be used to prepare the number of paper copies of the report needed for distribution at that location. Companies using such systems have found that the cost of using microfilm is generally considerably less than that of distributing bulky printout copies to remote locations.

Records Maintenance

The costs involved in records maintenance are staggering. One large aerospace company placed its records-keeping cost at 11 per cent of its entire overhead budget. The State of California, during the fiscal year 1959–60, placed the cost of records maintenance at $145 million. This figure is based upon (1) maintenance in active areas: 7,000 employees engaged in the maintenance of 600,000 cubic feet of records; and (2) maintenance of records in records centers: six employees involved in the maintenance of 72,000 cubic feet of records.

The experience of these two organizations is typical of most industrial and governmental organizations today and has led to the development of control techniques to minimize these costs. Recognizing fully that certain records must be retained if business is to be carried on, management is nevertheless taking a hard look at its records maintenance procedures and is destroying records as soon as their administrative, operating, and legal value is outlived. It is also re-examining its filing methods, making greater use of inactive records centers, and seeking standardization of filing equipment wherever possible. Finally, with the fear of a nuclear holocaust slightly lessened, as of this writing, management philosophy toward records protection procedures is changing.

While records maintenance has always been an expensive paperwork activity in the past, it has become even more so today, with computers producing paper records at speeds which astound the imagination. It is this sheer increase in the volume of records that must be filed which justifies our taking a closer look at the traditional control techniques of records maintenance to see just what the effect of automation has been upon them.

Files Management. Generally, most companies do their filing on a decentralized (or departmental) basis. While filing standards and systems may be established by a central authority, such as a records manager, the actual maintenance of the files remains the responsibility of the department whose records are in those files.

When a reference is required, the file clerk removes and delivers individual documents to the requester, who must then search through them for the information he desires. Normally, the file clerk does not attempt to search the documents himself for the information required by the requester; this remains the responsibility of the requester. Reference, therefore, is a slow, expensive, two-part operation. First the document must be found among the many contained in the file, and then the desired information must be extracted from the document.

With records being processed by computers and other high-speed data-processing systems, this situation has drastically changed. Many records are maintained, not in paper form, but on magnetic tape, tabulating cards, or other similar input media. When it is necessary to refer to a particular record contained in such files, it is possible to obtain the desired information directly. The requester may now ask a specific question—such as, "Which of our customers purchased 54-inch trampoline frames in quantities of a 100 or more during October 1964?" This question will then be converted into machine-acceptable language and fed into the data-processing system. The system quickly searches its file of magnetic tapes, tabulating cards, and so on and prints out the answer to the question. This information is then forwarded to the requester.

This is the greatest impact of computers and semiautomated and automated data-processing systems upon files management. Today a distinction has developed between "documents" and "information." Records stored in systems from which facts can be directly extracted are far more efficient and economical to maintain than filing systems in which only entire documents may be isolated. These documents must then be further examined for the desired data. Recognizing the advantages of storing information rather than documents, many companies are putting as many of their sales, accounting, and production records as possible on automatic data-processing systems. This practice has had a threefold effect on company records-keeping responsibility and organization:

1. It is drastically revising the records manager's responsibility for indexing and retrieving information.

2. It is leading to the centralization of information systems files.

3. It is diminishing the importance, except for legal purposes, of files in which document retrieval systems are used.

Each of these effects is of great importance and should be examined in greater detail.

Traditionally, the development of filing systems and the indexing and coding of documents filed in those systems have been a function of the records manager. However, the peculiarities and complexities of automated and semiautomated data-processing systems are causing this function to be taken over by data-processing technicians. This is, after all, a natural development, since—as experts in the operation of data-processing systems—the data-processing people generally are more knowledgeable on the subject of indexing and coding requirements for their equipment.

Techniques for high-speed electronic transmission of data are making it possible to send the vast volume of records needed for decision making or control purposes from plant and branch offices to a central location on a daily basis. Information is transmitted and received in machine-acceptable language and is automatically processed at the central location (a company data-processing center for example). This information is contained on tabulating cards, magnetic or punched paper tape, or some other machine-acceptable input media; and it forms a central file of data-processing input media. As required, these central files can turn out reports, or they can be quickly and economically searched with high-speed data-processing equipment.

The growth of centralized information-systems files has led to a downgrading of document systems files. With an ever-increasing number of operating and administrative files being placed on computer or other data-processing systems, document files are tending to become archival in nature; they hold records for statistical and legal purposes rather than for active business reference. This has brought constant pressure upon records managers to reduce maintenance costs for such files by eliminating them where possible, by transferring them to low-cost inactive records centers, or by microfilming (if their retention period is sufficiently long enough to justify the additional expense of microfilming).

However, there is one major exception to this situation. There is a growing need for efficient document files which are depositories of research information. Much of the material contained in research documents—graphs, charts, and so on—does not lend itself to efficient, economical conversion to machine-acceptable language. Therefore, it is better that such documents remain in their original hard-copy form or on microfilm and that they be filed and retrieved as integral documents rather than as bits of information. Yet even here computers and other high-speed data-processing systems can greatly increase the value of these document files by making the information they contain more accessible through in-depth indexing.

Documents are read, and the subjects discussed in them are noted by specially trained librarians. Referring to a predetermined "thesaurus of terms," one can determine which terms best describe the subjects discussed in the documents. These terms, each of which bears a constant numerical code, are fed into the data-processing system, along with the identification number of the research document. Whenever it is necessary to locate the documents which refer to a particular subject, the numeric code of the subject words best describing the information desired is fed into the data-processing system. For example, if one wanted to find out what side effects would result from the injection of a particular hormone, the words "hormone" and "side effects" would be fed into the system. The data-processing system will rapidly search its files of magnetic tapes or tabulating cards and prepare a listing of the accession or identification numbers of documents whose codes indicate they discuss both "hormones" and "side effects." The documents can then be removed from their files and examined further. This system, known as coordinate indexing, is indicative of how even documents filed in their original form have had their contents made more accessible and useful through the use of automatic data processing.

Filing Equipment and Standards. Until recent years, one of the most stable areas of records management was the file room. Office equipment manufacturers had developed several basic types of cabinets: These included letter- and legal-size files and the standard card files such as the 3×5, 5×8, and 4×6. Folders, file guides, and so on were also standardized. Aside from slight improvements and changes in materials used, this equipment varied very little. However, the advent of data-processing systems has created serious physical problems for this standardized equipment: The records no longer fit.

The major difficulty is readily apparent to anyone examining the typical records prepared by manual key-driven office machines and those prepared by a computer. Manual and office-machine records are of uniform sizes, generally sizes which can be economically cut from 17×22 and 17×24 sheets of paper. Records prepared by automatic printers are considerably larger, with 14-inch to 17-inch widths not uncommon. While this oversized format is desirable from an operating standpoint (since it allows more data to appear on the same line and, therefore, on a single page), it creates sizable filing problems. The maintenance of the input media of the computers and the other high-speed data-processing systems likewise causes difficulties. Punched cards, magnetic tapes, punched paper tapes, and the like simply could not be economically or efficiently filed in standard letter-, legal-, or card-sized cabinets.

Office equipment dealers have recognized the need for new equipment, geared to the storage of large, bulky printout and input media (tapes, tabulating cards, and the like). Today, entirely new lines of filing equipment and supplies, capable of efficiently storing the input and output of automated and semiautomated high-speed data-processing systems, are being offered by office equipment manufacturers. This equipment, however, must be carefully evaluated by the potential user to assure that it is best suited to his application. The equipment and performance standards, so carefully and precisely developed over the years for standard letter-, legal-, and card-sized file cabinets, will be of little assistance to the person seeking cabinets to house computer input and output. An entirely new set of standards of construction and performance for file equipment and supplies must be developed to assist the potential purchaser in selecting the equipment best suited to his application in the price range in which he wishes to buy.

Records Retention. Records retention programs evolved naturally over the years to control the growing volume of records that companies have found necessary to maintain. Through the systematic transfer of records from active office files to low-cost records storage areas and eventually to their final destruction, business and governmental organizations have long been controlling records maintenance costs by reducing expenditures for filing equipment, floor space, and supplies.

In the past, after a company established a records retention control program, it usually found that the volume of its records holdings tended to level off. It also discovered that the need for additional filing equipment and space was frequently eliminated, since one year's records were being transferred or destroyed before the next year's records were created. In addition, companies found that systematic transfer of records infrequently referred to from active files made it easier to refer to those records which were frequently used. This combination of cost reduction and better reference led to the almost universal acceptance of records retention controls.

But the postwar growth of the regulatory powers of the Federal and state governments has made careful controls a much more complicated, as well as a mandatory, activity for every business. Companies now have many additional requirements which make available a wide variety of records for examination. These requirements, coupled with the increased activity of the Justice Department and Congress in initiating antitrust actions, have made it imperative that companies develop systems to identify and make available those records that may be demanded.

In the area of governmental regulation and investigation of private enterprise, the computer poses a unique problem. Government has taken the view that a business record which it requires for examination may be put on computer as long as the normal audit trail is maintained and as long as the ability of the government to use the detail tapes is assured. This means that in addition to the tapes themselves, a company would have to retain the [software] package (the program tapes, wiring diagrams, and so on) as well; and if the computer was modified with special configurations, it might even have to make the computer available to the government.

Purely from a technical viewpoint, the increased use of mechanized data-processing systems poses several distinct records storage and retention problems which did not exist when records were prepared largely by hand and key-driven office machines. Considerable care must be taken to store tapes, microfilm, tabulating cards, and other such media in an area which is generally free of dust and excessive humidity and heat. Failure to do so will lead to their warping or general deterioration over a period of time.

The Federal Government has noticed that blemishes are appearing on some of its microfilm after 25 years of storage. These blemishes, in the form of tiny spots, do not prevent the production of enlarged paper copies from the microfilm, but they do make reading all the information on the blowups difficult. While it is still too early to tell whether these cases of "microfilm measles" are likely to reach the epidemic stage in number, this initial discovery of even partial deterioration has led many business and government organizations to carefully recheck the contents of their files.

The retention of information in digital computer memory, a situation which poses a records-keeping problem for many organizations, is typical of the records retention problems created by the increased usage of computers. Many of these records reflect completed transactions and require no updating. Yet they are cluttering the computer's memory. By printing this digital information out, and then microfilming the printout, it is possible for the memory core of the computer to be freed for the storage of digital information which requires updating or which is concerned with in-process transactions.

Microfilm and machine-language records storage are new techniques that have not been proved over a long period of time. For this reason, they require periodic checks on the physical condition of the records.

Vital-Records Protection. Perhaps no paperwork area has had its basic concept so drastically altered by automatic data-processing systems as has vital-records protection. When initially developed, vital-records protection programs had as their sole objective the identification and protection of those records needed by the organization in the event of disaster to: (1) protect its stockholders' interests, (2) reconstruct its basic operations, and (3) protect the organization's assets. The philosophy of vital-records protection was to protect only those records which contained information without which the organization could not go back into business the following day. Emphasis was on the protection of information, rather than of records. Therefore, companies attempted to identify and protect only those records essential to reconstruction. Records of historical or audit significance were not specially protected unless they contained information which was also essential to the reconstruction of the company.

The increased usage of microfilm, magnetic and paper tapes, discpacks, tabulating cards, and other such storage media has complicated this situation. With the need to reconstruct machine-language or microfilm records, it has become necessary not only to store the record itself but also to assure the continued availability of the means of processing and duplicating that record. For example, records stored on microfilm will require readers and printers if that microfilm is to be used quickly following a disaster such as a nuclear war; computer tapes to be usable in the event of destruction of the data-processing facility must also be accompanied by their [software] programs.

The lessening of world tensions has led to further changes in records protection thinking. Most vital-records protection programs initiated since World War II were designed for the ultimate in disaster—nuclear holocaust. Little by little, however, organizations now seem to be taking the view that the probability of such a disaster is too remote for important consideration. Therefore, they are becoming more concerned with providing adequate protection against natural disasters such as floods and earthquakes, as well as loss or damage of vital records through sabotage and pilferage. The recent theory that the only true vital-records protection was storage in a blast-proof, underground facility is losing ground. Increasing emphasis today is being given to in-process, on-site protection of records. We now find greater reliance upon storage of magnetic tapes, [software] packages, and other vital records and accessories in the plant in fire-resistant file cabinets and office safes. This trend is expected to continue through the near future.

The increasing use of computers and data-processing equipment has made radical changes necessary in the paperwork management techniques that were developed in the days when processing was done manually or by office machines. Considerable modification in management thinking as well as a realignment of responsibility for basic functions (the increasing authority of the data-processing manager) is necessary to assure that effective controls over costs are maintained.

The capacity of automatic data-processing systems will increase still further in the future. Uncontrolled, the cost of this output will eat into profits. Paperwork management techniques are the tools for controlling such costs.

Moreover, only careful scrutiny of the reasons for newly suggested records, efficient storage and destruction procedures, and forceful application of exception and tolerance reporting techniques can hold the volume of paperwork within bounds that allow time for the critical review by management of the hard information necessary for carrying out the function of managing.

Records managers today are trying to control the results of two trends which reinforce each other in creating formidable paperwork problems—(1) a growing centralization (particularly in government but also in business itself) that has brought with it requirements for more and more records and (2) the sometimes frightening power of computers to deliver an avalanche of printed information at the push of a button.

Computers and Paperwork*
Forest W. Horton, Jr.

Computers and their associated technologies are at once the most important and the most expensive information-handling tool in modern society. Paperwork may still be the most visible, and perhaps even the most pervasive form of information, but paperwork can no longer claim leadership as either the most important or the most expensive one. The computer has taken over! Eventually, some contend, we shall evolve into a paperless society. Already the electronic collection, transfer, and storage of data in banking, brokering, retailing and other important business sectors are commonplace. To be sure, significant data standardization, data ownership, and data confidentiality problems remain to be resolved. And these problems have important philosophical, legal, and even constitutional consequences. But the technological breakthroughs are already on hand, or in sight. The remaining technical barriers will most certainly be broken within the decade.

What consequence does the ascendancy of modern computer technologies over conventional ("manual") paperwork approaches portend for the Commission on Federal Paperwork and the prospect for reducing red tape?

First, because the unit cost of storing and processing data, using automated-capabilities, is cheaper than using paper media, particularly in the light of extraordinary speeds the machines are capable of, there are increasingly stronger economic incentives to switch from paper to electronics.

Second, because the knowledge explosion is generating more and more information, there is no shortage of "raw material" to feed the machines; quite the contrary.

Third, there is strong evidence that the switch to electronics and computers is creating more, newer, and different kinds of red tape problems than the conventional ones experienced with paper systems because:

—One cannot footnote or annotate a machine record; entire special "routines," as they are called, must be developed.
—People discontinue their old, informal "cuff" records slowly and painfully when new computer systems are installed. As a consequence, two

*Reprinted by permission of *The Bureaucrat.* Vol. 6, pp. 91–100, Fall 1977.

sets of records, often incompatible, exist side by side and compound the transition from the old manual system to the new computerized one.

—Capital investments in hardware, software, and human resource support staffs are substantially greater for most large computerized systems than those corresponding costs supporting equivalent conventional paperwork systems, even though unit costs may be substantially lower in automated systems.

Fourth, the computer offers substantial technical information-handling capabilities which are vastly superior to manual approaches or conventional machine-assisted approaches such as tabulating machines. These capabilities include computational powers, "logical" powers to edit, reorder, and correlate data, graphic display powers, search and retrieval powers, modeling and simulation powers, and extraordinary speeds that enable some operations (e.g., airline reservations) to be processed in "real time" (that is, as transactions occur by the clock). On the positive side, these exceptional capabilities provide the scientist and administrator with the means, theoretically at least, to help solve increasingly complex technical, scientific, and managerial problems. On the negative side these very same capabilities are creating enormous pressures on officials who are trying to manage their data resources judiciously. These pressures may take the form, for example, of imperatives to buy more capacity than may actually be needed "just in case," buy larger numbers of machines for use at lower and lower organizational levels with some loss of centralized control, and buy smaller modules of capabilities and fragment them into larger numbers of organizational units, with a similar loss not simply of control, but of the ability to integrate, correlate, and summarize comparable data.

Let us concentrate for a moment on the mixed blessings of this sophisticated tool in the context of the Paperwork Commission's mandate.

Perhaps the most important of these is that the sheer ability to process massive volumes of information cheaply and efficiently has sandtrapped officials into concentrating on data *processing* and data *systems* at the expense of *data management*. The glamor and excitement [have] been on speeds, capacity, and economies of scale, not how data and information can be organized and manipulated so that [they are] more *useful and relevant* to users. Oversimplifying and generalizing, since the advent of the decade of the seventies, managers and computer users have begun to focus seriously on effectiveness considerations. One could argue this situation has come about primarily because of tighter budgets and inflationary pressures, not because the problems were unforeseen, overlooked, or ignored. In short, data resources and data capabilities must be used more judiciously and circumspectly if the *information dollar* is a dollar well spent.

Next, source data automation techniques, such as the use of mark sensed tabulating cards or optical character recognition, does avoid, or at least minimizes, costs and errors associated with the transportation of data from hard copy source forms to key punched cards or typewritten form. However, preliminary commission research seems to indicate that the lion's share of costs is not in such transposition steps, but rather in the earlier stages of data capture and recordkeeping. Expressed in other words, the costs begin much earlier than when the respondent sits down to fill in the government form. They are heaviest in the actions that must be accomplished to locate, capture, organize and summarize raw data the government asks for on the forms.

Continuing, the temptations to collect all possible data "just in case" it might be needed have simply been too great for many organizations to resist. Because organizations have not planned their data needs carefully, or defined their problems carefully, the computer administrator has been subjected to the kind of pressure that runs along the lines "we don't have the time to define our problem carefully, but it really doesn't matter because the computer is such a powerful tool that we can collect and store all the information we could possibly need. And surely, on a hit or miss basis, enough of it will be useful. What isn't useful we don't care about, because it is so cheap to store anyway, who cares." The result? Data banks are not getting any smaller; more and more irrelevant, obsolete, and inaccurate data is clogging our storage and processing channels. This situation is not just a problem of expense. More importantly, we cannot quickly locate the data that is relevant, timely, and valid because there is so much of the irrelevant, untimely, and obsolete which we must first screen out and pass by to get to what we do need. The irony of the situation is that in many cases we do have the system capability to identify and "track" user identity, frequency, patterns of use, etc., but we don't feed back this intelligence to users.

As our social programs have reached further and more deeply into the lives of citizens, pressures to collect more and more detailed information on the personal lives of individuals have increased. Here again the computer has offered the powers and the capabilities to efficiently collect that data. While this paper does not propose to address all facets of the important issue of privacy, it must be pointed out that inevitably the collision between the right of privacy and the needs of data handling efficiency have enormously complicated orderly movement toward judicious information management. In its simplest form this problem is perhaps best represented by the need to foreclose sharing data between agencies, and thereby force the recollection of identical data, in order to protect the legitimate rights of citizens...to insure that information on their personal lives is not improperly and indiscriminately used by unauthorized persons and agencies.

Before addressing what the commission is doing about all of these problems, let us examine what the state of the art of information handling technology portends for us, both in the near and in the long term.

The mini- and microcomputer equipment and software is already upon us. Again we are being treated to a bewildering array of brand new bright bells and whistles that dazzle both the jaded computernik as well as the novice. It is no exaggeration to say that everyone now wants his or her personal computer, or at least terminal. Now an argument can be made, "so what?" Isn't that what technology is all about? Think of the implication of every scientist, technician, analyst and decision maker having his or her own data set at their elbow, with powers to call forth computational and manipulation routines enabling the quick and efficient resolution of problems as they come up. But such is the inevitable and inexorable consequence of this development that the endemic management problems attendant to fragmentation, specialization, and compartmentalization will most assuredly increase once again, perhaps geometrically.

Have we learned any lessons from the third generation of equipment now passing from the scene, that we might apply as we now move into the fourth?

One general lesson might be that moving information-handling technologies closer to their ultimate users does indeed heighten and sharpen the responsiveness of the technology to the user. At the same time it creates new problems that were not present when such capabilities were centralized and managed on a service concept basis. In the data and information area there are several such problems.

For one, the collection, storage, transfer, and dissemination of duplicative and potentially conflicting and incompatible data [are] compounded in proportion to the number of new units using the new capabilities.

For another, top management is confronted with the problem of how to deal with such conflicting and incompatible information. This problem has...dramatically surfaced in very large organizations, such as the Department of Defense, where the Secretary, until recently (since the creation of the new Information Directorate), was faced with the Military Services giving testimony to Congress, and releasing information to the media, using different sets of data (e.g., troop strength, missile numbers, budget figures, etc.) which were often inconsistent, or, in some cases, downright contradictory. Now, with minicomputer decentralization, the problem of tracking down, auditing, and reconciling differences in data sets without suitable controls is certainly going to be considerably more difficult. In some cases it may be that "incompatible" or "conflicting" data merely is data disparity due to dysynchronous cutoff, update dates, or the lack of data element standardization.

Continuing on a slightly different tack but still on the basic point, it is not just a problem of embarrassment that we face. The scientist in charge of the laboratory will have his assistants collecting and storing data used in vital experiments in health, safety, and security programs, which potentially is inconsistent, incompatible, and conflicting. Simply reconciling differences would seem to be a time-consuming and expensive job without adequate controls and policies, without considering the potential dangers that such irreconcilable information may pose. The reader is familiar with the various "horror stories" which every large federal agency already has in its files—cases where key officials didn't have access to the right information at the right time in the right form because it was buried in inaccessible places, and there was no "system" to retrieve it and surface it when needed.

Communication, even on simple matters and in routine fashion, is made inordinately difficult by the use of terms and phrases which are not standardized and uniformly defined in all parts of the organization's operations and activities. If the personnel department defines on-board strength as excluding temporary part-time employees as of the end of the reporting period, but the payroll department includes them in its definition, clearly time and money will be wasted in correcting the differences.

Another problem is miniaturization. The micrography technologies and the newer holographic technologies make storage of data cheaper and more accessible to use in textual form. In many cases these technologies complement and supplement computer technologies which may deal with data in digital or analog form. But another temptation is to collect, store, process, and disseminate data in *both* forms simply because "the technology is there," without carefully considering the *needs and uses* for handling data in multiple media forms. Certainly exercising both options in some data settings will make sense, but in most cases the use of both media will result in unnecessary redundancy that is expensive and time-consuming.

The telecommunication and satellite technologies must also come under our scrutiny. Without them we would be unable to move masses of data quickly and efficiently. It is difficult to quantify the value of ringing the earth with communication satellites that bring people and nations closer together and capture events of international scope as they occur. Multinational corporations and governments can communicate rapidly with their plants, ambassadors, and emissaries and give them instructions on the spot. But the reader will quickly recall the implications of "instant" problem solving and decision making. The results may be disastrous because actions taken were ill-considered, premature, or untimely. Again, the *temptation* because of the *mere existence and availability of cheap technology* has led to imprudent and irreversible action in many cases, in the political, social, economic, and commercial arenas.

The...areas—automation, micro-miniaturization, and telecommunications—are not the only information-handling technologies involved, but they are perhaps the most headline catching. There are groups hard at work in the pure sciences, and most notably in the information sciences, which are trying to help us harness the newer hardware technologies more efficiently and circumspectly, not just to serve individual users, but hopefully, society as a whole. Suffice it to allude to these groups only in passing.

Now what is the Commission on Federal Paperwork doing about these problems?

Public hearings have provided the means for commissioners to hear first hand from a wide variety of individuals, businesses, and representatives from institutions such as hospitals and universities, about the impact of automation technologies on them from a paperwork burden standpoint. As of July 9, 1976, in 12 public hearings, the commission had heard from 19 witnesses who made a variety of recommendations, or registered complaints, concerning the uses to which modern information-handling technology [was] being put in either helping, or frustrating efforts to reduce the paperwork burden. Two major categories of recommendations and/or complaints have been identified.

First, greater automation was recommended in forms handling to reduce paperwork at all stages, including collection, recording, processing, storing, and dissemination. Data requirements associated with federal program administration and management should be automated, to the extent it is feasible and cost effective.

Second, the "interface" between the computer and the persons, organizations, and methods for inputting data into the machine is poor. Controls should be strengthened to reduce transcription errors, minimize lost material, reduce garbled data, eliminate interpretation difficulties, and generally economize by using improved state-of-the-art techniques where cost effective. For example, computer output from large agencies, businesses and other respondent organizations should be in machine-sensible form where practical and cost effective, in order to directly transfer respondent computer output data to agency computer input data, bypassing dysfunctional and burdensome intermediate processing stages. Electrical Accounting Machine (EAM) or computer tape methods should be used in such cases in lieu of hard copy where possible.

A major study is underway to identify overlap and duplication between federal, state, and local forms and reports submitted by respondents to all levels of government. This study is focused not only at the document level, but also at the data element level. The results of this study are expected to be useful in identifying reforms and approaches to help resolve a wide variety of data coordination problems. For example:

—How critical is the duplication problem? Much has been written and many allegations have been made about its extent and consequence, but little hard evidence has been systematically accumulated to give us facts upon which we might make intelligent assessments and decisions.

—What kind of coordination system(s) at the federal, state and local levels might make sense to reduce duplication and overlap and at the same time get better, more timely, and more complete information into the hands of decision makers.

—At what level are the duplication problems found in agencies: among programs, specific forms and reports, or specific generic data element classes. Priorities should be established to resolve the most burdensome problem areas first, and defer the less important.

The data and information flow process has been documented in exhaustive detail. While no single flow process exists that would typify all the data flows in all organizations, situations, etc., nevertheless the process is very instructive and does illuminate leverage points where initiatives and incentives reduce and simplify information (and thereby paperwork) requirements. It also points up redundancy and overlap in processes, systems, and procedures which support the information flow. And it vividly illustrates the character of the overall process. The sheer number and complexity of individuals, organizations, steps, and subprocesses involved in the overall flow [are] overwhelming.

A study of the problems associated with safeguarding computer records is planned in collaboration with outside experts. Much is being written in this field and the difficulties are indeed legion. At the heart of the matter are two vital concerns: (1) the protection of legitimate needs for confidentiality, not just of citizen records, but of government's needs to protect state secrets and security information. The commission has received indication, however, that some duplication has resulted from "illegitimate" confidentiality claims. And (2) criteria to guide agencies in knowing when the collection and storage of redundant, duplicative data [are] essential even if not "efficient."

Additionally, the commission plans a number of special projects within the boundaries of various overall study charters that will address specific aspects of the computer's role in paperwork reduction. These will include: (1) small conferences with selected professional and trade groups and societies with expertise in this area to tap their experiences; (2) visits to selected key business firms and other organizations which have pioneered innovative approaches to harnessing computer and automation technologies to get on top of their paperwork problems; and (3) brainstorming sessions with selected groups of persons who have demonstrated competence and received recognition for their imaginative application of various ideas to reduce red tape.... While a whole range of paperwork reduction ideas should emerge from these sessions, the automation handling technologies will most certainly be given priority attention.

Finally, the commission is working with other public bodies which have an interest in this area. The Electronic Funds Transfer Commission and the National Commission on Libraries and Information Centers both have strong and direct interests in seeking ways to improve the uses of data and information, while at the same time minimizing causes and other dysfunctional problems....

Obviously, we are able to accomplish many things with computers which we could not do, or even think of doing, 20 years ago. And we can do them in a time period that is responsive to the problem-solving time frame. However, these capabilities have increased paperwork and its associated burdens. These burdens, large or small, must be juxtaposed against the information values with which they are associated.

With the application of advanced information technology and its powerful capabilities, we are demanding more and more information. Some is exploratory in nature and is used to seek out and identify problems which may not even be defined. Other information is collected with the hope that it may later reveal some relevance to an organizational objective.

It is when collected information has little or no value to a specified objective and to concrete results expected that the burden on citizens is the greatest. There is, in effect, a cost with no corresponding benefit—a burden with no corresponding value.

Occasionally there has been an overload in data collected, resulting in an inadequacy of relevant information. Relevant information has been submerged in a mass of irrelevant information. The exceptional ease in our ability to collect data and produce reports has led to the insidious tendency to give most attention to that which is *interesting* rather than that which is *essential.*

In summary, the problems the Paperwork Commission is addressing in the area of applying modern information-handling technologies to reduce the paperwork burden may be summarized as follows:

1. How to sharpen the focus on understanding these technologies and their uses in terms of not faster speeds and cheaper costs, so much as how the information's value can be enhanced in helping to achieve the organization's objectives. In short, less concern with *how* to manipulate information more efficiently and more concern with *what* is being manipulated and its effectiveness to goals and results.

2. The decline in costs for large scale data storage capacities and for increased throughput rates [has] made the information process relatively "cheap"; however, the burden on respondents has probably increased on a scale inverse to reduction in processing costs. Attendant to this shift has been an increasing insensitivity to problems outside the sphere of "the system." How, then, can a balance be reachieved in the "value/burden" ratio?

3. Misapplication of information technology, through a lack of understanding of both its capabilities and its limitations is a serious problem. Also, more and more reliance on technology to provide solutions, where less or few can realistically be provided, is an expectation which somehow must be lowered.

4. Improper application of technology has complicated many processes rather than made them simpler, and has, in some cases, increased costs. This has led to a situation where we are being enslaved by the tool rather than harnessing the tool to serve our needs. Who is the master?

5. Technology has become increasingly an excuse for human failures. This has obscured the real nature of problems and has delayed, if not in some cases totally voided, relevant solutions and solution seeking.

6. Information technology, or more correctly information-processing technology, has produced a brand new, large, and important segment in the professional labor force. The technology itself has partially replaced and substantially altered the character of another segment of the labor force consisting of clerical skills. This new segment of the labor force, unlike the older one, has vigorously advanced "its" technology and use of this technology is now essential to almost every aspect of large scale public sector programs—in its management, in its administration, and...in its routine operations. This trend will continue and broaden to encompass more user/quasi-technicians

with the advent of remote time sharing and simpler user command languages.

Finally, success or failure in the future, and the reduction of paperwork burdens, would seem to depend on how well we understand and apply our information resources. This challenge is equal to the challenge of understanding the potentials of the new technologies.

Coalescence: The Inevitable Fate of Data Processing*

C. W. Getz

Yankee ingenuity has changed the face of the world and is changing the world of MIS [management information systems]. Innovations and inventions in computer technology, telecommunications, circuitry, and related materials have meshed. Traditional divisions of labor and specialties in the organization are disappearing as the computer becomes a practical and economic tool used in a wide variety of applications and causes old skills to become obsolete and new ones to emerge. The historical development of these merging technologies is graphically displayed in Figure 1.

Amidst this technological uproar, the MIS manager must assess the future in a completely different way than in the past. As computer and communications devices and systems permeate all parts of the organization, even interfacing directly with customers, the problems of planning, budgeting, and controlling these systems are blurred in a mist of organizational confusion. There is only one common element that runs through this management maze, *the data resource*, the stuff that computers compute, communication devices communicate, word processors process, and the human resource uses or misuses. It is to the management of data that the manager must turn his attention; the alternative may be to see his influence eroded by other *data managers* in the organization.

The purpose of this paper is to present an overview, a new perspective if you will, of just what is happening to the MIS manager as a result of inventions and innovations that are happening faster than they can be assimilated into the organization. *At today's electric speeds, it is possible for a whole new professional field to be created, rise to power and become obsolete—within the span of one career lifetime.* Is this happening to the MIS profession? Is it possible that the term, *management information system,* needs redefinition in light of these changes? For the MIS manager with vision, management of *all* the firm's data resources may present the ultimate professional challenge.

*Reprinted by special permission from *MIS Quarterly*, Vol. 1, No. 2, pp. 21–30, June 1977. Copyright 1977 by The Society for Management Information Systems and the Management Information Systems Research Center.

The Data Resource

Data is the oldest of man's resources. From the moment of conception, the human anatomy is the perfect embodiment of a biological machine system that depends upon data to operate and survive. It could be termed a bioelectrical system, since it actually causes electrical charges to actuate its computing, communications and motor mechanism. According to Marshall McLuhan, "Our central nervous system is not merely an electric network, but it constitutes a single unified field of experience" [9, p. 348].

The history of the world has been influenced by data or the lack of it. Control of writing materials and control of writing skills formed societies, established social levels, created power structures, and shaped the moral and political fiber of nations. Of course, writing materials and the skill of writing are for the purpose of recording and communicating data. Professor Harold Innis made these points,[1] and believed that monopolies of knowledge developed and then lost influence in direct relation to the method of communication of the times. "A complex system of writing becomes the possession of a special class and tends to support aristocracies. . . . Inventions in communications compel realignments in the monopoly or oligopoly of knowledge" [5, p. 4].

Monopolies of writing skills and knowledge and their inherent power are found today. Persons who have the knowledge to communicate with the computer have become a special class of experts in the context of Innis. These specialists have held a monopoly over a field that is increasing in importance in all activities of human endeavor.

Specialists

Specialists in the organization present numerous problems. The brilliant and controversial Harold Laski believed the specialist (he used the name *expert*) sacrifices common sense insights to the *intensity of his experience* in his special field. Laski also believed the specialist will not test common sense in himself or others, because common sense is based on broad experience that goes beyond the field of special training [8, pp. 101-110]. The specialist often has an aversion to new ideas. Specialists in a field are often the first to oppose innovation. Specialists seldom see the whole problem. They sometimes assume their field of specialty is the center of importance and relate everything to it.

Some specialists have a feeling of superiority that is likely to be associated with the knowledge of being a specialist. The lack of humility often

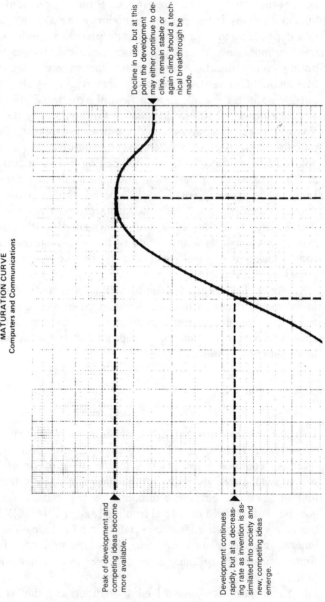

TECHNOLOGICAL
MATURATION CURVE
Computers and Communications

Decline in use, but at this point the development may either continue to decline, remain stable or again climb should a technical breakthrough be made.

Peak of development and competing ideas become more available.

Development continues rapidly, but at a decreasing rate as invention is assimilated into society and new, competing ideas emerge.

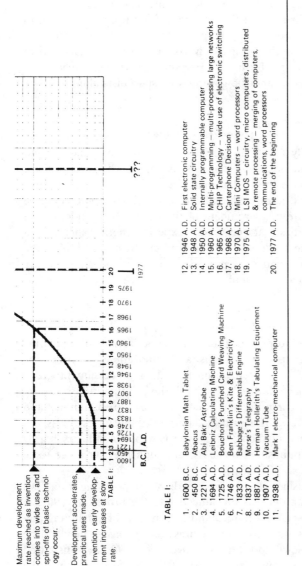

Maximum development rate reached as invention comes into wide use, and spin-offs of basic technology occur.

Development accelerates, practical uses made.

Invention, early development increases at slow rate.

TABLE I:

1.	1600 B.C.	Babylonian Math Tablet
2.	450 B.C.	Abacus
3.	1221 A.D.	Abi Bakr Astrolabe
4.	1694 A.D.	Leibniz Calculating Machine
5.	1725 A.D.	Bouchon's Punched Card Weaving Machine
6.	1746 A.D.	Ben Franklin's Kite & Electricity
7.	1833 A.D.	Babbage's Differential Engine
8.	1837 A.D.	Morse's Telegraphy
9.	1887 A.D.	Herman Hollerith's Tabulating Equipment
10.	1907 A.D.	Vacuum Tube
11.	1938 A.D.	Mark 1 electro-mechanical computer
12.	1946 A.D.	First electronic computer
13.	1948 A.D.	Solid state circuitry
14.	1950 A.D.	Internally programmable computer
15.	1960 A.D.	Multi-programming – multi-processing large networks
16.	1965 A.D.	CHIP Technology – wide use of electronic switching
17.	1968 A.D.	Carterphone Decision
18.	1970 A.D.	Mini Computers – word processors
19.	1975 A.D.	LSI MOS – circuitry, micro computers, distributed & remote processing – merging of computers, communications, word processors
20.	1977 A.D.	The end of the beginning

Figure 1   Technological maturation curve (computers and communications).

makes the specialist blind to the obvious. Specialists tend to have a strong identification with fellow specialists. Evidence and arguments suggested by non-specialists are usually viewed with suspicion. Specialists frequently keep the layman ignorant and assume that he is ignorant because he *is* a layman. A final point about specialists is that they sometimes confuse knowledge with wisdom. Wisdom is by no means the sole property of specialists. Specialists are necessary and inherent in the complex division of labor that characterizes our society. But, society, the business firm and government need both specialists and wisdom, and cannot be governed by specialists alone.

Specialized Data Organizations

Data specialists are usually found in specialized organizations and are not limited to automated data organizations. For example, when the scribes, oracles, and priests controlled the skill and materials of writing, they became the first publishers, the first librarians, and the first archivists, and could be found in the highly structured environment of the court, the temple, or the church. They were the earliest data processing experts. Another specialist, a statistician named Herman Hollerith, can be credited with establishing the forerunner of today's automated data processing organization and industry when he developed the techniques and machines to process the 1890 census data.

Printing Industry. The invention of movable type in the fifteenth century was also the birth of another kind of data processing organization—the printing industry—and more specialists. Inventions and innovations in the same technical fields that have influenced automated data processing progress, have also had a direct impact on developments in the printing industry: electricity, telegraphy, radio, computers (particularly the minicomputer), and circuitry, just to name a few. The printing, or publishing industry, as you prefer, has spawned its own offshoots; thus, the newspaper industry hardly relates itself to the book publishing business, although they have the same genesis.

Newspapers began using electronic, key-driven typesetting over two decades ago, and the computer was introduced into the process in 1961. A whole page can be composed on a minicomputer-driven CRT, including pictures, different font types, and formats; a press-ready master mat will be automatically produced. News stories from all over the world are transmitted instantly via satellite to newspapers everywhere. It is only a short step to the time when newspapers will be composed remotely and delivered to the home via a facsimile machine over fiber optic or laser beam telephone lines or satellites beaming into homes. Even now, libraries can be created on video tape units.

Then came xerography and new, cheap document binders. Every office could be in the publishing business. "The speed up of the printing process obsolesces the assembly line book...Xerox made everybody a reader and makes everybody a publisher" [10, p. 21]. Thus, still another group of specialists became collectors, producers, and communicators of data.

Communications Industry. Information is data made useful, and to be useful, information must be communicated. Communications is an integral part of any data processing system. The communications industry, with its many specialists, is of comparatively recent vintage, although one cannot arbitrarily eliminate smoke signals, drum beats, flag-waving, and the Pony Express from historical contention as early communications systems. Electricity made the Pony Express rider obsolete, but there were few objections from the horse. Marconi and Henry Ford are horse heroes. It is interesting to note that most early communication networks—except the horse—were digital. The invention of the telephone gave us the analog signal, but we are now rapidly going back to all digital networks, even in voice communications. This flip-flop in technology is discussed later.

The communications industry has traditionally been a combination of regulated oligopolies and non-regulated equipment vendors. Carterfone opened competition, but technology created competition. In the decade since the Carterfone decision, the technical inventions and innovations in communication devices and services stagger comprehension—fiber optic and laser beam voice circuits, satellite voice communications around the world, and data transmission speeds that can transmit William L. Shirer's monumental *The Rise and Fall of the Third Reich* in 1/10th of a second! Computers have been used in the communications industry for many years, but the process of coalescence began infiltrating telephone systems when, in recent years, the telephone company's main switching device became more of an electronic computer than an electro-mechanical switch. Electronic switchers and electric speeds have made the communications of data and information instantaneous—to match and merge the computation speeds of computers. Computers and communications are technological Siamese twins.

The speed of light is what is happening to your daily lives, and to the organization of our businesses. At the speed of light, you do not have any future. It is all right here and now. You cannot have a view of the future at electric speed, nor can you have a goal, at electric speed. It is already here. It is already realized...With electric speed...there is not transportation, but there is transformation. When I think of that in terms of your computers and programs, you are not transporting anything, but you are transforming everything. There is no transportation at electric speed. It is simultaneous everywhere [10, pp. 19–21].

Paperwork Management Organizations. There are two other data-related functions that have been performed by specialists in organizations for years before the computer, and were early efforts in data management. They are generally referred to as (1) *records and form management* (also called *paperwork management*), and (2) *reports management*. The former of these two functions has its own professional publications and societies, and is closely related to the *library sciences*. It is still a widespread activity in government and industry, and more will be said in paragraphs to follow.

The latter of these two functions, *reports management*, is of more recent origin. It is a product of the depression years and the proliferation of government agencies in the late 1930's.[2] Demands for reports from individuals and industrial organizations, often duplicating and complicated, caused reaction in Congress that finally resulted in passage of the Federal Reports Act of 1942. The results of such legislation were, first, to give new impetus to reports management and secondly, to create organizations with their experts to administer the new Act. But reports control was only the tip of the iceberg.

Paperwork management is the direct predecessor to data resources management. In the words of Joseph Kish and James Morris, "paperwork management is in transition" as a result of automatic data processing [7, p. 151]. They point out that most techniques in this respect emphasized the limitation of type, number, and distribution of forms, reports, and correspondence. These older techniques are still very much in evidence. These manual methods are measurable and savings could be seen. There was a wide acceptance of records control programs. The techniques were developed during a period when most data was processed either manually or by key-driven machinery. These older techniques are being critically reviewed in view of computer-driven, high-speed printers, computer-output microfilm, and computer-driven word processors.

Kish and Morris go even further and suggest that, as a result of the computer environment, "radical changes are needed to take place in the organization of the administrative function." They warned that the responsibility is shifting to the computer expert. Kish and Morris foresaw a complete revolution in the management of paperwork; one, they say, is already taking place. It is interesting to note that Kish and Morris wrote their prophetic words a decade ago and two decades after Executive Order 9784 was issued. This order recognized the burgeoning state of mountains of files of paper from World War II, and required Federal agencies to conduct *active, continuing programs for the effective management and disposition of records.* Not much was done, although succeeding Hoover commission reports in 1949 and 1955 gave impetus to paperwork management in the Government including passage of the Federal Records Acts of 1950 and 1976.

There are many estimates of what paperwork is costing the taxpayer. One estimate says over $15 billion a year [12, p. 1], and a more recent one says $40 billion a year for *both* government and private sector cost [1]! Whatever the figure, we know it is incomprehensible. Unfortunately, the organizations created to administer the Government's reports control program were not the same organizations charged with the paperwork management programs, including libraries: each group developed its own set of experts. There is presently a Federal Paperwork Commission chartered to study again this growing problem. From the information available, it appears this Commission is traveling down the same road as its predecessor: reduce the number of forms; manage the paperwork instead of managing the raw material that requires the paperwork—data! A refreshing change from this approach has been put forward by a member of the Commission, Forest "Woody" Horton, Jr. In a recent article in the Journal of Systems Management, he has advocated *the budgeting of the data and information resource* [2].

Flip-Flop Technology

There are two common elements in the changes underway in specialized data management organizations. First, that data, regardless of the name given to the organization responsible for it—whether a printing company, a library, or a data processing unit—is still essentially the same raw material used in different ways. Secondly, there is more and more dependence by these organizations upon the electronic computer as their principal data processing tool. As a result, organization patterns are changing as the computer takes on the day-to-day tasks of data clerks and forces new skills upon older arts.

Over the years, the various groups having responsibilities with data processing, reports control, libraries, publications, communications, or paperwork management, have formed into spheres of specialties, organized professional societies, developed jargons understandable only to their peers, and adopted all the other basic trappings of Laski's experts. With each major technological advance, even whole new industries and professional fields were created. In the words of Kish and Morris, "old skills became obsolete."

The scribes of the churches were wiped out by Gutenberg. The punch card of Jacquard eliminated the weaver. Babbage saved the world from eternal dependence upon the abacus and so on, and so forth. However, we live in a cyclical world. Wherein technology once divided us into many fields of specialty, we now find that technology is eliminating the need for some specialists and the generalist is on the rise again. As McLuhan said,

"What does this technology do to things that have been pushed out much earlier? Invention unexpectedly brings back something that had been pushed aside long ago...Every technology pushed to its limits, flips into the opposite form of what it began.

What has the computer flipped into as a result of being pushed?...The job becomes a role, the sequential becomes simultaneous, the visual becomes acoustic, and if I push bureaucracy up to very high speeds, what does the computer do? Anarchy. I have only to speed up any bureaucratic system to have complete anarchy...Inevitably, the man who is the center of decision-making does not wait for my delegation of authority. He is the electric model in action. I think you will find that he is everywhere today. In the highly informed world, you do not wait for delegated information" [10, p. 21].

Perhaps a more vivid example of this *flip-flop* caused by technology is the medical profession. At one time, a doctor performed all the medical tasks—the old country doctor image. But as medical knowledge expanded, a plethora of specialists emerged and it has become almost a self diagnosis problem to know which specialist to consult. In fact, there is a specialist to tell you which specialist to see! As a result, and just in the past decade, there has been a slow return to the family practitioner or generalist, *as a field of specialty!*

The data processing technology may also cause a flip-flop in the qualifications of the DP professional. In 1946 it was essential to be a physicist or mathematician to communicate with the computer. In 1977, you need only to know how to read and write, and even that knowledge can be very basic. As mini and micro processors become more common, the large processors will take on the more sophisticated tasks, and operating systems will become more complex in order to make the user-end simpler. Therefore, the DP professional will be found at the large centers where expert knowledge and skills are required.

The Coalescence of Functions

So, the coalescence or merging of different functional fields is progressing at McLuhan's electric speeds. It is straining the confining lines of conventional organization charts. The librarian is a computer specialist, the paperwork manager is a terminal operator, as is the newspaper typesetter, and the communicator is a data processor. IBM wants in to the communications carrier business. AT&T wants in to the data processing business. Both are being sued by the Government for antitrust. Western Union is in the post office business; the Post Office wants in to the electronic mail business. Everyone wants in to the publications business. Xerox builds printing presses. Xerox builds communication terminals; they used to build computers. Typewriters talk to each other. Electric speeds now make it possible to centralize and decentralize organizations simultaneously.

This entire coalescence process has been graphically portrayed by Artel Ricks in a previously unpublished *Information Wheel* (Figure 2).[3] The impact upon the organization has also reached current literature, but often with emphasis and domination of the computer-oriented expert [11]. A more pragmatic and nonparochial viewpoint of this coalescence process was taken by Paperwork Commission's Horton in an article, "Inter-disciplinary Approach Sought for Information Management" [3]. His *Information Solar System*, Figure 3, is another method of representing the coalescence of functions in the several data-related industries and professional fields.

The process of coalescence may be moving at electrical speeds, but it is also generating plenty of heat. In one procurement organization, as an example, there is a difference of opinion as to whether word processors should be bought by the same people who procure paper, pencils, and automobiles; or by the people who buy computers, communications equipment, and services. Among many agencies, there is a controversy about whether a facsimile machine is a communications device or an office machine, like a duplicator or typewriter. Debate continues on whether telecommunications management should be merged with data processing management and who should emerge as the leader in such a merger. The people who conduct paperwork management studies in still another agency cannot cross the boundary into automatic data processing—that is someone else's responsibility. And the proliferation of reports in the Government goes unchecked because responsibilities are unclear and controls ineffective.

Future of the Data Resource

It is worth repeating that there is one common thread to the coalescence of these diverse technologies and diverse functions—the data resource. It is *data* that is being collected, processed, published, filed, transmitted, used, and misused. It is *data*, man's oldest resource, that is causing paperwork

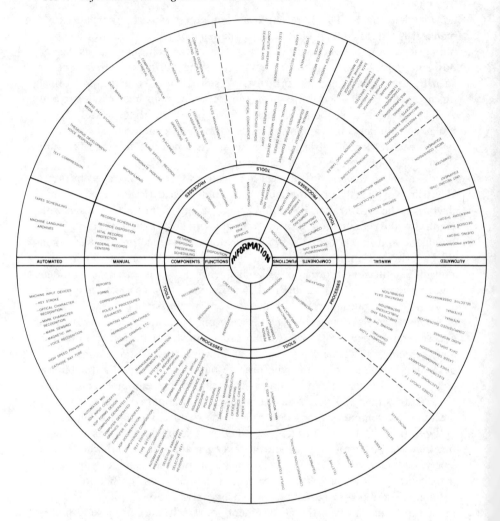

Figure 2   Information handling today. (Prepared by Artel Ricks.)

management problems. It is *data* that is demanding more and more of the company's resource dollar for capital investment. It is *data*, the raw material, that continues unmanaged, uncontrolled, and the subject of today's privacy issues.

	COMPUTERS & AUTOMATION	COMMUNICATIONS & TELECOMMUNICATIONS	PUBLISHING, PRINTING & REPLICATION	MICROFORM & MINIATURIZATION	STATISTICS & PROBABILITY	LIBRARY SCIENCE	MANAGEMENT & SYSTEMS	INFORMATION SCIENCE	INFORMATION ARTS
COMPUTERS & AUTOMATION	Mass data trsfr Auto msg switch networking Real time control Satellites								
COMMUNICATIONS & TELECOMMUNICATIONS	Phototypesetting Automated morgues Tex processing Page make-up	Remote editing Multiple editions national papers facsimile transm.							
PUBLISHING, PRINTING & REPLICATION	COM Direct text ref.	Video transmission document images	Micropublishing Microform report Condensed packaging collect.						
MICROFORM & MINIATURIZATION	Mini computing Random access Boolean algebra Linear program	Real time control Network structures	Report generators	Ultrafiche microminiaturization retrieval					
STATISTICS & PROBABILITY THEORY	KWIC indexing Auto. catalog Machine-read Biblio- search	Multiple facility access	Book catalogs Bibliographic systems	Microform holdings	Bibliometric analysis				
LIBRARY SCIENCE	Data base mgt. Process control MIS SDA	Teletransportation Laser technologies	Process Control printing	Photomicrography	Regression an. Monte Carlo Poisson Models/Simul.	Machine index. Auto. abs. & cat.			
MANAGEMENT & SYSTEMS SCIENCES	SDI Synth. long Cybernetics Machine trans.	Data reduction & compaction	Comprehensive & selective bibliographies	Holographic technology	Relevance & Access tech. Information Theory	Clearing houses Document Centers	OCR Lg. capacity storage Info. stnds.		
INFORMATION SCIENCES	Computer graph. CAJ Heuristic prog. Music scoring	Telelectures Teleconferencing Picture phones	Voice Visual-graphic Video cassette	Micrography	Dimensional and contour projections	"Please Ask"	Info. as resource Info. budget	Knowledge mgt.	
INFORMATION ARTS									

Reprinted from Information Action, February 1977 issue, with permission of the author and the Information Industry Association.

Figure 3 The information solar system.

Sometimes it is easier to predict what *will* happen than to accurately record or retrieve what *has* happened. It requires no surfeit of imagination to foresee the consequences of coalescence as discussed in this paper, and these predictions are plausible:

- From these technological *ashes of confusion* shall arise a new *Phoenix of organization*—the data resources management organization. The manager of this new area will be a generalist with a solid understanding of technology, but a better understanding of business conditions and needs. This data resources manager will be responsible for assuring that all elements of the organization are provided with the most effective and economical means to gather, process, and use the firm's data resources. Data will then be managed in the same sense that the other human and physical resources of the firm are managed.
- There will also be a coalescence of data-related legislation. The Privacy Act of 1974, the Federal Records Act of 1976, the Federal Reports Act of 1942, and other similar statutes, will be merged into a new Data Management Act, applicable to all Federal agencies.
- The efforts of the current Federal Paperwork Commission will result in only a modest reduction in Government paperwork. Like earlier efforts, there is too much concentration on the control of forms, a media for communicating or storing data, and not enough upon the data itself. It is encouraging to note that the Commission's director has been talking about *treating information as a resource and showing that, once identified, the normal management tools of budget appropriation and other controls can be brought to bear* [6, pp. 52–54]. Until Government managers are forced to budget and pay for the data they use, there will be no effective, long-lasting reduction in Government paperwork.
- And finally, all of these predictions will be accomplished within the next decade. *Coalescence is the inevitable fate of data processing, and it is also the inevitable fate of most data-related activities of the organization.* The message is quite clear; either the MIS manager will take the initiative to lead this merger of the firm's data resources activities and make some sense of their management, or some other data specialist outside of the MIS organization will do it for him. A good place for him to start is with Figures 2 and 3.

At the beginning of this paper, it was stated that data has influenced man from the beginning of time. It is now suggested, that management of the data resources has a much broader implication for the future. Data information and communications are resources that, when available and properly applied, raise the intellectual level of people. The result, as seen in history, is an improvement in material existence. This has bred pride, satisfied want, and provided people with the ability to contribute to society and not seek contributions from it. Thus, the technology associated with the data resource can accelerate these achievements into the remotest corners of the world. When viewed in this perspective, *data* is not only a basic resource of the organization, but a basic resource of mankind.

Much of the free world's success in using its human resources fully and with dignity can be laid to enlightened and progressive management...We have accomplished much, but we continue to have much to accomplish. Modern technology, which has been one of our most potent tools for advancement, has imposed in turn its own challenges in making old work skills obsolete, in making rigorous demands of high education standards, and in converting a static society into a mobile one...It is to managers who grow with the needs and resources of their times that we must continue to look for the new ideas and their implementation to meet the challenges of the future.

—John F. Kennedy

Notes

[1] Harold Adam Innis, the late author and professor at the University of Toronto. His books, *Empire and Communications* (Oxford: Clarendon Press, 1950) and *The Bias of Communication* (Toronto: University of Toronto Press, 1951) have had a profound impact on the thinking of scholars in the field of information theory and communications. Marshall McLuhan, author and professor at the University of Toronto, carried forward explorations of various earlier observers, including those of Innis, his fellow professor. He is the author of *The Gutenberg Galaxy* (Toronto: University of Toronto Press, 1962).

[2] The first real recognition of the paperwork burden began in May, 1938, when high level attention was turned to the large number of statistical and informational reports required from business and industry by the Federal agencies. Upon President Franklin D. Roosevelt's request, the Central Statistical Board, its findings based on studies made by the Committee on Government Statistics and Information Services (COGSIS) in the 1933–36 period, reported that, although most information collected by the decentralized and uncoordinated Federal statistical agencies was needed for the purpose of administration or regulation, there was some duplication and unnecessary reporting. As a result, the burden on the business community could be lightened "to some extent." Largely as a result of the vastly increasing "emergency" reporting brought about by World War II, these efforts resulted in legislation to be known as the Federal Reports Act (5 U.S.C. 139) which passed the wartime 77th Congress in

December 1942. U.S. Congress, House, Report of the Central Statistical Board, H. Doc. 27, 76th Cong., 1st sess., 1939, quoted in the Federal Paperwork Jungle, H.R. 31, 89th Cong., 1st sess., 1965, pp. 8–9.

[3] Artel Ricks, Regional Commissioner, National Archives & Records Service, General Services Administration, Region 9, San Francisco, CA.

References

1. Buhler, Warren. "Federal Paperwork Commission One Year Later," speech presented to the *American Records Management Association*, Denver, Colorado, October 13, 1976.
2. Horton, Forest, Jr. "Budgeting the Data and Information Resource," *Journal of Systems Management*, Vol. 28, No. 2, Issue 190 (February 1977) p. 12.
3. Horton, Forest, Jr. "Inter-Disciplinary Approach Sought for Information Management," *Information Action*, a member association of Information Industry Association, No. 2 (February 1977) p. 1.
4. Innis, Harold Adam. *Empire and Communication*, Clarendon Press, Oxford, 1950.
5. Innis, Harold Adam. *The Bias of Communication*, University of Toronto Press, Toronto, 1951.
6. Judge, John F. "Ripping Paperwork Out by the Roots," *The Government Executive*, Vol. 9, No. 1 (January 1977), pp. 52–54.
7. Kish, Joseph L. and Morris, James. *Paperwork Management in Transition*, American Management Association, New York, 1964.
8. Laski, Harold J. "The Limitations of the Expert," *Harper's Magazine*, Vol. CLXII (1930-31), pp. 101–110.
9. McLuhan, Marshall. *Understanding Media: The Extensions of Man*, McGraw-Hill Book Co., New York, 1964.
10. McLuhan, Marshall. Keynote address. *Proceedings of the 6th Annual Conference*, Society for Management Information Systems, San Francisco, California, 1974, University of Minnesota, MIS Research Center, 1976.
11. Pullen, Edward W. and Simko, Robert G. "Our Changing Industry," *Datamation*, Vol. 23, No. 1 (January 1977), pp. 49–55.
12. Staats, Elmer B. *Ways to Improve Records Management Practices in the Federal Government*, Report to the Congress, General Accounting Office, Washington, D.C., 1973.
13. U.S. Congress, House, Report of the Central Statistical Board, H. Doc. 27, 76th Congress, 1st sess., 1939, as quoted in the Federal Paperwork Jungle, H.R. 31, 89th Congress, 1st sess., 1965, pp. 8–9.

Managing Information Resources*
Commission on Federal Paperwork

The management process is a cyclical one: goals and objectives are continually revised in light of changing priorities and feedback from implementation of programs. Planning leads inevitably to evaluation and evaluation to more planning. Before a resource can be managed, its role, uses, limitations and opportunities must be understood. In the case of information, treating data as a resource means that Government must first understand the concept of the life cycle of information, and then construct the necessary tools and machinery to capitalize operationally on the concept.

The Information Life Cycle

The five stages of the information life cycle are requirements determination, collection, processing, use, and disposition. At each of these stages, information values must be estimated and measured, costed and accounted for, just as Government now does for any other resource.

Information requirements determination is the first step in the information life cycle. This step, too often overlooked in many agency data flows today, directly affects program development, management and design of information systems. When Congress passes a law establishing a new program, resource needs are routinely planned—the number and mix of personnel, the organizational structure needed, office space, supplies and equipment, and so on. But data and information needs are often left out of this process entirely. Where these needs are, in fact, addressed, they are rarely dealt with in an analytical benefit/cost framework.

If information is a valuable, manageable asset it then follows that information needs must be planned. It is in the planning phase that management must assess agency and program goals and objectives, and determine what information is needed and at what cost to support operation. This *information requirements determination* is an important leverage point where management can begin to control the paperwork and red tape problem.

*In: *Information Resources Management*. Washington, D.C., U.S. Government Printing Office, 1977, pp. 43-65.

Planning is a process because the steps or events which comprise it, although discrete and distinguishable, are interdependent, follow a logical order and build upon one another to form a whole. But planning is not simply a progression of steps leading directly to a conclusion; it continues throughout the life cycle of information. At each stage new evidence may be uncovered or old evidence seen in a new way, so that new or revised information may be required or data initially collected may no longer be needed.

Determining information requirements involves a set of interrelated tasks which, when completed, satisfies the information needs of a program. In planning for the achievement of any objective, the individual responsible must first identify the problem. What information is required by the legislation? What information is needed to manage or administer the program? The answers to these questions begin to establish the problem definition. Analysis follows. How can the data be obtained—by questionnaires, reports, applications? Are the data currently within the Federal Government? Can the information be obtained from another source, will it meet all the requirements, or are additional data required?

After identifying the problem and defining and analyzing it, a general solution will usually suggest several approaches to achieve objectives. The responsible planner must now examine crucial questions related to the solution, such as cost of the data, value of the data, and the burdens on the public and on Government. He or she must review such considerations as complete collection, sharing from other sources, new computer or reprographic equipment, and so on. Once this process has been completed, decisionmakers emerge with a coherent set of objectives, alternative approaches, and policies with which to make a choice of the optimal objective at desirable and affordable levels of achievement—the program information plan.

The information plan should be structured like the agency program plan and include at a minimum:

- An analysis of agency goals and objectives;
- An information requirements analysis;
- Time-phased schedules for meeting those requirements on a priority basis;
- Total costs over the expected lifetime of the use of the information, including both capital acquisition costs and annual operating costs; and
- A consideration of alternatives in satisfying the agency's information needs.

In developing the plan, areas of overlap and duplication, and instances where one agency's information could be used to satisfy another agency, should surface.

Beyond the agency information plan, Government-wide information plans must be developed which pull together information on major Federal program areas. One example is the energy information needs and resources plan currently established and operated by over forty executive departments and agencies.[1] A comprehensive Federal-wide plan should reduce overlap and duplication and identify gaps so that OMB could recommend the development of a single, multi-purpose information system, thus warding off the proliferation of narrow purpose information systems.

Information collection is the act of bringing information from one or more sources to a central processing point. This is the second stage of the information life cycle. Here again needs, values, uses, benefits and costs must be considered. And so it proceeds, through information processing, use and finally disposition.

Finally, with the foreknowledge of how the various information elements relate to each other in the life cycle, management can change directions as necessary to keep all activities on the most direct course toward objectives. Visibility, traceability and chargeability are thus indispensable to effective program evaluation and management. The degree to which they are present and available to management in a program situation is usually in direct proportion to the quality and level of information life cycle planning that has been carried out.

Costing and Accounting for Information

Throughout this report there are references to the "unknown" costs of data and information in the Federal Government as they affect the citizen. While many costs are hidden, there are fairly reliable figures available for computer costs, costs of reprographic equipment, etc. Generally, these are "hardware" costs only. But hidden costs are found in both program and overhead accounts. These are costs to both the respondent and Government associated with many human processes involved in information collection, processing, use and disposition.

In a recent Administration initiative to identify ways to hold down Government overhead costs and place maximum reliance on the private sector for goods and services needed to carry out Federal Government activities, these items were listed as overhead:

- Travel
- ADP practices
- Cash management
- Reproduction equipment
- Audiovisual activities
- Telephone equipment and usage
- Mailing practices
- Office space
- Records storage

Over half of these are information and paperwork-related. Nevertheless, the substance and language of the detailed guidelines which accompanied the target areas of the initiative were exhortational and oriented to "efficiency" questions (do it faster, cheaper, and so on). Rarely were agencies asked to look at either the causes of the costs or at questions of effectiveness: Does the expense help achieve goals and serve citizens and is it worth it?

The Commission expressly rejects the idea that reporting, recordkeeping and, more generally, paperwork are all "overhead" functions. Unlike rent, utilities and insurance, many paperwork costs are, in fact, an essential and integral part of direct program expenses. And yet Government (and for that matter much of private industry) tends to lump paperwork expenses into various overhead accounts, thus assuring their invisibility and intractability. It is no wonder, then, that the steady and astronomical rise in paperwork and information-related expenses has not been dealt with effectively; these costs cannot be seen and disaggregated, much less controlled.

These hidden costs must be made visible and broken into categories. The cost of information can be made visible and categorized in two ways: first, by developing and using an Information Object Classification, and second, by focusing on how information is actually used, the Information System of an agency. How will these two tools help us cost and account for information?

Information Object Classification. The Information Object Classification scheme would classify information-related expenses by the type of expense involved. The existing object classification structure used by the Federal Government establishes categories which are useful for the management of physical, material, human and financial resources, but not for information resources. The categories used—such as personnel compensation, contractual services, rent, and so forth—were expressly designed to help Congress and the President keep track of the magnitude and utilization of people, buildings, land, revenues collected, and so on, without regard to the statutes, programs, agencies or other "jurisdictional lines" through which, and across which, the resources were moved. For this purpose, they do a reasonably adequate job.

But information-related costs are observed in this existing object scheme because they permeate all of these other accounts. They must be made visible and broken out into categories which make sense to Federal and agency officials responsible for their authorization, management and audit—in both the executive and legislative branches. Moreover, information costs must be defined, classified and arrayed in useful tables and formats for review, including both the direct costs to the Government as well as the costs incurred by citizens and "third parties" who must respond to Government transactions. Too often the Government assumes the burdens and costs on these third parties are not its concern and therefore need not enter into the calculations. As a consequence, paperwork burdens are imposed on citizens, businesses, State and local governments, and others with what the Commission terms "fiscal impunity." This practice must stop. We do not allow such a thing to happen with respect to hiring personnel, or buying land or buildings, or investing Government-held funds in interest-bearing securities. There should be no "free lunch" when it comes to the need for Government to acquire information for its needs. This does not necessarily mean respondents should be reimbursed for every questionnaire the Census Bureau sends out, for example. But it does mean that both internal and external costs must be made an explicit part of the cost calculation backing up a Government proposal to collect information or impose a recordkeeping requirement on the public.

An Information Object Classification structure is the key. This is a new approach that cannot be developed overnight. We have very few standard information costs in Government (or private industry for that matter). Additional research must be conducted to identify these costs, categorize them and develop various methods and alternatives for aggregation, summarization and presentation. The development of *standard* information costs will eventually allow us to compare *actual* "information performance" with *expected* "information performance." In other words, the technique called "variance analysis" can be used here to help managers control information costs.

The Agency Information System. Next, let us look at the idea of the Information System. The Information System is simply another way of talking about the life cycle of information. Here we are concerned with the overall agency information system or the "total" information system of an orgainization. Ideally, information systems deliver the required timely information to the right place at the right time for the right purpose in an efficient manner. When the information system fails, decisionmakers get irrelevant, obsolete and untimely information. They therefore make inappropriate, wrong, or untimely decisions—or all of the above. Because information systems are designed with little thought to the roles of all the parties involved, the precise use to which the information is to be put, and the total costs to *all* parties weighed against expected benefits, many Government information systems are far too costly in both design and operation and do not serve useful purposes. Government officials soon become disgruntled and call for dismantling them; citizens are outraged that taxpayer monies are spent on such wasteful bureaucratic monstrosities.

The Commission has found that information systems are a crucial tool to both the Congress and the President in enacting good laws, designing effective programs, administering programs efficiently, and managing financial and other resources entrusted to them by citizen-taxpayers. As has been documented in other Commission studies, where laws, rules, regulations, programs and delivery systems overlap, are confusing and duplicative, paperwork and red tape flourish. In a very real sense, when Federal and agency information systems aren't working, the entire Federal system begins to unravel and weaken. The Commission believes this is precisely what has happened and cannot overstate the importance of information processes and resources to the nation's public administration system. It is why the Commission takes the view that a new approach is needed, one which the Commission calls "Service Management." But Service Management depends on good information resources management. Information resources management, in turn, depends on the development and use of an Information Object Classification scheme and a recognition of the role of sound Information Systems in the administrative process.

Defining Information-Related Expenses

We must begin by identifying and costing information. What are the building blocks? What is an "information-related" expense? One approach to costing information is to extract costs from the agency's basic chart of accounts. This approach would allow officials to look at costs as an information "line item" in the budget, without the need for a radical restructuring of either the agency or the Government-wide system. One procedure (a "bottom-up" approach) would:

- Identify and extract pre-identified data and information items and figures;
- Construct a total data and information cost for each product and service; and
- Conduct various analyses, such as relating costs to value; identifying information-intensive products and services; and identifying opportunities for cutting information-related costs.

Although this means that an accounting structure for *information resources* must be developed, it does not mean a radically new approach or major surgery to either budgeting or accounting structures and systems. However, the procedure does have limitations as some information costs may still remain hidden. Preliminary testing in both private industry and Government indicates that costing information may be accomplished with the existing overall chart of accounts, with possible minor changes.

The Commission experimented with a number of different approaches to the problem of identifying, measuring and costing information. One project was jointly undertaken with the National Association of State Information Systems, and the National Association of State Budget Officials. Another involved direct dealings with selected States, including Wyoming and Nebraska. A third involved looking at the costing of ADP resources and developmental work completed by the General Accounting Office. A fourth involved a detailed study of how information processing costs could be built up from personnel occupational titles and series.

Information costs include more than the direct expenses to the Government, such as preparing forms, processing responses, computer time, etc. There are substantial costs incurred by respondents in providing information. These costs include not only people's time and costs, but also computer programming and running time, and other costs associated with data processing.

There are three steps in the "bottom-up" development of an information resources accounting structure:

- Determine the *organizational elements* which are primarily "data service" in character (e.g. computer organizations);

- Identify those *primary activities* which are "data handling" in character (e.g. tabulating statistics); and
- Identify the specific object items of expense for 1 and 2 above (i.e. salaries, equipment, supplies, and so on).

Once costs have been identified and measured, an accounting framework must be developed to organize and classify the costs. In this study, "accounting" is defined in the broader sense of *value,* thus embracing conventional definitions of both physical and financial accounting, as well as the newer meanings assigned to that term by social accountants to assess human performance accountability.

If one considers material resources, for example, it is necessary to account for the cost of supplies financially, as a valued asset. It is also necessary to account for them physically, as items of supply—the inventory. Thus, as with any resource, we must be concerned with two types of accounting—financial (value) and item. With the information resource, item accounting is concerned with the extent to which the paperwork and information collected and used by an agency serves the purposes for which it was collected. Financial (value) accounting addresses the needs of higher level managers and financial staff officials for an analytical tool to tell them whether or not monies are being well spent, i.e. a good investment of capital.

Why is it necessary to account for information and information cost in this fashion? One important reason is that there are few standards against which to measure *actual* information performance versus *expected* information performance. Additional research is needed to develop classifications and standards for information use. The Commission had neither the resources nor the time to undertake an exhaustive study of this dimension of the information problem.

One approach which might be used to establish an accounting framework for information is a *use typology.* With the assistance of the National Association of State Information Systems and the National Association of Budget Officials, the Commission explored such an approach. A use typology includes five categories:

- Planning information uses;
- Using information to operate programs;
- Using information to manage and administer programs;
- Using information to evaluate program efficiency and effectiveness; and
- Use of general purpose information (general purpose statistics). [2]

Category 2—using information to operate programs—is considered the "core" information cost essential to the operation of any program, while the other four categories are considered "non-core" information costs, essential for management, but not for the actual operation of the program.

With these five categories, several projects explored alternative accounting techniques to identify and measure the cost of information. One project evolved the following procedure:

- For each agency or program (or both) studied, the foregoing five major functions would be identified "on the organizational chart";
- In those instances where two or more functions are subsumed within the same organizational unit, some scheme of proration would be used to estimate the distribution of functions for the total;
- Where an existing cost center structure already matches the functional classification scheme, the total cost involved could be computed relatively simply. Where there is no such ready match, and the functions are spread between two or more cost centers, then a prorata distribution approach would be taken;
- Continue the above procedure in interactive fashion; the total cost for functions 1, 3, 4, and 5 identified above would be aggregated into a single total;
- All costs associated with operating a program—function 2—would be placed in the numerator; and
- All other costs aggregated would be placed in a denominator. The direct costs associated with operating a program divided by the sum of all costs associated with information used to support a program (or an agency) yields an "information- or paperwork-intensity" ratio.

Inevitably the question arises as to the distinction between information used to operate a program and the other information used to support the program. "Core" information costs are those needed to accomplish *directly* the mission to which cost analysis is being applied. For example, take the case of a Social Security application form requiring information to determine an individual's eligibility to receive benefits. "Non-core" information costs would consist of "all other" information costs associated with the mission of providing benefits *but not directly* required to accomplish it, such as the time and attendance records of the Social Security staff operating the program.

Making the distinction between data needed to operate programs and data needed to support the program is, itself, a kind of action-forcing mechanism; it requires agency officials to define the basic, core information they need to operate their programs. This is a difficult task, more difficult for some programs than for others, particularly those which rely on qualitative rather than quantitative data. That is, programs which must rely more heavily upon data which is subjectively interpreted, rather than objectively assessed, may be constrained by wide differences of opinion.

Information needed to plan programs may be just as "essential" and "relevant" as information needed to operate programs. However, if we are to respond to the substantial complaint registered by the public at Commission hearings and in correspondence that "too much information is being collected by the Government for purposes which we believe are essentially irrelevant to the programs which are being administered allegedly to serve us," some attempt must be made to distinguish between information which is essential to operate programs and that which is merely "nice to know."

While helpful, this *"use typology"* is not a *universal panacea*. A series of experimental and research efforts might well be started to explore additional alternatives. (The other typologies which this study considered can be found in the volume of technical/staff reports available from the Commission. They include cost estimating techniques, cost finding aids, statistical sampling techniques, time and motion studies, work measurement methods, classical cost accounting approaches and others.) Whichever method(s) that are ultimately selected as promising must withstand the "test of time" and must couple the requirement that information be costed with the notion of organizational and individual accountability.

Visibility of Information Costs (Budgeting)

We have discussed planning for information requirements and costing and accounting for data using two tools: the Information Object Classification and the Information System. The next step is budgeting for information.

It was estimated in 1973 that "data processing"—which includes the costs of computers, terminals and computer services, time sharing, consulting, operating labor, and other associated services—cost U.S. organizations about $26 billion. Administrative processing—which includes typewriters, word processors, dictating equipment, telephones, copiers, etc.—cost another estimated $43 billion. The human element—the white-collar worker—now 22 percent of the total U.S. labor force, accounted for an estimated $350 billion.[3]

According to one authority, *the total estimated information processing* *base of the Gross National Product is at least $400 billion.* But how much of this is the cost of government paperwork on respondents? Government can identify the "hard" Information Object Classification costs fairly well, but as pointed out earlier, the "soft" Information System costs are more elusive.

While planning is the first step in the information process, in Government it is budgeting which substitutes for the marketplace in private industry. It is in the budgeting process that data costs can become visible. It has been the experience of many Government agencies that, despite all that is said about planning being the force that drives programs and then programs driving budgets, the budget usually is the real driving force. . . .

How Will Information Resources Management Reduce Paperwork and Red Tape?

We have tried to show that traditional "paperwork management" approaches to the control of paperwork and red tape, with their primary focus on controlling, simplifying and mechanizing documents, are not the whole answer. This approach, while essential to the management and control of files, correspondence, records and mail operations, has done little to get at the root causes of paperwork—the insensitivity of Government, uncoordinated programs and duplication in Federal information requests, and a general administrative environment that allows officials to collect whatever information they feel they need with very little constraint.

This study has pointed out that traditional paperwork and records management controls and programs should not be faulted for the failure to root out the causes of the information explosion. They are important, and without them the document explosion probably would have been worse. Records retention schedules, statistical sampling, auditing and other information management approaches are all essential. But they must be modernized, upgraded and redirected to incorporate the principles the Commission is putting forward here, and in its other studies, with respect to Information Resource Management, Service Management and other reforms.

The reader may well ask, "Exactly how will the 'new' Information Resources Management approach help alleviate the cost of paperwork, the insensitivity of Government, uncoordinated programs and duplication in Government information requests?" "How," the question continues, "do we know that we won't end up with simply another approach piled onto what we have now?" Here we recapitulate elements of the answer.

The Information Assessment Statement

The Commission's *Role of Congress* report pointed out that the beginnings of Information Resources Management must be in the early planning processes involving congressional committees, individual Congressmen, and perhaps some executive branch officials, who develop the very first blueprints of new laws and programs. They must incorporate an information assessment calculation into their deliberations, as is now required for projects which are expected to affect the environment. Detailed costs are not necessarily needed. Rather, there should be some indication of whether legislative drafters and authors have considered explicitly the extent to which alternative courses of action take into account the full and "true" costs of the planned program to everyone involved, not the Government alone. Less "paperwork-intensive" alternatives should be considered where they are feasible and cost-effective.

There is another important aspect to applying the best methodologies which goes beyond information resources. The Commission found many instances in which the information requirements which led to the development of an information system were themselves inadequately considered.

In designing a program, Congress and the agencies must recognize options, not only to request information but also to use other methods to meet program objectives. For instance, rather than requiring quarterly or annual reports, programs could be administered on the basis of audits or complaints which initiate actions. In other cases, the information requirements of one program become onerous, not because they poorly serve the program for which they were designed, but because program designers did not look for opportunities to lessen the burden by developing common administrative systems with other related programs. This Commission has made recommendations in several areas which, in effect, require the development of common administrative systems for multiple programs, thereby greatly reducing the burden imposed by these programs on respondents.

OMB has already initiated action by requiring, through OMB Circular A-11, that agencies include in their budget justification an analysis of the paperwork burden created for every new program initiative or expansion of an existing program.

The Information Plan

Once the Congress has acted and proposals take on the force of law, executive agencies must determine whether the information requirements of a new or revised program can be met by using sources already available, whether new sources must be tapped and new data flows established, and exactly what kinds of information instruments will be needed (e.g., questionnaires, reports, records, audits and so on). Again, agency planning systems must take into account the full and "true" costs to all parties involved, not just to themselves.

Thus far our discussions have dealt with developing an information component or plan for an agency program. Beyond the program plan, it is essential that each agency plan, manage, control and evaluate all its information requirements and resources, including both individual program and general, agency-wide administrative information needs. The agency plan should embrace a multi-year timeframe and provide an orderly and systematic framework for reviewing, improving, integrating and developing information requirements and resources. The overall agency information plan then is developed by accumulating all of the agency's individual program and administrative plans, sifting out duplication and overlap, and settling on the information actually needed to manage the agency and its programs. Each of these plans, the individual plans and the overall agency plan, will facilitate the zero-base review of all operational data and information flows, sharing of information, and the management of the information resource.

The Information Object Classification

One reason why information and paperwork costs have not been adequately taken into account in the past is that we have had no accounting for the nature of these costs; and the uses to which the information itself are put are rarely identified, measured, and costed. Any "information plan" which may exist is usually a hodge-podge of only the most visible and obvious major expenses—such as a new computer that may need to be purchased or a very large statistical survey. Except for the major statistical programs of Government, the nature of information expenses has not been systematically identified and classified in meaningful ways so that decisionmaking authorities might clearly see what these "hidden" costs are. The Information Object Classification scheme would lay out these costs just as we do now for personnel compensation, travel, equipment purchases and leases, rents, utilities and so forth. At present there is no such comprehensive object classification structure for information expenses.

The Information System

Once we have an Information Object Classification that reveals the magnitude and character of information-related expenses, we can begin to see whether the agency's information system is working or not. Without the classification structure, we tend to design, develop, test and install information systems without really knowing how the information is going to be used, or whether the cost of its collection, processing, storage and dissemination is going to be worth the investments. Now we have an opportunity to examine carefully deficiencies and weaknesses in information flows:

- Are officials getting the information they need?
- Are the most cost-effective means of delivering the data being employed; would perhaps a simple, manual system be superior to a complex, sophisticated and outmoded one?
- To what extent are paperwork-intensive and red tape reports, records and forms being used, where we should be using advanced electronic, microfiche or other methods?
- Does the information system also service the citizen either directly, or as a by-product; or does the system serve only the parochial needs of the government agency?

The need, therefore, is to recognize that the best use of information resources goes beyond merely designing the best information system for a program, to questions of how one program can best use information resources as opposed to other types of resources, such as personnel, and to how one program should be administered relative to other related programs. The logical way to address such issues is to place managers of information resources, as discussed above, within the organization responsible for such issues as organization, policy planning and management.

Furthermore, it is necessary to recognize that there are multiple areas where similar program responsibilities exist in several different agencies. For such situations, it is necessary to have an aggressive management unit capable of working with several agencies to assure that their similar administrative systems result in the least amount of burden possible. This central management unit, capable of dealing with management issues across agency lines, should also be given responsibility for dealing with issues that involve State and local governments as well as the Federal Government.

This Commission believes there has been a failure on the part of the Federal Government to manage programs across agency lines and across governmental lines. In the past, the limit of agency authority has set the limits for management. The Commission found that there are numerous interagency information committees within the Federal Government reviewing information requirements, respondent considerations, improved data processing through the application of technology, data sharing among agencies and administrative procedures for managing information. However, they have only minimal effect because there is no central coordination—no coordinating committee "to coordinate committees," and to direct Government-wide efforts. There is no excuse for permitting this lack of management attention to interagency and intergovernmental issues to continue.

Evaluation and Zero-Base Reviews

By using zero-base reporting methods as an integral part of evaluation, the fundamental goals and objectives of the paperwork associated with a given program can be systematically and periodically reviewed from the ground up. Zero-base reporting reviews would consist of an annual, three-tiered review of all of an agency's reports. The first review determines if a report can be eliminated and evaluates the impact of termination upon the agency's information system and decisionmaking process. The second review seeks alternative ways of gathering required information. For example, the information may be available in other agency reports or from other agencies, State or local government; also audits, sampling or other techniques may be used as an efficient way of getting needed information. And finally, the third review addresses the reporting burden being imposed upon the public. Factors considered at this review level are the ability of accounting and recordkeeping systems to yield the required information with the minimum of time and costs.

Just as the agency must reexamine basic program goals and objectives under zero-base budgeting procedures and sunset legislation, so the Commission is suggesting that the paperwork and information processes associated with those programs also be reexamined, possibly as an adjunct to the annual budget formulation and review process. After all, information handling technology is not standing still. Each month brings some new product, service or approach on the market that may well save the taxpayer money. Because an existing program may survive a zero-base budgeting review doesn't necessarily mean the administrative and delivery systems used by the program should automatically be continued.

The use of a zero-base reporting process could have the following effects on paperwork and red tape:

- Provide a sound base to support decisions that transfer the information cost/burden to the public;

- Reduce the inevitable conflict between competing information demands;
- Surface alternatives to information collection and reports and develop a better balance between the information resource and other resources; and
- Identify and possibly eliminate duplicate off-cycle reports and obsolete reports.

Annual Reports to the Congress

The executive branch has not done a very good job of reporting to the Congress on issues that relate to paperwork and red tape. Reports in the past, such as those of the Management Improvement and Cost Reduction programs that were in vogue in the 1960's and early 1970's, tended to be somewhat superficial and tended to relate to administrative considerations. For example, an agency might report that it eliminated "gold plating," or it "deferred" costs by not undertaking some phase of a program. Rarely did such reviews conclude that "the benefits of this program are now simply outweighed by the rising costs associated with its administration and management." Or, "the Congress should reconsider the basic thrust behind the program in the light of this finding, and reassess its continuance." Or, "the hassle and burden imposed on potential beneficiaries (applicants, licensees, etc.) has reached the point where eligible participants are not even taking advantage of the program. Alternatives must be found to reduce both the economic and psychological costs and burdens of the program if it is to be continued."

Other Information Resources Management Machinery

Beyond this, the Commission has put forward recommendations to design and install other, more specific tools for the reduction of paperwork, and to improve the services Government renders the people. The Federal Information Locator System, for example, not only will serve as a tool to help identify, and thereby reduce potential and existing overlap and duplication in agency information requirements, but also will serve the citizen, businesses, State and local governments, hospitals, academic institutions and others in locating information they need for their own purposes. In a recent compilation of executive branch information resources, the House Commission on Information Facilities identified *20 general information guides and sources, 11 budget and economic sources, 8 organization and management sources, 9 policy/program sources, and 14 statistical sources—a total of 63 information sources pertaining to more than one agency or mission.* This 1976 inventory also profiled key information for departments and agencies. For the Department of Agriculture, this "profile" required listing 20 major organizational elements, and 13 major "representative" data systems and sources for that one department alone.[4]

There is a substantial cost to society incurred by private individuals and organizations which "rediscover the wheel" because they simply are unaware of the knowledge that would prevent them from such a wasteful course. Because the Government is the single biggest collector, processor and depository of data, information and literature in the world, the Commission unhesitatingly concluded that the absence of an index to its vast information holdings was a very serious matter.

The designation of single focal agencies to serve as overall coordinators for the collection of similar information required by all Government agencies, on a permanent basis in lieu of an *an hoc* basis as is currently the case, is long overdue. Developing and using...multi-purpose Federal information systems or reference services, rather than proliferating narrow single-purpose systems, is a necessary policy to reduce the duplication and overlap in data, documents, files and record holdings within the Federal Government.

By redefining and recasting the role of reports clearance, and maximizing the decentralization of routine clearance actions to agencies, central policy-level management officials should have more time to look at broader, critical policy issues and concerns. Now they are consumed with technical details because they are inundated with hundreds of new reports every year. The Commission's Reports Clearance study shows how clearance, while still an important paperwork control, needs to be recast in the light of the present-day priorities and problems.

The Commission's other reports introduced innovative approaches to the design of more service-oriented delivery systems for the programs encompassed by their respective scopes. Such ideas as one-stop service, consolidated eligibility determination systems, comprehensive information systems and information indices, and "turn-around" forms all are important tools in the family of Information Resources Management and Service Management techniques and methods. All have one thing in common: they improve the way in which Government relates to and interacts with the people whom it serves....

Summary

The fundamental reforms and other machinery the Commission is advocating here will not come about overnight; many will take years to design, develop, test, and put into place. But, historically, the introduction of basic management reforms has been an evolutionary process, no matter what the nature of the reform.

The Commission urges prompt action to begin moving along this road, to develop the necessary framework and machinery, because a start is long overdue. Most recent paperwork study commissions, and other key paperwork reduction investigations such as those sponsored by OMB and GAO, have identified unbridled agency information requirements as an important root cause of excessive public paperwork burden. Yet all of these prior studies stopped short of forging the crucial link in the chain—namely, recommending that information be treated as a manageable resource. Until that critical link is made, bureaucrats will continue to treat data as virtually a free good.

Expressed another way, unless specific laws, policies and procedures *require* officials to plan, manage, and control their data resources according to established rules and standards, the costs of all this labor, equipment, and material needed to handle data will continue to be invisible—splintered and hidden in a wide variety of Government's overhead and program accounts. These costs *must be tallied, sorted, classified and pulled together* in Government's management systems (planning, accounting, budgeting, and so on). And the *values* Government receives from this information must be better defined and balanced against the *burdens and costs* incurred, not only costs incurred by Government, but also expenses to the citizen for both the direct costs involved in preparing and submitting the information and the indirect costs paid in the form of taxes to defray the costs of Government's handling of all of the information.

Strengthening management systems, developing and installing new control machinery and designing new accounting structures are not the whole answer. Without strong central direction and leadership, and clear and unequivocal authorities, the machinery will not function properly. . . .

The Commission has found repeatedly in its many studies that the reason so many programs are laden with poorly designed forms, attended by inefficient delivery systems and strangled in the red tape of overlapping and confusing instructions and procedures is because there is no single, central management authority charged with the responsiblity to look across administrative alternatives and make sure the best one is picked. This central management authority must be two-tiered at the Federal Government level and at the agency level. At the broader level, this authority must unify and integrate the information, paperwork and communications-related management functions and programs now dispersed.

The situation in the information and paperwork field today, in this regard, is very similar to what existed until very recently in the procurement field. The...Procurement Commission found that authorities and functions were strewn among many departments and agencies, including the Department of Defense, the General Services Administration, NASA, and others. The pattern of findings and conclusions reached by the Procurement Commission closely follows what this Commission has found in the paperwork area: the absence of strong, central policy leadership and direction resulted in weak, ineffective, confused and overlapping procurement standards, procedures and control machinery. The result was that the Government was losing money, vendors were displeased with their relationship with officials, supplies and equipment were not getting from vendors to users, and unnecessary inventories were building up in Government warehouses.

In the case of paperwork, the compartmentalization of policy and operating authorities and functions has resulted in the failure to consider systematically less paperwork-intensive alternatives, the costs involved to everyone when new programs are designed and implemented are not fully taken into account, and citizens are extremely dissatisfied with the manner in which they are served by and interact with their Government.

Therefore the Commission concludes that central policy and operating functions and authorities for Government's automatic data processing, statistical, public-use reporting, interagency reporting, forms, microform, word processing, telecommunications and related paperwork, information and communications programs should be brought together in a central management authority. Correspondingly, at the agency level, operating functions and authorities should be consolidated under the direction and control of an appropriate central management authority in each executive department and agency.

Notes

[1]Commission on Federal Paperwork report on Energy, April 1977.

[2]Report on the Joint Paperwork Task Force of the National Association for State Information Systems (NASIS), National Association of State Budget Officers (NASBO) submitted to the Commission, April 1977.

[3]Strassman, Paul A. "Managing the Costs of Information." *Harvard Business Review, 54*:133–142, September/October 1976.

[4]Committee Print, House Commission on Information and Facilities, Inventory of Information Resources, Part III, Executive Branch Resources, Washington, 1976.

Additional Readings

Arthur D. Little, Inc. *Telecommunications and Society: 1972-1991.* Washington, D.C., Office of Telecommunications Policy, 1976.

Bell, Daniel. "Communications Technology—For Better or for Worse." *Harvard Business Review,* 57:20-42, April 1979.

Bentley, Trevar J. *Information, Communication and the Paperwork Explosion.* London, McGraw-Hill, 1976.

Bryant, Edward C., and King, Donald W. *The Evaluation of Information Services and Products.* Washington D.C., Information Resources Press, 1971.

Commission on Federal Paperwork. *Reference Manual for Program and Information Officials.* Volumes I and II. Washington, D.C., 1977.

Dertouzas, Michael L., and Moses, Joel. *The Computer Age: A Twenty-Year View.* Cambridge, Mass., MIT Press, 1979.

Grossman, Lesli. *Fat Paper.* New York, McGraw-Hill, 1976.

Kraemer, Kenneth L., and King, John L. *Computers and Local Government.* Volumes 1 and 2. New York, Praeger,1979.

Kuttner, Monroe S. *Managing The Paperwork Pipeline.* New York, Wiley, 1978.

Meltzer, Morton F. *The Information Imperative.* New York, American Management Association, 1971.

Organization for Economic Cooperation and Development. *Automated Information Management in Public Administration.* Paris, 1973.

_____. *Computers and Telecommunications.* Paris, 1973.

Strassman, Paul A. "The Office of the Future: Information Management for the New Age." *Technology Review,* 82:54-65, December/January 1980.

U.S. Comptroller General. *Case Study of Department of Labor and Office of Management and Budget Activities Under the Federal Reports Act.* Washington, D.C., General Accounting Office, 1975.

Chapter 4

PLANNING, BUDGETING, AND ACCOUNTING FOR INFORMATION RESOURCES

[I]nformation is not a "free good."
  —Commission on Federal Paperwork, "Information Resources Management"

All the selections in Chapter 3 emphasized that organizations must manage information more effectively in response to the rapidly changing and integrating natures of various information technologies and the quickly rising expenditures for data, equipment, and information personnel and technicians. The selections in this chapter examine how organizations can manage data resources through planning, budgeting, and accounting. The task is not easy. Not only is information difficult to define, but, more important, the principles and approaches to managing information have not yet been articulated. How can we account for the costs of information in the government? How can we integrate cost accounting information with the budgeting process in public organizations? Finally, how can we orient program planning to accommodate the need to tie information resources to program decision-making requirements and objectives? Although the need for information resources management is clear, organizations are just beginning to develop the methods and tools to tackle the task.

In the first selection, "Budgeting the Data and Information Resources," Forest W. Horton, Jr. observes that the relative "invisibility" of information processing and resources in organizations has prevented effective use and management. Despite large amounts of data and growing expenditures for hardware and information and data-processing specialists, due to significant political, scientific, and humanistic reasons, organizations are far from developing an adequate doctrine of "data accountability." Recognizing these constraints, organizations must treat information as an accountable and budgetable resource. As Horton observes, this is required as an "actionforcing mechanism" to hold public managers and officials accountable for the efficient and effective use of data.

In the second and third selections, various approaches are given to accounting for and budgeting data resources. In "Budgeting Information Resources: Some Alternative Approaches," Donald A. Marchand and Charlie B. Tyer integrate the concern with how to budget information resources with the prevailing approaches to budgeting and cost accounting in the public sector. Any changes or modifications in the way an organization budgets and accounts for data must recognize current approaches to public budgeting and accounting and the advantages and disadvantages of altering these systems to accommodate budgeting and accounting for data resources. Like any new management function, information management implies changes in established policies and practices that will have to be balanced by the benefits of any new approach adopted. As Marchand and Tyer suggest, the magnitude of the benefits will vary with the method selected.

In the third selection, "Managing the Costs of Information," Paul A. Strassman discusses how a private firm can budget and account for data resources. As organizations begin to harness the full power of information technology, they must be concerned with the costs of administrative processing as well as with the costs of data processing. The information manager must develop a systematic approach to accounting for data resources and planning their uses more efficiently. Based on his extensive experience at Xerox Corporation, Strassman suggests a nine-step strategy for a firm to follow to improve the productivity of its information resources management. Although Strassman does not account for the difficulties of adopting his approach in the public sector, he remains sensitive to the need to tailor his method to an organization's requirements and preexisting accounting and budgeting processes.

In the final selection, "Our Shadow Government: The Hidden Cost of Government Paperwork, Information and Communication Costs to the Taxpayer," the Commission on Federal Paperwork tackles the problem of assessing the cost of government paperwork, information, and communication to the taxpayer. Using the Federal Government as a case study, the commission makes visible the total direct and indirect costs of paperwork, information, and communication as the first step in giving attention to the burdens and problems that agencies and citizens encounter. The commission observes that the true costs are "astronomical" and that "action must be taken on a number of fronts simultaneously to bring these costs under control."

Budgeting the Data and
Information Resource*

Forest W. Horton, Jr.

The information explosion, like the population explosion, is now old hat. But while many countries throughout the world are beginning to make progress with family planning, few beyond the Industrial West feel any need for data planning. For data, unlike people, is mostly invisible. And "out-of-sight, out-of-mind" seems like an appropriate aphorism.

But a paradox, with profound economic and public accountability consequences, is accelerating and forcing itself on our consciousness. On the one hand we are suffering from what some have called "information overload"—too much data is vying for our attention. On the other hand we are not getting all of the information we need. At the same time, the capital and operating expense investments we are making in collecting, storing and disseminating data resources are increasing steadily. Recent studies have begun to show that if one adds together all of the overhead and direct costs allocatable to information handling, ours is fast becoming an Information Economy.

In the Public Sector, government at all levels has relied heavily on the data resource. Of course the other resources—human, physical, financial and natural—all play their role too, but data and information are the only common denominator. Data links all resources together. Information is unique in that it can be either an abstract, mobilizing and catalytic agent, or it can be a physical commodity when it takes the form of a document, report, or record.

This uniqueness, this pervasiveness, this amorphous and intangible quality of information has created problems. Except perhaps for the librarian, the archivist or the historian, data has not traditionally been conceived of as a "resource" in the formal sense—to be treated and managed in the same way that we look upon people, typewriters, missile systems, dollars or an endangered species of wildlife.

Quite the contrary, until relatively recently, many businessmen and

*Reprinted by permission of the *Journal of Systems Management*, Vol. 7, pp. 12–14, February 1977.

government officials have tended to regard information as virtually a free good. To be sure the most obvious, tangible and concrete physical forms and expressions of data—the report, file, record or book, for example—have often been costed out and a price tag assigned at some point. Usually, however, only directly isolatable and attributable cost factors went into the calculation. Most information has escaped a rigorous cost accountability.

The Commission on Federal Paperwork has tentatively identified two root causes for this lack of accountability:

—First, separating the physical expressions of data from the abstract expressions is an enormously difficult philosophical task, much less [a] pragmatic one;

—Second, both the value and the need for information have traditionally been poorly defined and measured on scientific, political and humanistic grounds. The archivist, for example, resists measuring the value of data because he views all information as historically significant. He supports his position with the thesis that the true relevance of "current facts" can only be ascertained in some kind of historical context. The scientist resists measuring the value of data because he views all information as knowledge and admonishes those who would control, manage or destroy data as risking the destruction of knowledge and mankind's heritage. And, finally, the political scientist resists measuring the value of data because he calls our attention to the democratic rights of citizens in our free society....to access, retrieve and use public information when and in whatever form desired. The concomitant obligation of government is to store and furnish that data upon demand, subject only to limiting constitutional safeguards related to State secrets, business trade and financial secrets, and the protection of privacy.

The Paperwork Commission was charged by the Congress to seek ways of reducing the paperwork and red tape burden on the public. At the same time, our congressional mandate made clear that the information needs of officials must be met. Therefore, implicit in our congressional charge, and in every recommendation the Commission has made thus far or will make in the future, is a considered judgment, however fallible, that the burden imposed by a particular report, record, procedure, system, policy, or whatever paperwork requirement or instrument, is greater than the expected value of the information that would be received as a result of the continuance of the paperwork requirement or instrument.

This implicit judgment has, so far, been made on the basis of the in-

dividual merits of each case, taken one at a time, as it crops up and is analyzed. Clearly the Commission cannot forever escape generalizing its findings
and recommendations, not only because inevitably two situations are bound
to arise which are virtually identical and we should risk rampant inconsistency otherwise, but also because it must do more than merely "cut weeds."
The Commission must identify the root causes of paperwork and red tape,
and point to long term reforms which are government-wide in scope and applicability.

To that end a general hypothesis has begun to emerge. The hypothesis is
this: for the reasons and because of the dilemmas and difficulties already
mentioned, we've not looked upon data until now as a manageable or budgetable resource, and tried to package the data resource as a line item in the
budget the same way we've traditionally packaged human, physical, financial and even natural resources. As a result, we've never had what some
might call an "actionforcing mechanism" to hold managers and officials in
all branches, and at all levels of government accountable for the efficient and
effective use of the data resource.

For example, can anyone imagine that a legislator or an executive
agency official might hire, transfer, promote or fire his human resources in
any manner he chose? Hardly. There is a long, well established and detailed
set of rules, guidelines, sanctions and even rewards which tells us exactly how
we should accomplish those actions. Come budget time we are told precisely
how to define, measure and count bodies. We are directed to tally both positions authorized and on-board, as well as man-years, by a host of variables—
organizational sub-unit, object class, permanent vs. temporary, and on and
on. The Civil Service Commission at the Federal level has a whole body of
doctrine that pulls together all of these rules. At each successive level of government there are corresponding counterparts of doctrine.

Can anyone imagine that the accountable property officer would allow
us to requisition as many fancy chairs, tables, desks or typewriters as we
wanted and use them for whatever purpose we wanted? Of course not. We
have in this area tables of allowances and authorization schedules which
prescribe standards, criteria and formulas for exactly how many of which of
these commodities anyone is entitled to. The General Services Administration at the Federal level, like the Civil Service Commission, has promulgated
over a long period of time a detailed body of doctrine in the area of managing
and accounting for the use of assigned real and personal property resources.

The analogy can be extended to the financial and natural resources as
well without straining our imaginations too much. Certainly when it comes to
financial resources the rules of the game are perhaps even more inflexible,

immutable and the penalties and sanctions for misuse of public funds even more severe than they are for the other areas.

Why is it, then, when we come to the data and information resource area not only is there no central, cohesive body of doctrine but we don't always do a very good job in giving our officials informal guidance on a fragmented basis—a little bit for computers, a little bit for designing information systems, some for microform, some for reprography and so on. In rare cases do we have policies, much less procedures to guide officials in such areas as selecting possible handling media alternatives on a cost effective basis....

At present there is no Federally-prescribed set of rules that embraces the total information resource. At this point we can only exhort and admonish our clients. And, it doesn't do us any good, for example, to talk about computers under the physical resource heading. Computers may, and indeed do "obsolesce." But that obsolescence is on an entirely different character than a desk or a typewriter, or even a missile system. Unlike the other resource classifications, information resources—including the whole range of hardware, software, systems, services and products—are in a very real sense perpetually renewable. An economist might express it this way: the more we use data resources the "better" they become. Instead of being consumed in the process of being used, which is the prescribed economic outcome, information resources most often appreciate in value like an antique.

Surely not all information can be considered history or knowledge. With the advent of the new mini and microcomputers we now have the capacity to proliferate and splinter data all the way down to the level of personal control. The pressures against sharing and centralizing data are certainly increasing. On the plus side of the ledger, this may forebode well for flexibility and responsiveness. On the other side of the ledger, the problems of maintaining data integrity, consistency, comparability and compatibility are certainly becoming compounded.

One culprit here had been the rather insidious economy-of-scale argument. As long as individuals on the lowest organizational rungs are allowed to defend and justify their need for increasingly cheaper and more sophisticated information handling hardware on the grounds that the unit cost of collecting, recording, storing, retrieving and disseminating information is continually dropping, how can you—the data managers—enforce data accountability?

I'm saying that we can no longer afford to pose the...question in a rhetorical vein. The media tell of organizations that are considering throwing out their major information handling capability as a sunk cost.

Top officials are more and more complaining that they are trapped into incremental decisions to "buy and build bigger and better." Then, when things begin to go wrong, the problems are already too big and intractable to back down. They have, in a real sense, become a captive of this powerful but subtle technology. It is small solace to us or them to complain that top officials should have become more involved earlier, and more deeply in the decisions.

The Commission on Federal Paperwork is considering if the absence of a central body of doctrine addressed to the issues of data integrity and accountability might not be an important missing link in the chain.

If we are ever to realize the full potential of the new technologies we must make sure, particularly in this era of the tight budget dollar, that our monies are well spent. To unleash the full power of modern information handling technologies we must also plan the use of our data resources more judiciously. A doctrine of data accountability would, in my view, go a long way to helping us achieve that goal.

We must start somewhere with a plan establishing clear goals and objectives. And we must assign responsibilities, both general and specific for carrying out tasks.

Budgeting Information Resources: Some Alternative Approaches*

Donald A. Marchand and Charlie B. Tyer

Increasingly today attention is being turned to enhancing the responsiveness and responsibilities of public organizations. Implicit in this is a concern over the efficiency and effectiveness of public sector services. One area in particular has only recently begun to draw attention, however, as policy makers and managers strive to gain control over public expenditures—information resources. This paper attempts to focus upon the issue of budgeting information resources and the implications for the improvement of public services and management decisions.

Information resources include a variety of expenditures, such as computers, terminals, typewriters, word processors, telephones, copiers, microfilm, programming support, labor and consultants, to name only a few. Traditionally we have not viewed information as a resource to be managed as we have human resources and financial resources. With the rapid growth of information equipment and the need for better information to assist policy makers, we are becoming more aware of the costs of information and the need to budget for information services more wisely.

Traditional budgeting has focused upon resource information, or the inputs needed to perform activities, and not program information, i.e., what government does and the outcomes of activities. This grew out of an emphasis early in this century upon controlling public expenditures to promote economy and efficiency. This control emphasis resulted in the widespread use of line-item budgets to control spending and prevent improper spending. As government programs grew in scope and spending, concern developed over the efficiency of services. Thus, management concerns were raised and the budget was seen as a means of viewing the outputs of government spending to improve efficiency. More recently some emphasis has been placed upon not just the outputs of services but outcomes as well. Thus, some observers argue for more than resource information; program information is

*Reprinted from *International Journal of Public Administration*, Vol. 1, pp. 237–259, 1979 by courtesy of Marcel Dekker.

demanded in order to assess the effectiveness and appropriateness of government services.

It is within this framework that we view the need for budgeting information resources. Numerous studies have shown that the standard practice in government (and in private industry) has been to lump information resources into various accounts and overhead charges. Such accounts and charges include: automatic data processing services, reproduction equipment, audio-visual equipment and services, telephone charges, mail service and postage, and records storage. The problem is that viewing such resources as overhead expenses makes this resource invisible and intractable. Our thesis is that consideration should be given to making information resources visible, traceable and chargeable. The following sections discuss analytic options to achieve this goal followed by some critical comments based upon previous budget reform attempts.

Approaches to Decision-Making and Information Use

In a classic article in 1959 entitled "The Science of Muddling Through,"[1] Charles Lindblom identified two alternative forms of decision-making in organizations. Lindblom called one the rational-comprehensive approach and the other, the successive limited comparisons or incremental approach. He suggested that underlying our debates concerning budgetary decision-making and policy analysis in the public sector were the fundamental differences between these two methods. One, as Figure 1 suggests, was based on the clear linkage of means and ends and the other was highly dependent on informal negotiating and bargaining and on a step-by-step development of policies. What Lindblom did not articulate fully, but what is implicit in his discussion concerning alternative styles of decision-making, were certain basic orientations to information use. On the basis of such alternative styles of decision-making it is possible to identify two alternative methods of information use (see Figure 2): one we will call the input-oriented approach, the other, the output-oriented approach.

The input-oriented approach corresponds to Lindblom's incremental method of decision-making. The basic orientation of this approach is to use whatever information is available. Information is always partial and incomplete so the incremental method tries to make the most out of what is relatively easily accessible. New information is not introduced except when various organizations and individuals involved in the decision-making process feel that their interests are at stake and that additional kinds of information might make a difference in the informal bargaining process. The bias of

Rational-Comprehensive (Root)	Successive Limited Comparisons
1a. Clarification of values or objectives distinct from and usually prerequisite to empirical analysis of alternative policies.	1b. Selection of value, goals and empirical analysis of the needed action are not distinct from one another but are closely intertwined.
2a. Policy-formulation is therefore approached through means-end analysis: First the ends are isolated, then the means to achieve them are sought.	2b. Since means and ends are not distinct, means-end analysis is often inappropriate or limited.
3a. The test of a "good" policy is that it can be shown to be the most appropriate means to desired ends.	3b. The test of a "good" policy is typically that various analysts find themselves directly agreeing on a policy (without their agreeing that it is the most appropriate means to an agreed objective).
4a. Analysis is comprehensive; every important relevant factor is taken into account.	4b. Analysis is drastically limited: i) Important possible outcomes are neglected ii) Important alternative potential policies are neglected. iii) Important affected values are neglected.
5a. Theory is often heavily relied upon.	5b. A succession of comparisons greatly reduces or eliminates reliance on theory.

SOURCE: Charles Lindblom, "The Science of Muddling Through," *Public Administration Review, 19:*79–88, Spring 1959.

Figure 1   Approaches to decision-making.

this approach tends to focus on "tangible" resource accounting defined in terms of numbers of people and money spent on equipment, purchases and supplies. The aim of the decision-making and information process is decidedly retrospective and control-oriented.[2]

In contrast, the output-oriented approach is based on the assumption

Input-Oriented Approach	Output-Oriented Approach
—Use whatever information is available	—Need all the information one can get
—Information is always partial and incomplete	—It is possible (at least theoretically) to acquire all the data relevant to a decision
—Incremental decision-making makes the most out of whatever information is available	—New information is introduced as a result of conscious, systematic search
—New information is introduced when various organizations or individuals involved feel that their interests are at stake (i.e., in response to bargaining needs)	—Information collection and use reflects a prospective, programmatic or planning emphasis
—Information collection and use reflects a retrospective, fiscal accountability or control emphasis	—Information processing relies significantly on explicit and formal sources
—Information processing relies significantly on informal sources	

Figure 2   Orientations to information collection and use.

that the decision-maker needs all the relevant information he can get and that it is possible (at least theoretically) to get all the data relevant to a decision. New information is developed not as a result of the pressures and problems involved in the bargaining process but as a result of conscious systematic search. Information collection and use reflect a prospective, programmatic, output-oriented bias. For example, advocates of such an approach place heavy emphasis on the need to identify program and organizational objectives and to tie information requirements to these objectives.[3] This approach supports a style of decision-making which tends to be more formal, explicit and which devotes specific attention to the sytematic definition of information needs and requirements. Rather than being control-oriented, the output-oriented approach tends to place heavy emphasis on planning and performance evaluation and not simply on accountability for tangible resources expended.

The implications of these two approaches for information use in organizational decision-making are many and varied. In the context of our discussion of budgeting the data resources, it is possible to suggest four alternative modes of budgeting organizational data resources which can be deduced from our two general approaches.

Modes of Data Resource Budgeting

Figure 3 lists four modes of data resource budgeting: the incremental, adjusted incremental, value/use, and comprehensive modes. Two of these modes, the Incremental and Adjusted Incremental, are input-oriented approaches and two, the Value/Use mode and Comprehensive mode, are output-oriented approaches. Together these modes form a continuum ranging from incremental to comprehensive approaches. The continuum has been refined here by the addition of two intervening approaches. We will begin by identifying the basic characteristics of each mode of data resource budgeting and some of the more significant problems that are posed by each.

Input-Oriented Approaches. 1. Incremental mode. The incremental mode of budgeting can be defined as input-oriented budgeting which aggregates the costs of resources into general, easily comprehensible categories for policy makers and managers (see Figure 4). Typical accounting systems generally tend to lump together the tangible expenditures of the organization into objects of expenditure, or line-items, such as personnel, equipment, supplies, etc. For the purpose of top managers in an organization, the incremental mode of budgeting is heavily weighted in the direction of merely summarizing expenditures for the past fiscal year. The focus of the incremental decision-making process tends not to be on what has been spent, but on the difference between requested amounts and previous expenditures. Thus, decision-making does not demand detailed information concerning resource expenditures since the focus of the budgeting process is on changes at the margin, that is, on what *additional* resources are being requested and not on how past resources have been spent. In short, an analytical, programmatic focus is missing.

Input-Oriented Approach	(1) Incremental Mode
	(2) Adjusted Incremental Mode
Output-Oriented Approach	(3) Value/Use Mode
	(4) Comprehensive Mode

Figure 3 Modes of data resource budgeting and management.

—Personnel
—Equipment
—Supplies
—Physical Plant and Resources
—Rentals
—Contractual Services
—Employee Benefits

Figure 4   Typical object of expenditure categories for incremental mode of budgeting.

The incremental mode of line-item budgeting, therefore, raises several significant problems about the ability of an organization to account for its data resources. First, the object of expenditure categories of the typical line-item budget tend to obscure rather than highlight data resource expenditures. Because these categories are fairly broad in character, being organized on the basis of organizational entities, geographical area, function, time and so on, there is a tendency to lump expenditures into one category which affects more than one program or activity. For example, the category of equipment could contain expenditures for utensils, shovels, audio-visual equipment, typewriters and computers. The category of supplies could contain expenditures on pads, pencils, and paper as well as on food and beverages. Since the incremental line-item mode of budgeting does not focus on the purpose of expenditures, it is sufficient that all resource expenditures be accounted for. It is much less necessary for specific detail to be provided in other than the broadest categories since, in the incremental mode, maximum flexibility is retained for informal bargaining throughout the budget formation and implementation process.

A second problem raised by this mode of budgeting is that the cost-accounting or cost reporting systems developed to support this approach to budgeting do not pick up major aspects of data resource expenditures or do so only very indirectly. Thus, it is difficult, if not impossible, to assess what expenditures are being devoted to various kinds of paperwork and information handling and production tasks. Generally, the cost reporting systems in the incremental mode pick up the costs of only the largest data resource expenditures such as data processing, telephone, and printing costs. Other data resource expenditures for manual record-keeping systems, duplicating, microfilming, and word processing are accounted for only indirectly in such categories as supplies, equipment, rentals and contractual services.

2. *Adjusted incremental mode.* The incremental mode of budgeting as

it is carried out in most public agencies is seriously deficient in accounting for data resources. This is not to say, however, that this mode of budgeting cannot be significantly altered to "pick up" more specific information about data resource expenditures. Indeed, one of the advantages of the line-item approach is that the reporting system can be refined to whatever level of detail the organization feels is necessary. While such specification may not be needed for planning or policy-making, management can benefit a great deal from this kind of reporting.

A typical example of how the reporting system can be changed to reveal more clearly data resource costs is in the data processing item. Many organizations using the line-item approach tend to "lump" together all their data processing costs in one separate category which tends to reflect the direct costs of data processing for the organization's computer services group. In these cases, data processing hardware, such as terminals, which are located away from the main computer center may not be included in the data processing line-item. Viewed as overhead costs for the various units and divisions, these equipment costs might be listed under "office equipment," "educational equipment," or "rental or contractual services" categories. Thus, without some significant adjustment in this reporting system, the "true" cost of data processing tends to be obscured.

It is, however, possible to adjust this reporting system without doing away with the input-oriented approach. One way might be to account in a separate data processing line-item category for each unit or department within the organization. In this case, any data processing resource expenditures incurred apart from the central computer facility would be specifically accounted for. In addition, it would be possible to aggregate the separate data processing costs in the organization. Another approach might be to set up a cost-accounting system for the use of a central computer facility and on-line resources in each unit or program within the organization. In this case, the computer facility would not be regarded as a free good within the organization. Specific use figures and costs could be developed for all users of the facility. These adaptations are similar to what has been referred to elsewhere as establishing an Information Object Classification structure.[4]

While it is possible to move in the direction of adjusting the input-oriented cost reporting system to reflect more accurately the actual data resource expenditure, this mode of cost accounting is still deficient in several important ways.

First, a major problem arises precisely from its input-oriented bias. Despite the fact that the line-item approach can be adjusted to account for data resource expenditures in terms of personnel, supplies, equipment, etc., such an approach can reveal little concerning the relationship between information expenditures and information value. The adjusted incremental mode of budgeting still tends to be a "score card" approach aimed primarily at fiscal accountability.[5] The line-item budget in and of itself can indicate very little concerning the relationship between data collection, use, and value.

Secondly, because the line-item, or incremental, approach is retrospective in focus, one cannot easily relate past performance to any new or changing uses of data resources. This traditional approach is of only limited utility as a data resource planning tool since there is no attempt made to link programmatic goals and needs to actual expenditures and costs.[6]

3. *Value/use mode.* An alternative way of proceeding which differs from the previous input-oriented approaches to budgeting and accounting for data resources is to focus not on organizational inputs, but on outputs and the relationship between objectives and actual performance. A third mode of data resource budgeting which is output-oriented is what we call the value/use mode.

The aim of this approach is twofold: first, it is directed at integrating the cost of data resources with their use; second, it focuses on the key areas where information is of value for the organization.[7] No assumption is made that before one can identify problems of data resource use, one must understand comprehensively the organization's objectives, decision-making process and information systems. The value/use mode of data resource budgeting attempts to take a gradual approach to assessing the connection between data use and value rather than a comprehensive approach. It differs from the incremental modes of data resource budgeting because it is an output-oriented approach, that is, the key problem is to assess whether information that is collected is used and whether what is used is of value to individuals in the organization. Information value here includes not merely the costs of data resources but also the relationship between data resource costs and their utility to specific individuals, units or programs within the organization for either decision-making or analytical needs.

The value/use approach is based on coordination rather than the integration of the comprehensive mode or the "permissiveness" of the incremental modes.[8] It assumes that the appropriate response to the "do your own thing" style of data resource management implied in the incremental modes is not total integration, but a more appropriate degree of coordinated use of data resources in line with the needs of diverse individuals and units within the organization. Thus, the value/use mode aims at (1) identifying the demands or needs for information in the organization; (2) identifying the supplies of information/data in the organization; and (3) closing the gap between the demands/needs for information and the supply of information/data resources.[9]

In terms of methodology, the value/use mode is based, as Figure 5 notes, on four steps.[10]

The first step is a detailed inventory or survey of the organization's data resources. The aim is to identify the sources and types of data resources in the organization and the various kinds of supporting technologies employed.

A second step is to assess the actual costs of the data resources used by the organization in terms of personnel, equipment, supplies, etc. In contrast to the incremental modes of budgeting data resources, which assume that such resources can be costed if only we add additional categories to our object classification system, the value/use approach assumes that the primary problem is the identification of the data resources used. Only after a conscious search and analysis of such resources is completed can one attempt to assess the costs of such resources.

A third step in the value/use approach is to analyze the relationship between the cost and use of data resources in the organization and the value of the data resources to individuals or units in the organization for various types of decision-making and analysis. The aim is to begin reducing the divergence between data which is collected and used by the organization, but is of limited or no value, and to move to a situation where information that is collected and used is of value to individuals in the organization. This third step is perhaps the most difficult one confronting the effective adoption of the value/use mode since it demands an assessment of the complex and varied perceptions of data use and value in the information processes of an organization. Not only is this type of assessment likely to reveal a lack of consensus between individuals within an organization about what information is of value and what is not, but the fact that such questions of value/use are asked explicitly is likely to raise previously submerged or latent sources of conflict or disagreement over the collection, maintenance or dissemination of data resources.

1. Inventory and Catalogue Data Resources
2. Assess the Costs of Data Resources
3. Analyze the Relationship Between Data Resources and Their Use and Value to Individuals, Units and/or Top Management in the Organization
4. Develop a Coordinated Approach to Data Resource Management

Figure 5   Steps in the value/use mode.

Finally, the fourth aspect of the value/use approach is to begin moving toward the development of a coordinated approach to data resource management. Unlike the comprehensive mode of data resource budgeting, which suggests centralization of control and elimination of redundancy and overlap, the value/use approach is based on the assumption that it is neither necessary nor desirable to eliminate all redundancy and overlap. The key is to coordinate efforts at data resource management within existing organizational functions and structure. Changing the latter to meet the demands of the former is equivalent to letting the tail wag the dog. Coordinated data resource management does not depend on redesigning the organization, but rather aims at reducing those areas of data resource intensiveness which are unnecessary or inappropriate. Effective data resource management must be perceived as a gradual, step-by-step approach based on consensus-building within the organization over what should be done and how it can be done. No presumption is made that once the best alternative is identified, it should prevail. Rather, data resource management is perceived as essentially a learning process which can only be effectively adopted to the extent that it is understood and accepted by individuals in the organization.

While the value/use approach seems to hold out substantial benefits to the organization, there are, nevertheless, several problems with such an approach.

First, although the value/use mode is less costly in terms of personnel and time than the comprehensive mode, it is likely to be more costly than the incremental modes of budgeting. The latter approaches are unlikely to require the resources needed by the value/use approach.

Second, the value/use mode can be criticized as overly ambiguous. The *value* of information is an essentially undefinable aspect of this approach since it is likely to vary with each individual's articulation of his needs and wants. Therefore, it will be next to impossible to relate data value to data use. A possible retort to this objection in the context of the value/use mode might be that attempting to articulate the relationship between information value and use is at least an improvement over the current practice. At present, we simply assume that the information that is collected is used and what is used is of value. The value/use mode attempts to examine this assumption more carefully by focusing specific attention on the analysis of the uses and costs of data resources in relationship to whatever values can be defined, articulated or justified by organizational members and managers. While this may amount to a less than optimum approach, it nevertheless has the value of emphasizing what have previously been informal, ad hoc assumptions about data use and data value in organizations.

4. *Output-oriented approaches.* The fourth mode of data resource budgeting and second output-oriented approach is the comprehensive mode. This mode is based on the assumption that any assessment of data resource expenditures must be linked to the use of information to advance organizational or sub-unit goals and objectives. Thus, the only appropriate way to assess data resources is to define the relationship between the uses of information and the processes of decision-making and analysis that go on within the organization. In doing so one inevitably focuses on the outputs of data resource use and not simply on the inputs. That is, one moves from preoccupation with information efficiency to a concern with information effectiveness for decision-making and analytical needs.[11]

In terms of methodology, the comprehensive mode of data resource budgeting differs considerably from the incremental modes. Data resource budgeting in this mode would, as Figure 6 suggests, follow a series of discrete steps aimed at defining explicitly the relationship between organizational and program objectives and information needs and requirements. In this way, the most effective deployment of data resources can be planned for and defined.

While the comprehensive mode of data resource budgeting holds out the promise of large payoffs in terms of the most effective way of planning for data resource use and deployment, this mode does pose a number of serious problems.

First, this mode of data resource budgeting can be a very costly approach in terms of information and time. A large public organization may simply be unable to devote resources to such a task.

Second, the comprehensive mode of data resource budgeting may be politically unacceptable for two significant reasons. Such a mode of budgeting may demand a degree of centralization of organizational control that is incompatible with an organization's structure and traditions. The comprehensive mode of data resource budgeting is a decidedly "integrationist"

---

1. Define Organizational and Programmatic Objectives
2. Identify the Key Types of Decisions that Are Needed to Reach These Objectives
3. Assess the Information Needs for Decision-Making and Analysis
4. Define and Assess Alternative Ways of Meeting These Organizational Information Needs
5. Choose the Best Alternative in Meeting the Organization's Information Needs

---

Figure 6   Steps in the comprehensive mode of data resource budgeting.

mode of planning and control which, either implicitly or explicitly, will demand centralization of authority and resource control. In addition, this mode of data resource budgeting requires that organizational objectives and decision-making processes be clearly defined. In many organizations, such a demand for precise definitions and transparency may be unacceptable politically.[12]

Finally, the comprehensive mode of data resource budgeting may be inappropriate on methodological grounds. As we suggested above, this mode of planning and control demands that clear links be defined between objectives, decisions and information needs. Such a degree of formal definition is simply not compatible with the existing state of scientific knowledge concerning how to do so.[13] In addition, this mode of budgeting is dependent on an extensive cost reporting system which could fully reveal paperwork and other data resource costs. Such a reporting system would by itself constitute a significant paperwork burden since it would entail precise reporting, not simply at the program or unit level, but also at the individual level.

Policy and Program Implications

Budgeting information resources faces two problems which have traditionally confronted public budgeting. These are (1) the need for control over objects of expenditure together with grouping similar objects together so different levels of aggregation can be used; and (2) the need for assigning objects of expenditure to programs for meaningful information regarding outputs to facilitate evaluation and policy oversight. The first concern—control—can be met in large part by using the adjusted incremental mode of budgeting information resources discussed above. What is needed is an information accounting system. Existing accounting systems can be altered without major problems to identify (1) organizational elements which are "data service" in character, (2) activities which are "data processing" in character, and (3) object items of expense for (1) and (2).[14] Such alterations would make expenditures for information more visible, traceable and chargeable. It will not facilitate evaluations of effectiveness, however.

To focus upon the use of information and its contribution to programs' effectiveness means that one needs the information provided above as well as indications of the effective use of information to achieve program goals and objectives. This emphasis upon program information brings up the need for some type of program budget. Efforts to date with program budgets have encountered some problems.

Traditional budget classifications encountered focus upon organizational unit (agency, division, bureau, office, etc.), object of expenditure (travel, office supplies, etc.), function (health, education, etc.), time period, economic impact, activity and project. The program classification is probably the least well defined scheme. This is due to many factors, among the most important of which are: (1) Programs are "artificial" in that they are superimposed upon other classificatory schemes in order to combine activities (and associated costs) which are substitutes for each other, or to group complementary activities that contribute to a common objective. Thus, no "best way" exists to define programs. (2) Programs frequently cross agency lines and thus present problems in using common accounting systems or procedures and coordination between interagency personnel and organizational units. One must recall that government programs and services are provided by *organizational units* of agencies and *not* by program structures. Absent some drastic reorganization, an emphasis upon agencies and not programs is likely.

We should recall that emphasis upon programmatic decision-making with its attendant focus upon outputs and outcomes of programs is meant to have a real impact upon resource allocation decisions. Recasting information into program structures has no intrinsic value. While it may have some educational value—or a salutory effect on those involved in recasting the information, or provide more comprehensible documents to the layman—such changes reflect data manipulation and not substantial changes in the budget process.[15] The purpose for such an effort is to stimulate more systematic thinking about services, activities, programs and alternatives with the ultimate effect of impacting decisions and improving decision processes.

In short, problems with the program budget concept would seem to undermine our ability to budget information resources in a totally rational manner. As other resource allocation problems have shown, expenditures for an activity or equipment seldom contribute just to one program element. Thus, human judgements are used to apportion costs thereby reducing the reliability of expenditure data.

Finally, then, the most promise for budgeting the information resource may reside in the value/use mode. While it is output-oriented, this mode does not claim to be comprehensive or totally rational. It attempts to integrate the costs of data resources with their use and encourages us to focus upon areas where information is of value to an organization. In so doing it strives to examine the input costs of data resources and the relationships between the actual costs of data resources and their utility to users for decision-making. Thus, the value/use mode seeks to identify (1) the demands for information, (2) the supplies of information, and (3) close the gap between demands and needs.

The conflict between resource information and program information exists for information resources just as it does for other resources which contribute to providing public services. With increased attention, however, and a conscious awareness of information needs and costs, the quality of public management can be improved.

Notes

[1] Charles E. Lindblom, "The Science of Muddling Through," *Public Administration Review,* 19 (Spring 1959), 79–88.

[2] See Aaron Wildavsky, *The Politics of the Budgetary Process* (Boston: Little, Brown and Co., 1974), pp. 6–126.

[3] See, for example, Samuel M. Greenhouse, "PPBS: Rationale, Language, and Idea-Relationships," *Public Administration Review,* 26 (December, 1966), 271–277; Roland N. McKean, *Efficiency in Government Through Systems Analysis* (New York: John Wiley and Sons, Inc., 1958); and Peter A. Pyrr, "The Zero-Base Approach to Government Budgeting," *Public Administration Review,* 37 (January/February, 1977), 1–8. For the use of the output-oriented approach in information systems design, see Jan Forrester, *Industrial Dynamics* (Cambridge: MIT Press, 1961); Kenneth L. Kraemer, et. al., *Integrated Municipal Information Systems* (New York: Praeger, 1974); and Paul Siegel, *Strategic Planning of Management Information Systems* (New York: Petrocelli Books, 1975).

[4] Commission on Federal Paperwork, *Information Resources Management* (Washington, D.C.: Government Printing Office, 1977), p. 46.

[5] Herbert Simon et al., "Management Use of Figures," in *Public Budgeting and Finance,* edited by R. T. Golembiewski (Itasca, Ill.: Peacock Publishers, 1968), pp. 15–16.

[6] James T. Bonnen, "The Absence of Knowledge of Distributional Impacts: An Obstacle to Effective Policy Analysis and Decisions," in *Public Expenditures and Policy Analysis,* edited by R. H. Haveman and J. Margolis (Chicago, Ill.: Markham Publishing Co., 1970), pp. 246–270.

[7] See Adrian M. McDonough, *Information Economics and Management Systems* (New York: McGraw-Hill, 1963), pp. 7–18.

[8] Forest W. Horton, Jr., *How to Harness Information Resources: A Systems Approach* (Cleveland: Association for Systems Management, 1974), pp. 9–10.

[9] McDonough, op. cit., p. 77.

[10] The methodology of the value/use mode is adopted from Horton, op. cit., pp. 69–124.

[11] See Gerald Calderone, "Toward Measures of Information Efficiency and Effectiveness" (Unpublished Staff Paper, Commission on Federal Paperwork).

[12]See Aaron Wildavsky, "The Political Economy of Efficiency," *Public Administration Review*, 26 (December 1966), 292-310.

[13]Aaron Wildavsky, "The Budgetary Process Reconsidered," in *The Administrative Process and Democratic Theory*, edited by Louis C. Gawthrop (Boston: Houghton Mifflin Co., 1970), pp. 219-220.

[14]Commission on Federal Paperwork, *A Handbook for Managers*, vol. I (Washington, D.C.: The Commission, 1977), p. IV-3.

[15]S. Kenneth Howard, *Changing State Budgeting* (Lexington, Ky.: Council of State Governments, 1973), pp. 145-146.

Managing the Costs of Information*
Paul A. Strassman

Industries and governments all over the world are currently struggling to contain rising administrative and clerical overheads by automating information handling in the office. In the past 20 years, white-collar labor has been the fastest growing component of the work force in every industrialized country. Yet this labor segment consistently shows lower increases in productivity than such blue-collar employment sectors as farming, manufacturing, and mining, where the management of capital versus labor investments is much better understood.

If bureaucracy (in the most benign sense of the word) is indeed the premier growth industry of the foreseeable future, then the dollars spent on white-collar automation must assume prime importance, particularly for the top information systems executive in an organization. My purpose here is to show that managing information systems now goes far beyond just managing computers and to suggest a series of steps for managing this enlarged function effectively.

Information processing in today's large, complex organization really encompasses three sectors. The first is the by now well-understood and well-defined data processing sector. Aside from the costs of computers, terminals, and peripherals, this sector includes expenses for such things as computer services, time sharing, data processing supplies, data communication, programming support, operating labor, and consulting. It has been estimated that, in 1973, organizations in the United States spent about $26 billion in this area of information processing.

Now the problem is that all too many of today's information processing executives define their jobs largely within the context of data processing—they focus their energies on integrating the explosive data processing technologies into their organizations. This task has not been easy, but overemphasis on it has led managers into the trap of ignoring a second major sector of information processing, which for lack of a better term I call "ad-

*Reprinted by permission of *Harvard Business Review*, Vol. 54, pp. 133–142, September/October 1976. Copyright © 1976 by the President and Fellows of Harvard College; all rights reserved.

ministrative processing"—a sector on which an estimated $42 billion was spent in the United States in 1973.

This sector is rarely aggregated under a single expense heading, yet it accounts for the largest and most frequently used set of tools and facilities for handling information transactions. It includes everything from typewriters, word processors, and dictating equipment to telephone and Telex networks, recording devices, copiers and duplicators, facsimile-transmission devices, microfilm equipment, and even such relatively mundane necessities as office supplies, mail, and simple filing systems.

These adminstrative tools are quite diverse and often isolated from one another, so that the expense involved in their use tends to become highly diffused. Historically, little trade-off has been possible among such individual office "technologies."

Indeed, only rarely is an organization dedicated to the vital task of integrating these noncomputer aspects of information handling. But it is precisely here that the fastest expense growth is occurring in today's office environment; competition across several new administrative processing technologies is already here. This means that if we are to control rising expenditures for white-collar automation, careful expense accounting for these technologies must come under the rubric of information systems management.

The third sector of expense that should fall within the purview of the modern information systems manager involves people. After all, neither data processing nor administrative processing is an end in itself. The payoff from all sorts of office devices and facilities, from computers to mail rooms, lies in increasing the productivity of office labor—secretaries and typists, switchboard operators and clerks, administrative personnel and people who process applications, claims, orders, and inquiries of all sorts—that host of office employees classified as nonmanagerial and nonprofessional.

What makes the office labor sector so important for information systems people is the fact that it is the largest single occupational category—approximately 22%—in the U.S. labor force. What's more, in 1973 the total annual expense associated with such personnel, including benefits, pensions, office space, and other allocated overhead, has been estimated at about $350 billion.

The work that these people do, while vital to our organizations, represents almost entirely an overhead burden—and a fast growing one, too. From 1950 to 1970, the proportion of employees in these "overhead" categories as a percentage of the total U.S. labor force grew by more than 6%, while those in categories representing "direct" labor in areas of high productivity (for example, farming and manufacturing) decreased their share by more than 9%. Thus office labor represents a rich source of cost saving indeed for the information systems manager. If the myriad information transactions that this huge segment of our work force performs can be systematized and made efficient through modern information-handling techniques, the financial benefits will be great.

To accomplish this, we must abandon the traditional practice of managing excessive overhead labor growth by periodic pruning. Data processing, administrative processing, and the work that office labor does have become too intertwined and interdependent for the one-shot surgical approach to work anymore. Rather, we will have to design self-adaptive cost-control methods into each organization's systems and procedures. We must learn how to install advanced office automation techniques that will safeguard productivity improvements as conditions change.

In the face of uncertainties about the future volume of information transactions, the relative importance of various cost elements, rapid changes in technology, and shifting attitudes toward office automation by labor and government, we must harness the power of information technology through a more responsive control mechanism. Let us explore briefly the objectives of such a mechanism and then move on to the action I recommend to achieve it.

Once we accept the notion that the top information executive's job encompasses much more than managing data processing expense, we still have to articulate, in terms of precise objectives, just what the job calls for in today's business environment. In my view, the new job definition would include the following objectives:

Ensuring the integration of data processing, administrative processing, and office labor productivity programs.

Instituting accounting, cost-control, and budgeting innovations that will subject *all* information systems overhead activities to the disciplines traditionally applied to direct labor.

Subjecting office labor automation programs to analyses comparable to those applied to all other forms of capital investment.

Conceiving organizational designs that will permit information to be handled as a readily accessible and easily priced commodity rather than as a bureaucratic possession.

Creating within the organization an internal market for alternative information systems products, so that trade-off decisions, even technologically complex ones, can be decentralized into the hands of local user management.

Fostering a technique of pricing that will allow decisions on introducing new technology, or abandoning obsolete technology, to be made on a decentralized basis.

Installing and monitoring measurement methods that will protect improvements in productivity achieved by automation programs.

These objectives are far from easy to achieve. However, from experience with information systems in several large organizations, I have developed a set of nine guidelines, or steps, that have proved helpful in my work. They have been sufficiently tested to make me feel quite confident in offering them here as a practical route for any organization to follow in an effort to control its own information systems programs.

I should emphasize, however, that all of them may not be valid, or even acceptable, in every organization, for they do involve some major restructuring. Nor can they all be instituted quickly. Changing a whole organization's perspective on information systems managment to the broader view I have set out here must be a gradual process. Thus the steps outlined in the balance of this article constitute a rough road map to guide an organization toward the total management of its information resources.

Managing Costs

The sequence should start with the budgeting process. It must identify all of the components of information processing cost and segment them by (1) *function*, for example, the total cost of performing the billing function, from order entry until receivables are reconciled, (2) *technology*, for example, what portion of the billing cost is done clerically and what portion by computer, and (3) *organization*, for example, what the various billing systems of one organization are.

Step 1: Identify costs. Identifying computer and telecommunication costs is relatively easy. The tough part begins in identifying budget elements of corresponding administrative processing and office labor cost. Classifying expenses and people can be difficult, since organizational boundaries do not translate readily into functional or technological definitions. This step will probably require major modifications in the organization's job classification scheme, so that job categories for white-collar personnel become more detailed and comparable job functions become consistent across organizational lines.

In addition to this internally oriented, personnel cost analysis, careful attention must be paid to external purchases of services and technology. Because the budgeting process focuses on expense levels of a particular organizational element, costs incurred outside do not readily surface when an attempt is made at a functional profile of costs.

For instance, in arriving at the total cost of the billing function, you need to make sure that the costs of mail and banking services are included. The overall billing expense should include investment costs as well as new systems-programming or minicomputer-development expenses that are to be amortized over a period of years. Since for accounting purposes most information systems costs are now expensed rather than capitalized, it is important that your cost identification process discriminate between these different classes of costs.

Finally, a word of caution: step 1 is not an easy, one-shot effort. Depending on the size and complexity of the organization, it may take up to five years of continual changes in the budgeting process before consistent data are obtained. The new cost identification scheme must become the accepted way of looking at the cost structure of *all* information activities. And this takes time.

Step 2: Keep score on unit costs. Knowing what each information transaction costs is critically important for all that is to follow. It is the only way to monitor productivity trends independent of changes in volume, work element mix, and inflation.

After wrestling for years with the problem of getting comparable data on the consequences of computer automation, I have concluded that, to really control administrative costs, one must begin by tracking "real," deflated unit costs for discrete output end products. By these, I mean items like cost per service call, cost per payment, cost per purchase order, cost per printed page, and cost per inquiry. Only by keeping score over a number of years on such consistently defined unit output measures is it possible to observe real improvements in cost performance.

In unit costing, it is important to define the measurements in sufficient detail that assigning responsibility for them at the working level is easy. Defining a measurement too broadly forces excessively high aggregations such as one finds in divisional overhead-burden ratios, where little can be done to trace the consequences of specific productivity improvement programs.

Also, be sure to include total unit costs for each unit output measure you choose. For instance, the cost of management overhead, employee benefits, and capital must flow into unit transaction costs before you can make valid comparisons between various means of improving productivity through office automation.

In describing these first two steps, I am considering information processing services as an *industrial process* rather than as an undifferentiated overhead. This is quite deliberate, for in my experience it leads to a much better understanding of how costs can be controlled in this rather amorphous and "messy" domain.

Step 3: Establish standard costing. Setting a standard cost for each element of measured information output is essential for several reasons.

First, when cost reductions are planned, they must be locked into the planning and budgeting system by means of standards against which operating management can be measured. All too often, existing charge-out or full-cost-absorption costing systems disguise cause-and-effect relationships in expensive information processing activities and make it practically impossible to look at period variances from planned expense levels in a way that keeps management accountable for results.

Second, standard costing for information services is essential for making long-term commitments to users. If they have a predictable cost picture, users can feel more confident in making new investments and in decentralizing systems investment decisions.

A third reason for standard costing is its ability to reflect variability, so that the organization supplying information services can no longer cite "fixed costs" or "undisplaceable overhead commitments" as excuses for not achieving productivity improvements.

The basic tool for achieving standard costing is a job process sheet containing the cost profile for every resource used to create an output transaction. Each job step is costed out just as if it were part of a manufacturing assembly operation. The job process sheet should focus on all pertinent costs, such as those for handling, editing, output preparation, mailing, and reproduction or storage. In this way, analysts searching for cost reductions can do a thorough evaluation of the thousands of discrete activities that make up the total information processing budget.

In a well-run operation, such improvements do not come easily; saving a penny here or a nickel there is typical of most paper-work activities. This situation means that the basic tool—the job process sheet—must be designed with sufficient detail to permit an ongoing review of operating costs for every information transaction involved.

Aside from making it easier to track operating costs and thus to highlight opportunities for savings, the most important consequence of standard costing is that it changes the attitudes of managers supplying central information services. Standard costing also tends to shift the staff and planning people to the working levels of the organization, where they are closer to being a part of direct product cost. Also, such managers become more wary of commitments to fixed technology costs.

The reasons for both of these attitudinal changes lie in the imperatives of standard costing—that indirect overhead be kept small and that technology costs be responsive to changes in volume or to obsolescence in methods.

The experience with standard costing at Xerox has so far been good. We now operate over 40 internal information services groups that derive a large part or all of their revenues from standard revenue per unit of output. As a minimum, each of these groups must liquidate its entire cost structure, including all overheads and management charges, from a changing revenue mix. The overall result has been a sharpening of the ability of managers to respond to a changing information systems environment, while maintaining good accountability for cost performance.

Organizing Functions

The action steps discussed so far—identifying costs, tracking unit costs, and establishing standard costs—are all procedural aspects of information systems control. To be effective, they need an organizational focus. Cost-accountability centers, in which people engaged in functional office activities are assigned to product-oriented units, will provide this.

Step 4: Set up accountability centers. The rationale for this approach stems from the recent tendency in business, industry, and government to centralize information processing functions. Centralization, so goes the argument, puts the information processing specialist under one umbrella, consolidates the technology, and concentrates expert management—all this in the guise of "economies of scale."

But the real problem occurs after centralization takes place. Simply put, it is this: How do you manage large agglomerations of clerical and administrative people without sacrificing the attributes that make them effective in their local environments? For instance, how do you justify taking personal secretaries away from individual managers and grouping them into better equipped word-processing centers without losing in motivation what you gain from computerized text-editing typewriters?

The answer seems to lie in finding an organizational compromise between centralized efficiency and decentralized effectiveness of people. At Xerox, we have achieved this middle ground by creating small teams—sometimes as few as 10 people but never more than 50 to 80—to handle well-defined information-output tasks.

For example, our manager of the payroll processing center has complete control over his product, which is payroll checks and payroll-related reports. He is, in effect, an entrepreneur in the payroll processing business. He is responsible for his cost reductions per payroll check—weighed against error rates, document turnaround time, cash management, and so on. He sees himself, in turn, as being in a highly competitive payroll business, in which he must not only optimize his total resources but also aggressively seek opportunities for providing new and better services.

More important, we encourage this manager to make trade-off decisions among a variety of resource deployment choices that are available for improving his overall financial results. Thus he may trade off such options as training investments versus salary levels, information investments versus manpower expense, teleprocessing cost versus data processing expense, and in-house service versus external procurement.

In my view, the true test of "decentralization" is not an organizational one; rather, it is whether a manager responsible for an end product has the freedom to make trade-offs like those just cited in getting the job done. In such an environment, it is then possible to charter data processing or administrative processing activities without getting bogged down in organizational definitions. Output becomes the proper focus. When information processing functions become the accountability centers, they are in effect little businesses, buying and selling goods and services as needed.

For instance, our payroll processing center (to use the same example) "buys" batch-processing and time-sharing from our "centralized" computer service units, and "sells" the reports and analyses that are by-products of its payroll work to decentralized personnel departments within the company. Although people in computers and personnel may regard the payroll processing center as a centralized function, it operates in the independent, decentralized way I have described.

In short, one person's centralization becomes another's decentralization. The labels become meaningless after a while. In the end, it is accountability for the cost of information processed that matters.

Step 5. Apply competitive pricing. In information processing operations, it is not easy to establish standard costs and create accountability centers. There are two reasons for this: technologies can change radically, and the costs of computerization are hard to set realistically. Let me explain briefly what I mean.

When a new technology such as data base management software or time-sharing appears, the cost of converting to it, learning how to use it, and getting "customers" to employ it will make it appear noncompetitive with established methods. Thus the manager of an information processing operation may be reluctant to try the new technology. In contrast, obsolescent technologies always appear more attractive in the short run, since they are well established and it does not really cost much to add to the bag of tools already being used.

Comparing the cost of computerization with the cost of the human wages that will be displaced is also a very tricky business. Manpower is always valued at the going "market" rate for salaries plus benefits, whereas the cost of computerization varies according to the company's cost-accounting practices in allocating the initial introduction cost.

The up-front cost of buying a computer is usually written off separately, with the result that the price of computer time—at "marginal cost"—is almost always substantially lower than the market price offered by commercial service bureaus. We then have the incongruous situation that, when labor and machines compete, labor savings are valued at market price, whereas computer time is costed at a heavily subsidized level. It thus becomes impossible to compare the two costs realistically.

The solution to both of these difficulties—accommodating new technology and making valid cost comparisons—is to open internal information processing operations to competitive market forces by basing their revenues on prevailing competitive prices for equivalent services.

Establishing a market price for each information service rather than pricing it at "cost" accomplishes several ends: (1) it simplifies cost accounting by avoiding complex overhead allocations, since all automation facilities become fixed expenses if viewed from a sufficiently short-term standpoint; (2) it stimulates the introduction of new technologies because it permits cost averaging of such innovations over program life; and (3) it allows simulated "profit" objectives to be assigned to the lowest levels of an operation, so that even first- and second-level management has a clear understanding of what it can and cannot do.

An example of this last advantage is our experience with word-processing centers. When we first created them, we found it difficult to establish their scope and performance measures. Using competitive prices from local firms, we then allowed the text-preparation technicians (that is, the ex-secretaries who work in these centers) to charge their "clients" for secretarial services. The results were gratifying, because we found that, to remain competitive, we had to back off from many fancy technical solutions.

There are, however, two serious disadvantages to using market pricing formulas for internal transfer of information services. Automation opportunities may be turned down that would be justifiable under a marginal costing approach. Second, an efficient internal information processing operation may accumulate a large surplus of revenues over costs, and most bureaucracies simply do not have accounting conventions for dealing with internal profits.

The issue of too little automation can be easily resolved by regarding new automation investment opportunities as a part of the conventional capital funds budgeting process and applying the same criteria for choice used there. The recent progress in the technology of information processing suggests that there will be no dearth of automation investment opportunities over the next decade or so.

Establishing comparability between office automation and other capital investment opportunities should simplify the decisions on how to allocate scarce resources. The cutoff level between approved and disapproved automation projects will then be roughly consistent, regardless of the way investments are priced.

As for the issue of accumulated profits, each organization must resolve it within the context of its own rules. One way of looking at such profits is to use them as an indirect measure of how efficiently a particular service unit is investing in information technology over the long term. If it invests its funds wisely—in technology that makes its people really productive—the unit should not only be able to keep up with rapidly dropping market prices for information transactions (and thereby garner new customers) but also to use the accounting surpluses for making new investments (and thereby prepare for the future).

Step 6: Plan for the long term. Here I want to focus briefly on a basic dilemma facing the manager of an information systems department in a large organization. The people using the services he provides usually want some new task done right away—in three months or at most a year. The trouble is, meeting such a new demand often requires information technology or processing methods that take a long time to install.

This, plus the fact that total information processing costs can exceed 15% of a large organization's expense budget these days, is why the planning of long-term information strategies warrants the same processes as are applied to functions like marketing, manufacturing, distribution, procurement, and personnel.

In this step, therefore, I strongly recommend that information systems investment decisions be shifted from an annual funding basis to two- to five-year planning commitments initiated by the functional user departments in the organization. This suggestion means that the information systems department, even if it is completely decentralized, should not contend for corporate budget funds as an independent cost center.

Rather, its budget levels should be set through renewable long-range contracts with the *users* of its services, that is, with the people accountable for end product costs containing various elements of information transaction expense.

Step 7: Let the users control. This step is a logical outgrowth of the shift of planning initiatives regarding information systems from the suppliers of information services to the users. Users should control not only the initial procurement but the execution as well. After all, they are the ones who understand the trade-off opportunities between information and other variables in functions as diverse as manufacturing, engineering, marketing, personnel, and procurement. Computer people and administrative specialists like to claim that they know what is best for their clients, but information systems are just too important to the success of an organization to be left entirely in the hands of the suppliers of information services.

To achieve the necessary degree of control, I recommend that key aspects of information systems management—business analysis, methods planning, and applications training—be moved organizationally as close to the ultimate user as possible. This arrangement not only enables the user to make intelligent procurement of data processing and administrative processing services but also creates a powerful mechanism for balancing the business needs of the user against the claim of the information technicians.

I am frequently asked how to structure the user's organization to accommodate the systems planning and systems implementation personnel. There are many possible organizational combinations. However, my experience leads me to favor assigning business systems analysts to the planning mission for each functional area, since these are the people who are concerned about the future or about methods for changing the operating environment.

In preparing for new ways of doing business, we must increasingly rely on information systems as a means of achieving goals. Therefore, I am convinced that the user's planning area is the logical place to put information systems development and control staff.

Redirecting Emphasis

Over the past few years, I have become convinced that the greatest opportunities for lasting productivity in information processing lie in job redesign and job enrichment rather than in improving the efficiency of existing data processing operations. To be sure, new computer technology and new system approaches are frequently essential in improving the work done in offices. But there should be no mistake about what should come first—human work needs, not technology.

Step 8: Deemphasize the technology. I am recommending here a significant deemphasis of technology in information processing operations. This reorientation means that top information executives face a new challenge. Whereas their primary skills have been focused on technical management, the enlarged scope of information processing calls for a humanistic, nontechnical, and general management perspective rarely found among more specialized executives.

How can the transition from an excessive computer orientation be engineered? Perhaps our experience at Xerox can point the way. Recently, we have begun increasing our investments in methods, procedures, and training. For years, these activities atrophied as talent moved into the more glamorous and better paying computer-related activities.

The payoff from this redirection has been gratifying. For instance, in the information network we are currently installing, analysis of methods and work flow has shown that computer terminal access to central data bases allows us to rearrange accountability for work functions. Under the old system, work had to be broken up into specialties: accounts receivable specialists handled accounts receivable; equipment order entry clerks handled customer orders; credit was still another specialty. The new approach allows us to make versatile generalists out of narrow specialists. Since our people can now see the total results, job satisfaction has increased substantially.

Such a change is not free. I estimate that the costs involved in changing procedures, redesigning jobs, and training people to do them (all of which I call the "soft software") have exceeded the technical costs for setting up the computer terminals network itself (which I call the "hard software").

The important fact, however, is that the soft software aspects of the project have been given the same care and attention as the heretofore more glamorous hard software aspects. We have begun our own campaign of deemphasizing technology by increasing the importance and influence of the people who develop the soft software.

I should point out that deemphasizing technology in information processing operations does not necessarily mean getting rid of your technical people. It does mean, however, that you can shift many of them into administrative systems positions, where there is plenty of systems work to be done.

A goodly portion of the money formerly spent on computer problems can thus finance efforts to standardize technologies, to automate programming and testing tasks, to devise output measurements, and to improve quality control—all of which will increase the productivity of your technical resources. What this step comes down to, then, is a rebalancing of talent, not a purge.

Step 9: Use job enlargement. This recommendation elaborates a bit on the previous step. I single it out for emphasis because it calls for transforming our current rigidly designed information systems, with their emphasis on single-task work stations, into a different mode—one in which systems tasks are enlarged to include many of the attributes of computer-aided learning.

One of the problems I see in most existing information systems that rely mainly on computer terminals is their relatively narrow task orientation. People do not fit readily into such an environment. The training levels of individuals vary, and their attitudes toward work fluctuate. Therefore, designing terminal procedures to the lowest acceptable performance level, and leaving output volume as the only performance variable over which the operator has control, is clearly unsatisfactory, since it lessens productivity and discourages the operator.

For this reason, I recommended that terminal operating procedures be designed as a combination of tutorial and job execution devices—a combination that permits changes in both task content and job scope. As I see it, terminal systems should encourage people to deal with situations of increasing complexity as organizations and individuals continue to grow in their experiences.

As organizations perceive that increasing portions of their expense budgets are being devoted to information processing, judgments will have to be made about where to place the responsibility for overall information systems management. Making such decisions requires that both information systems executives and top management take time to reappraise their roles. To be specific:

Top management will have to decide whether to strengthen its control over increasing complexity and interdependence by gathering the functional costs related to information processing.

Explicit choices will have to be made among investments in computers, software development, training, methods development, telecommunications, job design, technologies available, and compensation levels.

Most important, top management will have to decide whether some of the steps presented in this article can be applied in their own organizations. Even if it is found, for example, that information processing cost-accountability centers and productivity improvement through job enlargement are desirable, will there be adequate management talent available in the existing information processing operation to support such a major change?

The information systems manager will also have to reappraise his role. Can he learn to delegate the management of technology to others? Can he break free of the disciplines that shaped his entire career and enter into competition with management generalists? Can he acquire the new skills needed to motivate white-collar workers toward greater involvement in their work? Can he broaden his background to include the complex economics of information handling?

There is no doubt that arriving at answers to such questions will be difficult. Initially, only a small number of organizations will find switching to information cost management sufficiently urgent to make these issues matters of central concern. In all likelihood, they will become central in information-intensive organizations like insurance companies, banks, credit card organizations, government social service agencies, income tax departments—places where information processing is a principal occupational concern. But as the pace of technology quickens and as shrinking margins make it necessary to employ resources more economically, most large organizations will have to consider the issues of information cost management as inseparable parts of overall business planning.

Our Shadow Government: The Hidden Cost of Government Paperwork, Information and Communication Costs to the Taxpayer*
Commission on Federal Paperwork

What Do We Mean by "Government Paperwork, Information and Communication" Costs?

The Definitional Problem. When the Commission undertook the study to determine the total cost of government paperwork, it immediately ran into definitional and measurement problems. Everywhere this commission turned to for a figure lay more questions than answers—"it all depends on who you ask"; "do you mean equipment, or people or both"; "are you talking about direct or indirect costs"; and "hard copy paper and printing costs are one thing, related processing and handling costs are quite another."

A number of efforts in both the public and private sectors have dealt with fractions of the total cost, but all of these efforts appear to understate the full magnitude and true character of the costs.

The term "paperwork" obviously has negative connotations. On the other hand, the terms "information" and "communication" are usually positive concepts. However, the Commission found that one man's "information" was another man's "paperwork," that the distinction between "good" paperwork and "bad" paperwork was often blurred. Therefore, we determined that both "good" and "bad" paperwork must be costed in the government's accounting system. Insofar as possible, the total cost of the communication process between citizens and their government must be captured.

A second definitional problem comes in distinguishing between "paperwork" as a narrow term taken to mean reports, records and other physical documents, versus the use of the word in a much broader sense to mean "information." The latter term connotes a broad array of government activities,

*Washington, D.C., U.S. Government Printing Office, 1977.

involving far more than the collection, processing, use and storage of physical documents. Information, in short, is more than documents. It involves the myriad *products and services involved in the communication process* between government and people; among and between governmental levels and agencies; and among and between units within the same agency.

The Commission decided that it must adopt the broader definition of paperwork, to include *information products, services and processes*, not just physical pieces of paper, their printing, and their replication. In adopting the broader definition, additional complications then present themselves.

For one, if we carry the definition of information cost in its broader, communication context, to the extreme, should we include, for example, the cost of the time of government officials spent on the telephone, or in meetings, talking with one another and with citizen-constituents? How about the time spent reading the morning mail, or technical reports, or newspapers? Or writing letters, dictating and giving oral instructions to subordinates? Or training, travel and conference costs? We have chosen not to include some of these costs because the figures would be so high as to be virtually meaningless.

The Costs We Must Pay. This study estimates the total *Federal Government* paperwork, information and communication costs imposed directly on the American taxpayer to be in excess of $43 billion a year. However, this tentative figure does not take into account the cost burden imposed directly on the public by State and local governments, estimated at an additional $17 billion (see Table 1). But even that resultant total still underestimates the full burden in a number of important ways.

For one, beyond the "direct" costs imposed by the Federal Government on you and me as taxpayers, there are five other major classes of cost burdens which we must bear, as shown in Table 1. First, there are the "indirect costs" incurred by the Federal Government. We certainly must pay for them in the form of taxes on us as citizens, but they are not discretely identifiable in government's accounting systems as expenses, for example, for postage or the salaries of government employees in tabulating statistics. Rather, they are "hidden" and "buried" in both overhead and program accounts, including some with labels like "Other Services."

Next, we must pay corresponding direct and indirect costs for paperwork, information and communication requirements imposed by State and local levels of government. Sometimes these levels of government are simply acting as intermediaries. For example, when they administer Federal grants. The revenues used to defray the costs of these activities are Federal revenues.

Table 1   Total Paperwork, Information and Communication Costs Imposed by Governments on the American Taxpayer[1] (in billions)

1. Direct Federal Government Costs (e.g. salaries, printing, postage, etc.)	$43
2. Direct State/Local Government Costs (paid from Federal funds)	11
3. Direct State/Local Government Costs (e.g. salaries, printing, postage, etc.)	17[2]
4. Indirect Federal ("Shadow Government") Costs (contractor documentation, "other services"; paid from Federal funds)	13[3]
5. Indirect State/Local Costs (corresponds to item 4 above; paid from State/Local revenues)	8[4]
6. Private Sector Costs directly incurred by Citizens and Businesses to pay for government paperwork	41[5]
7. State/Local Government as a respondent to Federal Information Requirements	9[6]
Total	$142

NOTES:

[1] Many cost estimates directly ascertainable from Federal income and expense accounts; many estimated by statistical sampling and statistical extrapolation.

[2] This estimate takes into account differences in the makeup of the State/Local government workforce and the Federal workforce (e.g. higher percentage of occupations and budget in education and law enforcement...).

[3] Excludes subcontractor costs incurred responding to paperwork requirements imposed by prime government contractors.

[4] Figure based in part on a ratio of the sum of items one and four to the sum of items three and five ($5 billion), supplemented by an additional amount, with supporting data, in the text.

[5] Includes $32 billion private industry, $8.7 billion for individuals, $.350 billion farmers and $.075 billion for labor organizations; see separate CFP Study on Paperwork Impact on Small and Large Business.

[6] Also see joint CFP-Academy for Contemporary Problems Study, separately available.

But in other cases State and local revenues are collected to pay for the programs.

Moreover, we must also pay taxes so that our own State and local levels of government can themselves respond to the Federal Government's information demands; we, as citizens, are not directly involved in these transactions. But we are taxed to pay for them of course.

And finally, we must directly bear the costs of filling out government forms and reports whenever, for example, the Census Bureau sends out a questionnaire, or a regulatory commission of government wants certain business and financial information, or we apply for a welfare, educational, veteran, or some other benefit to which we're entitled.

In short, the costs which we may pay are essentially of two types: (1) direct costs imposed on us as citizens, businesses and other members of the "private sector," and (2) taxes which are levied on us to defray the cost of governments' collecting, handling, disseminating and communicating paperwork and information. In the case of the direct costs, we may or may not be able to shift them to someone else. For example, if we are a businessman, shifting the cost onto a consumer in the form of higher prices. Or as a wholesaler, onto our retailers. And so on. In the case of taxes, our leverage must be in helping government wage its war on paperwork and joining in a partnership to seek less costly ways of administering government programs.

Inputs Versus Outputs. A third major definitional and measurement problem that crops up when one tries to compute a total government paperwork and red tape cost imposed on the American taxpayer comes about in trying to segregate and cost out paperwork and information "inputs." In his Ph.D. thesis, "The Information Economy," and in the nine volume report he authored for the Department of Commerce, "The Information Economy: Definition and Measurement," dated May, 1977 (OT Spec. Pub. 77-12), Marc Porat says "Part of the Federal Government's bureaucracy necessarily communicates with 'outside' entities—private firms and State and local governments. The bureaucracies 'talk' to each other in managing the economy. And that volume of bureaucratic chatter has grown to stupendous heights in the past 50 years." Porat characterized government as essentially an "information producing, distributing, and consuming organism. Bureaucracies plan, coordinate, command, evaluate, and communicate. They process information. They survey, gather intelligence, write reports."

Our difficulty arises in trying to distinguish which, and how much of this activity should properly be accounted for as "information input" (information resources) and how much under the program output.

Porat himself tallied the "information inputs" of the Federal Government, and said the total cost of information resources in 1967 was $50.5 billion, of which only $11.8 billion was in the form of direct purchases of goods and services from the primary information sector. One big item in the $50.5 billion figure is the cost of R&D to develop new weapons and space systems for the Department of Defense and NASA. Porat estimated that cost at $13.1 billion. Another big component was "employee compensation to information workers" which he said accounted for $16.6 billion in 1967. The latter figure he obtained from data produced by the Civil Service Commission on the occupational and compensation structure of Federal employees. This study followed a similar track and, as we will see later, Porat's figure gives us a basis with which to compare independently-derived Commission figures (see Figure 5).

Government Advertising? Dr. Porat estimated that in 1967 the Federal Government spent $11 million advertising itself, placing the amount somewhere between the amounts spent by Colgate-Palmolive Company and R. J. Reynolds Industries. This is in addition, he said, to the $260 million worth of advertising offered free as public service advertising. "The Government knows quite well that it is selling its output, even though no explicit market transaction occurs other than mandatory taxation."[1] Our study here estimates $147 million for DOD "recruiting advertising" alone.

George Beveridge, *Washington Star* Ombudsman, went further than Porat in discussing the legitimacy and justification for government spending in the area of public relations and advertising. In an article he authored April 19, 1976, published in the *Washington Star,* he alluded to a four-part series which appeared in the newspaper in preceding weeks, "Selling the Government" by John Fialka. Beveridge said (of the Fialka series):

(he, Fialka) described a Federal public relations colossus so uncontrolled and so dispersed in the bureaucracy that no one can accurately assess its true size or worth. The articles (in the series) questioned the degree to which some of the myriad "informational" activities of the government serve political self-interest rather than the public interest and how much of the taxpayer's money may be wasted in the process...But the article's main thrust was something quite different: That the current organizational morass of information activities is so diffused and so uncontrolled that it is difficult, if not impossible, to separate those vital, valid functions from the pure puffery and self-serving political material that pours out. What the issue boils down to, it seems to me, is that a clearer definition of what the government's public relations functions should—and should not—be is long overdue.[2]

Reference to the Beveridge commentary is included here because the Commission is calling attention to two problems. First, should advertising, promotion and public relations costs of government be considered "information and communication expenses"? And second, one of the serious problems in trying to get a handle on paperwork and information costs is that much of the "information activity" of government is hidden and buried. It is diffused and dispersed throughout many overhead and direct expense accounts at all government levels. For example, government agencies do not always give complete visibility to their "public relations and advertising costs." These expenses are oftentimes carried under some other heading.

In summary, the Treasury Department, the General Accounting Office, OMB and other central government management authorities which "oversee" agency financial and information management systems have not prescribed adequate guidelines and standards for determining what kind of component expenses should be carried under the heading "paperwork, information and communication expenses." Of course they cannot and should not be indicted on this score; no one may have asked them to. Agencies have tended to resist attempts to standardize such accounting definitions as "overhead" and "other services." But we know, certainly, that many paperwork, information and communication expenses must be *somewhere* in agency accounts; instead of trying to estimate their magnitude and character by indirect, deductive methods, why don't we tackle the problem head on and redefine the component expenses by direct methods?

The Ever-Increasing Growth of Federal Information Costs

In a brief study "Federal Information Increases 11.8 percent in 1976," Washington Researchers created a composite index of some 7 key indicators which they felt were "representative of the amount of data and information available by the Federal Government." The 7 indicators include: GPO spending; spending on congressional printing; spending on statistical programs; research and development; the number of computers; the number of *Federal Register* pages; and the number of NTIS publications. As Figure 1 shows, during the six year time span (1971-1976) when the Federal budget expenditures rose 19.1 percent, the "information index" rose 68.8 percent, or over three times as great.[3]

Another measure of the growth of Federal information can be obtained from the Special Analysis of the Federal Budget which deals with statistical programs of government. During this same six year period, 1971 to 1976, figures show that obligations for the principal major statistical programs rose from $161.2 million to $492.5 million.

A third estimate of the cost of Federal information comes from an analysis completed for the Commission's Value/Burden Study by Donald W. King. In his study "An Estimate of the Value of Scientific and Technical Information Derived from Federal Funds," King derived cost estimates based on what users are willing to pay for scientific and technical information published by such government organizations as the National Technical Informa-

Fiscal Year	*1971*	*1972*	*1973*	*1974*	*1975*	*1976*
Federal Information Index						
Fed. Register Pgs	21,864	26,053	33,284	42,372	44,847	59,600
Index	100	119.2	152.2	193.8	223.4	272.6
NTIS Publications	45,000	53,200	55,600	59,000	63,000	60,000
Index	100	116.4	121.7	129.1	137.9	131.3
No. of Computers	5,934	6,731	7,149	7,830	8,649	9,600
Index	100	113.4	120.5	132	145.8	161.8
GPO Spending (mil)	224	262	292	366	418	500
Index	100	109.7	118.9	140.0	147.7	173.4
Cong. Print. (mil)	41	48	54	62	74	85
Index	100	109.8	117.3	127.8	141.6	157.5
Spnd. Statistical Programs (mil)	204.8	237.6	280.8	371.9	428.1	498.4
Index	100	108.8	122.7	158.2	170.1	193.6
Spndg. R&D (mil)	15.1	16.4	17.8	18.3	19.5	21.3
Index	100	101.3	103.5	97.8	90.2	91.3
FED. INFO. INDEX	100	111.4	122.4	139.8	151	168.8
Federal Press Release Index						
Dept. Labor	100	116.7	128.2	117.5	106.4	144.5
Dept. State	100	93.3	109.2	139.3	161.6	170
Dept. HUD	100	95.9	72.8	49.	52.4	55.2
Dept. Transp.	100	100.3	92.3	97.5	87.1	70.2
Civ. Aer. Board	100	115.8	133.2	137.5	133.7	156
Small Bus. Admin.	100	90.1	61.4	77.2	50.5	76.3
Dept. Defense	100	91.9	65.7	52.7	60.7	52.5
Vet. Admin.	100	128	120	12.16	120.8	100
Dept. Commerce	100	115.2	106.1	114.8	85.9	103
FED. PRESS RELEASE INDEX	100	105.6	98.9	100.1	85.6	103.3

For computing an index, all dollar figures were converted into 1971 dollars by using the Federal Purchases Deflator.

Figure 1   Federal Information Index.

tion Service (NTIS) and the Government Printing Office (GPO). The information products studied were disseminated in 1976, based on R&D completed in 1975. The costs were estimates of the average price and number of subscriptions of scientific and technical journals as well as price and distribution of technical reports disseminated from NTIS and GPO. The costs determined by use were also estimated. Although King was more interested in getting at the "value" of information, his research is valuable from a cost standpoint as well.[4] The total cost of technical reports sponsored by the Federal Government came to an estimated $406.5 million. A rough estimate of value of scientific and technical information produced through Federal funding was estimated to be $4.7 billion. . . .

A fourth insight into government's increasing paperwork and information costs can be seen from Figure 2 which is a chart published by the Federal Highway Administration, Department of Transportation, in connection with the current wave of government requirements for public participation in governmental processes. In the stub column are listed "techniques," which means those governmental activities in which the public is requested to participate. Nearly all of these activities require paperwork.

The central point we're making here is that concomitantly with increasing public participation in the governmental process comes paperwork as an implicit requirement. And of course, someone must bear the cost. But increasingly the citizen, business or private sector entity is absorbing the cost of public participation in government directly, thereby shifting the burden from public sponsorship to private sponsorship. In Table 1, then, these costs would be embraced by Item 6, Private Sector costs. . . .

Methodology

Since there is no authoritative, agreed-upon methodology for computing an overall government information and paperwork cost to the taxpayer, it is necessary to use empirical methods. In general, two approaches were melded together.

The first of these methods goes back to the 1974 NARS Information and Records Costs Interim Report. . . . The data accumulated are developed on the principle that, in addition to salary, everything an employee requires to do the job of creating and processing information and records should be counted as a cost, including space, office equipment, office supplies, office machines, typewriters, adding machines, word processors, office furniture, printing, computers, communication, and so on. These costs are called "Direct Information and Record Costs."

Key: Planning Stage s: Systems c: Corridor D: Design o: Occasional use Technique	Action Plans	Alabama	Alaska	Arizona	Arkansas	California	Colorado
1. Public Hearing		S C D	C D	S C D	S C D	S C D	S C D
2. Information Meetings		S	S C D	S C	S C D	S C D	C D
3. Legal Notices		C D	C D	C D	S C D	S C D	S C D
4. Mass Media Advertisements		C D	C D	S	S	S	S C D
5. Mailing Lists		C D	C D	S C	S C D	S C D	C D
6. Citizens Committees		S	S		S	S	S C
7. Speaking Engagements with Interested Parties		S C D				C D	C
8. Circulate Project Reports		S C D	O				C
9. News Releases				S C D		C D	
10. Pre-hearing/ Post-hearing Meetings			C D				
11. Conduct Surveys			O			O	
12. Public Workshops			O	S C D		O	
13. Direct Contact with Affected Property Owners		C D					
14. Response Forms							

Figure 2 Public highway agency action plans (Department of Transportation).

15. Newsletter						
16. Personal Interviews			s			
17. Audio-Visual Presentations		o				
18. Public Forum			s	c		
19. Project Field Office					D	c
20. Publish Project Development Schedule				D	c	
21. Telephone Hotlines		o				
22. Televised Planning Discussions		o				
23. Project Field Review with Citizens						
24. Mass Mail-outs		o				
25. Citizen Band Radio Announcements		o				
26. Resource Base Analysis						
27. Announcements on Local Bulletin Boards						
28. Public Information Displays						
29. Billboard Advertisements near Project						
30. Press Conferences						

SOURCE: This chart was developed from material contained in the publication *Public Highway Agency Action Plans,* Volumes 1 & 2, prepared by the FHW.

Figure 2 (Continued)

Also included in this approach is "everything defined as records in the Federal Records Act—all material created or received regardless of physical format." This includes audiovisual records, scientific and technical reports, and publications other than the normal directives and agency administrative publications.

But as the 1974 NARS study points out "many costs related to processing of information and records are not obvious because they are placed under a budget category of 'Other Services,' and no civil service employees are involved." These costs, then, tend to be invisible, and have led to the Commission's use of the phrase "shadow government" in the title and text of this report. These costs, then, are a second major cost category and are called "Indirect Information and Records Costs," or more simply "shadow costs."

In the case of these "shadow costs" our research tried to "pick up the trail" from whatever source and place seemed useful. These included Congressional hearings on bills, public hearings, internal agency budget material, and many others.

Another approach pursued was to review major projects which were large enough to be "visible" and stand out as "line items" in planning and budget documents. Some of these are listed in Figure [3]. This makes it possible to track back to agency project managers and program officials and thereby obtain a reasonably authoritative judgment on that portion of the project's overall costs related to "information and records."

Additional notes on methodology are discussed under the various individual headings. . . .

Direct Information and Records Costs

Based on the Information and Records (I&R) approach, Figure [4] shows minimum annual costs of government information, communication and paperwork in excess of $40 billion. However, as both Figures [3] and [4] indicate, these costs are merely *examples* of *some* of the I&R costs of the Federal Government. They are not presented here as a definitive, all inclusive list of paperwork costs. Some of them are relatively "complete" for a particular area, such as personnel, printing, postage, etc. Other items are just partial costs for a particular area. This is true, for example, of "space costs," which represent *only* the office space under GSA/PBS control. And of the "communication costs of the civilian agencies," which, again, represent only those activities under GSA/ADTS control.

While the basic accounting data needed to estimate I&R costs is now maintained by most agencies, present systems do not permit easy extraction

	(Cost Estimate Millions)[1]
Library of Congress—James Madison Building	$123.
Commerce—NOAA—Automation of Field Operation and Services	46.5
Air Force Satellite Communications Program (AFSATCOM)	167.5
Defense Satellite Communications System—Space Segment (AF)	505.3
AF Satellite Data System	281.8
Army Defense Satellite Communications System—Grd Segment	902.8
Navy AN-UNK-5 Shipboard Management Information System Computer	31.4
Fleet Satellite Communication System	728.6
New Lister Hill National Center for Biomedical Communications	26.2
FBI Automated Identification Division System	57.2
Social Security Computer Center Building, Woodlawn, Maryland	73.
NASA Landsat C	47.9
NASA Seasat	70.5
VA Compensation, Pension and Education Computer Target System	81.7
	$3,143.4 or $3.1 billion

[1]The costs involved are included in various items in Figure [4].

Figure 3   Selected major projects relating to information, communication and records.

and aggregating of the cost data. The need for cost data is evident, for example, in the cross-cutting computations performed by OMB for the Special Analysis section of the President's Budget, using the internal cost accounts set up by some agencies for just such a purpose.

If true costs could be determined, in short, they would probably range *between $50–$60 billion*. But as Figure [4] indicates, even this amount does *not* include an additional estimated $11,476,200,000 of paperwork costs paid from Federal funds in carrying out Federal programs at the State and local level. Nor does it include an additional $13 billion for contractor paperwork burdens in major procurement actions, reimbursements to carriers for medicare, or a variety of information and record functions contracted out (consultants, graphics, composition, procedural manuals, etc.). And still other expenses are omitted.

1. Salaries of White Collar Workers Doing I&R Work $19,442,270,141
2. Salaries of Blue Collar Workers Doing I&R Work   860,744,844
3. Salaries of Military Personnel—Officers Doing I&R Work   1,326,935,608
4. Salaries of Military Personnel—Enlisted Doing I&R Work   2,552,291,772
5. Salaries of Foreign Nationals—Indirect Hires   414,500,000
6. Printing   951,000,000
7. Postage   549,673,000
8. Office Space (GSA controlled—SLUC only)   817,228,000
9. ADP Space (GSA controlled—SLUC only)   18,940,392
10. Communications Civilian Agencies (voice, data—GSA/
    ADTS control) (excludes personnel)   357,000,000
11. Communication DOD (voice, data satellite) (excludes
    personnel)   3,836,000,000
12. ADP Operations (excludes personnel) FY-76   6,120,966,000
13. Advertising (Recruiting—DOD) FY-76 (excludes person-
    nel)   147,330,000
14. DOD Publication of Newspapers and Periodicals (excludes
    personnel)   25,847,347
15. New Construction—"Information and Records" Buildings: 81,000,000
       *Library of Congress—James A. Madison Building
       *Social Security Computer Center, Woodlawn, Md.
       *Lister Hill Center for Biomedical Communications
        DOD Admin. Bldgs.
       (Cost prorated over 4 year average construction period)
16. Office Supplies and Equipment   1,100,000,000
17. Rents and Communications   1,337,000,000
18. Intelligence Information and Record Costs (including
    personnel)   3,300,000,000
                                                           TOTAL $43,238,727,104

Figure 4   Information communication and records (I&R) costs.[1]

[1]This does *not* include an additional $24 billion of paperwork costs paid from Federal funds ($11 Direct, $13 Indirect—See Table 1) in carrying out Federal programs at the State and local level, contractor paperwork burdens in major procurement, reimbursements to carriers for medicare, and a variety of information and record functions contracted out (consultants, graphics, composition, procedural manual, etc.)....

Salaries (1-5)*. The single largest item of expense in the Direct I&R category is the $24.5 billion in salaries and benefits paid to the 1,568,472 individuals (man-year equivalent) involved with I&R work for the Federal Government. This includes an estimated 382,014 man-years of uniformed personnel time.

   *These parenthetical numbers are keyed to Figure [4].

The total man-year equivalent time for I&R work was obtained through detailed analysis of civilian occupational services listed in the CSC Handbook of Occupational Groups and Series. The CSC handbook contains over 400 individual groups and series of classes of occupations of white collar workers. Nearly 300 of these series were reviewed in an attempt to determine their degree of involvement with Information and Records (I&R). Key terms looked for were such words as data, records, reviews, analyzes, processes, manages, plans,...coordinates, and similar words which offered clues as to whether the work was information or knowledge oriented as opposed to other types of work, where the major emphasis tended towards noninformation tasks (e.g., a pharmacist filling prescriptions; a laboratory assistant doing tests; guards and marshals guarding or protecting; inspectors grading meat, etc.).

...every occupational series can be classified into one of three groups: (1) a substantial, easily identifiable part of the work involves I&R; (2) a substantial, easily identifiable part of the work does *not* involve I&R; and (3) those series that required detailed study to arrive at a figure on the percent of time the work involves I&R.

While an attempt was made to be consistent in the analysis from series to series and group to group, the decisions were obviously subjective and therefore the possibility for a difference of opinion exists. In most cases, however, the "difficult decision" cases were relatively small in number of personnel (when compared to the total universe of nearly 2 million white collar workers) and high or low estimates tend to cancel each other out.

Discussions on questionable categories were held with knowledgeable personnel at the Commission on Federal Paperwork and with personnel of Federal agencies including the Civil Service Commission.

One of the problems encountered is that the occupational title frequently indicates the educational and professional background required rather than what is done by the individual. For example, comparatively few lawyers in the Federal Government actually appear before courts and most of these are in the Department of Justice. The bulk of lawyers are preparing, reviewing and coordinating regulations, legislation, etc; reviewing applications, claims, contracts or similar documents; and giving legal opinions or advice on assigned projects.

Similarly, many scientists are "desk" scientists rather than "bench" scientists. That is, they are helping *administer* or manage programs that are science oriented. For example, the National Science Foundation and National Institutes of Health have many professional personnel who are involved primarily with operating and managing grant programs. The professional may be classified as a mathematician, biologist, chemist, psychologist, oceanographer, dentist, etc., but the work he or she does in operating and managing a grants program is heavily paperwork and information-intensive.

Following the determination of the percentage of time each occupational service spent in I&R work, the remainder of the work was strictly computational. A summary by major occupational groups of civilian employees is shown in Figure [5].

A similar pattern was followed in arriving at I&R time for military occupations. The degree of comparability to civilian jobs ranged from "identical" to "quite different." To the extent that comparability could be determined an attempt was made to "cross match" the two and assign the same factor. However, the possibility for mistakes or errors in judgment is always present. Again, the size of the universe would tend to have high and low estimates cancel each other out. The lack of readily available data did not permit the same level of detailed analysis as in the civilian positions but it was sufficient to arrive at what we consider a reasonably accurate bottom line figure. See Figure [6] for a list of military occupational groups involved in I&R.

Summary

This study has tried to demonstrate that the aggregate paperwork, information and communication costs to the American taxpayer are truly astronomical and that action must be taken on a number of fronts simultaneously to help bring these costs under control. Most people are simply unaware that the country has entered the "Information Age." The terms "Information Society" and "Information Economy" have finally entered the lexicon of public speakers, after having been used for years by information professionals. But the implications of these notions to the "man in the street" have yet to be widely recognized, much less understood. Government, industry, the professions, academia and other groups all have a role to play in explaining, clarifying, interpreting and translating the meaning of this post-industrial information age to the citizen. This study contends that a good way to start would be to make visible total paperwork, information and communication costs to all parties concerned.

One of the major reasons government agencies may not accord full and appropriate attention to paperwork, information and communication costs is because these expenses are dispersed and submerged in a wide variety of program accounts, such as Social Security, Highway Safety, Pollution Control, and virtually thousands of other accounts. And in overhead accounts with such fuzzy labels as "Other Services."

POSITION GROUP	White Collar[1] Total	% of Time in I&R	I&R Personnel Man-Year Equiv.	Aver. Salary	I&R Salaries
Mis. Occupations	49,147	22	11,283	12,583	$141,973,989
Soc. Sc., Psy. Welfare	48,201	83	40,279	19,357	768,930,823
Pers. Mgmt. Ind. Relat.	43,830	90	39,559	15,790	630,952,610
Gen. Admin., Clerk Off. Ser.	472,157	100	472,157	12,428	5,867,992,052
Biological Sciences	45,615	24	11,252	15,851	178,355,452
Accounting & Budget	119,463	95	114,325	15,265	1,745,171,125
Med. Hosp. Den. Pub. Health	117,409	10	11,740	13,948	163,749,520
Veterinary Med. Science	2,828	10	282	21,438	6,045,516
Engineer & Architecture	151,560	45	68,879	10,843	1,435,644,997
Legal and Kindred	58,262	76	44,559	16,052	715,261,068
Information and Arts	20,358	86	17,656	17,508	309,121,248
Business & Industry	29,332	83	57,922	17,521	1,014,851,362
Copy-Patent	1,641	100	1,641	26,661	43,750,701
Physical Science	41,643	25	10,736	21,296	228,633,856
Library and Archives	9,173	100	9,173	14,921	136,870,333
Mathematics and Statistics	14,266	89	12,792	19,816	253,486,272
Equip. Facilities, Svc.	14,690	51	7,509	18,804	141,199,236
Education	28,160	42	11,951	15,208	181,750,808
Investigation	45,206	40	18,192	18,749	341,018,808
Qual. Assur. Inspection.	18,748	67	12,733	17,295	220,217,235
Transportation	43,509	60	26,840	19,110	512,912,400
Supply	62,390	91	56,978	13,116	747,232,448
Unspecified	8,559	10	855	19,071	16,305,705
Postal Group	489,638	15	73,445	14,045	1,031,535,025
TOTAL	1,935,785		1,142,456		$16,833,116,589
				10% of fringe benefits	1,683,331,165
					$18,516,447,754
				5% of salary increase (Oct. 1976)	925,882,387
					$19,442,270,141

[1]Based on data from U.S. Civil Service Commission.

Figure 5 White collar personnel involved in processing and use of information and records (I&R) Oct-1975.

	Enlisted Occupation	N	% I&R	M.Y. EQUIV.
15X	ADP Computers	7,455	100	7,455
16X	Teletype and Cryptographic Equipment	15,524	100	15,524
222	Air Traffic Controller	10,830	100	10,830
26X	Communications Center Operations	24,591	100	24,591
23&24	Communications—Other	31,882	100	31,882
40X	Photography	6,343	100	6,343
41X	Mapping	7,992	50	3,996
42X	Weather	5,713	20	1,142
496	Other Technical Specialists and Aides	462	50	232
500	Personnel, General	34,855	85	29,658
501	Recruiting and Counseling	7,750	50	3,875
510	Administration, General	65,137	85	55,368
511	Stenography	727	100	727
512	Legal	3,636	80	2,910
513	Medical	4,173	10	417
514	Transportation	10,186	90	9,168
515	Postal	2,733	100	2,733
516	Aviation Maintenance Records and Reports	6,977	100	6,977
517	Flight Operations	5,089	50	2,544
520	Combined Personnel and Admin., General	3,775	85	3,211
521	First Sergeants and Sergeants Major	4,006	85	3,406
531	Data Processing Operators/Analysts	10,884	100	10,884
532	Programmers	3,509	100	3,509
541	Auditing and Accounting	3,910	100	3,910
542	Disbursing	11,029	100	11,029
551	Supply Administration	61,000	90	54,900
552	Unit Supply	19,754	50	9,877
561	Chaplain's Assistants	2,425	10	242
562	Recreation and Welfare	3,137	10	313
570	Information and Education, General	6,160	50	3,080
740	Lithography, General	2,003	100	200
				300,133
	Officer Occupation			
3A,B,C	Communications	10,043	100	10,043
4J	Safety	770	50	385
5A	Physical Scientists	1,857	20	1,487
5B	Meteorologists	1,817	20	362
5C	Biological Scientists	441	20	88
5D	Social Scientists	219	80	175
5F	Legal	3,662	80	2,930
5J	Mathematicians and Statisticians	182	80	146
5K	Educators and Instructors	1,914	50	957
5L	Research and Development Coordinators	462	80	350
6E	General Nurses	6,331	10	633
6G	Veterinarians	704	10	70
7A	Administrators, General	8,451	90	7,606
7B	Training Administrators	3,160	90	2,844
7C	Manpower and Personnel	7,614	85	6,416
7D	Comptrollers and Fiscal	3,714	100	3,714
7E	Data Processing	3,661	100	3,661
7F	Pictorial	423	100	423
7G	Information	1,201	100	1,201
7H	Police	3,930	85	3,341
				46,899

Figure 6 Military personnel in I&R work.

But whatever the label of the account, and whether direct program or indirect overhead, the job of virtually every government worker (and for that matter every occupation in society in general), from Cabinet Secretary to Messenger, includes at least one common denominator: collecting, processing, using, disseminating and communicating information, and keeping a variety of records to get the job done. How well and how fast the job gets done depends, to a significant degree, on the policies and procedures related to the creation, processing, storing and retrieving of data, documents and literature.

Beyond government, there is increasing evidence that the percentage of time spent in information handling activities by the professions is also increasing. For example, a recent HEW study on nursing activity indicated that one-third of the nurse's work-day, whether in hospitals or ambulatory care settings, is devoted to information handling of one kind or another. "Many questions have been raised about the information burden that nurses have assumed, including its relevance and usefulness to decisionmaking."[5]

Note that although the HEW study quoted...states that ⅓ of a nurse's work-day is spent on information activities, we had used in this study the figure of 10 percent for nurses' time spent on I&R duties. This is an "underestimate," by comparison, of 23 percent.

Not only are information processing costs submerged and hidden in program operations, but as agencies have taken advantage of new information handling technologies, the very character of the communication process between government and the people it serves has changed. For example, much of the hard copy documentation previously sent through the mail in the form of letters or reports is now being sent by other means—magnetic tape, dataphones, microfilm reels, beamed via satellite transmissions, sent by facsimile methods, and so on. An image or representation of the data or document is sent, instead of the original data or documents themselves.

Also, paper records and file cabinets are being supplemented, and in many cases supplanted, by computers, video tape, word processing machines, microfilm machines, and other, even more advanced "hardware" and "software." While these technologies certainly have streamlined, sped up, miniaturized and in many cases made more cost effective existing communication processes, at the same time the changing technology of moving information around has made the traditional methods of costing information transmission (mail, correspondence, forms, reports, etc.) more difficult to use, and in some cases virtually obsolete.

For example, mail may be sent from one location to another electronically, by-passing the mail room entirely. Should dataphones be charged to telephone or mail? The "mail" object account is thus substantially understating the expenses connected with information transmission. "Mail," in short, is undergoing a complete transformation and accounting definitions and systems haven't kept up with this metamorphosis.

The same can be said of "postage," "utilities," "rents," and other traditional object classifications and definitions. They are rooted in hard copy media, and the traditional and conventional ways of dealing with information and communications twenty or thirty years ago. But beginning in the fifties, a radical transformation began to occur in the information and communication fields with the advent of the greatly expanded use of computers, telecommunications capabilities and other associated technologies.

Computers, for example, produce letters and address envelopes. Are these, then, "correspondence and mail costs" or "ADP costs"? Many reports are prepared by computers from data stored (filed) and then prepared in a variety of selected formats, also stored in the computer. Are these form costs, reporting costs or ADP costs?

Directives and regulations are stored on magnetic disks and drums, tapes and microfiche, as well as on and in other advanced media for ease of updating and distribution. Telephone lines are used both for transmitting data and voice communications. ADP operations require special space and auxiliary equipment, as well as a variety of highly specialized support personnel. Some agencies charge such support personnel to ADP functions; others do not.

In short, we have indeed entered the Information Age; we are, to be sure, an Information Economy; and ours is fast becoming an Information Society. But our accounting, budgeting, management and control structures and systems haven't kept up with this transformation. Consequently, we don't "see" what is happening. We must move now to effect the changes recommended in this report to keep the paperwork and information impact on the American taxpayer from getting completely out of hand.

References

1. Porat, Marc, Ph.D. thesis, "The Information Economy" and "The Information Economy Definition and Measurement," Department of Commerce, OT Special Publication 77-12(1), May 1977, GPO Stock No. 003-000-00512-7.
2. Beveridge, George, article in *Washington Star* 4/19/76.
3. Washington Researchers, News Release—Philip Hozenah—February 14, 1977.
4. King, Donald W., "An Estimate of the Value of Scientific and Technical Informa-

tion Derived from Federal Funds," April 1977 Study prepared for Commission on Federal Paperwork.
5. "Systematic Nursing Assessment, a Step Toward Automation," DHEW Publication No. (HRA) 74-17, research performed under Public Health Service Contract NIH 70-4132 (PH 108-69-17), Eugene Levine, Ph.D., Scientific Editor.

Additional Readings

Bernard, Dan; Emery, James C.; Nolan, Richard L.; and Scott, Robert H. *Charging for Computer Services: Principles and Guidelines.* New York, Petrocelli Books, 1977.

Dearden, John. "Computers and Profit Centers." In: *The Impact of Computers on Management.* Edited by Charles A. Meyers. Cambridge, Mass., MIT Press, 1967, pp. 174–203.

Dearden, John, and Nolan, Richard L. "How to Control the Computer Resources." *Harvard Business Review, 51:*68–78, November/December 1973.

Marshak, Jacob. "Economics of Information Systems." In: *Frontiers of Quantitative Economics.* Edited by M. D. Intrilligator. Amsterdam, North-Holland Publishing, 1972, pp. 32–106.

———. "Economics of Inquiry, Communications, Deciding." *American Economic Review, 58:*1–18, May 1968.

Nolan, Richard L. "Controlling the Costs of Data Services." *Harvard Business Review, 55:*144–124, July/August 1977.

———. "Managing the Crises in Data Processing." *Harvard Business Review, 57:*115–126, March/April 1979.

Knutsen, Eric K., and Nolan, Richard L. "Assessing Computer Costs and Benefits." *Journal of Systems Management, 25:*28–34, February 1974.

U.S. Comptroller General. *Illustrative Accounting Procedures for Federal Agencies—Guidelines for Accounting for Automated Data Processing Costs.* Washington, D.C. General Accounting Office, 1978.

Verhelst, M. "Elements of Information Economics for Management." *ICP Interface Administrative and Accounting, 1977:*14–18, Winter 1977.

Chapter 5

INFORMATION MANAGEMENT: POLICY FORMULATION, ANALYSIS, AND EVALUATION

Our most insistent social information processing problems are not a simple function of inadequate data. They stem from the inadequacy of the information processing structures that form our social systems.

—Edgar S. Dunn, Jr., *Social Information Processing and Statistical Systems—Change and Reform*

In recent years, the interests of practitioners and scholars in policy analysis have neglected the role of information in public policy. This statement seems puzzling until one understands certain attitudes.

In "The Role of Information in Policy Analysis," Mark E. Tompkins notes that although interest in and investigation of policy analysis have increased, the focus has been on the constraints on the various parties involved in political action and the development of decision-making models and tools, rather than on the uses of information to help or hinder public decision making and policy formulation. As Tompkins suggests, the process of producing information to support policy analysis and evaluation has been inadequately considered, affecting the ways in which information systems or services have been designed. Tompkins defines six information-based activities connected to policy analysis and examines the implications of each. He suggests that information is not neutral in the service of political interests and, therefore, is a key resource in skewing the biases of the decision-making process in various directions. Although such biases in data gathering can be expected, Tompkins suggests that there are systematic biases against collecting individually based information about externalities and negative victim-based impacts in the public policy process. Tompkins argues that these biases must be corrected by making policy analysis responsible to multiple rather than single constituents.

In the second selection, "Information Problem No. 2: The Symbolic Representation of Entities," Edgar S. Dunn, Jr. suggests that the most persistent information-processing problems are not caused simply by inadequate data but result from inadequacies in the way in which persons view the operations of complex social systems. Analysts and bureaucrats often rely on low-level information collection and processing to deal with high-level information requirements because they are unable to revise and alter their perspectives and values when rapid changes occur in their organizations or the outside world. "Entity fixation" occurs, which leads to the "reification" of data; that is, decision makers ask for more of the same data when they confront new problems and issues. In the statistical organization, this situation usually results in the collection of masses of traditional static indicators rather than dynamic performance measures that are more responsive to and appropriate for rapidly changing environments.

Managing information to support policy formulation, analysis, and evaluation is a challenging and complex task involving questions about the adequacy of human powers of perception, organization design, and the development of responsive information systems and services. In the final two selections, these questions are raised in the context of the information-processing needs and requirements of Congress and the state legislatures. In "Information Support for Congress: The Role of Technology," Robert Lee Chartrand surveys the evolution of the use of information technology by Congress since the early 1960s. Faced with increasing demands to deal with new and complex policy issues and problems, Congress has sought to utilize modern information technology to cope with its information needs. Chartrand observes that not only has Congress made significant use of information technology, especially in its administrative and housekeeping functions, but the members have become more receptive to developing new applications and to examining the effects that technology has on society.

The final selection, John J. Stucker's "Assessing the Role and Impact of Information Technology in the Legislative Environment," considers developments in the use of information technology by state legislatures. Stucker reviews past efforts to survey the use and impact of this technology in state legislatures and develops a typology for understanding the conditions for using the technology in legislative processes. Taking a less sanguine attitude than Chartrand, Stucker does not feel that the states are making optimal use of information technology. He identifies the preconditions necessary for members of legislatures and their staffs to use this technology as well as the major constraints and issues that have not really been examined. In the context of state legislatures, Stucker raises all the questions that Tompkins and Dunn suggested in recognizing the role of information in policy analysis, developing adequate organization structures and processes to elicit reliable information, and acknowledging the limits of a person's ability to deal with rapid and complex changes in his environment.

The Role of Information in Policy Analysis

Mark E. Tompkins

The increasing responsibility of the public sector in recent years has been met by society's increased interest in learning how successfully public organizations meet their demands. This concern has led to interest in policy analysis and in those persons who practice the craft. Academics now train professional policy analysts, bureaucracies hire them, and journals publish their research, while citizens and their representatives expect public programs to be "analyzed."[1] Policy analysis is still a young field, in which important issues are emerging. The critical role that information plays in focusing and limiting or enhancing policy analysis is one such issue that is often neglected.

Many investigations of policy analysis focus on the role played by diverse and conflicting interests or on the development of methods to improve decision making and the application of these methods to public problems. Although these investigations focus, limit, and enhance policy debates, available information does as well. Moreover, available or unavailable information affects the ability of interest groups to achieve their goals and constrains the use of these sophisticated methods. Consider, for example, the frequent, recent debates about national health insurance. The cost of a proposal is a central feature of any such debate. As a result, analyses must incorporate cost estimates; these estimates affect the chances of success of any proposal. Opponents of national health insurance have been aided by estimates of costs indicating that substantial new federal funding will be required. In turn, the analyses that produce these estimates have become more complex and controversial.

These issues are only touched on in other work. Organization theorists raise some issues in discussing "uncertainty." Their work often focuses on an organization's ability to adapt to its environment but neglects an organization's ability to shape its environment.[2] These limitations also appear in other work, such as research into the psychology of decision making.[3]

More attention should be paid to the link between information and policy analysis to help us appreciate the role of analysis in furthering particular political interests and in limiting their influence, to lead to more realistic expectations for analysis and the difference it will make, and to lead to a better understanding of how information services should be designed to serve the "art and craft" of policy analysis. In this reading, the role that information plays in this analysis effort will be examined.

Some groundwork must be laid for this review. *Policy* and *policy analysis* must be described. The description must account for the role of analysis in serving some interests and their causes at the expense of other interests. This role is connected with another, quite different instrumental role, which involves the common justification of analysis as a way to learn more about the world one hopes to improve or at least as a way to reduce uncertainty about it. For example, recall the problem facing analysts of national health insurance proposals. Better estimates of the costs of a particular proposal improve understanding, but they also aid opponents of the proposals. These intertwined roles emerge in the political process, of course, so that analysis typically strives for a middle ground between the desire for more knowledge and the service of particular political interests.[4] A better understanding of the dilemmas of analysis permits the investigation of the information that supports it. Information involves a variety of different phenomena, which are divided here into several distinctive processes. Only then can one investigate the various uses of analysis and the information included in it as well as the various users of analysis and information and the different interests they have in the process. This investigation produces some general conclusions about the consequences of particular ways of organizing information services, at least insofar as they affect policy analysis. These conclusions go beyond the simple prescriptions that now abound in the literature, which often argue either for "redundancy" and duplication as a rational strategy or for neat, integrated systems as an approach to information management.[5]

The Nature of Policy and Its Analysis

Closer study of policy and the policy process has made it increasingly clear that neither can be captured by simple, tidy descriptions. Policy emerges through activity that takes place in a number of settings, including the processes of legislation, administration, and adjudication: What happens in one setting often affects what occurs in another. Many different actors are involved in establishing policy, but their participation and influence vary. Their purposes are not always clear (even to them); in fact, they emerge and sometimes shift in the course of policymaking. For national health insurance proposals, proponents are now more interested in containing costs and phasing in federal responsibility.[6] Moreover, the participants' perspectives on the issues often differ; to understand their actions, one must appreciate these differences.

In studying policy in a particular area, another problem emerges. Policy evolves through a series of decisions and indecisions, rather than springs forth as a single, fully formed decision on a particular day. Therefore, the decision to study policy at a particular time matters.

If policy analysis is to succeed, it must focus and limit the field of inquiry. Yet the label seems to be casually applied to a variety of activities. Many different types of work use or attract the label. One can understand this diversity best by discussing a definition of policy analysis and highlighting two of its implications.

E. S. Quade offers a good working definition: Policy analysis is "any type of analysis that generates and presents information in such a way as to improve the basis for policy makers to exercise their judgement."[7] Heclo and Jones add to this definition by noting that some types of analysis frame issues, resolve questions of scope, and focus attention on certain relationships to the neglect of others.[8] At times, analysts have greater freedom of action than they do in other situations.[9] This definition focuses attention both on the fact that any analysis must eventually find a client whose judgment it affects and on the instrumental role that analysis plays. Although the clients for an analysis need not be immediately apparent, policy analysis that fails to find an interested party eventually loses value.

Purposive orientation is a critical feature of analysis. Because of the impact of an analysis on a person's judgment and perhaps decision, some interests are served at the expense of others;[8] those persons who favor the choice made have reason to be pleased, whereas those who oppose it do not.[9] Once acknowledged, purposive orientation raises a problem for analysis. How does analysis avoid becoming the unquestioning servant of those who see the world in a particular way? In that role, it would become an instrumental resource, serving those interests at the expense of the interests of persons who lacked access to these analytic resources. For example, Thomas L. McNauger found that the Army's traditional statement of the infantryman's role as a marksman focused the analysis of an experimental rifle, which eventually became the M-16, on its use for this mission, thus delaying appreciation of its value for other missions.[10]

A paradox exists here. The best policy analysis does not define its purposes too narrowly, since doing so would unduly limit its ability to improve the judgment of others whose purposes are defined differently. More successful analysis reduces the dependence of policy analysis on a particular client through the "publicness" of its processes. Good policy analysis "widens the area of informed judgement"[11] by aiding a number of actors in the policy process, notwithstanding their initial biases and presumptions. This action occurs "by making information available and laying bare hidden assumptions and value preferences,"[12] which opens up the technical choices made in the course of sophisticated methodologies for scrutiny by outside actors (where they concur, their confidence in conclusions is enhanced; where they disagree, attention is rightly directed to areas of disagreement). By exposing the analytic process and its product to critical scrutiny, the likelihood of the analysis affecting the judgment of the larger community is improved, since confidence in the findings will be increased if the community understands the process that led to them.[13]

Through its impact on judgment, analysis constrains the impact of the actions of narrow, conservative interests. One of the most effective counters to pleas for change is an appeal to "uncertainty," often made on behalf of those persons who prefer no action. Since any decision-making process (or, indeed, any process that leads to changes in the environment) that involves several actors and substantial resources will probably involve diverse, divergent, and diffuse interests, as well as interests in direct conflict, this uncertainty may play different roles for each of the actors. Opponents of national health insurance base their opposition on the uncertainties involved in estimating the costs of a proposal. Others view these problems as emerging from fundamental power relations (e.g., between doctor and patient) and argue that these relations should be restructured as part of any plan. Still others question the role played by new technology in the delivery costs of medicine; this leads them to raise other issues.

The uncertainty may be based on differing objectives (What is to be done?), levels of aspiration (How much should be done?), desired timing (When should it happen?), the means (How should it be done?), the perspective on external consequences (How much does one care about the effect that this action will have on others?), and the relationship between this problem and others. To the extent that actors disagree over objectives, aspirations, timing, or external consequences, analysis will do little except serve the narrow interests favored by its conclusions (these interests might involve a few individuals, an organization, or a group of actors agreed on a course of action). Analysis can do so by reducing the uncertainty about a particular action, by biasing knowledge in favor of an action (e.g., highlighting the benefits of that action or the costs associated with alternatives), or by resolving uncertainty in a way that favors one course of action or slights others.[14]

On the other hand, when disagreement occurs over the nature of a problem, then analysis may help resolve conflicts. Most analysis takes place on middle ground, where findings are not neutral in their implication; yet such findings can improve one's understanding of a problem. Any prescription for information services must be sensitive to the dual roles analysis plays in serving some interest and pursuing better understanding.

Still, the notion of *reduced uncertainty* may seem curious. Uncertainty generally implies a pervasive form of not knowing—not only is it unknown how likely particular alternatives are, but it also is uncertain what they are.[15] The first problem can be expected, since knowledge is often based on samples from the real world (raising one set of information-services questions). In making inferences from these samples to the larger world in which one works, one takes relatively well-understood risks. Uncertainty implies much more important gaps in understanding at the outset and less complete resolution of these gaps as a consequence of analysis. Still, policy analysts are generally agreed on the limitations of the enterprise and the focus of hopes. Carol Weiss presents a similar view in "Improving the Linkage Between Social Research and Public Policy":[16]

Research evidence does sometimes serve to reduce conflict by narrowing the zone of uncertainty. It establishes which variables are implicated in outcomes, something about their relative importance, and the interrelationships among them. It keeps people from arguing about what actually is, and saves them time to deal with the issue of values—with what ought to be. Although it does not resolve the policy issue, it focuses debate more sharply on its problematical and value-related facets.

Some examples will illustrate the point.

In considering the issue of "welfare policy," Lynn examines the evolution of the "income maintenance system" since the onset of the war on poverty. He concludes that "The sum total of experience with the existing system and the results of the research on poverty have irrevocably altered the content of the welfare reform debate."[17] The "cost" issue has become the key element in the debate over reform. Social experimentation, like that involved in the work-incentive experiments in which negative income tax proposals were actually tested, provides an immediate example of analysis that narrowed the terms of debate without ending it. In that case, Moynihan argues that the experiments served to defuse the potential issue of the effect that a "negative income tax" would have on the work behavior of clients.[18]

Discussions of proposals to provide a national health insurance program have increasingly focused on the interplay between the increase in demand that such an effort would involve and the constraints on supply.[19] This concern stems from consideration of the impact of earlier efforts to improve access to services, such as those involved in Medicare and Medicaid legislation.[20] Other, more specific analyses also focus debate and improve judgment but still leave important elements of uncertainty intact.[21]

Other human services present a similar picture. Wilson outlines several areas in which society's understanding of the "crime problem" has improved, but he remains pessimistic about society's ability to make more than modest progress in "solving" it.[22] An increasingly complex debate is emerging over the appropriate policy to follow in the quest for desegregation in education.[23] Analysis figures prominently in the debate about which risks are appropriate for workers to take in their workplaces and the role the Federal Government should play in limiting risks.[24]

The role of analysis is not confined to human-services programs. Walker discusses this point in an article focused on "wetlands preservation," arguing that "ecology is a particularly politicized field at this time"[25] and finding himself in a debate over the degree of politicization of information and the range of uncertainty. Years ago, Ashley Schiff examined the dual role of science and politics in the Forest Service.[26] In discussing regulatory policy, economists have developed a critique of current standard-setting practices, such as those used in pollution control, which depend on the presence of some, but not enough, information about the problems involved.[27] Enthoven and Smith, writing about the systems analysis revolution in the Defense Department, discuss the role of "analysis as the servant of judgement, not a replacement for it."[28]

Uncertainty figures in another argument made about gathering information to support analysis. This position suggests that the costs of gathering information are too high to support collecting data before its potential uses are known. How useful information is cannot be determined until it is known how it will be used. If information is collected before it is known whether it will be used, then resources might have been wasted on useless information. This view is identified with those who argue that "comprehensive rationality" is seldom possible in large social systems and that, as a result, most decisions are made through the "mutual adjustment" of diverse and divergent interests.[29] As a consequence, information should be gathered only to support someone's identified interest. Information serves partial interests (i.e., one group's wishes at the expense of another's), but the notion should be rejected that this is its only function. Besides diversity and divergence of interests, one should also expect some elements of common interest and understanding—where this is true, information will play a straightforward role in reducing uncertainties about desirable courses of action.[30]

An extreme version of this view—information is collected only when it serves an identified interest—neglects the important limiting consequences of this choice and ignores the possibility that information may stimulate the development of new interests,[31] catalyze the agreement of existing ones, or reshape the preferences of groups bent on another course of action. In short, analysis and its information foundation can be both causes and consequences. If the collection of information is limited to whatever serves identified interests, understanding will be biased in favor of the present situation and those with a stake in it.

Retrospective consideration of information involves important biases. After the fact, one recalls information selectively. Particular items are remembered as important, but one's judgment of importance is clouded by one's perceptions and by subsequent events. Information is lost because of the attention and inattention of those charged with its maintenance. Wohlstetter's examination of the attack on Pearl Harbor illustrates the problem: In analyses of the "failure," much attention was paid to information indicating an attack was likely, but little consideration was given to conflicting information that was available.[32] In the jargon of communication theorists, it is much easier to separate a "signal" from surrounding "noise" if it is known what the signal should be. It is hard to overestimate one's ability to interpret information as supporting preexisting hypotheses; thus, retrospective information gathering and processing are more likely to reinforce initial impressions.

The alternative of prospectively gathered information also involves biases that must be considered.[33] One of the most important biases is that prospective analysis appears to lead users to overstate their ability to control and manipulate events and to plan as though they can.[34] Still, gathered information may result in additional flexibility in analyses, since some information gathered and produced will prove useful in ways that users did not anticipate when they collected it. The risks involved, however, may complement those involved in retrospective information gathering. Whether or not they do, the alternative certainly constrains the use of information and aids some interests at the expense of others. Therefore, information services supporting analysis must strive for a balance between the costs of collecting information and the trade-offs inherent in its collection, either because an established group can use the information immediately or because the information may be useful in the future.

Policy analysis is judged by its service to persons involved in the policy process and by its contribution to their understanding and judgment. The role that information plays as a resource for analysis must be examined, since gaps in information become gaps in knowledge, and available information can be used to improve judgment in the future, if not now. Many elements are involved in producing information, however. These elements will be examined separately in the next section.

The Stages of Information Production

The five stages of information production are data gathering, data processing, information processing, attention focusing, and storage and retrieval.[35] Analyzing these stages will help develop the argument that follows. Action or inaction is possible in each stage; either will have consequences for subsequent decision making.[36] The consequences can be regarded as constraints because they limit debate, foreclose alternatives, define issues in particular ways, and provide selectively useful resources (in the form of knowledge) for use in the policy process.

1. Data gathering discretely represents a particular case along a dimension. Social-services clients are classified as "married" or "single," an organization delivers a particular number of units of service, or a geographic area is classified as a "wetland." These actions often result in several data points, for a number of cases, along several dimensions. Neither the descriptions of the individual cases (except for the common reference to a dimension) nor the various dimensions are related to each other at this stage and so are seldom useful for analysis. The descriptions are individualized and serve only to evoke ideas, such as the story of the Chicago "welfare mother" who illegally collected thousands of dollars in benefits; Ronald Reagan used this story during his 1976 presidential campaign.[37]

2. Data processing aggregates case data in a particular dimension. Symbolic representations,[38] data reduction and transformation strategies, and capacities all increase in importance (e.g., through requirements that the categories used in processing remain few enough to be manageable). Descriptive statistics also are an important tool at this stage. Social-services clients are summarized by the proportion with various marital statuses, the average number of service units delivered by an organization are reported, or a larger geographic area is described by the amount that is wetland. Data processing reduces the amount of information reported about a particular case (e.g., How long were the clients married? How did each organization perform? Exactly where are the wetlands?) so that researchers can obtain an easily summarized and understood result.

3. Information processing interrelates processed data. Interrelating data may lead to claims that one factor causes another (e.g., well-managed

organizations deliver more services) or to simpler claims that two or more factors are associated (e.g., social-services clients tend to be poor). Information processing may produce a summary describing several simpler dimensions (e.g., a wetland is land that is periodically inundated, with flora dependent on the inundation). Multivariate statistics and strategies now dominate information processing. Completely processed information often requires descriptions of the universe of application (e.g., the city of Chicago) and statements about the temporal context (e.g., in the last fiscal year). Some references may imply both, as when a rural area is classified as a region lacking modern transportation facilities.

4. Attention-focusing mechanisms (such as memos, meetings, briefings, and references to material) are the devices that lead to active consideration of the information involved. These devices should be separated because busy decision makers and analysts may ignore even available information. The crucial feature of these devices is their limited capacity, which holds true for both individuals and organizations.[39] Simon's statement of the problem is the most direct: "Attention is the chief bottleneck in organizational activity, and the bottleneck becomes narrower and narrower as we move to the tops of organizations...."[40] These constraints are compounded by the limited enthusiasm people and organizations show for searching for new information and for considering discordant information.[41] This problem is discussed in scholarly literature under several guises. Carol Weiss argued that dissemination of research results is limited, which leads to their neglect ("dissemination" is the problem of getting others to pay attention); Wohlstetter and Downs worried about the problem of "noise" in signaling (read this as a problem of the decision maker's neglect of some information as "mere noise" or useless); students of social systems sometimes focused on "overloads" (presumably produced by too much information) and how they are handled.[42]

5. Storage and memory systems retain material not currently being used. The systems may be files, data banks, libraries, human memory, storehouses, or any of several other items. Retrieval mechanisms, which enable the contents of a store to be recovered, are linked to the storage and memory systems. Retrieval mechanisms allow users to search the contents of a store and to recognize and highlight the appropriate material once they encounter it.

For the remainder of this analysis, these stages will be treated as though they were distinct, even though in practice they overlap. One should not assume, however, that the stages occur in a well-ordered sequence. Any product of the three stages of input processing (data gathering, data processing, and information processing) can be attended to immediately or stored to be retrieved later. At a future date, data can be retrieved for further processing. This model also implies that some data and information are stored without first receiving attention.[43]

One argument for separating the stages is that technological change has affected each stage differently. For example, in the context of organizational theory, Jay Galbraith suggested that when one considers information, new issues are added to the problems associated with designing organizations. Galbraith found that new technology has improved the ability of an information system to meet the demands placed on organizations by helping systems to avoid becoming loaded with more information than they can deal with.[44] Other changes affect information management, including increases in the amount of information handled and a person's interest in that information. These changes can be examined by a review of the five stages in information production.

The ability of organizations to gather data has improved. Among the innovations responsible are computer-read forms, audiotape and videotape, and reproduction technologies such as photoduplication. Although some scientific areas have experienced dramatic improvements,[45] the social sciences have shown only modest gains. Most of these have been incremental and orderly and have caused few disruptions. The enthusiasm for gathering data seems to have changed dramatically, however.[46] To account for this, other aspects of information production must be examined.

The ability of organizations to process data also has improved. Data processing used to involve tidy sequences taken one operation at a time and was limited by the capacity of the hardware. Now hardware capacity has expanded dramatically, and several processing operations can occur simultaneously.[47]

This "revolution" also has had important consequences for information processing. Statistics and other information-processing disciplines continue to advance, the pace accelerated by improvements in computer hardware and software. One example of technological improvement is the development of array processors, which can handle matrix manipulations much more efficiently than older hardware; this innovation, in turn, eases development of solutions to many important problems.[48]

Complexity is the most important characteristic of technological advances. As complexity increases, experts become more important as interpreters of the results. Advances threaten to outstrip even experts' ability to comprehend results. New disciplines, such as operations research, have emerged in response to advances in knowledge.[49] Because the new disciplines represent specialized bodies of knowledge and limited communities, their experts conduct analyses autonomously. Although the amount of knowledge will continue to grow, Winner warned that relative ignorance also will increase.[50] The number of persons who can understand what has happened and the portion of all knowledge that is widely shared are both shrinking.

Moreover, complex information processes can produce information that can be only partly understood. Although one may not know why a particular conclusion emerges, the conclusions are used and have consequences. An early discussion of PERT (the Performance Evaluation Review Technique used in the Polaris program) makes this fact clear by suggesting that one of PERT's benefits was its ability to reveal "interdependencies and problem areas which are either not obvious or not well defined by conventional planning methods."[51] Although the benefits may be real, they also involve risks because they rely on techniques and experts whose work is not widely understood.

Despite progress in other areas, there is no reason to believe that the capabilities of the attention-focusing mechanisms have changed much. Their limits seem to depend on individuals,[52] and organizations' limitations can be traced to individuals' limitations. Although the amount of information that one can consider has not changed greatly, the form of the information certainly has. Therefore, users must pay attention to processed information rather than to raw data. This means that they are studying more cases of data but are relying on other persons or methods to abstract, sample, transform, and select portions of the original universe of data for processing and subsequent presentation. Today, users can know about many subjects, but at the expense of knowing less about individual subjects. People can deal with complex notions about the relationship among items of data without knowing how the data were produced. For example, the Coleman Report findings on the impact of the educational system received much attention, but critiques of the methodologies used received far less consideration.[53]

The capacities of storage and memory systems have increased, and persons are more willing to create and use the systems.[54] Increases in capacity and use result from improvements in computer and reproduction technologies and, perhaps, from changes in society.[55] Because of technological improvements, small spaces no longer limit the amount of information that can be stored, which removes the need to prune record bases. Stores can be expected to grow, because less information will be eliminated from them than before. At the same time, users with access to a larger record base will have a new resource to use to influence analysis and decision making in their favor.

A more remarkable and significant result of technological improvement is that the capacity to retrieve stored material has increased. In addition to advances in computers and associated technology, improvements have occurred in indexing and scanning techniques. In indexing and scanning, another expert is required to retrieve information. Fragmentation of expertise increases the advantages of persons with access to experts in the decision-making process.

Like information processes in general, analysis is becoming more important and is being used by decision makers, despite its problems. But these problems do increase concerns about analysis. Analysis is built on an information foundation; as that foundation becomes more sophisticated and complex, it requires experts to a greater degree. If the information produced by information processes and experts is used uncritically, then the outcome of analysis may largely depend on their decisions. Decision makers cannot be expected to avoid using technology; indeed, it is hoped that they do use it to improve their judgment. One should, however, hold analysts accountable to an explicit standard and to explicit analytic decisions that can be subjected to critical scrutiny. If one does not, the risk is that decision makers and analysts will evade accountability by using the analysis process to rationalize decisions made on other grounds. If one does, then hopefully the judgment of all parties will improve.

Policy analysts also are interested in accountability. Without it, analysis becomes a political tool, serving established interests, and will always be viewed in this way; as a result, other functions of analysis will be neglected.[56]

Using the functions of analysis described and the aspects of information services identified earlier, one can discuss the role that information services play in analysis. This discussion is best conducted by describing various settings using analysis. The final section in this paper contains a description of organizations that issue various types of information and execute and use policy analysis. The description leads to conclusions about the forms of information services in organizations supporting policy analysis.

Information-Services Design

Although the distinctive features of information services have been considered, the organizations in which policy analysis is used and the issues raised by its use have not been examined. There are four different settings, each of which plays a role in policymaking, generating information and analysis but using them differently. If these contingencies are understood, then appropriate settings for the information services involved can be prescribed.

The four organization settings that must be examined include "provision organizations," such as social-service agencies and education institutions, which serve clients directly (persons or other organizations). The second type is "control organizations," which have authority over and accept responsibility for another organization's actions but are not immediately involved in its activity. Control organizations make decisions affecting the provision organization and sometimes focus on it, but they are not directly responsible for carrying out the decisions. The Department of Health and Human Services and the Department of Education are responsible for several programs within their purview that deliver human services. Regulatory agencies are responsible in varying degrees for the organizations they regulate. Environmental regulations are incomplete controls; one reason for limits on their authority is gaps in information. Although environmental regulators have authority to set standards, this authority can be undermined if someone shows that the standards are unreasonable. Environmental regulators cannot obtain all the information about a particular production process needed to make a conclusive judgment; even if they have the information, they lack the resources—including knowledge—that they need to use it wisely. These difficulties have lead to alternate approaches to the problem of incomplete control, for example, through incentives schemes.[57] The third type, "external organizations," has no direct responsibility or authority for the activities of other agencies. The Department of Defense has this relationship with several human-services agencies, for example. The reader should not infer that the actions of external organizations are irrelevant to the actions of other agencies (and vice versa); after all, many armed-services personnel use social services and receive benefits because of their low incomes. The fourth type, "diffuse organizations," is groups of persons who are interested in a course of action but are neither well organized nor able to articulate their view in the policy process.[58] Public interest groups try to transform individuals' interest in a common cause into a well-organized group effort that brings its resources to bear in the political process.

The interrelationship between information services and the organizations that use them can now be discussed. Data-gathering tasks are critical in producing information. All processing and analysis are built on this foundation; a gap can have crippling effects, which can only partly be overcome by estimation, inference, and guesswork. Data gathering is often affected by problems that influence the validity and reliability of subsequent results, but these flaws are seldom well understood. Persons who use the results are even further removed from the flawed process and less prepared to compensate for its effects.[59] This latter point is critical for the following discussion.

Data gathering within and by a provision organization involves many important issues, some strengthening and some weakening the data base produced. The most important strength is the close relationship between persons gathering data and the other functions of the provision organization. Weaknesses in the process, such as those involving gaps in the data, are likely to be well understood or readily discovered. The marginal costs of data gathering to the data collectors are likely to be low when costs can be added to the provision process. There are many problems as well. Provision organizations tend to view data gathering as producing "free goods," in the costs that they involve for the organizations' clients and in the time that their staff is required to spend on such activity. Data are not free, of course, but rather require time, effort, and other resources.[60]

Provision organizations can be expected to "overinvest" in data gathering. They probably overvalue the data collected, since the information is so close to the immediate experience of the persons providing services.[61] The data gathered probably describe the current state of affairs and are biased in favor of readily collected items.[62] Efforts are likely to neglect the collection of data on "external effects," particularly if those effects involve costs to others, since the effects are outside the organization's mission.[63] When one has considered all these biases, it can be seen that outsiders are likely to claim that the provision organization has gathered data only to defend its present activity. That view misses the problems produced by incentive and perspective.[64] As the problem for analysis is defined more broadly, for example, to include alternate approaches, this skewed view will become more limiting. If analysts are not working within the provision organization, they will probably encounter coordination problems because they will want data that the provision organization does not have and considers outside its mission.

Control organizations encompassing provision organizations are better able to integrate several sets of data (by enforcing common rules for their collection and by requiring collection of comparable data by several collectors). If a control organization's responsibilities include a particular effect, the organization may have incentives to enforce the collection of data on external effects. The problem can be highlighted by examining the role of a social-welfare agency. Although control organizations may hope to enforce commonality on the data collected, they are likely to continue to neglect the costs of data collection to the clients involved. The data may be used to demonstrate the impact of other forces on clients, however, as when unemployment increases. Control organizations are seldom in a position to collect data directly, since that would involve costs beyond those incurred by a provision organization.[65]

An external organization will probably have nearly insurmountable problems gaining access to the subjects of data gathering; it may be able to collect some information on external effects if it has an incentive to do so. Environmental groups provide many examples of this type of data gathering; clearly, external organizations are driven by incentives and interests different from those of provision and control organizations, which may be reluctant to release data that may be used against them. The incentives are thought to be powerful, illustrated by these organizations' treatment of employees who are whistleblowers.[66] Most data that these organizations obtain will be handicapped by "representativeness" issues (does this data represent the universe of cases involved in the problem?). Citizen lobby groups often encounter this difficulty, since they find information on specific problems, but must counter the claim that the instances are not typical of the overall problem. This type of data may serve as a catalyst in getting people to act, so it should not be downgraded unduly.

Finally, those persons involved in "diffuse organizations" lack the resources to gather data in any but the most fragmentary fashion. They face problems of access and lack the organization to obtain it. Further, they lack the resources required to perform the subsequent information processing. Available data may serve another catalytic function, providing the justification for organization. Policy analysis in the usual sense, involving comprehensive analysis, is unlikely to come from such a source.

One should recall the important role that data limitations play in policy analysis. If data are not available, collection may take years. In general, data that extend for a long period of time are desirable, especially with policy analysis, because policy intervention involves complex questions requiring sophisticated understanding that necessitates longitudinal analysis. Developing a complex information system takes several years.[67] From the viewpoint of persons who may wish to have data supporting policy analysis, institutional arrangements undervaluing data collection are more distressing.

Data and information processing can be addressed together, although their relationship varies across organizations. Organizations involved in executing a program would be expected to underinvest in both activities. They require the use of typically limited internal resources. For example, once providing information services becomes routine, staff time quickly becomes scarce, while hardware resources may not be constrained. Since Gresham's Law reminds us that programmed activity tends to drive out unprogrammed activity, routine work will dominate nonroutine work. Unless the analysis function is routine,[68] few resources will be devoted to it under ordinary circumstances. One common instance in which analysis is routine is in the monitoring process, which supports management activity.

In provision organizations, one would expect data and information processing to focus on simple tasks supporting the existing orientation and control functions in the organization. Complex inquiries are unlikely, and most activities will involve simple data processing, such as describing the levels of service provided and the populations served. These tasks involve ordinary management activities, of course, so they will be supported. On occasion, the information may prove useful in analysis with a larger scope. Still, the results will be constrained by the frame of reference of the provision organization, which limits critical inquiry.

Control organizations are in a better position to take on data and information processing. By exercising authority, they can enforce access to existing data bases and use them in analyzing broader questions. Because of their distance from data-gathering activities, control organizations may be ignorant or left ignorant of some limitations that these activities involve. Control organizations are likely to be the ultimate locus of any decision-making activity; therefore, not only can the analysis be broadened to meet their perspective, but also its timing can be made responsive to their schedules. This benefit is important, since a major explanation for unused analyses is that they were not available in time for use in decision making. Furthermore, specialized expertise can be incorporated into the analysis process, but now as the servant of the control organization's larger interests. Finally, these arrangements facilitate integration of fragmented data bases. When perspective is broadened, it is not unusual for several organizations to have data bearing on the issues under analysis. Solving all the problems raised may not be possible, since available data still limit analysis, but focusing on resolving these problems will be possible.

External organizations and diffuse organizations will be shut off from inquiry by the problem of data access. Occasionally, an external organization, at the sufferance of a control organization, may be permitted access; in these cases, it may function as an agent of the control organization. Still, both types of organizations may be able, through partial analyses, to perform an important political role in shaping perceptions and defining an agenda. Their actions are likely to involve some form of simplified analysis, broadening or redefining the focus of attention. This type of work will probably not stand alone in the decision process.

Attention focusing raises a distinctive set of problems. In essence, it involves the problem of making analysis relevant to policymaking. Attention is less a problem of information than one of framing, executing, and communicating the product of the analysis to someone in a position to make policy. Analysis done under the supervision of the decision maker raises issues such as the appropriateness of timing and decision premises (assumptions, goals, and so on), the feasibility of answering the questions examined, and the clearness of the results of the analysis. Once the analytic function is moved outside, it raises the additional problem of persuading the decision maker to invest scarce attention resources to considering its results.[69]

Another consideration is involved in attention focusing. Will analysis consider and use all relevant data and information already available? This problem becomes more important as the issues, the scope of government activity, and the fragmentation of knowledge become more important. An analyst who routinely works with a particular data and information base will be more likely to attend to it during analysis. Incentives can be created to affect analysts' interests in using a particular set of data. A client for an analysis often creates these incentives by expressing interest in a particular issue. As analysis becomes more defined as a profession, pressures within the community of peers will lead to such incentives.[70] Once again, the client's or potential client's interests focus this process, with provision organizations restricting the attention of analysts and organizations of greater scope broadening it. Apart from these incentives, however, the design of cataloging and retrieval systems remains critical, since they hinder or facilitate identification of data and information bases desired by analysts. If cataloging and retrieval systems are closely held, for example, by the provision organization, they constrain analysis. Control organizations and external organizations both have an interest in opening up the analysis process as a way of facilitating work that addresses their interests.

This leads to the last aspect of information services: design and location of storage and retrieval systems. This is most important for policy analysis. The data requirements of broad analysis are extensive in most cases, and therefore, data must be retained for a long time. The extent of this type of data increases the importance of documentation. When data collected several years ago must be used, analysts are unable to compensate for inadequate documentation by turning to the memory of those who originally collected the data. These issues of documentation will affect data and information processing quite directly. Analysis is usually conducted under serious time constraints, imposed by a decision maker's scheduling, which increases the role played by the "availability heuristic"—or concentration on the data available.[71] One curious aspect of changing technology is decreasing costs for data retention, coupled with increasing documentation requirements for data use. An organization heavily oriented to the present is less likely to pay either the costs of eliminating data or those of documenting data in anticipation of future use.[72]

Data gathering and its subsequent retention are often the focus of studies of abuses of personal rights.[73] When an information service system errs by retaining excessive amounts of data, it raises additional concerns over the proper use of case records in determining eligibility, entitlement, and liability, as well as the appropriate circumstances for disseminating data to other persons and organizations.[74] These concerns are best handled by considering the rights of the subjects of records and by designing incentives to limit abuses of those rights. Provision organizations are unlikely to address these on their own, however.

If provision organizations store the data, they are likely to retain excessive, inadequately documented information; however, attention will be focused because of the data's availability. Few resources will be devoted to data management, which will cause more problems with data use. These problems will be compounded by haphazard pruning of data. By definition, the retained data will be fragmented by the provision organization and less useful in broadly focused analysis.

Making systems for storing data the responsibility of control organizations provides a series of payoffs. One consequence of their transfer is creation of an additional opportunity and incentive for documentation, which should improve the prospects for subsequent attention to and retrieval of relevant data. A second consequence is magnification of the responsibility for retaining and releasing data.[75] Control organizations will determine the level of resources committed to this task as part of their larger commitment to analysis.[76] Since the two are linked anyway, this situation seems appropriate.

One should not expect systems for storing data to move outside the purview of control organizations. Apart from the concerns about potential abuses that this move would raise, it would limit the access of the more directly involved organizations to data and information that are involved in traditional management activities. Provisions and control organizations can be expected to resist such a move.

This investigation leads to several recommendations and to identification of a central issue about organization control. Analysis promotes purposive activity. As a result, those persons who hope to focus organizational activity must attempt to control the provision activities. These have been defined broadly, as has the control function, but the purpose of that is to highlight the key question: Who will take responsibility and exercise authority over public organizations? Whoever is involved will require the instrumental resources provided by policy analysis and, to obtain those, will have to construct the information foundation that it requires.

Conclusion

Several contingencies have been identified that define one's expectations for the design of information services and their impact on policy analysis. These contingencies can be organized on the basic components of information services and focused on the issue of the type of organization in which they are most appropriately housed.

Key stages in the data-gathering process are likely to take place in provision organizations. This should not be changed. When considering the broader mandate that analysis has, however, one should expect this to be supplemented by control organizations in two ways: by integrating data across several provision organizations and by supplementing analysis with data on external effects. Such data will come from external organizations, and occasionally from diffuse organizations, and will often highlight the dependencies of the control organization.

Once data have been gathered, however, control organizations should be expected to move the data to be retained to more directly controlled storage and retrieval systems. A typical solution—leaving them under the control of provision organizations—subjects the data to uncertainties and unsatisfactory incentives that will hinder analysis. More data may be obtained than are immediately useful, but the policy analyst will probably prefer this.

Analysis with immediate impact on decision making will be performed under the aegis of the control organization, which will draw the analyst's attention to data and information relevant to the control organization's interests and make the analysis process suitable to the needs of decision makers. Analysis may fill less immediate needs, which means that analysis performed by and for external and diffuse organizations, while often not so complete or sophisticated as that done for control organizations, is important and merits discussion.

The central activities directly involved in policy analysis in large organizations are data and information processing. These transform mere data into information or knowledge. Moreover, with the incomplete and widely shared control in the public sector and with related activity occurring in several settings in modern society, many actors are likely to have an interest in these functions.[77]

As a result, the process of analysis confronts the tensions of "multiple advocacy." Although a particular control organization may resist this, it will do so at its peril in a policy process characterized by diffuse and diverse interests. In a system with redundancies and duplications, interplay of the various interests serves as a.check on the potential bias of analysis performed for partial interests.[78] Katz and Kahn provide a succinct statement of this argument:[79]

Another means by which an organization can avoid corrupting or being corrupted by its own information channels is the astute use of multiple channels as check procedures...they can be set up so as to utilize various sources of information and process it in similar enough fashion to produce a consistent or inconsistent picture for decision makers.

This attitude is a return to regarding analysis as a servant of decision making: subject to the scrutiny of interested groups and improved by their critical review of crucial assumptions, limitations, and problematic decisions and intimately involved in resolving the interplay of interests and constraints of the real world as choices are made and avoided. This approach to policy analysis is not scientific in the traditional sense; "good policy analysis must deal with opinions, preferences, and values, but it does so in ways that are open and explicit and that allow different people with different opinions and values to use the same analysis as an aid in making their own decisions."[80] Although the conclusions reached may not be unambiguous—or conclusive—and may lead to failures, these "failures are rooted in structural problems that cannot be fully solved; they express universal dilemmas of organizational life."[81]

Notes

[1]Consider, as examples, journals such as *Public Policy, Policy Analysis, Policy Sciences,* and *Policy Studies Journal*; the development of policy analysis agencies at the state and national levels, marked, perhaps, by the McNamara revolution at the Department of Defense; and important graduate institutions that train policy analysis professionals, such as those at Berkeley, Harvard, and Michigan.

[2]Some examples include James D. Thompson, *Organizations in Action*, New York, McGraw-Hill, 1967; Jay R. Galbraith, *Organization Design,* Reading, Mass., Addison-Wesley Publishing Co., Chapter 3 (particularly pp. 35–39); and Daniel Katz and Robert L. Kahn, *The Social Psychology of Organization,* New York, Wiley, 1978, Chapter 5 (particularly pp. 130–139).

[3]These points are discussed, for example, in P. Slovic, B. Fischhoff, and S. Lichtenstein, "Behavioral Decision Theory," *Annual Review of Psychology, 28*:1–39, 1977.

[4]Arnold J. Meltsner's discussion of these tensions, as they appear in the roles adopted by analysts, is particularly useful; see his *Policy Analysts in the Bureaucracy,* Berkeley, University of California Press, 1976, Chapter 1.

[5]An example of the former appears in Martin Landau, "Redundancy, Rationality, and the Problem of Duplication and Overlap," *Public Administration Review, 21*:346–358, July/August 1969.

[6]A good description of the complexity of the policy process, and the problems that poses, can be found in George D. Greenberg, Jeffrey A. Miller, Lawrence B. Mohr, and Bruce C. Vladeck, "Developing Public Policy Theory: Perspectives from Em-

pirical Research," *The American Political Science Review, LXXI* (4):1532–1543, December 1977. The problems posed by multiple, shifting perspectives are illustrated by James G. March and Johan P. Olsen, *Ambiguity and Choice in Organizations,* Bergen, Norway Universitetsforlaget, 1976, particularly Chapters 1–6.

[7]See E. S. Quade, *Analysis for Public Decisions*, New York, American Elsevier Publishing Co., 1975, p. 4.

[8]See H. Hugh Heclo, "Review Article: Policy Analysis," *British Journal of Political Science, 2*:84–85, January 1972. Also see Charles O. Jones, *An Introduction to the Study of Public Policy*, 2nd Edition, North Scituate, Mass., Duxbury Press, 1977, pp. 4–5.

[9]Moreover, the role orientations of analysts affect their willingness and ability to test these constraints; see Meltsner, *Policy Analysts...*; also see Anthony Downs, *Inside Bureaucracy*, Boston, Little, Brown, 1967, in particular Chapters VIII and IX.

[10]See Thomas L. McNauger, "Marksmanship, McNamara and the M16 Rifle: Organizations, Analysis and Weapons Acquisition," paper prepared for delivery before the 20th annual convention of the International Studies Association, March 21–24, 1979, and published by the Rand Corporation as professional paper P-6306.

[11]See Quade, *Analysis for Public Decisions*, pp. 10–11.

[12]See Quade, *Analysis for Public Decisions*, pp. 10–11.

[13]The many themes tapped by this general comment are much more extensively examined in Carol H. Weiss, "Improving the Linkage Between Social Research and Public Policy," in: *Knowledge and Policy: The Uncertain Connection*, edited by Laurence E. Lynn, Jr., Washington, D.C., National Academy of Sciences, 1978, pp. 23–81.

[14]Notice the distinction: One can "remove" some uncertainty, skewing knowledge toward some courses of action (e.g., this particular national health insurance proposal will cost X billion dollars—too much), or one can "resolve" some uncertainties, which allows one to make decisions about a course of action without knowing the consequences, as when one assumes that the costs of the current health delivery system will be less than those of proposed changes.

[15]See Quade, *Analysis for Public Decisions*. Chapter 14 summarizes the differences; Quade distinguishes between "stochastic uncertainty" and "real uncertainty." Other authors refer to the former problem as involving "risk." By whatever name, "risk" is readily incorporated into decision-making algorithms, which presents analysts with a problem that can be reduced to a methodological question with which they are familiar.

[16]See Weiss, "Improving the Linkage...," p. 76.

[17]See Laurence E. Lynn, Jr., "A Decade of Policy Developments in the Income-Maintenance System", in: *A Decade of Federal Antipoverty Programs: Achievements, Failures, and Lessons*, edited by Robert H. Haveman, New York, Academic Press, 1977, p. 117.

[18]On the experiment, see *Work Incentives and Income Guarantees: The New Jersey Negative Income Tax Experiment*, edited by Joseph A. Pechman and P. Michael Timpane, Washington, D.C., The Brookings Institution, 1975. Daniel P. Moynihan's

views are set out in *The Politics of a Guaranteed Income: The Nixon Administration and the Family Assistance Plan*, New York, Vintage Books, 1973; in particular, see pp. 191-194.

[19]See, as an example, Karen Davis, *National Health Insurance: Benefits, Costs, and Consequences*, Washington, D.C., The Brookings Institution, 1975; in particular, see Chapters 4 and 6.

[20]See Robert S. Stevens and Rosemary Stevens, *Welfare Medicine in America: A Case Study of Medicaid*, New York, Free Press, 1974, for an excellent discussion of the emergence of the unexpected issues of supply and demand that the Medicaid program involved.

[21]As an example, see Richard C. Auger and Victor P. Goldberg, "Prepaid Health Plans and Moral Hazard," *Public Policy*, *22*(3):353-397, Summer 1974, where health maintenance organizations are discussed as an alternative delivery system. A less sanguine view of another aspect of health policy and the consequences of an attempt to manipulate the delivery system appear in Bruce C. Vladeck, *Unloving Care, The Nursing Home Tragedy*, New York, Basic Books, 1980. At an even more specific level, see *Costs, Risks, and Benefits of Surgery*, edited by John P. Bunker, Benjamin A. Barnes, and Frederick Mosteller, New York, Oxford University Press, 1977; in particular, see the chapters by Pliskin and Taylor, Neuhauser, Abt, Green, and Barnes.

[22]See James Q. Wilson, *Thinking About Crime*, New York, Vintage Books, 1975, pp. 222-224.

[23]For example, see Diane Ravitch, "The 'White Flight' Controversy," *The Public Interest*, *51*:135-149, Spring 1978.

[24]As an example, see Albert L. Nichols and Richard Zeckhauser, "Government Comes to the Workplace: An Assessment of O.S.H.A.," *The Public Interest*, *49*:39-69, Fall 1977.

[25]See Richard A. Walker, "Wetlands Preservation and Management on Chesapeake Bay: The Role of Science in Natural Resource Policy," *Coastal Zone Management Journal*, *1*(1):75-101, Fall 1973. The ensuing debate can be found in W. Odum and S. Skjei, "The Issue of Wetlands Preservation and Management: A Second View," and Richard A. Walker, "Comments," *Coastal Zone Management Journal*, *1*(2):227-233, Winter 1974.

[26]See Ashley L. Schiff, *Fire and Water: Scientific Heresy in the Forest Service*, New Haven, Conn., Yale University Press, 1962.

[27]The classic statement of the argument is found in Allen V. Kneese and Charles L. Schultze, *Pollution, Prices and Public Policy*, Washington, D.C., The Brookings Institution, 1975. Also see "Costs of Environmental Regulation Draw Criticism, Formal Assessment," *Science*, *201*:140-144, July 14, 1978.

[28]See Alain C. Enthoven and K. Wayne Smith, *How Much is Enough: Shaping the Defense Program: 1961-1969*, New York, Harper and Row, 1969, p. 322.

[29]The concept is generally attributed to Charles E. Lindblom; see, for example, his "The Science of Muddling Through," *Public Administration Review, XIX*, Spring 1959, in particular, pp. 85-86, and *Politics and Markets: The World's Political-Economic Systems*, New York, Basic Books, 1977.

[30]Weiss, in "Improving the Linkage...," discusses these issues, often in the context of identifying times when these commonalities break down.

[31]Consider, as an example, the role played by Rachel Carson's *Silent Spring*, or Ralph Nader's investigation of the Corvair.

[32]See Roberta Wohlstetter, *Pearl Harbor: Warning and Decision*, Stanford, Calif., Stanford University Press, 1962, Chapter 7 in particular.

[33]These biases are discussed in Davis B. Bobrow, "Policy Attention and Forecast Bias," paper presented at the annual meeting of the International Studies Association, February 25-29, 1976. A more general treatment can be found in Amos Tversky and Daniel Kahneman, "Judgement Under Uncertainty: Heuristics and Biases," *Science*, *185*:1124-1131, 1974.

[34]See Bobrow, "Policy Attention and Forecast Bias," p. 7. Also see Ellen J. Langer, "The Illusion of Control," *Journal of Personality and Social Psychology*, *32*(2):311-328, August 1975, where some suggestive data appear.

[35]Similar categories appear in the literature. For example, see the "information life cycle" proposed in *A Report of the Commission on Federal Paperwork: Information Resources Management*, Washington, D.C., U.S. Government Printing Office, 1977, p. 43. Wildavsky also points to these distinctions in "Policy Analysis Is What Information Systems Are Not," reprinted in Aaron Wildavsky, *Speaking Truth to Power: The Art and Craft of Policy Analysis*, Boston, Little, Brown, 1979, Chapter 1, where he suggests that most information systems contain little more than "raw data," which he argues only become knowledge through the application of subsequent analysis.

[36]In short, "nondecisions" may make a difference here, too; the concept can be traced to Peter Bachrach and Morton S. Baratz, "Decisions and Nondecisions, An Analytic Framework," *American Political Science Review*, *57*:632-642, September 1963.

[37]The incident is reported in Jules Witcover, *Marathon, The Pursuit of the Presidency, 1972-1976*, New York, New American Library, 1977, pp. 413-415.

[38]See the selection by Edgar S. Dunn, Jr. in this chapter for a more complete discussion of these problems.

[39]At the individual level, see Richard M. Shiffrin, "Capacity Limitations in Information Processing, Attention, and Memory," in: *Handbook of Learning and Cognitive Processes*, Vol. 4, *Attention and Memory*, edited by W. K. Estes, Hillsdale, N.J., Lawrence Erlbaum Associates, 1978. At the organizational level, see Herbert A. Simon, *Administrative Behavior*, 3rd Edition, New York, Free Press, 1976.

[40]See Simon, *Administrative Behavior...*, p. 294.

[41]A succinct statement of the problem is found in Irving L. Janis and Leon Mann, *Decision Making: A Psychological Analysis of Conflict, Choice, and Commitment*, New York, Free Press, 1977, Chapter 1.

[42]See Weiss, "Improving the Linkage...," p. 57, and Downs, *Inside Bureaucracy*, pp. 188-190. On the last point, see Karl W. Deutsch, *The Nerves of Government: Models of Political Communication and Control*, New York, Free Press, 1966, p. 137.

[43]The evidence is ambiguous, to some degree, at the individual level. Donald O. Norman, *Memory and Attention: An Introduction to Human Information Processing*,

2nd Edition, New York, Wiley, 1976, pp. 22-26, presents an overview of the issues posed by alternative models of the attention mechanism.

[44]See Galbraith, *Organization Design*, pp. 24-26 and p. 106.

[45]See a review of these in..."Advanced Technology," edited by Philip H. Abelson and Mary Dorfman, *Science*, *208*, May 23, 1980.

[46]These lead to arguments that "information" is becoming increasingly important in modern society; for example, see A. G. Oettinger, "Information Resources: Knowledge and Power in the 21st Century," *Science*, *204*:191-198, July 4, 1980.

[47]This is involved, for example, in the move to "distributed processing" in the management of computer resources.

[48]See Arthur L. Robinson, "Array Processors: Maxi-Number Crunching for a Mini-Price," *Science*, *203*:156-160, January 12, 1979.

[49]For a summary of the development of "operations research," see H. J. Miser, "Operations Research and Systems Analysis," *Science*, *204*:139-147, July 4, 1980.

[50]See Langdon Winner, *Autonomous Technology: Technics-Out-of-Control as a Theme in Political Thought*, Cambridge, MIT Press, 1977, p. 283.

[51]See Robert W. Miller, "How to Control and Plan with PERT," *Harvard Business Review*, *40*:107, March/April 1962.

[52]Recent evidence of this is provided by K. Anders Ericsson, William G. Chase, and Steve Faloon, "Acquisition of a Memory Skill," *Science*, *208*:1181-1182, June 6, 1980, where their work with a human subject enabled him to increase his memory for digit sequences dramatically, but apparently through cognitive reorganization, rather than by an increase by his baseline capability.

[53]For a discussion of this particular problem, see Glen G. Cain and Harold W. Watts, "Problems in Making Policy Inferences from the Coleman Report," and James S. Coleman, "Reply to Cain and Watts," *American Sociological Review*, *35*(2):228-242, April 1970.

[54]Still, this point should not be overstated. An obvious counterexample was provided by John K. Galbraith, the Archivo General de Indias in Seville, where some 400,000 regulations governing Spanish colonial affairs that had been generated by 1700 were housed; this situation reminds us of the timeless propensities of those persons with the authority to make rules. See John K. Galbraith, *The Age of Uncertainty*, Boston, Houghton Mifflin, 1977, p. 118.

[55]On the last point, the argument would be that increasing social complexity leads to a requirement that social relations become more formalized, thereby requiring more formal systems of rule making and precedent.

[56]See Meltsner, *Policy Analysts....*

[57]Consult, for example, John Dales, *Pollution, Property and Prices: An Essay in Policy-Making and Economics*, Toronto, University of Toronto Press, 1968, for a statement of alternative approaches to pollution regulation, including the first statement of the "market in rights to pollute" position.

[58]A particularly important statement of the problems involved here can be found in Frances Fox Piven and Richard A. Cloward, *Poor People's Movements, Why They Succeed, How They Fail*, New York, Vintage Books, 1977, Chapter 1.

[59]This problem is related to March and Simon's notion of "uncertainty absorption," James G. March and Herbert A. Simon, *Organizations*, New York, Wiley, 1958, pp. 164–169.

[60]This point is made, in a more general way, in *A Report of the Commission on Federal Paperwork: Information Resources Management*, September 9, 1977. Here, data gathering is generally viewed as "free," while the various processing tasks may not be (particularly as some of those resources, housed in the organization, become more scarce); the view is that "information" is often viewed as a "free good." See cover letter and p. 3 of the report.

[61]See the letter from Paul Feldman, director, Public Research Institute, July 14, 1975, cited in *A Report of the Commission on Federal Paperwork . . .*, p. 8.

[62]See the selection by Edgar S. Dunn, Jr. in this chapter.

[63]This point is made in a general way in the literature on externalities. Donald A. Marchand and Mark E. Tompkins have attempted to analyze the incentives facing public organizations in their handling of information elsewhere; one conclusion reached is that "external costs" will be undervalued, while "external benefits" will be overvalued. See "The Citizen and the Public Organization: Distributive Consequences of Information Management," unpublished manuscript, 1980.

[64]See Weiss's neat contingency perspective, based on "completeness of control," in "Improving the Linkage . . .," pp. 49–50.

[65]Most notable among these are the costs of sending a separate group of individuals into the field, instead of relying on service deliverers to gather data. Where control is incomplete, these data-gathering efforts may be resisted. For a complete statement of this argument, see Jeffrey Pfeffer and Gerald R. Salancik, *The External Control of Organizations: A Resource Dependence Perspective*, New York, Harper and Row, 1978, pp. 104–106.

[66]The classic analysis of the problem is found in Albert O. Hirschman, *Exit, Voice, and Loyalty, Responses to Decline in Firms, Organizations, and States*, Cambridge, Mass., Harvard University Press, 1970. Also see Edward Weisband and Thomas M. Franck, *Resignation in Protest . . .*, New York, Grossman, 1975, for examples of the problem.

[67]See Walter W. Haase, "Federal Government Information Needs," in *Information Systems for Management*, edited by Fred Gruenberger, Englewood Cliffs, N.J., Prentice-Hall, 1972, p. 45. For a stronger statement of the idea, see "Strategy Formulation and Information Systems: Setting Objectives," in: *The Information System Handbook*, edited by F. Warren McFarlan and Richard L. Nolan, Homewood, Ill., Dow-Jones Irwin, Inc., 1975.

[68]R. M. Cyert and James G. March discuss this possibility in "Organizational Design," in: *New Perspectives in Organization Research*, edited by W. W. Cooper et al., New York, Wiley, 1964, p. 565.

[69]See Laurence E. Lynn, Jr., "The Question of Relevance," in: *Knowledge and Policy . . .*, pp. 12–22.

[70]For treatment of this topic, see Meltsner's discussion in *Policy Analysts . . .* of the incentives facing the "technician."

[71] See note 33.

[72] See *A Report of the Commission on Federal Paperwork* . . . , p. 8.

[73] See Michael A. Baker, "Record Privacy as a Marginal Problem: The Limits of Consciousness and Concern," *The Columbia Human Rights Law Review,* 4:89-100, 1972.

[74] These concerns appear, for example, when one considers how a person's arrest record should be used in subsequent encounters with law enforcement. Should it be available (despite the presumption of innocence until guilt is established); if available, should it be used in screening functions, or only in establishing punishment for a subsequent crime?

[75] This finding springs from the change in function: Where the record-keeping function is primary, accountability should be more readily enforced.

[76] If these organizations are not committed to the analytic function, resources are not expended to make it possible. Organizations will expend those resources required to support the function where it is useful. In situations of incomplete control, or multiple layers of control, the contingencies are more complex, since organizations may wish to maintain a symbolic commitment to analysis, and the mutual adjustment process may be conducted in the language of analysis.

[77] The best overview of the types of problems involved appears in March and Olsen, *Ambiguity and Choice in Organizations* . . . .

[78] The "multiple advocacy model" is best described in Alexander L. George, "The Case for Multiple Advocacy in Making Foreign Policy," *The American Political Science Review,* LXVI(3):751-795, September 1972. (This article includes "Comment" by I. M. Destler and "Rejoinder" by George.)

[79] See Daniel Katz and Robert L. Kahn, *The Social Psychology of Organizations*, New York, Wiley, 1966, p. 255.

[80] See M. Granger Morgan, "Bad Science and Good Policy Analysis," *Science, 201*:971, September 15, 1978.

[81] See Harold Wilensky, *Organizational Intelligence, Knowledge and Policy in Government and Industry*, New York, Basic Books, 1967, p. 48.

Information Problem No. 2: The Symbolic Representation of Entities*

Edgar S. Dunn, Jr.

...Despite our awareness of our national problems and shortcomings, the critical, fundamental nature of information problems and information processes has been largely overlooked. These matters are related to the very survival of the social processes which serve the highest values to which our democratic social system is committed. *Our most insistent social information processing problems are not a simple function of inadequate data. They stem from the inadequacy of the information processing structures that form our social systems.*

This theme has been pursued to suggest that the information processing metaphor opens up a novel and enlightening view of social structures and processes. The implications of these concepts cannot appropriately be pursued further here. But our exposition, incomplete though it is, serves to emphasize that data and data systems must be seen in the light of their roles in supporting social processes and helping to resolve their critical information processing problems.

The Link Between Information Problems 1 and 2

The different levels of information processing required by adaptive situations are associated with different kinds of representational problems. These, in turn, yield problems of perception and data generation. The fact that we are currently plagued with low-level information processors in high-level adaptive situations is, therefore, associated with the fact that existing data systems are incapable of supporting higher levels of information processing. Behind every problem having to do with the appropriate structure of information processors is a problem having to do with the representation of its environment. A more thorough explanation of this link follows.

*In: *Social Information Processing and Statistical Systems—Change and Reform.* New York, Wiley, 1974, pp. 69–93. (Copyright © 1974 by John Wiley & Sons, Inc. Reprinted by permission of John Wiley & Sons, Inc.)

The first characteristic of human information processors is that they process symbols. They work exclusively with data that are symbolic representations of those entities of the real world *with which the information processor chooses to interact.*

The second characteristic identifies the purposive nature of human information processing. The activities and events that constitute the real world in any comprehensive sense (if indeed we can even know what this means) vastly exceed the capacity of any information processor to record them. Even if such an unbounded sensory capacity did exist, the resulting sensory register would contain all of the "proliferate variety" (to use Beer's term) and all of the "blooming, buzzing confusion" (to use Henry James' term) of the real world itself.

An information processor can extract meaning from this confusion only if it guides sensors to record those activities that generate meaning in relation to its purposes. We know this is not a process of passive induction, but a process of active interaction with elements of the environment that form a chosen operating environment. Thus, whatever an information processor deals with is partly a function of its own purpose-related structure. As it pursues its intentions through its interaction with its environment, mismatches call into question the adequacy of its structure, including the adequacy of its concepts of the entity "operating environment." Through repeated interactions of this sort, representations of the real world are developed.

Thus, whether an information processor's level of processing is adequate to serve its purposes does not depend entirely upon the norms and rule structures that make up its central processor. It also depends upon the adequacy of its concept of its operating environment and its capacity to represent that concept sufficiently well in symbolic form so that adaptive responses and further revisions in concept can be made.

Thus, the solution to the problem of low-level information processing rests in part upon the solution to the problem of generating adequate representations of environmental entities.

The Entity Concept

Establishing the link between information processing problems and the problems of symbolic representation is only the beginning of our task. In an important way the problems of symbolic representation lie in the nature of the entities that must be represented. We cannot deal with these without first dealing explicitly with the entity concept itself.

This matter requires emphasis because we all (public and private managers and social scientists alike) are heavily conditioned by our biological inheritance and language to overlook and oversimplify the task of perceiving and representing social environments. We have an inveterate tendency to *objectify* our world—to see it in terms of concrete objects.[1] We instinctively feel great empathy for the small boy who, when terrified by lightning and the clap of thunder, was visited by his father and calmed with the words, "Don't worry. Remember God is looking after us." Awakened a second time, the boy made his way to his father's bed and crept in, saying, "I want somebody with skin!" We face a similar predicament. Most of our abstractions, including information processors, social systems, and patterns of relationship have no "skin." Yet our own information processors are heavily conditioned by the fact that they work most naturally with "objects" accessible to direct perception, and we conceptualize and communicate with a language that exhibits a built-in "objectifying" bias.

We tend to overlook the true nature of the entities that social information processors must work with. There is a strong tendency to treat them as if they had "skin." It is hard to get it straight in mind that we don't "see" the social entities we work with; we invent them. They are creatures of our *"imagination"* (shades of Boulding, 1961). They are often given symbolic representation through the use of instrumental artifacts that may yield not a direct image of a set of relationships, but one only inferred from a fragmentary set of observations (as in the case where inferential statistical techniques are employed).

The entity concept is not my invention, but a concept in good standing in philosophy. More revealing is the way it is currently receiving emphasis. For example, Vickers (1967, 1968, 1970) spent the first twenty years of his professional career as a lawyer and the next twenty as a private and public social systems manager. In seeking to understand and evaluate the lessons of this experience since retirement, he has emphasized the importance of the entity concept as follows.

The entity is in fact a pattern of relationships, subject to change but recognizably extended in time. This way of regarding the objects of our attention helps to resolve the ancient dichotomy between the individual and society and many other pseudo-problems resulting from the tendency, built into our language, to regard the objects of our attention as "things," rather than systematically related sequences of events. (*Value Systems and Social Process* by Sir Geoffrey Vickers, © 1968 by Sir Geoffrey Vickers. Publishers: New York, Basic Books; London, Tavistock, p. 74.)

This need constantly to *restructure* problems makes novel demands upon [information processing]....Most of the discussion which goes into policy-making is directed to reaching agreement on how the situation can be most usefully regarded. (Vickers, 1968, p. 84. Italics added.)

Our inveterate tendency to objectify involves us in unreal problems of identity. . . . If we regarded events as a category more basic than objects—as I understand some languages do—we should save ourselves a lot of trouble. We should also be more nearly in accord with what we know about the way things are. We have never yet identified a particle so elementary that it just *is* and it seems most unlikely that we ever shall. . . . It looks as if objects were abstractions from events and relations, rather than the constituents of which these are built. So the subject-matter of science is a hierarchy of systems. . . .

Even at elementary levels, be it cell or even atom, the object of attention is a dynamic system, a configuration of forces. . . . The more highly developed such systems are, the more open they are and the more extensive is the net of mutual interdependence in which they are involved. But while everyone is familiar with the idea of dynamic systems open to energy exchange, we are so little accustomed to distinguishing openness to information that we have no word to describe it. Yet only openness to information makes possible the development of systems such as sociologists or even biologists study. (Vickers, 1968, p. 165.)

The world of represented contexts is, I suggest, the world within which we effectively live. It is our supreme mental achievement. Most of our communication is directed to developing it, servicing it, trying to reduce its inconsistencies, to test its accuracy and extend its scope. . . . I call it our appreciated world. . . . The appreciated world is selected by our interests. (Geoffrey Vickers: *Freedom in a Rocking Boat* (Allen Lane, 1970) p. 97 © Geoffrey Vickers, 1970.)

The same concept emerges from the recent concerns of psychologists and neurophysiologists studying the nature of human information processing. The neurophysiologist Maturana (1970) describes cognitive processes in general as a process of constructing and reconstructing entities. Anything beheld by an observer takes the form of an entity. But an entity is not defined or described in object language. It is depicted as a set of meaningful interactions perceived by an observer. An observer can describe an entity only if there is at least one other entity from which the observed entity can be distinguished. The primary reference is the observer himself—a human or social information processor with a sense of self as observer.[2]

In sum, an entity is formed by any set of relationships that yields meaning in terms of the purposes of observer system qua information processor. Thus, the operating environment is a set of quasi-ecological relationships which forms an entity. It is peopled by persons and organized activity systems which are entities. It is formed by an image that is a conceptual, symbolic entity, and "viewed" through the artifices of symbolic data that are representational entities. The psychological structures of human information processors are themselves functional entities evolved through human experience. In short, human information processing is a process of conceiving, perceiving, symbolizing, representing, constructing, operating, and interacting with entities. All of life is engaged in dealing with packages of relationships.

We close this section by noting a paradox. Although our understanding of these rudimentary principles is often obscured by the object bias of our language, the etymological roots of two terms indispensable for characterizing the entity concept make clear its fundamental nature. A specific entity must be *identified* by *designating* the relationships it manifests. These units are "id-*entified*" by "*design*-ating" relationships made meaningful by purpose. The process of "entification" is a creative (and even heuristic) design process carried out by a purposeful information processor.

The Variety of Entity Representations

The symbolized observations employed in the construction of operative representations of entities are data. The variety of the data that information processors must generate and process is, of course, as great as the variety of all the concepts and images about the world related to all of the purposes of all human and social information processors. The variety is unbounded.

However, the concepts that have been developed enable us to generalize the various roles that data play and the symbolic forms these roles require. These emerge from a consideration of the kinds of entity representations implicit in the nature of social information processing. These representational tasks are related (1) to the field of observation formed by orders of system hierarchy relative to an observer (or reference) system, and (2) to the levels of information processing required by the adaptive situation.

The Representational Task and Fields of Observation. The typical information processor is active in several fields of observation. The nature of the entities that an information processor must represent to itself, and therefore the nature of the representational task, is characteristically different for each. There are four such fields associated with four orders of system hierarchy relative to an observer system. It is useful to describe them briefly.

REPRESENTING INTERNAL OPERATING ENVIRONMENTS. We begin by designating a social information processor as an observer system. A processor of any complexity typically employs the services of specialized subsystems. The subentities emerge because they can be organized as quasi-autonomous information processors. The central observer thereby reduces the variety of relationships under its direct control or surveillance and, thus, reduces the scope of its direct information processing tasks. These quasi-autonomous subentities make up an observational field we may characterize as an *internal operating environment*. The central processor as observer system must form symbolic representations of these entities sufficient to support understanding and prediction leading to integrative regulation.

It will be apparent if we review the structure of an information processor, that there are three types of these subentities. First, there are those that perform specialized effector functions. These may be subdivided into two types. (1) There are those engaged in processing (transforming or transferring) material and energy elements of the environment. Sometimes the act is directed to shaping the external operating environment, as when a road is graded or a rose planted. At other times environmental resources are detached from their environmental roots and passed through a production process that transforms them into artifacts of human purpose, as when steel is produced, or a suit of clothing made. In either case, the information processors with which we are most widely familiar are those that manage such physical processes for the purpose of satisfying our material-economic needs. All of the machines, tools, trucks, trains, factories, etc., of the economy are components of specialized effector subsystems of some information processor—systems that act directly to change the physical environment or its detached resources. They are the "arms and legs" of social information processors. (2) There are effector subsystems that process (transform or transfer) symbols. These are brought into play when our intentions do not require us to act directly upon the physical aspects of an environment, but require us to communicate perceptions or concepts with other information processors.

Second, there are subentities that perform specialized perceptor functions. These are the "eyes and ears" of the information processors—the receivers rather than the transmitters. For example, organized social information processors of any complexity have accounting and statistical subsystems. Such subsystems employ the observational skills of persons along with myriad perceptual artifacts (thermometers, odometers, spectrometers, etc.) to count, measure and make qualitative observations that are converted into symbolic data amenable to further processing.

Third, information processors even employ specialized subentities that play a role in central processing functions. Libraries, filing systems, and computer records, and the organizational systems that manage them, augment the memories of central processors. Statistical clerks, actuaries, and computers add computational powers to central processors. We employ specialized symbol (as well as material) processors.

The point is that all of these specialized component entities form one kind of field of observation from the point of view of the designated observer—the central processor system, whatever its substantive purposes. Since many of the activities under its control are carried out indirectly by instrumental subentities, the regulation of their behavior is mediated by symbolic representations of them. The central processor-observer of any system regulates its component entities through the manipulation of a symbolic analogue of them. A primary field of observation for any social information processor is that formed by its quasi-autonomous internal components. They define one aspect of its representational tasks.

REPRESENTING EXTERNAL OPERATING ENVIRONMENTS. The entities which the observer system conceives and perceives in the process of designating its external operating environment manifest two kinds of relationships. Each confronts the observer system with representational problems different from those characteristic of its internal environment.

First, the observer system's external environment is peopled with organized information processors pursuing purposes that may or may not be related to its own. It develops direct functional links with some of these. For example, a manufacturer may develop strong transaction ties with his suppliers and buyers. In some cases these links are so strong, continuous, or formalized that the environmental entities almost partake the character of subsystems, and may be treated as such. The representational problems may not be vastly different.

Commonly, however, these relationships are much more contingent in nature. Retailers, for example, may maintain continuous relationships with a few "steady" buyers and intermittent and transitory relationships with a large number of "occasional" buyers. This population characteristic (here, of buyers) markedly affects the nature of the field of observation and the problems of representation. Statistical and probabilistic methods of environmental observation come more prominently into play. Quite apart from this, the external entities with which an observer system shares direct functional links are not creatures of its own design, as is often the case of subsystem entities. Transactions with them are not subject to the same degree of direct effect. The representational tasks are not directed to generating the kinds of data that support positive regulation of these systems. Rather, environmental representation forms the context for making reactive or anticipatory adaptations to the situations revealed.

There is a second kind of relationship characteristic of external operating environments. Patterns of relationships are formed by the transaction linkages among the organized social information processors that form the operating environment (also, depending upon the nature of the purposes of the observer system, among social information processors, human information processors, and even among biological and physical entities forming earthly and cosmic environments). These relationships do not form an image of another organized information processor. Rather they form an image of a set of quasi-ecological relationships. Representing these more generalized concepts of the operating environment is often desirable from the point of view of an observer because the indirect consequences of the coadaptations of a wider set of entities may be essential to guide its own purpose motivated behavior. Intelligent social regulation requires that we move from reactive adaptation to anticipatory adaptation, and the social problems themselves require that we bring patterns of ecological relationships under some form of regulation. Both problems underscore our need to generate these kinds of representations.

This is a representational problem of quite a different order. In the first place, the pattern of relationships to be represented is not defined by the behavioral intentions of an organized, purposive information processor operating at the level of the ecosystem. They can be observed only because the intentions and activities of a whole set of interrelated information processors and passive entities generate a pattern that is sufficiently stable for the moment, and sufficiently imbued with meaning, that they can be conceived and perceived.

Furthermore, these relationships are often so multifaceted and complex that they defy representation in detail. Observer systems are often required to deal with entities formed by the behavior of a population of similar and dissimilar component entities. The relational patterns represented must often be crude abstractions of underlying relationships. The representational task is complicated by the problem of identifying the levels of aggregation and abstraction that best serve the adaptive needs of the observer system.

In short, the external operating environment forms quite a different field of observation from an observer's internal operating environment. The representational tasks call for different forms of symbolic data, generated in different ways.

REPRESENTING EXTERNAL PERIPHERAL ENVIRONMENTS. Good information processors do not restrict their attention exclusively to their external operating environments. Just as a photograph acquires additional meaning because the "depth-of-field" representing its focused image is supplemented by a less sharp background, so also is the meaning of an information processor's operating environment augmented by some representation of its periphery. The representation of the periphery serves several purposes.

First, the same set of operating environmental observations may be interpreted differently against a different or changing background. For example, a change in the level of prices might be interpreted differently by a central banker or union labor negotiator if seen against a background of general economic expansion or contraction.

Second, this is the area within which unexpected disturbances arise that challenge the observer's designation of the operating environment, thus giving rise to information processing in the developmental mode. The wise information processor maintains a surveillance of the peripheral environment because these less-focused observations add to its adaptive sensitivity. The representational problems are relatively simpler in this field because often the roughest scalar or pattern representations are adequate.

SELF-REPRESENTATION. There is, finally, a fourth field of observation and one easily overlooked. An observer system requires the symbolic representation of the nature of its own central processor. Unless it can represent adequately to itself its own operative norms and rules, it has no means of considering their adaptive adequacy. The problems of representation are relatively greater in this field because they require more than a description of parameters. They require the designation of functions. They require more than the representation of the central processor's performance; they require the representation of its performance processes as well.

The Representational Task and the Adaptive Situation. Data assume different symbolic forms appropriate to differences in the representational tasks dictated by the adaptive situation encountered by an information processor. These differences also correspond to differences in levels of information processing. Our understanding of the variety of entities and entity representations will be further advanced by considering these factors.

STATE DESCRIPTIONS—REPRESENTATION OF THE RESULTS OF PERFORMANCE. The simplest form of symbolic data are those that designate the state (conditions), that characterize an entity at some point in time. They can be recorded by the simplest sensors, named or designated in the simplest form, stored in the simplest form, and used with the fewest complications. These data symbolize the results of the performances of behavioral systems—their concrete manifestations. They are the symbolic staples of information processors. They can be used to perform some quite simple as well as quite complex representational tasks.

In their simplest form such data are employed to represent a single characteristic of an entity at a point in time. Conventionally five "naming" components are required to fully designate this simplest symbolic element. It requires an identifier that names the entity being represented, a time descriptor that specifies the time of the observation, a space or place description, a descriptor that names the attribute under observation, and a quantifier or quality description that specifies the unit of measurement, count, or attribute quality. Several quantitative examples are indicated:

Example	Identifier	Attribute descriptor	Quantifier	Place descriptor	Time descriptor
1	"Y" Refinery	Inventory	26,000 bbls.	Dundalk, Md.	Dec. 31, 1972
2	Virginia	Population	6,732,435 people	(implied in identifier)	Apr. 15, 1970
3	U.S. economy	Index of prices	143 (on a 1960 base)	(implied in identifier)	Mar. 1, 1970

The first example describes the state of the inventory of a specified information (as well as petroleum) processor. The second describes the state of a geographically designated population aggregate. The third describes the state of the prices reflecting a set of socioeconomic ecological relationships. This further illustrates that this form of symbolic representation is applicable to all of the observational fields of an information processor. Moreover, this is also true of the other forms of symbolic representation that follow.

The examples also call attention to a fact that will have an important bearing upon our discussion later. When data are symbolized and recorded, some of the naming components essential for complete designation of an observation may be omitted. A place designation may be implied by the identifier, as indicated above. In some cases a space descriptor or time descriptor may be omitted altogether because they are not significant for the purposes for which the data were generated. Sometimes they are not recorded because they are given to the user by the context within which he is operating. This habit of frequently employing a kind of naming or symbolizing shorthand can create serious problems for someone who subsequently attempts to employ the same observation to perform a different representational task. The data turn out to be insufficiently designated for a different purpose. The context no longer supplies unrecorded attributes. This vastly complicates the problems of developing multiple-use statistical systems.

These elemental state descriptions can be employed in a variety of ways. They may be used in their simplest form or combined in ways to build up more complex representations.

In its simple form, for example, a population of the kind illustrated for Virginia may be highly useful for representing a common element in the peripheral environments of a number of processors, or it may serve more directly as a quantitative parameter in a public system information processor designed to allocate the seats in a representative legislature.

It is useful to emphasize some aspects of the organizational logic of hierarchically organized information processors in order to appreciate the enormously effective power such simple indicator signals can have *under appropriate conditions*. Consider the design of a simple automatic heating system.... The thermostat is the central processor of such a system. The heating system itself is a quasi-autonomous subsystem. While the thermostat rigidly determines when it operates, the heating system maintains autonomous control over how it operates. All the thermostat requires for the exercise of control are two simple state indicators and a comparison norm. One indicator represents the temperature of the closed environmental air space. The other represents the operating state of the heat source (on or off). When combined with a normative goal, and a few information processing rules, the thermostat can effectively induce an appropriate performance by the heat source *without any knowledge as a central processor of how the heat source subsystem processes either energy or information.* (It does both.) We previously noted that a tremendous amount of information conservation and amplification is inherent in the principle of the system hierarchy. This is emphasized here by the fact that the simplest state indicator is sufficient, under appropriate conditions, to represent operative aspects of systems that would require vastly more extensive data for a complete description.

The phrase "under appropriate conditions" should be underscored. As the internal and external operating environments become more complex, the simplest state indicators become inadequate. More complex representations of entity states must be developed. When state indicators are elaborated to represent patterns formed by multiple states of an entity, these patterns can take two forms.

The first involves simultaneous multiple observations. A more sophisticated heat regulator, for example, may monitor several air spaces at once and adapt simultaneously to different aspects of the represented pattern. The "Y" Refinery may break down its inventory into a variety of products. The population of the State of Virginia may be subdivided into counties or electoral districts. The price index may be differentiated into the prices of single products or products grouped in any of a number of categories. Such pattern representations are useful because the adaptive response of the information processor can be more selectively and sensitively adjusted to the states of more complex environments by employing more complex norms and rules. The "Y" Refinery can make a wide variety of adaptive responses to its inventory mix in response to changes in the patterns of their represented market prices.

The second form of pattern representation involves sequential multiple observations. State observations (based on the kind of state indicators discussed...) are continually or repeatedly made. It is not necessary, however for an information processor, employing such data to support reactive (ex post) adaptations, to make a long-term memory trace of them. Once the adaptive response is made, a specific state indicator has "informed" the system and loses its immediate relevance to the next emerging observation. The second form of pattern representation is concerned with something else. Information processors that simply adapt reactively to immediate observations often encounter time-related anomalies. The operation of central and subsystem information processes, particularly when it involves the activation of physical system effectors, may create a time lag that may result in the adaptation coming "on-line" at a time when a new state of the system calls for a different response. These time-related problems can appear in all kinds of operating variants. One classical case in economics is the lag involved when adaptive responses call for scale adaptations requiring capital investments.

Such situations induce information processors to practice anticipatory rather than reactive adaptation. They attempt to set time-lagged adaptations in motion in anticipation of future states of the operating environment. This leads the information processor to look for temporal patterns in retained memory traces of the individual state observations. Thus, time series formed by state indicators, and methods for educing pattern representations from them, become an important part of symbolic representation.

In the elaboration of entity representations which can be formed by state descriptions, one can take a third step by combining the first two. One can explore the way structural patterns (formed by multiple observations at a point in time) undergo structural transformations over time. Thus, labor-market analysts are well informed by the observation that, within the industrial pattern of employment, the relative share of service employment is being augmented in a persistent fashion over time.

The state descriptions formed by these elaborations become decidedly more complex than the five-element symbolic description of the simplest observation. These constructions are achieved by stringing together additional time and attribute descriptors for the same entity to form a more meaningful representation.

It turns out, however, that even these more elaborated state descriptions give adequate representations of the entity only *under appropriate conditions.* What constitutes "appropriate conditions" has to do with the stability and predictability of the activities or performances that generate the observed entity state and their changes over time.

This draws attention to the fact that state descriptions of the kind discussed provide no explicit representation of the performance or activities of the entities being described. There is a direct link, of course, because the observed states are a result of activities. This link sometimes permits us to infer from changes in state descriptions something about the activities that generated the change. Although we may not have observed directly and described symbolically the activities leading to the changes in state, we are rarely devoid of some inkling of what those activities may be. With reference to our illustrative cases, for example, we may not have observed the aspects of "Y" Refinery performance that generated an observed change in the scale and/or mixture of petroleum stocks, but we know from the change in state descriptions that such activities took place. We may also carry in "memory" an image of the kind of activities essential to generate the observed result and be able to infer their probable character. Similarly, all of the births, deaths, and changes of residence that generated an observed change in the population of Virginia may not have been observed and symbolized, but we know from an observed population change that they took place. We may also have a memory trace of the historical relationships of births, deaths, and changes of residence sufficient to support an inference about the nature of the activities behind the change. So it goes.

ACTIVITY DESCRIPTIONS—THE REPRESENTATION OF PERFORMANCE. We must return to our emphasis upon "appropriate conditions." We have already indicated that, in an organized system, the regulation of certain states generated by subsystem activities serves to regulate the underlying activities. This is true if there is a known deterministic relationship between the activity and the resultant state. But this is not always the case, particularly in complex systems. An effector subsystem, for example, may be able to effect the same resultant state by several different activity paths. Conceivably, which option obtains may not be a matter of concern to the central processor, but in many situations it may. If "Y" Refinery, for example, is really a collection of several subsystem processors forming a set of linked procedural sequences, what may be an indifferent choice of possible actions by the manager of subsystem "A" may be highly significant to the central processor engaged in trying to coordinate "A's" activities with those of subsystem "B," "C," etc. The coordination of multiple options requires that some representation of the activities themselves be made to the central processor. State descriptions may no longer be sufficient servants of purpose. . . .

Or consider changes in the population of Virginia. If one would like to project the population to support the anticipatory adaptation of governmental fiscal and operating activities, one might extrapolate the population time series. This could serve the intention adequately *providing the time pattern of the underlying activities and events* (i.e., of births, deaths, etc.) *is stable*. If it is not stable, this predictive purpose must have recourse to some record of activities and events so that the prediction can be based upon their changing time patterns. . . .

We should note that the designation of the most elemental act of an entity is more complex and difficult than the designation of one of its states. Every act involves either transforming or transferring some aspect of an entity from one state to another. It follows that the complete designation of the act involves the identification of the entity, the description of the nature of the act, the description of the relevant pre-act and post-act states of the entity, the specification of the time span or duration of the act, and the enumeration of such quantifiers or quality descriptions as may be appropriate. Thus, in diagrammatic form:

(identifier)	(activity description)	(quantifier)	(state descriptor)
The "Y" Refinery	shipped	1000 bbl.	of crude oil

(initial state)	(terminal state of transfer)
from the Port of Baltimore	to "Y" Refinery

(departure time)	(arrival time)
at 10:00 A.M. 11/5/73,	arriving at 4:32 P.M. 11/6/73.

The description of an elemental state or condition can be accomplished with a single identifier, quantifier, state descriptor, place descriptor, and time descriptor. Describing an elemental act adds an activity descriptor and often doubles the number of time, place, and state descriptors (as well as quantifiers) essential for complete designation of the act. Furthermore, acts (e.g., heating, fastening, moving, shaping) are more transitory phenomena than states, and often present different and more difficult sensing as well as symbolizing problems. The representation of performance demands far more of the perceptual and memory apparatus of information processors.

Single-act descriptions can be combined to construct representations of more complex entity performances in the same way that single-state descriptions are combined to construct more complex state representations. Thus, we may identify a set of acts that coincide in time (as when ten men simultaneously lift a heavy object, or a tax increase and interest rate increase are joined in an effort to reduce inflation), or we may identify a series of acts in time (as when a radio set is assembled, steel is refined and shaped, or a bill guided through a legislative process). Patterns of activities manifest in both "parallel" and "series" representation may be combined to yield still more complex patterns. Thus, one can elaborate the representations of acts into representations of performance patterns. This is a much more complex form of representation than can be shaped with state descriptors. A wider range of meaning may be represented and these represented acts can be employed to construct an explicit network of relationships.[3]

As in the case of state descriptions, activity descriptions are subject to some representational limitations. For all of their descriptive power, they yield no explicit representation of performance processes which underlie the activities and their patterns. Again, as in the case of state descriptions, the representation of these behavioral patterns can be used to infer something about the next higher level of entity representation *under appropriate conditions*. (It should by now be obvious that the same qualification is applicable to every level of representation.) The observation of recurrent activity patterns under similar conditions strongly implies that the pattern of activities is governed by some behavioral design or behavioral program. On the basis of prior knowledge of such processes, we may have an inkling of the structure of such an underlying program. But we can have no certain knowledge of the behavioral pattern that might emerge in a situation not yet observed. And we can project the same behavioral pattern under similar circumstances only if the underlying behavioral design is stable.

So, as we pursue the objective of entity representation we may once again run up against *conditions that are not appropriate* for higher-order inferences and must then turn to a third form of entity representation.

PROGRAMMATIC DESCRIPTIONS—THE REPRESENTATION OF PERFORMANCE PROCESSES AND PROCESSORS. The third form of entity representation involves the designation of the process (or the structure of the processor) that transforms patterned observations of environmental states and acts into adaptive actions designed to maintain or modify existing states. In recent years we have learned a great deal about the problems of representing these processes through accumulated experience with programming computers. This form of entity representation is precisely a *programmatic description*. It involves a description of the operating programs of an information processor (as well as any material-energy processors under its control).

Once again, the change in the level of representation requires the use of descriptive elements not previously encountered. Even if it is not made explicit, the designation of an operating environment is implicit in the design of any operating program—that is, the designation of the activity and state descriptions that constitute the potential parameters of its program. The designation of the program itself involves the identification and description of a structure formed by rules and norms specifying the simultaneous and sequential patterns of acts that shape adaptive responses.

Armed with this kind of data one can simulate the pattern of activities that ensue, given a different environmental situation than previously observed (or a projected future situation). As we have noted, this is impossible if one utilizes only activity descriptions.

Just as activity descriptions are more difficult to generate and employ than state descriptions, programmatic descriptions involve more difficult representational tasks than activity descriptions. Although much remains to be learned, we are reasonably successful in the representation of such processes when the field of observation is that of self-representation, or representation of the internal operating environment. The programmatic description of information processors making up the external operating environment—as individuals or populations—is much more difficult. Some progress has been made through the use of devices such as public opinion surveys. But this is an area of representation that requires much developmental work. It is also at this level of representation that we encounter vital issues of privacy and freedom in their most critical form.

DEVELOPMENTAL DESCRIPTIONS—THE REPRESENTATION OF LEARNING PROCESSES. The data generated by programmatic descriptions amplifies still further the information processing power of those processors structured to evaluate such data. Once again, there are limitations. It is true that programmatic description enables us to anticipate activity patterns (as well as state descriptions) that would be associated with previously unobserved situations, but this is true only *under appropriate conditions*. This familiar qualification reminds us that one can simulate the expected result only if two conditions prevail: (1) the environmental situation is one for which the processor contains a preprogrammed response, and (2) the structure of the processor remains stable. Where these conditions are not fulfilled the programmatic description is not adequate to support realistic inference.

One must then know whether—and how—the performance program can be redesigned to accommodate new modes of behavior. This requires a fourth form of representation that describes the developmental processes that design performance processors. One becomes engaged in the representation of the learning processes of social information processors. The anticipation of the probable performance of an entity rests upon some representation of its capacity to learn. It may have already occurred to the reader that the third form of representation involves the description of an information processor operating in a performance mode, and the fourth form involves a description of an information processor operating in a development mode.

This carries us to a level of information processing and a level of representation of fields of observation still highly undeveloped. Our stake in learning to function better at this level cannot be overemphasized. Our ability to evolve social systems capable of managing complexity, in a manner consistent with the maintenance of an open society may well rest upon our success in conceiving, perceiving, representing, designing, and operating developmental information processors.

There may be still higher levels of representation. The next level must involve the representation of the processes by means of which developmental processors learn to learn. Perhaps at this point we should leave the possibility of still other levels to metaphysics.

The presentation of this section has of necessity been cursory and limited. It could form the outline for an entire book. Hopefully, our discussion is sufficient to indicate the variety of forms that data can take, and the variety of representational tasks required for the designation of entities.

The Entity Problem

By now it should be clear that solutions to our information processing problems must rest upon our ability to generate adequate representations of operating entities and of the entities that make up the observational fields which constitute their internal and external operating environments. We have been at pains to make clear the meaning of the entity concept. We have outlined the nature of the representational tasks, and the perceptual fields within which they are exercised. Consider now the special nature of the representational problems that confront social information processors at this stage in our developmental history. We are confronted with an entity problem that is generic in character, but has been compounded by an information processing pathology endemic to our time.

General Aspects. The social information processing task of representing entities is a great deal more difficult when the entities are formed by human-social relationships than when they involve material and biological relationships that underlie social processes. This is because social entities are relatively more "skinless."

This has little to do with the fact that material and biological entities display "object" surfaces in some representational modes while social systems do not. Hopefully, the discussion of the entity concept makes it apparent to even the philosophically untutored that our most useful representations of material and biological entities designate "subsurface" relationships as well as those that often transcend surface. The psychological structures of human information processors previously discussed, for example, are made known by a conceptualization of subsurface relationships not accessible to object modes of perception. The term "father" designates a set of biological and social relationships that transcend the "skin" of the male animal. The phenomena of molecular "surface tension" that manifests system closure at one level of representation are often both literally and figuratively "immaterial" in designating major functional relationships. Our most important images—even of material systems—are "skinless" abstractions.

We speak now of a metaphorical "skin" that reduces to the concept of a degree of entity closure. Since no real-world entity is completely isolated from relationships with internal and external entities (or higher-order and lower-order entities), its designation requires specifying an arbitrary boundary between those relationships that describe one entity and those describing all other entities forming its environments. The "drawing" of this relative boundary is guided by the purposes and intentions of the observer. The relationships which the boundary circumscribes are more continuously engaged (in some sense related to purpose) and "densely" configured than those relegated to environmental status.

The metaphor indicates that abstract representations designating social entities may be different in important respects from those designating material and biological entities—different in ways that complicate the representational task. There are two aspects.

The first has to do with the fact that social entities tend to be less precisely bounded than material entities. The designation of the set of relationships forming a social entity is often more difficult and more arbitrary than the task of designating either material or biological entities. This is not because social entities are necessarily more complex; some biological entities, in particular, may display more functional variety or more complicated relational patterns than many social entities. The difficulty has more to do with the fact that the relational elements used to designate one social entity can, in many cases, also be employed to construct representations of other social entities with different meanings.

This stems from the fact that human-social entities are artifact constructs of human purpose.[4] Accordingly, they may be uncoupled and recoupled, on a part-by-part basis, to construct a variety of entities. The fact that instrumental systems may serve multiple purposes, and that central processors may be pursuing multiple purposes, leads to the consequence that social entities and their elements can be configured by concept in a variety of ways, depending upon which aspects of intention one wishes to serve. The sharing of common relational elements results in entities becoming less precisely bounded. (Put another way, this phenomenon yields a larger variety of purpose-related options.) Their symbolic representations require making increasingly difficult and arbitrary discriminations.[5]

There is a second important way in which social entities are different from material and biological entities. Social entities tend to be less permanent and stable in form.

We must be careful not to misunderstand this assertion. Social systems can be remarkably long-lasting. In some societies, the same institutions, organizational forms, and cultural traits have endured for generations, sometimes centuries. There are remarkably persistent elements of the traditional even in modern technological societies. Nor is it claimed that particular social entities may not be more long-lasting than particular physical or biological entities. The great advantage of the corporate form of business is that it transcends the life spans of its human components. The Catholic Church has endured longer than many of the physical liturgical artifacts it has employed over the centuries.

Precisely because social entities are artifacts of joint human behavior, they are repeatedly redesignated in response to adaptive encounters with changing environments, and to the transformations of technology and human purpose. Even the self-representations that designate the structure and purposes of central processors (and, hence, define their entity boundaries) are reformulated.

It is asserted that these transformations, leading to information processing in a developmental mode, have accelerated in recent history. Consequently, the social entities one seeks to represent tend to display stable forms over shorter periods of time. Not only must the representations of social entities be reworked more frequently, but, because of the nature of our adaptive problems, we must increasingly employ higher-order forms of representation. Inferences previously supported by state descriptions must now be supported by activity descriptions. Again, activity descriptions increasingly need to be augmented by programmatic descriptions. The problems peculiar to the task of representing social entities are being made progressively more difficult by the process of social evolution.[6] In sum, the observational fields within which social information processing takes place are being continuously transformed as the meaning and functional structure of each human-social entity is altered through a process of human-social learning. Social science and social management face a continuing need for reconceptualizing and redesignating their observational fields, and for developing new modes for generating and managing perceptual data.

Entity Fixation. Although the representational tasks required to support social adaptation are becoming more difficult, we have not become sufficiently sensitive to this fact. Our entity concepts and representations tend to become fixated in ways that obstruct appropriate responses to the entity problem. We are confronted with a vicious circle. Low-level information processors tend to work with fixated environmental representations which, in turn, tend to restrict information processors to relatively low levels of information processing.

Our information processing habits have become fixated in two ways. First, we tend to operate in such set social structures that valid data which can yield more useful representations tend to be ignored. How many of our critical social problems are being ignored by social scientists because they involve the representation of entities that do not correspond neatly to the concepts and representational tools of established disciplines? How many business enterprises have failed for want of a capacity for developmental information processing? There are many such examples of fixation. They are a product of our adherence to low-level performance modes of information processing in situations where they are inadequate. Maslow (1966) once said that if the only tool you have is a hammer, you tend to treat everything as if it were a nail. Similarly, since most of our behavioral systems are habituated to processing information in a performance mode, they tend to treat all problems as if they were amenable to the application of established performance techniques. This means that they also tend to see the world through a fixed set of "windows"—that is, they cling to established forms of symbolic data and fixed entity representations.

There is a way in which this kind of fixation is reinforced. Even where an information processor wishes to represent the entities of its operating environments differently, the ready accessibility of certain forms of symbolic data often reinforces the tendency to work with established representational images. This is particularly true in the case of representing external operating environments. This is the field of observation for which few information processors possess the resources to generate symbolic data to meet their needs. Therefore, they have a tendency to use symbolic data already available to perform representational tasks—to "see" entities in the patterns already "seen" by others.

We should note that entity fixation, in the face of the need to redesignate entities, tends to generate pathological responses. Furthermore, the nature of these difficulties is often misunderstood. In extreme form, entity fixation leads to the reification of data. When management is confronted by the fact that its traditional processes are not well enough informed to deal with current disturbances, it often demands more "information." This is often interpreted as a need for more of the same kinds of data accumulated in the same way. When coupled with the enlarged data processing capabilities of computers, the result can be a flood of detail leading to an actual reduction in meaning and to further loss of control *consequent to an overload of meaningless data*. All too frequently, information processors seek to resolve their problems by accumulating masses of traditional, easily available state indicators, when these problems might be much more easily resolved by acquiring a few well-selected activity descriptors.[7]

The Entity Problem Manifest in Statistical Organization

The symbolic data that social information processors require for both self-representation and the representation of their internal environments are predominantly data that each processor must generate through its own resources using its own perceptual apparatus. Typically these internal "entification" tasks require the generation of representations too detailed and too specialized to be of interest to other information processors.

In contrast, the symbolic data required for the representation of external environments are generated in a context that encourages the multiple use of some data. First, even though external environments typically require less detailed representation than internal environments, the very size and scope of these observational fields involve burdensome and difficult representational tasks. The representation of these environments often involves describing relationships that are ecological rather than organizational in character. Second, the external observational fields of different information processors are occasionally nearly identical and very often overlap. Thus, it happens that different information processors can employ the same symbolic data elements as components in both similar and different representational tasks.

This has encouraged the development of specialized multiple-use data systems. The foremost example of such systems is the Federal Statistical System, discussed earlier. Other examples are Dun and Bradstreet, the Gallup Poll, and the statistical agencies of state and local public systems.

...the entity problem is manifest in the present state of these organized statistical systems. They are ill equipped at present to substantially ameliorate our present and future representational problems. Indeed...limitations in the scope and availability of symbolic data tend to reinforce the entity problem. These organized statistical systems form a part of the problem.

A brief description of them will support this point. First, the symbolic data they generate are almost completely dominated by state descriptions.

Genuine activity descriptors are scarce. Therefore, the utility of these records is restricted almost exclusively to representational tasks that can be formed from state descriptors.

Second, even the use of these records to form state descriptions of entities is impaired. Time patterns of entity states are sometimes well represented where special attention has been paid to their construction and maintenance (e.g., price indices). There are formidable problems, however, if one picks any state description related to purpose, and attempts to construct a time series by matching it with identically formed descriptions for antecedent and subsequent time periods. Similarly, the arrangement of a set of simultaneous state observations into a pattern representation of an entity is sometimes carried out well by these statistical organizations (where special attention has been paid to their construction and maintenance). The national economic accounts and the occupational mix of the labor force are examples. In such cases, the time patterns of these structures may also be provided. However, if one wishes to construct patterned representations of an entity to serve different purposes, the task of assembling state descriptors into different composite descriptions becomes formidable indeed. To go further and construct the time path of such a structure is usually impossible.

Difficulties of this type can, of course, stem from the limited scope of observations represented in the file. More troublesome, however, is the fact that the symbolic elements are often designated in ways that limit their susceptibility to recombination. Rarely has any thought been given to the possibility of designating them in ways that facilitate their use in performing more than one representational task.

Third, these data are often made available only in the form of intermediate aggregates reflecting the combined states of a population of similar entities. This is one of the obstacles to recombining data elements in formulating a variety of entity representations, and it reinforces the limitations identified above.

Fourth, even in situations where adequate data elements may exist in the files, the fragmented and uncoordinated character of the administrative systems that manage these records commonly defeats their effective use.

... multiple-use statistical systems are currently in no position to aid the kind of representational tasks so essential to support higher, more complex levels of information processing. Again, the very nature of these systems is a part of the problem. Faced with the difficulty and expense of representing entity concepts with readily available symbolic data, we are generally content to view the world in established ways. We are often inclined to accept these canned observations as being more "real" in some sense, even when they yield entity representations that are unreal in terms of our intentions.

What, if anything, can be done to improve upon this situation depends upon our being able to view it as a problem in system design and development, guided by two kinds of information. (1) We need a representation of the kinds of data elements that can perform a variety of representational tasks and can, therefore, be justified as components of a multiple-purpose record. This requires a representation of the ways in which the observational fields and adaptive situations of the principal classes of information processors overlap. Some such image is not only essential to designate the scope and content of multiple-use archives, it is essential in indicating the ways in which the observations must be symbolized to facilitate their multiple use. Such a representation is essential to guide the appropriate organization of statistical records. (2) We need a set of images to guide the organization of the administrative and technical systems necessary to provide the flexible access to data elements essential for their use in a variety of entity representations. At issue are both technical and methodological problems.

The generation of these kinds of information services constitutes a social and information science research task of major proportions....

Notes

[1] Even Newell and Simon (1972) employ explicit "object" language to designate information processing structures.

[2] Arieti (1965) makes it clear that three basic modes of cognition are employed to carry symbolic representation beyond object *identification*. One may employ *contiguity* for perceiving linked events; *similarity*, for the classification of events as units of interaction; *pars-pro-toto*, for inferring from a set of events a total pattern or system of events that form a behavioral entity. Our understanding of this shadow world is a product of our power to project conceptual entities of relationship upon it, and then to validate and utilize these concept entities through the development of other entities (perceptual amplifers) constructed to generate representational entities. The entity concept is rooted in the nature of the cognitive aspects of human information processing.

[3] For example, in terms of the forms of graph theory, initial and terminal states can be symbolized by the vertices or nodes of a directed graph and the transforming or transferring action correspondingly symbolized by its edges. Thus depicted, the relationship of designated activities yields variants of the "tree," "forest," and "circuit" networks of graph theory.

[4] Including, by the way, all instrumental artifacts fashioned out of material or biological elements to serve as components of human-social systems.

[5] This does not imply that a designated element may not be a component of more than one biological life system because these entities are commonly hierarchically

related. (Thus, the ventricle can be "seen" as a component of the entity "heart," which is "seen" as a component of the entity "circulatory system," which can be "seen" as a component of something else, and so forth.) However, these are not often overlapping entities. The set of entities embracing a common element can be seen to form a simple "nested" hierarchy.

[6]Representations of physical systems involve relationships that are sufficiently stable, over prolonged periods of time, to develop laws of relationship that can survive the traditional falsification strategies of science. These relationships also display sufficiently high degrees of stability to permit their use in engineering physical-system artifacts. Biological systems, in contrast, yield only quasi-laws of relationships or probability predictions. (See Goudge, 1961, pp. 127–129; also Dunn, 1971a, pp. 125–136.) In an even more tentative way, human and social information processors operating in a strictly managerial mode may display somewhat stable relationships also yielding to generalization. But these generalizations are made highly contingent by a human capacity for creative social transformation not restricted to the tempo of cosmic, genetic, or ontogenetic processes.

[7]The Dana Corporation of Toledo went through just such a cycle of data proliferation, breakdown, and structural reformation. (See Dana Corporation, 1971.) Ackoff (1967), among many others, has also written about the tendency to proliferate irrelevant sources of data and the need for management to think in terms of the design of information processing systems.

References

Ackoff, Russell. "Management Misinformation Systems," *Management Science* (December 1967).

Arieti, Silvano. "Toward a Unifying Theory of Cognition." *General Systems Yearbook*, Vol. X, 1965, pp. 109–115.

Boulding, Kenneth E. *The Image*. Ann Arbor: University of Michigan Press, 1961.

Dana Corporation. "TV Replaces Stacks of Paperwork," *Business Week*, Vol. III (January 30, 1971).

Dunn, Edgar S., Jr. *Economic and Social Development: A Process of Social Learning*. Baltimore: Johns Hopkins Press. 1971(a)

Goudge, T. A. *The Ascent of Life*. Toronto: University of Toronto Press, 1961.

Maslow, Abraham. *The Psychology of Science*. New York: Harper and Row, 1966.

Maturana, Humberto. "Neurophysiology of Cognition," in Paul L. Garvin, ed., *Cognition: A Multiple View*. New York: Spartan Books, 1970.

Newell, Albert T., and Herbert A. Simon. *Human Problem Solving*. Englewood Cliffs, N.J., Prentice-Hall, 1972.

Vickers, Geoffrey. *Towards a Sociology of Management*. New York: Basic Books, 1967.

_____. *Value Systems and Social Process*. New York: Basic Books; London, Tavistock, 1968.

_____. *Freedom in a Rocking Boat*. London: Allen Lane, 1970.

Information Support for Congress: The Role of Technology
Robert Lee Chartrand

Congress has always had to respond to both creative proposals and crises. In many notable instances, Congress had to emphasize developing a synoptic capability, measuring the action alternatives, and striving to view the situation as a whole. Achieving this capability, which often involved engaging in political pyrotechnics, demanded valid information.

To cope with its enormous and ever-expanding information problem, Congress has been willing to explore numerous ameliorative approaches (several of which use advanced information technology), determined that its governing role would combine a perceptive, look-ahead approach with the ability to respond with alacrity to pressures from constituents or unanticipated calamities. The plethora of information on Capitol Hill is awesome. Despite a tripling of staff, which now numbers 23,000, and an annual expenditure of more than $50 million for computer costs—up from $4.8 million in 1970—the demand for narrative and statistical data continues to increase.

In the 1965 "Management Study of the U.S. Congress," which was commissioned by NBC News for its special television report "Congress Needs Help," the projected role of high-speed computers was spelled out: "The very nature of some analytical problems of Congress calls for flexible manipulation of massive data into many different arrangements to serve many different purposes." Toward that end, an array of technology-supported information systems has been created, sometimes in the face of a not-unexpected opposition to change. Misconceptions about what computers could do or about how these "wizard machines" could affect legislative workings included concerns such as these:

- Large numbers of staff members would be replaced by computers.
- Committee chairmen would lose control of confidential legislative information.
- Computers would assume some decision-making functions.
- Data bases would be the only source for needed data, with human specialists no longer available.

- Robotype letters would depersonalize congressman-constituent relationships to an unconscionable degree.

For the most part, these expectations have been unfounded. New devices and man-machine techniques have been incorporated into traditional committee and member office procedures; although some staff members have had to master a few new skills, disruption has been minimal in most cases.

Examination of actions initiated by Congress as a whole (or within an individual committee) reveals a determination to increase its efficiency and effectiveness. Starting with the Legislative Reorganization Act of 1970 (P.L. 91-510), continuing with the Congressional Budget and Impoundment Control Act of 1974 (P.L. 93-344), and augmented by the creation of sundry commissions and select committees, the emphasis has been on strengthening the legislative structure and selected procedures.

One salient facet of these intended improvements has been to enhance legislative information resources and services, especially through the use of automatic data processing (ADP) and micrographics devices, the increased reliance on telecommunications networks, and the willingness to experiment with audio and video technologies. Often, the reasons for introducing technology are simple: A computerized mailing system is adopted because the floor of the room where addressograph plates are stored is buckling; a terminal switching of information requests from point of receipt to research units is instituted because the human messengers can no longer distribute rush inquiries quickly enough. Corrective action usually results because of both inner and outer realities: pressures of those persons who must perform responsively and pressures from the leadership, which has an ill-defined but irrevocable feeling that changes are necessary.

The willingness of Congress to try innovative information-handling approaches stems from the desire to maintain mastery over its environment. In *The Ascent of Man*, Bronowski talks about man's ability to make "plans, inventions, new discoveries, by putting different talents together; and his discoveries become more subtle and penetrating, as he learns to combine his talents in more complex and intimate ways."

In the quest for improved information files and products, emphasis has been placed on the recurring questions, "What can it do for me?" "How much will it cost?" "Is it going to destroy my office routine?" "What will my constituents think?" Several carefully drawn surveys of member and staff information needs have helped identify and place in order of importance those legislative and constituent service areas that should receive prime consideration as funding and staff resources are allocated. For those persons charged with designing new or improved "systems," the old credo "something here, something now"—that is, provide useful deliverables en route to a total new capability—is still in vogue.

Although the pattern for developing such innovative systems has been chamber oriented or left to the various legislative support agencies—Congressional Research Service (CRS), General Accounting Office (GAO), Congressional Budget Office, Office of Technology Assessment—to implement, the realization has been reached that a mechanism is needed to monitor and guide these efforts. Early in 1977, CRS Director Gilbert Gude formally proposed to the Senate Committee on Rules and Administration and the Committee on House Administration that a Policy Coordination Group (PCG) be created "to coordinate the development of technology-supported information systems during the present and succeeding Congresses." The PCG would operate through a series of task forces, such as those responsible for developing the joint LEGIS (Legislative Information and Status) system capability, one focusing on the potential of microform technology, and another to establish and expand audio and video networks on Capitol Hill. Full approval of PCG was given by respective committee chairmen.

The House of Representatives, which began creating advanced information systems in 1969, has recently separated its policy formulation and operational responsibilities. A Policy Group on Information and Computers, chaired by Congressman Charlie Rose, fulfills the former role, while the 210-person House Information Systems (HIS) group provides daily service to the house members and committees.

Among the priority applications of ADP technology is handling bill content and status information by on-line LEGIS capability. Although originally the desired data could be obtained only by calling a central inquiry office, member offices increasingly have direct access to these computerized files. At present, more than 200 congressmen have either typewriter or videoscreen terminals in their Hill offices, and an increasing number are placing such units in their districts.

An experimental system using minicomputers and multiple terminal devices now performs combined composition and editing, allowing more expeditious entry of information on formal committee hearings into GPO's publishing operation. In the future, the same equipment and software will be used to support a bill-drafting system for the Office of the Legislative Counsel.

A broad spectrum of budget analysis and monitoring projects in support of the House Budget and Appropriations committees and the Congressional

Budget Office has been developed since passage of the Congressional Budget and Impoundment Control Act of 1974. The operating programs include

Budget Control System	Member Budget System
Budget Tracking System	Fiscal Data Base
Legislative Classification System	CBO Congressional Scorekeeping System
Project Control System	Rescissions and Deferrals

Comparative Statement of Budget Authority (CSBA)

An increasing number of computer-assisted models are used to help formulate policy alternatives, supported by packaged programs such as income modeling, statistical analysis, econometric forecasting, and income tax analysis. Perhaps in no other area has there been a more substantial congressional reinforcement of the concept, cogently set forth by Peter Drucker in *Landmarks and Tomorrow*, that "the only way to conserve is by innovating. The only stability possible is stability in motion."

A Member Information Network (MIN) gives offices access to various remote computerized files such as JURIS (Justice Retrieval and Inquiry System) and FAPRS (Federal Assistance Program Retrieval System) and to the 11 files of the Library of Congress SCORPIO (Subject-Content Oriented Retriever for Processing Information On-line) system. In addition, this network provides summary accounts of House floor activities, which are inserted by chamber reporters into the on-line Summary of Proceedings and Debate (SOPAD) system.

Other House applications of computers include the sophisticated electronic voting system used in the chamber, the terminals used by 18 committees in preparing their legislative calendars, and the computers used to perform several routine administrative functions (payroll and inventories). The potential of video technology is being assessed by the House Committee on Rules, based on a 90-day trial filming of House chamber activities conducted by the House Select Committee on Congressional Operations.

In the Senate, development of information systems is controlled in accordance with formal guidelines, by the Committee on Rules and Administration, but certain responsibilities are vested in the sergeant at arms, who manages the Senate computer center and trains Senate personnel to use various computerized services, and in the secretary of the Senate.

To "provide information and analysis to Senators and their staff to assist them in their legislative tasks," videoscreen terminals have been installed in 98 member offices and 46 other Senate locations. These screens allow quick access to the SCORPIO-served files such as the popular Major Issues System, a series of files containing bibliographic citations (from periodicals and books), and the Bill Digest files for the 93rd, 94th, and 95th Congresses.

In addition to cooperating with the House and Library of Congress in developing LEGIS, the Senate managers are actively supporting development of "full text retrieval" programming through the use of SCORPIO software, plans for a Senate meeting and hearing display system, and creation of data files featuring official information on Senators, Senate committees, and committee membership for use by the majority and minority secretaries.

Fiscal-budgetary support services have been started, including preparation of tables on budget targets, allocations, and ceilings and establishment of a library of analytical reports for the Senate Committee on the Budget. External services such as those provided by Chase Econometric and Wharton Econometric are also available to Senate committee users. ADP techniques help the Committee on Appropriations to prepare bill reports.

Another significant endeavor is the pilot Correspondence Management System (CMS), designed to help handle the voluminous correspondence that is a serious problem in most Senate offices. An Automated Index System has been created that permits office staff members to store basic identification data about a document only once and then use cross-referenced files to retrieve the data on the basis of name, date, city, and so forth.

Several Senate committees have had special computer-based services created for them. One of the most comprehensive efforts, for the Committee on Foreign Relations, features a retrieval system that contains a collection of indexing and abstracting records on committee documents such as charters, treaties, or international agreements, press releases, and reports required by law. An overview of computer services provided to committees and other Senate units can be seen in Figure 1.

Computers, microfilm, and other technological advances also are used by the Senate as it copes with massive addressing and mailing loads, receives and stores campaign expenditure data—in a manner similar to the House of Representatives—records vote tallies, and carries out several administrative functions (e.g., payroll).

Although all the legislative support organizations draw on the computer's flexibility and power, the CRS has pioneered its use. Commencing with computerization of the *Digest of Public General Bills and Resolutions* in 1968, CRS has sought to identify those priority congressional needs for information that could best be met by use of man-machine techniques. Through its Information Systems Group, which provides technical support to both CRS staff members and congressional clients, and an Information

	Scorpio	ATMS	Mail system	Budget analysis	New York Times data bank	Specialized services
Aeronautical and Space Sciences	*	*	*	**	**	
Agriculture and Forestry	*	*	**	**		
Appropriations	*	*	**	**		**
Armed Services	**	**		**		**
Banking, Housing, and Urban Affairs			**	**		**
Budget	*	*	**	**		**
Commerce	*	*	*	**	**	
District of Columbia	*	*		**		
Finance			**	**		
Foreign Relations	*	*	*	**	**	*
Multinational Corporations Subcommittee			**			
Government Operations	*	*	*	**		
Permanent Subcommittee on Investigations			**			
Intergovernmental Relations Subcommittee			**			
Interior and Insular Affairs		**		**		
Judiciary	*			**		
Improvements in Judicial Machinery			*			
Internal Security Subcommittee			**			
Separation of Powers Subcommittee			**			
Labor and Public Welfare	*	*		**		**
Post Office and Civil Service			**	**		
Public Works	*	*	**	**		
Rules and Administration				**	**	**
Computer Services Subcommittee	*	*	*	**		
Veterans' Affairs	*	*	**	**		
Select Committee on Small Business	*	**				
Select Committee on Standards and Conduct		**				
Select Committee on Nutrition and Human Needs				**		**
Select Committee to Study the Senate Committee System		**	**	**		**
Select Committee on Intelligence	*	*				
Special Committee on Aging				**		
Joint Economic Committee	**	**	**	**		**
Secretary of the Senate	**	**				**
Disbursing Office						**
Senate Library	**	**			**	
Legislative Counsel	**					**
Sergeant at Arms	**	**	**			
Radio and TV Gallery			**			
American Indian Policy Rev Commission			**			
Congressional Budget Office			**			
Office of Technology Assessment			**			
Democratic Policy Committee	**		**		**	**
Republican Policy Committee	**				**	**
Secretary for the Majority						**
Secretary for the Minority						**
Commission on Operation of Senate						**
Total	23	22	29	21	7	18

*Installed prior to 1976.
**Installed in 1976.

Figure 1 Computer services provided to committees, subcommittees, and other senate organizations. (Source: Subcommittee on Computer Services, *Report to the Committee on Rules and Administration, United States Senate,* Washington, D.C., U.S. Government Printing Office, 1977, p. 3.)

Sciences Section that consults with members and committees regarding research on topics dealing with the impact of information technology on society and government, CRS endeavors to meet the ever-changing requirements of its customer, Congress.

Other CRS services that use computer or microfilm support include the Major Issues System, featuring more than 200 specially written "briefs" available in paperform or displayed on a videoscreen, and the Bibliographic Citation File, which informs users of recent literature acquisitions. Congressional and CRS users of this latter file receive weekly notification cards describing items of possible interest, based on "profiles" prepared by the users themselves. All source documents are stored as microfiche and are available for quick delivery to the requesting office. A recent addition to the SCORPIO files is the computerized version of the *Congressional Record,* providing indexed abstracts.

Early in its program to broaden information resources and services, CRS management determined to use existing private-sector and government files. From the commercial marketplace, CRS draws on information in the New York Times Information Bank, the Congressional Information Service "CIS/Index," and the on-line, multiple-file offerings of the SDC Search Service and the Lockheed DIALOG information retrieval service. Although the FAPRS file and the National Technical Information Service (NTIS) citations—to name only two computerized government collections of interest to Congress—have been incorporated into one or more commercial services available to CRS, direct access is maintained to the National Library of Medicine MEDLINE file and the Department of Justice JURIS legal information retrieval system.

Although significant advancements have occurred in congressional management and use of information technology, as shown in Figure 2, the opportunity remains for enhancing support to that community of users. "Videoconferencing" by satellite, which was successfully demonstrated early in the 95th Congress, linked the Stevenson Subcommittee on Science and Space to witnesses in Springfield, Illinois who commented on artificial weather modification. Another session found Congressman Charlie Rose talking to a group of students in North Carolina. Audio and video technology are being considered not only to cover chamber and committee proceedings but also to convey to legislative users the gist of key issues in nonwritten form. Other identifiable resources, some of which are already being tested, include two-way portable audio units to enable members to stay in touch with their offices and a variety of computer-supported models that can quickly provide options to congressional planners and budgeteers.

1965–1966	Second Legislative Reorganization Act hearings
1966	First bill to create a congressional computer facility (H.R. 18428, 89th Congress)
1967	CRS automates Bill Digest information
1968	CRS computerizes first House calendar operation
1969	House acts on Brademas resolution by empowering Special Subcommittee on Electrical and Mechanical Office Equipment to study ADP uses
1970	Passage of Legislative Reorganization Act of 1970 (P.L. 91-510)
	Senate establishes Subcommittee on Computer Services; authorizes study of ADP uses
1971	House Information Systems office created
	Potter administrative survey of offices of the Secretary of Senate issued
1972	House and Senate campaign expenditure data systems implemented
	New House chamber voting procedures approved
	GAO "Budgetary and Fiscal Information Needs of the Congress" published
	Technology Assessment Act of 1972 creates OTA (P.L. 92-484)
1973	Senate commences pilot test of CRS on-line files
	House electronic voting system becomes operative
	CRS and Senate tie in to New York Times Information Bank
	CRS establishes links with MEDLINE and JURIS systems
1974	Congressional Budget and Impoundment Control Act of 1974 (P.L. 93-344) creates CBO and chamber Budget Committees
	House Select Committee on Committees makes recommendations (H.R. 988)
1975	House Commission on Information and Facilities establishes "pilot member information network"
	Senate provides terminals for all member offices
	House Committee Order No. 23 authorizes $1,000 monthly expenditure (from clerk-hire funds) by each member for computer services
	Temporary Commission on the Operation of the Senate established
1976	Temporary Select Committee to Study the Senate Committee System created House Commission on Administrative Review formed
	Expansion of Senate, House, and Library of Congress computer capabilities
1977	House Policy Group on Information and Computers established
	Trial videotaping of House chamber proceedings by Select Committee on Congressional Operations
	Policy Coordination Group authorized by Committee on House Administration and Senate Committee on Rules and Administration

Figure 2 Chronology of key steps toward improved congressional information support.

During the past decade, significant improvements have been made in legislative information support—not only the introduction of computers to Capitol Hill but also a discernible broadening of members' understanding of information technology as a major force in society. For example, a Department of Commerce study indicates that the "information industry" accounts for 46 percent of the U.S. work force and almost half the gross national product. A recent forecast predicts that in 1985, 70 percent of the U.S. labor force will depend on data processing to do its work. These patterns, reflecting the impingement of information technology, are undeniable and call to mind the reminder by Librarian of Congress Daniel Boorstin that "no device can be forgotten or erased from the arsenal of technology."

The growing consensus is that civilization has entered the "Age of Information," with all the benefits and dangers inherent in that evolution. The burden of planning, monitoring, and evaluating the roles of information must be borne by institutions such as Congress. The nation's responsibility is to protect and reinforce these social underpinnings, for, as John Gardner remarks in *The Recovery of Confidence,* "The swifter the pace of change, the more lovingly men must care for and criticize their institutions to keep them intact through the turbulent passages."

Assessing the Role and Impact of Information Technology in the Legislative Environment
John J. Stucker

Legislation remains an act of will and judgement, and information systems must be judged as they reinforce that fact.

—Senator John C. Culver (D-Iowa)

Form follows function.

—Louis S. Sullivan

Recently, much attention has been devoted to the process of "professionalizing" legislatures.[11] The question remains: What benefits have been derived from the trend during the past 15 years to modernize legislatures and their processes? Has the effort to modernize Congress and state legislatures improved the way in which these bodies function? Has this trend resulted in improved outputs from the legislative branch of government?

In this selection, one aspect of the modernization or professionalization of legislatures is addressed: the attempt to harness information technology for legislative purposes. Information technology includes not only the conventional forms of automated data processing but also the fields of telecommunications and microform, word-processing, and audiovisual technologies. The growth in legislative use of technology has been phenomenal. The total budget for computing services in Congress rose from $4.8 million in 1970 to more than $30 million in 1978, a sixfold increase in less than a decade. In the House of Representatives alone, the main support group, House Information Systems (HIS), began in early 1971 with a staff of one and a minuscule budget. For calendar year 1978, HIS operated with a $10.9 million budget and a staff of 225.[16]

State legislatures have not lagged far behind in implementing information technology. No reliable cost figures are available for all 50 states; however, the number of applications (e.g., for statutory retrieval, bill-drafting, bill status, photocomposition, fiscal-budgetary, and administrative systems) has grown more than 60 percent during the five-year period from 1972 to 1977. As of 1977, at least seven state legislatures had their own internal computer processor support.[14]

Several practices have initiated and sustained this growth during the past 15 years. First, adopting information technology represents an attempt to cope with increased workloads and longer sessions. Since the 1960s, both Congress and the state legislatures have had steadily increasing demands on their time, which has meant longer sessions, more committee work, and more meetings to attend. At the same time, many legislatures have not experienced a corresponding increase in support staff. Information technology is seen as a means of breaking through the legislative logjam and solving the time shortage that troubles individual members and legislatures as a whole.

Second, efforts have been made to give junior members more and better access to information traditionally controlled by committee chairpersons or senior staff. The coming of age of the baby-boom generation during the sixties and seventies brought about wholesale changes in the memberships of both state and federal legislative bodies. This new cohort has not always been satisfied with relying on the traditional information sources to carry out legislative responsibilities. This group has called for more orderly, systematic means of obtaining standardized public data regarding the programs, policies, and activities that they legislate. Many individuals see the computer as the means for providing accurate data in a timely manner.

Third, use of information technology has been a key component in reestablishing parity between the legislative and executive branches. Many legislators view the decline of legislative control and influence during this century as a result of the rise of executive influence and power. In their opinion, one manifestation of executive power has been extensive use by executive agencies of data-processing technology, which has given them an advantage in controlling the information needed for making decisions. Some legislators think that they will not be able to reassert their prerogatives until legislatures adopt computers as aggressively and extensively as executive agencies have.

Finally, increased reliance on information technology is symptomatic of a national secular trend—the growth of the "information society." Since World War II, there has been a steady growth in the development and spread of electronic information technology and the disciplines that have accompanied it (e.g., operations research, cybernetics, management science, etc.). This "technological imperative" has forced institutions to admit the existence of an information explosion and to adopt the artifacts of information technology to cope with ever-increasing data. It is not surprising that the legislature was one institution that resisted, longer than most, the temptation to "computerize." The imperative is so powerful, however, that by now most legislatures have incorporated at least some aspect of information technology.

The question remains: Has this investment of time, money, and resources really modernized legislatures? Information itself is an old and traditional commodity in the legislative process. Since legislative assemblies were first organized, information has been used by committee chairpersons, leaders, key staff persons, and even outsiders to influence outcomes. The relative supremacy of the executive branch in controlling information resources is an example of how information affects legislative processes. Another example is the claim by public interest groups that too often legislatures have passed special interest laws because the legislators have relied on special interest groups as their primary source of information about pending legislation.

The role of information has been analyzed by students of the legislative process.[7,8,12] The committee structure has been studied to determine its effects in fragmenting and channeling information in the decision-making process. Since the work of most committees follows agency-jurisdictional lines, policymaking is usually framed in institutional rather than programmatic terms. Another example has been articulation of a "deference model" to describe how legislators rely on key opinion leaders among their colleagues when they must make a decision (i.e., cast a vote).

The issue being addressed here is presumably not information; rather, it is the introduction to an institution of a technology (or technologies) to handle, process, and manage an otherwise conventional commodity. If adopting information technology is to be considered a modernizing force, it must be shown to have altered the dynamics described in the literature on legislative process. Adoption of information technology must have significantly changed the nature of the decisions made and/or how they are made and have improved the legislature's functioning.

Literature Review

Recently, many observers have indicated that students of legislative behavior have not given sufficient attention to the role of information technology in the legislature. Although I sympathize with that assessment, during the past 10 years, a considerable body of literature has been published on this subject (see Chartrand[1] for an extensive literature review). This literature can be dated from the late 1960s, when a group of political scientists first paid attention to the topic and wrote several books directed toward Congress.[2,4,5,13.]

The general thrust of those volumes was that Congress faced a crisis as a coequal branch of government. The workload for individual members was increasing, and members had to cope with this increase in the face of inadequate staff and other support. The nature and complexity of public policy issues were also changing. These developments would require a more sophisticated, information-rich decision-making capability than had previously existed in Congress. Finally, the presidency had achieved a dominant position in the Federal Government, seemingly dictating the terms of public policy decision making to the legislature.

The basic conclusion of these authors was that Congress had to modernize its procedures and institutional arrangements to regain its proper role in government. Information technology was a major vehicle for effecting this change because it could organize and provide rapid access to large bodies of information. Information technology could link data resources from both public and private sectors to ensure that Congress had access to all currently available relevant information. Information technology could also enable Congress to analyze past conditions and forecast or model future trends so that it could legislate policies and programs more responsive to social needs.

Note that these early volumes cannot be considered an assessment of the role or impact of information technology in Congress. At the time these books were written, information technology was almost nonexistent in Congress; rather, these volumes boost computers. With the premise that Congress needed reform and with certain assumptions about the usefulness of information technology, the authors argued that more extensive use of technology would help reform Congress.

By 1970, Congress had accelerated its efforts for general reform and reorganization, including adopting and using automatic data processing (ADP). Congress documented these latter developments in a series of internal reports beginning in 1969. The purposes of the initial studies were to identify the information needs of the Congress, to outline institutional goals, and to set priorities for developing and implementing technology.[15,18,20] When sufficient progress had been achieved, an overview report[17] was produced that not only described developments to date but also evaluated them. The report highlighted successful applications and discussed problem areas, noting the importance of integrating information technology into the legislative process rather than vice versa. The report also described activities of four major information support units for Congress—HIS, the Library of Congress, the General Accounting Office, and the Government Printing Office—and provided a brief overview of some of the developments in state legislatures.

Throughout this period, outside observers wrote about legislative information systems; however, they shifted their emphasis from that of earlier literature (previously cited) to a comparative assessment of the role of the technology in the states and at the federal level. Elkins[6] prepared a report entitled *A Survey of the Use of Electronic Data Processing by State Legislatures.* This report enumerated and described various computer applications initiated in state legislatures during the late 1960s. Elkins found that implementation of ADP applications was spotty and concentrated in the following areas: electronic voting systems, bill-drafting, and code revision systems. But the pace of development in the states was already increasing, and at the request of the Council of State Governments, Elkins updated his survey in 1971, 1972, and 1974. In these subsequent surveys, Elkins noted the use of information technology for statutory search and retrieval systems, reporting bill status, and photocomposition. Since 1974, the Council's survey efforts have been continued and the results given in the annual report of the National Association of State Information Systems, *Information Systems Technology in State Government.*[10] The data from these surveys show continuing emphasis on applications to support internal legislative functions.

In 1972, *Modern Information Technology in the State Legislatures*[19] was issued, the first of two reports prepared under the direction of Robert Lee Chartrand of the Congressional Research Service, Library of Congress. Like the Elkins–Council of State Governments surveys, the first Chartrand report noted that most applications of information technology supported basic legislative processes; however, Chartrand's data showed a growing interest in using technology to support fiscal-budgetary applications. In updating his survey five years later,[14] Chartrand noted a widespread use of technology by state legislatures to support fiscal accounting, budgeting and appropriations, and modeling applications. In both reports, Chartrand devoted attention to factors and constraints governing the adoption and use by legislatures of information technology. He thus helped move discussion of legislative information systems from a descriptive to an analytical level.

Growing interest in the use by state legislatures of computers to support budgeting and appropriations resulted in formation of the Fiscal Information Task Force by the National Conference of State Legislatures. During 1967–1977, this task force surveyed all the state legislatures to determine the level of automated legislative fiscal systems. The report *Legislative Fiscal Information Systems*[11] contains summary findings for all the states and in-depth profiles of five states. Review of this document suggests that interest in automated fiscal systems exceeds actual capabilities in most state legislatures; however, the profiles indicate that a few states have developed some sophisticated applications.

The final selection in this review is *Comparative Legislative Information Systems.*[21] Much of this volume is devoted to case studies of the development of legislative information systems in Congress, seven state legislatures, the Canadian House of Commons, and the British Parliament. Two chapters, however, contain an evaluation and assessment of the role of information technology in legislatures. Like Chartrand in his second report, the authors review the problems and pitfalls in using legislative information systems, attempt to isolate the factors leading to a legislature's successful adaptation of this technology, and explore the potential for future uses based on past experience.

Overview of the Literature. A summary of what this literature reveals about legislative information systems would be useful at this point. The surveys and inventories reported document the explosive growth in legislative uses of information technology. In the mid-1960s, computers were almost unknown in state legislatures; in Congress, information technology was limited to robotypewriters. By the late 1970s, however, information technology, in all its manifestations, was ubiquitous in Congress and in virtually all state legislatures.

The literature reviewed suggests that development of legislative information technology has followed a clear pattern. In almost every instance, the initial applications created support legislative and internal administrative functions, such as voting, bill status, bill drafting and code revision, committee calendars, payrolls and office accounts, and correspondence. Only after these initial systems have been successfully implemented do most legislatures develop decision-assisting and policy analysis applications. Examples of the latter applications include expenditure-tracking and budget systems and forecasting models and statistical analyses for performance assessment.

This development sequence is not surprising when one considers the differences between the two types of applications. In automated administrative or legislative process applications, the data input is accessible since it is all in-house. Furthermore, the procedures for processing that data and the expected outputs are well defined and often already embedded in the legislature's traditions and practices. Frequently, all that remains is to automate existing procedures. Of course, one should not think that there are no problems to overcome. There is the classic story of the elderly legislator who was shocked to discover that the new automated teller system, for which he voted approval, no longer permitted him to see his old friend in the clerk's office to change his roll-call vote a week after it had been recorded. But in most legislatures, implementing these applications has been a manageable task. As will be discussed later, however, manageability has not been the case with the second type of application.

Recent literature has gone beyond the descriptive and evaluated information technology in the legislature, primary emphasis being placed on assessing the preconditions for successful implementation. The findings on preconditions can be divided into the broad categories that follow.

The Role of Members. Successful adoption of information technology requires several members who neither are afraid to use it nor are oversold on its benefits—individuals who are realistic about technology's potential and limitations. These persons must also know what they want from technology and what to do with the results. It is preferable that the members be either chairmen of major committees or subcommittees or leaders. Such legislative positions offer two advantages: they not only increase the chances that the outputs of the technology will be used but also make it easier to secure the necessary (and usually substantial) resources needed for developing, maintaining, and operating the information systems.

Role of Staff. Next to members, the most important precondition is the role of staff. At least a few key staff persons should be knowledgeable and realistic about information technology and its uses and abuses. These persons play a critical role in helping translate member needs in support activities and must have not only a professional, realistic image of technology's capabilities and limitations but also the ability and willingness to use that perspective in dealing with members' requests. A major complaint about legislative information systems is that members either are undersold on the cost or are oversold on the potential performance of a proposed application. As the persons responsible for developing and implementing information systems, staff persons must ensure that their enthusiasm for technology does not result in systems that the legislature cannot afford or technology that does not meet needs.

Cooperation of External (Executive Branch) Agencies. Any information-processing system (technology based or not) requires steady input of relevant data to function properly. To implement information systems technology, the persons responsible must ensure that the necessary data input is available for the systems in question. As was noted in the discussion of administrative and legislative process applications, problems of data access can be minimized because data sources are within the legislative institution. The situation is quite different, however, in the case of fiscal, program, and policy applications because the legislature is then an information broker, not an information producer. The primary sources of relevant data for most of these matters are outside the legislature, usually within executive agencies. The legislature must ensure availability of the high-quality, accurate data needed. Legislative mandate is a traditional means of securing the necessary input from respondent agencies, but cooperation is also essential if data are to be reported accurately and on time.

Cooperation, however, extends beyond the substantive concern of data sources. With the exception of Congress and seven state legislatures, all other state legislatures that use automated information systems do not have a separate data-processing division to provide processor support but rely on outside agencies for this service. The legislatures usually justify this policy by claiming that they are only trying to take advantage of existing capacity in state government without adding a new operating division. Because standards and criteria for assessing costs and evaluating available capacity are usually poorly defined, the manager of the supporting division can seldom make simple, businesslike decisions regarding job scheduling, priorities for software development, and the like. As a result, conflicts emerge over which has priority: supporting legislative needs or dealing with other clients served by the operating division. Unless the legislative staff personnel responsible for the system's overall operation has a cooperative relationship with the external operating division, the legislature's processing requirements will not receive the priority that members assume they deserve.

Internal Organization. Most legislatures have assigned data processing to an older, more traditional group, such as a legislative counsel or a clerk's office, which is why most state legislatures have taken so long to innovate. Several leader states and the House of Representatives, however, have assigned data processing to a new group that reports to an oversight committee of members. Florida established the Joint Legislative Management Committee to oversee two sections, the Systems and Data Processing Division and the Information Division. Illinois formed the Legislative Information Systems Committee and assigned staff to that group.

Appointing a separate group to supervise the legislature's use of information technology has several advantages. This approach provides the proper framework for the key member–key staff roles described earlier. Group staff personnel can be given responsibility for managing technology without being burdened with conventional support activities. This arrangement helps the staff to implement and operate the information systems and to ensure that adequate security provisions are maintained for the systems and data bases. Linking the staff to a member oversight group makes the staff directly accountable to members, who can guide staff efforts and support activities.

Time Element. Successful introduction of information technology to a legislature requires experimental, evolutionary strategies that can identify "bugs" in the applications and account for the technology's effects on the legislature. Following a step-by-step strategy spreads development costs over time, allows the staff time to work out difficulties, and gives the staff a chance to identify and respond to unanticipated costs.

Because a time-phased, evolutionary approach has been emphasized, the reader should not think that this process will be random and unplanned. A long-range plan may be a good way to manage a time-phased process. For example, Illinois has adopted a five-year master plan for meeting its legislative information system requirements. The Illinois master plan expresses the legislature's goals and objectives for information resources and technology and identifies strategies for achieving them but does not dictate each step to be followed.

Impact of Information Technology on the Legislature

The literature on information technology in legislatures describes and evaluates the preconditions necessary for applying this technology in a legislative setting. But what does this literature tell about the impact of technology? What evidence is given to show that information technology has helped modernize legislatures? Although the literature has not ignored the subject, it has offered little insight. As Worthley[21] noted:

[T]here has been little effort by scholars and students of legislatures to integrate insights on legislative reform with the development of computerized legislative information systems. There is hardly a study available that analyzes the consequences of modern legislative information systems for the legislative process, for democratic government, for public policy making. (p. 21)

In reflecting on his own review of this literature, Chartrand[1] observed:

What emerges. . .is a *melange* of writings, sometimes casual, again more knowledgeable, but difficult to fathom unless one is inside the field. Where a specific application is concerned, however, the information presented tends to be more cogent. (p. 324)

Chartrand identified two interrelated aspects of the problem with this literature. The first aspect is that instead of beginning with the legislature and its requirements, the authors of this literature examine each application to determine which have been successfully implemented.

This approach leads to the question of what constitutes successful implementation of information technology in a legislature. Some of the case studies[11, 21] offer enough depth and perspective to enable the reader to determine the effects and judge the success of introducing information technology to a given legislature. But these studies and the number of legislatures considered are few. Most information on successful implementations is from surveys and inventories of state legislatures and Congress. The surveys usually consist of a mail questionnaire completed by a legislative staff person who is responsible for the applications being reported. Because in most cases the investigators do not visit the study sites, there is difficulty in controlling the natural tendency to overreport success by persons with a vested interest in the subject being studied. Success in these surveys is measured by the number of operating systems. The surveys seldom deal with how often and how well the systems are used.

The second aspect of the problem with this literature is the authors' backgrounds. Few of the authors are legislative analysts. Most have backgrounds in information science, operations research, or information technology from the perspective of public administration or management science, disciplines that do not always encounter the same problems that legislatures do when they introduce technology. The authors' institutional affiliations (as legislative members or staff) and their sources of support for research (e.g., National Science Foundation grants to help transfer technology to state government) may foster a partisan rather than a critical view of technology.

Because most authors do not go beyond preconditions and discuss the impact of technology on legislatures, the rest of this section reviews several major effects that should be investigated and analyzed and presents existing evidence of technology's impact on legislatures.

Varieties of Information Technology. Although this paper defines information technology in the broadest sense, most literature on information technology in legislatures focuses on large-scale computer systems. Therefore, several technological innovations have received little, if any, study. The growth of telecommunications improves access to data resources in the public and private sectors. But do legislators obtain better information to help them execute their responsibilities as a result of easier access to more data? How can telecommunications affect communication and data flow between the legislative and executive branches? What are the security requirements in a network containing data on legislative affairs, internal executive management concerns and private citizens?

The increased use of word-processing systems in both member offices and legislative support units alleviates the clerical workload. But what implications does stand-alone mini- and microcomputer technology have for the legislature? In most instances, computer access is tied to large-scale systems designed to serve the entire legislature. When an individual member obtains his own stand-alone processor, then he can design a unique set of systems and data bases with individualized logic. Can this development significantly alter the kinds of information a member has access to and thus alter the member's role in the legislative process?

Audiovisual technology is another area deserving study. Several states have established toll-free telephone systems to allow the public to inquire about the status of pending legislative business, and Congress has experimented with teleconferencing between remote sites throughout the country and Washington, D.C. The most widely discussed audiovisual application, however, is broadcasting legislative sessions. National Public Radio has broadcast sessions of both houses of Congress. Sessions of the Florida state legislature are broadcast live on a closed-circuit system throughout the capitol complex, and public television stations broadcast nightly summaries throughout the state. Canada and England now provide radio broadcasts of their Houses of Commons. Many legislators resisted efforts to broadcast their sessions because they feared that doing so could harm public opinion of the legislature. Proponents of broadcasting argued that it would bring people into closer contact with the legislature and thereby make the legislative process seem more democratic and representative. Now that the technology has been implemented, whose hopes and fears have been realized?

Impact on Individuals. A second area to be studied is the effect of information technology on individuals in the legislature, both members and staff. Many early justifications for adopting information technology promised benefits for individuals. For example, information technology would help members cope with increasing workloads, avoid large increases in support staff, and give junior members better access to information about the legislature's business. Now that the technology has been applied, some of the benefits can be studied to determine whether the observed matches the expected.

Evidence suggests that using information technology has significantly reduced the paperwork burden in certain areas of legislative activity and provided more data than before. What is not known is whether the additional data are relevant to members' needs. Some members are frustrated about what they consider information overload, but as yet no one has determined how widespread this feeling is among legislators.

In legislatures with highly developed technological capabilities, junior members have access to more and better information than do their counterparts in other assemblies; whether improved access has increased these members' influence is not known. If senior committee chairmen or leaders have been involved in design and maintenance of the systems used by the junior members, then the senior members have defined the kinds of data to which the junior members have access. What is unclear is whether the "control" of systems by senior members means that the relative access to information by junior members has been altered by the introduction of technology.

Cursory examination suggests that adopting information technology did not help to limit staff increases because most legislative staffs grew from the mid-1960s to the mid-1970s. Relying on such superficial evidence, however, could be misleading. The experience of most organizations indicates that introducing information technology seldom leads to staff reductions (at least on an organization-wide basis) for several reasons. First, existing staff members are often reassigned to duties and responsibilities that were previously unmet. Second, more employees must be hired to manage and operate the new technology. Third, technology can lead the organization into new areas of activity that require both personnel and technical resources for their support.

To date, changes in staffing levels have not been analyzed and related to the spread of information technology in legislatures. Some possible relationships could be investigated, however. In administrative and legislative applications, the processed workload has greatly increased, which is probably attributable to the technology far more than to staff increases. More correspondence is being handled than before (because of word-processing and correspondence management systems); more bills can be filed and acted on through committee, conference, and floor action stages (because of systems for bill drafting, bill status, and code revision); and more meetings and sessions can be scheduled with fewer conflicts for individual members (because of automated calendar systems). If staff increases have occurred in these areas, they are probably the result of nontechnical considerations. For example, in many state legislatures, legislators for the first time acquired a staff; in Congress, part of the increase in the staffs of individual members has been justified because of the rapid growth in constituent casework.

For decision making and policy analysis, important increments in legislative staff and the increased effectiveness of staff members are in some cases directly attributable to adopting technology. To implement technology successfully, the key staff person must not only translate member requests into feasible plans to develop useful systems but must also manage the output from the systems once they are developed and operating. The average legislator lacks both the time and expertise to deal with the output from complex information systems. The member needs an information service: a staff person who can synthesize and translate output into a form meaningful to the member. Most legislative support staff persons are not familiar with information technology; when advanced applications are adopted, experts must be hired to work with them. This situation leads to interesting, researchable questions: How do the technically skilled persons adapt to the legislative environment? What happens if a legislature relies instead on traditional staff personnel not skilled in the uses of technology? How do the two generations of staff—experts from outside and traditional legislative support personnel—interact? How do they complement each other? When do they come into conflict?

The Legislative Institution. A third area requiring study is the legislature as an institution. Three dimensions can be explored. The first dimension concerns the legislature's relationship to citizens. Has use of information technology by the legislature improved its representative function? Evidence is mixed, but by no means conclusive. Applications supporting individual member activities (e.g., systems for tracking correspondence and for providing district polling services) have increased members' contact with constituents, but are individual legislators better representatives of their districts, or have they just become more proficient ombudsmen in handling constituent casework?

There is no evidence suggesting that introducing phone inquiry systems has resulted in a deluge of calls from the public seeking information about the legislature's activities. On the contrary, what use phone inquiry systems have received seems to be limited to persons (e.g., bureaucrats and lobbyists) who have always monitored the legislature. As was already noted, no one is sure of the effect of broadcasting legislative sessions or summaries of sessions.

The second dimension concerns the relationship between the legislative and executive branches. The legislative branch's desire to expand its information technology capability to regain parity with the executive branch may have mixed consequences for the constitutional principle of separation of powers. There are several examples of the legislatures' encroachment on executive authority. The tradition is that the executive branch prepares a budget against which the legislative branch appropriates funds; the executive is then responsible for spending funds and accounting for expenditures. Lately, however, both federal and state legislatures have been formulating their own budgets (e.g., the Congressional Budget and Impoundment Act of 1974—P.L. 93-344) and requiring exhaustive accounting reports of executive agency expenditures. Oversight of the executive branch has been a traditional role of the legislature—a role that in the past was exercised on an ad hoc basis. Now, however, legislatures are mandating routine reporting requirements for executive agencies and undertaking detailed performance evaluations of the programs operated by these agencies.

Discussion of changes to the separation of powers raises some practical and constitutional issues that cannot be answered easily. Most of these changes stem from the legislature's lack of confidence (well founded in many instances) in the executive branch's ability to manage its own affairs in the public interest. If the legislature assumes responsibilities that parallel traditional executive functions and must rely on the executive branch not only for the data it uses but also for support for the information systems processing the data, how do these circumstances affect the legislature's ability to provide an independent check and balance on the executive branch? How do these changes in the separation of powers affect the legislature's ability to perform its unique functions?

Concern with the system of checks and balances leads to a consideration of the third dimension: the effects of information technology on the legislature's role in making public policy. Several aspects of the relationship between technology and public policy decisions bear examination. The first involves the way in which information technology relates to and supports decision making. Bureaucracy uses a problem-solving approach to make decisions about public policy. Taking this approach assumes that there is a "right" solution to a problem that can be determined if the problem can be defined properly and all the relevant facts can be reviewed and evaluated. This problem-solving approach contrasts with the consensus-building process that the legislature follows to make a decision. The goal of consensus building is to find any solution, as long as it satisfies the largest number of competing interests needed to win a vote. Defining the problem is not only irrelevant, it is usually avoided as being potentially harmful to achieving a successful outcome.

Most applications of information technology have been designed for engineers, administrators, or managers and take the problem-solving approach. It is not surprising that government executive agencies have been able to adopt information technology so readily. This fact also explains why relatively little progress has been made to date in implementing the decision-assisting and policy analysis applications for the legislature. Not enough applied models of information technology have been developed to support consensus building. Sullivan's dictum, "Form follows function," holds true. Users will not accept systems that do not meet their requirements.

Another aspect is the role of data in legislative policymaking. Data resources can answer questions, define the questions asked, and pose limits on what constitutes an acceptable answer. In terms of public policy, the data used by decision makers define the agenda of policy decisions to be made and the alternate outcomes to be permitted. When information technology is introduced, the requirements for standardizing the data resources and the processing steps can make these constraints even more rigorous.

As the legislature expands its use of information technology, the question raised is whose data resources the legislature relies on for its decision making. A reasonable assumption is that data systems developed by executive agencies are designed to support their own problem-solving requirements and to serve their bureaucratic self-interests (i.e., preserve and expand their responsibilities). If the technology applications that the legislature uses rely too heavily on the data resources of executive agencies, then the legislature has accepted the bureaucratic definition of the public policy decision-making agenda.

The problem of data access in an age of information technology can be considered in a broader context. If the legislative decision-making process consists of choosing acceptable solutions from several competing interests, then on any given policy issue the relevant executive agencies constitute one interest group and therefore one source of data. Institutions and groups in the private sector represent alternate interests from which the legislature should be able to access data. As information related to public policy becomes more closely related to technology, however, not all groups will have equal ability to secure and maintain data resources supported by information technology.

Access to automated data resources is heavily biased in favor of large, public and private bureaucratic organizations, not only because they can more readily afford the technology but also because the applications suit them. In this context, Senator John C. Culver's comment (quoted at the beginning of this section) assumes importance. If the legislature is to continue to discharge its policymaking responsibility, how can it correct for this bias? Can the legislature's appropriate use of technology help correct a bias in the policymaking process that was caused by this same technology?

Public Policy on Information Technology. The final topic to be considered is the public policy that the legislature has advanced in dealing with technology. This subject can serve as an important test of this section's original proposition. If technology has truly modernized legislatures, then presumably these institutions have legislated responsible policies to deal with the social issues involved in information technology and the information society.

To date, the record has been disappointing.[9] Most legislatures view information technology in the executive agencies as an item whose budget must be streamlined rather than as a resource that can be used to improve service delivery and control relative costs. The United States has been the industrial leader in developing and implementing information technology since World War II, but has lately been challenged by several nations seeking to build their own industrial capability to fulfill their own computing and communications needs and to undercut American industry's marketing position. Despite this challenge, Congress has not developed a policy defining national interest in information technology and outlining a strategy to protect the United States' industrial capability for meeting that interest.

Both federal and state government agencies continue to assemble large holdings of personal, proprietary, and fiscal data. Too often, however, systems are developed and maintained without adequate security to ensure the confidentiality and validity of these data resources. So far, not much legislative attention has been given to identifying standards for acceptable risk to govern the development of security programs in executive agencies.

Conclusion

Has the use of information technology improved the legislature's performance by modernizing its institutional makeup and processes? By now the reader should realize that the question cannot be answered, because the literature offers little evidence. Moreover, most of the studies reported were never designed to answer that question.

In fairness to the authors of the studies, it should be pointed out that they have made important contributions. The authors have provided descriptions of the information technology implemented by legislatures. They have also outlined the patterns characterizing adoption of this technology and given insights into why some development efforts have succeeded while others have failed. The more traditional students of legislative processes must now join forces with their colleagues in systems and information theory to explore some of the unanswered questions discussed in this section.

A basic strategy for investigating these questions should begin with the premise that information is a relative commodity. A particular item is information to a person only if it helps him form an opinion, reconfirm an understanding, make a decision, or take necessary action. A body of data is information only if it supports the functions a person or group wishes to perform. Therefore, any investigation should be based on a thorough review of the functions that legislatures and legislators currently perform. Identification of these functions will provide a basis for focusing on the various applications of information technology to determine how to serve legislator's information needs and will help to decide whether the technology helps some functions but hampers others, supports functions legislators want to perform, or leads to the performance of functions suited to the technology. The technology's usefulness must be judged not by how many systems a particular legislature has operating, but by whether the technology is serving the information requirements of the functions the legislature must perform.

References

1. Chartrand, Robert L. "Information Science in the Legislative Process." In: *Annual Review of Information Science and Technology.* Volume 11. Washington, D.C., American Society for Information Science, 1976, p. 332.

2. Chartrand, Robert L.; Janda, Kenneth; and Hugo, Michael, eds. *Information Support, Program Budgeting, and the Congress.* New York, Spartan Books, 1968.

3. Council of State Governments. *State Use of Electronic Data Processing.* Lexington, Ky., Council of State Governments, 1974.

4. Davidson, Roger H.; Kovenock, David M.; and O'Leary, Michael K. *Congress in Crisis: Politics and Congressional Reform.* Belmont, Calif., Wadsworth, 1966.

5. deGrazia, Alfred, ed. *Congress: the First Branch of Government.* Washington, D.C., American Enterprise Institute, 1966.

6. Elkins, James S., Jr. *A Survey of the Use of Electronic Data Processing by State Legislatures.* Athens, Institute of Government, University of Georgia, 1970. (Updated 1971, 1972, and 1974.)

7. Jewell, Malcolm E., and Patterson, Samuel C. *The Legislative Process in the United States.* 3rd Edition. New York, Random House, 1977.

8. Keefe, William J., and Ogul, Morris S. *The American Legislative Process: Congress and the States.* 4th Edition. Englewood Cliffs, N.J., Prentice-Hall, 1977.

9. Marchand, Donald A. *Privacy, Confidentiality and Computers: National and International Implications of United States Information Policy.* Columbia, Bureau of Governmental Research and Services and International Studies, University of South Carolina, June 1978.

10. National Association of State Information Systems. *Information Systems Technology in State Government.* Lexington, Ky., published annually.

11. National Conference of State Legislatures. *Legislative Fiscal Information Systems.* Denver, Colo., May 1977.

12. Ripley, Randall B., and Franklin, Grace A. *Congress, The Bureaucracy and Public Policy.* Homewood, Ill., Dorsey Press, 1976.

13. Saloma, John S., III. *Congress and the New Politics.* Boston, Little, Brown, 1969.

14. U.S. Congress, House, Commission on Administrative Review. *State Legislature Use of Information Technology.* 95th Congress, 1st Session. 1977.

15. U.S. Congress, House, Committee on House Administration. *First Progress Report of the Special Subcommittee on Electrical and Mechanical Office Equipment.* 91st Congress, 1st Session. 1969.

16. U.S. Congress, House, Committee on House Administration. *A Report to Accompany H.R. 977.* 95th Congress, 2nd Session. 1978.

17. U.S. Congress, House, Select Committee on Committees. *The Congress and Information Technology: Staff Report.* 93rd Congress, 2nd Session. 1974.

18. U.S. Congress, House, Select Committee on Committees. *Panel Discussions Before the Select Committee. Committee Organization in the House: An Inquiry Under the Authority of House Resolution 132.* Volume 2, Part 2. 93rd Congress, 1st Session. 1973.

19. U.S. Congress, Joint Committee on Congressional Operations. *Modern Information Technology in the State Legislatures.* 92nd Congress, 2nd Session. 1972.

20. U.S. Congress, Senate, Committee on Rules and Administration. *Automated Legislative Record Keeping System for the United States Senate: Feasibility Study.* 92nd Congress, 2nd Session. 1972.

21. Worthley, John A., ed. *Comparative Legislative Information Systems.* Washington, D.C., National Science Foundation, 1976.

Additional Readings

Boguslaw, Robert. *The New Utopians.* Englewood Cliffs, N.J., Prentice-Hall, 1965.

Brewer, Garry D. *Politicians, Bureaucrats, and the Consultant.* New York, Basic Books, 1973.

Chartrand, Robert C. *Computers and Political Campaigning.* New York, Spartan Books, 1972.

_____. "Congressional Management and Use of Information Technology." *Journal of Systems Management,* 29:10-15, August 1978.

_____. *Information Technology Serving Society.* London, Pergamon Press, 1979.

Dutton, William H., Danziger, James N., and Kraemer, Kenneth L. "Did the Policy Fail?: The Selective Use of Automated Information in the Policy-Making Process." In: *Why Policies Succeed or Fail.* Edited by Helen M. Inbram and Dean E. Mann. Beverly Hills, Calif., Sage Publications, 1980, pp. 163-184.

Dutton, William H., and Kraemer, Kenneth L. "Automating Bias." *Society,* 17:36-41, January/February 1980.

Heuer, Richard J., Jr. "Improving Intelligence Analysis: Some Insights on Data, Concepts, and Management in the Intelligence Community." *The Bureaucrat,* 8:2-11, Winter 1979-1980.

Hoos, Ida R. *Systems Analysis in Public Policy.* Berkeley, University of California Press, 1972.

Kraemer, Kenneth L., Danziger, James N., and Dutton, William H. "Automated Information Systems and Urban Decision Making." *Urban Systems,* 3:177-190, 1979.

Library of Congress, Congressional Research Service. *Library of Congress Information Resources and Services for the United States House of Representatives.* Washington, D.C., U.S. Government Printing Office, 1976.

_____. *State Legislative Use of Information Technology.* Washington, D.C., U.S. Government Printing Office, 1977.

Lynn, Laurence E., Jr., ed. *Knowledge and Policy: The Uncertain Connection.* Washington, D.C., National Academy of Sciences, 1978.

Meltsner, Arnold J. *Policy Analysts in the Bureaucracy.* Berkeley, University of California Press, 1976.

U.S. Commission on Federal Paperwork. *Statistics.* Washington, D.C., U.S. Government Printing Office, 1977.

U.S. Congress, Joint Committee on Congressional Operations. *Congressional Research Support and Information Services.* Washington, D.C., U.S. Government Printing Office, 1974.

Wilensky, Harold. *Organizational Intelligence.* New York, Basic Books, 1967.

Chapter 6

INFORMATION MANAGEMENT: IMPLICATIONS FOR ORGANIZATIONAL CHANGE

The principal mechanism for meeting the need for a unified approach to develop a national information policy should be the establishment of an Office of Information Policy in the Executive Office of the President.

—Staff Report of the Domestic Council Committee
on the Right to Privacy, *National Information Policy*

In the public sector, the attention being given to managing information as a resource is having at least two kinds of effects on organizational structures and processes. The first type of impact is the proliferation of information and the need to manage that information more effectively to reduce burdens on the public, private industry, and government and to distribute and use available information resources more effectively. The second kind of impact arises from the need to address a complex, diverse array of information-related problems and issues that currently demand resolution or may affect government and society in the future. Each of these impacts has major implications for how government structures and processes are organized to respond to current problems or to develop future public policy.

In this chapter, all the selections propose innovative ways to deal with major problems and concerns related to handling information as a resource in the public sector. All the authors suggest the need for developing coherent and consistent information policies and recommend various changes in organization designs and processes to solve current problems and to address significant concerns now on the horizon. Although the selections included here provide only a snapshot perspective on the vital challenges to improving government productivity and responsiveness in meeting contemporary needs and opportunities, they do highlight the scope and extensiveness of the organizational implications for government and society of treating information as a resource.

The first selection, "National Information Policy: Statement of the Problem and Recommendations," is drawn from a 1976 report to the President by the staff of the Domestic Council Committee on the Right to Privacy. This report was intended not only to focus on the need to clarify policies concerning personal record information in government but also to address this concern in the context of other related and interdependent public policy problems currently being raised, such as the rise of information technology, the growing convergence of information and telecommunications policies, and improvements in the use of scientific and technical information. The report suggests that dealing with these trends requires the need for a "National Information Policy" and a more active role by government in shaping and influencing that policy. The report notes that, in the past, government has had no clear focus for considering such matters. In both Congress and the executive branch, policy responsibilities have been diffuse and uncoordinated. The report recommends the need for a "unified approach" to information policy development and suggests several organizational alternatives in the Federal Government for addressing these matters.

In the second selection, "The Information Imperative," Forest W. Horton, Jr. reports on the activities and outcomes of a September 1973 National Environmental Information Symposium and suggests that the findings and recommendations of this conference are applicable to information production and dissemination in the public sector. Horton emphasizes that the major finding on which almost everyone at this conference agreed was that the principal constraint on environmental policymaking was the "lack of accessibility to data which has already been generated and stored" and that the principal need was for an information referral system that could identify information sources more effectively and disseminate such information to all interested parties nationwide. In such a finding, Horton perceives an "imperative" of the information age: the need to establish mechanisms by which new and existing information sources are identified when they emerge and are cataloged and maintained in cheap, easily accessible forms that permit tailored searches and inquiries. Horton concludes with the idea that establishing a one-stop information source service in government is today's information imperative.

In the next selection, the implications of the information imperative are discussed in the context of the accessibility of the nation's knowledge resources in libraries and repositories across the country. In a report entitled, "The Need for a National Program for Library and Information Services," the National Commission on Libraries and Information Science outlines its findings and recommendations for dealing with the challenge facing America: finding the means to distribute its vast information resources to those who need access and designing a means of coordination and cooperation among thousands of information sources and repositories throughout the nation. The commission recommends that a "National Program for Library and Information Services" be established to begin developing the means to treat information as a national resource and to achieve the total cooperation of all government and private parties involved.

The final selection identifies a specific area of information policy involving state and local government. In "Government by Program—The Key to Unlocking the Paperwork Burden," the Commission on Federal Paperwork looks at the paperwork burdens for state and local governments imposed by the thousands of distinct programs run by federal agencies and recommends ways to increase intergovernmental cooperation and reduce administrative burdens, redundancies, and overlap.

National Information Policy: Statement of the Problem and Recommendations*

Staff Report of the Domestic Council Committee on the Right to Privacy

Statement of the Problem

Q. *If we survive the technological crises, what should we then expect?*
      A. *We shall enter a post-industrial society...* "[1]

Continuing advances in computer and communications technology are raising new questions of public policy. The increasingly important role which such technologies play in the economic and commercial life of the United States lends a certain urgency to the answers to these questions.

Some of the more frequently asked of these questions include:

- What to do about our national postal network which is already retrenching in the face of spiraling costs and which faces the further loss of business to new information networks, such as electronic funds transfer systems?

- How to reconcile citizen demands for open government with the practical problems of administering freedom of information and Sunshine laws?

- How to preserve a sense of individuality and privacy against a massive government which demands more and more information from individuals and businesses, and which argues that its restricted use promotes efficiency?

- What to do about foreseeable dislocations brought on by the shift from an industrial to an information economy and the obsolescence in training and employment skills which could ensue?

*Washington, D.C., National Commission on Libraries and Information Science, 1976, pp. 1-19, 182-202.

Answers to these and the many other questions discussed in this report will, when taken together, constitute the national information policy of the United States. All such answers will not be arrived at simultaneously. Answers will not come from one source, nor will they come by government fiat. They will involve many participants in the Executive Branch, in Congress, in the independent agencies, in study commissions, in the state legislatures, in the courts and in the private sector. Answers will come through confrontation and through accommodation. They will come as part of the continuing process by which policy is shaped.

The report is both a part of that process and a blueprint for improving the contribution which the Executive Branch can make to it...

The Impact of Technology. The advent of computer and communications technology is causing a quiet revolution to occur in the field of information. It is quiet because the signs of change are subtle and not always visible. It is a revolution because the rate of change is very rapid. Our country now possesses new information technology that can retrieve and distribute information faster, with greater facility to more people than ever before in history. But information technology has brought problems as well as opportunities. Inadequate protection of the privacy of individuals, ineffective handling and retrieval of information, incompatibility of computerized information systems, and uncertain relationships between public and private sector groups involved in information activities, have all raised difficulties.

The consequences of this newly emerging information environment are poorly understood analytically, but they are destined to have an enormous impact on the Nation's economic growth, our social development, and our individual lives. How information is handled in this country determines, to a large extent, the quality of the decisions which our people make. Government must, therefore, be alert to the dynamics of change that are taking place. And, it should accept responsibility for facilitating the introduction of information technology and systems into our society in ways which conform to our democratic principles and respect our national ideals.

Some of the key characteristics of the new information environment created by information technology are as follows:

- *An exponential increase in the volume of information flow.* Critical observers expect a fourfold to sevenfold increase by the year 1985.

- *A shrinkage of time and distance constraints upon communications.* Satellite communications provide long distance capability to use computers and other information technology throughout the world.

- *Greater nationwide dependence upon information and communication services.* There are already nearly one million computer terminals in the United States which provide interactive, on-line information services to people across the country.

- *An increase in the interdependence of previously autonomous institutions and services.* For example, the National Commission on Libraries and Information Science has observed a definite trend in the linking of libraries and information centers into networks designed to share resources across traditional jurisdictional lines.[2]

- *Conceptual changes in economic, social, and political processes induced by increased information and communications.* The projected impact of a "checkless/cashless" society as a result of electronic funds transfer is a prime example.

- *A decrease in the "time cushion" between social and technical changes and their impact and consequences.* The introduction of devices such as the pocket calculator and citizen band radio have had immediate effects on the social environment in the United States. There is no longer time to anticipate the impact of information technology applications before they become part of our everyday lives.

- *Global shrinkage and its consequent pressures on increased international information exchange.* The Swedish government has passed legislation regulating personal information about Swedish citizens and various national interests have begun to anticipate more such laws.

During the last fifty years, communication by telephone passed from occasional into general use. Likewise, radio and television have become integral parts of our daily lives. Computer communication networks are now commonplace in business, scientific work, and government. Satellites circling the earth bring voice and pictures from other continents into homes and offices. Lasers and fiber optics are on the threshold of general use.

While the spectacular growth of computer technology and communications technology in the last thirty years has been notable, what is even more significant is the rapid way these technologies are merging....Computer and communication technology are not only merging but are also converging with related technologies such as printing and photography. When all of these elements are fully integrated, the resultant capability for information transfer and exchange could create a form of national information interdependence. Indeed, some believe the merger of computers and communications with other technologies will result in the development of a totally new information infra-structure for society. The possibility of networking local and regional information systems throughout the country or even ultimately throughout the world could greatly expand the citizen's access to the information needed to function effectively in tomorrow's technological and mobile society.

The Information Age. Collectively, these developments are seen by some of the most farsighted of our social commentators as ushering in a new period of human activity. In Daniel Bell's terminology, we are entering the "Post-Industrial Society."[3] This evolutionary stage of societal change is characterized by a shift in the composition of the vectors responsible for economic growth. The "Post-Industrial Society" is one in which economic growth is based on the expansion of a service economy built upon a sophisticated, information-based, capital-intensive production system rather than on technological innovation alone.

In the same vein, Peter Drucker describes the growth of a "knowledge economy":

The "knowledge industries" which produce and distribute ideas and information rather than goods and services, accounted in 1955 for one-quarter of the United States gross national product. This was already three times the proportion of the national product that the country had spent on the "knowledge sector" in 1900. Yet, by 1965, ten years later, the knowledge sector was taking one-third of a much bigger national product. In the late 1970s, it will account for one-half of the total national product. Every dollar earned and spent in the American economy will be earned by producing and distributing ideas and information, and will be spent on procuring ideas and information.

From an economy of goods, which America was as recently as World War II, we have changed into a knowledge economy.[4]

While economists struggle to improve their understanding of these developments and to refine their definitions and tools of analysis, it is nevertheless already clear that from one-third to one-half of the gross national product of the United States is currently attributable to the production and distribution of information and knowledge. Economists say that this trend signals a departure from a traditional economy of goods and that the United States is now entering the "Information Age." The economy will soon be one in which the production and application of knowledge will be the determining factor in competition. Just as the steam engine ushered in the Industrial Revolution and brought a host of public policy questions in its wake, the new information technology is ushering in the Information Age and its unique policy questions.

The Role Of Government in Shaping Information Policy. For more than three decades, observers in the United States have suggested the need for sharper governmental focus on information policy problems. Threaded through their reports are recommendations for the establishment of government policies that would contribute to orderly growth of information technology in the public and private sectors, to improve management of information resources, and so forth.

...numerous studies, Congressional documents, laws, other significant documentation, and technological advances...have appeared concerning various aspects of information.[5]...four major policy vectors—computers, communications, freedom of information and privacy, and science information—are rapidly converging....What is happening is that streams of policy development which have previously existed independently of each other have begun to come together. Individuals within such streams, often having diverse backgrounds and training, have begun to interact. And yet, sharp governmental focus has so far been elusive. Dr. Anthony Oettinger of the Harvard Program on Information Technology and Public Policy made the same point in a different way. He argues that there is currently no lack of information policy in the United States but that policy which is already in place is neither comprehensive nor coordinated.[6] Review of actions taken by Congress and Executive Branch agencies shed some light on how this has happened.

Legislative Branch Responses. The Congress has been frequently asked to resolve questions of information policy in recent years, although there is little indication that it has seen these questions in any related form.

Within the past few years, for example, the strong public outcry against potential threats to individual privacy from increased use of computerized data banks and from misuse of information maintained in Federal files prompted the passage of the Privacy Act of 1974. Pressures for more open government have also led to consideration of laws by the Congress such as the Freedom of Information Act[7] enacted in 1966 and the Sunshine proposal[8] recently passed by both Houses of Congress....

Thus information policies emerging from the Congress continue to be developed in an *ad hoc* piecemeal fashion by numerous Congressional committees struggling to frame responses without the benefit of a comprehensive overview of the field. And information issues have apparently been mounting beyond the Congressional capacity to respond. One result of this has been the proliferation of study commissions designed to look at some of the ticklish and distinct aspects of information policy issues. These commissions include:

- National Commission for Review of Federal and State Laws on Wiretapping and Electronic Surveillance, P.L. 90-351, June 19, 1968
- National Commission on Libraries and Information Science, P.L. 91-345, July 20, 1970
- Electronic Funds Transfer Commission, P.L. 93-495, October 28, 1974
- National Study Commission on Records and Documents of Federal Officials, P.L. 93-526, December 19, 1974
- National Historical Publications and Records Commission, P.L. 93-536, December 22, 1974
- Commission on Federal Paperwork, P.L. 93-556, December 27, 1974
- Privacy Protection Study Commission, P.L. 93-579, December 31, 1974
- National Commission on New Technological Uses of Copyrighted Works, P.L. 93-579, December 31, 1974

Such commissions are evidence of both growing interest and policy fragmentation. In some cases their jurisdictions overlap. There is a risk that they will themselves spawn new policies which may be in conflict. They also represent a Congressional attempt to delegate or postpone the resolution of difficult information policy issues. Such delegation is also reflected in issues left for judicial determination such as the balancing of open access and privacy considerations.

Executive Branch Responses. The same *ad hoc*, piecemeal approach which has characterized Congressional responses can also be found in the Executive Branch. Moreover, while institutional mechanisms which could have helped coordinate parts of the problem have occasionally existed, they have always been so beleaguered by constant proposals for their abolition, by inadequate resources and by limited authority that such a role has been impossible. Examples of such mechanisms are the Office of Telecommunications Policy, the Domestic Council Committee on the Right to Privacy, and the former Office of Presidential Science Advisor which once was the only locus in the Executive Office of the President concerned with information policy.

The present piecemeal approach to information policy has a historical antecedent in a similar and related area: the transportation infra-structure of the United States, which is a collection of *ad hoc* arrangements, many representing the overlay of new technology upon existing systems. The fact that they are interrelated has frequently been ignored, and as a result, transportation development in the United States has often been in disarray. A similar pattern could recur where the infra-structure is communications and the traffic is information, knowledge and ideas rather than people and goods.

One should be careful not to overstate these shortcomings in the information area. In the Executive Branch as in the Congress, the rapidity with which the issues of the Information Age have arrived has been the single biggest problem in framing coordinated and appropriate responses. In both branches, the focus has been on the immediate pressures generated by technology and by citizen demands. Moreover, developing a conceptual overview which will permit a government-wide perspective and improved coordination is difficult, at best, when issues are familiar; it is next to impossible to do in the abstract. But the past few years have provided considerable experience. That "critical mass" of issues, which clarifies the interrelationship of the problems may have been reached.

The signs that this is happening are numerous. The gradual awakening to this complex of issues is apparent in increased attention to the problems of coordination both on an inter-agency and an intra-agency basis.

As might be expected, the issues of current concern to the agencies reflect information problems attendant to their missions. These would include: difficulties encountered in implementation of the Privacy Act of 1974, the Freedom of Information Act (as amended), the Federal Advisory Committee Act, and the Federal Reports Act of 1942; the convergence of computers and communications technologies; burdens of reporting; need to ensure diversity of outlets of expression while preventing monopoly; content regulation in broadcasting; efficient use of data as a resource; ownership of information-handling services; export of information; and government subsidies. The agencies express concern about public trust in government, information-gathering, replacement of technologically outmoded information systems, standards and safeguards for Federal information managers, cost and responsibilities for information retention, effective flow of information between the Federal, state and local governments, improvement of data definitions and standards to improve the rapid and economical exchange of information, training of information personnel, clarification of policies regarding justification for data collection and exchange, impact of communication on the information sector, and better understanding of the information sector in socioeconomic terms.

Some Federal agencies report that they are undertaking a number of information policy studies internally and through contractors. Some of the subjects being studied include: impact on business if the Privacy Act is extended to the private sector; privacy and confidentiality as factors in research survey response; the information economy; the effect of growth in the information sector; issues and stakeholders in electronic transfer of information; and the need for a national research service to help crime laboratories identify evidence. Mention should also be made of several studies being undertaken by the Office of Telecommunications Policy (which were commissioned in the aftermath of the Presidential directive for this report); a study dealing with information policy for science and technology being conducted by the Division of Science Information at the National Science Foundation; studies by the National Commission on Libraries and Information Science in the library and information service areas; and, studies by other National Commissions in information-related areas.

Two agencies, the Department of Commerce and the Department of Justice, it should also be noted, have not only recognized the critical role of information, but they have also created high level bodies responsible for agency information policy. And the recently confirmed Director of the Office of Telecommunications Policy has announced that he is considering establishing an information policy capability within that office.

In summary, the Federal agencies have responded to information policy issues in reaction to specific stimuli, such as the Freedom of Information Act and the Privacy Act regulations. But as a general rule, they have not considered in any systematic way the impacts they are having on government-wide policy development or even the information needs of their own agencies.

The driving force of technological innovation, the convergence of previously diverse streams of policy development, and the attempts by government to respond to public demands for reform are elements that have given rise to the public policy issues of the Information Age....

Recommendations

Government alone cannot be equal to the task of guiding a major transformation of society that is essentially a phase in the cultural evolution of the human species. But government is the only institution competent to mediate the critical task of reassessing priorities, of redefining goals, and of devising the means toward the creation of a material and intellectual environment in which all other social institutions can play their respective roles in the transition. [9]

—Lynton K. Caldwell, 1975

To debate whether there should be a national information policy is pointless. There will be such a policy. It will be the result of the answers to the many questions raised...and the answers to other questions not yet foreseen. It will exist whether or not these answers are arrived at consciously or unconsciously, by commission or omission, carefully or haphazardly, in a comprehensive or in a piecemeal fashion.

The observations in a recent government report on communications issues apply as well to the broader issues which are the subject here:

In earlier times, the expansion of new technology was welcomed without too much concern for future impact. There was room to make up rules and develop policies on a case-by-case basis. Policy was often no more than an accumulation of regulatory decisions. But the quickening pace of technological advances in communications has now rendered the ad hoc method of policy formulation not only obsolete but dangerous. The conditions of today require cohesive planning for the future so that crises, such as those experienced in the energy field, can be anticipated and avoided. What is now needed in communications is a broad and enduring policy framework that will insure that the benefits of new technologies are effectively and expeditiously made available to the consuming public. [10]

The issue, therefore, is whether government will attempt to take a considered and coordinated approach in arriving at these answers. A key question is how to structure the policymaking process so that the country can begin to develop a national information policy that is comprehensive, sufficiently sensitive to new technology, and responsive to the implications of the Information Age. This report recommends that the first step toward structuring that process is the establishment of a policy organization within the Executive Office of the President to provide coordination and articulate a rational framework for a national information policy.

The Need for a Unified Approach . . . . Bringing together the threads of a national information policy in one policymaking location meets several needs:

(1) Information policy issues are interrelated so that actions taken in one area may impact others. Decisions directed at one specific problem may have consequences for other problems. Thus, the rules for dissemination of government-held information . . . affect the private information industry. . . . Changes in laws affecting copyright . . . and postal rates . . . , publication of government documents . . . , and legislation such as the Right of Privacy Act . . . and the Freedom of Information Act . . . , all affect the usefulness and accessibility of information, though these changes may have been initially prompted by discrete considerations. As Professor Oettinger has said in speaking of information policy, "Everything is related to everything else." [11] At present no unit of government has the authority to respond to that reality.

(2) Comprehensive attention to information policy issues provides the most efficient use of manpower and skills. A unified approach to these issues will permit the development of strong and sustained policy skills, take maximum advantage of related experiences, minimize duplication, and enhance the processes of coordination and policy development. In this regard, it is interesting to note that information policy is increasingly seen as a distinct academic discipline. The issues outlined in this report are, with varying degrees of emphasis, the subject of programs in several major universities. Numerous conferences organized by private sector groups in recent years have made information issues the theme of their program, even when the groups came from different places in the information sector. The general perception that these issues should be treated together is bringing about the development of approaches yielding cross-cutting skills which could benefit the Executive Branch.

(3) An organizational structure which has high visibility and adequate authority could prevent information concerns from being compromised and traded away for other concerns at the agency level (below the range of public visibility), which has often been the case in the past. This can probably be accomplished without changes in the statutory authority of existing agencies.

Organizational Alternatives. From time to time, institutional reorganizations have been advanced to provide better focus for some of the principal issues outlined in this report. One which has received considerable attention is the proposal for the creation of a Department of Communications. The limitations suggested by this name, it should be noted, narrow the broad focus for which this report argues. Therefore, for purposes of this discussion, it is assumed that any department would not take a broad policy approach.

One model which is often advanced is that based upon the Department of Transportation (DOT). It is particularly appropriate in the sense that, in addition to serving as the lead agency for the Executive Branch on transportation policy, DOT also co-exists with independent regulatory agencies (the Interstate Commerce Commission, the Federal Maritime Commission, and the Civil Aeronautics Board). Presumably a Department of Communications would co-exist with the Federal Communications Commission.

While such a Department might be appropriate at some future date, its establishment at this time would be premature. The departmental option entails a commitment beyond the size and scope needed at this time. Indeed, the policy analysis and groundwork which would warrant such a commitment has not yet been completed.

Other proposals have called for an independent agency to undertake the task of policy coordination with respect to information and communications issues. Those who prefer such a course stress the need to insulate those functions from partisan activity. While this is a worthy goal, such independence exacerbates an already prevalent problem in government policy formulation—the absence of accountability. At least to the extent that policy formulation involves establishing positions for the Executive Branch, the authority of the President should not be diluted. A President's ability to provide leadership and obtain a unified agency approach depends on clear lines of responsibility. It has been demonstrated that adequate checks and balances exist to cope with the possible misuse of authority. This is particularly true, as is the case here, where policy functions and not adjudicatory proceedings are involved.

Office of Information Policy. A national information policy is realizable through creation of an external committee and advisory structure and by a reallocation of resources within the Executive Office of the President. Financial and staff resource requirements to achieve this objective would be modest.

The principal mechanism for meeting the need for a unified approach to develop a national information policy should be the establishment of an Office of Information Policy (OIP) in the Executive Office of the President. This could be accomplished by structuring a new institutional entity within the Executive Office of the President or by refocusing and expanding responsibilities within any of several existing Executive Office of the President entities. The former would involve a larger investment of resources but would give impetus to the broadest focus on the critical issues. The latter would maximize use of existing expertise and experience and avoid increasing the size of the Executive Office.

Subject to the authority and control of the President, such an Office would perform the following types of general functions:

(1) Serve as the President's principal advisor on matters of information policy;

(2) Provide leadership for the Executive Branch through the initiation of programs of public benefit;

(3) Provide a structural framework for the resolution of competing interests and the balancing of competing values in the course of developing policies on behalf of the Executive Branch;

(4) Resolve conflicts between Federal agencies over policies for the Federal government and other sectors;

(5) Establish and refine priorities for dealing with issues of information policy;

(6) Develop technical and policy expertise with regard to information policy issues, contribute to the growth of a conceptual framework for dealing with these issues, and monitor developments relating to them;

(7) Provide a focal point for both the public and the private sector where proposals and problems can receive consideration;

(8) Develop recommendations for such further organizational changes as might be required over time and, where appropriate, work with the Congress to effect such changes; and,

(9) Provide a central location for the receipt of the reports of temporary study commissions dealing with information policy and, where appropriate, act on behalf of the Executive Branch concerning them.

Placing of the policy machinery in the Executive Office of the President is appropriate given the limitations which exist on the power of the Executive Branch to respond unilaterally to the issues of information policy raised in this report.

These issues are subject to the Constitutionally shared power between the Legislative and Executive Branches, and to a large extent have been historically divided among and between the two branches of government in a way that makes a fully coordinated approach especially difficult.

The degree to which Congress is already involved is apparent from the existing statutory schemes and potential legislative actions associated with each of the issue clusters. In other ways, the Congress has become uniquely involved in information policy questions. For example, both the Government Printing Office and the Copyright Office (within the Library of Congress) are part of the Legislative Branch and beyond the coordinating power of the Executive. The independence of FCC authority has the effect of isolating decisions from both Congress and the Executive Branch. Thus, cooperative arrangements will be necessary for policy development in almost all of these issue areas.

Before anything more is done, the Executive Branch needs to set its own activities and policy preferences in order. By establishing, at a sufficiently high level of authority, the means by which unified policies can be adequately considered and formulated, the Executive Branch can place itself in a position to provide leadership. This can best be done, given the importance of the issues and their government-wide effects, from within the Executive Office of the President.

Evolution of an Office. While the creation of a new office within the Executive Office of the President is one possible approach, such an office might also evolve out of the existing staff structures. The Office of Information Policy could conceivably be established as part of the Domestic Council or as part of the Office of Management and Budget. Another viable alternative for establishment of the Office could be through the Office of Telecommunications Policy.

When, in 1970, the Office of Telecommunications Policy was established pursuant to Presidential Reorganization Plan No. 1, a number of roles were envisioned for the new Office: to serve as the President's principal advisor on telecommunications policy; to help formulate government policies concerning a wide range of domestic and international telecommunication issues; and, to help develop plans and programs which take full advantage of the Nation's technological capabilities. The Presidential message accompanying the Plan noted that the speed of economic and technological advance in our time meant that new questions concerning communications are constantly arising, questions on which the government must be well informed and well advised.

In addition to its policy responsibilities vis-à-vis important telecommunications issues, OTP also reviews and coordinates Federal telecommunications planning procurement and manages the assignment of all Federal government radio frequencies. Executive Order 11556 of September 4, 1970 delineates all of OTP's functions and is the basic reference used in defining the Office's present mandate. The Office has a small professional staff but is supported by private contract research assistance and an operational unit within the Department of Commerce.

Much of the rationale and justification for the creation of the Office of Telecommunications Policy is similarly applicable to the constellation of issues outlined in this report, through the substitution of the broader focus of information for telecommunications. Among other things, the Office of Telecommunications Policy's activities in connection with electronic fund transfers, with FEDNET and other Federal networking proposals, and its close working relationship with the Domestic Council Committee on the Right to Privacy, have all shown the possibilities of such an expanded framework.

The issues which the Office of Telecommunications Policy is currently focusing upon are in many ways an information policy agenda.... The activities and concerns of any Office of Information Policy will, of course, be the result of the establishment of priorities based on public need and public demand. If properly organized, adequately supported, and thoroughly committed, the Office of Telecommunications Policy could undertake the broader agenda recommended by this report.

Council on Information Policy. As an adjunct to the operations of the Office of Information Policy, it is further recommended that there be established an inter-agency council, chaired by the Director of the Office, and consisting of designated high level officials in each agency. This body could be organized independently of the Domestic Council or as one of its committees.

The Council itself would meet only occasionally and then to serve as a forum in which government-wide problems could be aired. The Council and its members would serve as a framework for the organization of subcommittees and task forces to deal with specific problem areas. The members of such task forces might include the agency representatives; more frequently they would be drawn from among agency people with specific expertise.

Advisory Committee. An Advisory Committee should be established to assist the Office in the formulation of policy and should provide a medium of two way exchange between it and the private sector, state and local government interests who are concerned with information policy matters and the academic and professional disciplines which are active in these areas. Such a committee could serve the worthwhile purpose of bringing together the often disparate elements of the information community. Through creative use of the power of appointment, the President could establish a committee with wide representation and great potential for fruitful interaction. The seeds of cooperation thus planted could result in the more effective marshalling of the considerable resources in the private, state and local sectors in the service of the nation.

Relationship with the Office of Science and Technology Policy. The Congress has recently enacted legislation which re-establishes the position of Science Advisor to the President. The new Science Advisor (the Director of the Office of Science, Engineering, and Technology Policy) will be situated in the Executive Office of the President and provided with staff and membership on the Domestic Council. While the Science Advisor's mandate extends to the entire panoply of national scientific concerns, one specific area to which his attention is directed by the legislation is scientific information.

The subject of information policy, to the limited extent that is has been considered in prior years, has tended to be addressed in the context of scientific and technical information. This was the case during the 1960's, when the focal point within the government for the discussion of information policy was the Committee on Scientific and Technical Information (COSATI), located within the predecessor to the office of the Science Advisor. This continues to be the case in the OECD where information policy questions are all structurally under the aegis of the Committee on Scientific and Technical Policy (CSTP). Indeed, because of this history, the problems associated with scientific information have often crowded out other information policy problems, and have caused the narrower concern to receive the greater attention.

The reach of the information policy questions which now confront the government make such questions too broad to be the exclusive concern of the Science Advisor. However, the Science Advisor should be the primary focus of policy with respect to scientific information. This reflects his specialized expertise and concerns. But the exercise of this function should be tempered with the awareness that decisions which are made regarding scientific information can impact upon the broader field of information policy generally. Consequently, a close working relationship should be established between the Science Advisor and an Office of Information Policy with respect to such matters that might overlap.

Principles of Information Policy. One of the most difficult tasks confronting public officials who will grapple with the issues outlined in this report is the formulation of principles to guide them in making decisions. The issues discussed in this report present some of the most complicated and difficult choices facing government. An agreed upon set of principles entails overcoming semantic difficulties balancing competing interests, and reconciling contradictory objectives in an area where the intangibility and newness of the subject matter leads itself to imprecision and misunderstanding.

Despite these difficulties, the following principles are offered, if only as a starting point for debate. While they are general and incomparable, they indicate some directions which principles of information policy could take.

- Encourage access to information and information systems by all segments of society to meet the basic needs of people, to improve the quality of life and to enable the responsibilities of citizenship to be met.
- Safeguard the use of personal information about individuals and protect their right to personal privacy.
- Encourage systems that foster the creation and dissemination of knowledge.

- Maintain adequate control over the power information provides to government either through checks and balances, through diffusion of control, through decentralization, through Federal/state consortiums, or by other means.

- Encourage efficient resource allocation in the development of information systems and efficiency in their use through consistency in standards, practices and procedures, and through encouraging quality and accuracy.

- Maintain pluralism in information systems and strengthen the private sector so that, through competition, innovation can be encouraged.

- Adopt rules which will have some permanence and general applicability so that the private sector will be encouraged to invest in new systems and methods. . . .

Notes

[1]Herman Kahn in an interview by Edward Jay Epstein, "Good News from Mr. Bad News," *New York Magazine* (August 9, 1976) pp. 34–44.

[2]National Commission on Libraries and Information Science, *Toward a National Program for Library and Information Services: Goals for Action,* Washington, D.C.: Government Printing Office, 1975, pp. 31–35.

[3]Daniel Bell, "The Post-Industrial Society: A Speculative View," in *Scientific Progress and Human Values* (Hutchings, Edward and Hutchings, Elizabeth, eds.), New York: American Elsevier Publishing, 1967; see also Daniel Bell, *Coming of Post-Industrial Society: A Venture in Social Forecasting,* New York: Basic Books, 1973; *The Coming of Post-Industrial Society,* New York: Basic Books, 1976.

[4]Peter Drucker, *The Age of Discontinuity,* New York: Harper and Row, 1969, p. 263.

[5]Prepared by the staff of the Domestic Council Committee on the Right to Privacy.

[6]Anthony G. Oettinger, Remarks at Roundtable on Privacy and Information Policy, Washington, D.C., September 7–9, 1975.

[7]5 U.S.C. 522.

[8]Conference Report 94-1441.

[9]40 U.S.C. 759, P.L. 89-306 (October 30, 1965).

[10]47 U.S.C. 151 *et seq.*

[11]*Use of Carterfone Device in Message Toll Service* 13 FCC 2d 420 (1968); *Microwave Communications, Inc.,* 18 FCC 2d 953 (1969); *Specialized Carrier Inquiry,* 29 FCC 2d 870 (1971); *Establishment of Communications-Satellite Facilities by Non-Government Entities,* 35 FCC 2d 844 (1972).

The Information Imperative*
Forest W. Horton, Jr.

While some tried to argue that either the lack or glut of information available to deal with today's pressing social, environmental and economic problems should be the country's priority concern, the most universal need expressed by the Symposium[1] participants, regardless of attitudinal orientation, profession or affiliation, is for improved knowledge of and access to information and data. In short, the first question is "where is it, who has it, what is it, and how can I get my hands on it?"

The above quotation, slightly paraphrased, was at once the most startling and most vital conclusion reached by 1700 participants at a...national conference on information held in Cincinnati, Ohio and attended by scientists, administrators, legislators, citizen action groups, information technicians and many others. While the goal of this conference was primarily to provide a forum for bringing together concerned citizens, organized groups, trade associations, professional societies and governmental bodies to share objectives, concerns and interests as regards the production, use and dissemination of *environmental* information, it is the contention of this paper that the findings rendered by the conferees are applicable to the entire field of information production and dissemination. I would include in that category publishers, information and data centers, libraries, document service and referral activities, and the entire array of specialized organizations which deal with information as their primary product or service.

To offer some background, the Environmental Protection Agency in late 1971 was groping for ways to respond to widespread criticism that the Agency had not yet seized the initiative to "bring order out of chaos" to the ever-proliferating sources of information dealing with the environment. Information and data centers were springing up all over the country, each with its own distinct areas of concern and specialization, each with its special audience, but inevitably each with a certain amount of overlap with its neighbors. In the Federal Government alone, as a result of a special study authorized by the Office of Science and Technology to review sources of environmental data already extant or being established, over 75 different

*Reprinted by permission of the *Journal of Systems Management,* Vol. 24, pp. 8–12, June 1973.

sources of environmental information were identified. These sources involved the energies, resources and commitment of over a dozen different Federal agencies and departments.

Many critics pointed with varying degrees of relevancy and accuracy to certain historical parallels which had occurred in two fields often compared with the environmental field, in the sense that they emerge onto the national scene with a certain amount of suddenness and with very high priority.... These fields are atomic energy, in the decade of the forties, and space exploration in the decade of the fifties. The argument of these critics ran something like this: AEC (The Atomic Energy Commission) and NASA (The National Aeronautics and Space Administration) waited until it was too late to exercise their leadership position in ways that would constructively channel the evolution of information sources concerned with their respective fields. As a result, basic research efforts, the evolution of their offspring technologies, and the transfer of their technologies to other disciplines were seriously hampered by considerable duplication among producers, handlers and distributors of information concerned with their endeavors.

In addition to the history-minded accusers, EPA did not escape the wrath of other information malcontents. Most notably among these were certain articulate members of the Congress, including Congressman Dingell, Dem.-Mich., whose particular axe took the form of legislation he introduced in the First Session of the 92nd Congress "To amend the National Environmental Policy Act of 1969, to provide for a National Environmental Data System." Congressman Dingell's bill, H.R. 56, would establish a network of facilities which would coordinate the selection, storage, analysis, retrieval, and dissemination of environmental information, knowledge and data. The Director of this network would report to the Chairman of the Council on Environmental Quality and, in effect, act as a sort of czar in charge of environmental information....

Yet among the forefront of the challengers must be listed the media and the publishers. With newsletters, journals, news columns and a host of serials of all classifications springing up by the dozens with the emergence of the ecological problem onto the national consciousness, it was perhaps inevitable that the Environmental Protection Agency should come in for its share of hard knocks from this quarter as well. Journalists complained vehemently that they were not able to identify source materials quickly. Editors decried the lack of centralized facilities where they could expect to go and receive full and accurate briefings and information on whatever subject happened to hold their interest at the moment. And even that venerable institution—the librarian—with perhaps less malevolence in her voice, but nevertheless with firm and unwavering conviction, lamented the absence of a central EPA headquarters library from which she might seek her bibliographies, her indices, her abstracts and her book loans.

Finally, the afficionados of the information technology world also could not resist their arrows. From such distinguished groups as the National Science Foundation, the National Technical Information Service, the Smithsonian's Science Information Exchange and the Office of Science and Technology, came a barrage of exhortations and admonishments that the Environmental Protection Agency take the lead to stimulate and enlarge communication on environmental matters, both intergovernmentally and between the public and private sectors. Armed with these pleas, and coupled with the blessing of the Office of Management and Budget and the Council on Environmental Quality, the Environmental Protection Agency in March, 1972, decided to sponsor a national conference to take the first step in "bringing order out of chaos."

A steering committee was formed, composed of key officials from the various Federal agencies mentioned above—OMB, OST, NSF, and others. From the very first meeting of this group, which the author chaired, considerable differences of opinion as to what the goals and objectives of such a meeting should be, emerged and were debated. Some despaired that "environmental information" could ever be adequately defined to permit zeroing in on in the context of any kind of meaningful discussion. After all, it was argued, isn't the environment an interdisciplinary field and doesn't it trace its roots to virtually all of the physical sciences? Others took the view that there have already been too many fruitless meetings of this kind, resulting in studies and reports which no one ever read, much less took the time to act upon. And still others warned EPA that it risked raising expectations as to what might be theoretically possible, but practically impossible to attain, and therefore could not fulfill those expectations.

In the end, the program committee moved ahead and structured an agenda. It was decided that the basic structure of the conference would hinge on two groups of working sessions. On the one hand, *producers* of information on the environment would be called upon to present the various kinds of products and services they offered, arrangements for obtaining those services, and brief descriptions of the substantive content of the information produced. Then, following those presentations, *user panels* would stimulate participants to react—good and bad—to the producer/presentation sessions they had heard and try to articulate problems (and hopefully solutions) affecting the entire field of environmental information. The producer community was divided by "class of information" into four groups: scientific and technical; legal, legislative and regulatory; planning and management; and socioeconomic. The user panels were divided along affiliation lines: citizen action groups; press and publications; industry and trade associations; academic and professional institutions; and government. To liven things up a bit, distinguished speakers were interspersed with the working sessions, and included such personalities as William Ruckelshaus, Secretary Peter Peterson, Shirley Temple Black and Jules Bergman.

Despite advance notification as to the objectives of the conference, it became quickly apparent that the 1700 attendees had differing preconceptions and expectations. Some wandered the corridors, "session shopping," and mumbling that they had come to Cincinnati to "get their hands on hard facts on the environment," but in listening to producers, they came away even more bewildered than before they came—not only as to the excessive number of sources of such information, but the complexity of arrangements necessary to seek out the information stored by these institutions and organizations. "Could it be," one gentleman remarked, "that there is no single source of information on the environment to which I might go to find out what is available?"

Listening to this remark, the Federal information expert somewhat disgustedly responded with the comment "What do these people expect, to be handed information on a silver platter and spoon fed! They've got to *work at it,* just like I have for 25 years, to find out where all this stuff is!" The disgruntled lawyer and the cynical reporter, fed up with getting carefully edited and elegantly generalized bureaucratic "position papers" and news releases, loudly denounced not just EPA, but the Federal Government in general for the climate of closed decisionmaking which they alleged pervaded Washington, D.C. and manifested itself in carefully manipulated and controlled information management policies and practices. They advocated a much fuller right of access—not only to digested position papers and recommendations, but to support raw data and background research as well.

The private citizen in attendance, caught in this cross-fire of vested interest groups, managed to have his voice heard as well. Citizen action groups particularly felt strongly that the government should be obligated to provide cost-free data and information to all comers, regardless of level of detail or volume. Some tempered their criticism by indicating that it might be "fairer" if only the referral service that directed the citizen to information sources was provided free, while the substantive information sought, when finally obtained, might have nominal charges levied on the report, pamphlet, computer tape, microfilm or whatever.

While there were strong differences in viewpoints, there were also many common threads running through the discussions of all groups. Among these was the feeling that centralized information programs and services having one or but a few access points tend to fade from the consciousness of the average citizen or group working at the "local level," and over time become under-utilized because of lack of convenience and the difficulties in maintaining close contact with the managers/shapers of the systems which support these programs and services. Direct local access to information networks, most participants said, without going through intermediate channels to remote (though national) information sources and data banks, is the preferred approach. Closely related to this opinion was another firmly held belief that information must be tailored to local needs and the special conditions affecting regional problems and populations. Too many data banks, many complained, were simply highest common denominator repositories of data with little or no meaning to the ultimate user. This argument also tended to reinforce the recommendation that data and information facilities be decentralized to the maximum extent.

In the end, despite the sharp boundaries that were drawn between the various user community groups in attendance at the Cincinnati convocation, a strong majority expressed its view that steps should be taken by EPA and the Federal Government to establish a national environmental information referral network that should have the following functions and characteristics:

1. Provide reliable and comprehensive data on the location, content, form and availability of all environmental information services, nationwide, regardless of sponsorship;

2. Provide its services at nominal or no cost to the user, and with few or no restrictions placed on its accessibility or use. Confidentiality of certain data would, of course, be protected in the areas already so designated under the Freedom of Information Act, such as national defense material;

3. Provide search capabilities by subject, but service provided will be primarily in the form of *referrals to sources of information,* not substantive data per se;

4. Periodically publish general and specialized environmental information services directories, conveniently indexed by subject, for cost-free distribution to users;

5. Provide for the decentralized operation of components of the network system, in order to maximize the opportunity to tailor raw data to local needs and problems. But also recognize the need to aggregate and summarize data and information at higher geographic entity levels (regional and national) to

assist the needs of researchers, managers and other users operating at these levels;

6. Provide for user feedback at regular intervals. That is, refine central file entries based on periodic user evaluation reactions to use of referenced information services. To that end, establish appropriate user group mechanisms.

Other conclusions and recommendations were reached dealing with technical or special-purpose needs and arrangements which go beyond the scope of this paper. Certainly the...listed items associated with the establishment of the national referral center were the principle ones. Now at the beginning of this paper I generalized my thesis beyond the environmental field, and attempted to cite the experience of the Cincinnati Symposium to buttress some generalized points which I will now attempt.

Historically, the information technologist and information user alike have, for a wide variety of intuitive or well-intentioned reasons, believed that the information explosion (to use the well worn phrase) should not be approached from the premise that centralizing all information into one gigantic, monolithic system and data bank is the most effective way to move. I share that view, for some of the reasons stated...in this paper. But let us consider what has happened.

First, as Administrator Ruckelshaus said in his keynote address at the Information Symposium,

At this time, as at no other time in history, there are numerous and diverse studies, programs and projects generating data on the environment. A great store of information is already on record buried in file cabinets, notebooks, formal and informal reports and documents, and in computer systems. And yet this information is available to all too few of the decisionmakers at all levels of government and in private entities who are charged with meeting this Nation's pledge to preserve and improve the environment. The potential for optimum environmental management will be greatly enhanced if a method is found to improve the flow, analysis and utilization of this enormous resource base to and by all levels of government, universities and research institutions, private entities and the public. In addition, administrators in State and local agencies and other public and private organizations, who are often concerned with fiscal information only, would be exposed as well to substantive technical information. These decisionmakers, however, have neither the time nor the funds to conduct diligent searches for such information. They must know where to find the information and they must not be required to approach hundreds of different sources for it. Nearly everyone is in agreement that a principal road block to environmental policymaking is the *lack of accessibility to data which has already been generated and stored* [italics supplied]. The need for a central data system is widely recognized.

Could not Mr. Ruckelshaus' comments have as easily been applied to the Nation's crucial social problems, to urban technology, to mass transit problems and a host of others?

Second, information has come of age as an industry in its own right. In a publication entitled "Understanding Why You Are Disappointed, A Little Alone, A Little Afraid, And Nothing Seems Right Anymore, The Information Environment," a public interest program by the Communication Gap, 1971, Rollin and Marcha Pinza, some telling points are made.

If we want to change our nation's disastrous behavior toward our environments... and ourselves, we must first have enough information for each of us to change our own ideas and values about our environments. The real solution is in each of our minds and in our own attitudes and actions. If we hope to see the real causes of our problems and find intelligent answers for them, it is clear that the solutions lie more in the quality of our information than in the speed of our actions. Only by completing the information you are receiving about your environments, will you be able to intelligently separate problems which are the most visible from those which are the most urgent. As you, the public, have become better informed, you have become more important. Business and government have never been so responsive to your opinions and your demands. They want, and need to know, your opinions. Millions of dollars are spent by industry each year on research to find out what products you want to buy. Until everyone is as concerned about our environments as you are, we have little hope of improving them. Most important, make your voice heard to the people who can do the most to give the public the information they need.

I would argue with this quotation in only one way—*billions*, not millions of dollars are being spent today on the production, handling and dissemination of information. Some have predicted that by the end of this decade the information industry will be numbered among the top half dozen leaders. Although it has been slow in coming, at the national level information is now beginning to be treated as a major resource—no less important than dollars held in the Treasury, publicly held lands, our rivers and our roadbeds. The capital and operating investments this Nation has in its information facilities, its information handling equipment, and its information materials are enormous and growing almost geometrically. We are, in the language of the economist and the businessman, just at the beginning of the growth curve in the information product life cycle.

Third, technology spinoffs from modern science are increasing in number, complexity and rate. And the records associated with those spinoffs are increasing proportionately. Moreover, technologies are becoming increasingly interdisciplinary and interdependent. Pollution and the ecology crisis are perhaps the most recent and dramatic examples of this interdisciplinary characteristic of modern technologies. Information is needed from the physical, biological and chemical sciences to solve our air, water, solid waste, noise and other pollution problems. And this information must be correlatable across the traditional and conventional boundaries which have separated the disciplines. Indeed an entire new field—technology transfer—has emerged as an important scientific, technological and economic tool. There is, in short, widespread recognition of the commonality of interest among experts, joined together to work on society's common problems, that ranges all the way from the creation of agreed thesaurus terms for common use, to the formation of national bodies for periodic sharing of experiences and problems. Information science, and its associated technologies, is the key to dealing with this interdependency problem.

It would appear, then, that the information manager and technician alike, while heavily occupied with dealing with the control of this information vine, have at the same time not recognized that new roots have dropped to the ground and the plant now has contained within itself the seeds of its own destruction! I will not drench the reader with how many vines or roots there are; many authors have researched the increasing proliferation of technical periodicals, articles, information centers and the like. Suffice it to say that the sources of information have now reached astronomical proportions.

The Information Imperative, then, is *not:*

—The management or manipulation of information and data by the imposition of rigid controls on growth, restrictions on use, "quotas" or artificial limits; *nor*

—The quixotic quest for that magic formula that might permit us to "eliminate duplication," happily separate the relevant from the irrelevant, the factual from the inaccurate, the complete from the incomplete and the timely from the untimely; *nor*

—Faster computers, tinier microform media for storage, more sophisticated communication and handling methodologies, or breakthroughs in indexing, abstracting or thesauri schemes; *nor,* finally, and to the sad lament of our lawyers, members of the press and John Doe in the street,

—Greater reverence for the English language, burning of the Xerox machines or a fatter Yellow Pages directory.

The Imperative is simply this: we must establish the mechanisms whereby existing and new *sources,* the roots of the information vine, are recognized when they emerge, identified accurately and completely as to scope and content, catalogued under professionally acceptable but yet easily used and flexibly maintainable classification systems, and with efficient but cheap search and accessing capabilities that would permit tailoring to a universal audience of users whose inquiries would inevitably range widely in form and content. Eventually, source inventories could be linked together in clustered networks, based on priority of need, the degree of interdisciplinary interdependency and other criteria. The *form* of this imperative, the mechanism, might be referred to as an *"exchange."* That noun seems preferable to "systems," or "center," which carry somewhat different connotations.

In a word—the establishment of one-stop information source service is the information imperative. To establish a network of linked exchanges will require the most imaginative talents of our information scientists and engineers. It will also require the rethinking of policies and programs by our information managers—accustomed to doing business in a different way. And it will require resources—human, financial and material, to create the exchanges, link them together and operate them once established. I know of no greater challenge nor a more compelling one.

Note

[1]National Environmental Information Symposium, sponsored by the Environmental Protection Agency in Cincinnati, September 24–27, 1972.

The Need for a National Program for Library and Information Services*

National Commission on Libraries and Information Science

In establishing the National Commission on Libraries and Information Science (Public Law 91-345), Congress affirmed that "library and information services adequate to meet the needs of the people of the United States are essential to achieve national goals and to utilize most effectively the nation's educational resources." It called on the Federal Government to "cooperate with state and local governments and public and private agencies in assuring optimum provision of such services." Furthermore, the law authorized the National Commission to "promote research and development activities which will extend and improve the nation's library and information-handling capability as essential links in the national communication networks."

The Resources

Information, whether in the raw form of empirical data, or in the highly processed form we call "knowledge," has come to be regarded as a national resource as critical to the nation's well-being and security as any natural resource, such as water or coal. The wealth of popular, intellectual, scholarly and research resources in the libraries and information facilities of the United States is one of the great strengths of the nation. But like many natural resources, knowledge resources, uncoordinated in growth and usage, are in danger of being wasted and inefficiently utilized.

In advanced societies, a substantial part of the culture is handed down to successive generations in the form of recorded knowledge. This resource consists of books, journals, and other texts; of audio and visual materials; and of smaller units of information or data that can be separately manipulated, as by a computer. In recent years, these records have become increas-

---

*In: *Toward a National Program for Library and Information Sciences: Goals for Action.* Washington, D.C., U.S. Government Printing Office, 1975, pp. 1–11.

ingly varied—through technological extensions of written words, pictures and sounds. For example, a significant part of the country's information resource is now on film, on video tapes and in computer files. As the nation's knowledge grows and the number of records increases, our dependence on them increases, and the need to gain access to them becomes more crucial. "No society can advance beyond a certain point without effective access to its collective memory or record, or conversely, an advanced society that loses control of the record will regress."

In the United States information is created, stored, processed and distributed by a vast array of diverse information activities in the private and public sectors, employing millions of people and dealing with billions of dollars, using widely varying technologies to achieve equally widely varying objectives. The publishing industry, indexing and abstracting and other access services, the communications media, and private and public information services are just a few of the many and varied elements that make up the rich mosaic of the contemporary information scene. The more than 8,300 public libraries, thousands of school libraries in colleges and universities, armed forces, law, medical and religious libraries, special libraries, and information analysis centers, as well as other information facilities in the public and private sector, serve as custodians and dispensers of recorded knowledge in every form.

Libraries and other information facilities are the custodians of the part of our cultural heritage which is recorded. They must be adequately equipped, organized, financed and interconnected if their resources are to be made available to all the people of the United States. This, the Commission feels, can only be brought about with the help of the Federal Government, in full cooperation with state and local governments, and related public and private agencies and institutions. The Federal Government has a continuing responsibility to implement innovative, flexible measures that will ensure the continuing development of libraries and information services.

The Need for Access

Ready access to information and knowledge is indispensable to individual advancement as well as to national growth. The right information provided when it is needed, where it is needed, and in the form in which it is needed, improves the ability of an individual, a business, a government agency, or some other kind of organization, to make informed decisions and achieve particular goals.

Users are individuals, each with unique informational, educational, psychological, and social needs. A person may need "practical knowledge" to solve immediate problems in his daily life and work. There may be a need for "professional knowledge" to further his continuing education. Or there may be a need for "intellectual knowledge," the kind that furthers his understanding of the arts, humanities, and sciences, and which enriches the individual's personal life. Reading for pleasure, pursuing an innovative idea, or exploring knowledge just to satisfy one's innate curiosity, are other valid motives for reading, listening or looking. In addition, people feel the need for ethical, religious and philosophical insights.

Organizations, like individuals, need information and knowledge. Business organizations need facts and data to forecast a market, develop a new product, or adapt a new technology. Schools need information to improve and extend the learning process. Research organizations need information to synthesize new data with known facts as part of the creative process. Government needs information at every level to formulate plans, refine decision-making, and help government workers to anticipate and resolve problems.

The 93rd U.S. Congress accurately described the charter of the national information need in Senate Joint Resolution 40 (P.L. 93-568) which authorizes a White House Conference on Library and Information Services. The law states that "...access to information and ideas is indispensable to the development of human potential, the advancement of civilization, and the continuance of enlightened self-government."

It is almost impossible to generalize in assessing user needs. To understand the variety of user needs for library and information service and the extent to which they are being met, the Commission has conferred with many individuals and groups representing different constituencies. It is clear that library and information needs are felt at all levels of society, regardless of an individual's location, social condition, or level of intellectual achievement. Although library and information needs are not the same in all parts of the country, and although they vary widely among people by age, ethnic origin, educational achievement, work assignment, geographic location, and many other factors, most people feel some dependence on the availability of accurate and useful information.

User needs can be described from several perspectives. For example, the retarded, the illiterate, the blind, the visually handicapped, the physically handicapped, and the institutionalized require highly specialized resources and services. The immediate informational and library needs of young adults include easy access to library materials such as paperback books, phonograph records, reference materials, and audio-visual materials. Various ethnic groups, such as American Indians, Asian Americans, Black Americans, and Hispanic Americans require not only the traditional level of library and information service, but also various kinds of special help. For example, they need materials and services in their own language, or help in reading English, or specific knowledge such as where to go for a job. Users in the professions, such as the scientist, the researcher, the scholar, and the lawyer, require information for increasing their own productivity and for their continuing education. They often need information quickly, and some of them are accustomed to using computers, telecommunications, and other technology, if necessary, to get it. In addition, there are those whose information needs are affected by their location—the rural population and others in remote areas who do not have direct access to major resources as do their counterparts in metropolitan areas. Other user groups, such as senior citizens, the very young, and the poor, need still other kinds of services and resources.

The Commission is keenly aware that much more must be done to develop systematic understanding of the information needs of various special constituencies in the United States such as the economically disadvantaged, the uneducated and the handicapped. We need to know who they are, where they are, what they need, how fast they need it, and the cost and value—to them and to society—of increasing their access to information and knowledge. We also need to know who the nonusers are, what information services are important to them, why they do not use the existing facilities, and how to motivate and educate them so they will make use of such facilities.

The Challenge

America has an abundance of recorded information, not a shortage. However, this precious resource is concentrated in relatively few locations, often virtually inaccessible to millions of people, and is lying largely untapped. Thus, the challenge is to find the means for making these resources available to more people through an effective identification, location and distribution system. Many local library facilities and procedures designed for other times and conditions can no longer cope with the ever-increasing volume of information produced in this country and abroad—nor can they fully satisfy the rapidly-changing information needs of our society.

The information-dependent institutions in our society—business, industry, agriculture, education, government, professional societies, and others concerned with information service—are alarmed by the deteriorating ability of some information facilities to meet the essential needs of their constituents. In some fields, such as medicine, where the need is great and perhaps better understood, Congress has passed special legislation for development of information systems tailored to those specific requirements. These have been successful. In other fields, where the need is not less great, there has been little or no Federal activity. Local programs to improve libraries and provide better information services have usually been uncoordinated—lacking in continuity, overall leadership and sufficient funding. The nation must take steps now to strengthen and organize these resources into a coherent nationwide system, or it may soon face a form of information chaos which will sap the nation's intellectual energy and weaken its educational structure. Although information and knowledge exist in prodigious quantity in our country, they are unevenly distributed, and we often do not have the means to disseminate relevant information to those who need it at the time they need it.

New networks can be developed where required and existing ones can be extended to allow requisite information to be moved to individuals and groups, some of whom can scarcely be expected to travel to the established information resources available today. If this is not done, the nation's ability to adapt to changing environmental, societal and political conditions and to find solutions to major problems is diminished. Without valid and timely information, the economy can atrophy; without current and reliable information, society and government may falter; without relevant and useful information, individual development can languish; and without adequate means for distributing information, new knowledge backlogs.

Libraries and information centers in the United States are not developing according to any national plan, and consequently, from a systems viewpoint, their growth continues to be uneven and lacks cohesion. There are gross inequities in library service in the United States today. A new philosophy of library and information service is needed, one based on a common sense of direction and purpose, a commitment to national cooperative action, and a consistent program of equalization.

The scope of the Commission's charge by Congress encompasses the library and information needs of all the people of the United States. It is the Commission's view that the time to introduce remedial and innovative reforms is now, and not later when the information crisis has become worse. Consequently, the Commission has directed its efforts toward planning a new nationwide program for better, faster, and more effective library and information services, a program which would eventually provide people everywhere in the country with access to broad reserves of intellectual energy, so that they may lead full, satisfying, and productive lives as creative and responsible members of society.

The Influence of Technology

This nation's future capability to handle information effectively will, to an important degree, depend on how well and how rapidly we are able to integrate new technological methods and devices into the mainstream of our information activities.

Libraries are affected by four new technologies: computers, micrographics, telecommunications, and audio-visual media. The use of computers in libraries has already been pioneered. However, direct application of computers in libraries has been focused mainly on housekeeping functions; the computer's potential for recording, analyzing, and retrieving information has not yet been fully explored and realized. In addition, there are critical shortages of trained human resources and funds to help libraries convert from manual to machine methods.

The use of micrographics for preservation and compact storage is increasing but is far from widespread. While many publishers are making books, journals, and even entire libraries available on microfilm, there is still user resistance to materials in microform because special equipment is required for reading. In order for anyone to read the information in a small microphotograph, it must be magnified for viewing. Lack of an inexpensive portable reader, lack of standardized forms of film, and related equipment incompatibilities, have seriously slowed the rate of acceptance. It has become clear, however, that microfilm technology offers considerable potential for space and cost savings in libraries and represents a new era in information transfer. Together with the computer and telecommunications it promises to become a powerful force in shaping future library and information systems.

Libraries have been reasonably active in acquiring audio-visual materials: films, filmstrips, slides, audiocassettes, videotapes, video cassettes, and computer tapes. Unfortunately, capable personnel to handle such materials are in short supply, and the equipment is not only complex and expensive, but, in many cases, so little standardized that it causes difficulty and confusion to the user. A critical source of evaluation is needed to cope with the profusion of new and often incompatible devices that continually appear on the market.

Community Antenna Television (CATV), also known as cable television, is a technology still in its infancy. CATV stations have very powerful antennas that enable them to capture TV signals from many distant transmitters and retransmit the signals to the home through underground cables. Today, the technology embraces versatile broadband communication systems capable of providing the subscriber, by means of cable, with many channels and, potentially, two-way communication of both picture and sound, facsimile service and access to data processing. It thus becomes possible to bring sound and picture answers to information questions directly to individual home TV sets, over CATV educational channels reserved by Federal Communications Commission regulations for this purpose. Although there have been some library experiments exploring the possibilities for developing new library services and providing remote use of present services, much more needs to be done before the full potential of CATV for library applications is realized.

The potential for telefacsimile reproduction among libraries is very promising, but present costs per page of transmission and copyright considerations hamper its extensive use.

The joining of such diverse technologies as computers and telecommunications represents a new capability of great potential value to the United States. As yet, the nation has not perceived the far-reaching consequences of being able to distribute information to distant points with relative ease. CATV systems and computer data banks are just beginning to be used by libraries as means for information dissemination.

In the last decade, technology for the creation, processing and transmission of information has been vastly extended. Numerous on-line computer information systems are operating, and it is now realistic to consider harnessing the power of technology for new systems of organization, retrieval and distribution of information through networks. Advances in technology, and in information practices, occur each year. The Commission believes that the potential of the new technologies must be utilized to the fullest extent possible, and that this potential can be realized only by means of coordinated planning and adequate financing.

National planning for information technology is essential for several reasons. First, information technology is costly, and a long-range commitment from the Federal Government is required for sharing costs, contributing to research and development, and ensuring the stability of the program. Second, information technology is complex, and a common sense of technical direction at the national level is imperative, if all relevant agencies are to coordinate their activities effectively. Third, information technology is specialized, and its implementation will depend upon the technical education of the people who will work with it. And, finally, information technology breaks down former barriers to access.

Its introduction, therefore, invariably alters traditional ways of doing things and necessitates national concentrated attention on re-education of the specialist and the user.

There are two other important reasons to plan on the national level: (1) the rising cost of conventional library operations requires that information activities develop cooperative arrangements, which, if done outside of a national context, will be very difficult to interrelate; and (2) today's Federal policy decisions with respect to telecommunications can greatly affect information practices for many years to come.

A Threshold Issue

Resolution of the complex problem of copyright is crucial to the continuing development of cooperative programs and networks among libraries.

It was the Copyright Law which enabled the United States to achieve for its people the freest, the most uncensored, and the widest dissemination of information in history. Copyright is, in fact, the Constitutionally prescribed means for promoting the progress of science and the useful arts. It provides the creator a limited monopoly, not in the ideas, but in the form in which they are embodied.

In recent years, because of the widespread introduction of easy-to-operate copying machines and simplified means for distributing information electronically, the issues relating to copyright protection have grown increasingly complex. If the nation is to maintain the open and free society we enjoy today, with broad dissemination of information, then an updated system of copyright is absolutely essential.

Copyright issues are now before the Congress. An eventual solution must address the "threshold problem" of reconciling the rights and interests of authors, publishers, and other providers of information—in order to encourage the continuing creation and dissemination of their intellectual work—with the interests of the user in obtaining ready access to these works. The judicially constructed doctrine of "fair use" provides only a partial answer to this problem, and new solutions must be worked out which will maintain the economic viability of publishing in the context of new technological means of reproduction and electronic distribution.

The Commission believes that it is essential that the needs of networking systems should be among those considered by the Congress in devising new statutory provisions, and that a sound and clear copyright policy be worked out which retains incentives for those who create and disseminate cultural and intellectual materials.

Workable means must also be found whereby the library community can satisfy its legal and moral obligations to the author and publisher while meeting its institutional responsibilities to its patrons. In the meantime, the Commission encourages efforts to clarify the distinction between copying that does not require permission and compensation and that which does. It also encourages efforts to establish means by which permission, when required, can be readily obtained. Finally, it encourages efforts to establish cooperative arrangements between libraries and publishers, possibly with the use of computer networks for processing, for obtaining permission or licenses and accounting for usage.

The Rationale for Federal Involvement

While the Federal Government appears to be broadly aware of the part played by libraries and information centers in national growth and economic productivity, the Commission believes that now is the time for the Federal Government, in cooperation with state and local governments, to treat information as a national resource. The Commission believes that the concept of a National Program for Library and Information Services is a highly appropriate focus for governmental action because the concept is designed to blend:

user needs for information that are more pressing than ever before; with

information technology that is nowhere more strongly developed than in the United States.

It should be recognized that the United States, though it may now have an unusual opportunity to plan its "information economy," is not alone in this position. Japan, West Germany and other countries have published national information policies and networks. Norway has been working effectively for the last few years through its National Office for Research and Special Libraries, and in Great Britain, the British Library Board has made remarkable progress under its recent charter. If we, in this country, fail to link our resources together nationally so that all can use them, we will be neglecting a very significant contribution that we can make to the quality of our life and the productivity of our people. We may also be missing the opportunity to join other nations in sharing resources on an international level.

The implementation of a workable national program requires close cooperation between the Federal Government and the states, between state and local governments, and between the Federal and state governments and the private sector. Such cooperation is most appropriately fostered through Federal legislation that would adopt as its prime philosophical goal equal opportunity of access to the nation's library and information services. Practically, it would seek better organization, development, coordination and management of the nation's libraries and information facilities and services.

Government by Program—The Key to Unlocking the Paperwork Burden*
Commission on Federal Paperwork

...the changing roles and responsibilities of Federal, State and local governments are root causes of duplicative paperwork and red tape in our Federal system. This Section addresses the impact of Federal programs on the growth of paperwork and delineates those relationships between the Federal and State governments which are based largely on paper transactions. These relationships arise from the setting of national objectives, the transfer of funds from the Federal to State and local governments, the responsibility of the Federal Government for equitable and honest expenditures, and the complex relationships which developed when a plethora of individual programs were funded by the Federal Government.

This Section emphasizes the role played by States and their subunits of local government as administrators of Federal programs, for the potential for reducing paperwork is to be found within these role relationships. Further, the fact that States do play a primary role as governing entities in their own right offers hope for reducing the paperwork and red tape burden stemming from their role as "administrators" in the Federal system.

...growth of Federal programs has been ad hoc, uncoordinated and accelerating over the last half century. Growth of these programs fostered development of many separate interest groups, more committed to their individual program objectives than to the general welfare of the Nation and its citizens. These program interest groups are represented organizationally by programmatic bureaucracies whose constituencies include those individuals concerned with delivering the services and achieving the objectives of a particular program. The interest groups extend from congressional committees, through the Federal bureaucracies to delivery systems within State and local governments. The result has been, in effect, development of a *series* of governments, based not on geographic communities and their elected officials,

---

*In: *Federal/State/Local Cooperation*. Washington, D.C., U.S. Government Printing Office, 1977, pp. 35-53.

but on separate administrative governments intent on achieving particular program objectives. Our reports on health, education, and housing discuss the paperwork and red tape problems that enmesh these particular administrative governments and those who must deal with them. Our report on welfare emphasizes the unresponsiveness of the welfare program government to its own clients.

Even within each separate program, the administrative government's regulation, information and paperwork requirements have created enormous burdens. Each program and its bureaucracy developed its own information requirements, separate reporting and recordkeeping systems, individual financial management systems, distinctive audit systems, different accounting systems, and unique planning requirements.

We recognize that, as new needs are perceived and addressed at the national level, Congress will continue to enact responsive legislation authorizing new programs. We believe, however, that enactment of new programs should take place within a broad management framework which duly considers the role of categorical, bloc and revenue-sharing assistance, their attendant administrative requirements, and the burden of paperwork associated with each form of assistance.

The cumulative impact of separate program administrative governments upon State and local governments, and upon the citizens of those governments, is overwhelming. This Section describes the nature and extent of that impact upon State and local governments and identifies some systems which can be modified to reduce paperwork and red tape....

Impact of Program Paper. Governor Dan Evans of Washington has publicly stated that the States would accept a 10 percent reduction in Federal funds if categorical grants could be consolidated.[1] Many of the smaller jurisdictions within Los Angeles County turn their Federal Aid Urban Highway money entitlements over to the County for 50 cents on the dollar.[2]

According to tabulations issued by the Office of Management and Budget and the General Accounting Office, as of June 30, 1976, State and local governments were required to fill out 917 forms. The total (federally estimated) burden of these forms was 24,001,000 man-hours per year. On the basis of these figures, State and local governments fill out 17 percent of all forms cleared by OMB and GAO and carry 11 percent of the total burden, as measured by man-hours spent in filling out forms. As other reports of the Commission show, these figures may be seriously underestimated.

A study by the State of Oregon of forms selected at random[3] found that:

- The Oregon estimate of hours required to complete each form exceeded the Federal estimate in 19 of 22 cases.
- The most conservative judgment is that the Oregon estimates are at least four times higher than the Federal burden estimates.
- The Federal estimates do not appear to be valid relative measures capable of indicating which forms are more burdensome than others.

A study of the Comprehensive Employment and Training Act by Commission staff reported the following from the City of Los Angeles: "We estimate that 5,700 man-hours at a cost of $45,600 are required a year to prepare the Department of Labor (DOL) monthly and quarterly reports for the city and its subgrantees." The Federal estimate of burden per prime sponsor was 346 hours.[4]

In June 1976, the Texas State Department of Public Welfare conducted a cost-benefit study of Federal reports to determine the additional cost of preparing Federal reports, above the normal cost of acquiring information needed for the Department's own administrative purposes. Eighteen forms from the Social and Rehabilitation Service of the U.S. Department of Health, Education, and Welfare were analyzed. Of the 18 forms, only 9 were officially listed as having been cleared by OMB. Of these forms, the Texas estimate of burden exceeded the OMB estimates in eight of the nine cases, the Texas estimates being five to six times higher than the OMB estimates.[5]

During the course of this study many State and local officials were asked by the Commission to estimate that percentage of administrative costs in Federal programs under their administrative management which could be attributed to Federal information requests and paperwork. Estimates ranged from 5 to 75 percent. A study conducted by the General Services Administration with several other agencies in 1975 estimated administrative costs of Federal programs to be 25–30 percent.[6]

A study carried out by the Academy for Contemporary Problems for the Commission describes the paperwork burdens as "those costs that would not be incurred in the absence of a Federal information requirement." The study suggests further that:

...the paperwork costs for Federal assistance programs range between 1 and 10 percent. The costs are concentrated, however, between 3 and 7 percent of the grant amounts. Statistical analyses of State administrative costs indicate that the "threshold" burden of Federal paperwork is $70,000 for any federally supported program, plus an additional cost of just below 2 percent of the program grant.

This conclusion must be tentative because of the difficulty of measurement and the limited number of study sites. If, however, such paperwork costs were at the bottom of the range and accounted for 2 percent of the total State, local and Federal program costs—roughly $110 billion in fiscal 1977—the paperwork costs exceed $2 billion a year. If, as we suspect, the costs of this kind of paperwork are closer to 5 percent of total program costs, the annual cost is a little over $5 billion.

These estimates represent the minimum cost of Federal paperwork in federally assisted programs operated by State and local governments. They include only the costs to the primary governments and do not include costs that can be passed on to other governments, to private businesses, or to citizens.[7]

Approaches to program paperwork reduction which have been tried in recent years fit into five major categories:

- [attempting] to define the scope of Federal interest in an assisted activity;
- combining narrow programs into broader grants, including bloc grants and general revenue sharing;
- standardizing financial management and administrative management requirements;
- standardizing audit procedures;
- standardizing reporting requirements.

The paragraphs below assess progress to date through these approaches, document the problems they attempt to resolve, and offer some recommendations for specific changes that will make them more effective.

Defining the Federal Interest. The establishment of distinctions among grants as to the degree of Federal involvement they entail and the consolidation of programs into a larger functional grant are attempts to lessen the amount of paperwork associated with categorical grants. So-called categorical programs are based on the concept of providing Federal funds to achieve fairly narrow and specific national program objectives. They provide financial assistance to grantees and strong direction as to how program objectives are to be achieved. Because categorical programs tend to emphasize process objectives (how to manage) as well as narrow program objectives, they require extensive accountability reporting for both purposes.

Problems faced by State and local governments in administering categorical grant-in-aid programs have been studied intensively over the past 25 years. The Hoover Commission said in its 1949 report:

Grant programs are unrelated; they are uncoordinated; and they have developed in a haphazard manner without one agency—Federal or State—concerned with the overall impact and the overall effects of grants-in-aid upon the general operations of Government.[8]

Categorical grants have been the basic vehicle for development of the program administrative governments which have had such adverse impact upon State and local general purpose governments. Each categorical program has its own record retention requirements, bonding and insurance requirements, method of payment requirements, and audit requirements. A grantee must conform to every requirement to be in compliance with the program as a whole.

Although large communities (more than 500,000 population) and large States usually can absorb the resultant compliance costs—personnel, storage space, reproduction of information, etc.—small communities (under 25,000 population) generally are hard pressed and unable to comply. In the interest of assuring uniformity, no allowance in program compliance requirements is made for size of community. Small communities suffer disproportionately, as do small companies in the private sector, from the impact of program information compliance requests.

Governor Philip Noel of Rhode Island expressed his resentment at the failure of the Federal Government to recognize the diversity among States and localities, as follows:

Many Federal categorical aid programs are so rigid that they try to paint a universal solution across this vast and diverse Nation, when in some parts of the country those kinds of problems are not even identifiable.[9]

Governor James Holshouser of North Carolina was blunter in his reaction:

The best thing the Federal Government could do to help State and local governments would be to get some of the regulations out of our hair and let us do the job.[10]

An explanation of the reason for the continuation of categorical programs was set forth in the *National Journal:*

Congressional committees favor a categorical approach to problems because it is easier to track the program, and enactment of a specific bill to address identifiable needs hold[s] far more political appeal than a bloc grant.[11]

Federal officials have other reasons for advocating continued use of the categorical grant. In the case of research and demonstration programs, tightly structured project operations and objectives are considered necessary to obtain useful results. Categorical grants are also considered necessary in cases where the Federal Government believes that a specific, narrowly defined need will not be met without strong Federal intervention. Categorical grants are useful tools for one-time projects, such as construction, where only some of the otherwise eligible recipients have need for the funds. Categorical project grants are often used when funding for the program will not suffice for all potentially eligible recipients. . . .

The Commission supports the proposed Federal Grant and Cooperative Agreement Act (S. 431 and H.R. 1503 in the 95th Congress) as an approach to reducing the red tape and paperwork associated with categorical grants-in-aid. Essentially, this measure calls for Federal agency grant administrators to determine, for each Federal assistance transaction:

- the level of Federal involvement needed to carry out the transaction;
- who the actual beneficiary of the transaction will be; and
- whether the transaction represents a procurement or assistance relationship.

If the transaction basically represents a procurement relationship, a procurement contract should be used. If the transaction basically represents an assistance relationship, and if a substantial degree of Federal involvement is required to assure performance, a cooperative agreement should be used. If the transaction represents an assistance relationship and a minimum degree of Federal involvement is required, a grant should be used.

Section 8 of the bill calls for a two-year effort by OMB to study further methods of implementing the concepts and to determine the feasibility of a comprehensive system of guidance for Federal assistance programs. The Academy for Contemporary Problems, in its report to the Commission, *Impact of Federal Paperwork on State and Local Governments: An Assessment,* recommended, similarly, that Federal assistance programs be classified on the basis of Federal interest and involvement and that Federal reporting requirements be reduced in programs where the Federal interest is not paramount.

The concept of standardizing Federal assistance relationships and classifying them according to the degree of Federal involvement necessary to attain program objectives seems to be a valid approach to the reduction of unnecessary paperwork.

However, much research remains to be done to establish guidelines for such an approach.

Recommendation. . .
A central policy unit in the Executive Office of the President should undertake a study to establish criteria for the degree of Federal involvement ap-

propriate in assistance activities, taking into account such factors as the ultimate user of the assisted activity, the amount of Federal funds involved, and whether the assisted activity is essentially State or local in character, or has interstate or national implications.

Combining Programs. Five identifiable bloc grant programs currently are authorized:

- Comprehensive Planning and Public Health Service Act (commonly known as the Partnership for Health Act) of 1966;
- Omnibus Crime Control and Safe Streets Act of 1968;
- Comprehensive Employment and Training Act of 1973 (CETA);
- Housing and Community Development Act of 1974; and
- Title XX of the Social Security Act (1975).

Bloc grants are broader in purpose than categorical grants and, in at least four of the acts cited...combine categorical grants into broader programmatic areas. The result of such combination is to decrease the necessity for separate paperwork-intensive program compliance reporting and to provide more flexibility for State and local program administrators to respond to State and local problems within the program areas covered by the bloc grants. Administrative costs appear to be less for at least some bloc grants than for the total of categorical grants previously provided by the Federal Government because accounting, recordkeeping, personnel, etc., systems can be combined. State and local officials prefer bloc to categorical grants because they lower administrative costs, reduce paper compliance, and allow program decisions to be made on the basis of program problems identified rather than achievement of national program objectives. However, testimony of many State and local witnesses makes it evident that, although bloc grants initially accomplished a lessening in red tape and paperwork, a "recategorization" process is now underway.

For example, the original Crime Control statute contained these words:

Congress finds further that crime is essentially a local problem that must be dealt with by State and local governments...therefore the declared policy of the Congress [is] to assist State and local governments in strengthening and improving law enforcement at every level by national assistance.[12]

These were very meaningful words to the small staff who began to award grants to State planning agencies in 1968. They were dedicated to the objective of allowing the States and local units of government to determine their needs and to fund those needs so long as they met the comprehensive requirements of the legislation. Apparently, information requirements for administering the program have grown. The Commission was told in a June 1976 hearing that one particular participant's application had grown in length from 3 pages in 1975 to 25 pages in 1976.[13] Other restrictions since the original enactment include a State assurance that 20 percent of the funds go to corrections projects (unless the State files a lengthy waiver request), a specific earmarking of funds for juvenile justice, and the addition of co-matching requirements.

Our reports on grants for social services under Title XX of the Social Security Act and on the administration of CETA document the existence of excessive paperwork in both these programs, particularly in planning documents and accountability reporting.[14]

This process of recategorization and the addition of planning and reporting requirements over time demonstrate the inherent tendency of Congress and the Federal agencies to expand beyond the original intent of bloc grants. Thus, despite the original intent that bloc grants would provide substitutes for broad management reforms and uniform administrative requirements, bloc grants now entail many of the same paperwork and red tape burdens as categorical grants. Nevertheless, the Commission believes that they represent an improvement over categorical programs.

Recommendation...
Congress and the President should continue to review program assistance areas to identify opportunities for combining categorical programs into bloc grants.

Standardizing Requirements. Under the State and Local Fiscal Assistance Act of 1972, Federal assistance is provided to State and local governments with minimal compliance and regulation reporting and recordkeeping requirements. Some reporting requirements under the legislation are burdensome, nevertheless, such as reports on nondiscrimination and citizen participation which are discussed separately in this section.

Revenue sharing dramatically decreases compliance and financial reporting. For example, a letter of credit is used for transferring funds; certification by chief executives in lieu of frequent reporting is used to assure compliance with fiscal requirements; and two reports, one denoting planned and the other actual use of funds, substitute for the large number of recurring reports required by other types of programs. Amendments to the act in October 1976 eliminated the planned use report and required use hearings in each jurisdiction instead.

The types of administrative and compliance requirements outlined... in the general revenue sharing program point the way to similar reforms which might be proposed for other financial assistance programs.

The Intergovernmental Cooperation Act of 1968 was the first statute directed specifically to improving the administration of Federal assistance programs. Included among its provisions are the following standardization elements:

- No grant-in-aid to a State shall be required to be deposited in a separate bank account.

- States shall not be held accountable for interest earned on grant-in-aid funds.

- Permission is granted to "the head of any Federal department or agency" to waive single State agency provisions upon request of the State.

The most recent attempt by the Congress to standardize Federal assistance arrangements was the Federal Grant and Cooperative Agreements Act of 1977, discussed [earlier]. . . .

The Joint Funding Simplification Act of 1974, initially introduced in 1967, proposes actions by which Federal agencies may combine to support common applications, joint use of funds and project management. Although there has been little experience with Joint Funding Simplification, it is not dissimilar to, and in fact is based on, the Integrated Grants Administration (IGA) experiment.

Implementation of the IGA was hindered by the reluctance of managers from separate program areas to work together, because each program manager fears loss of control over his own program. One local official reported his experience in trying to use the statute to jointly fund a sewer project in his city. Three Federal agencies were involved. One of the three agencies pulled out of the project when it was unable to persuade the other two agencies to accept a particular program requirement.[15]

Santa Fe, New Mexico, had a similar problem in using the act to develop a project jointly funded by HEW and HUD:

HEW required simply a donor's agreement for the funds—what they call a donor's agreement—a real simple thing of about two pages. HUD required a contract. We had to pay back $84,000 because our HUD auditor said you had this money and it was not under contract and they did not accept the donor's agreement. HEW would say, heck no, the donor's agreement is all we require. The money was spent wisely. $84,000 down the drain from the general fund of the city.[16]

As the act is currently written, its major provisions defer to existing legislation, so that program managers who do not wish to combine their program funds and administrative requirements may refuse to participate on the grounds that their enabling legislation prohibits their doing so.

A procedure is needed whereby Congress can expeditiously consider necessary administrative changes. One procedure used by Presidents since the 1930's allows the President to submit reorganization plans to Congress, subject to a 60-day resolution of disapproval. If Congress does not disapprove a proposed plan within 60 days, the plan would automatically take effect. A similar procedure should be authorized for administrative changes in statutes which the President determines will enhance the administration of Federal programs, while not effecting substantive change. Such a procedure would have to be embodied in a statute giving the President administrative reform authority.

Recommendation...
The Joint Funding Simplification Act should be amended to permit the President to propose administrative reform plans to Congress where administrative provisions of program-enabling statutes prevent joint funding. Such administrative reform plans would consist of permanent conforming amendments to statute and should receive expedited treatment similar to the procedures available under executive reorganization authority.

Management Circulars. In addition to these three pieces of legislation concerned with standardizing the provision of Federal assistance, a number of Office of Management and Budget circulars have been issued. They include the following:

- A-87 (now FMC 74-4). Sets standards of cost allowability for grant-in-aid programs.
- A-102 (now FMC 74-7). Promulgates common rules and regulations for administering grant programs and provides a common application form and reporting forms.
- FMC 73-2. Calls for the coordination of Federal/State/local audit requirements to the maximum extent feasible.

Federal Management Circulars 74-4 and 74-7 represent an approach to the reduction of paperwork through the standardization of financial and administrative requirements associated with grants-in-aid. Together, the circulars set standards of cost allowability, establish common approaches to 15 areas of grant administration for all assistance programs, and provide for common application and reporting forms among the various Federal programs. They have strong support from State and local officials, who generally believe they have led to improvements in grants administration. There is general support for the concept among Federal program officials as well.

However, as administrative directives, they must defer to any statutory requirements. In addition to specific requirements which cannot be overridden and about which there has been no question, Federal officials rely on general language, such as "the Secretary may prescribe," to ignore circular provisions, particularly in new programs. Deferral to program statutes effectively inhibits the implementation of standard financial and administrative management procedures which would relieve some of the burden of paperwork associated with Federal grants-in-aid. If more standard approaches to the administrative management of assistance programs are to be applied by the Federal Government, the Commission believes that such approaches as those taken in Circulars 74-4 and 74-7 will have to supersede the administrative procedures of program-enabling statutes. Such provisions can be changed through administrative reform plans.

Recommendation...
The President and Congress should consider the use of administrative reform plans to establish standard administrative and financial management requirements for Federal assistance to State and local governments.

Recommendation...
A central policy management unit in the Executive Office of the President should be authorized by Congress to issue appropriate rules and regulations to implement such legislation.

Treasury Circular 1075. This circular, establishing guidelines for the use of single and central letters-of-credit in transferring Federal funds to State and local governments, was issued in May 1964. It has been endorsed by the Congress and has been implemented by some departments, particularly HEW, as a way of reducing paperwork involved in providing advances and/or reimbursements to State and local governments who administer Federally funded programs. A report of the Joint Financial Management Improvement Program points out the benefits of the letter-of-credit approach:

It is of interest to note that the letter-of-credit procedure has been looked upon favorably by the Select Committee on Government Research of the House of Representatives. That committee examined the procedure during its review of the administration of the Government's research and development program. The committee stated, in this connection that: "...The simplicity of the process is perhaps its surest guarantee of success, eliminating a number of hitherto unavoidable, laborious and time-consuming steps: the filing of a request for a payment; the examination of the request; the issuance of a voucher to the Treasury for a check to be issued; the issuance of the check. This is the point at which the procedure begins. The draft or payment voucher is the equivalent of the former check. The grantee deposits it in its own bank just as it did the check; the draft, in its course from the grantee's bank to the Treasurer of the United States, follows a course very similar to that of a Treasury check."[17]

It is important to note that use of the letter-of-credit can be limited by program-enabling statutes that may prescribe specific methods of payment. The circular defers to such laws. The method is currently limited to amounts over $250,000. Although programs which disburse smaller amounts of money are excluded from using the letter-of-credit method, the Commission has found that paperwork savings do result from the use of the method, and its use should be more widely encouraged.

Recommendation...
The Department of the Treasury should actively encourage use of the letter-of-credit method of payment, where possible, and should further encourage the use of a single letter-of-credit combining programs fund transfers to State and local governments, wherever possible.

Recommendation...
The President and Congress should consider use of administrative reform plans to permit use of the letter-of-credit.

Standardizing Audit Procedures. The increase in Federal assistance programs for State and local governments in recent years has resulted in heavy reliance on the audit function both to assure the proper use of Federal funds and to measure program effectiveness. Because Federal financial assistance is usually granted on a Federal-State or Federal-local matching formula, both participating levels of government share responsibility for assuring that funds are used properly. However, uncertainty and conflict frequently characterize the intergovernmental audit function because of overlapping jurisdiction, undefined audit responsibilities, and dual program administration and duplication.

The problem of intergovernmental audits was recognized as early as 1965, when OMB issued a circular encouraging the sharing of audit findings among Federal, State, and local governments. A two-year effort by OMB,

GAO, and Federal agencies resulted in the GAO *Standards for Audit of Governmental Organizations, Programs, Activities and Functions,* published in 1972. The following year, GSA issued FMC 73-2, *Audit of Operations and Programs by Executive Branch Agencies,* which requires that:

Federal agencies coordinate their audit requirements and approaches with these organizations (State and local governments) to the maximum extent possible. The scope of individual audits will give full recognition to the non-Federal audit effort. Reports prepared by non-Federal auditors will be used in lieu of Federal audits if the reports and supporting work papers are available for review by the Federal agencies, if testing by the Federal agencies indicates the audits are performed in accordance with generally accepted auditing standards, and if the audits otherwise meet the requirements of the Federal agencies.

Despite this policy, which encourages the standardization of audit procedures and increased reliance on State and local audits, a GAO report, *Increased Intergovernmental Cooperation Is Needed for More Effective, Less Costly Auditing of Government Programs,* says that "most Federal auditors said they generally do not rely on State and local audits because of the Federal Government's different legal requirements, interests, audit guidelines and reporting methods."[18]

Recommendation...
The Joint Financial Management Improvement Program should investigate issues arising from the assignment of a central Federal agency with the responsibility for establishing minimum standards for audit performance. This study should include methods whereby a single Federal agency may determine whether individual State audit divisions have the technical capability of performing audits of Federally assisted programs.

Recommendation...
Federal agencies should seek assistance from the General Accounting Office Data Bank File before burdening State Central Auditors with inquiries concerning State audit programs. The GAO should further publicize the existence of this data bank and continue to update the material.

Recommendation...
To the maximum practical extent, Federal agencies should be required to accept audits of Federally assisted programs by States and localities. Such acceptance should apply unless either:

   a. State auditors decide that they do not wish to perform a given audit, or

b. *The agency involved determines that a particular State does not have the capability to perform an audit in accordance with its established guidelines.*

Recommendation...
The Joint Financial Management Improvement Program should investigate the possibility of strengthening Federal Management Circular 73-2 or adopting legislation which would accomplish the following:

a. *State auditors should be given first right of refusal regarding audit of Federal assistance programs provided the State has been found to be capable of properly performing audits of Federal programs.*
b. *In those cases where audits are performed by Federal auditors, including GAO, work papers and audit findings will be made available to State auditors.*
c. *In those cases where audits are performed by Federal auditors, those auditors must advise legislative audit authorities, Statewide central audit authorities, and other affected parties of the particulars of said visits.*

Recommendation...
The Joint Financial Management Improvement Program should investigate the issues involved in requiring Federal agencies to conduct training seminars for State officials and pay for all costs including per diem and travel for such training, in those cases where Federal agency audit guidelines for a particular program must differ from the standardized audit guidelines.

Recommendation...
The Joint Financial Management Improvement Program should investigate the issues involved in Federal Government reimbursement of the States for that share of the costs incurred during a program audit which arise from additional work performed to satisfy those Federal requirements which are over and above normal State audit procedures.

Recommendation...
The Joint Financial Management Improvement Program should investigate the need for the Congress to authorize Federal programs to reimburse State and local governments for audit work. The reimbursement would cover that share of the costs incurred during an audit which arise from the additional work performed to satisfy the Federal requirements over and above normal State and local audit procedures. The JFMIP should also investigate the need for Congress to appropriate funds for this purpose.

Recommendation...
Congress should consider measures whereby specific compliance standards
would be eliminated from legislation. Where certain compliance standards
were deemed necessary, they should be standardized so that all programs
may be audited within the parameters of a single standardized Federal audit
guideline....

Notes

[1]*National Journal,* "Federalism Report/State, Local Officials Hit Unnecessary Federal Regulations," by Neal Peirce, Vol. 8, No. 2, January 10, 1976, p. 46.

[2]Los Angeles County Road Department, *Red Tape, A Diversion of Transportation Funds.* Los Angeles, California, March 1973, p. 1.

[3]*People or Paper?* Department of Health, Education and Welfare—National Reporting/Monitoring Study—1977, Draft, Prepared by HEW-Region X, March 7, 1977.

[4]*The Comprehensive Employment and Training Act [CETA],* Analysis of Selected Paperwork Components, Commission on Federal Paperwork, Program Studies, February 25, 1977.

[5]Study contained in letter to Terrance E. Swanson from Raymond W. Vowell, Commissioner, Texas State Department of Public Welfare, dated November 2, 1976, in files of the Commission on Federal Paperwork.

[6]*Administrative Costs in Federally-Aided Domestic Programs,* General Services Administration, Washington, D.C., 1975.

[7]*Impact of Federal Paperwork on State and Local Governments: An Assessment,* Academy for Contemporary Problems for the Commission on Federal Paperwork, May 1977.

[8]The Commission on the Organization of the Executive Branch of the Government, Concluding Report, *A Report to the Congress,* May, 1949, p. 31.

[9]*National Journal, op. cit.,* p. 47.

[10]*Ibid.,* p. 48.

[11]*Ibid.,* p. 46.

[12]P.L. 90-351, The Omnibus Crime Control and Safe Streets Act of 1968, June 19, 1968, 82 Stat. 197.

[13]Testimony of Michael A. Carroll, Deputy Mayor of Indianapolis, Indiana, at hearings of the Commission on Federal Paperwork, June 2, 1976.

[14]Report of the Commission on Federal Paperwork, *Title XX: Federal Demands, State Impact, and Recommendations for Reform,* May 1977.

[15]Testimony of Charles Graham, Deputy City Manager, Pueblo, Colorado, at Commission on Federal Paperwork Intergovernmental Studies Workshop, Denver, Colorado, September 21-22, 1976.

[16]Testimony of Philip Baca, City Manager, Santa Fe, New Mexico at Commission

on Federal Paperwork Intergovernmental Studies Workshop, Denver, Colorado, September 23-24, 1976.

[17]Report of the Joint Financial Management Improvement Program, 1964, as quoted in GAO Report, *Opportunities for Savings in Interest Cost through Improved Letter-of-Credit Methods in Federal Grant Programs,* April 29, 1975, p. 22.

[18]GAO Report—*Increased Intergovernmental Cooperation Is Needed for More Effective, Less Costly Auditing of Government Programs.* No. B-176544, April 8, 1974, p. 2.

Additional Readings

Aines, Andrew, and Day, Melvin S. "National Planning of Information Services." In: *Annual Review of Information Science and Technology.* Edited by Carlos Cuadra and Ann Luke. Washington, D.C., American Society for Information Science, 1975, pp. 3-42.

Arthur D. Little, Inc. *Passing the Threshold into the Information Age: Perspective for Federal Action on Information.* Washington, D.C., National Science Foundation, 1978.

Horton, Forest W., Jr. "The Federal Locator System: A Presidential Mandate." *Government Data Systems,* 9:15-16, 19, January/February, 1980.

Kraemer, Kenneth L., and King, John L. "In City Information: A Critique of Federal Involvement." *Government Data Systems,* 7:12, 16-17, July/August 1977.

Laudon, Kenneth C. *Computers and Bureaucratic Reform.* New York, Wiley, 1974.

Office of Management and Budget. *Paperwork and Red Tape: New Perspectives— New Directions.* Washington, D.C., U.S. Government Printing Office, 1978.

Simon, Herbert. "Applying Information Technology to Organization Design." *Public Administration Review, 33*:268-278, May/June 1973.

U.S. Commission on Federal Paperwork. *Final Summary Report.* Washington, D.C., U.S. Government Printing Office, 1977.

———. *The Information Locator System.* Washington, D.C., U.S. Government Printing Office, 1977.

U.S. Comptroller General. *Program to Follow Up Federal Paperwork Commission Is in Trouble.* Washington, D.C., U.S. General Accounting Office, 1980.

U.S. Congress, House, Committee on Government Operations. *Paperwork Reduction Act of 1980.* Report No. 96-835, 96th Congress, 2nd Session, March 19, 1980.

———, Subcommittee on *Legislation and National Security. Paperwork Reduction Act of 1980.* Hearings, 96th Congress, 2nd Session, February 7, 21, 26, 1980.

Chapter 7

INFORMATION MANAGEMENT: THE IMPACT ON CITIZENS

Disadvantaged people are often into their own subculture. This removes them from the flow of popular information that exists in society at large. Their information universe is a closed system. The disadvantaged individual needs large remedial doses of information in order to bring him up to "information par" with the rest of society.

—Thomas Childers, *The Information Poor in America*

Citizens in a democratic society are schooled in the principles of democratic morality, which suggest that citizen participation is vital to the success of a democracy. For such participation to be meaningful, it must be informed. Citizens must be given the necessary educational tools and information to participate effectively in collective action. Citizens in a democratic society are taught that government should be limited and have constraints on its right to intrude on private lives. Citizens are inculcated with the view that government should affect their lives in the least burdensome and obtrusive manner possible. Although few persons would argue about the appropriateness of such notions on the general level, the selections in this chapter indicate that substantial difficulties and problems arise over the ways these principles are applied in the use and management of information in public organizations and over how these information policies and practices affect citizens. In recent years, however, significant efforts have been made to study the effects on citizens of information management and use in the public sector, and some interesting recommendations for change have been put forward.

The readings in this chapter detail four different adverse effects on citizens: paperwork burdens and distributive, privacy, and political impacts. In each case, questions are raised about the ease with which public organizations can impose economic, political, and social costs on citizens by the way they control and use information.

In the first selection, "The Burdens of Paperwork," the Commission on Federal Paperwork reviews the economic, psychological, and cumulative burdens of "bad" management of paperwork and reports on citizens and private groups and organizations. The commission notes that, until recently, public agencies tended to disregard such costs of paperwork. If this trend is to be reversed, several significant steps must be taken, including full cost accounting for paperwork and information requirements on outsiders and improved efforts by Congress and public agencies to define more carefully reporting requirements embedded in legislation. Finally, the commission advocates increased activity by citizens and public and private interest groups to make agencies more aware of burdens on respondents and more responsive in initiating efforts to minimize these costs.

The second paper, "Information and the Disadvantaged: Overview," by Thomas Childers, discusses the problems of "information poverty" in the United States and the difficulties that the disadvantaged have in acquiring and using information to improve their situations. Not only are the disadvantaged locked into a culture that inhibits them from collecting information appropriate to their needs, but these needs differ significantly from those of the middle class. Childers concludes by drawing a "portrait" of the information-deficient and disadvantaged American that emphasizes that the information such individuals do receive from television and informal sources is largely inappropriate for defining the individuals' real problems and difficulties.

In the third reading, "Record Privacy as a Marginal Problem: The Limits of Consciousness and Concern," Michael A. Baker turns to the effects on privacy of information management in the public sector. He suggests that information privacy is a marginal concern for public managers because record keeping is a low-visibility activity in an organization. Thus, the tendency is to overlook information policies and practices that may cause privacy problems for citizens. Baker also suggests that current laws and policies relying excessively on the individual as the main action-forcing mechanism overlook the low visibility of information problems and difficulties for individuals as well.

In the fourth selection, "Government Secrecy: Exchanges, Intermediaries and Middlemen," Itzhak Galnoor highlights the political impacts of administrative secrecy by focusing on information exchanges between interest groups and public officials. Basing his analysis on information as a political resource, Galnoor examines the different uses of information by "established," "less-established," and "non-established" lobbies. Galnoor observes that despite laws governing the status accorded information in the government, such as the Freedom of Information Act and confidentiality statutes, administrative secrecy is "situational." Rarely is there a need for absolute secrecy in government. The usual situation is one in which information is used as a resource and shared selectively by public officials and those interested in agency programs and activities. Galnoor suggests that this sharing often works to the disadvantage of "less-established" or "non-established" lobbies, particularly individual citizens or public interest groups.

The Burdens of Paperwork*
Commission on Federal Paperwork

The very nature of government tends to be paperwork-bound. Our forefathers started us on a course that is paperwork-intensive from both a political and economic standpoint. The separation of powers, checks and balances, the Bill of Rights, the due process clauses of our Constitution, and our Federal structure necessitate a tremendous amount of paperwork. Checks and balances, along with the separation of powers, frequently require the executive branch, Congress and the courts to engage in similar information activities in the process of developing independent positions on the same issues. The Bill of Rights and the due process clauses, designed to protect the rights of the individual and business, generate considerable paperwork in the attempt to respect privacy and insure confidentiality.

...two changes have occurred that bear directly on the Commission's work: first, there has been a dramatic buildup in information activities; ours has become an Information Society. In part, this is attributable to the long-term trend towards service industries, such as government, that are information-intensive. Another part of this information explosion is attributable to our greater capability to process information. In a sense, we have a case of computer capability creating its own information demands. Second, as social concerns other than economic growth assume importance, we have increasingly become a regulated society. Unfortunately, the "regulation explosion" has also increased information demands. It now seems clear that, at least in terms of information activities, steps must be taken to "regulate the regulators."

In short, government by its very nature tends to be paperwork-bound; all paperwork imposes some type and some degree of burden; when paperwork results in little value—to the imposer or the respondent—the burdens are emphasized or magnified. This kind of paperwork the Commission calls "bad" paperwork, and it is on this category, not all paperwork in general, that the Commission has focused its attention.

The Commission was able to distinguish three types of burden: eco-

---

*In: *Information Value/Burden Assessment*. Washington, D.C., U.S. Government Printing Office, 1977, pp. 3–20.

nomic, psychological and cumulative. This distinction is important because the Commission found that past efforts to deal with the paperwork problem have overstated the significance of the economic dimension and understated the importance of the psychological and cumulative categories (if, indeed, they addressed them at all).

Economic Burden. DIRECT COST BURDENS. Direct economic costs associated with Federal paperwork include: (1) costs of information collection; (2) information processing costs; (3) storage costs; (4) interaction costs such as the cost of a taxi to the Social Security office; (5) professional and legal costs, such as payment for notarization of a document. Costs associated with any of these activities may be absorbed by the Government, or they may be assigned, in whole or in part, by the Government to the respondent, the regulated entity, or the individual or organization seeking benefits. For example, in one program the Government may require that records be kept and transmitted quarterly to the Government, with the Government thus bearing storage costs. In another program, the Government may require that the records be retained by the other party, thus requiring the respondent to bear storage costs.

DECISION DELAY BURDENS. In some cases, the paperwork is so extensive that timely decisions are delayed for years. Frequently, during the years of such indecision, business investments that should be made are either delayed or decided against. As a result, valuable economic resources may be lost, crippled, or misdirected. The most expedient path—that is, the one with the least amount of paperwork—will take precedence over the paper-encumbered one.

Concomitantly, information gathered by an agency or program manager may be so voluminous that the totality clogs the decision-making process. A mountain of available information may discourage agencies and individuals from searching existing data systems. Two negative consequences may result: (1) A decision may be made to act without benefit of available information, or (2) a new data collection effort may be initiated because the agency concludes that it would be cheaper to ignore what exists and simply collect new information.

Psychological Burden. Responding to an information request may also give rise to burdens which are not quantifiable in strictly economic terms but yet are of sufficient import to be considered in an overall burden assessment. These can be called psychological burdens. Psychological burden is defined to include all negative attitudinal reactions to Federal paperwork/information activities. These negative attitudes can have behavioral effects which are adverse to the Government, such as small business not seeking Federal contracts.

Information requests do not necessarily elicit negative reactions. For example, the Government-wide effort to generate greater citizen participation is based, in part, on the premise that citizens like to have a voice (that is, provide information) on policy matters. As a further example, there is evidence that some people enjoy providing information when they are interviewed personally. These examples make it clear that by focusing strictly on economic burdens, one might either underestimate or overestimate the overall burden.

Second, it is important to note that, while the psychological effect is registered by the individual (organizations do not have attitudes), there are different roles in which individuals might be affected by Federal information practices. As a member of a society, one might be bothered by the belief that information is being collected by the Government for undesirable purpose. As an employee of a firm, one might be frustrated by having to compile information that one considers redundant or irrelevant. And finally, as an individual, one might be bothered by not being able to understand a form or by fearing that one does not have sufficiently accurate information with which to respond.

The significance of the multiple ways in which individuals can be reached by Federal information practices is that ultimately a large number of people are affected by Federal paperwork in one way or another. Hearings have brought to light the following negative attitudinal reactions to Federal paperwork.

- **Invasion of Privacy**. An important value of the Anglo-American tradition is privacy. The American political system is founded on the premise that the individual and society are, at times, separate spheres, and that there must be limits to the right of government or any other social institution or group to intrude into the personal affairs of individuals.

- **Dehumanization** is a concept that is of central concern in studying the non-economic burden of Federal paperwork. An individual can be considered dehumanized whenever he is not treated as a human being, with dignity. In this instance, we are talking about the filling out of information requests for anonymous users and machines.

- **Information Misuse Burdens**. Unfortunately it cannot be guaranteed that information once collected will lead to beneficial results. Sometimes the wrong information is collected, sometimes it is improperly analyzed, and sometimes it is improperly used. In all cases, citizens are ultimately burdened.

- **Legitimacy**. The legitimacy of a person, social role, institution, ideology, political system or other subject is established by giving abstract, generalized moral approval to the subject. The importance of such moral approval is that it serves as a foundation for the exercise of power or influence. Note that legitimacy or moral approval of a subject is not the same thing as satisfaction with the subject's performance. Moral approval is, more precisely, assent to the subject's right to perform a prescribed social function.

Numerous examples of situations in which U.S. citizens question the legitimate functions of the Federal Government can be readily cited from CEP hearings.

Gerald Thorton, General Counsel and Vice President of Administrative Services, Inc.:

FCC does not have statutory authority to regulate programming, but they do. Instead of doing the job of administering a law that they [Government agencies and Departments] have, they all get into the social reform business, and they don't just collect taxes, they get into the home situation business. They get into all sorts of things.

Ashley deShazor, Corporate Manager, Vice President, Consumer Credit, Montgomery Ward and Company, Chicago, Illinois:

Time and time again I have had complaints from businessmen swamped with patently unnecessary paperwork requirements from Federal regulatory agencies. At times, these intrusions constitute a virtual infringement of their basic rights.

Cumulative Burdens. The total paperwork burden is important because even one series of justifiable requests for information can result in an excessive economic and psychological burden. This can occur when multiple Federal agencies and layers of government each impose reporting requirements on the same respondent. In such cases, the individual burdens of Federal forms from a particular agency need to be considered in the context of the greater cumulative burden and the ability of the respondent to meet those reporting requests.

The cumulative psychological burden is most evident today in the widespread feeling of alienation, that is, the belief that information compiled in ever increasing amounts stifles society. Unlike the specific types of psychological burden that can be related to a particular information request, alienation is a pervasive burden that emerges out of the aggregate of specifics. Alienation comes on gradually as specific is added to specific. In essence, it occurs at a point where quantity becomes so great as to produce a qualitative change.

Examples of Burden. Here are some of the burdens complained of by citizens and others at public Commission hearings and in correspondence with the Commission's Ombudsmen:

- **Forms/Reports Are Difficult/Complex**. Various Government forms and reports prepared by respondents appear to be unnecessarily complicated, and difficult to complete. They should be simplified, streamlined and consolidated.

- **Costs Are Excessive**. The guidance the Government gives agency officials for estimating costs incurred by respondents in filling out forms is inadequate. Both the nature of the costs and their full magnitude are substantially understated. These guidelines need to be expanded, updated and strengthened in terms of their coverage and usefulness.

- **Regulations Are Too Complex**. Government regulations lack simplicity and are difficult to understand. As a result, citizens spend an inordinate amount of time just trying to figure out what they mean. Regulations need to be greatly simplified.

- **Over-Regulation**. There are too many overlapping and duplicative regulations imposed by local, State and Federal agencies, with heavy associated paperwork and red tape burdens. These should be consolidated, synchronized and simplified.

- **Reporting Is Too Frequent**. Government reports are required to be furnished too often; frequency should be reduced, where possible to an "as needed" basis, such as from weekly to monthly, monthly to biannually, biannually to annually, and so forth. Better yet, they should be requested "as required," on no fixed cycle.

- **Irregular Reporting Periods**. Reporting periods differ between local, State and Federal agencies for the same information; or governmentally-prescribed reporting cycles and cut-off dates do not coincide with normal business practice, thereby causing duplicative sets of books to be kept and confusion in bookkeeping.

- **Filing Dates Not Staggered**. The same due dates are imposed for many different reports and information, such as the first of the month, the end of the year, etc. Peak workloads are therefore a real problem. Submission dates should be staggered where possible to balance the workload.

- **Continuous/Intensive Reporting in Lieu of Sampling**. Consideration should be given to the use of statistical sampling, where scientifically and technically acceptable and practicable, in lieu of 100 percent reporting. Policies should be developed to identify and reduce the burden on "high impact" respondent groups like farmers and small businessmen.

- **Unrealistic Timeframes**. Current reporting timeframes prescribed by statute are too compressed to obtain accurate and complete data. For example, the first reporting data [are] often set too soon after enactment of legislation to permit obtaining the required information accurately and completely and without incurring excessive costs.

- **Unrealistic Review Times**. Too much time is taken by an agency to review data collected, particularly in areas where fairly quick resultant action is required, such as in the administration of grant programs. As a consequence, data become outdated, untimely and unreliable and must sometimes be recollected.

- **Audits Are Excessive**. Too many audits are required, by the same or different agencies, apparently for identical or closely related programs and purposes. Consequently, the associated paperwork burdens are excessive. Agencies should coordinate their audit programs more closely.

- **Excessive Number of Copies**. Too many copies are required of the same documents and reports. Agencies should explore assuming this burden if cost-effective, including reproduction costs, or sharing copies, or routing information in tandem instead of acting in parallel (which is often why extra copies are justified).

- **No Data Interchange**. Information is apparently not efficiently and effectively interchanged between and among local, State and Federal level agencies, even when such interchange capabilities are known to exist and there are no overriding considerations of confidentiality or technical "hardware" or "software" problems. Consequently, there is a great deal of overlap and duplication when agencies require information which is slightly different in timing, format, and so on. We should shift attention to unnecessary *differences* in agency requirements and away from similarities.

- **Duplication of Data**. This burden is closely related to the preceding item. The absence of effective and efficient data interchange capabilities, intergovernmentally and at each level of government, is itself a primary cause of duplication and excessive burden. A locator system is critically needed at each level of government, particularly the Federal level. Such a system would identify exactly what information government has, where it is located, and so on. Data...would *not* be contained in the locator.

- **Little Intergovernmental Cooperation**. Again, this burden is closely related to the preceding two. Local, State and Federal agencies do not appear to be working together as effectively and efficiently as they could to coordinate their requirements for information. The recommendations of the Commissions's *Federal/State/Local Cooperation* report call for important remedies in this area.

- **Lack of Centralized Control**. There is no central policy or operating authority at the Federal level which controls and manages overall requirements for information collected from the public. Citizens complain that the absence of such central authorities...and the absence of overall information management policies...are an important cause of burdensome requirements.

- **No Central Data Files**. Many respondent-complainants told the Commission they felt that data base technologies had reached the point where consolidating agency data bases was both feasible and cost-effective. Until such consolidation was effected, they said, duplication could not be effectively controlled. Although in fairness the Commission acknowledges that the absence of a Government-wide, integrated data base might be considered as a cause of the paperwork burden, past attempts at data centralization (for example, the idea of a National Data Bank and the FEDNET proposal of the early 1970's) were abandoned because of the problems of privacy, confidentiality and data security. Instead of moving in this direction, the Commission recommends the locator idea to establish a finding aid, not data centralization.

- **No Standard Definitions**. Standard definitions for common-use terms, names and abbreviations and their symbolic codes either do not exist, or exist but are not used. Consequently, there is confusion, incompatibility and duplication. The Commission squarely addresses this particular burden in its recommendation for the establishment of a data element dictionary (see the *Federal Information Locator System* report).

- **No Standard Forms**. Respondent-complainants furnished the Commission with hundreds of examples of forms which overlap in purpose, content, format and so forth (even forms from the same branch or division within an agency). Though there was sometimes justification for these differences, usually it was lacking. The Government's Standard and Optional Forms Program at one time offered promise of providing a major point of leverage for attacking the forms duplication and overlap problem. Unfortunately, it has never lived up to this promise. Too often forms are approved perfunctorily; there is little relationship between forms management and reports management or records management, and "standard" doesn't mean standard at all, but simply the stamping of a forms request with an official number.

- **Lack of Coordination Between Forms and Regulations**. Regulations require information which is not always contained on the implementing forms. Conversely, forms may contain information not required by the regulations. Either way, a burden is imposed.

- **Forms of the Same Length Regardless of Respondent Size and Capability**. A common and serious complaint of respondents is that the Government sends out requests for information without making any attempt to assess the capability of respondents to comply with the request, particularly those with limited economic capabilities. In short, a Mom and Pop grocery store is hardly in the same position as IBM to respond to a fifty-page questionnaire or survey.

- **Programs, Systems and Policies Are Not Standard**. Data requirement specifications (both content and format) imposed by different levels of government, and by agencies within the same level, are different, even for the same kind of information. Standard administrative and program delivery systems should be developed and used. This problem figured centrally in several of the Commission's major reports, includ[ing] those of an *Income Security, Health, Housing, Procurement,* and *Federal/State/Local Cooperation*.

- **Retention/Storage of Records**. Records retention and storage requirements oftentimes do not exist, imposing extensive burdens on citizens, businesses and others who must hold onto these records long after the time they serve any useful purpose. Retention standards and schedules should be prescribed where they are needed. The Records Management Act amendments of 1976 supported by the Commission would in part correct this deficiency and enable the National Archives and Records Service of the General Services Administration, which oversees the

Government's records program, to help agencies establish such standards and criteria.

- **Irregular Form Sizes and Other Specifications**. Finally, there is the problem of a profusion of Government standards and specifications for paper sizes, form sizes, layout specifications, and a host of related technical problems. Businessmen, in particular, are dismayed at the irregular sizes and specifications for paper and forms used by the Government, often standards and specifications which are not consistent with conventional industry standards and practices. Many Federal specifications do not agree with standards set by the American National Standards Institute and other national and international standards organizations with respect to paper, forms and records. Considerable work needs to be done in this area, and the Commission has met with the Public Printer, the Joint Committee on Printing, and the National Bureau of Standards to identify what steps could and should be taken.

- **Invasions of Privacy**. This serious problem was the central subject of a major Commission report on *Privacy/Confidentiality*. Sometimes Government asks questions which cause the respondent to feel apprehensive, embarrassed or even humiliated, and in extreme cases, questions and probes can be "dehumanizing." The Privacy Protection Study Commission has documented instances of this kind of burden and made its recommendations. In brief, the Commission on Federal Paperwork believes that some kind of sensitivity classification scheme needs to be developed, which distinguishes between (1) data on individuals which, by its very nature, tends to be highly personal and therefore sensitive, and (2) information which tends to be relatively impersonal, the disclosure of which the individual resents less strongly. Also, there is the very real problem of agencies asking for such information which may turn out to be irrelevant or not very useful, which compounds the difficulty.

- **Disclosures of Confidential Information**. Closely related is the problem of unauthorized disclosure of certain kinds of business and trade information which, under statute, is considered to be privileged information, not disclosable to government agencies. And yet—sometimes intentionally, sometimes inadvertently—agencies have gone to companies, universities and colleges, hospitals, and other institutions, seeking the release of this kind of information. In a few cases they have done so using the mandatory reporting provisions of the Federal Reports Act of 1942. This may constitute a form of economic burden, of course, but more importantly, it is often seen by the business community and others as a form of harassment.

- **Discriminatory Laws, Rules, Regulations or Administrative Procedures.**
  Sometimes a respondent is faced with Government requirements for information which he or she believes [are] discriminatory, by reason of age, sex, religion, ethnicity, national origin, or some other factor. Such a requirement may or may not expressly be a violation of existing statutes; in many areas the law has not kept up with this kind of discrimination. Like the privacy and confidentiality areas, the discrimination area is still an evolving body of doctrine and is by no means "settled law."

- **Unhelpful Behaviors and Attitudes of Public Servants.** Another psychological burden has to do with the interaction between citizens and their Government via direct contact with public officials and public agencies with whom they do business, whether to obtain a license, apply for food stamps, or follow up on a lost Social Security check, or whatever. Sometimes officials and agencies are helpful, constructive and positive in their behavior and in their attitude toward the citizen, business or other party. But too often the citizen gets "turned off" because officials are inconsiderate, ignorant of rules or facts, careless, or officious. In extreme cases they may even be arrogant and totally unresponsive. This is where the Commission has said there may be a "hassle," where the citizen simply cannot obtain the services to which he may be lawfully entitled without going to extraordinary lengths in complying with Government eligibility rules and operating procedures or meeting the idiosyncratic needs of a "petty bureaucrat." Fortunately, there are far more instances of a responsive bureaucracy than an unresponsive one; but the number of cases reported to the Commission in the latter category is disquieting, obliging us to list this complaint as an important psychological burden.

- **Inadequate Training and Skills of Public Servants.** Whether in private industry or in Government, the "customer" expects a certain level of professional competence from the organization to which he [or] she goes for help. A number of citizens and businesses to whom the Commission talked said they believed the level and quality of assistance, service, advice and instruction they received from public officials is oftentimes below par. This in turn translates, for them at least, into a certain amount of confusion, ambiguity and misunderstanding that properly can be classified as a psychological burden.

- **Information Misuse Burdens.** As mentioned, unfortunately, it cannot be guaranteed that information, once collected, will lead to beneficial results. A very large amount of information is collected for one purpose but used for another, unknown to the respondent.

In preparing an information request or developing an information requirement, attention to all of these factors can do much to minimize unnecessary burden. For example, a report form requesting substantial detail will by definition be burdensome; it is incumbent that careful examination be made of the need for such detail. It may indeed be necessary, but at least the burden has been acknowledged and considered. Examination of information requirements against the indicators of burden can provide program managers with initial opportunities for reduction of burden within programs.

Estimating Burden. Having pinpointed the three major primary burdens of Federal paperwork and illustrated specific kinds of burdens, the question is: are these burdens measurable? The tools and methodology for estimating economic burden data exist. However, the Commission's investigations show that existing guidance, such as OMB Circular A-40, which implements the Federal Reports Act of 1942, as amended, and the technical guidance issued by the National Archives and Records Service entitled "Guidelines to Estimating Reporting Costs," are seriously deficient on several counts:

- They do not provide for a full cost accounting of all of the burdens and costs to all parties concerned, not just to Government.
- They do not provide for psychological burden estimation, or cumulative burden estimation.
- They do not interrelate the dynamic aspects of how burdens and costs can be shifted back and forth between Government and respondents, between respondents and "third parties" (for example, customers, in the case of business).
- They do not provide for capitalizing on the full power and capabilities of modern information handling technologies; such guidance does exist in some areas, separately, but it is fragmented and the total technology is not harnessed effectively to reduce the paperwork burden on the American public.
- They do not provide for adequate management controls such that both agency and Federal paperwork management authorities are made aware of the character and full magnitude of the paperwork burden; controls are inadequate and deficient in a number of ways and need to be strengthened.

The Commission has made a number of major recommendations with respect to each of these areas; they are outlined in the following sections.

Primary Ways of Minimizing Burden. Now that we've examined the nature of the burdens, reviewed existing methods of estimating and controlling them, and tried to analyze deficiencies in all of this machinery, the next question is, what can be done to minimize the burdens? Basic to any long-range reforms is the need for a full and accurate accounting of just what these burdens are. Such an accounting, which is now absent from the control machinery, is probably the biggest defect of all. Costs must be "captured," properly identified, measured, summarized, and quantified where possible for:

- all of the parties involved, not just the Government;
- all of the types of expenses involved, including equipment, supplies, personnel costs, communication, and many others;
- each of the steps involved in the information process.

The Commission found that there are basically two leverage points for minimizing paperwork and red tape burdens. The first of these is the goal-setting stage. That is, when Congress enacts new laws and establishes new programs the Government's *information requirements* are first formulated. It is here where alternatives to paperwork-intensive courses of action should be brought into focus, thereby nipping in the bud the long chain of executive branch action that so often leads to red tape and excessive paperwork.

The second leverage point is when an agency begins to think about the kind of *information system* it believes is necessary to collect and bring to bear the data needed to satisfy the information requirements established during the goal-setting stage. Too often agencies bring into being gigantic, automated management information systems, which is akin to using the proverbial sledge hammer to dispatch a fly. Sometimes, quite often as a matter of fact, a simple "manual" system is far more effective and enormously cheaper. Of course, the choice may depend on the efficient coordination mechanisms and many other reforms which the Commission recommends in its reports.

Many of the specific leverage points provide opportunities for minimizing burdens; others for maximizing values; and a few for both. In the following discussion, we try to point out which of these opportunities is involved, in what way, and how to capitalize on them.

DESIGNING INFORMATION REQUIREMENTS. Here is the first point where leverage can be exerted to minimize the paperwork burden. It is at this stage, in the program planning process, where the specific needs for data are articulated. Sometimes requirements are constrained by language in the governing statute itself, but, more often, agencies have wide latitude and authority to establish the nature, level, character and form of the information they need. Opportunities which the Commission has identified here include:

- Congressional use of a *Paperwork Assessment Statement*, to serve both as a checklist for bill drafters to insure that the paperwork impact of proposed legislation is adequately considered, and as a guideline to the cognizant Federal agency when developing programs to implement the law. It may also help oversight committees establish criteria for measuring agency performance. The Commission has issued a "Paperwork Assessment Checklist" to assist those charged with developing paperwork assessment statements in both the executive and the legislative branches.

- **Agency Information Plans**. The Commission has recommended the establishment and use of an Agency Information Plan as a fundamental management framework for reviewing, improving, integrating and developing program information requirements and resources for all agency programs, embracing a multiyear timeframe consistent with the agency's budget. Determining whether agency information requirements are reasonable and feasible is a complex and continuing process. It begins with contacting potential respondents to solicit their views, as well as the views of other agency and outside parties who have interests in and will be affected by the proposed information collections. The Commission has proposed such a Plan in its *Information Resources Management* report; details are included in a separate study entitled "Guidelines for Managing Information Requirements and Resources in the Federal Government."

- **Strengthened Guidelines and Standards for the Clearance Process**. A third major improvement which the Commission is recommending at this first, and most important, opportunity point for minimizing burden is the development of strengthened administrative and information standards and guidelines in such areas as: a working definition for duplication; developing multi-purpose Federal information systems instead of narrow, single-purpose systems; uniform definitions for common-use terms and abbreviations; consolidated program eligibility requirements; and others. GSA, the Department of Commerce, OMB and GAO, as well as other agencies, all have authorities and responsibilities in this area. The details of this recommendation are in the Commission's *Information Resources Management* report.

- **The Need for a Central Federal Information Locator and a Central Registry of Forms**. Finally, the Commission recommends the establishment of a central information locator system as a finding tool so that, for example, if agency X needs information it can quickly and efficiently locate existing information and data bases throughout Government and determine whether existing information can meet its needs, thereby avoiding the recollection of duplicative information. Moreover, the Commission is also recommending that all agencies, even those currently exempt from the provisions of the Federal Reports Act of 1942, be required to register all of their reports with the central locator office to insure that the data base is comprehensive.

COLLECTING INFORMATION. The next leverage point is information collection. Here again there are significant opportunities for minimizing burden.

- **Pre-Testing**. The Commission has recommended that surveys and other information collection instruments be pre-tested, without formal clearance, with a maximum of thirty respondents. Respondents, both individually and as represented by many professional, trade and industry spokesmen, strongly urged the Commission to recommend far greater use of the pre-test as a means of testing the technical specifications of collection instruments as well as other considerations such as respondent capability, information utility, "normal business practice," cultural and ethnic language biases (for example, words used and value-laden questions) and similar problems.

- **Strengthened Quality Assurance Measures**. The Commission's report on *Statistics* addresses a wide range of information quality control problems, particularly those that contribute to paperwork burdens on citizens and others. These include: better methods for updating various indices to reduce the long delays often associated with processing the massive amounts of data involved in the big economic indicators, such as the Consumer Price Index (CPI); the use of rotating cycles to spread the respondent burden across the respondent spectrum (for example, in housing surveys); standardizing terminology, which is a problem that currently prevents some agencies from using data already collected by another agency without extensive adjustments; and advance notice to "high impact"/"low response capability" groups, such as schools, farmers, small businessmen, small colleges, local government and others, to provide them with adequate lead time to collect the required information in their normal cycles, instead of requiring them to mount enormous, costly and bothersome ad hoc efforts to respond to Government's requests.

PROCESSING INFORMATION. The third stage...is processing—which means recordation, analysis and summarization:

- **GSA Authority to Monitor and Advise Federal Agencies on Retention Schedules for Publicly-Maintained Records.** The Commission has recommended amendments to existing records management laws to give GSA/NARS authority to monitor and advise Federal agencies on the retention schedules they set for records that must be kept by State and local governments, industry and the general public. Citizens at the Commission's public hearings, and businessmen in correspondence and personal visits to the Commission, complained bitterly of recordkeeping requirements which were unreasonable and ineffective. Citizens and businesses are sometimes required to maintain records which are not in accordance with "normal business practice," appear to serve no useful purpose, are very costly to establish and maintain, and often duplicate the records usually maintained.

- **Using Modern Information Handling Technologies.** The Commission points out in its *Information Resources Management* report that dramatic advancements in computers and automated information handling technologies in the last twenty years have been a mixed blessing. On the one hand this capability has made possible the provision of services to citizens which, if done on a manual basis, would be prohibitively costly (for example, the computation, printing, sorting and mailing of Social Security checks), but the very existence of this technology has tempted agencies and officials to collect more information than they need or can use. Achieving a proper balance, then, requires the establishment of a new function and a new position in agencies, the information resources management function and the information resources management official, who can serve as the "go-between"—between the user and the computer analyst—a mediator to insure that information needs and uses are properly matched to computer technology.

- **Using Microdocumentation, Including Microfilm.** It is at the processing stage that microdocumentation technology offers its greatest opportunity for reducing the paperwork burden, both to the citizen and to Government agencies which must process and store such enormous quantities of data. The Commission found that this technology has not even been tapped in some areas. With property, warehousing and utility costs rising, it makes sense in many applications to transform hard copy paper records to micromedia. In addition to saving money, the transformation from hard copy to a micromedium offers the opportunity for purging obsolete, inactive and useless holdings. It also offers the opportunity for setting up a much improved information storage and retrieval system, so that such records and holdings become accessible to a far broader spectrum of users, including the public. Too often agency information systems are inaccessible because of technical hardware and software barriers.

- **Selective Dissemination Profiles.** One of the most exciting new technologies the Commission examined for enhancing the value of information collected by government, and simultaneously reducing the burden is the use of Selective Dissemination [of] Information (SDI) "profiles." Briefly, this approach permits an agency official (or citizen) to predetermine his or her special information needs, interests and uses. A "profile" of these requirements is prepared, with the help of information specialists. This profile is then "loaded" into a machine or handled manually in a screening process. As new information comes into the agency, it is "scanned" by the program, and when a subject is found which matches the predetermined profile, it can be extracted and routed directly to the user. Sometimes this technology is called a "computer reading list." It has other names as well. Clearly the technology offers great promise in enhancing the value of information because it makes information available to a much wider array of potential users faster and more efficiently. As more and more of our data flows become automated, the feasibility of this technique will be extended.

USE OF INFORMATION. The fourth stage of the information cycle is use. The Commission has made a number of suggestions in this area.

- **Practical Utility.** Beginning with the FY 1978 budget, the Office of Management [and Budget] incorporated a new requirement for agency reporting systems; that is, requests for new reporting systems must contain a review of the "practical utility" of the information to be collected. Agencies are admonished that, if data [are] not used for reasons beyond the agency's control, they should not collect data, even though [data] may be "needed." The Commission endorses this new "test" and urges the expansion of its application beyond the reporting context. For example, the practical utility test is one which the Commission believes should be addressed very early, in information planning stages. Accordingly, the need is addressed in its recommendations (already discussed...) for the establishment and use of a Paperwork Assessment Statement by the Congress and again in the Agency Information Plan. Finally, the practical utility test is an integral part of the Commission's call for substantial strengthening of the whole evaluation process.

- **Zero-Based Reporting (ZBR)**. The Commission jointly pilot-tested the notion of a zero-based reporting system with the Environmental Protection Agency. The purpose was to develop a schedule for reviewing agency reports (public-use, interagency and internal) periodically, "from the ground up." Too often, the Commission found, reporting requirements remain on the books long after the need for which they were originally justified has disappeared, and yet the report goes on and on. When queried as to their utility, the official replies: "We've always gotten that report; I don't really need it, but I've assumed someone else does." The Commission has recommended that the ZBR concept be further pilot-tested beyond EPA and that the prototype system jointly developed with that agency be further refined as necessary to extend its utility to other agencies. Also, it should be tied in with the Administration's Zero-Based Budgeting System.

DISPOSITION OF INFORMATION. The last step in the information cycle is disposition, or disposal. The problem, the Commission learned, is that the Government has never addressed itself to the overall problem of *information disposal* (as opposed to *records disposition*). *The distinction is crucial to reducing the paperwork burden, certainly on the public directly but, most importantly, within Government (and thus on the taxpayer indirectly). Too often the Government's unused information is left lying around in archives, records centers, document depositories, and other places, costing money to keep but serving little purpose. The Commission has addressed this problem in several contexts.*

- **Recycling Information**. Information resources are not recycled the way we recycle other resources. Of course information cannot simply be dispensed with on benefit/cost grounds. There are important Constitutional, statutory and other requirements to keep records and information. Any recycling program must take these factors into account. But when one considers the enormous capital and operating investments the Federal Government has made, and is making, in its data and information holdings, simply jettisoning data systems and data which become "obsolete" when a program is discontinued, cut back, or subsumed into another program seems shortsighted and costly. The Commission has suggested that the availability of such data be made known to all agencies via the same kind of process which is currently used for excess and surplus property and supplies. That is, that the central information authority should prepare and circularize a comprehensive list of such information, identifying its subject, location, form and such other specifications as are necessary to permit its efficient retrieval. Of course, special precautions and safeguards are required where data holdings involve personal or proprietary or other sensitive material, in which case the various protections the Commission advances in its *Privacy/Confidentiality* report would apply.

* **Clearinghouses and Strengthened Intergovernmental and Interagency Data Interchange**. The Commission's *Federal/State/Local Cooperation* report made a number of recommendations in this area. The problems of interchange of information between levels of government remain much the same as those identified by the Joint Intergovernmental Task Force on Information Systems, an effort in which OMB, the Advisory Committee on Intergovernmental Relations (ACIR), the various public interest groups, and others participated in 1968. Among these are: no efficient machinery exists for interchanging information of interest to multiple levels of government; there is inadequate consultation by the Federal Government with State and local governments in the development of information requirements (particularly those program requirements which burden the other levels of government heavily); and duplicative and overlapping program and information requirements exist because of statutory, administrative or technical barriers which foreclose effective and efficient intergovernmental information interchange. In the Commission's *Federal/State/Local Cooperation* report, recommendations were made for putting new and strengthened interchange machinery in place; for example, the greater use of clearinghouses that might specialize in certain broad classes of information and take responsibility for keeping abreast of new developments, acquisitions, storage and dissemination.

Other Ways to Minimize Burden. Beyond the steps identified above, there are still other ways the paperwork and red tape burden can be effectively addressed and dealt with. In our discussion above, we considered primarily the direct, quantifiable and more obvious factors which contribute to burden, but there are many less quantifiable, more indirect and less tangible kinds of burdens which are no less significant.

CITIZEN INTERACTION COSTS. Sometimes the disabled forego services to which they are entitled because the Government's delivery system forces them to incur costs, both economic and psychological, which, in their view at least, outweigh the benefits they are seeking. Sometimes the cost of a taxi to the local welfare office may make the difference between meeting this week's bills or risking default on a payment. Transportation costs to citizens, particularly those in the various disadvantaged categories, [are] a critical consideration.

PROFESSIONAL FEES. Citizens often must seek commercial and professional assistance to fulfill their obligations under the law (or to apply for optional benefits). Entire industries, such as tax consultation, have emerged because of this kind of burden. Beyond tax consulting, professional assistance is often required of certified public accountants, auditors, lawyers, physicians, information bureaus, research organizations, and many other kinds of specialists in order to understand, process, complete and submit various forms, reports, records, applications and other Government requirements. These are sometimes provided to specially disadvantaged citizens at minimal cost, but for most citizens they must be obtained at prevailing market rates. Usually the Government does not provide compensatory relief, such as rebates, tax credits or direct payments.

PROCESSING DELAY COSTS. This is a very important problem, but a difficult one to deal with. Delay costs heavily. Delay means missed opportunities. Delay means taking on added risks. Delay means missed business investments. Too often government is insensitive to this critical factor and, in the words of one respondent, "takes its own sweet time" in responding to citizen needs. Yet agencies are often in a position to improve their administrative and delivery systems by employing relatively simple and inexpensive control devices, such as suspense dating or "tickler" systems as they are sometimes called. Due dates, action notices, follow-up phone calls and other actions can be predetermined in many cases and adequate means provided for insuring that they take place on a timely basis.

Recommendation...
The Office of Management and Budget should provide for further research on the nature of burdens imposed by Federal paperwork, with the goal of establishing measures of burden for use by those developing information requirements...

Information and the Disadvantaged: Overview*
Thomas Childers

The Culture of Information Poverty

Disadvantaged people share some characteristics that affect their information universe. These characteristics constitute barriers to their felt need for information, their search for it, their acceptance of it, or their use of it.

First, disadvantaged groups are typically disadvantaged by the level of processing skills at their command. Reading ability is very low. Hearing or eyesight may be impaired. English may be a second language. Communication skills, such as those involved in bargaining for a house or budgeting, are not conventional knowledge for them as they are for the mainstream of society.

Second, they are often locked into their own subculture. This removes them from the flow of popular information that exists in society at large. In effect they live in an information ghetto. Their information universe is a closed system, harboring an inordinate amount of unawareness and misinformation (myth, rumor, folk lore). While they do have information contacts with the rest of society, these contacts are very often one-way information flows, via the mass media, from the greater society. It can be expected, where the cultural uniqueness of the group is substantial, that the imported one-way communication runs the risk of being irrelevant or wrongly interpreted. Even more specifically, reliance on television as the primary mass medium—a one-way channel emphasizing entertainment rather than information—may result in an information void.[1,2] While the group may be very rich in certain kinds of internally generated information, it is deficient in the information shared by the larger society.

A study of female public housing tenants in a large northeast city may offer a partial explanation. It was concluded that the poor, even when politically oriented, tend to interact with others largely in a highly personalized or local social milieu. They are not accustomed to dealing with a complex system of specialized role behavior such as a bureaucracy. Thus their interac-

---

*In: *The Information Poor in America.* Metuchen, N.J., Scarecrow Press, 1975, pp. 32–43. (Reprinted by permission of the publisher.)

tion with agencies is inhibited, and a potentially important source of information remains relatively unused.[3] There is a weaker system of information within the disadvantaged community. Just like most people with a felt need for information, the disadvantage person turns first to the informal network, the friends, neighbors and relatives who might know. Some of the people who are turned to are "opinion leaders" in the community. Yet while they are indeed more informed than is the person who seeks them out, and do indeed transfer information into the community from outside, even opinion leaders are hindered in fulfilling their role by the social barriers that are drawn up around the community. Although opinion leaders in disadvantaged communities play the same role as gatekeepers in advantaged communities, the former cannot play it as effectively, for their access to outside information is curtailed.

Internally generated information or information specifically aimed at the disadvantaged may accumulate and get disseminated in the disadvantaged community just as it does in every other community. But there is a kind of social embargo against a great body of externally generated information. It is the information that is typically communicated through informal channels outside the disadvantaged communities, or through the printed mass media. It is the information that helps you get to the proper source of help, wield your political power, demand your entitlements—the information that imparts the knowledge needed to secure a share of the standard American dream, to which even the person at the lower end of this society aspires.[1,4]

The third major barrier to information is a composite of attitudes and philosophies that we will call predisposition. Report after report portrays the various disadvantaged populations as despairing, fatalistic people with a pervasive sense of helplessness. The *least* disadvantaged individual—suffering from one disadvantage, such as poverty—maintains some hope in the future and is confident that some things, perhaps even things within his power, can be done to alleviate his problem. The *most* disadvantaged is the one on whom several social and personal disadvantages converge, such as poverty plus poor education plus social isolation plus ethnic discrimination—and who has never known any other way of life. He is the one who is resigned to those conditions of life, convinced that no act of his own will alter them [this discussion draws heavily on a taxonomy of disadvantagedness[5]...].

Mendelsohn claims that residents of a Denver housing project aspire to what middle-class America aspires to.[4] Assume for the moment that these findings are generalizable to most of the country's populations, including all disadvantaged groups: we would expect that the more disadvantaged an individual is—the greater his sense of helplessness, the greater his acceptance of fate—the less effective these standard middle-class aspirations will be in motivating him to act in his own behalf. There is some support for this expectation in the Warner report. In that study of a sizeable urban sample, it was found that the poorer and older groups perceive fewer problems or questions that need to be dealt with to ameliorate their lives. Those who could be considered personally and socially *advantaged* express significantly more problems.[6] The same study indicates that even for those problems/questions that they did state, the poorer and older groups tend to see the problem/question as a need for information less often than the general population.

It is clear that the disadvantaged are not as predisposed as the general population to alter the undesirable conditions of their lives, or to see information as an instrument of their salvation.

Information Needs

In today's complex society—especially in a large urban area like St. Louis with its many social service agencies and programs—ignorance is one of the chief barriers to utilizing the resources that are available to meet human needs. (p. 33)[7]

It is sometimes claimed that the disadvantaged have information needs just like anyone else. This is only broadly true. If we look hard enough, we can detect information needs that are different both in degree and in kind from the information needs of the general adult population.

Study after study attests to the disadvantaged adult's widespread lack of information when compared with his "average" counterpart on any number of topics. The studies suggest that all people need essentially the same kind of information to survive in this society, but the disadvantaged individual needs large remedial doses of information in order to bring him up to "information par" with the rest of society.

And, as we define "information need" more and more specifically, a few differences in *kind* do begin to show up. Those who are disadvantaged, even though they aspire to the standard American dream, are impelled by physical, cultural and personal realities to need slightly different kinds of information. There is some information that he will be inclined not to need. There is some, and this is the important stuff, that he will have a greater than average use for.

Considering all people, there are two kinds of information need: kinetic and potential. Kinetic needs are the ones dictated by a given situation or condition in the life of the individual. They move and change from moment to moment. If a kinetic need is a felt one, the individual may try to respond to it by seeking out information that will correct a *specific* problem, alter a *particular* reality.

Kinetic needs themselves can be divided into two finer categories: crisis and non-crisis. Examples of crisis needs might be "Where can I get some food for my family this weekend?" or "A rat just bit my hand; what do I do?" or "My neighbors have left their infant children alone for the past three days and nights; where do I get help for them?" Non-crisis needs might be something like "Is there a reading program for adults in my area?" or "Where can I find a job?" or "What is the address of the welfare department?" Obviously, crisis and non-crisis needs can be equally important in the life of the needy person; the difference between the two lies in the immediacy of the need. They are both kinetic; they are dictated by a given condition or situation.

Potential needs, on the other hand, are only loosely defined by the present or short range realities. Instead, they are determined by the longer range anticipations of the individual. To a large extent, they remain unconscious, hidden under layers of attitudes, impulses and values that influence the behavior—and specifically the information-related behavior—of the individual. It is a potential need that impels a person to find out who his senator is, just in case; to learn the name of a bail bondsman, just in case; to inform himself on the future of the local job market, or get a physical check-up regularly. Information acquired in response to a potential information need may never be put into action. And, being generally long-range in nature, a potential need can be expected to last somewhat longer than a kinetic need.

Back to the disadvantaged adult. His actions, including his information-seeking activities, are directed by his kinetic needs. His unwillingness to delay gratification or plan for even the short-term future militates against his acting on a potential information need. Instead, he will respond to needs that are of crisis or near-crisis nature, for instance, he may seek new housing only after being evicted. He is not disposed to recognize or respond to his own potential (long-term) needs.

More than the average, he feels a need for coping information. Coping with life in the disadvantaged ghetto—urban, rural, black, white, Indian, aged, whatever. This information is the kind that will help him acquire the basic necessities in pursuit of that standard American dream. The information is not frivolous. It is an increment toward action of some sort.

More often than others of course, disadvantaged people have information needs related to public assistance: subsidized housing, welfare benefits, free school lunch, medical care, etc. Closely allied are needs in the area of individual rights—what am I entitled to?, how do I go about getting it?, how do I protect myself legally? etc. And there are needs associated with remedial adult education and public day care. While they are not, strictly speaking, unique to disadvantaged Americans, these needs do pervade their lives out of all proportion.

Information-Seeking Behavior

There are two kinds of channels by which information is received: formal and informal. Friends, neighbors, and relatives—that is, personally known individuals—comprise the informal, or interpersonal, channels. The formal channels consist of all other sources of information: the mass media, social agents and agencies, private enterprises—any commodity or activity in society, private or public, that is not related to individuals personally known to the receiver of information.

In one degree or another, channels of both types are available to everyone in society, and everyone uses them both. Is the nature of channel use different for the disadvantaged American?

Mostly, no. Somewhat, yes. Like others, the disadvantaged adult prefers to tap the informal network when he needs a specific piece of information. For some subjects, such as housing, grocery shopping, or job hunting, he may prefer formal sources.[2] When he does perceive a need for information and opts to seek it, his search is often less active (intense) than others.[6]

On the other hand, the average adult is exposed to great quantities of information that he does not actively seek out for a specific problem of his own. Television, newspapers, magazines, films, and books provide a large portion of this unsolicited information. The agents and agencies operating in society provide another part. The informal network, friends, relatives, neighbors, provide still another.

Does he absorb all the information from these sources? Of course not. We have very little hard knowledge about the extent to which such unsolicited information is retained by the individual. But we can be sure without doubt that not all of it is. And based on the evidence of a few studies, we can speculate that what a person knows is a function of the channels to which he is exposed, since some channels are richer in information content than others. Typically, study after study attributes high levels of informedness or awareness to high levels of readership. People who read more know more. They are more prepared to solve their problems.

It is true that the average American adult spends more time with the electronic than with the print media. But it is also true that the urban disadvantaged adult spends even more of his time with the electronic media than the average adult. Unlike his "average" counterpart, he relies on television to the exclusion of other media, expecially newspapers, magazines, and books, that are higher in information value.[2] And he puts more faith than the "average" adult in what television presents.[8]

Warner has categorized information as either "ends" information or "means" information—that which relates to what you want to achieve, and that which relates to how to achieve it. Ordinarily, the electronic media contain more "ends" information; the print media, more "means"information.[6] Television, radio and movies provide information on commodities or life styles that can be striven for; magazines, newspapers and books contain the information that will help acquire the commodities or life styles that we choose to strive for. Remembering that the disadvantaged adult relies on the electronic media significantly more than the average adult, we can see another way in which his information universe is circumscribed by his habits of media use. He is overexposed to "ends" information through television and radio, and sorely underexposed to the kind of information that might help him achieve the ends that he desires.

Again and again, studies point out that disadvantaged people in general are significantly unaware of the social services that might be tapped for the solution of their problems.[9,10,11] Not only are the names of the agencies relatively unknown; so are the programs and responsibilities of the agencies. On the other hand, where there is "knowledge" of social helping programs, that knowledge is frequently wrong: one investigation found that welfare recipients consistently underestimate their own welfare entitlements and overestimate the welfare agent's authority.[12]

Building on such data, some studies have found that the strong nonprint orientation of the disadvantaged adult is a primary cause of his relatively greater ignorance of where to turn.

There are indications, though, that seeking a solution to a problem is very largely a matter of the intensity of the felt need.[13] A few studies, particularly in the area of employment, conclude that in certain situations the disadvantaged adult will turn to formal channels of information more than the average adult. This may spring from his realization that the informal channels of communication to which he has access are inadequate for his particular need. The patterns of job-seeking, described [earlier]...provide the best illustration of this point.

The Impact of Information

The writings that deal with the impact of information on the disadvantaged American present a picture of uncoordinated, scattered and tentative research whose results are largely not comparable. It is tempting to speculate on impact from the many surveys of expressed information need and use, and channel use. However, there is no reason to assume that an *expressed* use of information is an *actual* use, or that an *expressed* impact is an *actual* impact.

Without risking such assumptions, some assorted tentative observations on impact can be gleaned from the literature: A study of some CBS-TV programming concludes that credibility of the information source is directly related to the durability of impact.[14] There is indication that among ghetto populations 50 percent or more would use only commercial or in-ghetto sources or their own resources for information in problem solving.[2]

Donohew and Singh report the conclusion that the innovator in the community is *not* necessarily exposed to the mass media more than his non-innovating counterpart.[15,16] Yet Warner found that the respondents who were more "successful" in solving their problems/questions were the ones who (1) used more overall information sources, (2) used personal contacts more, and (3) used magazines more as an information source than the average.[6] Voos reports on a study of farmers indicating that the innovator, unlike the "early adaptor, early majority, late majority and laggards," utilizes channels of information that transcend the community.[17]

There are suggestions that the purchasing behavior of the urban black or white (not necessarily disadvantaged) is influenced more by information from the white-oriented mass media than by personal contacts.[18] Voos asserts that pragmatic information (i.e., comparative value) is not as important in making purchase decisions as behavioristic information—color, scent, salesman, etc.[17] In some contrast, though, one consumer study has found that a shopper with additional pragmatic information (a shopping list prepared at home) spends $5 less per week on groceries than a shopper without that information.[18]

It is uncertain what impact information has. Little is known about:

How the quality of life of the individual or community changes in the short or long term as the result of information

The impact of information on individual and community demands on social and private service agencies

How information affects actual decisions made

How it affects the decision-making or problem-solving processes

The relative impact of information from various channels

The relative importance of information in making decisions in various areas

How forces within and around the individual influence him to act or not act on new information.

Portrait of the Disadvantaged American in His
Natural Information Habitat

The prototypal disadvantaged American, more than his average counterpart:

Does not know which formal channels to tap in order to solve his problems, or what specific programs exist to respond to his needs

Watches many hours of television daily, seldom reads newspapers and magazines and never reads books

Does not see his problems as information needs

Is not a very active information seeker, even when he does undertake a search

May lean heavily on formal channels of information if it becomes apparent that the informal channels are inadequate and if his need is strongly felt

Is locked into an informal information network that is deficient in the information that is ordinarily available to the rest of society. . . .

Notes

[1]Dervin, Brenda L. "Communication Behaviors as Related to Information Control Behaviors of Black Low-Income Adults." (Unpublished Ph.D. dissertation, Michigan State University, 1971.)

[2]_____, and Bradley S. Greenberg. *The Communication Environment of the Urban Poor.* East Lansing: Michigan State University, Department of Communication, 1972. (CUP Report No. 15)

[3]Levin, Jack, and Gerald Taube. "Bureaucracy and the Socially Handicapped: A Study of Lower-Status Tenants in Public Housing," *Sociology and Social Research* 54:209–219, January 1970.

[4]Mendelsohn, Harold, and others. *Operation Gap-Stop, a Study of the Application of Communications Techniques in Reaching the Unreachable Poor. Final Report.* Denver: University of Denver, 1968. 2 vols. (ERIC ED 024 788 and ED 024 816)

[5]Hayes, Ann P., and George W. Eyster. "Proposal for an Institute for Training in

Librarianship: Developing Public Library Services to Disadvantaged Adults" (unpublished). Morehead, Ky.: Morehead State University, March 1973.

[6]Warner, Edward S., Ann D. Murray, and Vernon E. Palmour. *Information Needs of Urban Residents.* Baltimore: Regional Planning Council, April 1973. 2 vols. (Draft)

[7]*Aging in St. Louis: A Study of the Aging Information and Direction Service.* St. Louis: Health and Welfare Council of Metropolitan St. Louis, 1970.

[8]Greenberg, Bradley, and Brenda Dervin. *Use of the Mass Media by the Urban Poor.* New York: Praeger, 1970.

[9]Cornely, Paul B., and Stanley K. Bigman. "Acquaintance with Municipal Government Health Services in a Low-Income Urban Population," *American Journal of Public Health* 52:1877-1886, November 1962.

[10]Duke Law Journal Staff. "The Legal Problems of the Rural Poor," *Duke Law Journal* 1969:495-621, June 1969.

[11]Tibbles, Lance, and John H. Hollands. *Buffalo Citizen's Administrative Service: An Ombudsman Demonstration Project.* Berkeley: University of California, Institute of Governmental Studies, 1970.

[12]Briar, Scott. "Welfare from Below: Recipients' Views of the Public Welfare System," *California Law Review* 54:370-385, 1966.

[13]Levine, Felice J., and Elizabeth Preston. "Community Resource Orientation among Low Income Groups," *Wisconsin Law Review* 1970:80-113, issue no. 1, 1970.

[14]Alper, S. W., and T. R. Leidy. "Impact of Information Transmission through Television," *Public Opinion Quarterly* 33:556-562, Winter 1969-70.

[15]Donohew, Lewis, and B. Krishna Singh. "Communication and Life Styles in Appalachia," *Journal of Communication* 19:202-216, September 1969.

[16]_____, and _____. "Poverty 'Types' and Their Sources of Information about New Practices." Paper presented at the International Communication Division, Association for Education in Journalism, Boulder, Colorado, August 27-31, 1967.

[17]Voos, Henry. *Information Needs in Urban Areas: A Summary of Research in Methodology.* New Brunswick, N.J.: Rutgers University Press, 1969.

[18]Block, Carl E., and others. *The Badge of Poverty, the St. Louis Report.* Columbia: University of Missouri, Regional Rehabilitation Research Institute, 1970. (Research Series #4)

Record Privacy as a Marginal Problem: The Limits of Consciousness and Concern*

Michael A. Baker

In this essay I would like to place what are broadly called *record privacy* problems in the context of organizational routines and everyday personal experiences, arguing that the manner in which record-keeping is embedded in the background of most individual and organizational existence has real rather than trivial implications for how we deal with confidentiality and due process problems.

Specifically, I will suggest that what we can expect in the way of self-protective action on the part of individual citizens is severely limited by the fact that record-keeping practices are of relatively low visibility to and salience for the individual. Second, I will suggest that managers typically find privacy protection something on the order of a nuisance organizationally, and that we do not find attention to privacy *built into* record-keeping practices; in fact, there is often a strain in the direction of ignoring civil liberties protections.

Let us begin with some scene setting. We live in a world in which organizations are the principal consumers of recorded knowledge about individuals and in which they are the principal determiners of what is gathered and how the data will be used and shared. Theoretically, the individual can refuse to share information about himself with organizations, but there are three important conditions operating to reduce individual control in this area: (A) Much of what an organization (say a police department or a market research body) wants to know about citizens or potential customers is available totally without their cooperation; (B) For the individual to refuse to cooperate in a record-keeping process often means giving up whatever that record-keeping is in support of—rather considerable deprivation where, say, welfare or medical care is concerned or where a job is at stake. The similarity of record-keeping practices among organizations of the same type makes it difficult in

---

*Reprinted by permission of *Columbia Human Rights Law Review,* Vol. 4, pp. 89–100, 1972.

many cases to *shop around* for goods or services offered with what you consider to be an appropriate level of intrusion into your life and decided by means of what you consider to be legitimate criteria; (C) Where an individual is in a position to control certain aspects of the record-keeping process, it is usually only through the ability to marshall the support of another organization. Part of the meaning of living in an *organization society* is that, implied in the relations between organization and customer, citizen or client is a set of relations with other organizations whose aid the individual may invoke. That this is the individual's principal source of power as far as record privacy is concerned means that the ownership and control of record identities is for the most part firmly in the hands of organizations. It is an important truism that the individual, *qua* individual, has little real power.

It is important to keep in mind that significant aspects of the privacy-and-records problem are built into the record-keeping process. Invasions of privacy are rarely accidental and do not usually reflect a *breakdown* of organizational practices in any sense. Instead, they grow out of such processes.

In the following section I would like first to suggest that a number of features of organizational record-keeping and decision-making about individuals make for a lack of managerial consciousness and concern about civil liberties problems and for a critical dearth of knowledge about record-keeping processes on the part of the individual.

In some of what appear to be the more hackneyed statements about the conditions for a free society, civil liberties protections are described as the underpinning for a decent human existence. Rather than being ends in themselves, constitutionally protected liberties are an important set of means. As such they may exist in the background of political life, for the most part taken for granted. By way of noting that there is something of real importance in such a description, however, I suggest that the *background* character of civil liberties concerns and record-keeping practices produces some of the most important features of what we have come to call the *privacy-and-records* problems.

Record Privacy as a Nuisance

In some form, privacy, confidentiality and due process issues are important within most organizations, and a degree of *organizational awareness* exists with respect to them. In most cases, however, a manager's orientation to record privacy issues does not reflect an abstract commitment to civil liberties protections; it is tied instead to concrete features of the organizational environment in which he works. The kind of awareness one encounters in record-keeping organizations is the practical concern of the managers for the implications of civil liberties claims and challenges. This concern is typically embedded in a complex of operating procedures and cost considerations and reflects both organizational structure and external legal and social pressures.

Having to take into account the privacy rights of those on whom they store and use records is something akin to a nuisance for many organizations. There are several reasons why this frequently turns out to be the case. First, record-keeping is a means for most organizations and in some respects goes on in the background of the organization's daily activites. Resolving civil liberties problems in the interests of individuals may at some points require managers to attend to aspects of their record processing to which little time and attention would otherwise be given. In many organizations, for instance, management has little systematic knowledge concerning the accuracy of personal records. The organization *gets by* with a level of accuracy acceptable to its own goals and comes to recognize that an *accuracy problem* exists only when its own operations are disturbed in some way.

Second, many organizations are by their very nature manipulative of clients, customers, citizens, research subjects, students, suspects, etc. Whether their goal is therapy, education, law-and-order or marketing, they are more or less oriented to the individual as an object rather than as a citizen-with-rights. This is especially true for large organizations which *batch process* clients or citizens through a series of operations designed to transform them into fully *acceptable* members of society and to keep them manageable during a period of custody. Providing civil liberties for such people may be seen as *technically* unnecessary. Erving Goffman, in his work on *total institutions,* notes that in many respects processing people is like processing things; certain minimum conditions have to be met (*e.g.,* the temperature of the *warehouse*) if the *material* is to be kept in good shape to be worked upon. But unlike non-human objects, he notes:

Persons are almost always considered to be ends in themselves, according to the broad moral principle of a total institution's environing society. Almost always, then, we find that some technically unnecessary standards of handling must be maintained with human materials. The maintenance of what we call "humane" standards comes to be defined as part of the "responsibility" of the institution, and presumably is one of the things the institution guarantees the inmate in exchange for his liberty.[1]

There is built into the structure of some processing organizations, then, "constant conflict between humane standards on the one hand, and institutional efficiency on the other."[2]

Finally, for some organizations the protection of individual privacy may mean a loss of highly cherished autonomy, since recognizing such rights implies that the individual may invoke the aid of courts, legislatures, guardian groups and other organizations when his expectations as to data gathering, sharing, access and use are not met. Prior to the passage of fair credit reporting acts at the state and federal level, for instance, individuals had virtually no relationship with the commercial organizations which compiled credit, pre-employment and pre-insurance reports on them. Individuals were quite literally the *objects* of a report and little more. Passage of these laws has given individuals covered in the files of consumer reporting agencies a formal relationship with these organizations, backed up by regulatory agencies and the courts.

The significance of these features of organizational processing for the record privacy question is that we cannot expect from organizations a high level of awareness and concern about civil liberties problems unless coincidental internal needs make for privacy protections or external pressures place privacy protections among the courses of action in the interest of the organization to pursue.

Record-Keeping as Invisible

Like many processes which are means rather than ends, much of the record-keeping which affects individuals goes on in the background of social life and is for this reason of low visibility to the individuals concerned. On a given person there may be upwards of 100 files maintained in various organizations. These range in visibility from those in which data gathering, use and sharing goes on completely behind closed doors (*e.g.,* intelligence files) to those in which the individual has some knowledge about content and use but little, if any, knowledge about the data sharing which goes on from his file (as in the case of a bank which routinely shares account experience information with local credit bureaus). In very few settings is the individual fully knowledgeable about the content, use or sharing of *his* record, and in almost all cases there are some aspects of the record process (*e.g.,* who worked on the records; what is the likelihood of an error in my record; in how many locations is the information duplicated once I give it to an organization?). For instance, one of the central problems in attempts to control and update arrest record circulation is that a single arrest may generate records in many locations as the arresting agency establishes its own set of records on the event and passes on fingerprint and arrest information to other organizations such as the FBI, state identification agencies or the courts. "It is virtually impossible for any person to know what happens to his criminal record. For example, one study made by the Oakland Police Department revealed that as many as 40 separate documents of an arrest record, with a minimum of 71 copies are routinely made."[3] To fully communicate the plethora of records and record transactions in which the individual citizen is involved or by which he is affected, detailed examples would need to be drawn from perhaps twenty different areas of information about the individual, including credit, physical and emotional health, vital statistics, military service, voting, employment and religious activity. Further complicating the problems of public knowledge about record-keeping practices is the fact that people are often in no position to know very much about the computer systems which are increasingly used to store and process records about them. Sometimes the fact of computerization—to say nothing of the details of its impact on civil liberties—is not even visible.[4]

For the most part, the low visibility aspects of the record process do not arise out of the intentions of managers; as we will see... record-keeping goes on in the background of the organization's life as well, often without conscious attempts on the part of managers and officials to hide it. But as the history of the privacy and records debate makes plain, there are record-keeping operations intentionally carried on with as low a profile as possible. Much of the informal exchanges of personal information which characterize the *information buddy system* in fields such as law enforcement and personnel administration frequently are accomplished with the understanding that the *record subject* will have no knowledge of the occurrence or content of the transaction. As another example, the credit reporting industry managed to keep itself out of the public eye for better than fifty years of its growth, until the privacy debate of the 1960's focused attention on this important piece of the record-keeping world.

The civil liberties import of the general lack of visibility which characterizes record-keeping processes has been displayed over and over again in the course of the privacy and records debate of the 1960's and early 1970's. Whether by happenstance or managerial intention, individuals did indeed have their rights abridged without their knowledge. And most of those who came forward to tell their story of being hurt through record-keeping policies or errors reported that they did not at first know about the data gathering and use which was the source of their trouble and that they had not been concerned in a general way about privacy problems prior to their difficulties.

As important as the sheer visibility of record processes is, the matter of how salient they are to the individual while he is in the course of some transaction with an organization is perhaps even more important. Civil liberties problems in record systems are often generated at points in our lives when, compared to other events taking place simultaneously, they must occupy relatively low positions on our list of priorities as to what is deserving of worry and attention.

Arrested on an armed robbery charge, a New York City youth discovered a rather important record error: another youth had given this young man's name and address on two occasions when arrested in order to avoid having a record on himself. The name and fingerprints were forwarded to the appropriate agency, but since neither youth had a record at that time, there was no way for this piece of duplicity to be uncovered. When the court requested the youth's record for arraignment proceedings, a garbled return was forthcoming, since there was a match on name and address (and on some others, by unhappy coincidence: age, sex, height and color of hair), but no match on fingerprints. But garbled or not, the possibility that this youth had been arrested twice before was enough to convince the court that the charges being made against him by a storeowner were plausible. The young man claimed that he had never been arrested before (true) and that he had had no part whatsoever in the robbery (also true). A very high bail was set.

What is important in this example is that the young man came to know of his record problem at a point of crisis and that it was pointed out to him that there were well established procedures by which he could go about getting his record straightened out. But given the problem of dealing with the armed robbery charge (and of surviving the experience of incarceration at Riker's Island awaiting trial), the record problem receded into the background of his concerns. Further, while he had a lawyer for the more important function of dealing with this indictment (all charges were eventually dropped), he did not have assistance afterwards for dealing with the rather complicated process of getting records expunged and corrected. The state had come through with a lawyer for the important event, but had left him with a nagging record problem which he was in no position to solve without devoting a great deal of time and energy to it.

More mundane examples point to the same feature of the record privacy problem. While the individual may challenge the record when something in it seems to be barring him from some right or privilege, he is far less likely to question practices which are not of immediate import. In the process of getting medical care, insurance, or credit an individual may feel reluctant to inquire about the meaning of the waiver he signs authorizing the physician or firm to seek more information about him. Even if curious or worried about what exactly he is giving up by signing, his more or less dependent position may encourage him not to risk challenging questions. Problems of confidentiality are often problems for the future in just this way. Some vague worry may surface in the course of a record transaction, only to be submerged by more important uncertainties of the moment.

There are of course situations in which worry about the future of a record affects present behavior considerably, as for instance the case of the pre-law student who might want to be officially active in a given political group on campus, but who is *chilled* from this course of action by the prospect of having future trouble with the gamekeepers of his profession. But, as I think became quite clear during the McCarthy period, people may worry about their future presentation-of-self, but still do not mold their lives around each and every record possibility of the future.

Overall, many record-keeping tasks have the character of an errand—frequent enough to annoy us and claim a good deal of our time, but so trivial, given the larger events for which they represent a means, as to warrant little of our concerned attention.[5]

A related problem arises when the meaning of recorded information is not clear to us because we are not in a position to know what criteria are being used in decisions about us. The civil liberties implications here of course are that knowledge about how information is used is critical to most privacy and confidentiality complaints. Underlying our ideas about what data should be collected and shared are fears about the eventual use of such information. In addition to the more obvious kinds of problems, such as discrimination on the basis of age, sex or race, are situations in which a record system appears to *make sense,* as far as its function is concerned, but where it in fact has a very different relationship to a decision about us than we imagine. The manager of a branch bank, for instance, may be told that he must keep employee costs down. At the same time, he knows that there are very few opportunities for promotion within the bank for the employees he supervises. He does not want to lose his trained tellers and other personnel, so instead of telling them why he cannot give them very much in the way of a raise, and why he cannot promote them, he refers with great manipulative skill to their record, suggesting that "if you had a little bit more on the education side, I might be able to help you." For some employees, this is a *sensible* explanation, given their notions as to how one gets ahead in the world and the fact that they are not in a position to see that the very few who are promoted have no more education than they do. In other settings, such as a university, the same technique of using what are thought to be *sensible* criteria as a screen, is employed to hide the real reasons for not granting tenure to a faculty member. Even where individuals see through such an organizational ruse, they remain powerless against such techniques because it is difficult to demonstrate in the appropriate forums for appeal that such tactics are being employed.

There is in the privacy area a small but interesting body of public opinion literature, and one of the clear pictures which comes through this material is that, even where record processes are visible to the citizen, he often has little clear picture of what his formal civil liberties are. Popular concepts of individual *rights* often correspond poorly to the civil libertarian's view of constitutional guarantees, and particularly where private organizations are involved, an individual's claim that a certain kind of *decent* treatment is *rightfully his* may have little basis in law or tradition. This is not to suggest that citizens typically claim more rights than they are in fact provided by constitution and courts; in fact, the task of convincing people that they should vigorously pursue their rights has frequently fallen to civil liberties spokesmen, and often involves, as a first step, informing the public as to what these rights are. A further problem is that citizens differ in the extent to which they have experienced situations which might raise the issue of some specific constitutional protection. Often, it is difficult for citizens to identify with those in the society whose rights may be in jeopardy, and this blocks recognition of how some official practices might threaten their own rights. An almost classic civil liberties dilemma arises when a legislature moves with public support in ways that threaten the liberties of some segment of the population—with little apparent worry on the part of the general public that the damaging legislation might be turned against themselves at some future time.

It is quite clear I think that at a number of points in American history, a national referendum might well have failed to approve the Bill of Rights. That consciousness of civil liberties is neither sharp nor self-protective in anticipatory ways, represents still another respect in which record privacy problems remain on the margin of everyday existence.

On the more specific matter of privacy, many commentators have noted that in law this is one of our least clearly articulated rights. In the public mind, it is a concept that is less clear still, and as a result, it is difficult to measure the strength of the set of values we have come to label *privacy*. Under the simplest kind of questioning, virtually everyone declares himself *for privacy*; the Friends-of-Big Brother Association is a trifle short of admitted members in contemporary America. But this generalized allegiance to privacy, confidentiality and due process protections devolves into a complicated set of opinions as the focus of questioning becomes more specific and the balance between individual liberties and the practical needs of organizations is introduced as an issue. Most individuals do not appear to have the kind of strong consciousness of their own civil liberties interests which might serve as a resource for beginning to deal with record privacy problems. While there may be some room to expand this consciousness, it seems more likely that civil liberties issues in general and privacy issues in particular will remain matters of strong conscious concern to only a minority of citizens.

This is an organizational society in which the presentation of self through records is commonplace. But it is not a world in which individuals are thoroughly comfortable with the knowledgeable concerning the record errands which are part of their daily rounds of existence. We cannot assume that individuals are entirely document-wise, especially where this is precluded by the fact that they do not know decision criteria are in play where services, rights and benefits are being allocated. Sometimes the gulf between individual capacities and the requirements for informed citizenship is very wide indeed. In his study of record-keeping in a West Coast social welfare agency, Don Zimmerman recounts an instance where an old woman became an object of amusement to social workers who were well built into the world of documents-as-proof. She reported that she could not find the citizenship papers required as proof of age but that she did recall having copied down her age on a piece of paper at one time. She handed over a rumpled piece of paper with that date written on it—a document not official but no less authentic from her perspective. It was of course not acceptable, and the story, when related to fellow workers, was greeted with great amusement.[6]

Lest we think that such misunderstanding of formal record-keeping processes is a problem only of the poor and less educated, remember that several decades of credit bureau activity took place before middle class critics—who had been the objects of much of this commercial reporting—discovered the existence of their local credit bureau and national giants like Retail Credit Company of Atlanta, and began the process of dragging this industry into the critical glare of journalistic and congressional exposure, and into a modicum of public accountability. In many cases, differences in knowledge between citizens of different socioeconomic status are probably meaningless as far as their level of control over record privacy problems is concerned.

That both record-keeping and civil liberties occupy only the margins of individual consciousness would not matter at all if records were at most points accurate reflections of our qualities and activities. Under fire for their record-keeping practices, organizational managers are fond of the defense that individuals *make their own records* and *have nothing to fear if they have behaved appropriately* with respect to credit, educational, citizenship and other responsibilities. But we know all too well at this point in the history of the privacy and records debate that record-keeping is by no means a *neutral* process. Though used in the background, the manner in which the record is constructed, its completeness and accuracy and its particular relationship to information gathered on a face-to-face basis can affect the outcome of decision processes markedly.

The Problem of Remedies

With this reminder, we come to the question of remedies. Drawing together the ideas that people are not generally knowledgeable about the record-keeping practices of organizations with which they deal and that they may not have a sense of either what their own rights are or when these are being trod upon, we derive a picture of the individual as a poor candidate for self-protection where record privacy problems are concerned. As things currently stand for most record-keeping situations, the range of corrective action we can expect on the part of the individual himself is quite limited. In my view, we can for the most part expect this built-in predicament to remain for the future as well. We may be able to engage in some productive consciousness-raising aimed at record privacy problems. But we are dealing in most cases with a zero-sum situation, and given the amount of complex and detailed information about record-keeping which the individual would be required to absorb if he were to genuinely *take charge* of records about himself, it does not seem likely that we can expect self-protective vigilance from more than a few dedicated citizens who will apportion to record privacy matters some substantial part of their resources. As Wenglinsky notes in his discussion of this as a broader issue, *solutions* to problems of the citizens or consumer often come at their own expense, rather than out of some reallocation of institutional resources:

...just as caveat emptor was a doctrine which placed the burden on the consumer beyond his ability to challenge the offers of the powerful, so contemporary law and usage places a burden on the errand-runner far beyond his ability to contend with the powerful who manipulate and create the errands. Indeed, so ingrained is the legitimacy of unequal resources between seller and consumer, that legislation supposes that fairness in the relationship is achieved through giving extra errands to the consumer. In unit pricing, for example, as in much legislation of the New Deal variety, the consumer is given information that allows comparison shopping only if he adds more time, effort and skill in computation to the errands of the supermarket. It is as if the resources for errands on the part of the consumer are inexhaustibly elastic and can be drawn upon without compensation.[7]

In the tradition of *informed* consent, it is possible that we can build-in some real choice for the individual with respect to what information about him is gathered, used and shared. But we have to beware of establishing remedies which turn out to be fictional because they require daily acts of minor heroism on the part of the individual, as he challenges clerks, managers and officials on record-keeping matters and works to grasp the significance for his interests of each record-related choice he is given. There are a number of situations in which it is probably impossible to create the conditions under which genuinely *free* individual choices are possible. *Requesting* the cooperation of a public housing tenant in government sponsored evaluation research, for instance, or asking a welfare applicant to "voluntarily" supply his Social Security number for more efficient record processing, do not seem to be the kind of measures which reflect real life in this organizational society. Several suggestions have been made for remedies which embody the notion that organizations will keep each citizen continuously informed of the content and use of his record and allow him to approve all record transactions for which he has not given previous consent. Aside from the immense logistical problems such remedies would entail for record-keeping organizations (of some concern where the public purse would shoulder this burden), it is not at all clear that, used on a wide scale, such programs would resolve very many serious record privacy problems without creating problems of even greater moment for the citizen.

Neither record-keeping nor civil liberties concerns are likely to move from the background of individual daily existence into the forefront of attention. This means that we must look beyond the individual himself for creative solutions, and beyond the kind of arrangements that will involve substantial commitments of time and energy on the part of individuals perhaps already overburdened with adapting to the needs of the organizations which process or serve them. Along these lines, it is clear that while allowing the individual access to his own record should be the rule in all but a very few instances, the most important aspect of this access process will be the procedures for challenges to and correction of the individual's record. If such remedies are to be of real significance, they have to be structured into the record process so as to prove almost effortless for the individual. Similarly, the destruction of records after appropriate periods of time really needs to be an automatic weeding process, rather than one which waits upon requests from individuals. Further, enforcement for record privacy protections has to be a matter of routine that lies for the most part outside the individual's responsibility, since court challenges and even regulatory proceedings are out of reach for most individuals psychologically and financially and in terms of their time.

Wherever it does prove possible to increase the level of individual consciousness about record privacy problems, public reactions may serve as a resource out of which some policy can be derived as to what information organizations are allowed to gather and use in their decision-making about individuals. We have learned over the years that, however much organizations foster the appearance of necessity and rationality with respect to their information needs, these needs remain quite negotiable. Organizations rarely fail to even falter because of restrictions on their data gathering, storage, sharing or use. This is perhaps the most difficult route to take in handling record privacy problems, since organizations resist strongly intrusions upon their autonomy in this area, and since it is is often difficult to demonstrate either the relevance or the irrelevance of personal information for a particular decision. But there are occasions on which the approach of challenging information needs may still prove fruitful.

Finally, some record privacy problems are principally a reflection of an organization's *attitude* towards its record subjects. If such attitudes change (for instance in the case of the status of school children or prisoners as full-fledged members of society), we may see some record privacy problems disappear or become amenable to genuine individual control. Barring this, however, solutions to record privacy problems are going to have to come from outside the record-keeping organization itself, and be accomplished primarily for, not by, the individual—a *paternalism* which, while perhaps not welcome, does reflect the individual's position in this society and his existential relationship to record-keeping processes.

Notes

[1] Erving Goffman, *Asylums* 76 (1961).

[2] *Id.*

[3] Hearings on National Penitentiaries Before the Subcommittee on National Penitentiaries of the Senate Committee on the Judiciary, 92d Cong. 2d Sess. (1972) (statements by Aryeh Neier and John Shattuck, at 14–15).

[4] For a full study of the impact of computer technology on civil liberties in record systems, see the...report, A. F. Westin & M. A. Baker, *Data Banks in a Free Society* (1972).

[5] Martin Wenglinsky discusses the concept of errands as a special type of social activity in...*Into the Ordinary* (A. Birnbaum & F. Sagarin ed.) (1972).

[6] D. Zimmerman, "Paperwork and People Work: A Study of a Public Assistance Agency," 1966 (unpublished dissertation, Department of Sociology, University of California at Los Angeles).

[7] Wenglinsky, *supra* note 5.

Government Secrecy: Exchanges, Intermediaries and Middlemen*

Itzhak Galnoor

Secrecy in public affairs is said to be needed in order to protect a public interest which is judged to be, on balance, more important than other public interests. In external affairs the public interest to be protected is usually national security and the effective conduct of diplomatic relations with other countries. In the context of government activities related to domestic affairs—which is the subject of this article—the important public interests to be protected are usually the efficiency of the governing process and the privacy of individuals, groups, and organizations. Here is an example reported in a British newspaper:[1]

White and Coloured Youth Gangs Riot for Four Nights

Senior police officers, members and officials of Liverpool City Council, and community relations held an emergency conference tonight to discuss rioting during the past four nights in the Edge Hill District.

Disturbances between white and coloured communities involving the throwing of bricks, bottles and at least one petrol bomb and the erection of barricades were disclosed only late last night.

...The silence of the police over the events which began on Friday and which the local residents say were at their worst on Saturday and Sunday can be put to their desire to stop the rioting from spreading.

The example reveals the conflicting elements of the secrecy dilemma. On one hand the police justification for withholding information was based on an important consideration: premature disclosure might encourage disturbances in other places. This public interest was judged to be more important than that of satisfying the curiosity of the *Times* readers in London who were kept from knowing about the events in Liverpool for four days. On the other hand, immediate disclosure also could have served important public interests: people should have been allowed to know what was happen-

*Reprinted by permission of *Public Administration Review,* Vol. 35, pp. 32–42, January/February 1975.

ing because they have relatives in Liverpool, have plans to visit the city, or because they could have used the information to evaluate and influence the way the authorities handled the situation. Besides, accurate and timely information could have replaced the rumors that may have led to the outbreak of violence.

These typical arguments about secrecy lead to the obvious conclusion that the merit of privileged information is in the eyes (and ears) of the beholder. But "situational secrecy" leaves the people's right to know dangling in the air and does not provide answers for those who are seeking normative solutions to the problem posed by the government's propensity to withhold information.

What are the remedies commonly suggested for dealing with government secrecy? First, the democratic principle of the people's right to know. Liberal theory regards secrecy as an evil necessity imposed upon free citizens as a result of some imperfection in human affairs.[2] The assumption is that only regrettable, temporary measures require tampering with the free flow of information. Secrecy, accordingly, will ultimately wither away: when there is international peace, the rules of the democratic game will be firmly established and the electorate will be sufficiently enlightened. There will be no reason then for government to conceal in the public interest.

These tacit assumptions in liberal democratic theory are further reinforced by the separation between politics and administration doctrine. Elected politicians are considered to be the main safeguard for maintaining the people's right to know. The information that they obtain from appointed officials should enable them to exercise their guidance and oversight responsibilities. This information, as well as their activities as representatives of the public interest, are reported to the public thus establishing a two-way communication channel between constituencies and government. Administrators, in turn, are assumed to be responsible only for implementing policies, and their contact with the public should be restricted to the delivery of services. The professional integrity of civil servants can be maintained by keeping them out of the politics of secrecy. This is the basis of the British principle of "ministerial responsibility," according to which civil servants should maintain their anonymity and be relieved from the task of explaining policies, informing the public, and keeping contacts with outsiders.

It is perhaps not a mere coincidence that the same scholar who formulated the theory of politics-administration separation also emphasized the need for openness in government and advocated later on, this time as President of the United States, the need for international agreements "openly arrived at."[3] We need not explain here why President Wilson could not and did not practice openness in the peace negotiations in Versailles. As Friedrich has shown, dubious practices such as secrecy, propaganda, corruption, violence, and betrayal have been always present in political life.[4] The point is that the theoretical dead ends of both the principle of the people's right to know and the politics-administration dichotomy are related and have important ramifications for the dilemma of secrecy in democracies. Both stop short of tackling two questions: Who decides when intentional withholding of information is more beneficial than disclosure? And from whom is information to be kept secret?

The second approach, or suggested remedy, focuses on the legal and formal measures that will support citizens and officials, respectively, in an encounter over access to information. Secrecy then becomes a problem of defendant-claimant relationships to be solved whenever the right to possess information or to gain access is disputed. Public information is regarded as a tangible property: documents, written memoranda, tapes, transcripts, exhibits, and other materials that can exchange hands, or are submittable as evidence in court.

There are basically two categories of constitutional and legal provisions. The first aims at guiding officials in determining what constitutes an official secret and at preventing disclosure to unauthorized persons.[5] It includes civil service oaths of allegiance, official secrets acts, espionage statutes, document classification, censorship laws, and Crown or executive privilege doctrines. The second category aims at establishing the principle that disclosure by government is the general rule, not the exception, and that whatever government does is public, unless legally restricted. It tries to shift the burden of proof from the citizen to the government, from the need to know practice to the need to conceal justification. The two famous examples in this category are the Swedish constitutionally guaranteed right of access which dates back to 1766 and the American Freedom of Information Act, enacted in 1967.

The experience in the operation of the American Act...shows the limitation of the legal approach.[6] Those who believe in legal remedies as an independent vehicle for change tend to ignore the observable phenomenon that unless formal arrangements codify norms and reflect existing or evolving practices, their ability to affect the flow of public information is marginal. This does not mean that "legality" in itself does not have a symbolic value of high importance, especially in periods of transition and social tension.[7] However, the clearly illegal cases of secrecy are relatively few and far between. The space for government maneuvering within the legal confines of secrecy remains broad in both foreign and domestic affairs. Administrative discretion is inevitable and the desirable equilibrium between publicity and secrecy cannot be achieved by statute alone.

The Information Marketplace

A functional way to look at public information is to regard it as a commodity in the political and administrative marketplace where various suppliers and customers operate.[8] Government, albeit a major supplier of information, is also a customer of the information required for policy making, feedback, and support. Demand for public information is based, therefore, on the need to know, and the "price" paid for it is determined by the benefits that the receiver expects to derive.

This approach emphasizes above all norms of fair play. The information marketplace can work only if there is a general commitment to the people's right to know, freedom of the press, freedom of expression, and the rules of the democratic game. Group *pluralism* as a supplement to democratic representation is the theoretical basis of this approach: the interplay of interests in which everybody has an equal opportunity to form a pressure group and try to influence government. Contacts between government and groups and the trading of information [are] a necessity because of the complexity of modern life and the intensity of government involvement in social services. Groups and organizations need intelligence about government operations not to satisfy curiosity, but in order to survive. This is happening not only in the planned or welfare economies of France, Britain, and Sweden, but also in the strongholds of private enterprise in Washington and Bonn.[9]

Government, on the other hand, cannot survive without close cooperation from private groups. The task of governing has become too complex and public officials have a critical need to exchange information and maintain alliance with non-governmental groups. In short, the exchange marketplace is functional and it makes government more responsive.

This approach to government secrecy obviously comes close to describing reality. As a normative paradigm, however, it ignores well-known "imperfections" in the information marketplace. One thinks of the CIA, a covert use of traveling scholars to gather intelligence in foreign countries, the contacts of housing departments with private contractors about public housing projects, or the disclosure of private information by the Internal Revenue Service to unauthorized persons.

In more general terms this approach ignores the fact that secrecy is the *added value* of the information commodity in the exchange marketplace. Access, rather than being an absolute right or a legally defined property, is a process whereby data become a means of influence and power. The value of information fluctuates according to (a) circulation and the number of knowers, and (b) inflationary pressures which reduce the exchange rate for information—usually as a result of extraordinary events (the Profumo affair in Britain, and Watergate in the United States). Questions arise as to who are the people in these circles? How do they gain access? Why they and not others?

Practical Arrangements for Exchanges

Practically it can be argued that there is no such thing as government secrecy. Only a small amount of information pertaining to military plans or diplomatic negotiations is totally monopolized by a few authorized officials. Even in sacred areas of security and foreign affairs, most of the classified information is known to "outsiders" such as foreign adversaries or trusted confidants.[10] The clandestine bombing of Cambodia by the United States up to May 1970 was no secret to the people in the area when the bombs started to fall; French officials knew about the secret preparations in Britain for the Suez Campaign in 1956; the International Telephone and Telegraph Company (ITT) seems to have had access to classified government information when it became involved in the election in Chile in 1970. All of these transactions are reciprocal and access to information is gained on an exchange basis. Officials are prevented from disclosing information by organizational loyalty and secrecy oaths, but have numerous opportunities to circumvent these restrictions by leaks, the cultivation of clientele groups, or as a last resort—thunderous resignations.

In domestic affairs the need of officials to share information is even more acute, and few things can be kept secret for very long. Information as such is not secret. The context of a certain piece of information in the policy-making process and the additional pieces which can solve the jigsaw puzzle—these are the commodities that administrators can bring to the exchange marketplace. We can also witness a tendency toward secrecy within the executive itself. Not only are "second opinions" not sought by one department from another, but also vital information is mutually concealed, or used for manipulations. The ability to withhold information from the other governing bodies and to determine with whom to share it is one of the strongest manipulative powers of the executive in modern democratic states.

At the same time, an important phenomenon has been observed by students of pressure groups: the really significant public will consists, as far as government departments are concerned, of opinions articulated by recognized groups.[11] Consequently, a new kind of government machinery not yet fully explored by students of public administration has emerged. It consists of complex systems of private and public organizations, of providers and consumers of public services in areas such as defense, transportation, education, housing, and health. As we noted before, neither libertarian democratic theory nor constitutional and legal provisions can reveal much about the functioning of these modern systems. The new democratic Leviathan, according to Dahl, is based on a consensus of professional leaders in highly organized elites who constitute a small part of the citizen body, as well as on compromises ironed out by a process of technical bargains.[12]

The very basis of justifying some measure of administrative discretion has been eroded when preliminary consultations are carried out within inner circles that include selected outsiders. Government cannot claim executive privilege for information which it is willing to disclose to co-opted or self-appointed guardians of particular interests. If this system worked perfectly, each legitimate interest would have found its place within the overlapping networks. But the very basis of these communications is the *selectivity* of organizations, groups, and members of the mass media. The ability to exclude establishes these networks as formidable gate keepers armed with the political power which goes with it.

In pluralistic terms, lobbying entails an everpresent conflict between adversary and cooperative relationships with governments. But there are some groups which have "made it" and became established. A group becomes established when the option of open conflict has been replaced by some form of mutual accommodation with government decision makers. The first commandment of the lobby, wrote S. Finer, is: "get advance intelligence."[13] The established groups can afford to be concerned with the second commandment of lobbying: direct influence. Exclusiveness (and the secrecy which makes it possible) is the chief concern of the established lobby.

The less-established lobby operates in an environment where there are still no dominating arrangements with government, no prescribed channels of communications, and no fixed commitments on either side. In some cases the groups will offer information, money, prestige, or votes in exchange for information (and influence), secretly provided. In other cases, a cooperative relationship is rejected and access is attempted through pressure tactics and public campaigns.

However, there are also organizations, groups, and individuals which are out of the information exchange marketplace altogether. They cannot or do not want to have discrete relationships with government. The reasons for a group's position at this end of the lobbying continuum vary. Some groups such as Bertrand Russell's anti-nuclear society (SANE) simply refuse to "discuss" their position with government because of their uncompromising demands.[14] Others, such as environment groups in the United States up to the mid-1960s, could not even start influencing policy making because they did not possess anything important to offer in exchange for government information.

The boundaries between these clusters are blurred and the shape of these networks changes frequently. Moreover, one can hardly separate the process of *obtaining* information from the process of *using* it for political and administrative leverage. Nevertheless, some practical insights can be gained by focusing on the dynamics of secrecy within the "performance domain" of government-lobby relationships.

The Established Lobby

Within the established lobby there are certain groups which have opted for a formal role in government decision making and have become in fact part of the administrative machinery. The Ministry of Agriculture in Britain is controlled by the farmers mainly through their National Farmers Union. The same can be said of the Labor and Commerce Departments and the Veterans Administration in the U.S. In these cases, interest groups share not only information, but also responsibility for government policies and secrecy procedures. They are ready to trade independence for direct influence and are willing to forego the option of exerting public pressure for greater control of their special interests. They sometimes find it extremely difficult to switch back to conventional lobbying and pressure campaigns because of their public image as an accessory of government. [15]

In Britain, there seems to be more tolerance of political lobbying and of MPs representing special interests in Parliament. [16] At the same time, a certain aura of conspiracy surrounds the functioning of the lobby within the administrative machinery. The exchange relationships in Britain are more institutionalized and those groups which have made it can be regarded almost as H. M. Loyal Lobby. But the essence of these exchanges are quite similar to those in the United States and equally secretive. There are "continual day-to-day contacts between public bureaucrats in government departments and private bureaucrats in the offices of the great pressure groups." [17] In Britain this is quite surprising in view of the draconian prohibitions of the Official Secret Act on passing official information to outsiders.

Closely aligned with the established lobby is the machinery of advisory bodies. These organizations are formally outside of government, but for all practical purposes serve as a meeting ground for government and special interests. "What the government basically wants from advisory committees," observed Seidman, "is not 'expert' advice, although occasionally this is a factor, but support." [18] In the same vein, what the constituencies want from advisory bodies is access to rule-making information and direct influence. A special study prepared for a House subcommittee conducting hearings on access to public information lists 1,940 advisory committees, panels, boards, councils, and commissions within the federal Executive Branch alone.[19] They include presidential advisory committees such as the National Aeronautics and Space Council, and the President's Commission on School Finance; as well as departmental committees such as the prestigious Defense Department Science Board, the powerful Business Advisory Board to the Commerce Department, and the State Department Committee on Art in Embassies. A British study reports the same phenomenon in scope and substance.[20]

This expansion of the administrative machinery represents an institutionalization of the symbiotic relationship between groups and government whereby exchange relationships become legal, fluid channels of communications become prescribed, and confrontations are removed from the public arena into closed chambers. The American Study found out that many meetings held by advisory committees were not announced, only 51 per cent of them were open to the public, 68 per cent of the committees failed to transcribe their proceedings, and not all committees which had transcripts made them available to the public.[21]

Modern democracies are also characterized by a great number of professional mediators who interact between the citizen and the government. They are the middlemen who have become familiar faces in the corridors of power. They sell accessibility to public officials to those who can afford the costs involved.

In developing countries these exchanges are well documented.[22] Government officials are accessible and provide information if they are approached by recognized arbitrators. This is done as a favor, especially if nepotism exists, or on a give-and-take basis. If corruption prevails, the fee paid by the interested party is shared by the officials and the middleman. The same phenomena, only on a much more sophisticated level, can be observed also in developed countries. There are fewer studies of the role of middlemen in the U.S. and British governments. The private detective who exchanges information with the police officer, or the scientist discussing research funds with the head of the grant institution in a private club appear mainly in fiction and popular movies, perhaps because they know how to conceal their secrets.

Some professional middlemen tend to become generalists and establish themselves as Whitehall or White House liaisons and deal only with matters of high importance, while others utilize the whole array of their contacts as former government employees. Middlemen may also restrict their services to functional areas, such as health, education, energy, and even poverty.

The best preparation for this kind of career is apparently legal training. It has been estimated that the majority of professional lobbyists in the U.S.A. are lawyers.[23] Watergate has revealed the extent of their involvement as secret emissaries between government and outside groups. When it became necessary, another group of lawyers stepped forward to do the cleaning up. In addition to lawyers, we can find a host of other middlemen with professional training in public relations and marketing; finance, accounting, banking, and taxation; journalism and communications; labor relations and other forms of arbitration.

Independent intermediaries, willing to sell their services to whoever requires it, are less common in Britain. It goes against the highly structured nature of contacts between public administrators and pressure groups and the disciplinary restraint imposed by political parties and ideologies. The British liaison experts have to work within the established networks in which government departments, political parties, and pressure groups operate.[24] Their success is measured by their ability to ring up their "opposite numbers" in Whitehall and exchange information on a first name basis.[25] Government officials tend to respond favorably to this development because it facilitates their dealing with the public and confines communication to a few knowledgeable people. Instead of an anonymous and annoying citizen, they deal with a reliable expert in the same way they deal with other interest groups. This arrangement also creates ample opportunities for information exchanges and the manipulation of outsiders. Favorable reaction by public officials is by no means universal. In some cases the middlemen are felt to be too strong, while in others the department cherishes its direct contact with the public. The department may then decide to employ its own spokesmen who serve as information brokers for middlemen and for the public.

We cannot conclude this section on the established lobby without noting the direct and unheralded access that certain interests have to the centers of power. John A. McCone, the former head of the CIA and now a director of the ITT Corporation, did not need formal representation in either government departments or advisory groups, or for that matter the services of middlemen, to gain access to information pertaining to his corporation's interests.[26] Needless to say, being discrete is the absolute rule of such direct access.

This function is performed in many Western democracies by political parties when political affiliations are the most important channels for administrators, legislators, interest groups, and influential individuals. In Britain, the Cabinet system makes room for strong influence by the parties on the executive, but there is some evidence that the role of parties as information channels is declining. Even MPs may get better access to government in their capacity as members of pressure groups.[27] Furthermore, interest groups prefer to direct their lobbying efforts to government and not to Parliament.[28]

In the United States, the institutionalized role of political parties is overshadowed by their function as a clearinghouse for campaign contributions. Between elections the established lobby, notably private business and multinational corporations, can bypass the parties and enjoy direct contacts with the centers of power. Their lobbying activities are not covered by the Legislative Reorganization Act of 1946. Organizations such as General Motors, Ford, the American Banking Association, and the National Rifle Association are not registered as lobbying associations in Washington.[29] The fact that there are fewer studies of their "liaison offices" in Washington is quite indicative of their more secretive deliberations with the government.

The Less-Established Lobby

In this cluster we find groups and organizations faced with the conflict between symbiotic and independent relationships with government. "Pure" lobbying needs a free democratic process where interests can obtain information and exert influence openly and in accordance with their moral, social, and political merits. It is this role of outside groups in a pluralistic society which so impressed de Tocqueville: "intermediary bodies stand between the isolated individual and the tyrannical potential of the majority or the state."[30]

But the political price of independence may be intolerably high. Some groups are not "established" simply because they have not been recognized as responsible or respectable enough to share government confidence. They may encounter great difficulties in merely finding out what is going on. The various small groups supporting some form of national health insurance in the U.S.A. are a good example of this case.[31] Government may be willing to share relevant information if a group agrees to join the inner circle and the group may be willing to do so. The trouble with this perfectly normal political process is that at a certain point the balance may tip overwhelmingly in the direction of the executive and its satellites. At this point, more information (and influence) will be denied to outsiders and higher prices will have to be paid in order to become established. Another example is the process whereby scientific and research groups gain exclusive access to governmental information sources (and their financial resources). Thus, a majority of the consultants to the National Institutes of Health were also members of organizations which received most of NIH grants.[32] The transcripts and minutes of these bodies were regularly withheld from the public.[33] We should note in passing that government dominance is not necessarily the outcome of symbiotic relations. Collaboration between the executive and interest groups may turn into colonization of the former by the latter.

Occasionally, an established pressure group is forced to engage in an open debate enabling the public to catch a glimpse of the hidden part of the lobbying iceberg. In 1969 Robert H. Finch, the Secretary of Health, Education and Welfare, wanted to nominate Dr. John H. Knowles as Assistant Secretary. Knowles was known for his support of federal involvement in health insurance—a position which was strongly opposed by the American Medical Association (AMA).[34] The Secretary's choice was known for five months and was apparently made with the President's approval. Then, in four days the final stage of the confrontation surfaced in what was described as "one of the most outstanding displays of the behind-the-scenes wrangling."[35]

On June 27 Secretary Finch announced the withdrawal of Knowles' candidacy. On June 28 the President's press secretary announced the nomination of Dr. Roger O. Egeberg for the post. The reports attributed the sudden change to the AMA's pressure, promises made by the President during the election campaign, and White House attempts to get conservative votes for the pending proposal to extend the income tax surcharge. Some interesting questions remain unanswered in the published reports on the episode: Why could not the AMA exert its influence behind the scenes and avoid the initial attempt to nominate Knowles? What really happened in the four days when the decision was changed?

The real stuff of government-groups interaction is usually not exposed. The prevailing rule of confidentiality is observed as long as it serves both sides. As noted by Rourke: "...secrecy is not exclusively advantageous to bureaucratic organizations themselves. It serves the interests of a wide variety of groups outside the government, and its continuation is in no small measure sustained in their support."[36]

The mass media also belong to this cluster through their role as brokers of information between the government and the attentive publics. The mass media and every individual newsman face the dilemma of cooperative versus adversary relationship with the executive. To the degree that the first is chosen, we find more informed newsmen and more confidential information passed on to them "off the record," or as "backgrounders." If the adversary relationship predominates, the mass media encounter greater difficulties in securing access and tend to use publicity as their main pressure device. The phenomenon is well-known and has recently received some documentation.[37]

The mass media profit professionally and economically from access to public officials. They can use information to sell advertisements and to make a profit. They also have a vested interest in secrecy because it raises the value of published information. Secrecy is sometimes the process whereby trivial information becomes valuable news. The same piece of concealed information which serves as a source of bureaucratic power can serve as a source of media power when published as inside information, leaks, and scoops. Media can become fully "established" if fully controlled by government. By contrast, a free press retains the ability to use the weapon of publicity to prevent government domination. The Nixon Administration was not known for its close friendship with the media, but one remarkable aspect of the discussion revealed in the White House transcripts is the repetitive reference to "cultivation of the press." Mutual cultivation is a good description of the two-sided relationships between the media and public officials. Mass media organizations, like other pressure groups, can exchange independence for private knowledge as well as publicity for the prestige and other benefits that go with belonging to the inner circle. Another danger, not entirely unimaginable in a modern society, is the formation of an interest amalgamation, with the media as part of it. In such cases reporting concentrates on "purely" governmental affairs (usually foreign relations), or on crime and sex, thus providing little information on the real happenings of governmental activities through and with other interest groups.

In the same way, the mass media's crusade on behalf of the people's right to know can take place in either type of relationship with government. As an outsider, the mass media crusade may aim at establishing an alternative route for opening up the mouths and files of government officials. As an insider, it may only pay lip service to professional values.

The media's position is also influenced by the general political and administrative culture in a country. For instance, newsmen covering Whitehall are usually deprived of the excitement that their colleagues in Washington enjoy—being used as tools in fights between officials and departments of the same government. Moreover, "the automatic instinct of the British citizen is to identify not with the Press, but rather with the victims of its curiosity—be they public figures or (much more understandably) private individuals."[38] In contrast, the mass media in the United States have revealed both the negative and the positive potentiality of the cooperative-advisory nexus.[39] On the one hand, established relationships may turn the media into an instrument of propaganda.[40] It makes little difference, in this respect, whether the propaganda originates in the government, other pressure groups, or the mass media themselves. Dependence is disguised and very little is known about the mass media's policies and campaign decisions.[41] On the other hand, the position of the mass media as a powerful mediator between government and the public enables the mass media to become extremely useful watchdogs of democratic processes in general and of administrators' behavior in particular.

The Non-Established Lobby

This cluster includes groups and individuals which are not engaged in exchange relationships with the guardians of public information. A distinction should be made between those that are too ignorant to know the exchange game or too weak to play it, and those who decided to use publicity instead of secret cooperation.

The first category includes groups and individual citizens whose interests are not organized, whose awareness of political and administrative procedures is uncertain, and whose demands for information are inexact. They are the new "politically illiterate" masses whom the right to know is supposed to protect.[42] In a different context these groups have been identified by Edelman as those who are more interested in the symbolic values of politics and administration.[43] Deprived of access to operational information and the tangible benefits that come with it, their quiescence is secured by the appearance and images of democratic processes. Thus, dramatic moves such as the enactment of a new freedom of information act substitute real change with symbolic reassurances. By adjusting to symbolic values these groups become defenders of a system which favors the more organized groups.[44]

Studies of public opinion, mass communications, and participation have refuted time and again the notion that citizens in democracies are capable of indicating "where the shoe pinches." It takes access, advance intelligence, and familiarity with bureaucratic networks to turn citizen complaints into public policy.

These requirements raise the question about the effectiveness of the other type of groups in this cluster—promotional groups, civic associations and public interest groups. By definition these groups have no definite clientele. They try to articulate the public interest by promoting policies that are not of exclusive benefits to their members only. They also try to make governments more open by using the whip of publicity. Citizens can write letters to newspapers, send complaints to their representatives, or use formal procedures such as the ombudsman or the courts. Sometimes the mere threat of publicity is enough to start a cycle of disclosure. In many cases, however, government is immune to these pressures, based as they are on partial information that can be easily ignored.

What the British call "cause groups" is not a new phenomenon. The National Council for Civil Liberties was established in the 1930s to articulate demands of the disadvantaged or aggrieved.[45] A 1962 study by the Fabian Society lists several of these groups and reports that 58 per cent of their members responding to a questionnaire did not really understand what was going on in their organization.[46] The British groups are more promotional in nature and less involved in direct confrontations with government. A British Ralph Nader will probably not go as far as advocating that civil servants should "blow the whistle" and reveal government secrets whenever they think it is morally right to do so.[47]

In the United States the emergence of the "citizens lobby" is aimed at counter balancing the dominant influence of the established private interest groups. The purpose of Public Citizen Inc., an organization established by Ralph Nader, is to help citizens acquire know-how to protect themselves against private industry and government bureaucracies.[48] The targets of Common Cause's activities are "politicians who ignore the people, unresponsive bureaucracies, and behind-the-scenes betrayals of the public interest."[49] The following two are among the lines of citizen's actions that are suggested:[50]

—enact laws prohibiting secret meeting of all public bodies and enabling public access to legislatures, committees, advisory boards, commissions, etc.
—enact lobbying disclosure laws requiring registration of any lobbyist and middleman who communicates with legislators or public officials with the purpose of influencing their actions.

As noted..., the practical impact of legal remedies is circumstantial. New laws such as those listed above can be circumvented as easily as the old ones. They may also have their strongest impact on the symbolic rather than the pragmatic level. But in addition to using legal remedies, groups like Common Cause try to exert direct pressure on government operations. They are also engaged in specific projects aimed at spreading information that a problem exists. The main difference between these efforts and traditional lobbying is the attempt to conduct them publicly. It is a serious effort to change the mode of government interaction with groups and it therefore goes to the heart of the matter. An organization that can effectively use the publicity weapon to call attention to latent interests of various neglected groups is operating in the political and administrative marketplace. The initial success of the environmental coalition that supported the discontinuance of federal funding for the supersonic transport (SST) in 1971 indicates the possibilites in this area. More important perhaps is the fact that this coalition defeated an intensive campaign by SST supporters led by the AFL-CIO, the Aerospace Industries Association, the United Steel Workers of America, and the Air Line Pilots Association.[51] So far most of the efforts of public interest groups have been aimed at reforming the law and changing the behavior of legislators. Changing the secretive mode of operations of the executive and the established lobbyists might prove to be much more difficult.

Summary: The Unwritten Rules of Government Secrecy

In our presentation we have examined the postulates that a citizen should be able to exercise his right to know because: (a) it is a principle of democracy; and/or (b) it is a constitutional or legal right; and/or (c) it is functional. Let us now place these assumptions in the context of a hypothetical, but practical encounter.

Imagine the reaction of a public official (say, a police officer in the example presented at the beginning of this article) when approached by a citizen who demands to know what is going on in his department and cites the right to know as a justification for this request. What is the startled official most likely to do? We may assume that he would not use the occasion to lecture the citizen about situational secrecy; about the right of the public to exercise control through publicity not being an absolute right; or about the need for discreet and confidential deliberation. More likely, the official would choose one or more of the following options.

Being practical, he will try to find out why, and what specific information is requested ("Who sent you? What is bothering you? Are you a journalist?"). For him the general democratic stipulation about the right to know has to be translated into pragmatic "need to know" reasons. Hence the first unwritten rule of government secrecy reads:

Information requests will be denied on the threshold unless accompanied by specific need to know justifications.

Being cautious or uninterested, the official may refuse to answer, quoting the civil service code, or other regulations and laws. He will then probably refer the concerned citizen to an official spokesman, the Information Bureau, or the Complaint Department ("they handle public relations, besides, I am too busy"). In this case, the citizen's legal right (if any) can be easily countered with government legal provisions for withholding information, or with practical arrangements providing free access. The second unwritten rule thus reads:

Legal provisions and regulations aimed at preventing disclosure of official information are used whenever an exchange process does not take place.

Being interested, the official may try to find out what he, his group, or his organization can get in exchange for divulging information. ("I will tell you if you promise to keep it secret and support us when the news breaks out; I will tell you, but off the record," etc.) Thus, the encounter turns into a barter and the citizen, although he is an outsider according to the official definition of "authorized personnel," may gain access by virtue of his ability to reciprocate. Excluding the illegal cases in which official information is traded for money and other tangible goods, the exchanges we are referring to are functional and are aimed at facilitating the governing process. The third unwritten rule reads:

Regardless of the legal provisions, official information is divulged to selected confidants in return for some equivalent and on the basis of mutual interests.

Finally, the reference to official channels for disseminating information to the public reflects the fact that a great deal of information about government activities gets published. But this is not necessarily a result of democratic principles or constitutional and legal provisions aimed at securing freedom of information. Government can supply public information *independently* of demand, for purposes of educating the people, public relations, propaganda, or brainwashing. At the same time, the effectiveness of citizens' demands is usually a function of their ability to mobilize attractive political resources and exchange them for otherwise undisclosed information. This tends to discriminate against those citizens whose interests are diffused, more intangible, and less organized.

Hence, attacks on government secrecy as an isolated phenomenon miss the point and will result in marginal changes only. The broader context of secrecy is the political and administrative culture of the governing process.[52] As the laws we have described operate, there is a high probability that the aggregation of information which circulates as a result of demand and supply will not add up to the desirable equilibrium between secrecy and publicity in democracies.

Notes

[1]*The Times,* August 9, 1972, pp. 1, 2.

[2]For a discussion of government secrecy in democratic countries see Itzhak Galnoor (ed.), *Government Secrecy: An International Perspective* (New York: Harper & Row, 1975).

[3]Woodrow Wilson, "The Study of Administration," *Political Science Quarterly,* Vol. 56, No. 2 (June 1887), pp. 481–506. See also discussion in Arthur M. Schlesinger, Jr., *The Imperial Presidency* (Boston: Houghton Mifflin Co., 1973), p. 336.

[4]Carl Friedrich, *The Pathology of Politics* (New York: Harper & Row, 1972), p. 232.

[5]For a full review of legal provisions in Britain, Canada, and the United States, see Thomas M. Franck and Edward Weisband (eds.), *Secrecy and Foreign Policy* (New York: Oxford University Press, 1974).

[6]Harold C. Relyea, "Opening Government to Public Scrutiny: A Decade of Federal Efforts," *Public Administration Review,* 35(1):3–9, January/February 1975.

[7]Charles E. Merriam, *Political Power* (Glencoe: The Free Press, 1950), p. 13.

[8]For a discussion of information as a political resource, see Warren F. Hehman and Norman T. Uphoff, *The Political Economy of Change* (Berkeley: University of California Press, 1971), p. 67.

[9]See Andrew Shonfeld, *Modern Capitalism* (London: Oxford University Press, 1965); Edwin M. Epstein, *The Corporation in American Politics* (Englewood Cliffs, N.J.: Prentice-Hall, 1969), pp. 67–86.

[10]Attempts to really do something secretly in government require extraordinary precaution. In the July 1963 negotiations with the Soviet Union over a nuclear test ban treaty, a special cable system had to be installed in order to keep it secret within the State Department secrecy apparatus. See David Wise, *The Politics of Lying* (New York: Random House, 1973), p. 77.

[11]Graeme C. Moddie and Gerald Studdert-Kennedy, *Opinions, Publics and Pressure Groups* (London: Allen & Unwin, 1970), pp. 95–96; Lester W. Milbrath, *Washington Lobbyist* (Chicago: Rand McNally), 1963.

[12]Robert A. Dahl (ed.), *Political Oppositions in Western Democracies* (New Haven: Yale University Press, 1966), pp. 399–400.

[13]S. E. Finer, *Anonymous Empire* (London: Pall Mall Press, 2nd edition, 1966), p. 56.

[14]For an account of this group encounter with the British Official Secrets Act, see David Williams, *Not in the Public Interest: The Problem of Security in Democracy* (London: Hutchinson, 1965), p. 78.

[15]David Truman, *The Governmental Process* (New York: Alfred A. Knopf, 1964), p. 461.

[16]Samuel H. Beer, "Pressure Groups and Parties in Britain," *The American Political Science Review,* Vol. 40, No. 1 (March 1956), p. 5.

[17]*Ibid.,* p. 7.

[18]Harold Seidman, *Politics, Position and Power* (New York: Oxford University Press, 1970), p. 239.

[19]House Committee on Government Operations, *Public Access to Information From Executive Branch Advisory Groups,* 92nd Congress, 2nd Session (Washington, D.C.: U.S. Government Printing Office, Part 9, June 6, 8 and 19, 1972), p. 3424.

[20]PEP, *Advisory Committees in British Government* (London: Allen & Unwin, 1961).

[21]House Committee on Government Operations, *Public Access to Information, op. cit.,* p. 3424.

[22]See, for instance, Lucian W. Pye, "Administrators, Agitators and Brokers," *Public Opinion Quarterly,* Vol. 22 (Fall 1958).

[23]*The Washington Lobby* (Washington D.C.: Congressional Quarterly Inc., 1971), p. 3.

[24]Committee on Intermediaries, *Report* (London: HMSO, Cmnd. 7904, March 1950), para. 6.

[25]Beer, *op. cit.*, p. 8.

[26]See his testimony before a special subcommittee of the Senate Foreign Relations Committee as reported in *The New York Times,* March 21-22, 1973.

[27]See R. T. McKenzie, "Parties, Pressure Groups & British Political Process," *Political Quarterly,* Vol. XXIX (1958); and S. H. Beer, *Modern British Politics* (London: Faber, 1965).

[28]Anthony Barker and Michael Rush, *The Member of Parliament and His Information* (London: Allen & Unwin, 1970), pp. 119-121.

[29]Lawrence Gilson, *Money and Secrecy* (New York: Praeger Publications, 1972), p. 9.

[30]Alexis de Tocqueville, *Democracy in America* (New York: Alfred A. Knopf, 1945), p. 191.

[31]For a recent survey, see Alice M. Rivlin, "Agreed: Here Comes National Health Insurance," *The New York Times Magazine,* July 21, 1974.

[32]House Committee on Government Operations, *The Administration of Research Grants in the Public Health Service,* House Report No. 800, 90th Congress, 1st Session (Washington, D.C.: U.S. Government Printing Office, 1967), pp. 61-62.

[33]Gilson, *op. cit.*, p. 24.

[34]All the accounts are from *The New York Times,* June 27-29, 1969, and CBS Evening News, June 28, 1969.

[35]*The New York Times,* Editorial, June 28, 1969.

[36]Francis E. Rourke, "Bureaucratic Secrecy and Its Constituents," *The Bureaucrat,* Vol. 1, No. 2 (Summer 1972), p. 119.

[37]See for instance, Ben H. Bagdikian, *The Effete Conspiracy and Other Crimes by the Press* (New York: Harper & Row, 1972).

[38]Anthony Howard, "Behind the Bureaucratic Curtain," *The New York Times Magazine,* October 23, 1966, p. 94.

[39]Edward A. Shils, *The Torment of Secrecy* (Glencoe, Ill.: The Free Press, 1956), p. 52.

[40]See Carl Friedrich, *op. cit.,* pp. 196, 206-207.

[41]Wilbur L. River and Wilbur Schram, *Responsibility in Mass Communication* (New York: Harper & Row, revised ed., 1969), p. 54. See also Jerome A. Baron, "Access to the Press—A New First Amendment Right," *Harvard Law Review,* Vol. LXXX (June 1967), pp. 1644-1678.

[42]Stein Rokkan, *Citizens, Elections, Parties* (New York: McKay, 1970), pp. 31-32.

[43]Murray Edelman, *The Symbolic Uses of Politics* (Urbana: University of Illinois Press, 1964), pp. 35-36.

[44]*Ibid.,* p. 40

[45]See Robert Benewick, "British Pressure Group Politics: The National Council for Civil Liberties," *The Annals of the American Academy of Political and Social Sciences,* Vol. 413 (May 1974), pp. 145-157.

[46]Peggy Crane, *Participation in Democracy* (London: The Fabian Society, December 1962), p. 5.

[47]Ralph Nader, *et al.* (eds.), *Whistle Blowing* (New York: Bantam, 1972).

[48]For instance, Donald K. Ross, *A Public Citizen's Action Manual* (New York: Grossman Publishers, 1973).

[49]John W. Gardner, "Introduction," in Gilson, *op. cit.,* p. XIII.

[50]*Ibid., passim.*

[51]For a full report see *The Washington Lobby, op. cit.,* pp. 108–112.

[52]See Rourke's careful treatment of this subject: "In arriving at such a point of equilibrium in the field of government information practices, it is important to consider not only the claims that need to be weighed in the balance . . . but also the degree to which each of these conflicting interests is effectively represented in the process of pressure and counterpressure through which public policy in a democracy is so largely hammered out." In: *Secrecy and Publicity* (Baltimore: Johns Hopkins Press, 1961), pp. 15–16.

Additional Readings

Commission on Federal Paperwork. *Confidentiality and Privacy*. Washington, D.C., U.S. Government Printing Office, 1977.

_____. *Service Management*. Washington, D.C., U.S. Government Printing Office, 1977.

Galnoor, Itzhak, ed. *Government Secrecy in Democracies*. New York, Harper and Row, 1977.

Henderson, Hazel. "Information and the New Movements for Citizen Participation." *The Annals of the American Academy of Political and Social Science, 412*:34–43, March 1974.

Homet, Roland S., Jr. *Politics, Cultures and Communications*. New York, Praeger, 1979.

Kraus, Sidney, and Davis, Dennis. *The Effects of Mass Communications on Political Behavior*. University Park, Pennsylvannia State University Press, 1976.

Marchand, Donald A. "Privacy, Confidentiality and Computers: National and International Implications of U.S. Information Policy." *Telecommunications Policy, 3*:237–259, September 1979.

_____. *The Politics of Privacy, Computers, and Criminal Justice Records: Controlling the Social Costs of Technological Change*. Arlington, Va., Information Resources Press, 1980.

Mowshowitz, Abbe. *The Conquest of Will: Information Processing in Human Affairs*. Reading, Mass., Addison-Wesley, 1976.

Nora, Simon, and Minc, Alain. *The Computerization of Society*. Cambridge, MIT Press, 1980.

O'Brien, David. *Privacy, Law and Public Policy*. New York, Praeger, 1979.

Privacy Protection Study Commission. *Personal Privacy in an Information Society*. Washington, D.C., U.S. Government Printing Office, 1977.

_____. *Technology and Privacy*. Washington, D.C., U.S. Government Printing Office, 1977.

Smith, Robert Ellis. *Privacy*. Garden City, N.Y., Anchor Press, 1979.

U.S. Department of Health, Education and Welfare, Secretary's Advisory Committee on Automated Personal Data Systems. *Records, Computers and the Rights of Citizens*. Washington, D.C., U.S. Government Printing Office, 1973.

Westin, Alan F., and Baker, Michael A. *Databanks in a Free Society*. New York, Quadrangle Books, 1972.

Winner, Langdon. *Autonomous Technology*. Cambridge, MIT Press, 1977.

Chapter 8

INFORMATION AND KNOWLEDGE MANAGEMENT

In the face of increasing uncertainty born of organized social complexity, planning and policy formulation set the stage quite as much for learning as for action.
—Todd R. La Porte, *Complexity and Uncertainty: Challenge to Action*

In other parts of this book, the editors have observed that the ultimate role of information management is to increase the value of information for decision making and analysis. Knowledge (the ability to have insight into and assess current problems, puzzlements, and conjectures) is based on one's capacity to search for, acquire, process, and disseminate information. A close and direct relationship exists between information management (the ability to manage information and supporting technologies to increase the value and use of this resource) and knowledge management (the ability to search for, have insight into, analyze, and synthesize questions, problems, and alternatives in different ways to resolve, if not solve, significant needs, concerns, and interests). Information management is necessary for the generation and use of knowledge, whereas knowledge management involves both the individual acts of analysis and synthesis and the collective act of creating the conditions in organizations and government for analysis and synthesis to take place. Thus, in theoretical and practical discussions, finding a convergence of information management and knowledge management is not surprising.

The selections in this chapter explore the reasons for and the implications of this convergence. Interesting questions are raised about the role and impact of information and knowledge management on the role and functions of public administrators in organizations whose uniqueness derives from the combination of knowledge, power, and technology in the pursuit of specialized tasks.

In the first selection, "Complexity and Uncertainty: Challenge to

Action," Todd R. La Porte highlights the role of "organized social complexity" in enhancing individual and collective uncertainty about both the means and ends of actions. Such uncertainty leads to error proneness in choice and action; that is, as social complexity and interdependence increase, so does the probability that any choice made or action undertaken will have both positive and negative unanticipated consequences. Thus, developing policy increasingly assumes the character of error detection and avoidance rather than the advocacy of "possibilities." La Porte suggests that public organizations must be structured to detect errors and not suppress them. Centralized, hierarchical organizations are inadequate for this purpose. Decentralized and collegial organizations may be more appropriate, along with a basic change in attitude to foster open recognition of errors rather than their suppression.

In the second selection, "Managing Knowledge as a Corporate Resource," James F. Berry and Craig M. Cook move inside the organization and discuss the role of knowledge in producing public goods and services. Berry and Cook view knowledge as a vital resource whose role must be understood before it can be effectively managed. In addition to developing a "taxonomy" of knowledge in the organization, Berry and Cook emphasize that appropriate use of computers and information technologies depends on the organization members' conception of the role and value of knowledge.

In contrast to the previous analysis, Amitai Etzioni examines the relationship between knowledge and power. Although political elites emphasize building "consensus" to maximize their ends and values, Etzioni suggests that the real need is for fundamental criticism that reaches the basic values, structures, and processes of a society. Rather than playing only a negative role in society, criticism can be constructive. To play this positive role, however, the "critics" must be protected from immediate social pressures to conform. Thus, Etzioni suggests that "unattached intellectuals" can engage in such criticism. For him, knowledge and power are in an uneasy tension and must remain so. Social decision making must be based on fundamental criticism and reality testing if it is to be truly responsive to social needs and demands and not just a reflection of elite consensus-building efforts.

In the final selection, "Bureaucracy, Technology, and Knowledge

Management," Nicholas Henry poses the ultimate political challenge for knowledge management and public administration. He suggests that technology and bureaucracy have undermined the basic assumptions of pluralism. This fact poses a basic constitutional question: How does one integrate technology and bureaucracy into the framework of democratic government and society? The solution rests with knowledge management. For Henry, public administration is a unique field. The key to its uniqueness "lies in its conception of the role knowledge plays in the bureaucratic policy-making process in technological societies." The significance of this role lies in two directions: the development of public policies for knowledge management and the proper reorientation of education for public administrators. Henry argues that future public administrators must be oriented to synthesis in their thinking and not to specialization. "Bit orientations" to policy development must be discouraged, since the proper role for public administration in our government and society involves a holistic approach to knowledge management and public policy.

Complexity and Uncertainty: Challenge to Action*

Todd R. La Porte

The Politics of Uncertainty and Psychic Reassurance

Increasingly complex social organization poses a difficult situation for legislators, executives, and political leaders. It seems clear that there is a growing uneasiness in the public mind about the behavior of our governing institutions. We must still assume that through these institutions we have a great capacity to achieve what we seek; but mounting evidence of failure and unexpected social problems surrounds us. Thus, as relative control seems to decline and adequate foresight dims, the sense of social, economic, and personal uncertainty grows. Days no longer bring with them a bright sense of possibility.

We give the name "politics" to the process of dialogue and action carried on in pursuit of social privilege and personal advantage, equity and opportunity, social order and justice. Contemporary politics is the scrambling process of vying for the access to scarce social and economic resources. In the recent past, a great deal has been made of the notion that we joust over establishing certain orderings of political preference: what I want opposes what you want unless we want the same thing. Popular political rhetoric, often with echoes in political science writing, seems to suggest that if we could, collectively, just agree on what we want we would arrive at a happy state of consensus. Then, after achieving agreement about goals, we could get on with carrying out the means to those collective ends. The implicit assumption is that we have sure confidence in our knowledge of means. But the *means* themselves have also become the object of uncertainty. What, then, is the character of politics in the face of increasing personal and collective uncertainty about *both ends and means?*[1] In such a situation we can expect agreement only that our national experience is far from our liking and beyond our understanding. When the disjuncture between experience and

*Excerpts from Todd R. La Porte (ed.), *Organized Social Complexity: Challenge to Politics and Policy*, (Copyright © 1975 by Princeton University Press, pp. 345–356. Reprinted by permission of Princeton University Press.)

understanding widens, the sense of political and social ambiguity grows. As it reaches high level, thresholds of psychic pain and anxiety are approached arousing in many people vague but disquieting fears. At the same time, attempts are made to reduce incongruities and decrease the confusion between our values and beliefs and our experience. Translated into political modes of action, these attempts take on the character of the *politics of psychic reassurance.*

Attempts to bridge the gulf between experience and understanding can be made in at least two ways. We could attempt to change political and social reality "back" to fit our conceptions of it; that is, work to make the political institutions and popular values consonant with past values and with the cause-effect beliefs we have held about the world. Conversely, we could attempt to alter our values and/or our beliefs about the way things work so that they accord more with what appears to be going on "out there" in society. Advocates of either of these responses can try to achieve their aims through existing institutions or by attempting to establish new ones. Either way, political activity is characterized by arguments, persuasions, and proposed actions that promise to reduce uncertainty. Leaders on the right find a willing ear among the public when they urge upon us policies that "will make things more sensible," and advise us to act or concur in actions that will make the world "more like it ought to be," that is, as they remember it to have been.[2] New leaders on the Left take the other tack. They propose programs which promise the confused that another ideology will allow a view of the world as it *really* is and thus will provide a better basis for action. Many of the young are now attempting to change their consciousness and actions to find a better fit with their sense experience. But many people with a more crystallized perspective resist the costs of such wholesale mind-bending. They seek to turn political and social institutions toward a sensibility to personal experience. Figure 1 roughly partitions these various responses. Insofar as each perspective illustrated in Figure 1 is based essentially on simplicity assuming conceptions about the world, so each is subject to stumbling error and promises of reassurance. Nevertheless, the popular appeal of a Ronald Reagan or a George McGovern, a Guru Maharaji or a Billy Graham bespeaks both the various styles of attempted reassurance and the intensity of the search for it.

Policy Implementation as Error Making: Planning as Learning

As conceptions of the political world become more error prone, policy implementation becomes tantamount to error making. No matter what the policies or action guides established in the management of a large-scale

THE OBJECT OF CHANGE

		Values and Cause/Effect Beliefs	Social Experience
MODES OF RESPONSE	Political	Liberal movements Radical left	Conservative movements Radical right
	Social	Youth culture Communes Mysticism	Traditional social groups Fundamentalist religions

Figure 1 Types of response in the politics of psychic reassurance.

organization, a government, or its economy, they are likely to be more productive of problems than they will be of solutions. Given the limitations on
human foresight and the growing uncertainty about the *adequacy* of political
and social values sought and the means to seek them, policy makers and
planners must take a new perspective.

Much has been written about the policy process—its development and
its analysis. A good deal of this work seems at bottom to be showing how certain types of procedures are destined either to succeed or fail in the formulating of a rational decision or policy depending on how close they come to
effecting an orderly arrangement of information. These analyses, invariably
computer based, seem to be founded mainly on the logic of information arrangement, as if clever structuring of information were adequate for investing data with the *meaning* necessary for clear understanding. But the
substantive notions of organizational dynamics, political development, or
social change, in areas such as elementary education or social welfare, remain largely implicit. Some policy analysis, especially that using computer
models, leaves one with the strong impression that its authors consider the
assiduous application of information technology a sensible substitute for conceptual thought about the social world.[3] It seems to be generated by an unquestioning belief that moving ahead with this or that policy will turn out all
right just as long as it is supported by quantities of data and many social indicators. It is difficult for us to share this faith. Other literature probes policy
development and shows that behind it all lurks the scaly head of politics

subverting the process and bestowing advantage to one group or another under the guise of the "rational thing to do."[4]

Likewise, much has been written about the proper ends of public policy.[5] Everyone has his favorite policy position, assigning top priority to equity in the public service, or to the recovery of a healthy environment, or to peace with honor, economic growth, no growth, and so on. But whatever values become the touchstones of policy, we still must act it out, even as we remain unconvinced and uncertain about the methods of action available to us.

Policy and Planning in a New Mood. In the face of increasing uncertainty born of organized social complexity, planning and policy formulation set the stage quite as much for learning as for action. The underlying conceptions of social reality that informs policy analysts seem often to miss the interdependent character of the social or institutional situations thought to be the source of a particular problem. To the extent that they do, we can expect errors to follow, sometimes of remarkable proportion. Thus, surprises occur frequently in the process of implementing plans and policies, surprises from which a good deal could be learned, if only learning were considered as important as fixing blame. As the probability of policy induced error and failure increases, many of the expectations generally held for public policy lose their semblance of common sense. Public expectation for lasting solutions certainly should not be encouraged. Nor should particular confidence persist in sweeping comprehensive programs promising improvements in a single stroke. When errors are highly likely no matter what planners do to prevent them, the most valuable features of proposed plans and policies are those which work to reduce the relative costs of those errors. And if policy errors become occasions for posing questions, rather than for immediately assigning blame, invaluable learning will take place.

If unanticipated mistakes are going to persist, then actions which have *reversible* consequences should be encouraged over actions which have *irreversible* results. This reasoning suggests that the more irreversible the physical, economic, and social consequences of a particular public policy, the more hesitant we should be in making final commitments to it. Thus policy proposals or plans should be judged in terms of the relative costs of undoing as well as doing what is proposed.[6] A good deal of the intensity characterizing the environmentalists' objection to large, technically based programs, such as Mineral King, the Alaskan pipeline, and the development of oil shale sites, seems to be based on such a recognition. So too does the controversy about the effects of nuclear radiation upon plant and animal life.

While the reversibility criterion is logically sensible, precision in determining degrees of potential irreversibility must await greatly improved conceptualizations and empirical work on the longer term consequences of large-scale programs. And we still are some distance away from having the theoretical or descriptive materials upon which to base reliable estimates.

In such a situation, another quality of policy takes on added importance. In some instances there is evidence that *multiple pathways* to a common policy outcome have been more or less systematically employed. The early day "Model Cities" planning is one such instance. Conceding that the "one best way" will always remain elusive, planners should develop several avenues for achieving the desired outcome. This strategy could be called *functional redundancy*, after the work of Landau. . . . Policies and plans that explicitly establish patterns of activities which include redundancy of function will be much less likely to precipitate harmful long-term consequences unknowingly. Multiple efforts in attacking the same problem area are much more likely to discover a wider range of benefits and to reduce the numbers of surprises than programs which are based on essentially preconceived single-minded solutions. This principle applies as much to economic programs as to social welfare; to technological programs as much as to governmental reorganization.

The criteria of both reversibility and redundancy can be used in evaluating policies which tend either toward the incremental or comprehensive. . . . While it is probable that incremental policies are more often "reversible" than comprehensive ones, this characteristic probably varies considerably within both types. There is no reason to suppose that incremental efforts are in principle more reversible than comprehensive ones. Nor is there reason to suppose that, given advances in concept and in research techniques, there could not be considerable reversibility designed into aspects of synoptic policies. On the other hand, greater systematic attention to functional redundancy in comprehensive policy development is more likely to prove effective than are piecemeal attempts at incremental improvement. But, in this regard, there is no intrinsic reason for these two types of policy perspectives to differ in principle. Various combinations of the three variables are presented in Figure 2 with some illustrations of policy programs which seem to be described by the various cells. We leave it to the reader to supply other examples and/or to refine the implications of this way of perceiving policy formation.

Finally, to the degree that policy formulation and implementation are carried out in the face of increasing uncertainty, a substantial change within policy formulation and action groups is necessary. In the past, we believed

POLICY MAKING STRATEGY

Effect of Policy		Incremental		Comprehensive	
		Reversible	Irreversible	Reversible	Irreversible
CHARACTER OF POLICY REDUNDANCY	Functional	Tax policies	Energy resource depletion	Community mental health planning Environmental protection	New town development Large-scale urban renewal
	Dysfunctional or Absent	Interest rate adjustments	Public works investments		Metropolitan mass transit and land-use planning

Figure 2   Types of policy perspectives and criteria in a new mood.

that we could know enough about social, economic, and political dynamics to "go for" the one best single policy. In effect this meant that it was sensible to expect a policy analyst to find the best way. If many mistakes were made in the process of implementing a policy, or if the policy itself turned out to be a disaster, then clearly the analyst's duplicity or incompetence should be held responsible. Policy failure need not have occurred. It did so only because some individual or some group was corrupted or lacked the competence they should have had. But in a policy world where our conception of the social and economic is much too simplistic, the making of errors is due not only to particular incompetencies or loss of nerve or ethics; rather, error-making is endemic to any policy forming or advising role.

In a growing number of areas, the quality of conceptions does not lend much predictive confidence to policy formulation. Self-interest or ineptitude on part of the analyst is rarely to blame; on the contrary, the best...are bound to err. Thus, in organizational situations where the major mode of dealing with errors is punitive, most of those responsible for making errors attempt to avoid detection. Hence there is very little shared learning about the situation which produced the error or about what might be done to avoid it in the future.[7] To camouflage error in the face of increasing uncertainty is often a successful way of dodging blame. It is almost always a missed opportunity to learn. What attributes define a policy group for which inevitable error becomes an occasion for collective learning? What are the conditions associated with a group in which the reporting on one's personal errors is rewarded and valued by other members?

Probably the most important characteristic of such a group is its general recognition that errors are inevitable and that delay in reporting or acknowledging them will prove very costly to the *collective* operation. Such a recognition is slow in coming as an official organizational norm, for it implies modes of interpersonal relationships which run counter to most of what is informally learned in organization life.[8] It means that groups understand that they must become error exploring rather than error camouflaging, error embracing rather than error punishing.[9] Interpersonal relationships within organizations are seldom characterized by that relative trust and openness required to induce members to reveal that they have made a mistake or have been responsible for a miscalculation. Rather, the predominant mode is "punishment centered"; to acknowledge mistakes is to open oneself to informal ridicule or formal punishment.[10] Generally, only in those organizations based on quite sophisticated technologies, such as some R & D groups, is there sufficiently recognized interdependence to make the acknowledgment of errors and debriefing on them valued activities.

As a complement to error embracing, sustained internal self-criticism is required to discover in advance of policy implementation as many potential surprises as possible. In a sense, this practice is part and parcel of the scientific method as applied to policy work and is already incorporated into many policy groups. Again, the support of such a climate of interaction requires that conceptual gaps or blind spots be acknowledged by the persons who have them. The corollaries to this requirement are that personal conceptual growth should be sought and then rewarded by others in the group and that a corporate spirit of experimentation is necessary in order for individual members to endure the anxieties often associated with revealing personal limitations. But in an organizational and policy world in which the expectation of adequate knowledge is less and less sensible, what sense remains in punishing the conceptual limitations which afflict us all? What ought to be subject to blame or praise is the individual member's propensity to learn from error and to engage in those reciprocal exchanges which enhance participants' capacities mutually to reduce uncertainty.

Organization in Response to Complexity. The making of plans signals action, but without cooperative effort plans remain paper hopes. Complex organizations have in a modern technological age become the crucial requirement for action. Yet as organized social complexity increases so does our uncertainty about how to sustain effective cooperative effort. Surprises issue from group action as well as from personal action. Our confidence in centralized authority declines. Weber's assertion that bureaucratic forms are the most efficient rings hollow in our ears, and reliable alternatives to the once trusted hierarchical structure of large organizations are clearly being sought.

Executive expectations of a fixed and effective organizational structure are the grounding for bureaucratic forms. These expectations assume that the substantive requirements of problem solving in one or another area will remain relatively stable and can be known. Such expectations also assume that directions and goals can be known and that new opportunities and pitfalls are foreseeable. Thus a particular organizational structure is, in essence, a hypothesis about the technical and coordinative requirements of the future. But the burden of our entire argument is that neither problems nor task requirements can be known in advance with very much confidence. The skeins of interdependences matched against the limited conceptions we employ give us little basis for confidently moving into the future. Most situations far outstrip our capacities to identify crucial factors and control them. We cannot expect stability of an organization's environment nor depend upon hierarchical authority structure for effective control. What then are sensible organizational responses? For we must continue to cooperate and act. One of the responses most likely to occur is the devolution and modification of authority structures.

In cases of relatively simple organized complexity, executives can meet the requisites of centralized authority dispensed through "tree-like" hierarchies of command and communication. It has been possible to construct chain-of-command and technical arrangements more or less adequate for the task and character of the environment of certain "simple" organizations. In effect, someone in a position of centralized authority could usually tell when a subordinate made a significant error and probably knew enough himself to direct corrective measures with some confidence. As it becomes more difficult to specify how to *avoid* errors, dependence upon technically skilled subordinates must increase. When it also becomes difficult to *discover* errors, the fundamental conditions which underlie all firmly centralized hierarchical organizational arrangements collapse. Hierarchy runs amok; tasks are not coordinated well, problems are not anticipated correctly, and the necessary modes of information exchanged are not developed.[11]

At least two modifications are in order as hierarchy becomes problematic: One, the *professionalization* of organizations, is obvious to most managers and embraced by them everywhere; the other, organizational *decentralization*, is occurring but is generally resisted by managers.[12] Both professionalization and decentralization lead to a dramatic increase in the "semilatticelike" structure of complex organizations. Together, these two changes suggest that we need to alter significantly our expectations for authority styles and our notions of efficient operations and organizational design.

As management's knowledge limitations become more obvious, "professionals" are recruited in increasing numbers, clearly in an effort to reduce the uncertainties felt by executives.[13] Competition between and among public and private organizations then becomes as much a technical rivalry as it is a market or political one. Such technical rivalry means that the dominance of managers over technical subordinates declines in proportion to the needs managers feel for specialized information and knowledge. After a point, it seems clear that professional specialists, while resolving technically rooted uncertainty, become themselves a new source of organizational uncertainty. By and large, executives have seized on the benefits of specialists' knowledge, but at the expense of their own autonomy. At the extreme, the top executive becomes very dependent upon the expertise of his own subordinates. Certainly as professionalization pervades more levels of an organization, we would expect significant changes in authority style. The highly directive authoritarian mode has all but disappeared from complex organizations. It is being replaced by a much more consultative one, in some R & D organizations approaching collegiality. When consultation is limited and the situation complex, we could expect great and often unpleasant surprise. The troubles of Nixon's White House seem an apt case in point.

With increasing numbers of professionals necessary for technical effectiveness, extreme centralization is increasingly difficult to maintain. Pressures for decentralization often follow quickly when tasks are delegated to technical groups. Almost always it is argued that those close to the "real work" of the organization know better both what the problems are and the most probable solutions. But as this inevitable decentralization takes place, it does so often at the expense of coordination of various specialties. In effect, it increases differentiation without the necessary increase in perceived interdependence.[14] The issue of technical knowledge versus organizational control is joined, in part, due to deeply held notions of efficiency. Often it is believed that parallel or overlapping activities, i.e., redundancy, are wasteful. It is also tacitly felt that investment in communicating to others about what is going on in a group is at best a necessary inconvenience and possibly dangerous to professional autonomy. Thus, efforts to cut down overlap and generally to avoid "overinforming" others (through paperwork) about activities within a group are believed to be undertaken for the sake of "efficiency." And indeed they are when ultimate goals are clear, the problem well defined, and the solution well established. They are not when simplicity escapes us and neither goals nor means nor consequences are very clear.

These observable trends offer an important lesson for organizational designers. Instead of grudgingly accepting professionalization and decentralization and resisting efforts to achieve close coordination, people in organizations confronted with high levels of organized complexity must develop new patterns of delegation and redundancy. Searching out apt sites for functional redundancy and for situations in which decentralization would benefit everyone in the organization is crucial for maintaining the technical and social capacities provided by cooperation in changing complex environments. It is possible to alter authority and communication patterns so that everyone involved feels an increased control over those things that affect their work.[15] A much more positive and sustained search for organizational arrangements and guidelines that increase both *actual* and *perceived* interdependence is crucial for the future. Were this to occur, relationships within institutions or organizations as well as those among them would begin to take on the qualities of "normative complexity" discussed by Wilson....[16] Technical and executive arrangements that lead from a clear recognition that individual members need each other for mutual exchange and benefit must accompany such a development, for in effect it means that trust among members becomes recognized as functional and necessary and that the winning of relative short-term advantage may result in longer-term hurt.

But entering a period of mutually recognized interdependence can occur only if there are very significant shifts in the tone and character of social exchange within and between organizations. At present mutual dependence is not rewarded; often it becomes a liability to those attempting it. What is rewarded are separate, quite plural, competitive activities within organizations—the very behavior which reduces the likelihood of mutually recognized interdependence.

It seems quite clear that the opportunities as well as the challenges of increasing organized social complexity will stimulate the development of new organizational and political forms. Optimistically, this could be an adventure in discovery and enrichment. It is also possible that our response to uncertainty could result in terrible social violence if we simplify unwisely. In any event meeting both challenge and opportunity will result in unfamiliar patterns of cooperative complex public and private organizations as they try to cope with a more complex future. To cope successfully will require at minimum those policies and new sensibilities which foster an organizational and social ambience of openness to new possibilities. Recruitment and advancement policies and programs of evaluating groups and individuals have to be reviewed and changed, so that any liabilities attached to social interdependence can be avoided. Formal incentives designed to elicit group attitudes that will encourage mutual exchange and trust among members should be instituted. On balance, it is most likely that advances toward the opportunities of social complexity will be made by those people who combine highly competent technical skills with keen sensitivity in interpersonal and group relationships. Our mutual challenge is to live in such a way that the ambience of openness to new possibilities which is crucial for the risky and demanding business before us may be realized. . . .

Notes

[1] For an extension of this discussion related to agreement on organizational means and ends and the resulting decision strategies, see James D. Thompson and Arthur Tuden, "Strategies, Structures and Processes of Organizational Decision" in *Comparative Studies in Administration,* ed. Thompson *et al.* (Pittsburgh: University of Pittsburgh Press, 1959) and J. D. Thompson, *Organizations in Action,* Ch. 8. For an extended example of managerial behavior in conditions of intense uncertainty, see Jay D. Starling, "The Miracle of City Government: Five Loaves and Two Fishes Equals One Fishwich," unpubl. dissertation, University of California, Berkeley (1973).

[2] See Garry Wills, *Nixon Agonistes: The Crisis of the Self-Made Man* (Boston: Houghton-Mifflin, 1970) for an example of this "conservative" mode of political behavior.

[3] See Garry D. Brewer, *Politicians, Bureaucrats, and the Consultant* (New York: Basic Books, 1973) for a deeply probing critique, set within the context of organized complexity, of the use of computer models, and the men who sell them.

[4] . . . see Alan Altshuler, *The City Planning Process: A Political Analysis* (Ithaca: Cornell University Press, 1965) and Aaron Wildavsky, *The Politics of the Budgetary Process* (Boston: Little, Brown, 1964).

[5] See esp. Alan Altshuler, "The Goals of Comprehensive Planning," *Journal of the American Institute of Planners,* 31 (1965), 186–195; Melvin Webber, "Comprehensive Planning and Social Responsibility," *Journal of the American Institute of Planners,* 29 (1963); and C. West Churchman, *The Systems Approach* (New York: Delacorte, 1968).

[6] See the discussion in National Academy of Science, *Technology: Processes of Assessment and Choice* (Washington, D.C.: Government Printing Office, 1969). See also Don K. Price, *The Scientific Estate* (Cambridge: Harvard University Press, 1965), pp. 144–156.

[7] For a discussion of the difficulties of hierarchy in this situation, see Lawrence Spence, "Social Epistemology: An Essay in the Politics of Knowledge," unpubl. dissertation, University of California, Berkeley (1973). See also Harold Wilensky, *Organizational Intelligence: Knowledge and Policy and Government and Industry* (New York: Basic Books, 1967).

[8]For a discussion of the psychological climate surrounding executives, see Chris Argyris, *Integrating the Individual and the Organization* (New York: Wiley, 1967), Ch. 5.

[9]See esp. Donald Michael, *On the Social Psychology of Learning to Plan—And Planning to Learn* (San Francisco: Jossey-Bass, 1974).

[10]See Alvin Gouldner, *Patterns of Industrial Bureaucracy* (Glencoe, Ill.: Free Press, 1954).

[11]See esp. Wilensky, *Organizational Intelligence*; Victor Thompson, *Modern Organizations* (New York: Knopf, 1961); James D. Thompson, *Organizations in Action*; and Theodore Caplow, *Principles of Organization* (New York: Harcourt, Brace, 1964).

[12]For an expanded discussion of this reaction, see Todd R. La Porte, "Organizational Responses to Complexity: Research and Development as Organized Inquiry and Action," Part I. Working Paper no. 141 (January, 1971), Center for Planning and Development Research, Institute of Urban and Regional Development, University of California, Berkeley, Ch. 1.

[13]See, for example, K. S. Lynn, ed., *The Professions in America* (Boston: Houghton Mifflin, 1965); Mark Abrahamson, ed., *The Professional in the Organization* (Chicago: Rand McNally, 1967); Corinne Gilb, *Hidden Hierarchies: The Professions and Government* (New York: Harper & Row, 1966); and W. Kornhauser, *Scientists in Industry: Conflict and Accommodation* (Berkeley: University of California Press, 1962).

[14]See the necessary distinction made in Chapter I [*Organized Social Complexity*. Edited by Todd R. La Porte. Princeton, N.J., Princeton University Press, 1975] of *perceived* interdependence, p. 6.

[15]Arnold Tannenbaum, ed., *Control in Organizations* (New York: McGraw-Hill, 1968).

[16]A comparison of *normative complexity* to *coercive complexity* is drawn in [Chapter IX], along with a discussion of some of the implications associated with perceiving complexity relations in one frame or the other....

Managing Knowledge as a Corporate Resource

James F. Berry and Craig M. Cook

Industrial corporations and private companies produce products (steel, automobiles, or clothing) or provide services (construction, maintenance, or repair). For their efforts these organizations earn profits or incur losses that can be used to measure their effectiveness. Government, on the other hand, produces "public goods" meant to serve society's general needs. Sometimes public goods are tangible (roads or dams). Such engineering feats are generally well defined and their costs and benefits quantifiable. All levels of government, however, also deal with complex social and economic problems. In these cases, the public goods sometimes are vague concepts ("strong" defense, "better" health care, "improved" transportation systems, or the elimination of "poverty"). The cost of producing public goods in these complex and subjective areas is generally well known, but the benefits obtained are hard to quantify. Hence, measuring the effectiveness of government is difficult. In fact, many citizens feel that government is not effective. Kermit Gordon, president of The Brookings Institution and budget director under Kennedy and Johnson, has said that the waning of faith in government is the product of "the government's losing struggle to cope with the crisis of convulsive change in which we live."[6] Harold Seidman, in noting these problems, has said, "If they are to be resolved, [it will] demand radically new approaches."[12] This reading introduces one such new approach: a reexamination of the key components involved in producing most public goods.

Knowledge of relevant facts, of appropriate techniques, and of the goals the organization is attempting to achieve is essential to federal departments and agencies in producing public goods. Without such knowledge, little would be accomplished and few public goods would be produced. Many federal departments or agencies may be called "knowledge agencies" because their primary product or public good is knowledge, be it factual knowledge about particular subject areas (health, food, housing, energy, environment, or transportation), procedural knowledge about how economic, environmental, social, or political factors affect these areas, or judgmental knowledge used to set policy and to determine the allocation of resources that the department controls. The manner in which a department manages and uses its knowledge determines how successful or effective it is in carrying out its mission. A more structured view of knowledge is required, however, before substantial improvements in knowledge use and management may be realized in the Federal Government. This section proposes a philosophy for public administration based on the assumption that knowledge is an important basic resource of the Federal Government's various departments and agencies. Implementation of this philosophy requires a sound theoretical definition of an organization's knowledge, appropriate managerial structures for managing this resource, and effective schemes for knowledge acquisition, use, and preservation. In this section, some definitions of knowledge are introduced and briefly explored, and some implications are given for computerized information system design. These and other issues have been discussed by us in greater detail in earlier works.[1,2,3]

Knowledge in recent years (especially within the Federal Government) has become linked with the use of computers; as a result, knowledge problems and computer problems have become interrelated. These interrelationships presented relatively few difficulties in supporting traditional government activities, such as collecting and disbursing monies. As computer-based systems have spread to areas involving complex social issues, however, the knowledge dimensions of the problems have changed. Conventional computer and information system approaches are inadequate to support the sophisticated knowledge processing required in these more subjective areas. Further, the tendency has been to relegate the design and development of such systems to computer specialists who are trained to understand the technology but not necessarily the mission that the system is intended to support.

This section attempts to develop a vocabulary for and an explanation of the knowledge that a department may use to fulfill its mission. The technological capabilities and shortcomings of current computer systems are then discussed in relation to the kind of knowledge they can process.

In his probing essay, "1984 and Beyond: Social Engineering or Political Values?" Don K. Price[10] identified three dilemmas significant to modern government administrators: "The first is the dilemma posed by the apparent conflict between science and values; the second by the conflict between the generalist and the specialist; and the third between an elite meritocracy and participatory democracy." In terms of the public knowledge maintained by a department (and especially that portion relegated to computer-based systems), these dilemmas are raised in the following questions that public administrators should ask their computerized information systems:

1. Can facts collected on housing, food, transportation, or any other major social problem really be value free? Are values not used in selecting which facts to collect, for example?

2. If the highly technical knowledge held by a department is incomprehensible to those who must use it to make public policy, what is the knowledge worth? What good is collecting data if employees cannot have the information when they need it, or if they do not have all the relevant facts for interpreting the data correctly?

3. Can the knowledge held by a department be developed so that it can be widely shared, or will it be tightly held by a small group of bureaucrats (even within the department itself?)

These questions address significant problems encountered with current information systems in collecting, organizing, interpreting, and sharing data. The work described in this section is an initial step toward categorizing the kinds of knowledge processing that computers, given the current technology, can reasonably be expected to perform well and those functions that had best be left to humans.

Knowledge Classification

To manage knowledge as a resource, a department or agency must understand the kinds of knowledge it uses to fill its roles. Knowledge has many aspects and means different things to different people. We have not developed a theory for all forms of human knowledge; rather, this discussion of knowledge is limited to the areas most relevant to a government department or agency. Two approaches to classifying knowledge have been selected: a functional taxonomy and a domain taxonomy. From the functional viewpoint, knowledge includes what the department knows (i.e., facts), what it knows how to do (i.e., skills), and what it knows about what it should and should not be doing (i.e., wisdom). To discuss these kinds of knowledge and to understand the interplay between them, we have developed a generalized functional taxonomy that can describe the knowledge possessed by any government department or agency or any company or corporation of any size.

Figure 1 shows the authors' functional classification of knowledge into three types: factual, procedural, and judgmental. Factual knowledge is the data about the world that interest a given department. Procedural knowledge concerns the operations used to organize factual knowledge better or to transform it to a more usable form. Judgmental knowledge involves guiding

KNOWLEDGE TYPE:	PERTAINING TO:
FACTUAL KNOWLEDGE	BEING (WHAT)
Data	Perceiving
Metadata	Describing
Relationships	Structuring
Semantics	Interpreting
PROCEDURAL KNOWLEDGE	DOING (HOW)
Algorithmic	Data processing
Heuristic	Problem solving
JUDGMENTAL KNOWLEDGE	DIRECTING (WHY)
Constraints	Evaluating
Goals	Planning

Figure 1 Functional knowledge taxonomy.

principles and value systems that explain why an enterprise does what it does.

Besides classifying knowledge into general types, it is also useful to consider the subject matter (or context) to which the knowledge pertains. The primary advantage of recognizing various contexts is the conceptual separation of subject matter according to the needs and purposes of the individual using the knowledge. Understanding the different types and contexts of knowledge is important in developing computer systems to help manage knowledge. In the past, developers of computerized information systems have often failed to recognize these differences; as a result, the departments have spent much time and money to develop systems that cannot possibly meet the intended users' differing needs.

Functional Taxonomy. FACTUAL KNOWLEDGE. The factual knowledge of a department or agency concerns notations about objects of interest (what they are, what they are made of, what they are part of, etc.). It consists of *data* (representations in some storage medium about the perception of an object), *metadata* (data about other data, e.g., descriptions of data elements), *relationships* (associations or groupings of sets of data that impart some structure to the data), and *semantics* (interpretations of the data, metadata, and relationships as having some meaning for objects in the real world).

Factual knowledge can be processed or used to guide processing but cannot do any processing itself. In that sense, factual knowledge is passive. This observation is not meant to imply, however, that factual knowledge is static. Depending on the enterprise and the nature of its mission, factual knowledge may be dynamic: Data may be entered or deleted, descriptions may change, relationships may be established or destroyed, and interpretations of the meaning of various pieces of factual knowledge may be altered over time.

There are important conceptual differences between conventional data-processing notions (which emphasize only data) and the concepts of factual knowledge that may operate on higher-level knowledge as well. For example, some more advanced systems may allow access to metadata relationships, or semantics, without getting involved in the voluminous number of instances that might occur in a factual data base. Thus, the answer to a query such as, "Do we have any information on food production in Asia?" could be obtained by accessing these higher-level knowledge bases alone without accessing the actual facts in the data bases. If the answer is "No," then no access to the potentially large facts data bases would be required. If the answer is "Yes," then specific factual data bases (say, on rice production in Cambodia during 1975) would need to be accessed to obtain specific facts. (Even so, the higher-level knowledge can be used to preselect only those data bases likely to contain relevant facts on food production in Asia.) Traditional computer techniques (file processing) deal primarily with data, while more modern approaches (data-base management and data dictionaries) address metadata and relationships. Unfortunately, few techniques can adequately handle the semantics of the data being processed (although there are many research activities in this area).

PROCEDURAL KNOWLEDGE. Procedural knowledge concerns the "how" component of a department's aggregate knowledge. It deals with the skills the department employs to use its factual knowledge or to implement its judgmental knowledge. In the taxonomy, two categories of procedural knowledge can be identified: algorithmic and heuristic. Algorithmic procedural knowledge is used whenever problems can be solved by repeatedly applying rules or procedures. Use of this knowledge implies a complete and detailed understanding of the problem and its solution. Algorithmic knowledge can be expressed in a computer program in which a programmer is able to specify explicitly the passing of control from one section of program code to another. Every instruction to the computer must be understood and carefully placed in the proper sequence. In the past, the government has succeeded in computerizing algorithmic knowledge. Unfortunately, not all problems can be solved this way. Analysts also employ heuristics or rules-of-thumb that they have compiled during years of experience in their analytic discipline to solve problems, to determine which algorithms are relevant, or to construct new algorithms as warranted.

Heuristic procedural knowledge is used to solve problems or to react to situations when prespecifying a particular algorithmic solution is not possible. Heuristic knowledge is generally specific to skill areas such as health systems, economic statistics, and transportation, but it can also involve commonsense reasoning. Heuristic procedural knowledge depends heavily on the existence of the metadata, relationships, and semantics mentioned earlier, to "prune" a given problem to a manageable size. Specific heuristic knowledge is used to guide solutions or reactions. It may be expressed in either goal-driven ("to accomplish this, do that") or event-driven ("if this happens, do that") terms. Heuristic knowledge is flexible and capable of dealing with a variety of problems and situations. It is the most common form of knowledge used by government analysts, but very little, if any, of this knowledge is presently computerized. The traditional emphasis in computer programming has been on encoding algorithmic knowledge; few tools have been developed to facilitate the encoding of more heuristic forms of procedural knowledge.

Procedural knowledge is active; that is, procedural knowledge acts on knowledge of all types to produce new knowledge ("information") for the department. Procedural knowledge may be static or dynamic—depending on how rapidly the department acquires new skills and techniques.

JUDGMENTAL KNOWLEDGE. Judgmental knowledge includes the "why" component of a department's aggregate knowledge. It deals with the wisdom used to determine which factual and procedural knowledge is relevant to a given decision, and it motivates and directs the making of that decision. Exercise of judgmental knowledge also includes consideration of moral and legal issues before a decision is made. There are two types of judgmental knowledge: constraints (which contain values and regulations) and goals (which include objectives). Constraints are used to evaluate proposed actions, whereas goals are used to motivate planning for new actions. Values are a form of knowledge obtained from society and experience (morals, ethics, etc.). Values do not carry the force of law and cannot be used as legal grounds to justify a decision. Regulations are a form of knowledge similar to values but written as statutes or rules of conduct that carry the force of law and judicial action. Goals are a form of knowledge pertaining to the broad mission of a department. Objectives relate to the specific actions or tasks that are to be completed in connection with particular goals.

The importance of including moral and legal considerations in the decision-making process has been underlined by recent events involving all branches of government (e.g., privacy legislation), which have stressed the importance of ethics in government activity. Given today's computer technology, decisions involving judgmental knowledge are exercised solely by human beings. In addition to this judgmental knowledge, however, decision makers require a solid basis of support (factual and procedural knowledge) before they can reach their conclusions. This latter type of support can be provided by computerized systems. The model given here is an attempt to organize this support to enhance the decision-making process. Attempts to automate the decision-making process by incorporating large amounts of judgmental knowledge should be recognized as experimental research, which runs a higher risk of failure.

No single item of knowledge is very useful by itself. Facts without procedures to manipulate them or without goals to satisfy are worth little. Skills without raw material (facts) to work on accomplish nothing. Wisdom without the means to carry out policies or to meet goals is futile. Hence, large amounts of knowledge of different types (factual, procedural, and judgmental) are necessary before useful work can be performed by a department. Without a diversity of knowledge (today, largely stored in employees' heads), a department may be in danger of becoming merely a data collector with no goals or sense of direction for effectively using data to produce useful results.

Domain Taxonomy. There are many ways of categorizing the knowledge employed by an enterprise. The functional taxonomy (factual, procedural, and judgmental) considers the knowledge itself and how it is used irrespective of the subject matter to which the knowledge pertains. An equally important method of classification categorizes knowledge according to subject domains (transportation, agriculture, education, computers, accounting, management, etc.). Of course, the list of categories or domains is potentially very large (consider all the specialty branches in a federal department or all the academic departments in a modern university). Often these domains are organized into a hierarchy of subjects, ranging from most general knowledge (theories, general principles, laws of science, etc.) down through increasing specificity to specific facts or techniques. The decision as to which domains are important or how they should be organized usually rests with the enterprise and its own special interests.

KNOWLEDGE CONTEXTS. Because of the potentially vast number of subject domains, attempting a general-domain taxonomy is not productive; however, departmental knowledge can be divided into three broad contexts: mission, support, and direction. (These contexts are similar to the policy, resource, and program management classifications of the Study Committee on Policy Management Assistance.[14]) Each of these three contexts can be divided into general knowledge of the appropriate subjects (such as economics or programming) and further divided into more specific knowledge (such as food production in Asia or FORTRAN programming on an IBM 370 computer). These subjects, of course, consist of factual, procedural, and judgmental knowledge that are relevant to the particular subject. Figure 2 depicts, in a Venn diagram, this organization of a department's knowledge contexts. Where a particular item of knowledge falls on this diagram is determined largely by the degree of relevance the item has to one of the three contexts (i.e., what is considered to be the mission of an enterprise, and what is seen

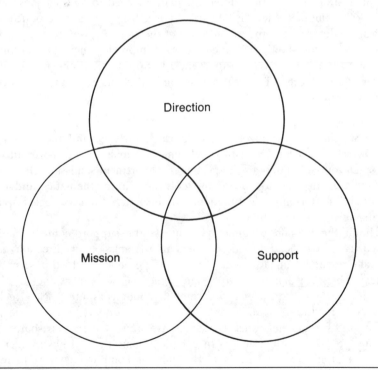

Figure 2 Knowledge contexts.

as essentially a supporting activity?). The amount of overlap among the contexts for a given enterprise indicates the amount of common knowledge there must be between mission-oriented and support-oriented personnel for the enterprise to function effectively.

1. *Mission context*

Knowledge in the mission context involves the basic facts, skills, and wisdom needed to perform the main mission of the organization. Medicine and economics are examples of general domains used by the National Institutes of Health and the Department of Agriculture Economics Statistics and Cooperatives Service. These domains are further divided into activities frequently called "applications." Analysts with specialized skills (e.g., an Economics Statistics and Cooperatives Service economist skilled in basic forecasting techniques) use the wisdom they have acquired through experience in the mission to determine which factual knowledge about their application (food and fiber production in the United States) they need to do their jobs. Their basic skills combined with their factual knowledge are used to produce forecasts on food and fiber production. Most of the training given to analysts who work on a mission should be directed toward improving their mission knowledge (e.g., forecasting facts on food and fiber production) and not toward a deeper understanding of the support context (e.g., how to run various computer programs).

2. *Support context*

The support context involves procedural knowledge and factual knowledge, which deal primarily with developing and maintaining tools and with the organizational functions supporting a department's mission. Examples of these activities include providing tools such as mathematics and computers and performing the functions of personnel, finance, logistics, and maintenance.

From the mission or direction context, the support context is often viewed as an overhead function. Users in the mission or direction areas generally resent having to master the knowledge relevant to this secondary context. The result has been strong and sometimes vocal resistance by these users to learning "extraneous" information about computers. New techniques are needed to allow those persons trained in support to define the support algorithms and heuristics so that many different users can share them (sharing procedural knowledge). In a typical computerized environment, a mission analyst must first navigate through the computer context to reach the appropriate mission knowledge stored on the computer. Such navigation must appear transparent if this burden is to be lifted from those persons who wish to work exclusively in the mission or direction areas.

3. *Direction context*

The direction (or management) context spans both the mission and the support contexts. Three types of management can be identified: management of missions, of support (in particular, computers), and of other managers. As with the other knowledge contexts, the direction context involves both procedural and factual knowledge. Skills such as budgeting and personnel usually apply to all forms of management, regardless of the unit being managed. To manage properly, an effective manager will require specialized knowledge about the organization, project, or operation. Wisdom in the context of direction, of course, is the most visible form of knowledge, because it is in this context that department-wide policies and goals are established. Supporting this kind of activity has long been the intention of classic management information systems.

Metaknowledge. Of particular importance to any department's attempt to manage its knowledge as a resource in the production of public goods is adequate knowledge about the knowledge itself (i.e., knowing what knowledge is available, knowing how to use it, and knowing why certain information has been accumulated and stored in particular locations, such as computers, filing cabinets, or people's heads). Knowledge about the knowledge of a department is called *metaknowledge* and is central to successfully managing knowledge as a resource.

Metaknowledge for a department will probably be factual (e.g., information about data contained in various data bases, characteristics of various programs and procedures available, or the meaning of certain internal rules in light of external laws and policies). Included under metaknowledge are data and program dictionaries and directories and hierarchies of goals and objectives. Factual metaknowledge about procedural knowledge addresses issues such as what programming language the program is written in, what machine it runs on, what parameters it expects, what the relationship is between procedures A and B, and what the execution of a procedure means (as opposed to what it does).

Of primary importance is notation about the method of representing the knowledge (e.g., files, data bases, sets, programs, semantic networks, predicate calculus, production rules, and frames[16]). Each representation has certain advantages and disadvantages, and an enterprise may use several representations.

Metaknowledge may have forms other than factual. Knowing how to use factual metaknowledge (e.g., how to use a dictionary) is procedural, as is knowing how to determine why a department follows a certain policy. Knowing why data obtained from one source may be considered more valid than data obtained from another source and why a particular statistical process should not be applied to a given data set are judgmental metaknowledge. Hierarchies of metaknowledge (about other metaknowledge) form an essential (albeit complex) part of the total knowledge possessed by a department.

As a department begins to manage its knowledge as a basic resource with increased emphasis on sharing knowledge and avoiding unnecessary duplication, the role of metaknowledge becomes more important. Metaknowledge must be managed if a department's members (people and machines) are to have a reasonable chance at succeeding in sharing their individual knowledge with other members. Metaknowledge management is a new endeavor warranting considerable concentration to develop new and better techniques for sharing knowledge.

Technological advances in computer science and information management do not yet include fully automating the storage and processing of all an organization's knowledge. How far machines can go in representing and employing knowledge in support of a department's mission is questionable.[17] For example, will machines ever be able to establish what a department's mission should be? On the other hand, machines have been shown to be effective tools in supporting human endeavors, and proliferation of such tools is one reason why metaknowledge management is needed to keep track of what tools are available, what they can do, how to use them, and where to find them.

Metaknowledge need not be limited to knowledge about only the information stored in or manipulated by computers. Manual systems (such as libraries or filing cabinets) or systems involving humans (such as "John Doe is the resident expert on rice production in Southeast Asia") can also be included as legitimate and valuable metaknowledge. This metaknowledge may be automated to yield a more complete system for a department.

At present, organizations do little to manage metaknowledge. Data dictionaries and directories are just now receiving widespread use in conjunction with data-base management systems. Occasionally, program libraries are organized and indexed to assist the user who is unknowledgeable about the computer context of what programs are available and where they are located. Activities such as analyzing a user's query and automatically determining which of several data bases should be accessed (or even how to access them) are still in the research stage, and the automatic retrieval and correlation of

knowledge from a variety of sources and in a variety of representations may be in the distant future.

There are functions that human beings perform readily (if not always rapidly) under often adverse conditions. Consistent, effective management of even a portion of the metaknowledge that these persons need to fulfill their roles could increase their effectiveness and reduce costs by making it easier for them to understand how to use metaknowledge.

When viewing the knowledge of a department, a person may choose to look at all the factual knowledge, say, possessed by the department, or at a particular subject and ask what knowledge the enterprise has about this subject. The former approach might reflect the interest of a data-base administrator or a program administrator for performance or capacity considerations, whereas the latter approach might reflect the viewpoint of an analyst with a specific mission to accomplish. From either view, adequate metaknowledge about the location and contents of the various knowledge bases is central to effective use.

Knowledge Independence. The key idea behind managing knowledge as a basic resource of a department is that such knowledge can be shared among the various authorized members of the enterprise. To share, department members must understand what is being shared, how it is constructed, what it means, and how it should or should not be used. This is the role of metaknowledge.

Recently, the data-processing industry has begun to realize the importance of maintaining data separate from the procedures that manipulate information. The notion of *data independence* has become prominent with respect to data bases and data-base management systems. A direct result of attempts to achieve data independence has been recognition of the need to include metadata and relationships among items in the data base and not in the many applications programs that may access the data.

During the last few years, a parallel movement has occurred in software engineering advocating "modular" and "top-down" design of computer programs. In this design, the metaknowledge of how various routines are to be called and how they function is separated from the routines themselves and made available to all routines that may need the functions they perform.

Finally, the government emphasis on management programs such as Management by Objectives and Zero Based Budgeting indicates a renewed interest in overtly identifying the goals and constraints of the departments and agencies. Management by Objectives and Zero Based Budgeting are attempts to extract portions of the judgmental knowledge being followed by

government managers and to make them available to the department work forces. Explaining these policies requires metaknowledge (descriptions, relationships, meanings, how the information should be used, etc.) that cannot be buried in the goals themselves.

These concepts are similar in that they attempt to separate metaknowledge from the knowledge it describes and to allow department members to share knowledge (data, programs, and goals) by providing them with adequate metaknowledge to interpret correctly the knowledge resource and to use it effectively. The separation of knowledge items and the necessary metaknowledge to identify the items can be called *knowledge independence.*

One characteristic of knowledge independence is separation of the various types of knowledge identified in the taxonomy. Factual knowledge must be separated from the procedural knowledge used to access or employ that information and from the judgmental knowledge used to direct the organization's activities. Such separation is important to the long-term survivability and usefulness of an organization's knowledge resource. If knowledge independence is provided, facts will be more readily usable by multiple procedures (data sharing), and procedures should be more amenable to running with multiple sets of facts (tool flexibility). Separation of algorithmic from heuristic knowledge can provide a rational basis for understanding the kinds of procedures that may be translated into software for computer systems. Heuristic procedures are expected to change frequently and thus need to be implemented in forms that are easy to change. Algorithmic procedures, on the other hand, should remain relatively stable. Therefore, recognition of the critical differences between the stability of heuristic and algorithmic procedures can lead to the design of information systems that can accommodate both types of knowledge. Such designs can help control mounting software costs by overtly recognizing those programs that are more likely to change and handling them appropriately. Recognition of the importance of the human role in managing judgmental knowledge is crucial in any attempt to automate procedures that rely heavily on this type of knowledge.

A second characteristic of knowledge independence is the need to separate the three contexts of direction, mission, and support so that individuals can concentrate on their areas of specialization without wasting valuable time learning extraneous details (facts, procedures, goals, jargon, etc.) from another context. For example, additional knowledge about computers can be helpful to economists (mission analysts), but the valuable time spent in training economists to function effectively in the computer context could perhaps be better used in improving their forecasting skills (procedural knowledge) or in acquiring more factual knowledge on food and fiber production. The distinction must be made between that portion of the analyst's time spent ac-

quiring specialized mission knowledge and the time spent wrestling with awkward computer protocols and computer languages (the support context). Some understanding of other contexts is both useful and desirable for most members of an organization, but requiring too much understanding (especially knowledge of computers) can be counterproductive.

The principles of knowledge independence embody important criteria with which public administrators can evaluate the effectiveness of their computerized information systems. Controls must be exercised over the degree with which knowledge types or domains overlap in a given system, because the overlap will probably occur in the human portions of the systems (i.e., the users and systems programmers). Not only is such a configuration suboptimal in effectively using employees but it can also breed resentment and discontent at their being forced to learn knowledge from a second domain. Individual employees are not permanent members of any system, and when they depart they may take irreplaceable knowledge with them. If such knowledge can be captured in the computerized portion of the system, such a loss need not occur.

The Organizational Knowledge Resource

As described in this selection, knowledge is a valuable organizational resource that must be actively and overtly managed. In trying to manage knowledge as a resource, agencies and departments are seeking to organize their knowledge acquisition, use, maintenance, and preservation process. Unavailability to decision makers of the "right" knowledge at critical times can spell disaster for a department's mission, which can, in turn, affect the entire nation. The key to managing knowledge effectively seems to be to concentrate on managing the metaknowledge that describes it.

Throughout history, knowledge, as well as the reasons why it is important and should be preserved, has been stored in human minds. Transmittal of knowledge from one individual to another in government is growing more expensive, because the amount of knowledge required for a department to function is growing at an ever-increasing rate. Furthermore, the cost of "human storage" (in the form of employees' minds) is also increasing. Perhaps the most pressing knowledge-related problem is the departure from the government of many of the most respected and knowledgeable experts. These losses underscore the need to capture the experts' unique knowledge before it is gone forever. Publications, school courses, textbooks, lectures, and protégé teaching all help, but increasing amounts of the knowledge needed for daily operations are being "preserved" by algorithmic computer programs. Although computers are performing information processing more frequently, computer programs are currently an awkward (and incomplete) form for storing many kinds of knowledge.

Something more is needed to ensure proper retention and use of a department's unique knowledge. Organizations should begin to use formal mechanisms for representing, acquiring, and applying knowledge. New generations of metaknowledge management tools can aid by providing human decision makers with better access to the vast storehouse of knowledge so painstakingly garnered by the employees and management of the various departments. Such knowledge-access assistance is already being provided in medicine and chemistry, where "knowledge-based systems" have begun to demonstrate remarkable capabilities.[5,13] The availability and use of such capabilities by government departments is essential if those organizations are to improve their use of knowledge.

Knowledge-Processing Tools

Today's knowledge-processing tools can be grouped into several categories that differ from one another primarily in the degree of logical structuring and independence of knowledge that each type of system can accommodate. Figure 3 shows a continuum of knowledge processors running from the standard file system supplied with a computer's operating system, through file management systems and data-base management systems, to knowledge-based systems, and finally to a new kind of system (to be developed) called a *knowledge-based management system*. These five kinds of systems differ in their purpose, function, capabilities, and view of knowledge they provide to users. They also differ in the ability to support the needs of metaknowledge management (the separation of knowledge contexts and of knowledge forms). Many varieties of the knowledge managers described in Figure 3 are currently available and are found in different agencies today. What is missing is a framework for connecting those systems so that the knowledge they manage can be shared most effectively among the systems and with the human users they serve (i.e., a framework for metaknowledge management).

The standard file system (SFS) contains the basic access methods provided by the computer's operating system. A file management system (FMS) begins to allow rudimentary data description in the form of files, records within files, and fields within records. A data-base management system (DBMS) maintains and provides access to an integrated data base of many interrelated data aggregates. Provision is made for logical structuring of the data to reflect both abstract and physical relationships. This structure is made explicit in the data base itself and is available to the DBMS.

Physical   Logical

←——→

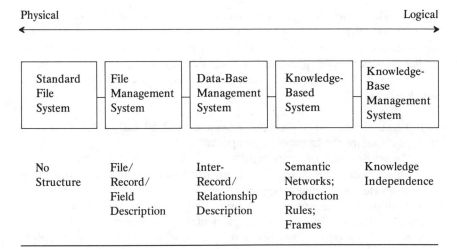

Standard File System	File Management System	Data-Base Management System	Knowledge-Based System	Knowledge-Base Management System
No Structure	File/ Record/ Field Description	Inter- Record/ Relationship Description	Semantic Networks; Production Rules; Frames	Knowledge Independence

Figure 3   Knowledge-processing tool continuum.

A knowledge-based sytem (KBS) allows for the representation of rules of logic and conditions for the application of these rules to be placed within the knowledge base and accessible to the KBS (see Davis and King[4]). One advantage of representing knowledge in a rule form is the ease with which the rules can be changed as the user's perception of the problem changes (meta-knowledge management). Another advantage is the potential capability for the KBS to explain in terms understandable to the user why it is doing what it is doing. Alternative representations to rule sets include semantic networks[11] and frames.[9] The KBS needs a data base and metadata against which to apply its rules. Most current implementations include a specialized DBMS built for the particular knowledge-based system. In this regard, the factual knowledge and procedural knowledge are not clearly separated, thus making it difficult to share these kinds of knowledge with other applications.

A knowledge-base management system (KBMS) is an extension of the knowledge-based philosophy to include the concept of knowledge independence. Organizing and representing knowledge separately from the applications that use it is a positive step toward formally preserving it for future users. A knowledge-base management system uses all the other types of knowledge-processing software consistently to try to maintain the independence of various forms of knowledge. A KBMS thus makes knowledge available to various applications. The failure of current systems to make knowledge available to multiple applications leads to the redundant redesign of systems. This point is a legitimate part of the life-cycle cost of a software system, but one that is rarely measured today. A KBMS is also the foundation on which a department can build and manage its knowledge resource. In our earlier papers,[1,2,3] we presented a preliminary systems architecture for a knowledge-base management system. Several key aspects of this design are listed here.

1. Requirements for any proposed system must be gathered with a clear understanding of the knowledge components.

2. Knowledge independence must play a key role in the design.

3. One aspect of knowledge independence is the separation of user interfaces from the knowledge processors.

4. Multiple user interfaces are required to provide the appropriate view of knowledge that is most natural to a particular user category.

5. Multiple knowledge processors are needed to provide adequate capabilities to meet the users' requirements.

6. Some sort of canonical representation of knowledge (at least for each form) will be required for knowledge sharing among distributed systems.

7. Some facility will be required to assist in the navigation of a distributed knowledge base.

Further work, of course, is needed to determine the exact characteristics of such a system.

Conclusions

The premise of this paper is that knowledge is already a basic resource of most federal departments (whether or not it is formally recognized as such). Many federal departments may even be regarded as knowledge agencies. Their primary product is knowledge, be it factual knowledge about health, food, or housing; procedural knowledge about techniques to obtain or produce information; or judgmental knowledge to monitor and direct the organization's behavior. Combined knowledge is central to an organization's existence and should be formally recognized as a basic resource. Organizations would do well to adopt a philosophy that will allow them to understand and then manage this valuable resource. This paper has summarized and clarified ideas developed by us.[1,2,3] The sections that follow review the conclusions reached in those earlier works.

Knowledge Is a Basic Resource. Formal recognition of knowledge as an organization's basic resource will have widespread ramifications. The most visible effect, perhaps, will be creation of an executive for metaknowledge management to maintain the top-level view of the knowledge resource and to ensure compatibility among all programs and projects. Consistent with this philosophy is the need for program and project managers to reorganize their approach to knowledge applications and systems design. Knowledge independence (the formal separation and specification of knowledge types and contexts) is essential. Authority over knowledge applications should not be removed from those persons with expertise, but organization-wide controls and guidelines must be maintained over representing and sharing the knowledge used by the various applications. For a program of this magnitude and wide-reaching impact, top management's full support is necessary.

Knowledge Independence Is Important. Several aspects of the issue of knowledge independence should be considered by systems analysts in designing future systems for the various departments. A crucial step in the design is to separate the factual knowledge (data management function) from the procedural knowledge (application program function) and the judgmental knowledge (user interface and decision support functions) and to provide a translation and control mechanism to allow multiple knowledge applications to access multiple facts data bases. This approach to knowledge independence offers the advantages of permitting data sharing (really knowledge sharing) among applications, supplying a limited number of (standardized) user interfaces to the knowledge resource, and providing a central point from which to monitor and understand the flow of knowledge among various elements of the organization. Heuristic procedural knowledge must also be recognized and separated from algorithmic procedural knowledge. Recognition of this separation can lead to significant changes in current methods of designing systems and writing software. The second aspect of knowledge independence is recognizing the need to separate, where appropriate, the mission, direction, and support contexts to reduce training costs and to promote knowledge sharing.

Task Forces for Metaknowledge Management Are Needed. The departments of the Federal Government will have to develop methodologies for achieving metaknowledge management. Much more specific thinking is required before the knowledge resource philosophy can be effectively introduced into ongoing and future projects. Task forces should be appointed to study and expand the definition of a knowledge resource philosophy. These task forces should identify the short-range and long-range consequences of embracing the refined philosophy. Finally, plans should be developed to identify the actions needed to manage knowledge resources in different departments.

Experimentation with Knowledge-Based Systems Is Needed. Considerable research will be required in both the supervisory and technical aspects of metaknowledge management. An area warranting extensive investigation in the near future is knowledge-based systems. An extensive program of testing this technology against knowledge applications is needed to gain valuable expertise in their use and a deeper understanding of the problems involved. Normal personnel turnover and the associated departure of key experts in different government departments emphasize the need for a means by which a department can organize and retain at least part of its employees' invaluable expertise. Knowledge-based systems might serve that function, but experts must be available to supply the appropriate knowledge to the system in a process that now can take several years to accomplish. In addition, knowledge-based systems might provide the basis for the systems architecture required by the knowledge-base management system mentioned in this paper.

Joint Efforts Are Essential. No department should attempt by itself to convert to metaknowledge management. The expected cost of such an endeavor (indeed, a cost-benefits trade-off analysis should be performed) has not been mentioned, but one department should not have to incur all the research and development costs. In addition to seeking other sources of funding, an organization should collaborate with other agencies that might benefit from a policy for managing knowledge. Indeed, one organization's development of a knowledge resource is of limited worth without the ability to communicate that knowledge to other organizations. Agencies can supply valuable knowledge to assist one another in their tasks, but a coordinated methodology is required. Experiences with present-day computer networks attest to the usefulness and difficulty of knowledge sharing among agencies. We believe that the ideas outlined in this paper can serve as the basis for that methodology.

Much work is necessary to refine and experiment with the idea of maintaining a knowledge resource for an enterprise. Political, managerial, and technological issues must be investigated; a successful solution for any enterprise will combine aspects of each. Many of the problems departments face are not new; organizations have always worried about managing their knowledge resources. The advent of the computer and related technologies, however, has solved some problems but created others. The capacity to store electronically trillions of characters of data and to manipulate millions of these characters every second has provided some technical relief to the "information explosion" while simultaneously encouraging organizations to collect and attempt to process data at an ever-increasing rate. The challenge of the 1970s was to build machines that could store and manipulate enormous quantities of data and procedures at fantastic rates. The challenge of the 1980s is for enterprises to gain control over their knowledge-processing capabilities, to direct these capabilities to support production of public goods, and to free humans to conduct the true mission of the enterprise. The philosophy of a knowledge resource is a step in that direction.

References

1. Berry, J. F., and Cook, C. M. *Managing Knowledge as an Agency Resource.* March 1977. (Special access required.)
2. _____. *Managing Knowledge as a Corporate Resource.* July 1976. NTIS No. AD-A029891.
3. _____.*Viewing Knowledge as a Resource Within Departments of the Federal Government.* September 1977. NTIS No. PB-271 925.
4. Davis, R., and King, J. *An Overview of Production Systems.* Stanford, Calif., Computer Science Department, Stanford University, October 1975.
5. Feigenbaum, E. A. et al. "On Generality and Problem Solving: A Case Study of the DENDRAL Program." In: *Machine Intelligence 6.* Edited by B. Metzler and D. Michie. Edinburgh, Scotland, Edinburgh University Press, 1971.
6. Gordon, K. *The Brookings Institution Annual Report.* Washington, D.C., The Brookings Institution, 1970.
7. Kent, W. *Describing Information,* TR 03.012. Palo Alto, Calif., IBM General Products Division, May 1975.
8. Langefors, B., and Sundgren, B. *Information Systems Architecture.* New York, Petrocelli Books, 1975.
9. Minsky, M. "A Framework for Representing Knowledge." In: *The Psychology of Computer Vision.* Edited by P. Winston. New York, McGraw-Hill, 1975.
10. Price, D. K. "1984 and Beyond: Social Engineering or Political Values?" In: *American Public Administration: Past, Present, Future.* Birmingham, University of Alabama Press, 1975.
11. Quillian, M. R. "Semantic Memory." In: *Semantic Information Processing.* Edited by M. Minsky. Cambridge, Mass., MIT Press, 1968.
12. Seidman, H. *Politics, Position, and Power: The Dynamics of Federal Reorganization.* New York, Oxford University Press, 1975.
13. Shortliffe, E. H. *Computer-Based Medical Consultations: MYCIN.* New York, American Elsevier Publishing Co., 1976.

14. Study Committee on Policy Management Assistance. "Executive Summary (Executive Summary of Volume II of the Study Committee on Policy Management Assistance Report, 'Strengthening Public Management in the Intergovernmental System')." *Public Administration Review,* *35*:700–705, December 1975. [Special Issue]

15. Sundgren, B. *Theory of Data Bases.* New York, Petrocelli Books, 1975.

16. System Development Corporation. *Knowledge-Based Systems: A Tutorial.* June 1977. NTIS No. AD-A044883.

17. Weizenbaum, J. *Computer Power and Human Reason: From Judgment to Calculation.* San Francisco, W. H. Freeman, 1976.

Knowledge and Power*
Amitai Etzioni

As is well known, kings do not make philosophers and philosophers do not make kings. Or, as a modern-day sociologist would put it, the functional prerequisites of power and of knowledge are incompatible. Beginning with the structural differentiation of the two, we ask—how does the relationship between the centers of societal control and the societal units which specialize in the production of knowledge affect societal activeness? The answer, we shall see, is affected by the organization of the production of knowledge itself, by the structure of access to power, and by the provision for fundamental overview. The main actors involved seem to be political elites, intellectuals, experts, and the various publics. Their mutual relations must be taken into account in any study of knowledge and power.

The Interaction Between Knowledge and Control

An analysis of the relationships between units that specialize in the production and processing of knowledge and units that head the controlling overlayers of societies may benefit from the combination of cybernetic analysis with the study of power hierarchies which has been developed in the analysis of complex organizations.[1] It has been suggested that (a) the authority of knowledge and the authority of control are best kept structurally segregated and (b) the specific nature of the relations between the two kinds of authority significantly affects the efficacy of complex organizations.[2] Here we explore the relations between knowledge and control on the societal level. While these are examined in structural-organizational terms, the normative implications of varying arrangements are evident.

Segregation of the Two Knowledge Functions. According to a widely held organizational viewpoint, the quality of societal knowledge is considerably affected by the degree to which the societal services devoted to reality-testing

---

and evaluative interpretation are segregated, and by the ways in which the units that specialize in serving these functions are linked.[3] Primitive actors—including not only preliterate tribes, but also collectivities in post-modern societies which have poor knowledge-facilities—are said to keep the services of the two functions meshed. The elders, be they tribal chiefs or leaders of old-fashioned labor unions,[4] are the source of collective information about what the world is like, how it functions, *and* how it should be collectively interpreted.

A high degree of segregation, it is suggested, makes for greater division of labor, thus allowing for greater specialization. The segregation of staff from line and of collectors and assessors of intelligence from policy makers has been advocated for complex organizations.[5] On the societal level, modernization has been said to require the segregation of academic and professional ("expert") elites from their political counterparts.[6]

In this structural segregation—along functional rather than collectivity lines—the knowledge elites, as the centers of societal reality-testing, are viewed as dealing primarily with information, while political decision-makers (with the help of ideological elites) are more concerned with societal interpretations. It is often suggested in this context that the immunity of professionals and the academic community from political and economic sanctions is a prerequisite for their unconstrained testing of reality; this defers the responsibility for dealing with societal needs, values, and power to the political elites.[7] Finally, it is proposed that societal units are more effective if, as autonomous as the knowledge elites may be, the political elites have a clearly superior rank, since they are in charge of the encompassing societal action.[8]

This widely held model has two limitations. First, it stresses the problem of segregation but underemphasizes the means by which information and evaluative interpretation are to be related (other than by granting superiority to one kind of elite over another).[9] Second, it is too abstract to provide a productive model for describing the effects of inter-elite relations on the societal use of knowledge, as it is primarily a prescriptive scheme which defines the way things ought to be. It expresses the value of freeing scientists from a concern with the societal implications of their findings and legitimates the decision-making elites' claim that they ought to maintain superior rank. This model also suggests that the reduction of conflicts between the knowledge and power elites can occur through this sharp segregation of the sides which rarely view the world within the same contextuating orientations.

The actual pattern of relations between key sources of new information, new interpretations, and decision-making is itself a major subject on which only a few illustrative observations can be made here. First, while the segregation model may prescribe the societal conditions most favorable to basic research, most of the information used by post-modern societies is "applied" and only indirectly based on basic research. If federal obligations for research are taken as a rough indicator, the United States committed $1,689.9 millions in 1965 to basic research and $12,909.7 millions to applied research and development.[10] Most of the applied information is gathered and used by engineers, x-ray technicians, social workers, and so on, whose norms and needs differ greatly from those of the basic researchers. A considerable degree of contextuating control seems to inflict surprisingly little damage on their work. Applied research has been carried out quite effectively even in totalitarian societies.[11] Political supervision of and intervention in such work, even in Stalin's day, may be less stringent than was once believed but are much greater than the amounts which the segregation model assumes that research can tolerate.[12]

Second, there is also significantly less segregation on the opposite score: As the custodians of reality-testing, the producers of information participate much more actively in recasting political orientations than the segregation model suggests.[13] New information is introduced into the political process through numerous mechanisms other than the ubiquitous, non-directive, classified, expert's report left on the decision-maker's desk.

Experts are able to support almost any side in most political contests with testimony before executive or legislative committees, sometimes by drawing on different sets of facts, but much more commonly by giving different cognitive and evaluative interpretations to available facts. Conflicting interpretations about the danger of fallout from thermonuclear bombs, the probabilities of surviving a nuclear attack, and the effects of medicare are among the better-known examples.[14] The Armed Services support advisory corporations, whose studies support and sometimes even extend the basic contextual positions of the Services, even though they may differ about details.[15] Industries maintain public relations divisions to magnify and interpret "their" experts' findings on cancer and tobacco, vitamins and growth, drugs and pregnancy.[16] The effectiveness of experts, somewhat like that of attorneys, is determined not only by the amount of their evidence but also by the skill with which they present it, the resources they command, and the acuteness of their political perceptions.[17] Therefore, it is not that one group of experts presents the facts and the other perpetrates falsehoods, but rather that matters often involve questions which, even if an impartial and expertly trained judge were available, cannot be readily decided on the basis of information alone.[18]

It might be argued that while the predictions and advice of experts generally cannot be evaluated when they are first given, those experts who are proved correct gradually acquire more status and following, while those who are shown to be wrong are rejected. Although such societal "editing" of experts has not been systematically studied, we suggest that even *post hoc* selection is more limited in extent and efficacy than is often assumed. Occasionally, a clear test of a highly specific problem is possible, and some experts are shown to be correct while others are discredited—e.g., Admiral Rickover's arguments in favor of the feasibility of building nuclear-powered submarines. Knowledge concerning societal actors and their properties, however, tends to be far less verifiable and more time-consuming in its testing. Therefore, a "wrong" approach often outlives the experts who advocated it. The differences between "right" and "wrong" approaches are not clearly defined but are usually a matter of being less or more effective. The tests of the relative effectiveness of such matters as foreign aid, civil rights legislation, or police codes are, as a rule, difficult to establish, ambiguous, and open to different expert interpretations.[19] Because of the high costs of allowing "their" experts to be discredited, political elites tend not only to defend them partisanly but even attempt to prevent their evaluations.[20] The politicalization of the "editing" of experts who have access to power also works in reverse: Effective experts go unheard while less knowledgeable ones receive an audience because of such outright political factors as the change of an administration or the majority in a legislature. We do not argue that uninformed men usually serve as counselors while experts are ignored. We simply submit that the selection of the experts whose advice is introduced into the societal decision-making processes is a complex, partly evaluative and partly political process. Structurally, the processes of societal reality-testing and evaluation are interwoven rather than segregated, just as information and interpretation as symbolic systems are mixed in the societal mind.

Pluralistic Input. What, then, leads to a more effective societal organization of knowledge input? One frequently given answer posits pluralism both in production and in input. It is suggested, all other things being equal, that as one knowledge-elite (or school of thought) increasingly monopolizes either the production of knowledge in a particular field or the access to a decision-making elite, the actor's reality-testing will tend to become less effective. In organizational terms, this means that the less restricted the *participation* in the contest among knowledge producers which have political access, the more effective will be the knowledge *supply*; and the less politically-based the decisions regarding the *outcomes* of the knowledge contest, the more effective will be the societal course followed. It cannot be stressed enough, however, that this is a matter of degree; given the concern with societal needs other than reality-testing, considerable politicalization of the knowledge supply and of decision-making is to be expected even among comparatively effective actors.

It is also necessary to recognize that the pluralism of the production of knowledge rests on more than the institutionalization of the proper values. It is not only affected by "background" conditions, such as Calvinism or free enterprise economics, but it is also affected by the societal organization, especially by the distribution of relevant resources. For instance, the proposal to establish a cabinet-level United States Department of Science has not received wide approval because it would too greatly concentrate the sources of support for the production of knowledge.[21] A scientist who is refused support from one agency should always have another source of support to which he can turn, although, of course, the mere existence of two or more sources of support does not suffice if one school of thought controls the allocation of resources by all the sources. Thus, not only does a degree of pluralism in regard to sources of support, training, and affiliation seem a prerequisite for the relatively effective use of knowledge, but also a measure of conflict among the various sources of support seems necessary.

Furthermore, the position which favors pluralistic input is held not only for the societal organization of knowledge production; it is advanced for the intra-governmental production of knowledge as well. One of the arguments for intelligence collection by the three Armed Forces, the CIA, and the State Department is that combining these services into one intelligence agency would undermine the pluralistic production of this form of knowledge. (We, of course, do not imply that the number of agencies must be large or that some additional coordination of their efforts would be detrimental to the quality of the knowledge produced.)

The significance of the distributive patterns of knowledge-producing resources should not be underestimated. While a great mind might generate a great idea under most conditions, there seems to be a positive association—especially in the applied fields—between investment (not only of funds but also of the number and quality of personnel and organizational talents and efforts) and the level and quality of knowledge output. This is not to suggest that by merely increasing investment in, let us say, cancer research, the problem would be solved more quickly. Some areas of research are already "flooded," while in others some basic questions must be answered before much additional progress can be anticipated. But while there is no one-to-one correlation between investment and results, in many cases the amount of investment does make a significant difference.[22]

Second, pluralism cannot be maintained when one area is given all the resources it needs while the others starve. The knowledge contest then becomes like a court fight between a battery of corporation lawyers and a young man from the Legal Aid Society. That is, if the case is an open-and-shut one, the latter man may win, but under most circumstances—when experience, the capacity to gather evidence, and the power of the presentation matter— he is more likely to lose because of his lower capacity either to amass the necessary facts or to make them visible and accessible to the judge and jury— i.e., to the decision-makers.

More active units, we suggest, have a more egalitarian pattern of investment in the various areas as well as of access to control centers of the various knowledge-producing units than is prescribed by the prevailing goal-priorities and societal power-relations. This serves as a guarantee that alternatives which have no immediate appeal and little power but may have merit will not be drowned out and also allows for anticipation. Thus, the access to decision-making centers of societies is so organized that deprived collectivities are heard long before they command sufficient power to force attention. Such societies also organize their knowledge input so that they are aware of gathering clouds on the international horizon long before the storm is blowing down their gates. Those actors who are unable to study, understand, and deal with systems whose patterns differ from their own priorities and power structures are precisely those who are untransformable, while those actors whose knowledge production is relatively detached from their existing societal structures are those one would expect to be most able to anticipate, recast, survive, and grow.

The pluralistic organization of knowledge production and of its input into the societal decision-making process is expected to be more effective than monopolization not only for societal reality-testing but also for evaluative interpretation. Focusing on one substantive issue—the structural-organizational base of societal criticism—we now turn to explore the organization of knowledge from this second functional viewpoint.

Communities-of-Assumptions. Societal actors, as we have seen, tend to view the world and themselves with contextuating eyes. While "lack of enclosure" is an institutionalized value for the knowledge collectivities themselves (academic communities, learned societies), consensus has an instrumental value for the political elites, aside from the degree of validity of the knowledge. A major task of any political elite is to construct a whole from societal parts; dissensus is costly and hinders the elite's ability to fulfill this function. And while consensus is not necessarily favorable to an elite in power, dissensus rarely is, for fragmentation of the political base and conflict within it tend to weaken the elite's capacity to guide.

When a societal unit faces a crisis which threatens some of its main values or its survival, pressure to cling to interpretations which had previously gained elite and/or majority support often increases, even though such a crisis may highlight the unreality of these interpretations. That is, we expect that societal actors, like persons, will often become increasingly ritualistic rather than innovative under pressure. This will express itself in the repetition of acts that have already failed and in an obsessive rejection of criticism.[23]

The elites of most modernized societal units are influential in determining whether or not a particular situation is a crisis, e.g., how dangerous are city riots or the gold outflow. And, one major reason for identifying crises is the elites' concern with their own positions. There is, therefore, pressure to limit new interpretations to those which fit the prevailing context not just during a crisis imposed on the system from outside but also in the course of pseudocrises generated by an elite and by its interpretation of the situation.

The contextuating pressure of the control centers is directed above all toward knowledge and communication units which are able to provide and spread conflicting interpretations. It is not that political elites do not desire more valid and encompassing knowledge; some leaders, such as Roosevelt, are reported to have encouraged conflict among their staffs to increase the quality of the knowledge with which they were provided.[24] But whenever such conflicts reach a level which challenges the basic interpretive assumptions of an elite or of the societal unit, there tends to be resistance to basic innovations which may transform the prevailing context. This pressure for preserving the basic consensus is even further accentuated because the criteria for distinguishing the valid from the invalid are more vague on the contextual level than when bits are considered. Such vagueness increases the desire for a "community-of-assumptions" within which interpretations are confined.

A *community-of-assumptions* may be defined as the set of assumptions shared by the members of a societal unit which sets a context for its view of the world and itself.[25] A community-of-assumptions differs from a context in that a context is a symbolic system while a community-of-assumptions is a combined societal and symbolic one; that is, a community-of-assumptions is a context internalized and institutionalized by a societal unit. A context may be held by only a few leaders or by a small sub-unit of the members, but a community-of-assumptions exists only if it is shared at least by the elites and the active members of a societal unit. There are often several contexts in the symbolic world of any societal unit but only one or two communities-of-assumptions.

A community-of-assumptions may be limited by subject. Such communities may define the context for viewing only the external world or the internal world as well. However, we expect them to aim the orientation toward outsiders more than toward members, whether it be the orientation of the United States toward other nations (as compared to the United States' orientation toward sub-societies), or the orientation of one ethnic group toward others—e.g., Negroes toward whites as compared to Negro sub-groupings. Intimacy makes enclosure difficult. While this makes the transformation of internal (and self) images easier than the transformation of images of outsiders, it also means that internal (and self) images are more vague and less agreed upon. This is one factor that hampers self-oriented action as compared to action oriented toward others.

Some social scientists have suggested that a community-of-assumptions is a prerequisite for an effectively integrated elite or a cohesive societal unit; others have pointed out that those in control of the United States Armed Services, for instance, have no shared "mentality," and, hence, elites do not require a community-of-assumptions.[26] We suggest that the answer may lie in between these two positions. While not all elites also constitute communities-of-assumptions, even about external images, and while different bits may be held by members of an elite or by elites and their publics, they may nonetheless share a community-of-assumptions. Thus, the three Armed Services may have conflicting estimates of a potential enemy's capacities, and some generals may be Democrats while others are Republicans, but the fact that most share the Cold War perspective is sufficient for them to be able to work effectively in unison. And those elites which do not share a community-of-assumptions may exist but are less effective controlling agents.

Communities-of-assumptions are usually held without awareness* of their hypothetical nature. Many actors assume that the world really is the way their internalized and institutionalized images depict it; they do not see their images as a set of assumptions shared by their community but of undetermined validity.† The presence of some diversity of interpretation(s)

---

*"... what is most surprising to a new arrival in Saigon is the general unawareness, almost innocence, of how what 'we' are doing could look to an outsider." Mary McCarthy, "Report from Vietnam: I. The Home Program," *The New York Review of Books*, Vol. 8 (April 20, 1967), pp. 5–11, quoted from p. 5.

†The mechanisms which enforce a community-of-assumptions are not different from other

within the community-of-assumptions itself further obscures the community's existence, since concepts, views, and facts which appear subject to dissent conceal that dissent is tolerated only within the limits of fundamentally the same interpretations. It is difficult to determine the extent to which such communities act as blindfolds of which the elites as well as the active publics are unaware. However, it is likely that the elites who generated these communities-of-assumptions are themselves caught up in them to some extent; *and*, in addition, the elites often seem bound into a community-of-assumptions which substantively differs from that of their subjects but is similar in its constricting effect. Not the least of these communities is the elites' contextuating view of what their subjects believe and will tolerate and what courses of action they view as out-of-context and, therefore, as unacceptable.

A community-of-assumptions is not necessarily a dysfunctional phenomenon. Given the high number of possible basic positions and sub-positions, decision-making elites would obviously be overloaded and paralyzed if they had to examine the full range of policy alternatives each time they acted. The same holds for the publics. It is very difficult to work out a consensus about assumptions among the various Armed Services, governmental agencies, Congress, and publics on any given line of policy. And when such a consensus is finally reached, undoing it is an expensive process. Actually, the costs are usually so high that it "pays" a societal unit to lose some of its reality-adjusting capacity and to maintain a set of assumptions that do not "fit" well rather than to change them frequently. Only when the community-of-assumptions prevents learning long after the reality has changed significantly is a point reached at which the community's costs in terms of a loss of reality-testing outweigh its gains in terms of reduction of conflict and reinforcement of solidarity and "meaning."

It may seem that the more active societal units are those which more successfully determine the stage at which the costs of maintaining the community-of-assumptions outweigh the gains. This capacity, however,

---

aspects of societal control. Discussing the ways in which scientists are kept from exploring topics "too far off," despite a formal ideology of unrestricted freedom to explore, a *Science* reporter stated: "It appears that a major influence in keeping an investigator from being carried too far off the track of relevant research is, as Baker put it, 'the cultural influence of the community.' Getting the glazed-eye treatment from colleagues is an effective way of keeping researchers from going too far afield." John Walsh, "Bell Labs: A System Approach to Innovation Is the Main Thing," *Science*, July 22, 1966, p. 395.

assumes (a) that the actor is aware of the existence of the community-of-assumptions, (b) a highly refined analytic ability to determine the relative costs and gains, and (c) the availability of an alternative set of assumptions to replace the old ones when their costs become unacceptable.

Actually, societal actors per se rarely calculate in this manner. Societal units that are effective from this viewpoint seem to be those *whose organization of knowledge includes an institutionalized provision for revision of the community-of-assumptions*. Such organization requires one or more structural positions whose functions are (a) to remain outside the community-of-assumptions in order to be able to analyze and evaluate information on the basis of *different sets of assumptions*, and (b) to exert pressure on elites and/or publics to *change* the communities-of-assumptions, especially as their relations to reality become more distant. The point is that the process by which new orientations enter and become established is a political one. Ideas per se have no societal power, and new ideas, especially contextuating ideas that may serve as the basis of a community-of-assumptions, do not enter into a societal system because the elites or active publics suddenly feel that new contextuating orientations are needed or are more valid or meaningful than the established ones. The process tends rather to be one of a societal conflict between the elites in power and the knowledge-producing elites that promote alternative assumptions (often in coalition with competing political elites). As a result, the sub-units charged with maintaining alternative orientations and "opening" communities-of-assumptions have a mobilization function as well as a symbolic-interpretative one. While we shall see that a considerable amount of such mobilization is carried out by other sub-units, the critics themselves must give their criticism enough of a societal push to get it off the ground before even favorable winds can carry it.

In short, it is unlikely that societal actors will act effectively without communities-of-assumptions, for, while such communities delay reality-testing, they contribute to consensus building, and thus, to action in unison. Therefore rather than seeking the conditions under which there will be no such communities, a task which seems utopian as well as unconducive to an active orientation, we explore, instead, the conditions under which communities-of-assumptions are kept relatively "flexible" and transformable. The answer is given in morphological rather than genetic terms; that is, it seems to lie in the availability of a particular kind of knowledge-producing sub-unit—one that is outside the community-of-assumptions, able to exert pressure on the societal unit (or its elites), and is a permanent feature of the societal organization of knowledge.

The Societal Need for Fundamental Criticism

Fundamental criticism is the function of those sub-units whose task is to overview the communities-of-assumptions and challenge them when they become detached from reality. Since such criticism challenges not bits—which could be changed within the existing community-of-assumptions—but the context, we refer to it as fundamental criticism ("radical" criticism would also be an appropriate term). The function of bit-criticism differs from that of fundamental criticism: When the disparity between reality and a community-of-assumptions is not great, bit-criticism enhances reality-testing within the limits of a community-of-assumptions and, thus, strengthens the community in the sense that the "same" context is shown capable of adaptation. When the community's detachment from reality is considerable, however, bit-criticism is dysfunctional because it tends to conceal the disparity and to delay overdue transformation.

Two main structural conditions seem necessary for the provision of fundamental criticism: (a) the critical sub-units must operate even when there is no need or opportunity for the transformation of a community-of-assumptions. Effective societal guidance systems, like other effective systems, require a measure of redundancy, that is, some duplication is required if the relevant function is to be fulfilled. The reason for "redundancy" in this particular case is that the system most in need of fundamental criticism is also likely to be most resistant to it and least inclined to make the structural arrangements necessary for the cultivation of such criticism. To the degree that these arrangements are available, they seem to have been institutionalized before a loss-of-reality crisis occurred.... the availability of alternative fundamental interpretations (i.e., potential communities-of-assumptions) when the prevailing one is broken or weakened requires their preparation *before* the event, which, in turn, necessitates prolonged efforts to synthesize large bodies of knowledge and mobilize initial support.

(b) A value of tolerance for such criticism must be included as part of the *established* community-of-assumptions—a tolerance for basically divergent viewpoints and institutions outside of the community. Scientific metatheories do, to a degree, maintain such assumptions. They are rarely maintained in political systems, however, although liberal and social-democratic ideologies do have some such notions.

The function of fundamental criticism differs according to the state of the societal unit and of its community-of-assumptions. Units that are well integrated by other criteria are also likely to have communities-of-assumptions promoted by and supporting the elites in power. In this kind of unit, the promotion of an alternative set of assumptions takes the form of criticism. In less integrated units, fundamental criticism is often part of the competition over which assumptions should serve as the community-of-assumptions. In the process of nation-building, this is often closely related to the struggle over national identity. Criticism here serves to guard against premature enclosure and the quick acceptance of older assumptions as a basis for the new community. Thus, both when there is an established community-of-assumptions and when one is just being evolved, fundamental societal criticism has a central function.

Intellectuals, Experts, and Political Elites

Post-Modern Criticism: A Morphological Perspective. The critical function requires one or more sub-units relatively immune from societal pressure which allow for and even reward the questioning of a supra-unit's basic assumptions. Such immunity may be the accidental out-growth of other arrangements; for instance, the granting of relative autonomy and access to the centers of power to units engaged in long-run planning or research and development (R&D), tends to provide the sociological conditions under which fundamental criticism may be institutionalized. In the courts of kings in earlier periods, some religious functionaries and jesters had such an institutionalized role.[27]

Which societal sub-units are likely to fulfill the critical function in the post-modern period? The answer varies with the kind of society. In pluralistic societies, the fourth estate, the free press, was viewed as the depository of the function of fundamental criticism, but there is little empirical research on the degree to which it fulfills this function.[28] We know, however, that the greater part of the space in most newspapers in post-modern pluralistic societies is devoted to advertising. Much of the remaining space is used for what may be classified as tension-reduction purposes, including personal feature stories, crime and sex "news," etc. By providing escapist outlets for the tensions generated by the societal structure and by providing individualistic interpretations of them, this kind of journalism reduces the receptivity to fundamental criticism and the pressure for transformation. Only part of the remaining newspaper space is devoted to political and societal information, and only a fraction of this deals with interpretation and fundamental criticism. Furthermore, the norms upheld by most professional newspapermen seem to discourage a view of societal criticism as their proper function; "straight news" is encouraged instead.

The situation is different for a very small number of newspapers, the so-called elite newspapers[29] such as *The New York Times*, but even here the basic priorities with regard to space are as specified above. The major difference is that elite newspapers devote more space to information and less to tension-reduction; "crusading" is, nevertheless, rare and discouraged, and there is little fundamental criticism. Loyalty to the establishment curbs not so much the facts printed as the interpretation given to them.[30] The critical function is much more highly represented in such periodicals as *The New Republic* and *The Nation*, but their circulation is small even among the active publics and elites.[31] And many of the critical articles that are published in these journals are not written by professional journalists but by intellectuals whose structural base is not the press.

A second structural foundation for the critical function is national legislatures. While they undoubtedly have such a function, many have argued that it has been declining since the advent of the post-modern period.[32] Parliaments seem to exercise their critical function to a greater extent for domestic matters than for external ones in a period in which the importance of foreign affairs has greatly increased. The facilities of parliaments have grown little, while the societal and political activities—that is, the scope of what needs to be surveyed—have considerably increased.[33] While the units which need to be reviewed critically—governmental agencies and corporations, armed services, and school systems—have developed sizeable organs for the collection, synthesis, and promotion of knowledge, *legislatures have only very small knowledge-collecting-and-processing units and depend largely on knowledge provided and interpreted for them by either executive or partisan interests.*[34] Attempts at encompassing overviews are few and ineffectual.[35] Proposals to reform the fragmented budgetary processes of the United States national government, for example, have been generally unsuccessful. The Legislative Reorganization Act of 1946 created a joint committee on the budget which was to report to each house a legislative budget which would include an estimate of all Federal receipts and expenditures for the coming fiscal year.[36] We suggest that *unless legislatures are provided with greatly increased staffs and with large-scale and autonomous capacities to collect and process knowledge, their already low critical capacity will continue to diminish.*

While it is difficult to test statements about the relative roles of institutions in fulfilling a societal function, we suggest that in the post-modern, pluralistic societies the unattached intellectuals play a more important critical role than the press, the legislature, and probably both combined. By "unattached" intellectuals we mean those who have no institutional commitment to any elite; they are to be found in such societal enclaves as the bohemian quarters, autonomous policy-research centers, and the universities. Intellectuals, as opposed to experts, have two attributes: They are concerned with contextual matters, while experts are more bit-oriented, and they deal more with evaluative interpretations, while experts are more concerned with reality-testing and cognitive interpretation. Clearly, not everyone who works with symbols or his intellect is an intellectual; those who are not may be referred to as intellect-workers.[37] Intellectuals maintain a wholistic evaluative stance, and those who are unattached are more likely than others to maintain a critical one.[38]

Much of the criticism carried by the press or brought before the national legislatures originates in the autonomous centers which house these intellectuals. An important study would be to identify the main critical ideas of the last decades and to trace their origins and paths into the political system. University committees and individual scholars, for example, have dealt with the fundamental aspects of United States foreign policy; Michael Harrington has often been credited with calling elite and public attention to the realities of poverty in the United States.[39] The United States educational system was roundly criticized by a Harvard President and by a free-lance bohemian.[40] The university played the key role in introducing the notions of a rich economy and an impoverished public sector (the original conception of the Affluent Society),[41] of the American inability to guide the foreign world,[42] and of redefining the mentally ill and criminals as sick people.[43] Each of these deserves study in terms of the methods by which established assumptions were challenged, the extent to which the change was overdue, and other forces in favor of the transformation of the orientation.

The relative contributions of the three main loci of unattached intellectuals—bohemia, the unaffiliated policy-research center, and the university— have not been determined and may be changing. The structural-organizational conditions of each are of some interest.

The university provides, on the one hand, the necessary socio-political conditions for generating fundamental criticism; the tenure faculty has the necessary basic autonomy from undue economic and political pressures, at least in the leading universities. The rise of the government as a main source of funds, however, has generated numerous intra-university pressures against such criticism. Rather than direct pressures on the content of the intellectual's work or life, these pressures are often subtle, involving differences in the possibilities of obtaining a summer salary, secretarial and research assistance, or travel grants.[44]

University faculty members tend to have both the training and the tools, from libraries to computers, required for the production and interpretation of new knowledge. In pre-modern periods, it was easier to fulfill the critical function in less institutionalized settings, as fewer tools were necessary; coffee houses, patrons' homes, and small magazines served it well.[45] While these have not disappeared, fundamental criticism in post-modern societies may require training and facilities that are more available at universities than on the Left Bank, in Greenwich Village, in Munich's Schwabing, or in their sociological equivalents in other countries.[46] It also seems that post-modern societies find criticism more acceptable when it appears in the guise of science or information. There appears to be little place in post-modern society for the charismatic, purely normative, true prophet.[47]

Criticism emanating from bohemia or from unaffiliated policy-research centers is often more broad-scoped and radical than much of the criticism emanating from the universities. On the average, however, it is less "professional" in both appearance and substance.[48]

The products of these centers may, however, complement more empirical work by adding a stronger evaluative component and by appealing to segments of the active publics, even when such criticisms are less attuned to the elites. There seems also to be a tense but productive relationship between these centers and the universities, in that the centers act as the critics of the university in general and reinforce its critical function in particular.[49] In this sense, the unaffiliated critical centers serve as a third-order reviewing unit, with the universities as second-order and the government as first-order ones.

A common fallacy is the suggestion that the critics are ineffective because there is no consensus among them about what is faulty or what needs to be done to correct it. Further, it has been argued that consensus, when it does occur, is often based on a community-of-assumptions of the intellectuals which is no more tested and often no more testable than that of the political elites.[50] We suggest, on the contrary, first, that intellectuals' communities-of-assumptions are *relatively* more open to innovative interpretation and empirical testing than political ones or those of the public, because of the institutionalization of the value of truth and because the pressure of extrinsic interests and norms is relatively less. (There is, however, one factor which works in the opposite direction: Political elites are held accountable, in the long run, for the consequences of their positions, while this is much less true for the unaffiliated intellectuals.)

...consensus among intellectuals is not a prerequisite for the effective discharge of their critical function, which requires that the established communities-of-assumptions be challenged and that alternative ones be provided. It is not the function of the intellectuals to provide consensus, an agreed-upon line of action; *that* is the function of the political process. The intellectuals' role is to pry open the walls in which society tends to box itself and suggest various directions which the freed prisoner may take; which ones are preferred is to be decided by the community as a whole. To demand consensus from the intellectuals is to assume that the questions involved can be selected empirically and rationally while actually they are, in part, normative issues, and to assume that they can be settled by an elite while actually they must be worked out in societal consensus-building. The intellectuals enrich the debate, both on the elite and the public level, and often are needed to keep it alive, but this can be fully achieved, even better achieved, without consensus among the intellectuals.

The Societal Input of Criticism. The active orientation is most effectively sustained if societal decision-making, inevitably a political process, is subject to fundamental criticism *and* to empirical reality-testing. The degree to which the services of the political, critical, and empirical functions are articulated is considerably affected by the relations among three kinds of societal elites—political, intellectual, and expert. The service of any one function is not limited to any one kind of elite; political elites are somewhat concerned with empirical considerations, experts deal with fundamental criticisms to some extent, and intellectuals take empirical matters into account. Still, there is a tendency toward specialization, with each function being fulfilled largely by one of the three kinds of elites.

It seems productive to view the relations among the three elites as a three-filter screen through which new contextuating orientations are projected to guide societal efforts. The intellectual filter is the most open one; ideas are approved with comparative ease, especially if they are not in open conflict with a major body of known facts. Intellectual screening is more evaluative than empirical and more concerned with value-relevancy and "coverage" than with reality-testing. The expert filter is considerably less open and admits mainly ideas that withstand some kind of empirical test.[51] The political filter is the most narrow for it allows only one or two alternatives to pass through it—those which the elite will seek to implement.

The analytic schema whereby the three filters can be distinguished serves as only the first step in a morphological study of the input of fundamental criticism into societal decision making. This is the case because societal actors vary significantly in the degree to which (a) the filters are structurally segregated and their respective functional needs served; (b) the units which provide the major structural anchorages for the three filters are protected from interpenetration; and (c) a balance is kept among the three.

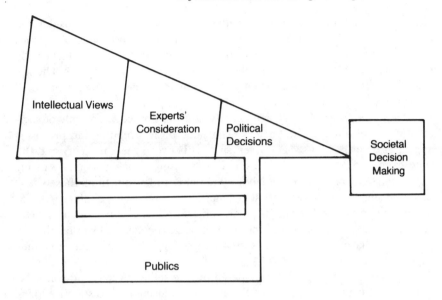

Limited structural segregation of the three filters is most evident in pre-modern societies in which the political elites attempted to carry out all three functions (though some delegation of the critical and expert functions to members of the courts' lay and clerical staff did occur).[52] In modern and post-modern societies, a lack of resources or other facilities so that the units in service of a given filter cannot function adequately poses greater difficulties than an insufficient segregation of the filters. Thus, as suggested above, the critical function cannot be carried out effectively if the unaffiliated intellectuals are not granted economic security, immunity from political and societal pressures, and access to the two other kinds of elites. Underdeveloped nations are often more deficient with respect to the second filter than with regard to the first or the third; ideas, thus, travel readily from the intellectual to the political elites without sufficient expert screening and, hence, empirical testing.

Even when the three kinds of units are segregated and resources are provided for them, some mixing of functions and interpenetration are to be expected. Thus, seeking to participate in or affect the societal evaluative trends, political elites penetrate into the intellectual realm; unaffiliated intellectuals become "co-opted" by or actually share in the margins of power; and experts get involved in intellectual criticism and anticipation of political considerations, pre-empting both roles and, to a degree, neglecting their own.[53] In comparison to earlier societies, which suffered from considerable political penetration into the expert realm, pluralistic post-modern societies often suffer from a *lack* of sufficient political guidance for experts (especially in the relations between civilian political elites and military experts). The active society requires the reassertion of the primacy of political guidance over the experts' view of the world.

The three filters' funnel significantly affects knowledge not only of society but also of other societal actors. The same basic structure and processes appear also on the sub-societal level, such as between the University and the state capital in Madison, Wisconsin; East Lansing, Michigan; and Austin, Texas; the body of a church; a labor movement, and so on. In all these situations, we suggest, a division of labor among the three kinds of elites is functional, and some conflict among them is inevitable and also functional. The critic, like the true prophet, cannot expect to be the court's favorite; the expert cannot have the intellectual's prerogatives; and the policy maker cannot hope to please both.

The critical function is not hindered by inter-elite tensions and conflicts; instead such conflict may prevent the elites from losing their distinctive identities and the members from excessive interaction across elite boundaries rather than with members of their own elite. Tension and conflict become dysfunctional only when they rise to a level at which access is blocked and the conditions for work and for autonomy are undermined.

The Roles of the Publics. The interaction among the three kinds of elites does not take place in a societal vacuum; elites affect and are affected by the publics, especially the active ones. First, the deliberations of the political elites are inevitably affected by the publics' views of reality and their subsequent evaluations, and therefore by the degree to which the new expert findings and intellectual orientations (evaluations) are accepted.[54] Second, because the publics affect the structural relations among the three kinds of elites, the degrees to which there are tolerance for intellectuals, respect for experts, and support for the elites in power have a contextuating impact on both the actions and relations of the three kinds of elites.

Basically, there are two channels from the loci of societal criticism to the loci of political power. One is contact between intellectuals and political elites, either direct or mediated by experts.[55] Second, there is the more indirect route of appeals to the publics and to the political opposition—i.e., attempts to transform the communities-of-assumptions of the publics and to mobilize political support in order to force a change in the assumptions of the political elites.

The more institutionalized politics are, the more the first channel would be expected to be open, although we expect to find strong barriers en route in even the most effectively institutionalized political system because the political filter must be much more narrow than the intellectual one. Societies can be compared according to their relative reliance on the two channels; as a smaller amount of criticism travels through one channel, a greater burden is placed on the other. For instance, the United States may be seen as having moved toward a greater opening of the direct channel if the last generations of the modern age are compared with the first post-modern generation, though different national administrations can be ranked differently on this account.[56] But at the same time, the two channels should not be viewed as mutually exclusive alternatives; progress in one is often related to progress in the other. The public paid more attention to Michael Harrington's book about poverty in the United States after it became known that President Kennedy had read it with interest.[57]

The foregoing discussion of the interaction between the elites and the membership of societal units...focused upon publics rather than collectivities and political organizations. The publics referred to here are often the members of one or more collectivities and their political organizations. "Active public," then, refers to the active members of a collectivity, and "passive public" refers to the other members. Active and passive publics are often bound together in one collectivity and/or political organization, with the more active members leading the more passive ones. The analysis of knowledge processes, though, can proceed, as we attempt here, without specifying at each step the morphological bases of each public and of the relations among them, because the knowledge held by the members, we suggest, is relatively more independent of structural position and organizational activation than their values and especially their interests. Therefore we have deferred analysis of the relations among elites, collectivities, and political organizations until the concepts of commitment and power are introduced.

Our purpose here is not to construct a full macro-sociology of knowledge but to illustrate the directions in which it may evolve if a societal guidance perspective is maintained. The three kinds of filters and the relations among the units that specialize in their services and between these units and the publics seem to be the most essential components to be considered. Two conclusions seem to emerge from this preliminary exploration: (a) The often-repeated emphasis on the need for pluralism in the production of societal knowledge points to only one (though major) functional prerequisite for an active society. The systematic provision for the three filters—intellectual, expert, and political—and for their articulation with each other and with the publics is essential. (b) A society that is free to test its ideas and to try out fundamentally new ones cannot be restricted to approaching the world and itself merely through the narrow political filter of the elites in power: such a society must provide for fundamental criticism and be open to it. Such a self-critical society—active in its use of societal knowledge—cannot be brought about unless the post-modern society is transformed by a fuller exercise of the critical function.

Notes

[1] Cf. Tom Burns who proceeds in the opposite direction, using the theory of the state to study corporations. "Micropolitics: Mechanisms of Institutional Change," *Administrative Science Quarterly*, Vol. 6 (1961), pp. 257-281.

[2] Leonard Reissman, "A Study of Role Conceptions in Bureaucracy," *Social Forces*, Vol. 27 (1949), pp. 305-310. See also Etzioni, *Modern Organizations, op. cit.*, pp. 77 ff.

[3] This is a central thesis of Don K. Price, *The Scientific Estate* (Cambridge, Mass.: Belknap Press of Harvard University Press, 1965).

[4] Harold L. Wilensky, *Intellectuals in Labor Unions* (New York: Free Press, 1956).

[5] Hilsman, *Strategic Intelligence and National Decisions, op. cit.*, Ch. VIII; Robert Dubin (ed.), *Human Relations in Administration* (Englewood Cliffs, N.J.: Prentice-Hall, 1951), pp. 121-123; and William Kornhauser with the assistance of Warren O. Hagstrom, *Scientists in Industry: Conflict and Accommodation* (Berkeley: University of California, 1962).

[6] See Fred W. Riggs, *Administration in Developing Countries: The Theory of Prismatic Society* (Boston: Houghton Mifflin, 1964), pp. 21-23; and James R. Townsend, *Political Participation in Communist China* (Berkeley: University of California Press, 1967), p. 215.

[7] "There is a division of labor between science, which seeks truth, and politics, which is concerned with power, purpose, and responsibility," Kenneth E. Boulding, summarizing Don K. Price, in a review of his book in *Scientific American*, Vol. 214 (April, 1966), pp. 131-134, quoted from p. 131.

[8] See Sheldon S. Wolin, *Politics and Vision: Continuity and Innovation in Western Political Thought* (Boston: Little, Brown, 1960), pp. 352-434.

[9] On the point of relations, see Riggs, *Administration in Developing Countries....*, *op. cit.*, pp. 63-67, and esp. pp. 436-441.

[10] Data on federal obligations for basic research and applied research and development are for fiscal year 1965 and are taken from the National Science Foundation Report, *Federal Funds for Research, Development, and Other Scientific Activities: Fiscal Years 1965, 1966 and 1967*, Vol. 15 (Washington, D.C.: Government Printing Office, 1966), p. 77, Table C-1. The figure for applied research and development excludes plant costs.

[11] Leo A. Orleans, "Research and Development in Communist China," *Science*, Vol. 157 (July 28, 1967), pp. 392-400. See also P. H. Abelson et al., "Science in the U.S.S.R.," *Science*, Vol. 126 (Nov. 19, 1957), pp. 1095-1099.

[12] See Bernard Barber, *Science and the Social Order* (New York: Collier, 1962), pp. 115-120.

[13] For the main works on this subject, see Don K. Price, *Government and Science* (New York: New York University Press, 1954), pp. 134 ff.; Ralph E. Lapp, *The New Priesthood* (New York: Harper & Row, 1965), *passim*; and Wiesner, *Where Science and Politics Meet, op. cit.* See also C. P. Snow, *Science and Government* (Cambridge, Mass.: Harvard University Press, 1961) and Robert Gilpin and Christopher Wright (eds.), *Scientists and National Policy-Making* (New York: Columbia University Press, 1964), esp. essays by Bernard Brodie and Warner R. Schilling.

[14] On the effects of fallout, for instance, compare Herman Kahn, *On Thermonuclear War* (Princeton, N.J.: Princeton University Press, 1961), pp. 3-116 with Robert A. Dentler and Phillips Cutright, *Hostage America* (Boston: Beacon Press, 1963), pp. 1-76. On the likelihood of nuclear war, C. P. Snow predicted in 1960 that "Within, at the most, ten years, some of these bombs are going off. I am saying this as responsibly as I can. That is the certainty...a certainty of disaster." *The New York Times*, December 14, 1960, p. 14. Kahn's estimate is much lower. See *On Thermonuclear War, op. cit.*, pp. 208-209.

[15] For a fine study which reveals the inadequacy of the segregation model, see: Bruce L. R. Smith's description of the very active role which RAND plays in Air Force policy formation. "Strategic Expertise and National Security Policy: A Case Study," in John D. Montgomery and Arthur Smithies (eds.), *Public Policy*, Vol. 13 (1964), pp. 69-106. See also Albert Wohlstetter, "Scientists, Seers, and Strategy," *Foreign Affairs*, Vol. 41 (1963), pp. 466-478, and Edward S. Flash, Jr., "The Knowledge-Power Relationship," in his *Economic Advice and Presidential Leadership* (New York: Columbia University Press, 1965), pp. 308-325. Flash deals with the political advice the United States economists gave United States presidents. For additional elaboration of our position, see Amitai Etzioni, "Knowledge and Power," *The New York Times Book Review*, July 31, 1966.

[16] On the need to promote new knowledge, even if valid, see discussion of the fluoridation fights and the failure to reduce smoking on a wide scale. For a study and references to other works, see Donald B. Rosenthal and Robert L. Crain, "Executive Leadership and Community Innovation: the Fluoridation Experience," *Urban Affairs Quarterly*, Vol. 1 (March, 1966), pp. 39-57. See also Stanley Joel Reiser, "Smoking and Health: The Congress and Causality," in Sanford A. Lakoff (ed.), *Knowledge and Power* (New York: Free Press, 1966), pp. 293-311.

[17] "The sophisticated public servant knows not only that there is 'another' point of view on almost any scientific issue which bears on an important policy question, but he knows quite matter of factly to whom to turn to get it." Lawrence Cranberg, "Ethical Problems of Scientists," *The Educational Record*, Vol. 46 (1965), p. 289. Jerome B. Wiesner and Herbert F. York wrote an article on "National Security and the Nuclear Test Ban," *Scientific American*, Vol. 211 (Oct., 1964), pp. 27-31. In the arti-

cle they characterized themselves as "scientists," and stated that they discussed "the matter from the point of view of our country's national interest." But a reporter, specializing in science affairs, suggested that "since 1964 was an election year, one must consider this article in another light. Drs. Wiesner and York wrote for the country's most influential, semipopular technical magazine one month before an election in which the role of nuclear arms was an issue." David Warren Burkett, *Writing Science News for the Mass Media* (Houston, Texas: Gulf, 1965), pp. 3-4. He also pointed out that Wiesner was identified in the same magazine as one of two organizers of a bipartisan committee enlisting scientists and engineers in support of President Johnson. See also Nathan K. Rickles, "The Battle of the Experts," *Corrective Psychiatry and Journal of Social Therapy*, Vol. 10 (1964), pp. 232-240 and Richard J. Barber, *The Politics of Research* (Washington, D.C.: Public Affairs Press, 1966).

[18] H. L. Nieburg, *In the Name of Science* (Chicago: Quadrangle, 1966), esp. pp. 131-134.

[19] For a detailed discussion of the difficulties attendant with measuring progress in many areas of societal efforts, see Albert D. Biderman, "Social Indicators and Goals," in Raymond A. Bauer (ed.), *Social Indicators* (Cambridge, Mass.: MIT Press, 1966), pp. 68-153; see also Amitai Etzioni and Edward W. Lehman, "Some Dangers in 'Valid' Social Measurements," in Bertram Gross (ed.), *The Annals of Social and Political Sciences* (September, 1967). Vol. 373, pp. 1-15.

[20] Much material to support this statement is included in James L. Penick, Jr., et al. (eds.), *The Politics of American Science, 1939 to the Present* (Chicago: Rand McNally, 1965), see esp. pp. 34-48; 54-72; and 148-161.

[21] Wallace S. Sayre, "Scientists and American Science Policy," in Gilpin and Wright, *Scientists and National Policy-making, op. cit.*, pp. 105-106.

[22] Jacob Schmookler, *Invention and Economic Growth* (Cambridge, Mass.: Harvard University Press, 1966).

[23] A moderate level of pressure rather than a high level, it has been suggested, is more conducive to learning. James G. March and Herbert A. Simon, *Organizations* (New York: Wiley & Sons, 1958), pp. 182-184.

[24] Richard Neustadt, *Presidential Power, The Politics of Leadership* (New York: Wiley, 1960), pp. 157-158.

[25] The danger of "tabu problems" is discussed by Klaus Knorr and Oskar Morgenstern, "Conjecturing about our Military and Political Future," *University*, No. 26 (Fall, 1965), pp. 33-34.

[26] For a critique of C. Wright Mills' *The Power Elite*, see Daniel Bell, "Is There a Ruling Class in America? The Power Elite Reconsidered," in his *The End of Ideology* (New York: Free Press, 1960), pp. 43-67. See also Morris Janowitz, *The Professional Soldier* (New York: Free Press, 1960), pp. 233-255. Cf. J. Blondel, *Voters, Parties and Leaders: The Social Fabric of British Politics* (Baltimore: Penguin, rev. ed., 1965), pp. 234 ff.

[27] Humor, especially satire, is, of course, a well-known instrument of criticism. On the one hand, it is relatively "safe," i.e., allows one to criticize and live, to see another

occasion for criticism *and* to be heard ("he is just joking" or "one must be able to take it"). On the other hand, there is a danger that the humorous criticism may not be taken seriously. Criticism which becomes a form of entertainment, such as Hollywood movies about nuclear war, risks a generic danger. *Failsafe*, for instance, has much less critical value than *Dr. Strangelove* precisely because the former closely resembles conventional entertainment while the latter attempts to satirize—to shock the viewer into critical reflection. (The mad scientist and the infantile president, at the center of power, achieve this effect.)

[28] For a discussion of the role of the press as "observer," "participant," and "catalyst," see Bernard C. Cohen, *The Press and Foreign Policy* (Princeton, N.J.: Princeton University Press, 1963). On the opportunities for and limitations on thoughtful criticism and comprehensive reporting by the press, see James Reston, *The Artillery of the Press: Its Influence on American Foreign Policy* (New York: Harper & Row, 1967).

[29] For a discussion of elite newspapers in Great Britain, France, the United States, Russia, and Germany, see Ithiel de Sola Pool with the collaboration of Harold D. Lasswell, Daniel Lerner, et al., *The "Prestige Papers," A Survey of Their Editorials* (Stanford, Calif.: Stanford University Press, 1952).

[30] For a critique of American journalism in general and *The New York Times* in particular, see Irving Kristol, "The Underdeveloped Profession," *The Public Interest*, No. 6 (Winter, 1967), pp. 36-52. For *Times* Managing Editor Clifton Daniel's reply and Kristol's rejoinder, see *The Public Interest*, No. 7 (Spring, 1968), pp. 119-123. For additional discussion, see George Lichtheim, "All the News That's Fit to Print: Reflections on The New York Times," *Commentary*, Vol. 40 (September, 1965), pp. 33-46.

[31] The average circulation of *The New Republic* for a six-month period in 1966 was 120,290 while that of *The Nation* was 29,470. *Ayer Directory of Newspapers and Periodicals* (Philadelphia: Ayer & Son, Inc., 1967), pp. 190, 757. For a discussion of the limitations of these publications, see Robert Lekachman, ". . . No, But I Read the Reviews," *Columbia University Forum*, Vol. 7 (Winter, 1964), pp. 4-9. See also Louis M. Lyons, "Chain-Store Journalism," *The Reporter* (Dec. 8, 1960), pp. 60-63.

[32] For a discussion of this point and references, see Chapter 17, FNOQ, pp. 488-489, and Note 53.

[33] Philip Donham and Robert Fahey, *Congress Needs Help* (New York: Random House, 1966). For specific suggestions to overcome this weakness, see Kenneth Janda, "Information Systems for Congress," in Cornelius P. Cotter, et al., *Twelve Studies of the Organization of Congress* (Washington, D.C.: The American Enterprise Institute for Public Policy Research, 1966), pp. 415-456, and Daniel P. Moynihan, "A Crisis of Confidence?" *The Public Interest*, No. 7 (Spring, 1967), pp. 3-10.

[34] For reference, see [Amitai Etzioni, *The Active Society*, New York: Free Press, 1968], Chapter 16, Footnote 54.

[35] For discussion and some documentation of this point, see [*The Active Society*], Chapter 11 . . . pp. 268 ff.

[36] "By 1949 it was obvious that the plan was not accomplishing its purpose, and the joint committee has not functioned since then." Joseph P. Harris, *Congressional Control of Administration* (Washington, D.C.: The Brookings Institution, 1964), p. 108.

[37] For an elaboration of the distinction between intellectuals and intellect-workers, see Paul A. Baran, "The Commitment of the Intellectual," *Monthly Review,* Vol. 13 (May, 1961), pp. 8–18.

[38] Raymond Aron reluctantly concurs that "there remains...a basis of truth in the hackneyed notion, which has been taken up in a more subtle form by certain sociologists (J. Schumpeter, for example), of the intellectuals as revolutionaries by profession." Raymond Aron, *The Opium of the Intellectuals* (Garden City, N.Y.: Doubleday, 1957), p. 209. On similar views of the intellectuals, see George Lichtheim, "The Role of the Intellectuals," *Commentary*, Vol. 29 (1960), pp. 295–307; Edward A. Shils, "The Intellectuals and the Powers: Some Perspectives for Comparative Analysis," *Comparative Studies in Society and History,* Vol. I (1958), pp. 5–22, and by the same author, *The Intellectual Between Tradition and Modernity: The Indian Situation* (The Hague: Mouton, 1961), esp. pp. 17–21. See also Bennett M. Berger, "Sociology and the Intellectuals: An Analysis of a Stereotype," in Seymour Martin Lipset and Neal J. Smelser (eds.), *Sociology: The Progress of a Decade* (Englewood Cliffs, N.J.: Prentice-Hall, 1961), pp. 37–46.

[39] Michael Harrington's influential book is *The Other America: Poverty in the United States* (New York: Macmillan, 1962). It is reported to have called the attention of President Kennedy to the issue and to have initiated the war on poverty. See note 57 below.

[40] James B. Conant, *The American High School Today* (New York: McGraw-Hill, 1959). Paul Goodman, *Compulsory Mis-education* (New York: Horizon Press, 1964).

[41] John Kenneth Galbraith, *The Affluent Society* (Boston: Houghton Mifflin, 1958).

[42] William J. Lederer and Eugene Burdick, *The Ugly American* (New York: Norton, 1958).

[43] Gregory Zilboorg, M.D., in collaboration with George W. Henry, M.D., *A History of Medical Psychology* (New York: Norton, 1941), pp. 175–244, 479–510. See also Michel Foucault, *Madness and Civilization: A History of Insanity in the Age of Reason*, translated from the French by Richard Howard (New York: Pantheon Books, 1965), which traces the attitude of Western European Society towards madness from the Middle Ages to the beginning of the nineteenth century.

[44] Clark Kerr, *The Uses of the University* (Cambridge, Mass.: Harvard University Press, 1964), pp. 57 ff. In regard to Kerr's de-emphasis of the university's intellectual and moral identity, see Harold Taylor's review in *Commentary*, Vol. 38 (1964), pp. 68–73. For an analysis of the impact of federal financing of research on universities, see Charles V. Kidd, *American Universities and Federal Research* (Cambridge, Mass.: Belknap Press of Harvard University Press, 1959). For additional comment, see Joseph Ben-David and Awraham Zloczower, "Universities and Academic Systems in Modern Societies," *European Journal of Sociology*, Vol. 3 (1962), pp. 45–84; A. H. Halsey, "British Universities and Intellectual Life," *Universities Quarterly*, Vol. 12

(1958), pp. 141-152; A. H. Halsey, "The Changing Functions of Universities in Advanced Industrial Societies," *Harvard Educational Review*, Vol. XXX (Spring, 1960), pp. 119-127. See also Jason Epstein, "The CIA and the Intellectuals," *The New York Review of Books,* April 20, 1967, pp. 16-21.

[45] See Lewis A. Coser, *Men of Ideas: A Sociologist's View* (New York: Free Press, 1965), pp. 11 ff.

[46] For the sociological bases and limitations involved see Caroline F. Ware, *Greenwich Village, 1920-1930* (Boston: Houghton Mifflin, 1935); Malcolm Cowley, *Exile's Return* (New York: Viking, 1961); and Allen Churchill, *The Improper Bohemians: A Re-creation of Greenwich Village in Its Heyday* (New York: Dutton, 1959).

[47] Max Weber in *Ancient Judaism*, translated and edited by Hans H. Gerth and Don Martindale (New York: Free Press, 1952), analyzed the critical function of true prophets as distinct from the false, court-retained, ones. Weber's thesis of a disestablished, independent prophecy has been questioned by recent research. See Peter L. Berger, "Charisma and Religious Innovation: The Social Location of Israelite Prophecy," *American Sociological Review*, Vol. 28 (1963), pp. 940-950.

[48] Paul Goodman of the Institute of Policy Studies has suggested that television networks be decentralized "as much as possible, on any plausible principle, to municipalities, colleges, local newspapers, ad hoc associations. With many hundreds of centers of responsibility and initiative, there will occur many opportunities for direct local audience demand and participation, and for the honest and inventive to get a hearing and try to win their way." See Goodman's "The Continuing Disaster," *The New Republic*, Vol. 148 (January 26, 1963), pp. 24-26, quoted from p. 26. In a letter in reply, newscaster David Brinkley noted that with the exception of municipalities, the local groups of which Goodman spoke "are the very groups owning the television stations now—including some of the worst of them." Brinkley adds, "Does Mr. Goodman believe that, without networks, we could expect to see honest examinations of the civil rights story on stations controlled by Southern municipalities, which is to say Southern local politicians?" For Brinkley's letter, see *The New Republic,* Vol. 148 (March 23, 1963), p. 39.

Also see the exchange between Donald N. Michael of the Institute of Policy Studies, and Daniel Bell of Columbia University, over the factual basis of the alarmist approach to automation. *New York Review of Books* (Nov. 25, 1965), pp. 36-38, and *ibid.*, August 26, 1965, pp. 23-25. See also Amitai Etzioni, "Speaking of Books: Protesting with Facts and Figures," *The New York Times Book Review,* March 14, 1965, and the following exchange with Paul Goodman (*ibid.*, April 4, 1965). On the need for "reasoned criticism in the fullest sense," see Christopher Lasch's "The Banality of Liberalism," a review of Hans Morgenthau's *The Crossroad Papers* and Paul Goodman's (ed.), *Seeds of Liberation* in *New York Review of Books* (September 30, 1965), pp. 4-6. For critiques of Lasch's review, see letters to the editor by Paul Seabury, John F. Withey, and E. Jeffrey Ludwig and Lasch's reply, *ibid.*, November 11, 1965, pp. 36-37.

[49] See Arthur A. Cohen (ed.), *Humanistic Education and Western Civilization:*

Essays for Robert M. Hutchins (New York: Holt, Rinehart & Winston, 1964), esp. essays by David Riesman and Arthur A. Cohen. Robert M. Hutchins, *The University of Utopia* (Chicago: University of Chicago Press, 1953).

[50] Barber, "Resistance by Scientists to Scientific Discovery," *op. cit.*, pp. 596–602.

[51] Methodology is to a considerable extent also a part of a community-of-assumptions, as different communities of experts make divergent assumptions as to what constitutes validation. For instance, propositions which psychiatrists consider as well-tested, experimental psychologists hardly view as tested at all. See, for example, H. J. Eysenck, "The Effects of Psychotherapy: An Evaluation," *Journal of Consulting Psychology*, Vol. 16 (1952), pp. 319–324.

[52] See, for example, T. F. Tout, "The Emergence of a Bureaucracy," in Robert K. Merton, Ailsa P. Gray, Barbara Hockey, and Hanan C. Selvin (eds.), *Reader in Bureaucracy* (New York: Free Press, 1952), pp. 68–79.

[53] See Harold K. Jacobson and Eric Stein, *Diplomats, Scientists, and Politicians* (Ann Arbor, Mich.: University of Michigan Press, 1966). See Wiesner, *Where Science and Politics Meet, op. cit.*, and Barber, *The Politics of Research, op. cit.* [Note 17]. On the mobilization of a group of scientists in an attempt to prevent the dropping of the first atomic bomb, see James R. Newman, "Big Science, Bad Science," *New York Review of Books*, August 5, 1965, pp. 10–12. See also footnote 55.

[54] The dynamics of this process were discussed...in Chapter 7 [*The Active Society*].

[55] On this point, see Adam Yarmolinsky, "Shadow and Substance in Politics (2): Ideas Into Programs," *The Public Interest*, No. 2 (Winter, 1966), pp. 70–79. For an intellectual's interpretation of the problems of Negro family life and the ramifications of his report in both governmental and non-governmental circles alike, see Lee Rainwater and William L. Yancey, *The Moynihan Report and the Politics of Controversy* (Cambridge, Mass.: Massachusetts Institute of Technology Press, 1967); for more discussion of the same point, see Cecil H. Uyehara, "Scientific Advice and the Nuclear Test Ban Treaty," in Lakoff, *Knowledge and Power: Essays on Science and Government, op. cit.*, pp. 112–161, and Francis L. Loewenheim (ed.), *The Historian and the Diplomat: The Role of History and Historians in American Foreign Policy* (New York: Harper & Row, 1967). Joan W. Moore and Burton M. Moore, "The Role of the Scientific Elite in the Decision to Use the Atomic Bomb," *Social Problems*, Vol. 6 (Summer, 1958), pp. 78–85. See also note 53.

[56] Discussing the role of intellectuals, Seymour Martin Lipset cites *Harper's* Editor John Fischer's comment that "The Eisenhower administration employs more professors than the New Deal ever did." See Lipset's *Political Man: The Social Bases of Politics* (Garden City, N.Y.: Doubleday, 1960), p. 333.

[57] Arthur M. Schlesinger, Jr., *A Thousand Days, op cit.*, pp. 667 ff.

Bureaucracy, Technology, and Knowledge Management*

Nicholas Henry

It is remarkable how unappreciated the significance of the bureaucracy is among America's political thinkers. It is evident from reading *The Federalist* that the country's most original contributors to the world's political literature did not anticipate the rise of the public bureaucracy, much less its institutional dominance in the public policy-making process, nor the fact that by the middle of the 20th century there would be more Americans earning their livelihoods by working for it than there were Americans living when the Constitution was written. Less understandably, our current generation of political thinkers—those who are ensconced in the political science departments of universities and colleges—also have failed to appreciate the importance of the public bureaucracy, despite its awesome magnitude, its growing administrative reliance on the techniques of social science, and its financial support of their own academic research. By way of indication, a recent survey of the five major political science journals of a non-specialized nature revealed that only four per cent of all the articles published in them during an 11-year period between 1960 and 1970 dealt with "bureaucratic politics," which was the only one of 15 categories concerned with the public bureaucracy.[1] Moreover, the four per cent figure appeared to be declining over time.

Is there a reason behind the disregard for and disinterest in the public bureaucracy that is exhibited by the bulk of modern political thinkers? One can conjure several possibilities, including that of rampant stupidity, but in this article I shall offer only one hypothesis. It is: The bureaucracy, as a public policy-making institution in a technological society, is antithetical to the pluralist paradigm of the democratic process originally conceived by James Madison and perpetrated by most of his intellectual progeny in political science departments. More pointedly, the Madisonian notion that the interests of the public will be best served in a democracy by the policy of

*Reprinted from *Public Administration Review*, Vol. 35, pp. 572–578, November/December 1975. Copyright © 1975 by The American Society for Public Administration, 1225 Connecticut Avenue, N.W., Washington, D.C. All rights reserved.

compromise emerging from the contentions of interest groups (which "represent" those "publics" affected by the policy resolution) is of dubious validity in a techno-bureaucratic state. In brief, two overwhelming factors of modern culture—technology and bureaucracy—undermine what one political scientist has described as the "hydraulic theory" of the democratic process.[2] The hydraulic thesis constitutes the basis of the pluralist paradigm shared by mainstream political scientists, and it is apparent, given the short shrift accorded the public bureaucracy, public administration, and technology assessment by political scientists as objects of study, that few scholars interested in politics are capable of denying interest-group pluralism as an apologia for how the public interest is achieved in a democracy.

Perhaps the hydraulic thesis still "works" (*i.e.*, interest group compromises are indeed in the public interest) in legislative and adjudicative policy settings, and perhaps its "provability" in these settings accounts for why political scientists much prefer studying voting behavior, legislative committees, lobbyists, and the judicial process in contrast to "bureaucratic politics." But in order to "work," the hydraulic thesis by necessity rests on at least three implicit assumptions concerning the political process: that (1) all publics affected by a particular policy question are aware that its resolution will affect them, (2) all affected publics have a reasonable understanding of the policy question, and (3) if the affected publics are unaware of the policy question, it is only a matter of time before they find out about it and join in the policy-making fray in order to protect their interests.

These assumptions, combined with some strictly enforced rules of the game, such as freedom of the press, provided a rational foundation on which the hydraulic thesis could be constructed as an explanation of the policy-making process in a democracy—at least in the 18th century. Yet, in the 20th century, the interlaced forces of bureaucracy and technology deny these assumptions. For its part, bureaucracy denies assumptions #1 and #3. The well-documented penchant of bureaucrats for secrecy,[3] and the mounting evidence that neither bureaucrats nor the citizenry always act on their "most rational" self-interest[4] undercut the premises that people *know*, that people are *informed*, of what matters, and that they will act on what matters.

Technology denies assumption #2. Technology, or what is perceived by the people as being science "applied" for the rectification of their problems, is not simple. Technology is complicated, and it becomes more complicated when, as public bureaucrats are wont to do, technology is cast into the context of systems analysis in an effort to inhibit the proliferation of its socially dysfunctional side effects. Technology and its social assessment, by their very complexity, deny understanding to the people of what their problems are.

Such concepts as "technocracy," "professionalism," "politics of expertise," "technipol," "systems politics," "noetic authority," and "participatory technology" represent intellectual efforts to address the enormous political problems of bureaucracy and technology not considered in the Madisonian pluralist paradigm—nor, for that matter, in the Constitution that Madison largely wrote. Yet, if democratic political processes are to be retained under the Constitution, bureaucracy and technology must be integrated into its framework, for the twin factors may be, in their essence, antithetical to democratic values.

Bureaucracy, Technology, and Public Administration

If we accept the argument that bureaucracy and technology are at best "nonconstitutional" and at worst unconstitutional, at least in terms of the social pathologies to which they give birth, then we must turn to a consideration of the problem of how to convey a sense of the public interest to these twin phenomena. Traditionally, of course, bureaucracy and technology have been perceived as being entities of a totally empirical (*i.e.*, anormative) nature. Ironically, advocates of bureaucracy and technology have seen their mutual empiricism as "good," in that their innate "objectivity" resulted in a more rational society. Max Weber, for example, perceived monocratic, *wertfrei* bureaucracy as the only genuine control over the "Kadijustice" whirling throughout the romantic, irrational society beyond the bureaucracy's confines, while Buckminster Fuller and Pierre Teilhard de Chardin have embraced the omnirationality of technology as a liberating force for mankind. In the late 1940s, however, bureaucracy as an apolitical and amoral concept came under its first serious questioning by intellectuals, and by the early 1960s technology as a value-free entity was being similarly challenged.[5]

Public administration as an academic field responded to these two largely discrete challenges in two discrete ways. We shall consider the problem of a political bureaucracy first. When it became commonly accepted by public administrationists that the "politics/administration dichotomy" was no longer a functional distinction, and that bureaucracy did indeed concern itself with political and normative dimensions, scholars in the field responded by becoming, or trying to become, mainstream political scientists. The concept of "the administrative process" was redefined into terms of "the political process," the "nuts and bolts" of budgeting evolved into "the politics of the budgetary process," public personnel administration likely as not became "bureaucratic politics," and so it went. While there was an essential truth in this new orientation of public administration during the

1950s and 1960s, there were at least two dysfunctions. One dysfunction was that public administration as a field lost its definitional identity. Writings during the period spoke of public administration as an "emphasis" or as a "synonym" of political science.[6] Simply in terms of academic prestige, public administration plummeted to a new nadir.[7]

The other dysfunction was related but more profound, and goes back to our original thesis concerning the questionable validity of the pluralist political paradigm in bureaucratic and technological societies. In their effort to be "just as good" as any other subfield of political science, public administrationists adopted the implicit assumption of the pluralist concept: i.e., that the infighting and pressures of competing special interests would result in a public policy approximating the public interest because all citizens and policy makers germane to the policy question were adequately knowledgeable about the policy issues. While public administrationists undoubtedly were correct in their new-found belief that values and politics were at the center of the bureaucratic process, it was a dubious case at best that the hydraulic thesis of the political process either explained how public policies were made in bureaucracies or justified the resulting policy outputs as exemplary of the best of all possible worlds.

While public administrationists responded to the conceptual dilemma of a political bureaucracy by plunging into mainstream political science (and banging their skulls on a few rocks in the process), they reacted to the intellectual problem of a politicized technology quite differently. Instead of merging, they separated, and became increasingly interested in the broadly interdisciplinary topic of "science, technology, and public policy." By the late 1960s, there were about 50 such programs and they were situated for the most part in the top academic institutions of the country. It was largely this new focus of science, technology, and public policy that gave those public administrationists connected with political science departments any claim to intellectual distinction during the 1960s, and helped offset the loss of a disciplinary identity that then beset public administration as a result of its abandonment of the politics/administration dichotomy. This renewed identity came in part because the focus of science, technology, and public policy did not (and does not) rely conceptually on the hydraulic thesis favored by political science. Instead, the focus is elitist rather than pluralist, synthesizing rather than specializing, and hierarchical rather than communal.

Recently, those public administrationists who have been concerned with the impact of science and technology on society have become increasingly aware that the core issues of the technology/polity interface can be understood more profoundly when cast in terms of information and knowledge. As economist Donald M. Lamberton has observed, at least three new conceptual insights have served to generate a realization among public administrationists that the role of knowledge in politics is closer to the theoretical essence of bureaucratic policy making in technological societies than is the more amorphous concept of science and public policy. These realizations all are reflective of a broader concept of information. First, knowledge from the social sciences was seen as being as relevant as knowledge from science and technology; second, a systems approach was perceived as being needed; and third, "attention focussed on the new information technologies—for example, computers and satellites—which seemed to symbolize the movement of society into a new industrial revolution: the information revolution."[8]

In short, a diad of forces has pushed the field, broadly conceived, to (1) an implicit rejection of the hydraulic thesis of the public policy-making process in the bureaucracies of technological societies, and (2) more specifically framed, an acceptance of the notion that an understanding of the distribution of knowledge in the bureaucracy and the polity goes far in comprehending how bureaucratic decisions are made in technological societies. The emergence of the phrase "knowledge management" in public administration circles—a term inclusive of such phenomena as new information technologies, the rationalist policy-making model, "public interest law" and "public interest science," consumerism, technology assessment, environmental administration, and bureaucratic secrecy, as well as more traditional concerns of the discipline—expresses this combined rejection and acceptance.

Two Foci of Knowledge Management: Policy and Education

While the emerging focus of knowledge management can take and is taking a plethora of directions, there are two broad orientations that appear to be of particular and immediate import to the field of public administration that I would like to consider here. One is the area of public policies for knowledge management. This orientation is "external" in the sense that it chiefly concerns the public organization's relations with its society. The other is the area of higher education for public administration. This orientation is "internal" in that it principally deals with the formulation of the decision premises (which are, by definition, knowledge-based) of future public administrators.

Public Policies for Knowledge Management (Or, Was President Nixon an Esoteric Box?). In this orientation we are considering questions of informational equity. In the rubric of knowledge management, who *knows* what assumes more importance in the bureaucratic decision-making process than who *has* what. In the most profound sense of that overworked cliché, knowledge is power. Hence, we find ourselves studying the dynamics of such public policies as the Copyright Act, the Administrative Procedure Act, the Freedom of Information Act, the National Environmental Policy Act, the Fair Credit Reporting Act, and the Federal Advisory Committee Act, as well as the sundry agency policies dealing with computers, security, and citizen participation in organizational decision making. The commonality in all these policies (as well as many others) is that they rest on the assumption that those with knowledge have power, and, as policies, they attempt to redistribute knowledge throughout the polity in such a way as to give a greater number of citizens more knowledge with which they can influence the policy-making process.

Public administrationists can and should have a greater social voice in prescribing...public policy for knowledge management. To achieve this, they would be well advised to give greater recognition to the role of information theory in their analysis of the general polity. Cybernetist Stafford Beer provides a useful insight along these lines. Beer contends that knowledge itself is distributed throughout a social network of "esoteric boxes." The esoteric box is "an identifiable social institution," such as a firm, a profession, or a social service, that is "internally autonomous and self-organizing and self-regulating." Esoteric boxes have their own histories and recondite mores; they process things (including people), yet remain unaltered themselves because each esoteric box "is a strongly robust system in equilibrium." Esoteric boxes, rather than responding to changes in the religious, legal, and moral framework around them, instead "are putting up the shutters and seeking to maintain themselves as integral systems.... This will not work." Linkages between esoteric boxes (e.g., credit systems and balances of payments, which comprise linkages between the "boxes" of economics, banking, and business) are as tenuous and unstable as the boxes themselves are robust and stable. This situation has contributed to a condition of "social clonus," or, put vividly, political and administrative spasticity. Because our esoteric boxes are putting up their shutters and keeping out external stimuli, society is developing "wildly overreactive reflexes" to those stimuli that do manage to slip inside. (Consider, in light of Beer's analysis, the White House and its reaction to Watergate.) Thus, any knowledge management policy must be metasystemic in design; that is, it must be constructed in such a fashion as to define and institutionalize the "strings and networks" between esoteric boxes in order to bring about a degree of social stability.[9]

In essence, Beer's analysis represents a rejection of the hydraulic thesis of public policy making from the standpoint of information theory. Each "esoteric box" constitutes a system closed to pressures from the "outside," and the "outside" in this construct means all the other institutions and interests of society. The tighter the boxes "put up their shutters," the more the polity becomes atomized at an institutional and professional level. Hence, the topic of public policies for knowledge management becomes a matter of some significance in any academic effort to make government more responsive to the governed. We are talking about, to borrow Yehezkel Dror's term, "metapolicy," or policies for policy-making procedures,[10] but on an extremely broad scale.

Education for Public Administration. Perhaps a facet of knowledge management even more germane to public administrationists than that of prescribing for public policy is the education of public administrators, if for no other reason than education represents an area in which the efforts of scholars can be felt with greater immediacy. While the subject of education for the public service is elusive, it is reasonable to argue that the concept of knowledge in public administration is fundamentally different in kind from the concept of knowledge prevalent in the more traditional academic disciplines. The traditional concept of knowledge in the university is one of specialization. Public administration must, by necessity, break with this interpretation in order to offer a viable curriculum to public decision makers. The acquisition of knowledge in public administration must be perceived as a synthesizing exercise rather than as a specializing one. To do otherwise is simply to deny the validity not only of information theory as it pertains to the administration of society, but the ecological concepts extant in the physical sciences as well.

In an insightful essay on information and citizen participation that is reflective of Beer's analysis, Hazel Henderson contends that,

All this uncoordinated institutional activity in the United States today is based on the atomistic Cartesian view of the world which has held sway in our minds for three centuries. This Cartesian world view is predicated on the idea that we can comprehend whole systems by analyzing their parts. This has led not only to the growth of narrow-purpose structures and reductionism in our academic disciplines, but has in turn over-rewarded analysis, while discouraging synthesis...[and] fostered unrealistic mental dichotomies....This Cartesian view has colored all our perceptions and caused us to focus on objects and entities, while ignoring their fields of interplay....We are now witnessing this collapse of policies based on this Cartesian world view.[11]

If Henderson is correct, and I think she is, then public administration must adopt forthrightly a holistic concept of the meaning of knowledge in order to help rebuild those public policies that are tumbling down because they are constructed on a narrow and tottering conceptual foundation. This means, in effect, rejecting the specialized notion of knowledge extant not only in political science (along with its hydraulic interpretation of the political process), but which also prevails in the great majority of university departments.

In making the case that public administration must integrate a systemic concept of knowledge into its curricular design, I am not advocating that public administrationists "farm out" their students to pertinent courses in other parts of the university, such as social psychology and business management. While there is a limited place in public administration programs for such curricular techniques, at least in those programs not situated in autonomous schools of public affairs, it is far more vital that the field undertake the task of interpreting and redefining knowledge from many disciplines in terms useful to public administrators and to the public. Herbert Simon urged almost a quarter century ago that this exercise be started in the field, and his argument remains valid—particularly so in its implicit definition of knowledge and its management.[12]

I have suggested in this article that public administration is a unique field, and that a key to its uniqueness lies in its conception of the role knowledge plays in the bureaucratic policy-making process in technological societies. I have contended that bureaucracy and technology are overriding facts of American life in the 20th century, and that the notion of "knowledge management" provides a useful intellectual perspective in analyzing the public's problems as they relate to bureaucracy and technology.

It is not yet clear that all public administrationists recognize and value the uniqueness of their own enterprise. Recent texts in the field relate more to political science and its underlying hydraulic paradigm than to the distinctive variables of bureaucracy, technology, and holistic knowledge.[13] But, if public administration is to be responsive and responsible to its society, it must capitalize on its own uniqueness. Knowledge management is one intellectual tool for beginning this task.

Notes

[1]Jack L. Walker, "Brother, Can You Paradigm?" *PS,* Vol. 5 (Fall 1972), pp. 419–422.

[2]Harmon Ziegler relies on this term in his *Interest Groups in American Society* (Englewood Cliffs, N.J.: Prentice-Hall, 1964). There are, of course, exceptions among political scientists to the hydraulic theory of power conception of the policy-making

process. An example of note is Michael Parenti's "Power and Pluralism: A View from the Bottom," *Journal of Politics*, Vol. 32 (August 1970), pp. 501–530. In this case, however, the exception proves the rule.

[3]Max Weber argued some 70 years ago that "Every bureaucracy seeks to increase the superiority of the professionally informed by keeping their knowledge and intentions secret...in so far as it can, it hides its knowledge and action from criticism." The phenomena of Watergate and the Pentagon Papers would appear to be ample evidence of the continuing validity of Weber's point although more updated interpretations of the pathology of bureaucratic secrecy may be found in Harold L. Wilensky, *Organizational Intelligence: Knowledge and Policy in Government and Industry* (New York: Basic Books, 1967), and David Wise, *The Politics of Lying: Government Deception, Secrecy, and Power* (New York: Random House, 1973). The quotation from Weber can be found in Max Weber, *From Max Weber: Essays in Sociology*, edited and translated by H. H. Gerth and C. Wright Mills (New York: Oxford University Press, 1946), p. 233.

[4]The realization that people behave in ways which indicate that there may be more to life than a series of political economies constitutes, of course, a major hypothesis of 20th-century social science and an implicit rejection of Madison's view of man as a political actor; that is, as an omnirational "economic man." Herbert Simon has cast this insight into organizational terms with his "administrative man," who was a cross between "economic man" and "Freudian man." See his classic, *Administrative Behavior: A Study of Decision-Making Processes in Administration Organization*, 2nd ed. (New York: Free Press, 1959). In terms of those concerns favored by political scientists, the numerous public opinion and voting behavior studies are among the most reflective of the idea that people do not always act "rationally." See, for example, the major work by Angus Campbell et al., *The American Voter* (New York: John Wiley, 1964).

[5]As I note later in the article, this questioning of the bureaucracy as an apolitical institution assumed the form of an intellectual attack on the traditional "politics/administration dichotomy," which then was a principal defining pillar of public administration as an academic field. Notable contributions in this attack during the late 1940s were John Merriman Gaus (ed.), *Reflections on Public Administration* (Tuscaloosa: University of Alabama Press, 1947); Robert H. Dahl, "The Science of Public Administration: Three Problems," *Public Administrative Review*, Vol. 7 (Winter 1947), pp. 1–11; Fritz von Marstein-Marx (ed.), *Elements of Public Administration* (Englewood Cliffs, N.J.: Prentice-Hall, 1946); Dwight Waldo, *The Administrative State* (New York: Ronald, 1948); and Simon, *op. cit.* The notion that technology was value-free came under the gun during the early 1960s (although, of course, anti-technological rumblings can be traced back well into the 19th century). Among the more notable works in terms of their subsequent impact on current American political thought that appeared during this period are: Jacques Ellul, *The Technological Society*, translated by John Wilkinson (New York: Knopf, 1964); Pierre Teilhard de Chardin, *The Future of Man* (London: Fontana Books, 1964); Donald N. Michael, *The Next Generation* (New York: Vintage, 1964); Robert Gilpin and Chris-

topher Wright (eds.), *Scientists and National Policy-Making* (New York: Columbia University Press, 1964); James Lucian McCamy, *Science and Public Administration* (University, Ala.: University of Alabama Press, 1960); and Don K. Price, *The Scientific Estate* (Cambridge: Harvard University Press, 1965).

[6]A worthwhile review of this posture of public administration relative to political science is in Martin Landau, "The Concept of Decision-Making in the 'Field' of Public Administration," *Concepts and Issues in Administrative Behavior*, Sidney Mailick and Edward H. Van Ness (eds.) (Englewood Cliffs, N.J.: Prentice-Hall, 1962), pp. 1–29. Perhaps the element of public administration which most readily adopted the hydraulic thesis of power during this period was the subfield of comparative public administration, which was and is prone to examine societal phenomena beyond the confines of the bureaucracy.

[7]Dwight Waldo's searing attack on political science recounts public administration's decline of status during the 1960s. See his "Scope of the Theory of Public Administration," *Theory and Practice of Public Administration: Scope, Objectives and Methods*, James C. Charlesworth, (ed.) (Philadelphia: American Academy of Political and Social Science), 1968, pp. 1–26. In it, Waldo notes (p. 8) that "We are now hardly welcome in the house of our youth."

[8]Donald M. Lamberton, "National Information Policy," *The Annals of the American Academy of Political and Social Science*, Donald M. Lamberton (special ed.), "The Information Revolution," Vol. 412 (March 1974), pp. 147–148.

[9]Stafford Beer, "Managing Modern Complexity," *The Management of Information and Knowledge*, Panel on Science and Technology (Eleventh Meeting), Proceedings before the Committee on Science and Astronautics, U.S. House of Representatives, 91st Congress, 2nd Session, January 27, 1970, No. 15 (Washington, D.C.: U.S. Government Printing Office, 1970), pp. 60–61.

[10]Yehezkel Dror, *Public Policymaking Reexamined* (Scranton: Chandler, 1968), p. 8.

[11]Hazel Henderson, "Information and the New Movements for Citizen Participation," in Lamberton, *op. cit.*, p. 36.

[12]Herbert A. Simon, "A Comment on 'The Science of Public Administration,'" *Public Administration Review*, Vol. 7 (Summer 1947), pp. 200–203. In this relatively obscure article, Simon was impressively foreseeing about the meaning of public administration. Simon urged that, on the one hand, public administration be concerned with "prescribing for public policy," an "applied" task which would "condemn a narrow specialization in any one area of political science, or even in the whole of it, in favor of both a broad and a deep training in political science, economics, and sociology," and, on the other hand, the field seek to develop "a pure science of human behavior in organizations—and, in particular, governmental organizations," grounded in the concepts of social psychology (p. 202). This combination, Simon argued, was unique and rested on a unique, holistic concept of knowledge: "Public administration...cannot be conceived as a purely passive field that accepts the conclusions of psychiatrists and sociologists....The only really satisfactory synthesis of specialities takes place within the intricate mechanism of the individual human brain" (p. 203).

[13]Examples in this regard are: Ira Sharkansky, *Public Administration: Policy-Making in Government Agencies* (Chicago: Markham, 2nd ed., 1972); James W. Davis, Jr., *An Introduction to Public Administration: Politics, Policy, and Bureaucracy* (New York: Free Press, 1974); and John Rehfuss, *Public Administration as Political Process* (New York: Charles Scribner's Sons, 1973). All these texts relate exclusively to the political science version of the policy-making process. Interestingly, the authors appear to be cognizant of and uncomfortable about the inadequacy of this premise as a basis for a satisfactory discussion of public administration. Consider Sharkansky, who states...that his book "concentrates on those components that appear to be most relevant to the political process and that have received the most attention from political scientists" because his "primary goal is to make the study of public administration relevant and interesting for the student of political science." Similarly, Davis states..."this book represents only the political-science part of public administration...."

Additional Readings

Bell, Daniel. *The Coming of Post-Industrial Society.* New York, Basic Books, 1974.

Breed, Warren. *The Self-Guiding Society.* New York, Free Press, 1971.

Carroll, James D., and Henry, Nicholas L., eds. "A Symposium: Knowledge Management." *Public Administration Review, 35*:567–602, November/December 1975.

Deutsch, Karl W. *The Nerves of Government.* New York, Macmillan, 1966.

Drucker, Peter F. *The Age of Discontinuity.* New York, Harper and Row, 1969.

Etzioni, Amitai. *Social Problems.* Englewood Cliffs, N.J., Prentice-Hall, 1972.

Hayek, F. A. "The Use of Knowledge in Society." *American Economic Review, 35*: 519–530, 1945.

Henry, Nicholas L. *Copyright, Information Technology, Public Policy,* Part I—*Copyright-Public Policies*; Part II—*Public Policies, Information Technology.* New York, Marcel Dekker, 1976.

———. *Public Administration and Public Affairs.* Englewood Cliffs, N.J., Prentice-Hall, 1979.

Moore, Willert E., and Tumin, Melvin M. "Some Social Functions of Ignorance." *American Sociological Review, 10*:787–795, 1945.

Oettinger, Anthony. "Information Resources: Knowledge and Power in the 21st Century." *Science, 209*:191–198, July 4, 1980.

U.S. Congress, House. *Management of Information and Knowledge.* 91st Congress, 1st Session, January 1970.

Westin, Alan F. *Information Technology in a Democracy.* Cambridge, Mass., Harvard University Press, 1971.

Chapter 9

CONCLUSION AND RESOURCE GUIDE

The purpose of this book has been to explore the significance and implications of information management in public administration. We have tried to report the status of trends in diverse academic disciplines and practical interests and needs. We have been interested in raising broad issues and questions as well as strictly administrative and technical concerns. Our overall aim has been to encourage scholars and practitioners in a variety of disciplines and organizations to consider seriously the questions, issues, and concerns raised in this emerging subject.

Information management in public administration is a broad, interdisciplinary topic that demands not only specialized technical expertise but also a generalist perspective. If we have enabled the reader to develop this perspective, then we have succeeded, since the key to understanding is the ability to ask the right questions and define the problems appropriately. Before we can claim success, however, we must address several significant arguments against information management in public administration.

THE CASE AGAINST INFORMATION MANAGEMENT
IN PUBLIC ADMINISTRATION

The four arguments against the concern for information management in public administration suggest that it is not needed, is unrealistic, is too late, and is dangerous. Although we do not wish to be alarmists, we think that these arguments have some merit and that there are good reasons for concern about information management in public administration.

1. *Current information policies and practices in the public sector are adequate.*

This argument suggests that existing government policies concerning reports, files, and paperwork management, as well as approaches to managing the use of computer, word processor, reprographic, micrographic, and printing technologies, are adequate. All these technologies have developed independently for good reasons. Integrating these technical specialties into a broader context will not make it easier to manage information.

Clearly, this argument is not supported by extensive and increasing evidence, which suggests that current government information policies and practices are inadequate and create more problems than they solve. Failure to perceive the growing convergence of information technologies also has serious effects on the effectiveness of government programs. During the last 10 years, several commissions and government study groups have highlighted serious problems in paperwork; information technology; research and development; and library, scientific, and technical information management. Even a cursory reading of commission and group reports suggests the need for an integrative view of information management. Thus, evidence indicates serious deficiencies, although organizational, economic, and political interests may be more concerned with minimizing change to protect current policies.

2. *Information cannot be managed.*

This argument suggests that information cannot be managed because of its intangible and process-oriented nature. One response to this argument is empirical. Government and private efforts to manage research and development are based on the assumption that information is and can be managed. Therefore, the real issue is how well information is currently being managed. To what extent should government define the relationship of the cost of this resource to use and value? The questions raised are similar to those suggested by advocates of personnel or financial management in the early twentieth century. What methods are needed to permit information to compete effectively with other resources in the decision-making process? Should not the field of public administration treat this resource as effectively as human, financial, equipment, space, and natural resources?

3. *Is it too late to change government policies and practices in this area?*

Some persons claim that it is too late to do much about the problems because enormous operating investments and budgets are already committed to computerized information networks including communication linkages. To transform hardware, software, and procedural systems into compatible linkages, both within a single organization and between geographically dispersed units of multifaceted organizations, would be prohibitively expensive. These changes would cause such disruption in the ranks that top management would reconsider because they were afraid of causing irreversible damage to the dynamics of their organizations.

Critics point to the extraordinary sluggishness with which international, national, federal, and other efforts to standardize commonly used names, terms, abbreviations, and symbols have moved forward. Despite a decade of intensive work in the Federal Government, for example, there are only a half dozen standard codes and abbreviations for such obvious entities as the 50 states, time designations, Congressional districts, countries, metric and customary units, and a few others. Members of the many groups that labor daily in the International Standards Organization, the American National Standards Institute, and the Federal Information Processing Standards program of the National Bureau of Standards are told "We must go slowly because information technology is at the bottom of the growth and learning curves, and prematurely standardizing our communications would inhibit the flow of creative ideas."

Of course, that argument contains both truths and falsehoods. Computer and communication technologies are evolving and may have a significant impact on the economies of all nations. For example, to what extent might increased use of computers and information networks in government and industry lead to increased centralization and control over economic systems? Will computers continue to contribute to the flight of industry from central cities? What might improve the outcome of the computer's revolutionary impact on society?

We must address still another dimension before making a forecast: the human predilection for resisting innovations such as the management of information and using the bulk of paper generated to cover up inactivity (particularly in bureaucratic environments). Sometimes these are the same persons who exhort us to avoid excessive paperwork and produce lucid, concise, up-to-the-minute reports. Attempts to "manage" paperwork by reducing the opportunities to collect, move, and proliferate it must take into account the human tendency to lean on paperwork as a crutch.

4. *Information management means information manipulation and control, which will stifle creativity and open inquiry and threaten individual privacy rights.*

Although this argument is the most compelling to confront, it is based on an erroneous assumption; that is, the current situation, in which information proliferation and the inability to acquire relevant information are the rule, does more to stifle creativity and open inquiry than any attempts to manage information as a resource. Even though information manipulation that abuses individual rights and distorts the search for evidence for public problems is always possible, information management policies and practices can also *prevent* abusive control. More viable policies in government make information difficult to manipulate. Making information more easily accessible to researchers and analysts can enhance open inquiry and creativity. Clearly, whether information management will be used for unreasonable information manipulation and control depends on the values and perspectives of those who advocate change in this area.

These arguments represent the case against information management in public administration. Although they have some relevance, the case for information management in public administration has a number of compelling aspects.

As we suggested earlier, information management does not have to mean a controlled society in the sense of Orwell or Huxley, in which some persons dominate others' lives by spoon-feeding and suppressing information. We prefer the alternative, an information society in which individuals are given enough information to control their own lives and fulfill their own potential for self-growth. Effective alterations in interpersonal, intergroup, and citizen-government relationships occur only when individuals are involved in making decisions in all facets of their lives.

Author, futurist, and planning consultant Robert Theobald told a Senate panel exploring the quality of life that the United States is emerging from the industrial era into a new communications era, in which the values, laws, institutions, and styles shaped by the industrial era are fast becoming obsolete. Theobald said,

We cannot hope to deal with the issues which actually confront us in the 20th century in this way. . . . We must somehow find more effective decision-making techniques if we are to have any hope of changing the values, laws, institutions and styles which have been made obsolete by the on-going change from the industrial era to the communications era.

Theobald argued that we have reached a turning point in humanity's history; we must change from doing the things that seem directly and immediately desirable to learning how to manage the world in accordance with the realities of a finite universe. Failure to accept and act immediately on this reality, he said, "will ensure that there is continued degradation in our quality of life and an eventual breakdown in American and world socioeconomic systems."

In less grand terms, we must better educate and inform citizens of local, regional, and national issues and policies. Only in this way will a larger, informed citizenry be able to interact and participate in the democratic process effectively and intelligently.

Moreover, another goal of information management in public administration should be to encourage the citizen to read, listen, and share his thoughts and ideas with others on the issues and problems that concern them both, either as individuals or as members of some social, religious, economic, or political group. The job of information management is to make known many of these applicable approaches and techniques.

But citizen participation in the democratic process is only part of our concern. Public officials must have the data and information they need to make sound policy and effective decisions. We would certainly count officials among the first to agree with the saying, "The more you know, the more you know what you don't know."

There are many ways to express the difficulty of applying information management more effectively to the problems of public administration. We need to embark on a carefully conceived course of policy research on using modern information technologies to solve problems of policymaking and program management, including resource management. Several authors in this book touched on this topic, and we shall begin our forecast by reaffirming this important need.

The Federal Government must establish a substantial research program to apply technological advances and approaches to problems. Different approaches should be tested, including directly funded, discrete research projects and in-house programs and activities using available government-controlled resources and structures.

We must provide our administrators with tangible mechanisms to fill their information needs. The authors in this book have made several innovative suggestions in this regard. The Commission on Federal Paperwork, the Privacy Protection Study Commission, the Electronic Funds Transfer Commission, the Public Documents Commission, and other public bodies have made many recommendations regarding information management on issues such as the personal right to privacy, the public's right to know, the government's need for accurate information, and the government's obligation to meet its information needs at a minimum cost to the citizen. In addition, universities have been expanding their library and information science curricula to strengthen the interdisciplinary focus of their traditional programs by incorporating modern concepts of information management.

The focus of previously mentioned study groups was negative. The key words were "minimize burden," "protection," and so forth. Although we would certainly agree that these are imperatives in the "Information Age," we must address the positive dimensions of the "Information Explosion": How can we maximize the value of information already collected, enhance our information-seeking techniques and tools, strengthen our information-exchanging methods, and recycle our tremendous information investments? Those problems, we contend, are the real challenge and are the focus of this book.

Resource Guide

The purpose of including references and sources in a book of this kind is as much to raise consciousness as to provide useful tools—that is, to alert legislators, teachers, officials, and analysts to the versatile and powerful array of information organizations, brokers, technologies, and techniques. The materials have been carefully selected to illustrate sources, services, products, and systems that information managers need and use. Of course, like most bibliographies and listings, ours is illustrative, not definitive. The choices were not randomly made, however. We followed three criteria. The entries must

1. Meet the special interests of public administrators; teachers of government; federal, state, and local officials; and information managers, analysts, and researchers in public and private organizations
2. Have practical value in helping readers find the data, information, and knowledge they may need to solve problems and make decisions
3. Point to innovative sources, services, products, and systems

Like all editors, we could not escape the problems of obsolescence and change. Therefore, some names, addresses, telephone numbers, and other data may have been changed or deleted since we compiled the references. We hope that the inconvenience is not critical.

TRAINING, EDUCATION, AND CAREER-ENHANCEMENT OPPORTUNITIES

Agencies, Associations, and Firms

AMERICAN INSTITUTE OF INDUSTRIAL ENGINEERS
Computer and Information Systems
  Division
AIIE Seminars
P.O. Box 3727
Santa Monica, CA 90403

AMERICAN SOCIETY FOR INFORMATION SCIENCE
Special Interest Groups
1010 16th St., NW
Washington, DC 20036

**AMERICAN SOCIETY FOR
    PUBLIC ADMINISTRATION**
Training Programs
1225 Connecticut Ave., NW
Washington, DC 20036

**ASSOCIATED INFORMATION
    MANAGERS**
Information Industry Association
316 Pennsylvania Ave., SE, Suite 400
Washington, DC 20003

**ASSOCIATION FOR SYSTEMS
    MANAGEMENT**
Training and Seminar Programs
24587 Bagley Rd.
Cleveland, OH 44138

BECKER AND HAYES, INC.
Seminar Programs
11661 San Vicente Blvd., Suite 907
Los Angeles, CA 90049

BUREAU OF TRAINING
Office of Personnel Management
1900 E St., NW
Washington, DC 20415

**CERTIFIED RECORDS MANAGERS
    PROGRAM**
Association for Records Managers and
    Administrators
P.O. Box 10208
Tallahassee, FL 32302

CUADRA ASSOCIATES
Seminar Programs
1523 Sixth St., Suite 12
Santa Monica, CA 90401

DATA COURIER, INC.
Seminar Programs
620 S. Fifth St.
Louisville, KY 40202

DATA FLOW SYSTEMS, INC.
Training Session Program
7758 Wisconsin Ave.
Bethesda, MD 20814

**DATA RESOURCE MANAGEMENT
    ASSOCIATES**
19 Orchard Way N.
Rockville, MD 20854

DYNAQUEST, INC.
Training and Seminar Programs
P.O. Box 15995
San Diego, CA 92115

FEDERAL EXECUTIVE INSTITUTE
Route 29 N.
Charlottesville, VA 22903

FROST & SULLIVAN, INC.
Seminar Programs
106 Fulton St.
New York, NY 10038

**GRADUATE SCHOOL SPECIAL
    PROGRAMS**
Department of Agriculture
277 National Press Bldg.
529 14th St., NW
Washington, DC 20045

**INSTITUTE FOR CERTIFICATION
    OF COMPUTER PROFESSIONALS**
304 E. 45th St.
New York, NY 10017

MICRONET, INC.
Seminar, Forum and Workshop
    Program
2551 Virginia Ave., NW
Washington, DC 20037

NATIONAL MICROGRAPHICS
  ASSOCIATION
Training and Seminar Program
8728 Colesville Rd.
Silver Spring, MD 20910

OFFICE OF RECORDS
  MANAGEMENT (RM)
Training and Seminar Programs
National Archives and Records Service
General Services Administration
Washington, DC 20408

SCIENCE INFORMATION
  ASSOCIATION
3514 Plyers Mill Rd.
Kensington, MD 20795

SOCIETY FOR MANAGEMENT
  INFORMATION SYSTEMS
Seminar Program
111 E. Wacker Dr., Suite 600
Chicago, IL 60601

Universities

UNIVERSITY OF CALIFORNIA,
  BERKELEY
School of Library and Information
  Studies
Graduate School of Business
  Administration

UNIVERSITY OF CALIFORNIA,
  IRVINE
Public Policy Research Organization

UNIVERSITY OF CALIFORNIA,
  LOS ANGELES
Graduate School of Library and
  Information Science
Graduate School of Management

UNIVERSITY OF SOUTHERN
  CALIFORNIA
Annenberg School of Communications

CARNEGIE-MELLON UNIVERSITY
Graduate School of Industrial
  Administration

CASE WESTERN RESERVE
  UNIVERSITY
School of Library Science

UNIVERSITY OF CHICAGO
Graduate Library School

DREXEL UNIVERSITY
School of Library and Information
  Science

GEORGIA INSTITUTE OF
  TECHNOLOGY
School of Information and Computer
  Science

HARVARD UNIVERSITY
Program on Information Resources
  Policy
Master of Information Science Program

UNIVERSITY OF MARYLAND
College of Library and Information
  Services
Information Systems Management
  Department

MASSACHUSETTS INSTITUTE OF
  TECHNOLOGY
Sloan School of Management
Center for Information Systems
  Research

MICHIGAN STATE UNIVERSITY
Department of Communication

UNIVERSITY OF MINNESOTA
School of Business Administration
Management Information Systems
  Program

NEW YORK UNIVERSITY
Graduate School of Business
  Administration

**STATE UNIVERSITY OF NEW
  YORK AT ALBANY**
School of Library and Information
  Science

OHIO STATE UNIVERSITY
Department of Computer and
  Information Science

UNIVERSITY OF PENNSYLVANIA
The Wharton School of Business
Decision Sciences Department

UNIVERSITY OF PITTSBURGH
Graduate School of Library and
  Information Sciences

PRATT INSTITUTE
Graduate School of Library and
  Information Science

**UNIVERSITY OF SOUTH
  CAROLINA**
Bureau of Governmental Research
  and Service
Program on Information Management
  and Technology in the Public Sector

STANFORD UNIVERSITY
Graduate School of Business
Institute for Communication Research

SYRACUSE UNIVERSITY
School of Information Studies

UNIVERSITY OF TEXAS
Graduate School of Business
Graduate School of Library Science

UNIVERSITY OF WASHINGTON
School of Communications

PERIODICALS AND NEWSLETTERS

Administrative Management
Advanced Technology/Libraries
*American Federation of Information
  Processing Societies Headquarters
  Newsletter*
*Bulletin of the American Society for
  Information Science*
Business Automation
Business Horizons
Business Week
*Communications of the Association of
  Computing Machinery*

*Computer and Communications
  Industry Association Industry
  Service Memo*
Computers and Automation
Computerworld
Database
Datamation
Data Processing Digest
EDP Analyzer
Fortune
Harvard Business Review
Information and Management

Information and Records Management
Information Hotline
Information Industry Association
  Friday Memo
Information on Information
The Information Report
Information Times
Information World
Infosystems
Journal of the American Society
  for Information Science
Journal of Systems Management
Management Adviser

Management Review
Management Science
The Office
Online
R & R, Business Advisory Council
  on Federal Reports
Regulatory Eye
S.A.M. Advanced Management Journal
Sloan Management Review
Special Libraries
Transnational Data Report
Technotec Newsline
Update

ON-LINE VENDORS, LIBRARY NETWORKS, AND
TELECOMMUNICATION NETWORKS

ARPANET NETWORK
INFORMATION CENTER
SRI International
333 Ravenswood Ave.
Menlo Park, CA 94025

BIBLIOGRAPHIC RETRIEVAL
SERVICES
1200 Route 7
Latham, NY 12110

DIALOG INFORMATION
RETRIEVAL SYSTEMS
3460 Hillview Ave.
Palo Alto, CA 94304

FEDERAL LIBRARY
INFORMATION NETWORK
Navy Yard Annex, Room 400
Library of Congress
Washington, DC 20540

INFONET
Computer Sciences Corporation
650 N. Sepulveda Blvd.
El Segundo, CA 90245

NATIONAL LIBRARY OF
MEDICINE
8600 Rockville Pike
Bethesda, MD 20209

THE NEW YORK TIMES
INFORMATION BANK
1719A Rte. 10
Parsippany, NJ 07054

OHIO STATE LIBRARY CENTER
1125 Kinnear Rd.
Columbus, OH 43212

RESEARCH LIBRARIES GROUP
45 South Main St.
Branford, CT 06405

SDC SEARCH SERVICE
Systems Development Corporation
2500 Colorado Ave.
Santa Monica, CA 90406

TELENET COMMUNICATIONS CORPORATION
8330 Old Courthouse Rd.
Vienna, VA 22810

TECHNOTEC
Control Data Corporation
8100 34th Ave. S.
Minneapolis, MN 55440

GOVERNMENT PUBLICATIONS

Bicentennial Statistics
Superintendent of Documents
Government Printing Office
Washington, DC 20402

Budget of the United States Government (Year)
Superintendent of Documents
Government Printing Office
Washington, DC 20402

Budget of the United States Government (Year)
Appendix
Superintendent of Documents
Government Printing Office
Washington, DC 20402

Budget of the United States Government (Year)
Budget in Brief
Superintendent of Documents
Government Printing Office
Washington, DC 20402

Budget of the United States Government (Year)
Special Analyses
Superintendent of Documents
Government Printing Office
Washington, DC 20402

Catalogue of Federal Domestic Assistance (Year)
Office of Management and Budget
Executive Office of the President
Washington, DC 20502

A Citizen's Guide on How to Use the Freedom of Information Act and the Privacy Act in Requesting Government Documents
House Report No. 95-793, 95th Congress, 1st Session
Superintendent of Documents
Government Printing Office
Washington, DC 20402

Commerce America
Department of Commerce
Washington, DC 20230

**Computer-Based Information Resources
for the U.S. House of Representatives**
Committee Print, 94th Congress, 1st
  Session, September 1, 1975
Committee on House Administration
Superintendent of Documents
Government Printing Office
Washington, DC 20402

Congressional Directory (Session of
  Congress) (Year)
Superintendent of Documents
Government Printing Office
Washington, DC 20402

County and City Data Book
Superintendent of Documents
Government Printing Office
Washington, DC 20402

**Current Survey Statistics Available
  from the Bureau of the Census**
Data Access Description No. 38
Bureau of the Census
Department of Commerce
Washington, DC 20233

Current Wage Developments
Department of Labor
Washington, DC 20210

Data User News
Bureau of the Census
Department of Commerce
Washington, DC 20233

**Digest of General Public Bills and
  Resolutions**
("Bill Digest")
Library of Congress
Washington, DC 20540

**A Directory of Computerized Data
  Files, Software and Related
  Technical Reports**
National Technical Information Service
Department of Commerce
5285 Port Royal Rd.
Springfield, VA 22161

**Directory of Federal Agency Education
  Data Tapes**
National Center for Educational
  Statistics
Department of Education
Washington, DC 20202

**Directory of Federal Energy Data
  Sources**
Department of Energy
Washington, DC 20545

**Directory of Federal Statistics for
  Local Areas**
Bureau of the Census
Department of Commerce
Washington, DC 20233

**Directory of Federal Technology
  Transfer**
Federal Council for Science and
  Technology
National Science Foundation
Washington, DC 20550

Economic Report of the President
(Year)
Superintendent of Documents (Stock
No. 040-000-00376-2)
Government Printing Office
Washington, DC 20402

Employment and Earnings
Department of Labor
Washington, DC 20210

Export Mailing List Service
Department of Commerce
Washington, DC 20233

**Federal Information Sources and
Systems** (Year)
Congressional Sourcebook Series
(General Accounting Office)
Superintendent of Documents
Government Printing Office
Washington, DC 20402

Federal Program Evaluations (Year)
Congressional Sourcebook Series
(General Accounting Office)
Superintendent of Documents
Government Printing Office
Washington, DC 20402

Federal Statistical Directory
Superintendent of Documents (Stock
No. 4101-00098)
Government Printing Office
Washington, DC 20402

Foreign Market Reports
Department of Commerce
Washington, DC 20233

Global Market Surveys
Department of Commerce
Washington, DC 20233

**Government Reports Announcements
and Index**
National Technical Information
Service
Department of Commerce
5285 Port Royal Rd.
Springfield, VA 22161

Handbook of Labor Statistics
Department of Labor
Washington, DC 20210

**Information Policy: Public Laws from
the 95th Congress**
(For the U.S. House of Representatives,
Committee Print, January 31, 1979)
Superintendent of Documents
Government Printing Office
Washington, DC 20402

LC Science Tracer Bullet
Science and Technology Division
Library of Congress
Washington, DC 20540

**Major Collective Bargaining
Agreements: Safety and Health
Provisions**
Department of Labor
Washington, DC 20210

**Mini-Guide for the 1972 Economic
Censuses**
Bureau of the Census
Department of Commerce
Washington, DC 20233

Monthly Labor Review
Department of Labor
Washington, DC 20210

NASIS Report (Year) **Info Systems Technology in State Government**
National Association of State Information Systems
Iron Works Pike
Lexington, KY 40511

Occupational Outlook Handbook
Department of Labor
Washington, DC 20210

Occupational Outlook Quarterly
Department of Labor
Washington, DC 20210

Population Profile of the United States: 1976 Series P-20, No. 307
Catalog No. C3.186:P-20/No. 307
Superintendent of Documents
Government Printing Office
Washington, DC 20402

Recurring Reports to Congress (Year)
Congressional Sourcebook Series (General Accounting Office)
Superintendent of Documents
Government Printing Office
Washington, DC 20402

Reference Manual on Population and Housing Statistics
Bureau of the Census
Department of Commerce
Washington, DC 20233

Standard Industrial Classification Manual (Year)
Superintendent of Documents
Government Printing Office
Washington, DC 20402

Statistical Abstract of the United States
Superintendent of Documents (Stock No. 003-24-01173-5)
Government Printing Office
Washington, DC 20402

Statistical Pocketbook—World Statistics in Brief
United Nations Statistical Office
New York, NY 10017

Statistical Services of the U.S. Government
Superintendent of Documents (Stock No. 041-001-00100-1)
Government Printing Office
Washington, DC 20402

Statistical Yearbook
United Nations Statistical Office
New York, NY 10017

United States Government Manual (Year)
Superintendent of Documents
Government Printing Office
Washington, DC 20402

Urban Atlas
Superintendent of Documents (Stock No. 003-024-00732-1)
Government Printing Office
Washington, DC 20402

U.S. Industrial Outlook (Year)
Superintendent of Documents (Stock No. 003-008-00174-2)
Government Printing Office
Washington, DC 20402

U.S. Workers and Their Jobs: The Changing Picture
Department of Labor
Washington, DC 20210

FEDERAL GOVERNMENT SUBJECT-MATTER EXPERTS
AND KEY TELEPHONE NUMBERS

AGRICULTURAL PRICES
Department of Agriculture
(202) 447-3570

BANKING DATA (Money Stock)
Federal Reserve Board
(202) 452-3591

BUILDING PERMITS
Bureau of the Census
(301) 763-7244

BUILDING TECHNOLOGY
Department of Commerce
(301) 921-2816

CAPITOL HILL SWITCHBOARD
U.S. Congress
(202) 224-3121

CENSUS, DECENNIAL, GENERAL INFORMATION
Bureau of the Census
(301) 765-2748

CENSUS, DECENNIAL, MINORITY STATISTICS
Bureau of the Census
(301) 765-5169

CENSUS, POPULATION
Bureau of the Census
(301) 765-5161

CENTRAL CITY PROFILES
Bureau of the Census
(301) 765-5173

CLAIMS COURT (U.S.) DECISIONS
Clerk
(202) 382-1984

CONGRESSIONAL DISTRICT DATA
Bureau of the Census
(301) 765-5475

CONGRESSIONAL INFORMATION SERVICES
Library of Congress
(202) 287-5700

CONSTRUCTION STARTS
Bureau of the Census
(301) 763-5731

CONSUMER CREDIT
Federal Reserve Board
(202) 452-2458

CONSUMER PRICE INDEX
Department of Labor
(202) 523-7827

CONSUMER PRODUCT SAFETY
Consumer Product Safety Commission
(202) 492-6544

CONSUMER SURVEYS
Department of Agriculture
(202) 447-9200

COUNTY AND CITY DATA
Bureau of the Census
(301) 765-5475

COUNTY BUSINESS PATTERNS
Bureau of the Census
(301) 765-7642

CRIMINAL JUSTICE STATISTICS
Bureau of the Census
(301) 765-2842

CROP STATISTICS
Bureau of the Census
(301) 765-1939

Department of Agriculture
(202) 447-2127

CURRENT POPULATION SURVEY
Bureau of the Census
(301) 765-2773

**CUSTOMS AND PATENT APPEALS
COURT DECISIONS**
Clerk
(202) 347-1552

DISASTER ASSISTANCE
Department of Housing and Urban
  Development
(202) 634-6666

**EDUCATION AND SCHOOL
ENROLLMENTS**
Bureau of the Census
(301) 765-5050

Department of Commerce
(301) 763-7273

**EMPLOYMENT AND
UNEMPLOYMENT**
Bureau of the Census
(301) 765-2825

Department of Commerce
(301) 763-7273

ENERGY CONSERVATION
Department of Commerce
(202) 377-4703

Department of Energy
(202) 254-3910

ENVIRONMENTAL POLLUTION
Bureau of the Census
(301) 765-5616

Department of Commerce
(301) 921-2435

**FARM POPULATIONS AND
ECONOMICS**
Bureau of the Census
(301) 765-5161

Department of Agriculture
(202) 447-4830

Department of Commerce
(301) 763-7487

**FIRE PROTECTION, PREVENTION
AND CONTROL**
Department of Commerce
(202) 634-7663

National Fire Prevention and Control
  Council
(202) 634-7561

FISH AND WILDLIFE
Department of the Interior
(202) 343-5634

**FOREIGN TRADE, EXPORT AND
IMPORT**
Bureau of the Census
(301) 765-5140

Department of Commerce
(202) 377-2253

Agency for International Development
(202) 632-0674

Department of Agriculture
(202) 447-8261

HOUSE BILL STATUS
U.S. Congress
(202) 225-1772

HOUSE CLOAKROOM
U.S. Congress
Democrats
(202) 225-7400

Republicans
(202) 225-7430

HOUSING CONSTRUCTION
Bureau of the Census
(301) 765-2873

Department of Commerce
(301) 763-7273

INDIAN (U.S.) AFFAIRS
Department of the Interior
(202) 343-6342

INDUSTRY AND OCCUPATION STATISTICS
Bureau of the Census
(301) 765-5144

LAND, GEODETIC
Bureau of the Census
(301) 765-5161

Department of Commerce
(301) 443-8708

Department of Agriculture
(202) 447-6578

LIVESTOCK STATISTICS
Bureau of the Census
(301) 765-1974

Department of Agriculture
(202) 447-4289

MIGRATION, MOBILITY
Bureau of the Census
(301) 765-5255

MILITARY APPEALS COURT DECISIONS
Clerk
(202) 693-1922

MINORITY BUSINESS PROGRAMS
Department of Commerce
(202) 377-4597

Small Business Administration
(202) 653-6526

OCCUPATIONAL SAFETY AND HEALTH
Department of Health and Human Services
(301) 443-2140

PARKS
Department of the Interior
(202) 343-6843

POLICE, FIRE AND SCHOOL DISTRICT STATISTICS
Bureau of the Census
(301) 765-5050

POVERTY STATISTICS
Bureau of the Census
(301) 765-5790

RADIATION
Department of Commerce
(301) 921-2435

Nuclear Regulatory Commission
(202) 492-7000

REVENUE SHARING
Bureau of the Census
(301) 765-5179

SCHOOL DISTRICTS
Bureau of the Census
(301) 765-5050

SENATE BILL STATUS OFFICE
U.S. Congress
(202) 224-2971

SENATE CLOAKROOM
U.S. Congress
Democrats
(202) 224-8541

Republicans
(202) 224-8601

SOIL AND WATER
Department of Agriculture
(202) 447-7157

SUPREME COURT DECISIONS
Clerk
(202) 393-1640

TAX COURT (U.S.) DECISIONS
Clerk
(202) 376-2751

**TOURISM AND TRAVEL,
    DOMESTIC AND
    INTERNATIONAL**
Department of Commerce
(202) 377-4987

TRAVEL SURVEYS
Bureau of the Census
(301) 765-1798

VETERANS STATISTICS
Bureau of the Census
(301) 765-5050

Veterans Administration
(202) 389-2423

VOTING AND REGISTRATION
Bureau of the Census
(301) 765-5050

WHITE HOUSE SWITCHBOARD
(202) 456-1414

WHOLESALE PRICE INDEX
Department of Labor
(202) 523-1080

WOMEN'S RIGHTS
Advisory Council on the Status of
    Women Citizens
(202) 523-6538

SOURCES OF INFORMATION (INSTITUTIONAL)

**ADMINISTRATIVE OFFICE OF
    THE U.S. COURTS**
Supreme Court Bldg.
1st and Maryland Ave., NE
Washington, DC 20544

AFL-CIO
AFL-CIO Bldg.
815 16th St., NW
Washington, DC 20006

**AMERICAN ASSOCIATION OF
    SCHOOL ADMINISTRATORS**
1801 N. Moore St.
Arlington, VA 22209

**AMERICAN ASSOCIATION OF
    STATE COLLEGES AND
    UNIVERSITIES**
One Dupont Circle, NW
Washington, DC 20036

**AMERICAN ASSOCIATION OF
UNIVERSITY PROFESSORS**
One Dupont Circle, NW
Washington, DC 20036

AMERICAN BAR ASSOCIATION
Government Relations Office
1705 DeSales St., NW
Washington, DC 20036

**AMERICAN CHAMBER OF
COMMERCE EXECUTIVES**
1133 15th St., NW, Suite 620
Washington, DC 20005

**AMERICANS FOR DEMOCRATIC
ACTION**
1424 16th St., NW
Washington, DC 20036

**AMERICAN ENTERPRISE
INSTITUTE**
Institute for Public Policy Research
1150 17th St., NW
Washington, DC 20036

**AMERICAN FEDERATION OF
GOVERNMENT EMPLOYEES**
1325 Massachusetts Ave., NW
Washington, DC 20005

**AMERICAN FEDERATION OF
INFORMATION PROCESSING
SOCIETIES**
210 Summit Ave.
Montvale, NJ 07645

In Washington:
1815 N. Lynn St., Suite 805
Arlington, VA 22209

**AMERICAN FEDERATION OF
STATE, COUNTY AND
MUNICIPAL EMPLOYEES**
1625 L St., NW
Washington, DC 20036

In New York:
140 Park Place
New York, NY 10007

AMERICAN FILM INSTITUTE
The John F. Kennedy Center for the
  Performing Arts
Washington, DC 20566

**AMERICAN LAWYERS
ASSOCIATION**
292 Madison Ave.
New York, NY 10017

**AMERICAN LIBRARY
ASSOCIATION**
110 Maryland Ave., NE
Washington, DC 20002

**AMERICAN NEWSPAPER
PUBLISHERS ASSOCIATION**
11600 Sunrise Valley Dr.
Reston, VA 22091

**AMERICAN POLITICAL SCIENCE
ASSOCIATION**
1527 New Hampshire Ave., NW
Washington, DC 20006

**AMERICAN POSTAL WORKERS
UNION**
817 14th St., NW
Washington, DC 20005

**AMERICAN SOCIETY FOR
INFORMATION SCIENCE**
1155 16th St., NW, Suite 210
Washington, DC 20036

AMERICAN SOCIETY OF
ASSOCIATION EXECUTIVES
Information Center
1101 16th St., NW
Washington, DC 20036

ASSOCIATION FOR
EDUCATIONAL DATA
SYSTEMS
1201 16th St., NW
Washington, DC 20036

ASSOCIATION OF AMERICAN
LAW SCHOOLS
One Dupont Circle, NW
Washington, DC 20036

ASSOCIATION OF AMERICAN
MEDICAL COLLEGES
One Dupont Circle, NW
Washington, DC 20036

ASSOCIATION OF AMERICAN
UNIVERSITIES
One Dupont Circle, NW
Washington, DC 20036

ASSOCIATION OF FARM
WORKER OPPORTUNITY
PROGRAMS
418 C St., NE
Washington, DC 20002

ASSOCIATION OF GOVERNMENT
ACCOUNTANTS
727 N. 23rd St.
Arlington, VA 22207

ASSOCIATION OF INDEPENDENT
COLLEGES AND SCHOOLS
1730 M St., NW
Washington, DC 20037

ASSOCIATION OF INSTITUTIONS
OF HIGHER EDUCATION
2311 M St., NW
Washington, DC 20036

ASSOCIATION OF PUBLIC DATA
USERS
The Urban Institute
2100 M St., NW
Washington, DC 20037

ASSOCIATION OF RECORDS
MANAGERS AND
ADMINISTRATORS
1901 N. Fort Myer Dr.
Arlington, VA 22209

ASSOCIATION OF RESEARCH
LIBRARIES
1527 New Hampshire Ave., NW
Washington, DC 20036

ASSOCIATION OF SCIENCE-
TECHNOLOGY CENTERS
2100 Pennsylvania Ave., NW
Washington, DC 20036

ASSOCIATION OF STATE AND
TERRITORIAL HEALTH
OFFICERS
101 2nd St., SE
Washington, DC 20003

ASSOCIATION PRESS
1029 Vermont Ave., NW
Washington, DC 20005

THE BROOKINGS INSTITUTION
1775 Massachusetts Ave., NW
Washington, DC 20036

BUREAU OF SOCIAL SCIENCE
RESEARCH, INC.
1990 M St., NW
Washington, DC 20036

**CHAMBER OF COMMERCE
OF THE UNITED STATES**
1615 H St., NW
Washington, DC 20062

**CLEARINGHOUSE LIBRARY
CIVIL RIGHTS COMMISSION**
1121 Vermont Ave., Room 709
Washington, DC 20452

**COALITION OF AMERICAN
PUBLIC EMPLOYEES**
1126 16th St., NW, Suite 213
Washington, DC 20006

THE CONFERENCE BOARD, INC.
845 3rd Ave.
New York, NY 10022

**CONGRESSIONAL
CLEARINGHOUSE ON
THE FUTURE**
House Annex No. 2, Room 3692
300 D St., SW
Washington, DC 20515

**CONGRESSIONAL
CLEARINGHOUSE ON
WOMEN'S RIGHTS**
722 House Annex No. 1
300 New Jersey Ave., SE
Washington, DC 20515

**CONSUMER PRODUCT SAFETY
COMMISSION**
Library
5401 Westbard Ave.
Washington, DC 20207

**COUNCIL FOR PUBLIC INTEREST
LAW**
1250 Connecticut Ave., NW, Suite 120
Washington, DC 20036

**COUNCIL FOR STATE
CHAMBERS OF COMMERCE**
1028 Connecticut Ave., NW
Room 1018
Washington, DC 20036

**COUNCIL ON LIBRARY
RESOURCES, INC.**
One Dupont Circle, NW
Washington, DC 20036

**DEFENSE DOCUMENTATION
CENTER**
Defense Supply Agency
Cameron Station, Bldg. 5
Alexandria, VA 22314

**ERIC CLEARINGHOUSE FOR
JUNIOR COLLEGES**
National Institute of Education
Office of Dissemination and Resources
96 Powell Library Bldg.
University of California at Los Angeles
Los Angeles, CA 90024

**ERIC CLEARINGHOUSE FOR
SOCIAL STUDIES/SOCIAL
SCIENCE EDUCATION**
National Institute of Education
855 Broadway
Boulder, CO 80302

**ERIC CLEARINGHOUSE ON
HIGHER EDUCATION**
National Institute of Education
George Washington University
One Dupont Circle, NW, Suite 630
Washington, DC 20036

**ERIC CLEARINGHOUSE ON
INFORMATION RESOURCES**
National Institute of Education
130 Huntington Hall
Syracuse University
Syracuse, NY 13210

**ERIC CLEARINGHOUSE ON
READING AND
COMMUNICATION SKILLS**
National Institute of Education
National Council of Teachers of English
1111 Kenyon Rd.
Urbana, IL 61801

**ERIC CLEARINGHOUSE ON
URBAN EDUCATION**
Teachers College
Columbia University
525 W. 120th St.
New York, NY 10027

**EXPORT INFORMATION
REFERENCE ROOM**
Bureau of International Commerce,
Room 1063
Department of Commerce
14th and Constitution Ave., NW
Washington, DC 20230

FEDERAL BAR ASSOCIATION
1818 H St., NW
Washington, DC 20006

**FEDERAL INFORMATION
CENTERS**
General Services Administration
7th and D Sts., SW
Washington, DC 20407

FEDERAL JUDICIARY CENTER
1520 H St., NW
Washington, DC 20005

**FEDERAL STATISTICS USERS
CONFERENCE**
1523 L St., NW
Washington, DC 20005

FIRE REFERENCE SERVICE
National Fire Data Center
National Fire Prevention and Control
Administration
Department of Commerce
Washington, DC 20230

GEOLOGICAL SURVEY
National Center
12201 Sunrise Valley Rd.
Reston, VA 22092

**GOVERNMENTAL AFFAIRS
INSTITUTE**
1776 Massachusetts Ave., NW
Washington, DC 20036

**INDUSTRY AND TRADE
ADMINISTRATION**
Bureau of Domestic Business
Development
Department of Commerce
14th and Constitution Ave., NW
Washington, DC 20230

INFONET
Automated Data and
Telecommunications Service
General Services Administration
Washington, DC 20405

INFORMATION CENTER
Office of Minority Business Enterprise,
Room 5600
Department of Commerce
14th and Constitution Ave., NW
Washington, DC 20230

**INFORMATION CENTER
COMPLEX**
Oak Ridge National Laboratory
Box X
Oak Ridge, TN 37830

INFORMATION CENTRAL
American Society of Association
  Executives
1101 16th St., NW
Washington, DC 20036

**INFORMATION INDUSTRY
ASSOCIATION**
316 Pennsylvania Ave., SE, Suite 400
Washington, DC 20003

INSTITUTE FOR POLICY STUDIES
1520 New Hampshire Ave., NW
Washington, DC 20036

**INTERNATIONAL CITY
MANAGERS ASSOCIATION**
1140 Connecticut Ave., NW
Washington, DC 20036

**INTERNATIONAL CONFERENCE
OF POLICE ASSOCIATIONS**
1239 Pennsylvania Ave., SE
Washington, DC 20003

**INTERNATIONAL DEMOGRAPHIC
DATA CENTER**
Bureau of the Census
Department of Commerce
Washington, DC 20233

**LEAGUE OF WOMEN VOTERS
OF THE U.S.**
1730 M St., NW
Washington, DC 20036

**LIBRARY OF CONGRESS
COMPUTERIZED CATALOG**
Library of Congress
Washington, DC 20540

**NATIONAL ALLIANCE OF
BUSINESSMEN**
1730 K St., NW
Washington, DC 20006

In New York:
380 Madison Ave.
New York, NY 10017

**NATIONAL ALLIANCE OF POSTAL
EMPLOYEES**
200 W. 135th St.
New York, NY 10030

NATIONAL ARCHIVES
National Archives and Records Service
General Services Administration
8th St. and Pennsylvania Ave., NW
Washington, DC 20408

**NATIONAL ASSOCIATION FOR
COMMUNITY DEVELOPMENT**
1424 16th St., NW, Room 106
Washington, DC 20036

**NATIONAL ASSOCIATION OF
BROADCASTERS**
1771 N St., NW
Washington, DC 20036

**NATIONAL ASSOCIATION OF
COUNTIES**
1735 New York Ave., NW
Washington, DC 20006

**NATIONAL ASSOCIATION OF
GOVERNMENT ENGINEERS**
818 15th St., NW, Suite 711
Washington, DC 20005

**NATIONAL ASSOCIATION OF
LETTER CARRIERS**
100 Indiana Ave., NW
Washington, DC 20001

NATIONAL ASSOCIATION OF POSTMASTERS OF THE U.S.
490 L'Enfant Plaza East, SW
Suite 4200
Washington, DC 20024

NATIONAL ASSOCIATION OF SCHOOLS OF PUBLIC AFFAIRS AND ADMINISTRATION
1225 Connecticut Ave., NW
Washington, DC 20036

NATIONAL ASSOCIATION OF STATE UNIVERSITY AND LAND GRANT COLLEGES
One Dupont Circle, NW
Washington, DC 20036

NATIONAL CENTER FOR EDUCATIONAL STATISTICS
Department of Education
400 Maryland Ave., SW, Room 3001
Washington, DC 20202

NATIONAL CENTER FOR HEALTH STATISTICS
Department of Health and Human Services
3700 East-West Highway
Hyattsville, MD 20782

NATIONAL CIVIL RIGHTS CLEARINGHOUSE LIBRARY
Commission on Civil Rights
1121 Vermont Ave., NW, Room 709
Washington, DC 20425

NATIONAL CLEARINGHOUSE FOR MENTAL HEALTH INFORMATION
Department of Health and Human Services
5600 Fishers Lane
Rockville, MD 20857

NATIONAL CLEARINGHOUSE ON ELECTION ADMINISTRATION
Federal Elections Commission
1325 K St., NW
Washington, DC 20463

NATIONAL COUNCIL OF STATE EDUCATION ASSOCIATIONS
1201 16th St., NW
Washington, DC 20036

NATIONAL CRIMINAL JUSTICE REFERENCE SERVICE
P.O. Box 6000
Rockville, MD 20850

NATIONAL DEMOCRATIC COMMITTEE
1625 Massachusetts Ave., NW
Washington, DC 20036

NATIONAL EDUCATION ASSOCIATION
1201 16th St., NW
Washington, DC 20036

NATIONAL ENERGY INFORMATION CENTER
Department of Energy
1200 Pennsylvania Ave., NW
Room 1404
Washington, DC 20461

NATIONAL FEDERATION OF FEDERAL EMPLOYEES
1737 H St., NW
Washington, DC 20006

NATIONAL FEDERATION OF INDEPENDENT BUSINESS, INC.
490 L'Enfant Plaza East, SW
Suite 3206
Washington, DC 20024

NATIONAL INFORMATION BUREAU, INC.
419 Park Ave. S.
New York, NY 10016

NATIONAL INSTITUTE OF GOVERNMENTAL PURCHASING
1001 Connecticut Ave., NW
Washington, DC 20036

NATIONAL INSTITUTE OF LAW ENFORCEMENT AND CRIMINAL JUSTICE
633 Indiana Ave., NW
Washington, DC 20531

NATIONAL INSTITUTE OF MUNICIPAL LAW OFFICERS
839 17th St., NW
Washington, DC 20006

NATIONAL INSTITUTE OF PUBLIC AFFAIRS
1225 Connecticut Ave., NW
Washington, DC 20036

NATIONAL LAWYERS CLUB
1818 H St., NW
Washington, DC 20006

NATIONAL LEAGUE OF CITIES
1620 I St., NW
Washington, DC 20006

NATIONAL MICROFILM ASSOCIATION
8728 Colesville Rd., Suite 1101
Silver Spring, MD 20910

NATIONAL NEWSPAPER ASSOCIATION
1627 K St., NW
Washington, DC 20006

NATIONAL NEWSPAPER PUBLISHERS ASSOCIATION
National Press Bldg.
529 14th St., NW
Washington, DC 20045

NATIONAL PRESS CLUB
National Press Bldg.
529 14th St., NW
Washington, DC 20045

NATIONAL REFERRAL CENTER
Library of Congress
Washington, DC 20540

NATIONAL SHERIFFS ASSOCIATION
1250 Connecticut Ave., NW
Washington, DC 20036

NATIONAL SMALL BUSINESS ASSOCIATION
1225 19th St., NW
Washington, DC 20036

NATIONAL SOCIETY OF PUBLIC ACCOUNTANTS
1717 Pennsylvania Ave., NW
Washington, DC 20006

NATIONAL TECHNICAL INFORMATION SERVICE
5258 Port Royal Rd.
Springfield, VA 22161

NATIONWIDE COMMITTEE ON IMPORT-EXPORT POLICY
815 15th St., NW, Suite 711
Washington, DC 20005

THE NEW YORK TIMES
229 W. 43rd St.
New York, NY 10036

OFFICE OF THE OMBUDSMAN
Department of Commerce
14th and E Sts., NW, Room 3800
Washington, DC 20230

PATENT OFFICE SEARCH ROOM
Department of Commerce
2021 Jefferson Davis Highway
Arlington, VA 22202

**POPULATION REFERENCE
  BUREAU**
1337 Connecticut Ave., NW
Washington, DC 20036

PRESS GALLERIES OF CONGRESS
U.S. Capitol
Washington, DC 20510

PROJECT SHAPE
Department of Health and Human
  Services
Box 2309
Hamilton, VA 22068

PROJECT SHARE
P.O. Box 2309
Rockville, MD 20852

PUBLIC DOCUMENT ROOM
Department of Energy
20 Massachusetts Ave., NW
Room 1223
Washington, DC 20545

PUBLIC INFORMATION OFFICE
Bureau of the Census
Department of Commerce
Federal Office Bldg. 3, Room 2089
Suitland, MD 20233

**PUBLIC INFORMATION
  REFERENCE UNIT**
Environmental Protection Agency
401 M St., SW (PM 213)
Washington, DC 20460

PUBLIC REFERENCE ROOM
Consumer Product Safety Commission
1111 18th St., NW, Room 825
Washington, DC 20006

**REPUBLICAN NATIONAL
  COMMITTEE**
301 1st St., SE
Washington, DC 20003

**RESEARCH APPLIED TO
NATIONAL NEEDS DOCUMENTS
CENTER**
National Science Foundation
1800 G St., NW, Room 1241
Washington, DC 20550

RURAL AMERICA
1346 Connecticut Ave., NW, Suite 500
Washington, DC 20036

**SMITHSONIAN SCIENCE
  INFORMATION EXCHANGE**
1730 M St., NW, Room 300
Washington, DC 20036

**STATISTICAL REPORTING
  SERVICE**
Department of Agriculture
Washington, DC 20250

TRADEMARK SEARCH ROOM
Patent Office
Department of Commerce
2011 Jefferson Davis Highway
Arlington, VA 22202

THE URBAN INSTITUTE
2100 M St., NW
Washington, DC 20037

THE URBAN LAND INSTITUTE
1200 18th St., NW
Washington, DC 20036

U.S. CONFERENCE OF MAYORS
1620 I St., NW
Washington, DC 20006

THE WALL STREET JOURNAL
22 Cortlandt St.
New York, NY 10007

THE WASHINGTON POST
1150 15th St., NW
Washington, DC 20071

WATER RESOURCES SCIENTIFIC
 INFORMATION CENTER
Office of Water Resources and
  Technology
Department of the Interior
Washington, DC 20240

WHITE HOUSE NEWS
 PHOTOGRAPHERS
 ASSOCIATION
7809 Lewinsville Rd.
McLean, VA 22101

WOMEN'S NATIONAL
 DEMOCRATIC CLUB
1526 New Hampshire Ave., NW
Washington, DC 20036

Appendix

PAPERWORK REDUCTION ACT OF 1980

Public Law 96–511
96th Congress

An Act

Dec. 11, 1980
[H.R. 6410]

To reduce paperwork and enhance the economy and efficiency of the Government and the private sector by improving Federal information policymaking, and for other purposes.

Be it enacted by the Senate and House of Representatives of the United States of America in Congress assembled, That this Act may be cited as the "Paperwork Reduction Act of 1980".

Paperwork
Reduction Act of
1980.
44 USC 101 note.

SEC. 2. (a) Chapter 35 of title 44, United States Code, is amended to read as follows:

"CHAPTER 35—COORDINATION OF FEDERAL INFORMATION POLICY

44 USC 3501.

"§ 3501. Purpose

"The purpose of this chapter is—
"(1) to minimize the Federal paperwork burden for individuals, small businesses, State and local governments, and other persons;
"(2) to minimize the cost to the Federal Government of collecting, maintaining, using, and disseminating information;
"(3) to maximize the usefulness of information collected by the Federal Government;
"(4) to coordinate, integrate and, to the extent practicable and appropriate, make uniform Federal information policies and practices;
"(5) to ensure that automatic data processing and telecommunications technologies are acquired and used by the Federal Government in a manner which improves service delivery and program management, increases productivity, reduces waste and fraud, and, wherever practicable and appropriate, reduces the

information processing burden for the Federal Government and for persons who provide information to the Federal Government; and

"(6) to ensure that the collection, maintenance, use and dissemination of information by the Federal Government is consistent with applicable laws relating to confidentiality, including section 552a of title 5, United States Code, known as the Privacy Act.

"§ 3502. Definitions   44 USC 3502.

"As used in this chapter—

"(1) the term 'agency' means any executive department, military department, Government corporation, Government controlled corporation, or other establishment in the executive branch of the Government (including the Executive Office of the President), or any independent regulatory agency, but does not include the General Accounting Office, Federal Election Commission, the governments of the District of Columbia and of the territories and possessions of the United States, and their various subdivisions, or Government-owned contractor-operated facilities including laboratories engaged in national defense research and production activities;

"(2) the terms 'automatic data processing,' 'automatic data processing equipment,' and 'telecommunications' do not include any data processing or telecommunications system or equipment, the function, operation or use of which—

"(A) involves intelligence activities;

"(B) involves cryptologic activities related to national security;

"(C) involves the direct command and control of military forces;

"(D) involves equipment which is an integral part of a weapon or weapons system; or

"(E) is critical to the direct fulfillment of military or intelligence missions, provided that this exclusion shall not include automatic data processing or telecommunications equipment used for routine administrative and business applications such as payroll, finance, logistics, and personnel management;

"(3) the term 'burden' means the time, effort, or financial resources expended by persons to provide information to a Federal agency;

"(4) the term 'collection of information' means the obtaining or soliciting of facts or opinions by an agency through the use of written report forms, application forms, schedules, questionnaires, reporting or recordkeeping requirements, or other similar methods calling for either—

"(A) answers to identical questions posed to, or identical reporting or recordkeeping requirements imposed on, ten or more persons, other than agencies, instrumentalities, or employees of the United States; or

"(B) answers to questions posed to agencies, instrumentalities, or employees of the United States which are to be used for general statistical purposes;

"(5) the term 'data element' means a distinct piece of information such as a name, term, number, abbreviation, or symbol;

"(6) the term 'data element dictionary' means a system containing standard and uniform definitions and cross references for commonly used data elements;

"(7) the term 'data profile' means a synopsis of the questions contained in an information collection request and the official name of the request, the location of information obtained or to be obtained through the request, a description of any compilations, analyses, or reports derived or to be derived from such information, any record retention requirements associated with the request, the agency responsible for the request, the statute authorizing the request, and any other information necessary to identify, obtain, or use the data contained in such information;

"(8) the term 'Director' means the Director of the Office of Management and Budget;

"(9) the term 'directory of information resources' means a catalog of information collection requests, containing a data profile for each request;

"(10) the term 'independent regulatory agency' means the Board of Governors of the Federal Reserve System, the Civil Aeronautics Board, the Commodity Futures Trading Commission, the Consumer Product Safety Commission, the Federal Communications Commission, the Federal Deposit Insurance Corporation, the Federal Energy Regulatory Commission, the Federal Home Loan Bank Board, the Federal Maritime Commission, the Federal Trade Commission, the Interstate Commerce Commission, the Mine Enforcement Safety and Health Review Commission, the National Labor Relations Board, the Nuclear Regulatory Commission, the Occupational Safety and Health Review Commission, the Postal Rate Commission, the Securities and Exchange Commission, and any other similar agency designated by statute as a Federal independent regulatory agency or commission;

"(11) the term 'information collection request' means a written report form, application form, schedule, questionnaire, reporting or recordkeeping requirement, or other similar method calling for the collection of information;

"(12) the term 'information referral service' means the function that assists officials and persons in obtaining access to the Federal Information Locator System;

"(13) the term 'information systems' means management information systems;

"(14) the term 'person' means an individual, partnership, association, corporation, business trust, or legal representative, an organized group of individuals, a State, territorial, or local government or branch thereof, or a political subdivision of a State, territory, or local government or a branch of a political subdivision;

"(15) the term 'practical utility' means the ability of an agency to use information it collects, particularly the capability to process such information in a timely and useful fashion; and

"(16) the term 'recordkeeping requirement' means a requirement imposed by an agency on persons to maintain specified records.

44 USC 3503.

Establishment.

"§ 3503. Office of Information and Regulatory Affairs

"(a) There is established in the Office of Management and Budget an office to be known as the Office of Information and Regulatory Affairs.

"(b) There shall be at the head of the Office an Administrator who shall be appointed by, and who shall report directly to, the Director. The Director shall delegate to the Administrator the authority to administer all functions under this chapter, except that any such delegation shall not relieve the Director of responsibility for the administration of such functions. The Administrator shall serve as principal adviser to the Director on Federal information policy.

Administrator, appointment.

"§ 3504. Authority and functions of Director

44 USC 3504.

"(a) The Director shall develop and implement Federal information policies, principles, standards, and guidelines and shall provide direction and oversee the review and approval of information collection requests, the reduction of the paperwork burden, Federal statistical activities, records management activities, privacy of records, interagency sharing of information, and acquisition and use of automatic data processing telecommunications, and other technology for managing information resources. The authority under this section shall be exercised consistent with applicable law.

"(b) The general information policy functions of the Director shall include—

"(1) developing and implementing uniform and consistent information resources management policies and overseeing the development of information management principles, standards, and guidelines and promoting their use;

"(2) initiating and reviewing proposals for changes in legislation, regulations, and agency procedures to improve information practices, and informing the President and the Congress on the progress made therein;

"(3) coordinating, through the review of budget proposals and as otherwise provided in this section, agency information practices;

"(4) promoting, through the use of the Federal Information Locator System, the review of budget proposals and other methods, greater sharing of information by agencies;

"(5) evaluating agency information management practices to determine their adequacy and efficiency, and to determine compliance of such practices with the policies, principles, standards, and guidelines promulgated by the Director; and

"(6) overseeing planning for, and conduct of research with respect to, Federal collection, processing, storage, transmission, and use of information.

"(c) The information collection request clearance and other paperwork control functions of the Director shall include—

Paperwork. Control functions.

"(1) reviewing and approving information collection requests proposed by agencies;

"(2) determining whether the collection of information by an agency is necessary for the proper performance of the functions of the agency, including whether the information will have practical utility for the agency;

"(3) ensuring that all information collection requests—

"(A) are inventoried, display a control number and, when appropriate, an expiration date;

"(B) indicate the request is in accordance with the clearance requirements of section 3507; and

Post, p. 2819.

"(C) contain a statement to inform the person receiving the request why the information is being collected, how it is to be used, and whether responses to the request are voluntary, required to obtain a benefit, or mandatory;

"(4) designating as appropriate, in accordance with section 3509, a collection agency to obtain information for two or more agencies;

Post, p. 2820.

"(5) setting goals for reduction of the burdens of Federal information collection requests;

"(6) overseeing action on the recommendations of the Commission on Federal Paperwork; and

"(7) designing and operating, in accordance with section 3511, the Federal Information Locator System.

Post, p. 2822.

"(d) The statistical policy and coordination functions of the Director shall include—

"(1) developing long range plans for the improved performance of Federal statistical activities and programs;

"(2) coordinating, through the review of budget proposals and as otherwise provided in this section, the functions of the Federal Government with respect to gathering, interpreting, and disseminating statistics and statistical information;

"(3) developing and implementing Government-wide policies, principles, standards, and guidelines concerning statistical collection procedures and methods, statistical data classifications, and statistical information presentation and dissemination; and

"(4) evaluating statistical program performance and agency compliance with Government-wide policies, principles, standards, and guidelines.

"(e) The records management functions of the Director shall include—

"(1) providing advice and assistance to the Administrator of General Services in order to promote coordination in the administration of chapters 29, 31, and 33 of this title with the information policies, principles, standards, and guidelines established under this chapter;

44 USC 2901 *et seq.*, 3101 *et seq.*, 3301 *et seq.*

"(2) reviewing compliance by agencies with the requirements of chapters 29, 31, and 33 of this title and with regulations promulgated by the Administrator of General Services thereunder; and

"(3) coordinating records management policies and programs with related information programs such as information collection, statistics, automatic data processing and telecommunications, and similar activities.

"(f) The privacy functions of the Director shall include—

"(1) developing and implementing policies, principles, standards, and guidelines on information disclosure and confidentiality, and on safeguarding the security of information collected or maintained by or on behalf of agencies;

"(2) providing agencies with advice and guidance about information security, restriction, exchange, and disclosure; and

"(3) monitoring compliance with section 552a of title 5, United States Code, and related information management laws.

"(g) The Federal automatic data processing and telecommunications functions of the Director shall include—

"(1) developing and implementing policies, principles, standards, and guidelines for automatic data processing and telecommunications functions and activities of the Federal Government, and overseeing the establishment of standards under section 111(f) of the Federal Property and Administrative Services Act of 1949;

40 USC 759.

"(2) monitoring the effectiveness of, and compliance with, directives issued pursuant to sections 110 and 111 of such Act of

1949 and reviewing proposed determinations under section 111(g)   40 USC 757, 759.
of such Act;

"(3) providing advice and guidance on the acquisition and use of automatic data processing and telecommunications equipment, and coordinating, through the review of budget proposals and other methods, agency proposals for acquisition and use of such equipment;

"(4) promoting the use of automatic data processing and telecommunications equipment by the Federal Government to improve the effectiveness of the use and dissemination of data in the operation of Federal programs; and

"(5) initiating and reviewing proposals for changes in legislation, regulations, and agency procedures to improve automatic data processing and telecommunications practices, and informing the President and the Congress of the progress made therein.

"(h)(1) As soon as practicable, but no later than publication of a notice of proposed rulemaking in the Federal Register, each agency shall forward to the Director a copy of any proposed rule which contains a collection of information requirement and upon request, information necessary to make the determination required pursuant to this section.

"(2) Within sixty days after the notice of proposed rulemaking is published in the Federal Register, the Director may file public comments pursuant to the standards set forth in section 3508 on the   *Post,* p. 2821.
collection of information requirement contained in the proposed rule.

"(3) When a final rule is published in the Federal Register, the agency shall explain how any collection of information requirement contained in the final rule responds to the comments, if any, filed by the Director or the public, or explain why it rejected those comments.

"(4) The Director has no authority to disapprove any collection of information requirement specifically contained in an agency rule, if he has received notice and failed to comment on the rule within sixty days of the notice of proposed rulemaking.

"(5) Nothing in this section prevents the Director, in his discretion—

"(A) from disapproving any information collection request which was not specifically required by an agency rule;

"(B) from disapproving any collection of information requirement contained in an agency rule, if the agency failed to comply with the requirements of paragraph (1) of this subsection; or

"(C) from disapproving any collection of information requirement contained in a final agency rule, if the Director finds within sixty days of the publication of the final rule that the agency's response to his comments filed pursuant to paragraph (2) of this subsection was unreasonable.

"(D) from disapproving any collection of information requirement where the Director determines that the agency has substantially modified in the final rule the collection of information requirement contained in the proposed rule where the agency has not given the Director the information required in paragraph (1), with respect to the modified collection of information requirement, at least sixty days before the issuance of the final rule.

"(6) The Director shall make publicly available any decision to disapprove a collection of information requirement contained in an agency rule, together with the reasons for such decision.

"(7) The authority of the Director under this subsection is subject to the provisions of section 3507(c).   *Post,* 2819.

"(8) This subsection shall apply only when an agency publishes a notice of proposed rulemaking and requests public comments.

"(9) There shall be no judicial review of any kind of the Director's decision to approve or not to act upon a collection of information requirement contained in an agency rule.

"§ 3505. Assignment of tasks and deadlines

"In carrying out the functions under this chapter, the Director shall—

"(1) upon enactment of this Act—

"(A) set a goal to reduce the then existing burden of Federal collections of information by 15 per centum by October 1, 1982; and

"(B) for the year following, set a goal to reduce the burden which existed upon enactment by an additional 10 per centum;

"(2) within one year after the effective date of this Act—

"(A) establish standards and requirements for agency audits of all major information systems and assign responsibility for conducting Government-wide or multiagency audits, except the Director shall not assign such responsibility for the audit of major information systems used for the conduct of criminal investigations or intelligence activities as defined in section 4-206 of Executive Order 12036, issued January 24, 1978, or successor orders, or for cryptologic activities that are communications security activities;

"(B) establish the Federal Information Locator System;

"(C) identify areas of duplication in information collection requests and develop a schedule and methods for eliminating duplication;

"(D) develop a proposal to augment the Federal Information Locator System to include data profiles of major information holdings of agencies (used in the conduct of their operations) which are not otherwise required by this chapter to be included in the System; and

"(E) identify initiatives which may achieve a 10 per centum reduction in the burden of Federal collections of information associated with the administration of Federal grant programs; and

"(3) within two years after the effective date of this Act—

"(A) establish a schedule and a management control system to ensure that practices and programs of information handling disciplines, including records management, are appropriately integrated with the information policies mandated by this chapter;

"(B) identify initiatives to improve productivity in Federal operations using information processing technology;

"(C) develop a program to (i) enforce Federal information processing standards, particularly software language standards, at all Federal installations; and (ii) revitalize the standards development program established pursuant to section 759(f)(2) of title 40, United States Code, separating it from peripheral technical assistance functions and directing it to the most productive areas;

"(D) complete action on recommendations of the Commission on Federal Paperwork by implementing, implementing with modification or rejecting such recommendations including, where necessary, development of legislation to implement such recommendations;

"(E) develop, in consultation with the Administrator of General Services, a five-year plan for meeting the automatic data processing and telecommunications needs of the Federal Government in accordance with the requirements of section 111 of the Federal Property and Administrative Services Act of 1949 (40 U.S.C. 759) and the purposes of this chapter; and

Five-year plan.

"(F) submit to the President and the Congress legislative proposals to remove inconsistencies in laws and practices involving privacy, confidentiality, and disclosure of information.

"§ 3506. Federal agency responsibilities

44 USC 3506.

"(a) Each agency shall be responsible for carrying out its information management activities in an efficient, effective, and economical manner, and for complying with the information policies, principles, standards, and guidelines prescribed by the Director.

"(b) The head of each agency shall designate, within three months after the effective date of this Act, a senior official or, in the case of military departments, and the Office of the Secretary of Defense, officials who report directly to such agency head to carry out the responsibilities of the agency under this chapter. If more than one official is appointed for the military departments the respective duties of the officials shall be clearly delineated.

"(c) Each agency shall—

"(1) systematically inventory its major information systems and periodically review its information management activities, including planning, budgeting, organizing, directing, training, promoting, controlling, and other managerial activities involving the collection, use, and dissemination of information;

"(2) ensure its information systems do not overlap each other or duplicate the systems of other agencies;

"(3) develop procedures for assessing the paperwork and reporting burden of proposed legislation affecting such agency;

"(4) assign to the official designated under subsection (b) the responsibility for the conduct of and accountability for any acquisitions made pursuant to a delegation of authority under section 111 of the Federal Property and Administrative Services Act of 1949 (40 U.S.C. 759); and

"(5) ensure that information collection requests required by law or to obtain a benefit, and submitted to nine or fewer persons, contain a statement to inform the person receiving the request that the request is not subject to the requirements of section 3507 of this chapter.

Infra.

"(d) The head of each agency shall establish such procedures as necessary to ensure the compliance of the agency with the requirements of the Federal Information Locator System, including necessary screening and compliance activities.

Procedures, establishment.

"§ 3507. Public information collection activities—submission to Director; approval and delegation

44 USC 3507.

"(a) An agency shall not conduct or sponsor the collection of information unless, in advance of the adoption or revision of the request for collection of such information—

"(1) the agency has taken actions, including consultation with the Director, to—

"(A) eliminate, through the use of the Federal Information Locator System and other means, information collections which seek to obtain information available from another source within the Federal Government;

"(B) reduce to the extent practicable and appropriate the burden on persons who will provide information to the agency; and

"(C) formulate plans for tabulating the information in a manner which will enhance its usefulness to other agencies and to the public;

"(2) the agency (A) has submitted to the Director the proposed information collection request, copies of pertinent regulations and other related materials as the Director may specify, and an explanation of actions taken to carry out paragraph (1) of this subsection, and (B) has prepared a notice to be published in the Federal Register stating that the agency has made such submission; and

"(3) the Director has approved the proposed information collection request, or the period for review of information collection requests by the Director provided under subsection (b) has elapsed.

"(b) The Director shall, within sixty days of receipt of a proposed information collection request, notify the agency involved of the decision to approve or disapprove the request and shall make such decisions publicly available. If the Director determines that a request submitted for review cannot be reviewed within sixty days, the Director may, after notice to the agency involved, extend the review period for an additional thirty days. If the Director does not notify the agency of an extension, denial, or approval within sixty days (or, if the Director has extended the review period for an additional thirty days and does not notify the agency of a denial or approval within the time of the extension), a control number shall be assigned without further delay, the approval may be inferred, and the agency may collect the information for not more than one year.

Ante, p. 2815; *post,* p. 2821.

"(c) Any disapproval by the Director, in whole or in part, of a proposed information collection request of an independent regulatory agency, or an exercise of authority under section 3504(h) or 3509 concerning such an agency, may be voided, if the agency by a majority vote of its members overrides the Director's disapproval or exercise of authority. The agency shall certify each override to the Director, shall explain the reasons for exercising the override authority. Where the override concerns an information collection request, the Director shall without further delay assign a control number to such request, and such override shall be valid for a period of three years.

"(d) The Director may not approve an information collection request for a period in excess of three years.

Ante, p. 2819.

"(e) If the Director finds that a senior official of an agency designated pursuant to section 3506(b) is sufficiently independent of program responsibility to evaluate fairly whether proposed information collection requests should be approved and has sufficient resources to carry out this responsibility effectively, the Director may, by rule in accordance with the notice and comment provisions of

5 USC 500 *et seq.*

chapter 5 of title 5, United States Code, delegate to such official the authority to approve proposed requests in specific program areas, for specific purposes, or for all agency purposes. A delegation by the Director under this section shall not preclude the Director from reviewing individual information collection requests if the Director determines that circumstances warrant such a review. The Director shall retain authority to revoke such delegations, both in general and with regard to any specific matter. In acting for the Director, any official to whom approval authority has been delegated under this section shall comply fully with the rules and regulations promulgated by the Director.

"(f) An agency shall not engage in a collection of information without obtaining from the Director a control number to be displayed upon the information collection request.

"(g) If an agency head determines a collection of information (1) is needed prior to the expiration of the sixty-day period for the review of information collection requests established pursuant to subsection (b), (2) is essential to the mission of the agency, and (3) the agency cannot reasonably comply with the provisions of this chapter within such sixty-day period because (A) public harm will result if normal clearance procedures are followed, or (B) an unanticipated event has occurred and the use of normal clearance procedures will prevent or disrupt the collection of information related to the event or will cause a statutory deadline to be missed, the agency head may request the Director to authorize such collection of information prior to expiration of such sixty-day period. The Director shall approve or disapprove any such authorization request within the time requested by the agency head and, if approved, shall assign the information collection request a control number. Any collection of information conducted pursuant to this subsection may be conducted without compliance with the provisions of this chapter for a maximum of ninety days after the date on which the Director received the request to authorize such collection.

"§ 3508. Determination of necessity for information; hearing

44 USC 3508.

"Before approving a proposed information collection request, the Director shall determine whether the collection of information by an agency is necessary for the proper performance of the functions of the agency, including whether the information will have practical utility. Before making a determination the Director may give the agency and other interested persons an opportunity to be heard or to submit statements in writing. To the extent, if any, that the Director determines that the collection of information by an agency is unnecessary, for any reason, the agency may not engage in the collection of the information.

"§ 3509. Designation of central collection agency

44 USC 3509.

"The Director may designate a central collection agency to obtain information for two or more agencies if the Director determines that the needs of such agencies for information will be adequately served by a single collection agency, and such sharing of data is not inconsistent with any applicable law. In such cases the Director shall prescribe (with reference to the collection of information) the duties and functions of the collection agency so designated and of the agencies for which it is to act as agent (including reimbursement for costs). While the designation is in effect, an agency covered by it may not obtain for itself information which it is the duty of the collection agency to obtain. The Director may modify the designation from time to time as circumstances require. The authority herein is subject to the provisions of section 3507(c) of this chapter.

Ante, p. 2819.

44 USC 3510.

"§ 3510. Cooperation of agencies in making information available

"(a) The Director may direct an agency to make available to another agency, or an agency may make available to another agency, information obtained pursuant to an information collection request if the disclosure is not inconsistent with any applicable law.

"(b) If information obtained by an agency is released by that agency to another agency, all the provisions of law (including penalties which relate to the unlawful disclosure of information) apply to the officers and employees of the agency to which information is released to the same extent and in the same manner as the provisions apply to the officers and employees of the agency which originally obtained the information. The officers and employees of the agency to which the information is released, in addition, shall be subject to the same provisions of law, including penalties, relating to the unlawful disclosure of information as if the information had been collected directly by that agency.

44 USC 3511.

"§ 3511. Establishment and operation of Federal Information Locator System

"(a) There is established in the Office of Information and Regulatory Affairs a Federal Information Locator System (hereafter in this section referred to as the 'System') which shall be composed of a directory of information resources, a data element dictionary, and an information referral service. The System shall serve as the authoritative register of all information collection requests.

Functions.

"(b) In designing and operating the System, the Director shall—

"(1) design and operate an indexing system for the System;

"(2) require the head of each agency to prepare in a form specified by the Director, and to submit to the Director for inclusion in the System, a data profile for each information collection request of such agency;

"(3) compare data profiles for proposed information collection requests against existing profiles in the System, and make available the results of such comparison to—

"(A) agency officials who are planning new information collection activities; and

"(B) on request, members of the general public; and

"(4) ensure that no actual data, except descriptive data profiles necessary to identify duplicative data or to locate information, are contained within the System.

44 USC 3512.

"§ 3512. Public protection

"Notwithstanding any other provision of law, no person shall be subject to any penalty for failing to maintain or provide information to any agency if the information collection request involved was made after December 31, 1981, and does not display a current control number assigned by the Director, or fails to state that such request is not subject to this chapter.

44 USC 3513.

"§ 3513. Director review of agency activities; reporting; agency response

"(a) The Director shall, with the advice and assistance of the Administrator of General Services, selectively review, at least once every three years, the information management activities of each agency to ascertain their adequacy and efficiency. In evaluating the adequacy and efficiency of such activities, the Director shall pay particular attention to whether the agency has complied with section 3506.

Ante, p. 2819.

"(b) The Director shall report the results of the reviews to the appropriate agency head, the House Committee on Government Operations, the Senate Committee on Governmental Affairs, the House and Senate Committees on Appropriations, and the committees of the Congress having jurisdiction over legislation relating to the operations of the agency involved.

Report to congressional committees.

"(c) Each agency which receives a report pursuant to subsection (b) shall, within sixty days after receipt of such report, prepare and transmit to the Director, the House Committee on Government Operations, the Senate Committee on Governmental Affairs, the House and Senate Committees on Appropriations, and the committees of the Congress having jurisdiction over legislation relating to the operations of the agency, a written statement responding to the Director's report, including a description of any measures taken to alleviate or remove any problems or deficiencies identified in such report.

Written statement, submittal to congressional committees.

"§ 3514. Responsiveness to Congress

44 USC 3514.

"(a) The Director shall keep the Congress and its committees fully and currently informed of the major activities under this chapter, and shall submit a report thereon to the President of the Senate and the Speaker of the House of Representatives annually and at such other times as the Director determines necessary. The Director shall include in any such report—

Report to President of the Senate and Speaker of the House.

"(1) proposals for legislative action needed to improve Federal information management, including, with respect to information collection, recommendations to reduce the burden on individuals, small businesses, State and local governments, and other persons;

"(2) a compilation of legislative impediments to the collection of information which the Director concludes that an agency needs but does not have authority to collect;

"(3) an analysis by agency, and by categories the Director finds useful and practicable, describing the estimated reporting hours required of persons by information collection requests, including to the extent practicable the direct budgetary costs of the agencies and identification of statutes and regulations which impose the greatest number of reporting hours;

"(4) a summary of accomplishments and planned initiatives to reduce burdens of Federal information collection requests;

"(5) a tabulation of areas of duplication in agency information collection requests identified during the preceding year and efforts made to preclude the collection of duplicate information, including designations of central collection agencies;

"(6) a list of each instance in which an agency engaged in the collection of information under the authority of section 3507(g) and an identification of each agency involved;

Ante, p. 2819.

"(7) a list of all violations of provisions of this chapter and rules, regulations, guidelines, policies, and procedures issued pursuant to this chapter; and

"(8) with respect to recommendations of the Commission on Federal Paperwork—

"(A) a description of the specific actions taken on or planned for each recommendation;

"(B) a target date for implementing each recommendation accepted but not implemented; and

"(C) an explanation of the reasons for any delay in completing action on such recommendations.

"(b) The preparation of any report required by this section shall not increase the collection of information burden on persons outside the Federal Government.

44 USC 3515.

"§ 3515. Administrative powers

"Upon the request of the Director, each agency (other than an independent regulatory agency) shall, to the extent practicable, make its services, personnel, and facilities available to the Director for the performance of functions under this chapter.

44 USC 3516.

"§ 3516. Rules and regulations

"The Director shall promulgate rules, regulations, or procedures necessary to exercise the authority provided by this chapter.

44 USC 3517.

"§ 3517. Consultation with other agencies and the public

"In development of information policies, plans, rules, regulations, procedures, and guidelines and in reviewing information collection requests, the Director shall provide interested agencies and persons early and meaningful opportunity to comment.

44 USC 3518.

"§ 3518. Effect on existing laws and regulations

"(a) Except as otherwise provided in this chapter, the authority of an agency under any other law to prescribe policies, rules, regulations, and procedures for Federal information activities is subject to the authority conferred on the Director by this chapter.

"(b) Nothing in this chapter shall be deemed to affect or reduce the authority of the Secretary of Commerce or the Director of the Office of Management and Budget pursuant to Reorganization Plan No. 1 of 1977 (as amended) and Executive order, relating to telecommunications and information policy, procurement and management of telecommunications and information systems, spectrum use, and related matters.

5 USC app.; 3 CFR 1978 Comp., p. 158.

"(c)(1) Except as provided in paragraph (2), this chapter does not apply to the collection of information—

"(A) during the conduct of a Federal criminal investigation or prosecution, or during the disposition of a particular criminal matter;

"(B) during the conduct of (i) a civil action to which the United States or any official or agency thereof is a party or (ii) an administrative action or investigation involving an agency against specific individuals or entities;

15 USC 1311 note. *Ante,* p. 380.

"(C) by compulsory process pursuant to the Antitrust Civil Process Act and section 13 of the Federal Trade Commission Improvements Act of 1980; or

50 USC 401 note.

"(D) during the conduct of intelligence activities as defined in section 4-206 of Executive Order 12036, issued January 24, 1978, or successor orders, or during the conduct of cryptologic activities that are communications security activities.

"(2) This chapter applies to the collection of information during the conduct of general investigations (other than information collected in an antitrust investigation to the extent provided in subparagraph (C) of paragraph (1)) undertaken with reference to a category of individuals or entities such as a class of licensees or an entire industry.

40 USC 759.

"(d) Nothing in this chapter shall be interpreted as increasing or decreasing the authority conferred by Public Law 89-306 on the Administrator of the General Services Administration, the Secretary of Commerce, or the Director of the Office of Management and Budget.

"(e) Nothing in this chapter shall be interpreted as increasing or decreasing the authority of the President, the Office of Management and Budget or the Director thereof, under the laws of the United States, with respect to the substantive policies and programs of departments, agencies and offices, including the substantive authority of any Federal agency to enforce the civil rights laws.

"§ 3519. Access to information

44 USC 3519.

"Under the conditions and procedures prescribed in section 313 of the Budget and Accounting Act of 1921, as amended, the Director and personnel in the Office of Information and Regulatory Affairs shall furnish such information as the Comptroller General may require for the discharge of his responsibilities. For this purpose, the Comptroller General or representatives thereof shall have access to all books, documents, papers and records of the Office.

Ante, p. 312.

"§ 3520. Authorization of appropriations

44 USC 3520.

"There are hereby authorized to be appropriated to carry out the provisions of this chapter, and for no other purpose, sums—
    "(1) not to exceed $8,000,000 for the fiscal year ending September 30, 1981;
    "(2) not to exceed $8,500,000 for the fiscal year ending September 30, 1982; and
    "(3) not to exceed $9,000,000 for the fiscal year ending September 30, 1983."

(b) The item relating to chapter 35 in the table of chapters for such title is amended to read as follows:

"35. Coordination of Federal Information Policy.".

(c)(1) Section 2904(10) of such title is amended to read as follows:
    "(10) report to the appropriate oversight and appropriations committees of the Congress and to the Director of the Office of Management and Budget annually and at such other times as the Administrator deems desirable (A) on the results of activities conducted pursuant to paragraphs (1) through (9) of this section, (B) on evaluations of responses by Federal agencies to any recommendations resulting from inspections or studies conducted under paragraphs (8) and (9) of this section, and (C) to the extent practicable, estimates of costs to the Federal Government resulting from the failure of agencies to implement such recommendations."

44 USC 2904.

(2) Section 2905 of such title is amended by redesignating the text thereof as subsection (a) and by adding at the end of such section the following new subsection:
    "(b) The Administrator of General Services shall assist the Administrator for the Office of Information and Regulatory Affairs in conducting studies and developing standards relating to record retention requirements imposed on the public and on State and local governments by Federal agencies.".

44 USC 2905.

Studies.

SEC. 3. (a) The President and the Director of the Office of Management and Budget shall delegate to the Administrator for the Office of Information and Regulatory Affairs all functions, authority, and responsibility under section 103 of the Budget and Accounting Procedures Act of 1950 (31 U.S.C. 18b).

44 USC 3503 note.

(b) The Director of the Office of Management and Budget shall delegate to the Administrator for the Office of Information and

3 CFR 1978
Comp., p. 158; 5
USC app.

20 USC 1221-3.

Regulatory Affairs all functions, authority, and responsibility of the Director under section 552a of title 5, United States Code, under Executive Order 12046 and Reorganization Plan No. 1 for telecommunications, and under section 111 of the Federal Property and Administrative Services Act of 1949 (40 U.S.C. 759).

SEC. 4. (a) Section 400A of the General Education Provisions Act is amended by (1) striking out "and" after "institutions" in subsection (a)(1)(A) and inserting in lieu thereof "or", and (2) by amending subsection (a)(3)(B) to read as follows:

"(B) No collection of information or data acquisition activity subject to such procedures shall be subject to any other review, coordination, or approval procedure outside of the relevant Federal agency, except as required by this subsection and by the Director of the Office of Management and Budget under the rules and regulations established pursuant to chapter 35 of title 44, United States

Ante, p. 2812.

Ante, p. 2819.

Repeal.

Code. If a requirement for information is submitted pursuant to this Act for review, the timetable for the Director's approval established in section 3507 of the Paperwork Reduction Act of 1980 shall commence on the date the request is submitted, and no independent submission to the Director shall be required under such Act.".

(b) Section 201(e) of the Surface Mining Control and Reclamation Act of 1977 (30 U.S.C. 1211) is repealed.

(c) Section 708(f) of the Public Health Service Act (42 U.S.C. 292h(f)) is repealed.

(d) Section 5315 of title 5, United States Code, is amended by adding at the end thereof the following:

    "Administrator, Office of Information and Regulatory Affairs, Office of Management and Budget.".

Effective date.
44 USC 3501
note.

SEC. 5. This Act shall take effect on April 1, 1981.

Approved December 11, 1980.

LEGISLATIVE HISTORY:

HOUSE REPORT No. 96-835 (Comm. on Government Operations).
SENATE REPORT No. 96-930 accompanying S. 1411 (Comm. on Governmental Affairs).
CONGRESSIONAL RECORD, Vol. 126 (1980):
    Mar. 24, considered and passed House.
    Nov. 19, S. 1411 considered and passed Senate; passage vacated and H.R. 6410, amended, passed in lieu.
    Dec. 1, House concurred in Senate amendments.
WEEKLY COMPILATION OF PRESIDENTIAL DOCUMENTS, Vol. 16, No. 50:
    Dec. 11, Presidential statement.

○

INDEX